ADVANCED INDUSTRIAL ECONOMICS

ADVANCED INDUSTRIAL ECONOMICS

Second Edition

STEPHEN MARTIN

University of Amsterdam

First edition published 1993

Second edition published 2002

2 4 6 8 10 9 7 5 3 1

Blackwell Publishers Inc.
350 Main Street
Malden, Massachusetts 02148
USA

Blackwell Publishers Ltd
108 Cowley Road
Oxford OX4 1JF
UK

Library of Congress Cataloging-in-Publication Data

Martin, Stephen, 1961–
    Advanced industrial economics / Stephen Martin.—2nd ed.
      p. cm.
    Includes bibliographical references and index.
    ISBN 0-631-21756-8 (alk. paper)—ISBN 0-631-21757-6 (pb.: alk. paper)
      1. Industrial organization (Economic theory) I. Title.

    HD2326 .M348 2001
    338.8—dc21
                                                                  2001018474

British Library Cataloguing in Publication Data
A CIP catalogue record for this book is available from the British Library.

Typeset in 10 on 11½ Ehrhardt
by Newgen Imaging Systems (P) Ltd, Chennai, India

Printed in Great Britain by TJ International, Padstow, Cornwall

This book is printed on acid-free paper.

CONTENTS

PREFACE

It is an act of ego and presumption to write a book, more so to write a textbook, even more so to write a graduate textbook, and even more so squared to write a graduate textbook in industrial economics. The scope of the field is so wide that no person can be its master; the rate of progress is so rapid that any manuscript must be out of date by the time it is published. Those of you who read this book, and survive, will learn to regularly download working papers from the Internet to try to keep up.

I ought therefore to offer you some reason for devoting that most scarce of all commodities, time, to the perusal of this book, in addition to (after all, industrial economists ought to believe that product differentiation can improve welfare) its excellent competitors. The reasons I put forward are rooted in the evolution of the field and in the kind of book I have tried to write.

My first contact with industrial economics was in winter 1968. The field has changed immensely since then, both substantively and methodologically. There are many things we know now that we did not know then. There are many things we knew then that we now take to be false. I have tried to write a textbook that makes clear the relation between the old truths and the new ones, because I think either one is incomplete without the other.

The most dramatic changes in industrial economics have involved techniques. Conversational game theory is an essential skill for the adult industrial economist. I provide an appendix that aims to supply the tools necessary to acquire the requisite fluency at the book's companion web site (http://www.fee.uva.nl/fo/sm/aie2/linkaie2.htm).

In discussing theoretical models, I have tried to give as many details of proofs as possible. Steps that can be omitted in journals (where it is safe to assume that the reader will be able to provide them) should if possible be included in textbooks (where it must be assumed that the reader is still acquiring the skills needed to pole vault over omitted steps). In some cases, considerations of space make a thorough outline of derivations impossible. In such cases I have placed supplementary lecture notes at the book's companion web site.

In discussing empirical work, I have tried to give enough of a description of data sets and methodology to transmit the flavor and quality of the results. Be warned: it is not possible to appreciate the limitations of the theory without working through the proofs; it is not possible to appreciate the limitations of the empirical work without training in econometrics and, if at all possible, some experience with empirical analysis.

In preparing the second edition, I have completely revised the treatment of basic oligopoly models, which now occupies chapters 2–4 rather than chapters 2 and 10. I have chosen to present much of this material in terms of general functional forms rather than the linear inverse demand, constant marginal cost framework that I relied upon almost exclusively in the first edition. In part, this change is because I came to feel that Bertrand's (1883, pp. 499–500) slap at Canard[1] hit too close to home (despite, and perhaps because of, the continued widespread use of the simpler framework in industrial economics). In part, this change reflects the judgment that the marginal cost of using the more general formulation is modest, and the marginal benefit substantial.

To conserve page space, I have omitted the chapter on the theory of contestable markets that appeared in the first edition. It is available, with a few updated references, at the book's companion web site.[2]

New material in chapter 2 includes an extensive treatment of the neoclassical understanding of the Cournot model, as well as three examples of Cournot duopoly when the inverse demand curve is not linear and marginal cost is not constant. Chapter 3 includes an expanded discussion of the consistent-conjectures literature and a presentation of the differences between the Bowley and Shubik–Levitan representative consumer models of product differentiation, differences which it seems to me are not as much appreciated as they might be. I also introduce a four-graph diagram to illustrate the Cournot and Bertrand models with product differentiation that I hope will be found to be useful.[3] Chapter 3 also contains discussions of the supply function oligopoly model, the Kreps and Scheinkman model with product differentiation, and the Güth–Maggi extension of the Kreps and Scheinkman model.[4]

Chapter 4 collects and expands the first-edition discussion of the Hotelling model and models of vertical product differentiation. Here I introduce figure 4.2 to illustrate the problem of nonexistence of equilibrium in the second stage of the Hotelling model. There is now a treatment of the Mussa–Rosen duopoly model of vertical product differentiation.[5]

The three chapters on empirical studies of market power now immediately follow the three chapters on the foundations of oligopoly theory. Chapter 5 has been shortened. Chapter 6 includes an expanded discussion of the firm effects versus industry effects literature. Chapter 7 now includes expanded discussions of the new empirical industrial organization, Solow residual, and event study literatures.

---

[1] Bertrand (1883, pp. 499–500; Friedman's 1988 translation, p. 74):

> Citizen Canard, although a professor of mathematics, is unaware of or forgot the elements of the calculus of functions. $B + Ax$ is, in effect, according to Canard, the model for all functions which are increasing in the variable x, and $B' - A'x$, for all decreasing functions.

[2] I have also omitted the chapters on industrial economics and macroeconomics, and industrial economics and international trade. I may post versions of these chapters at the book's companion web site.

[3] I have not seen this diagram elsewhere; the idea came to me thinking about a four-graph diagrammatic exposition of the IS/LM model which I associate with Dernburg and McDougall (1976).

[4] The details of the K–S and G–M models are tedious; both are the subjects of lecture notes that may be downloaded from the web site to support this book.

[5] Also supplemented by a set of lecture notes that may be downloaded from the book's companion web site.

The material in chapter 11, on market structure, has been updated. Chapter 12 consolidates the discussions of firm structure, mergers, and joint ventures that appeared in two separate chapters in the first edition. Chapter 9, on advertising, is somewhat shorter than its predecessor in the first edition, largely because I have moved some of the material on advertising to other chapters. I have revised chapter 14 to cover the exponentially expanding literature on R&D cooperation, including a comparison of the d'Aspremont–Jacquemin and Kamien–Muller–Zang models and a discussion of the absorptive capacity literature. There is much of interest in this field that space considerations have not permitted me to discuss.

I am grateful for comments received on various parts of the first edition from Elettra Agliardi, Stephen Davies, Simon Domberger, James Friedman, Ron Harstad, Claudia Keser, Paul Klemperer, Marvin Lieberman, Peter Møllgaard, Louis Phlips, Warren Samuels, Alexander Schrader, Paul Segerstrom, Margaret Slade, Oliver Stehman, and Robert Waldmann. I am also grateful for comments on revised versions of parts of the second edition from Simon Anderson, Werner Güth, Jeroen Hinloopen, Hans Theo Normann, John T. Scott, and Xavier Wauthy.

In another place (Martin, 1988c) I compared the process of writing a book with that of having a child. I am now in a position to note yet another similarity. Immediately after confronting the fuss and bother of having a child, few couples willingly contemplate going through the process again. Yet only children are a small minority of the human race. In this spirit, I dedicate this book to Beth, Rose, Anna, and Tess.

Stephen Martin
January 2001

CHAPTER ONE

INTRODUCTION

Once a student researching a classic military problem which de Gaulle had set his class happened in the library on de Gaulle's own solution produced in his days as a cadet. He copied it and submitted it to de Gaulle as his own. He was given 7/20 and gated for the weekend. In protest he pointed out that it was de Gaulle's own answer and had been given top marks. "I was aware of that," replied the Captain coldly. "But now it is out of date."

Ledwidge, *De Gaulle* (1982, p. 28)

1.1 THE SCOPE OF THE FIELD

The roots of industrial economics are commonly traced to work that Mason (1939) and Bain (1949a) called "price and production policy."[1] Their inspiration lay in the Chamberlinian monopolistic competition revolution (1933),[2] and their emphasis was on markets within which competition was imperfect (Mason, 1939, p. 61):

> In perfect markets, whether monopolistic or competitive, price is hardly a matter of judgment and where there is no judgment there is no policy. The area of price policy . . . embraces the deliberate action of buyers and sellers to influence price . . . .

They argued that the assumptions of the classroom model of competitive markets – price-taking buyers and sellers – did not match the markets that they saw around them (Bain, 1949a,

---

[1] For discussions, see Grether (1970), Comanor (1971), Fuchs (1972), Stigler (1974), Phillips and Stevenson (1974), Schmalensee (1982, 1987a, 1988), Bresnahan and Schmalensee (1987), Bonanno and Brandolini (1990), and Pitelis (1990).

[2] As well as Robinson (1933); but see Stigler (1949) and Fisher (1989, fn. 2). For a provocative essay on the relation of Chamberlin's work to the development of industrial economics, see Ekelund and Hébert (1990b). It seems likely that Ekelund and Hébert are better students of Chamberlin than most industrial economists. But their description of mainstream industrial economics is quite restrictive, and their characterization of the Chicago school as a "new approach" is out of step with the field. See also Peltzman (1991, p. 202).

p. 136):

> studies of American market structure (indicate) . . .
> (1) that concentration of output among relatively few large sellers is the dominant pattern,
> (2) that fewness of buyers is common in producer goods markets,
> (3) that product differentiation is significant for practically all consumer goods and a number of producer goods,
> (4) that there are potentially many significant sub-varieties of "fewness" and concentration which would logically fall within the bounds of . . . oligopoly . . . ,
> (5) that there are additional market characteristics . . . upon the basis of which markets might be meaningfully distinguished.

The general emphasis of industrial economics on imperfectly competitive markets remains a defining characteristic of the field (Phillips and Stevenson, 1974, p. 324):

> Judging from the research of those willing to be classified as industrial organization economists, the principal concerns of industrial organization relate to the application of microeconomics to the problems of monopoly, restraints of trade, and the public regulation and ownership of enterprise.

and (Schmalensee, 1987a, p. 803)

> industrial organization . . . may be broadly defined as the field of economics concerned with markets that cannot easily be analyzed using the standard textbook competitive model.

But if industrial economics deals with the analysis of imperfectly competitive markets, it is clear that the roots of the field are to be found earlier than the 1940s. Writing on "Monopolies in the United States" in what one supposes must now be called *The Old Palgrave*, Jenks (1925–6; 1963, pp. 804–5) argued

> (1) that the causes of industrial monopoly lay in the great capital investment required by modern industry;
> (2) that such concentrations permitted cost savings and efficiencies of various types;
> (3) that such cost savings would allow monopolies to lower prices to consumers;
> (4) but that monopolies had in fact preferred to raise price;
> (5) although their ability to do so was limited by the fact that supra-competitive prices would attract new rivals.

This is a set of topics, and a chain of reasoning, that falls clearly within the confines of what is now called industrial economics.

Similarly, contemporary scholarship associates the theory of countervailing power with Galbraith (1952) and the theory of creative destruction with Schumpeter (1943/75). But both topics, and many others that remain of interest to industrial economists, appear in Marshall's (1920, ch. XIV) discussion of monopoly.[3]

Descriptions and analyses of various aspects of imperfectly competitive markets pepper works on microeconomics from *The Wealth of Nations* onward. With some justification,

---

[3] See Phillips and Stevenson (1974, pp. 326–7) for a discussion of Marshall's contributions to industrial economics.

therefore, Stigler (1968, p. 1) could argue that industrial economics did not exist as a distinct subfield of economics but coincides with conventional price theory.[4]

Economists, however, remain faithful to Adam Smith's dictum that productivity increases with the division of labor. Industrial economics is now regarded as a distinct branch of price theory (Schmalensee, 1988, pp. 643–4),

> best defined by three main topical foci . . .
> determinants of the behaviour, scale, scope, and organisation of *business firms* . . .
> *imperfect competition* . . . how do market *conduct* and *performance* depend on relatively stable observed variables – that is, on market *structure*, broadly defined?
> *public policy toward business.*

1.2 THEORY VERSUS EMPIRICISM

At the roots of mainstream industrial economics lies a methodological debate about the relationship between theoretical and empirical analysis, a debate that continues to the present day.[5] Bain's description of "price policy" shows the continuity of the field (1949a, p. 129):

> even the earliest treatments were in general concerned with all of what we currently regard as the primary issues: (1) the structure, organization, and ownership of business; (2) the competitive behavior and price policies of enterprise – including motives, strategy, and tactics; (3) the price, output, and associated results of this behavior; and (4) the public policy issues raised by such structure, behavior, and results.

The industrial economists of that time felt that their work marked a break with the past, which they viewed as insufficiently guided by economic theory (Bain, 1949a, p. 130):

> Much of the work prior to 1930 . . . featured simple description and superficial interpretation of financial organization, structural change and competitive tactics, and in evaluating behavior emphasized the norms of law rather than those of economics. . . . there was frequently a lack of close or extended analysis of price–output results, or of how observed market structure and competitive behavior affected the determination of prices and outputs . . . . These limitations . . . arose primarily from a general lack of rapport with the corresponding field of "economic theory" . . . .

They regarded their own work as motivated by the Chamberlinian revolution (Bain, 1949a, p. 130):

> Chamberlin's work seems to have been by all odds the most important It related the theory of pricing specifically to the institutional framework and practice of the real economy – to concentration, product differentiation and its legal framework, collusive activities, trade practices, and barriers to entry . . . .

---

[4] Commenting on his own survey of experts in the field, Grether (1970, p. 86) remarks that the diversity of responses "supports the view that industrial organization is not a clearly defined homogeneous entity." It seems unlikely that this has changed.

[5] The scope of this debate is not, of course, is not limited to industrial economics. See Morgan (1988).

At the same time, they rejected the development of theory for theory's sake (Mason, 1939, p. 62):[6]

> Some theorists, pursuing their analysis on a high plane, refer to their work as "tool making" rather than "tool using." A "toolmaker," however, who constructs tools which no "tool user" can use is making a contribution of limited significance. Some knowledge of the use of tools is probably indispensable to their effective fabrication.

Their view was that the formal, mathematical expositions of economic theory of the day did not provide testable hypotheses for the analysis of imperfectly competitive markets (Bain, 1949a, pp. 158–9):

> "Degree of monopoly" classifications . . . like those advanced by Lerner and Rothschild rest upon practically non-ascertainable sellers' demand curves and cannot be considered as objective or empirically applicable.

The general feeling was that the role of theory was limited to defining the relevant questions. Answers would have to come from empirical research (Phillips and Stevenson, 1974, p. 337):[7]

> Mason's model evidenced a curious blend of the use of theory and empiricism. Theory could be useful in identifying the relevant structural and performance variables. But the relationship between variables would have to be established by empirical analysis.

Beginning with this premise, Mason's students produced a series of case studies that tended (Bain, 1949a, pp. 142–3)[8]

> to accept the terms of Chamberlinian and post-Chamberlinian price theory at least as an orientation and sometimes as a specific formula for verification. Thus the "full-dress" industry study . . . pays attention to the character and historical origins of market structure – including concentration, product differentiation, entry, technological and legal conditions, and geographical relationships – to the resultant conditions of demand and supply for the industry and for firms, to the character of price calculation and of rivalrous and collusive behavior, and to price results including profits, efficiency, selling costs, progressiveness, price rigidity, price discrimination, and so forth.

As might be expected, given the public policy orientation of the field, such studies often originated in the analysis of antitrust cases. Many of these studies still repay a careful reading.

---

[6] Mason's contemporaries would have recognized the allusion to Pigou's 1929 description of "Edgeworth, the tool-maker, [who] gloried in his tools" (Pigou and Robertson, 1931, p. 3).

[7] For a curious echo of this position, see Coase (1972, pp. 70–1):

> it is unlikely that we shall see significant advances in our theory of the organization of industry until we know more about what it is that we must explain. An inspired theoretician might do as well without such empirical work, but my own feeling is that the inspiration is most likely to come through the stimulus provided by the patterns, puzzles, and anomalies revealed by systematic data-gathering.

[8] Wallace (1937), Kaysen (1956), and Adelman (1966) are examples.

At the end of the 1940s, the case study was well established, but its limitations were recognized (Bain, 1949a, p. 167):

> The method of the extensive case study, frequently repeated, seems the best yet discovered for this field. But each case study takes a long time, and many of them are required to permit effective generalization. The prospect of getting general results in the near future is not promising.

It was Bain himself who initiated industrial economics' 25-year infatuation with cross-section analysis. His (1956) *Barriers to New Competition* contained detailed descriptions of market structure and large-firm performance in 20 industries, and an analysis of the relation between differences in industry characteristics and differences in performance.[9]

Bain's empirical work was descriptive rather than econometric. But his use of small samples and a limited number of variables was ideally suited to the econometric techniques of the 1960s, and such studies were not slow to appear. The late 1960s saw a switch to the use of large cross-sections of industry data, usually based on information originally collected by a government agency. Analysis of such data absorbed the energy of industrial economists through the early 1970s. The structure–conduct–performance paradigm provided the intellectual framework within which this analysis took place.

1.3 BARRIERS TO ENTRY AND THE STRUCTURE–CONDUCT–PERFORMANCE PARADIGM

The methodology of the structure–conduct–performance framework dominated industrial economics throughout the quarter century following the Second World War. Researchers sought to explain the degree to which industries approached the competitive ideal in terms of market characteristics and firm behavior. "Market characteristics" included the ease or difficulty with which new firms could come into the market. From Bain onward, "barriers to entry" were central to the structure–conduct–performance paradigm (Bain, 1956, pp. v–vi):

> The present work reports on a modest effort in the continuing endeavor to ascertain the extent and character of the association of industrial market structures to market performance. It concerns the nature and effects of one potentially strategic dimension of market structure – the "condition of entry," or the relative ease or difficulty of entry of new competitors to an industry. In other terms, it seeks to measure the varying force among industries of "potential" competition, or threatened new entry, and to inquire whether and in what way variations in this force influence the market performance of established firms.

In retrospect, it seems likely that much intellectual dithering might have been avoided if the term "cost of entry" had been used instead of "barrier to entry" (see section 11.2.5).

Barriers to entry were regarded as a necessary condition for the exercise of market power (Scherer, 1970, p. 10):

> It is conventional . . . to add several additional characteristics in describing the "ideal" competitive market of economic theory . . . . The most important is the absence of barriers to the

---

[9] Shepherd (1976), and chapter 5.

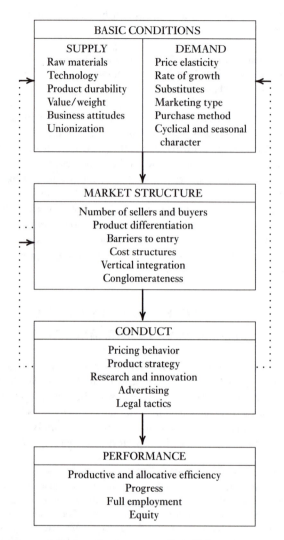

Figure 1.1 The structure–conduct–performance paradigm (Scherer, 1970, p. 5).

entry of new firms...Conversely, significant entry barriers are the *sine qua non* of monopoly and oligopoly ... sellers have little or no enduring power over price when entry barriers are non-existent.

Bain sought to explain the condition of entry in terms of underlying technological and demand factors – principally, minimum efficient scale, absolute capital requirements, and product differentiation. Influential schematic outlines of the structure–conduct–performance paradigm, like that of Scherer (1970, p. 5), reproduced in figure 1.1, also showed

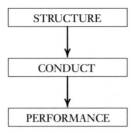

Figure 1.2 Stripped-down structure–conduct–performance diagram.

barriers to entry, and other elements of market structure, as depending on underlying demand and supply conditions. Within this framework, causal relationships flowed up and down the SCP chain.[10]

But mainstream industrial economics was sometimes portrayed as employing a stripped-down version of the structure–conduct–performance framework (figure 1.2). In this caricature, causal relations went in one direction only (Phillips, 1974, pp. 409–10):

> [The model] says that industries have various structural characteristics S – the number of firms, size of firms, entry conditions, cost conditions, what demand looks like, and things of that sort. The model says that (somehow or other) out of structure the conduct of firms, C, is determined. Conduct covers the degree of collusiveness, R&D behavior, behavior relating to broad innovation, price–output policies, advertising, and so forth. Market performance, P, ultimately depends on structure alone, since conduct is itself seen as uniquely related to structure.

1.4   A DECADE OF HIGH THEORY

The developers of the structure–conduct–performance paradigm sought to provide a new theoretical framework for what they perceived as having been a descriptive, nonanalytic field. They were successful, but because they rejected contemporary microeconomics as simply not up to the task of analyzing real-world markets, the theoretical framework that they developed evolved on its own path, largely independent of ongoing refinements of formal models of imperfectly competitive markets.

For roughly 35 years after Mason's (1939) seminal essay, research in industrial economics progressed in a discursive way, using informal theoretical arguments to explore the relationships between market structure, firm conduct, and market performance (Shubik and Levitan, 1980, p. 21):[11]

> There is a history of mathematical models of oligopolistic competition dating from Cournot (1838) to the theory of games. There is also a literature generated by institutional economists,

---

[10] Thus (Caves, 1998, pp. 1963–4): "In the SCP paradigm, sellers' concentration is thought to affect their behavior patterns but also to depend on their past conduct."

[11] Questioning the formal mathematical approach to economic analysis is nothing new; see the discussions of Marshall's attitude toward mathematics in Pigou (1955, pp. 5–12), Samuelson (1967, pp. 22–6), and more generally, see Lazear (2000).

lawyers, and administrators interested in formulating and implementing public policy. It has been the tendency of these groups to work almost as though the other did not exist.

Over time, the structure–conduct–performance paradigm itself came to be perceived as descriptive and nonanalytic. Current research in industrial economics, theoretical and empirical, is based on formal oligopoly models, not on the structure–conduct–performance paradigm. Three factors favored this development.

First, although the structure–conduct–performance school and the formal microeconomic analysis of imperfect markets developed along different paths, the paths were largely parallel. As we shall see, formal models of the influence of the number of firms and the degree of product differentiation on equilibrium prices and outputs have the advantages of making essential assumptions precise and of suggesting explicit functional forms for hypothesis testing. But the conclusions that they yield are not qualitatively different from those of the structure–conduct–performance paradigm.

Econometric testing of structure–conduct–performance hypotheses is a second factor behind the rise of formal theory in industrial economics. Economists who do empirical research, by and large, are trained as regression-runners. They formulate hypotheses in terms of the signs and magnitudes of particular parameters in specific structural models, and they test these hypotheses by estimating the equations of the structural model using some more or less appropriate data set. One consequence of this work was the view that market structure should be treated as an endogenous element in a larger system (figure 1.1), not as something exogenous (figure 1.2) with respect to firm conduct and market performance. Once industrial economists began to formulate empirical tests in terms of specific structural models, it was inevitable that they should work backward and seek formal theoretical foundations for the structural equations that were being tested. The natural foundation was found by elaborating received models of oligopoly.

The third factor in the theoretical reformulation of industrial economics was the quantum leap forward in the application of game theory to oligopoly models, providing industrial economists with a formal tool for the analysis of the strategic interactions that are central to the determination of market performance in oligopoly. Oligopoly theory has replaced structure–conduct–performance as the organizing framework for industrial economics because it has grown up enough to answer the questions that it could not answer in the 1940s.

The period from the early 1970s to the early 1980s marked a golden age of theoretical development in industrial economics. In some cases, this work recast structure–conduct–performance arguments in formal terms. In other cases (predatory pricing, for example), theoretical analyses provided clear advances in results as well as in techniques over previous approaches.

On the surface, the most striking difference between the structure–conduct–performance approach and current mainstream industrial economics is the latter's embrace of formal theory. Below the surface, there is what may come to be seen as an even more fundamental difference. Whatever else the structure–conduct–performance framework was, it was a *general* analytic framework. It drew on empirical regularities observed in many industries and offered correspondingly broad policy advice.

Market performance was expected to be better, all else equal, the more firms supplied the market. For this reason, mergers were viewed with suspicion, as was advertising (held to make it more difficult for rivals to compete). Agreements among rivals to limit competition were condemned; agreements between manufacturers and their distributors to limit competition were viewed with suspicion, largely by analogy with horizontal collusive agreements. In these and other areas, what was lacking was an analytic framework able to assess the welfare-enhancing and welfare-reducing consequences of specific types of market structure or firm conduct in a precise way and to indicate whether the net effect was positive or negative.

The extensive collection of game-theoretic models of imperfectly competitive markets developed in the 1980s does not share this limitation. Such models generate very precise assessments of positive and negative aspects of market performance. But the game-theoretic framework does not aspire to generality. Game-theoretic models are defined by quite specific assumptions and their predictions about equilibrium behavior are correspondingly specific, often not at all robust to seemingly minor changes in underlying assumptions.

The 1980s saw not only the formalization of theoretical industrial economics but also its fractalization: the literature of industrial economics now consists of a labyrinth of highly refined, highly specific models, each yielding conclusions that apply, in principle, only when the assumptions of the model are met. Generalizations must be drawn by reading between the lines – and by searching for regularities in the results of empirical tests of the formal models.

Industrial economics has always been a fundamentally empirical field. In spite of, or perhaps because of, the theoretical revolution of the 1970s and 1980s, from the early 1980s onward there has been a renewed interest in empirical work in industrial economics. Much recent work involves econometric industry studies, which test theoretical models developed in the 1970s and 1980s with modern econometric methods applied to the kind of industry-specific data first studied in the 1940s (Bresnahan and Schmalensee, 1987).

1.5 AN OUTLINE OF THE BOOK

Chapters 2, 3, and 4 review the fundamental oligopoly models that are widely applied to the research questions of industrial economics. Chapter 2 presents the Cournot model, as it was understood by the first economists who became aware of it and as it came to be understood by classical oligopoly theorists. Chapter 3 confronts the classical Cournot model with its game-theoretic relative and discusses the classical literature on conjectural variations from a game-theoretic perspective. It is in chapter 3 that we introduce representative consumer models of product differentiation and examine versions of the Cournot and Bertrand models with differentiated products. Chapter 3 also includes discussions of supply function oligopoly, as well as a version of the Kreps and Scheinkman model with differentiated products, and of the Güth–Maggi extension of that model.

Much of chapter 4 is devoted to the Hotelling spatial model of oligopoly and to some of its many extensions. Here we also discuss models of oligopoly with vertical product differentiation.

Chapters 5 and 6 deal with mainstream empirical work in industrial economics from the 1950s through the 1970s, and perhaps a little beyond. It is necessary to know about the research covered in chapter 5 – by Joe Bain and his immediate followers – to understand the issues in the 1970s debates over the empirical analysis of market power that are the subject of chapter 6. It is necessary to understand the 1970s debates to understand contemporary empirical studies of market power, which are the subject of chapter 7.

The topic of chapter 8 is strategic behavior, including the strategic use of excess capacity, oligopoly behavior in the presence of switching costs, as well as models of predation and of limit pricing. Chapter 9 deals with advertising. Chapter 10 covers theoretical models of collusion, including facilitating practices, and empirical studies of collusion.

Chapters 11 and 12 deal with the determinants of market structure and firm structure, respectively. Chapter 13 covers vertical restraints, including tying and bundling.

In chapter 14 we turn to the economics of innovation. There are discussions of the empirical literature on rates of return to R&D and of R&D spillovers, as well as of the literature on R&D joint ventures. We also review deterministic and stochastic models of innovation and the literature on patent design.

CHAPTER TWO
FOUNDATIONS OF OLIGOPOLY THEORY I

I propose to show in this essay that the solution of the general questions which arise from the theory of wealth, depends essentially not on elementary algebra, but on that branch of analysis which comprises arbitrary functions, which are merely restricted to satisfying certain conditions.

Cournot (1838/1927, p. 4)

2.1 INTRODUCTION

Our starting point is what Schumpeter (1954, p. 980) called "the backbone of all further work on oligopoly," the Cournot model of homogeneous product, quantity-setting duopoly which, in its extensions and variations, has been used to address an astonishing range of questions in industrial economics.

It cannot be said that Cournot sprang full-grown from the brow of Zeus. He was familiar with the mainstream economic literature of his day, and with attempts to cast mainstream theories in mathematical form. But his own work was so far in advance of that of his contemporaries that it remained without influence, as if sealed in a time capsule, until the profession matured sufficiently to comprehend it.[1]

2.2 COURNOT IN HIS OWN WORDS

After discussing the case of a monopoly supplier of mineral water who picked price to maximize profit, Cournot wrote (1838/1927, p. 79; emphasis in original):

> Let us now imagine two proprietors and two springs of which the qualities are identical, and which, on account of their similar positions, supply the same market in competition. In this case the price is necessarily the same for each proprietor. If p is this price, $D = F(p)$ the total sales, D_1 the sales from the spring (1) and D_2 the sales from the spring (2), then $D_1 + D_2 = D$. If, to

---

[1] For analytic biographies, see Edgeworth (1925–6) and Shubik (1987).

begin with, we neglect the cost of production, the respective incomes of the proprietors will be pD_1 and pD_2; and *each of them independently* will seek to make this income as large as possible.

Much ink has been spilt over the words

> Instead of adopting $D = F(p)$ as before, in this case it will be convenient to adopt the inverse notation $p = f(D) \ldots$

and

> Proprietor (1) can have no direct influence on the determination of D_2; all that he can do, when D_2 has been determined by proprietor (2), is to choose for D_1 the value which is best for him. This he will be able to accomplish by properly adjusting his price, except as proprietor (2), who, seeing himself forced to accept this price and this value of D_1, may adopt a new value for D_2, more favourable to his interests than the preceding one.

which appear on the following page.

Despite having adopted output as the decision variable, and explicitly using a notation that makes price a function of total output, Cournot writes of proprietor 1 adjusting *his price*. This is inexact on two counts, first because it speaks of proprietor 1 adjusting price and second for the reference to "his" price, since with a homogeneous product there is only one price (and it is $p = f(D)$).

2.3   THE CLASSICAL OLIGOPOLY THEORY FORMULATION

It may be correct to say that French economists ignored Cournot's book; economists outside France were simply unaware of it. The earliest known review is by Cherriman (1857). It and a review by de Fontenay (1864) seem to have passed unnoticed. Marshall apparently read Cournot sometime between 1867 and 1870 (Pigou, 1956, p. 19), and acknowledges his debts to Cournot in the preface to the first edition of his *Principles*. Jevons writes in the preface to the second (1879) edition of *Theory of Political Economy* that he had obtained a copy of Cournot's *Recherches* in 1872, "but have only recently studied it." In the preface to the fourth (1926) edition of his *Elements*, Walras notes that the first (1877) edition, as well as Jevons' work and that of Cournot, had been translated into Italian at about the same time; he credits Cournot as his source for the idea of using calculus in economic analysis.

Thus Cournot's 1838 book surfaced in the 1870s.[2] Bertrand's (1883) critical review (see section 3.8) set the tone for professional assessment of Cournot's contribution for the second 45 years of its life, in which Cournot went from being unknown to being unloved. Cournot was given credit for pioneering the application of mathematical techniques to economic analysis, but his conclusions were rejected. Edgeworth's (1925, p. 111) comment is representative:

> The theory of monopoly in the ordinary sense of the term is connected with the theory of two-sided monopoly or "duopoly." Cournot had represented the transactions between two parties to

---

[2] For discussions of Cournot's passage out of the wilderness, see Ekelund and Hébert (1990a), Magnan de Bornier (1992), and Dimand (1995).

be determinate in the same sense as competitive prices. But heavy blows had been dealt on this part of his system by Bertrand in the *Journal des Savants*, 1883, and by Marshall, in an early edition of his *Principles of Economics*. Still in 1897 much of Cournot's construction remained standing; the large part which is based on the supposition that the monopolist's expenses of production obey the law of diminishing returns. Now the demolition of Cournot's theory is generally accepted. Professor Amoroso is singular in his fidelity to Cournot.

In the 30 years that followed Bertrand's review, the economics profession reached a common understanding of the Cournot model, which is presented in Fisher (1898a,b), Edgeworth (1925–6), and elsewhere. The main elements of this understanding were that the Cournot model has a stable equilibrium, with price and output between the monopoly and the perfectly competitive levels, and that Cournot equilibrium output rises toward the long-run equilibrium output of a perfectly competitive industry as the number of firms increases. It was generally accepted that Cournot's conclusions followed in a logically correct way from his assumptions. It was the assumptions that were rejected, as we will see in chapter 3 when we take up the subject of price-setting oligopoly models. Before reaching that point, however, we examine the classical and modern understandings of the Cournot model.

2.3.1 Graphical exposition

Cournot's model is of a market for a standardized product, supplied by two firms, each observing the output of the other and picking its own output to maximize its own profit. The market is in equilibrium if each producer selects the output expected by the other.

Figure 2.1, which is drawn for a linear inverse demand curve and constant marginal cost, shows the traditional graphical analysis of the output decision of one of the two firms – in this case, firm 1. Subtracting firm 2's output from the market demand curve gives firm 1's residual demand curve. With this residual demand curve comes a residual marginal revenue curve, and in the usual way[3] firm 1's profit-maximizing output is that which makes its residual marginal revenue equal to its marginal cost.

Repeating this process for different levels of firm 2's output allows us to trace out firm 1's *best-response curve* – in traditional usage, referred to as firm 1's *reaction curve*. The best-response curve is the locus of points that shows firm 1's profit-maximizing output level for any output of firm 2. Firm 1's best-response curve is drawn in figure 2.2(b), along with firm 2's best-response curve, which is derived in the same way as that of firm 1.

The general configuration of the best-response curves in figure 2.2(b) can be explained in economic terms by comparing monopoly output and output under perfect competition (Cournot, 1838; 1927, p. 82; Fisher, 1898, p. 240). Assume, as did Cournot, that firms have identical unit costs. Firm 1's profit-maximizing output is zero at the vertical-axis intercept of its best-response curve. In order for firm 1 to be maximizing profit with zero output, firm 2's output at this point must make price equal to firm 1's marginal cost; otherwise, firm 1 could earn a profit with positive output. The output that makes price equal to marginal cost is the

---

[3] Cournot was the first to characterize profit maximization in terms of the equality of marginal revenue and marginal cost. It was once common to refer to the intersection of the marginal revenue and marginal cost curves as the "Cournot point" (Edgeworth, 1922, p. 401; Stackelberg, 1952, p. 175; Schneider, 1962, p. 113), but this usage has been lost as the concept has become second nature to the profession.

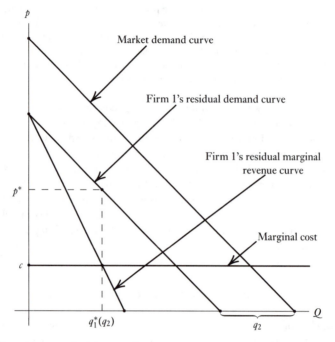

Figure 2.1 Firm 1's output decision, q_2 given.

long-run equilibrium output of a perfectly competitive industry. Hence firm 2's output at the vertical axis of firm 1's best-response curve is the long-run equilibrium output of a perfectly competitive industry.

Firm 1's output is also zero at the vertical-axis intercept of firm 2's best-response function. If firm 1 produces nothing, firm 2 is a monopolist, and firm 2 will maximize its profit by producing the monopoly output. Hence firm 2's output at the vertical-axis intercept of its best-response curve is the monopoly output.

Monopoly output is less than the long-run equilibrium output of a perfectly competitive industry. It follows that the vertical-axis intercept of firm 2's best-response curve must lie below the vertical-axis intercept of firm 1's best-response curve.

A corresponding argument establishes that the horizontal-axis intercept of firm 1's best-response curve (at which firm 2 produces nothing and firm 1 produces its monopoly output) lies to the left of the horizontal-axis intercept of firm 2's best-response function (at which firm 1 produces an output that makes price equal to firm 2's marginal cost and firm 2 produces nothing).

With continuous best-response curves, this argument shows that the best-response curves intersect at a point like the one shown in figure 2.2(b). At this point, each firm is maximizing profit, given the observed output of the other. Thus output q_1^C in figure 2.2(d) makes firm 1's residual marginal revenue equal to its marginal cost, and the output–price pair (q_1^C, p^C) lies

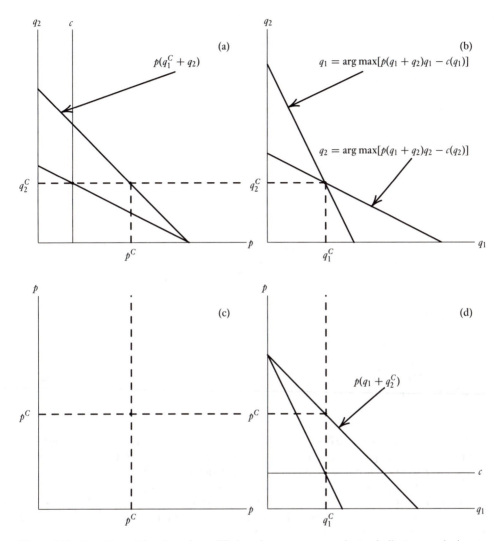

Figure 2.2 Quantity-setting duopoly equilibrium, homogeneous product. c indicates marginal cost, and superscript C indicates the Cournot equilibrium value. (a) Firm 2's equilibrium residual demand curve; (b) quantity best-response curves; (c) price space; (d) firm 1's equilibrium residual demand curve.

on firm 1's residual demand curve. The same applies to output q_2^C and the output–price pair (q_2^C, p^C) in figure 2.2(a).[4]

---

[4] For consistency with figure 2.2(b), figure 2.2(a) is drawn with output on the vertical axis and price on the horizontal axis, contrary to usual practice.

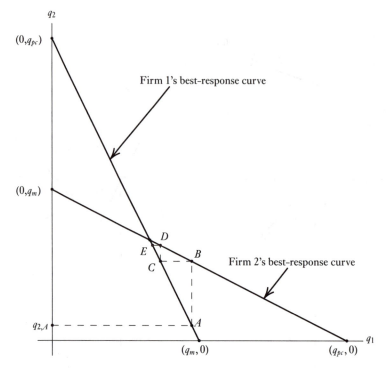

Figure 2.3 The Cournot stairstep stability diagram. q_m = monopoly output; q_{pc} = long-run equilibrium output of a perfectly competitive industry.

Projecting price down from figure 2.2(a) and left from figure 2.2(d) to figure 2.2(c) identifies the point (p^C, p^C) in price space. The price-space segment of the diagram assumes a more interesting role in the presence of product differentiation (section 3.2).

The output pair (q_1^C, q_2^C) is an equilibrium because, at this point, each firm is maximizing its profit, given the output of the other. With Cournot's other assumptions of independent decision-making and profit maximization, neither firm would have any incentive to depart from the (q_1^C, q_2^C) output combination.

In the classical interpretation of the Cournot model, a firm's own behavior is inconsistent with the beliefs that it is assumed to maintain about the behavior of its rival. In the Cournot model, each firm treats the other's output as independent of its actions, while selecting its own output based on the other's observed output (Kamien and Schwartz, 1983, p. 193). We consider classical attempts to confront this inconsistency in section 3.4.

Classical oligopoly theorists also regarded the output pair (q_1^C, q_2^C) as an equilibrium, because under Cournot's assumptions the outputs of the two firms would return to that point if somehow they found themselves away from it. This is shown, following Cournot's figure 2, in figure 2.3. If firm 1 should observe firm 2 producing an arbitrary output $q_{2,A}$, firm 1 would maximize profit by producing at point A on its best-response curve. If firm 2 were to observe firm 1 producing at point A, firm 2 would maximize profit at point B on its best-response curve. But then firm 1 would maximize profit by producing at point C on its best-response curve. Continuing in the same way, outputs converge to the Cournot equilibrium pair at the intersection of the best-response curves.

Cournot recognized that the intersection of the best-response curves would not be a stable equilibrium if the best-response curves crossed "the wrong way" (in contrast to figure 2.3) with firm 2's best-response curve moving from above to below firm 1's best-response function moving from left to right in the neighborhood of the intersection (Cournot's figure 3 and discussion thereof). He dismissed this possibility, relying on the argument given above about the relative size of monopoly and perfectly competitive output.

To this point, we have reviewed the classical arguments that the Cournot equilibrium would exist and be stable. A graphical argument shows that under the conditions considered by classical oligopoly theorists, Cournot equilibrium output will be greater than monopoly output and less than long-run perfectly competitive equilibrium output.

In figure 2.3, a straight line connecting the points $(0, q_m)$ and $(q_m, 0)$ (not drawn in the figure) shows all combinations of outputs by the two firms that make total output equal to monopoly output. At points below this line, total output is less than monopoly output; at points above this line, total output is greater than monopoly output. Because the Cournot equilibrium point (q_1^C, q_2^C) is farther away from the origin than this monopoly output line, Cournot equilibrium output $q_1^C + q_2^C$ is greater than monopoly output.

In the same way, a straight line in figure 2.3 connecting the points $(0, q_{pc})$ and $(q_{pc}, 0)$ shows all combinations of output by the two firms that make total output equal to the long-run equilibrium output of a perfectly competitive industry. At points below this line, total output is less than long-run competitive equilibrium output; at points above this line, total output is greater than long-run competitive equilibrium output. Because the Cournot equilibrium point (q_1^C, q_2^C) is inside the long-run competitive equilibrium output line, Cournot equilibrium output $q_1^C + q_2^C$ is less than long-run competitive equilibrium output.[5]

2.3.2 Mathematical exposition

Classical oligopoly theorists relied on a combined graphical and mathematical argument to conclude that, as the number of firms rises, the Cournot equilibrium price falls, from the monopoly price for a single firm, and approaches in the limit the long-run equilibrium price of a perfectly competitive industry as the number of firms goes to infinity.

To present this argument, we use the classical mathematical version of the Cournot model.[6] Let the inverse demand function for the duopoly market be

$$p = p(Q) = p(q_1 + q_2), \qquad (2.1)$$

and let firm i's total cost function be

$$c_i(q_i), \qquad (2.2)$$

---

[5] Classical oligopoly theorists did not make this graphical argument, relying instead on the argument accompanying figure 2.4. See, however, Fellner (1949, pp. 59–60).
[6] See, for example, Allen (1938).

for $i = 1, 2$. The demand and cost functions are continuous and have continuous first and second derivatives and other properties to be specified as needed.

Firm 1's profit is

$$\pi_1(q_1, q_2) = p(q_1 + q_2)q_1 - c_1(q_1). \tag{2.3}$$

For a given value of q_2, this is maximized for the output q_1 that solves

$$\frac{\partial \pi_1(q_1, q_2)}{\partial q_1} = p(q_1 + q_2) + q_1 \frac{dp}{dQ} - \frac{dc_1(q_1)}{dq_1} \equiv 0, \tag{2.4}$$

provided that the second-order condition for a maximum is satisfied.

A sufficient second-order condition for a maximum is

$$\frac{\partial^2 \pi_1(q_1, q_2)}{\partial q_1^2} = 2 \frac{dp}{dQ} + q_1 \frac{d^2 p}{dQ^2} - \frac{d^2 c_1(q_1)}{dq_1^2} < 0. \tag{2.5}$$

This is satisfied, for example, for linear inverse demand and constant marginal cost (in which case, the second and third terms in the center of (2.5) are both zero). It is also satisfied if the inverse demand curve is concave ($d^2 p/dQ^2 < 0$) and the cost function convex ($d^2 c_1(q_1)/dq_1^2 > 0$).

Alternatively, the second-order condition can be written

$$\frac{dMR(Q)}{dQ} < \frac{dMC(q_1)}{dq_1}. \tag{2.6}$$

In the normal case, marginal revenue falls as output rises. The second-order condition is then automatically satisfied if marginal cost is constant or rising as output rises. If marginal cost falls as output rises, so that both terms in (2.6) are negative, the second-order condition requires that the slope of the marginal revenue curve be greater in magnitude than the slope of the marginal cost curve – that the marginal revenue curve slope downward more steeply than the marginal cost curve.

Classical oligopoly theorists assumed that the second-order condition was satisfied (often without explicit discussion). Equation (2.4) then implicitly defines firm 1's best-response function.

At this point, follow Cournot and assume that firms produce at zero cost. The critical aspect of this assumption is not that cost is zero, but that it is constant and the same for all firms. Then all firms will produce the same output in equilibrium, and the first-order condition (2.4) can be written in condensed form as

$$p(Q_2) + \frac{Q_2}{2} \frac{dp(Q_2)}{dQ} \equiv 0, \tag{2.7}$$

where Q_2 denotes Cournot duopoly equilibrium output.

Rewrite (2.7) as

$$2p_2 = -\frac{Q_2(p_2)}{dQ(p_2)/dp}, \tag{2.8}$$

where $p_2 \equiv p(Q_2)$ is the Cournot duopoly equilibrium price.

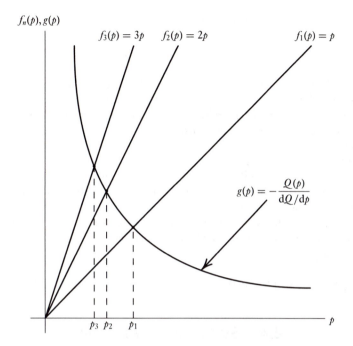

Figure 2.4 Number of firms – the Cournot equilibrium price relationship.

Going through the same steps with n firms rather than 2, we obtain

$$np_n = -\frac{Q_n(p_n)}{\mathrm{d}Q(p_n)/\mathrm{d}p} \tag{2.9}$$

as an implication of symmetric Cournot equilibrium.

Figure 2.4 illustrates the solution to (2.9) – the Cournot equilibrium price with n identical firms – as the intersection of two curves, $f_n(p) = np$ and $g(p) = -Q(p)/(\mathrm{d}Q/\mathrm{d}p)$, each a function of price.[7]

The straight line with equation $f_n(p) = np$ slopes upward, and is steeper as n is larger. The curve with equation $g(p) = -Q(p)/(\mathrm{d}Q/\mathrm{d}p)$ is taken to slope downward. We could go into this more deeply,[8] but simply note that it is correct for a linear demand curve (in which case $-Q(p)/(\mathrm{d}Q/\mathrm{d}p)$ is a straight line with slope -1).

As shown in figure 2.4, the Cournot equilibrium price falls as the number of identical firms operating in the market increases. In the limit, with infinitely many firms, the Cournot equilibrium price is marginal cost, zero, the long-run equilibrium price of a perfectly competitive industry.

---

[7] See Cournot's figure 4 and the discussion thereof.
[8] The condition that must be satisfied is $1 - \left[Q/(\mathrm{d}Q/\mathrm{d}p)^2\right]\mathrm{d}^2Q/\mathrm{d}p^2 > 0$.

2.3.3   Recapitulation

Thus we have the classical understanding of the Cournot model:

- Independent profit-maximizing behavior can be described in terms of best-response curves that slope downward "under normal conditions" (Allen, 1938, p. 201).[9]
- The best-response curves intersect at a point that is a stable equilibrium in the sense that if outputs are somehow away from that point, firms' decisions will return the market there.
- Equilibrium duopoly output exceeds monopoly output but falls short of long-run perfectly competitive equilibrium output, with the corresponding result that equilibrium duopoly price will be less than monopoly price but above the long-run perfectly competitive equilibrium price.
- As the number of firms in Cournot oligopoly increases, Cournot output, price, and market performance approach the long-run perfectly competitive equilibrium values in the limit.

We now turn to an examination of modern understanding of each of these issues.

2.4   BEST-RESPONSE FUNCTIONS

Differentiating the equation of firm 1's first-order condition, (2.4), gives an expression for the slope of firm 1's best-response function:

$$\frac{\partial^2 \pi_1(q_1, q_2)}{\partial q_1^2} \frac{dq_1}{dq_2}\bigg|_{\text{foc}} + \frac{\partial^2 \pi_1(q_1, q_2)}{\partial q_1 \partial q_2} = 0$$

$$\Rightarrow \quad \frac{dq_1}{dq_2}\bigg|_{\text{foc}} = \frac{\partial^2 \pi_1(q_1, q_2)/\partial q_1 \partial q_2}{\left[-\partial^2 \pi_1(q_1, q_2)/\partial q_1^2\right]}. \tag{2.10}$$

The denominator on the right in (2.10) is positive by the second-order condition. It follows that the slope of firm 1's best-response function has the same sign as the numerator,

$$\frac{\partial^2 \pi_1(q_1, q_2)}{\partial q_1 \partial q_2} = \frac{\partial}{\partial q_2}\left[\frac{\partial \pi_1(q_1, q_2)}{\partial q_1}\right] = \frac{dp}{dQ} + q_1 \frac{d^2 p}{dQ^2}. \tag{2.11}$$

The first term on the right in (2.11), the slope of the demand curve, is negative. The second term, $d^2 p/dQ^2$, is negative for a concave inverse demand function, and zero for a linear inverse demand function. In such cases, the second-order cross-derivative (2.11) and the slope of the quantity best-response function are negative.[10] If the inverse demand

---

[9] Stackelberg (1934) developed an elaborate classification of configurations of best-response curves, upward- and downward-sloping. For reviews in English, see Hayward (1941), Peacock (1950), and Scherer (1996).

[10] Allen (1938, p. 346). For linear inverse demand, see figure 2.3 and Problem 2.1.

function is convex, d^2p/dQ^2 is positive and the slope of the quantity best-response function may be positive.

Following Bulow et al. (1985b), firm 2's output is defined to be a *strategic substitute* for firm 1's output if an increase in firm 2's output reduces firm 1's marginal profitability – if the second-order cross-derivative (2.11) is negative – and firm 2's output is defined to be a *strategic complement* to firm 1's output if an increase in firm 2's output increases firm 2's marginal profitability – if the second-order cross-derivative (2.11) is positive. From (2.10), firm 1's best-response curve slopes downward if outputs are strategic substitutes, upward if outputs are strategic complements.[11] The nature of strategic relationships among firms' choice variables is often a central factor determining the properties of oligopoly models.

There is a tendency to regard strategic substitutes and downward-sloping best-response curves as the normal case for quantity-setting oligopoly. It is certainly the most familiar case, holding for the widely used specification of linear demand and constant marginal cost.

But the three examples that follow show that it cannot be taken for granted that outputs are strategic substitutes, and best-response functions downward-sloping, in quantity-setting oligopoly. The first two examples involve well-behaved inverse demand curves and cost functions that yield quantity best-response curves that are upward-sloping over part or all of the relevant output range.[12] The final example pairs a well-behaved inverse demand function with a fourth-degree cost function to generate a model with multiple equilibria in which, in equilibrium, the best-response curve of one firm slopes upward while the best-response curve of the other firm slopes downward. In general, the nature of strategic relationships should be verified on a case-by-case basis.

2.4.1 Constant elasticity of demand

Let the equation of the inverse demand curve for a market supplied by two firms be

$$p = \left(\frac{a}{Q}\right)^{1/\varepsilon} = \left(\frac{a}{q_1 + q_2}\right)^{1/\varepsilon}, \tag{2.12}$$

for $\varepsilon > 1$.

If marginal and average cost are a constant c per unit, firm 1's profit is

$$\pi_1 = \left[\left(\frac{a}{q_1 + q_2}\right)^{1/\varepsilon} - c\right] q_1. \tag{2.13}$$

The first-order condition to maximize π_1 can be written (Problem 2.3):

$$\left(\frac{1}{q_1 + q_2}\right)^{1/\varepsilon} \left(1 - \frac{1}{\varepsilon}\frac{q_1}{q_1 + q_2}\right) = \frac{c}{a^{1/\varepsilon}}. \tag{2.14}$$

---

[11] The connection between strategic relationships and the properties of best-response functions was noted at various places in the literature before Bulow et al. (1985) highlighted its importance; see, for example, Scherer (1967, pp. 378–9).

[12] See Problem 2.5 for another such example.

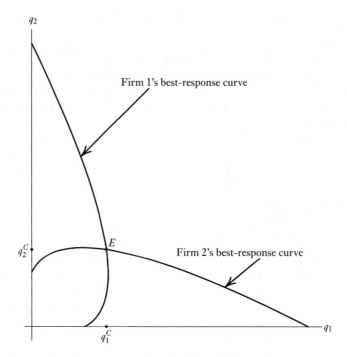

Figure 2.5 Cournot duopoly, constant price elasticity of demand. $a = 10$, $\varepsilon = 1.5$, $c = 1$; superscript C denotes the Cournot equilibrium value.

The second own-output derivative of π_1 is negative, so the second-order condition for profit maximization is satisfied. The second-order cross-output derivative is

$$\frac{\partial^2 \pi_1}{\partial q_1 \partial q_2} = \left(\frac{a}{q_1 + q_2}\right)^{1/\varepsilon} \frac{q_1 - \varepsilon q_2}{\varepsilon^2 (q_1 + q_2)^2}. \tag{2.15}$$

Equations (2.10) and (2.15) imply that the slope of firm 1's best-response curve has the same sign as $q_1 - \varepsilon q_2$. This is positive at the horizontal axis intercept ($q_2 = 0$), zero where the best-response curve intersects the line $q_1 = \varepsilon q_2$, and negative at the vertical axis ($q_1 = 0$). Imposing symmetry in (2.15), best-response curves are downward-sloping at the equilibrium output pair. These properties are illustrated in figure 2.5.[13]

2.4.2 Stackelberg example

Now consider the inverse exponential inverse demand function

$$p(Q) = 100e^{-(1/10)\sqrt{Q}} \tag{2.16}$$

[13] See Puu (1998) for discussion of Cournot and related oligopoly models when demand has constant price elasticity.

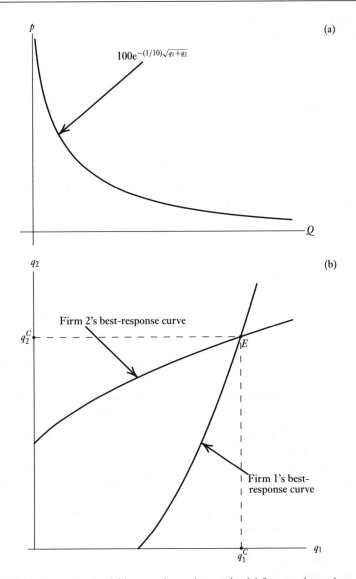

Figure 2.6 Stackelberg exponential inverse demand example. (a) Inverse demand curve; (b) best-response curves.

for $Q = q_1 + q_2$, from an example of Stackelberg (1934, pp. 126–30). Let average and marginal cost be zero. Figure 2.6(a) shows the inverse demand curve, which is convex.

Firm 1's profit is

$$\pi_1(q_1, q_2) = \left(100e^{-(1/10)\sqrt{q_1 + q_2}} \right) q_1. \tag{2.17}$$

With some manipulation (see Problem 2.4) the first-order condition to maximize π_1 gives the equation of firm 1's best-response function:

$$q_1 = 200 + 20\sqrt{100 + q_2}. \tag{2.18}$$

The upward-sloping best-response curves are shown in figure 2.6(b). Imposing symmetry in (2.18), equilibrium outputs are $q_1 = q_2 = 800$.

2.4.3   Amoroso example

This example is due to Amoroso (1921, pp. 258–63), and is discussed by Edgeworth (1922).[14] In a duopoly market, let the equation of the inverse demand curve be

$$p(Q) = \frac{450}{2 + Q}, \tag{2.19}$$

for $Q = q_1 + q_2$. The inverse demand curve is shown in figure 2.7(a).

Let the two firms have the same cost function,

$$c(q) = 30q - q^2 + \tfrac{1}{4}(q - 5)^2(q - 8)^2 = 400 - 230q + \tfrac{245}{4}q^2 - \tfrac{13}{2}q^3 + \tfrac{1}{4}q^4. \tag{2.20}$$

The implied average and marginal cost curves are shown in figure 2.7(b). The average cost curve appears to be well-behaved, and indeed has a shape that resembles common empirical results: average cost falls sharply as output rises for low output levels, and then is approximately level over a long range, eventually rising at high output levels. Marginal cost is negative at low output levels, and this might lead one to argue that the example should not be used to model behavior when output is in this range. Amoroso himself (1921, p. 258) limits the domain of the cost function to outputs greater than or equal to three. As we will see, equilibrium output levels lie outside the range over which marginal cost is negative.

Firm 1's profit function is a surface in (π_1, q_1, q_2)-space. Three cross-sections of this surface, for $q_2 = 2.5, 5, 8$, are shown in figure 2.8. Over this output range, firm 1's profit function has two local maxima. The global maximum is at a low output level when firm 2 produces either low (figure 2.8(a)) or high (figure 2.8(c)) output. Firm 1's profit is maximized for a high output level when firm 2 produces an intermediate output level (figure 2.8(b)).

The implied best-response function, shown in figure 2.9, shifts discontinuously upward at $q_2 = 2.66$ and discontinuously downward at $q_2 = 7.01$. The lower and middle sheaves of the best-response function are upward-sloping; the upper sheaf is downward-sloping.

Classical oligopoly theorists were inclined to assume continuity. Marshall put the phrase "Nature does not make leaps" on the title page of his *Principles*, in which he also wrote (1920, p. 409n) "In economics, as in physics, changes are generally continuous." In his seminal discussion of spatial duopoly, Hotelling (1929, p. 44) wrote that "a discontinuity, like a vacuum, is abhorred by nature."[15] In the Amoroso example, demand and cost change in a continuous way – as q_2 rises from low levels, the payoff at the left-hand local maximum falls

---

[14] The results of this section are obtained by numerical analysis.

[15] It is ironic that a central result of this paper is itself affected by an unrecognized discontinuity; see chapter 4.

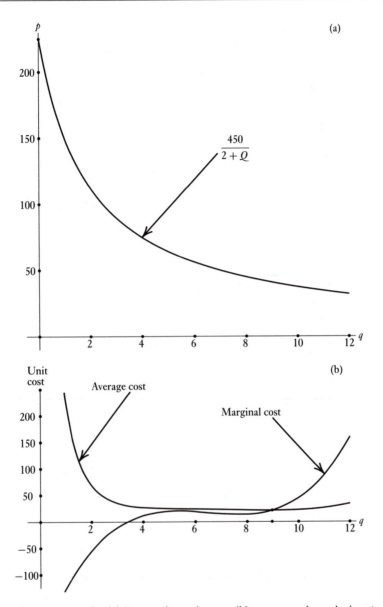

Figure 2.7 Amoroso example. (a) Inverse demand curve; (b) average and marginal cost curves.

continuously, and the payoff at the right-hand local maximum rises continuously. It is the behavior of the firm, taking these continuous changes into account, that is discontinuous.

This example has two pure-strategy Cournot equilibria, $(q_1, q_2) = (5, 8)$ and $(q_1, q_2) = (8, 5)$, as shown in figure 2.10. In each case, one firm produces along the upper sheaf of its best-response curve, while the other produces along the middle sheaf of its best-response

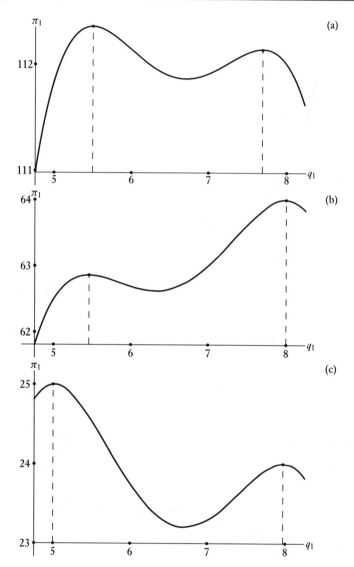

Figure 2.8 Firm 1's profit function, alternative q_2 levels, Amoroso example. (a) $q_2 = 2.5$; (b) $q_2 = 5$; (c) $q_2 = 8$.

curve. Thus at the $(q_1, q_2) = (8, 5)$ equilibrium, firm 1 is producing on the middle, positively sloped segment of its best-response curve; firm 2's output is a strategic complement for firm 1's output. Firm 2 operates on the right, downward-sloping segment of its best-response function: firm 1's output is a strategic substitute for firm 2's output. At the $(q_1, q_2) = (5, 8)$ equilibrium, these strategic relationships are reversed.

Multiple equilibria render the Cournot notion of equilibrium problematic. The two equilibria are symmetric and equivalent from the point of view of market performance, but the

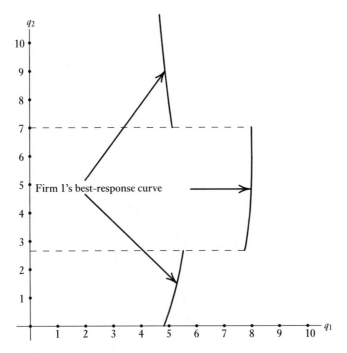

Figure 2.9   Firm 1's best-response curve, Amoroso example.

two equilibria are not equivalent as far as the firms are concerned: the firm that produces eight units of output makes a profit of 64, while the firm that produces five units of output makes a profit of 25.

How will one or the other output combination be settled upon? In the context of the classical interpretation of the Cournot model, one might appeal to the stairstep adjustment process (figure 2.3) as a local explanation for the choice among equilibria. This is satisfactory only in a limited sense: a large shock to outputs might cause the stairstep adjustment process to lead firms to jump discontinuously from one equilibrium to another.

The questions raised by the presence of multiple equilibria are equally troubling when the classical Cournot model is reformulated as a one-shot game; we take up this topic in section 3.2.

2.5   EXISTENCE

Industrial economists usually work with models in which it is natural to assume continuous cost and demand functions. Reasonable additional assumptions normally suffice to ensure the existence of a pure-strategy Cournot equilibrium.[16]

[16] In addition to the papers discussed in this section, see also McManus (1962, 1964b), Gabay and Moulin (1980), Kolstad and Mathiesen (1987), Balder (1995), and Svizzero (1997).

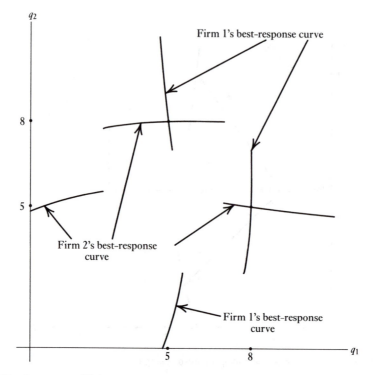

Figure 2.10 Cournot equilibria, Amoroso example.

The main assumptions of Frank and Quandt (1963) are that:

- there is a standardized product, the inverse demand function for which is continuous and bounded (there is a finite sales level at and above which price is zero)
- the cost function is continuous and strictly increasing
- firms' profit functions are concave

They apply the Kakutani fixed point theorem to show the existence of a Cournot equilibrium.[17]

Szidarovszky and Yakowitz (1977) prove the existence of equilibrium under the assumptions that inverse demand is downward-sloping and concave, while the cost function is increasing and convex. These assumptions together imply that the firm's profit function is concave.

Novshek's (1985) principal assumption is that a firm's marginal revenue falls as the output of all other firms rises. This assumption was made by Hahn (1962) in a discussion of stability

---

[17] MacManus (1964a–c) and Frank and Quandt (1964) debate whether a requirement to characterize an equilibrium as involving *n* firms should be that all *n* firms have positive output, an issue that is also touched upon by Fisher (1961).

in the Cournot model. Considering (2.11), the Hahn–Novshek assumption is equivalent to assuming that outputs are strategic substitutes.

Collie (1992) examines the question of existence of equilibrium for international trade in imperfectly competitive markets – segmented Cournot markets supplied by firms based in two countries. This approach has applications beyond the specific context in which it is developed, applying whenever firms fall into well-defined groups (vertically integrated and not; patent-holding and not; cartel member or fringe member). His assumptions are as follows:

- continuous, twice differentiable inverse demand with bounded industry revenue
- a condition on the curvature of demand that is weaker than strict concavity[18]
- stability

Although the kinds of assumptions mentioned will not be restrictive in basic models, existence cannot be taken for granted. Novshek (1985) gives examples of the failure of existence of equilibrium in Cournot models when inverse demand is not concave and cost functions are not convex.[19]

2.6 STABILITY

Stability analysis is of interest for its own sake. It is also a source of restrictions that allow one to sign the comparative static properties of oligopoly equilibrium (Seade, 1980a, p. 483):[20]

> It is natural to disregard unstable equilibria as being unobservable, in particular in the context of a comparative-statics exercise, where any possible initial unstable equilibrium would be lost when perturbed and would not be regained subsequently.

We review two versions of continuous-time[21] local stability analysis.

---

[18] This curvature condition is independently derived by Schlee (1993a,b).

[19] For examination of conditions for the existence of a Cournot equilibrium when payoff functions are not concave, see Roberts and Sonnenschein (1976).

[20] For a critique of this position, see Friedman (1983b, p. 40), who argues in favor of carrying out stability analysis in fully formulated dynamic models:

> It has been common in economics to investigate the stability of static models. Such analysis inherently involves a logical contradiction, because stability is a dynamic property. Therefore, it cannot actually be studied in a static setting. This problem is dodged by the unsatisfactory expedient of grafting ad hoc dynamic assumptions onto the static model and examining the stability property of the resulting ill-formed dynamic model.

[21] The Cournot adjustment process has a tendency to instability in discrete-time models; see Theocharis (1959–60), Fisher (1961), Hahn (1962), and Bishop (1962).

2.6.1 Adjustment to equilibrium

Let (q_1^*, q_2^*) be a Cournot equilibrium pair of outputs. Suppose that if firms are producing outputs (q_1, q_2) in the neighborhood of (q_1^*, q_2^*), firm i changes its output over time at a rate proportional to its marginal profitability,

$$\frac{dq_i}{dt} = k_i \frac{\partial \pi_i(q_1, q_2)}{\partial q_i}, \tag{2.21}$$

for $k_i > 0$ and $i = 1, 2$. That is, if it is profitable to expand output, the firm expands output, at a rate that is proportional to marginal profitability.

Let $i = 1$ and take a local linear approximation to (2.21) around (q_1^*, q_2^*):[22]

$$\frac{dq_1}{dt} = k_1 \frac{\partial \pi_1(q_1^*, q_2^*)}{\partial q_1} + k_1 \left[\frac{\partial^2 \pi_1(q_1^*, q_2^*)}{\partial q_1^2}(q_1 - q_1^*) + \frac{\partial^2 \pi_1(q_1^*, q_2^*)}{\partial q_1 \partial q_2}(q_2 - q_2^*) \right]. \tag{2.22}$$

The first term on the right in (2.22) is zero by the first-order condition. Proceeding in the same way for $i = 2$, the system of adjustment equations can be written in matrix form as

$$\begin{pmatrix} dq_1/dt \\ dq_2/dt \end{pmatrix} = \begin{pmatrix} k_1 & 0 \\ 0 & k_2 \end{pmatrix} \begin{pmatrix} \dfrac{\partial^2 \pi_1(q_1^*, q_2^*)}{\partial q_1^2} & \dfrac{\partial^2 \pi_1(q_1^*, q_2^*)}{\partial q_1 \partial q_2} \\ \dfrac{\partial^2 \pi_2(q_1^*, q_2^*)}{\partial q_1 \partial q_2} & \dfrac{\partial^2 \pi_2(q_1^*, q_2^*)}{\partial q_2^2} \end{pmatrix} \begin{pmatrix} q_1 - q_1^* \\ q_2 - q_2^* \end{pmatrix}. \tag{2.23}$$

Stability requires that the Jacobian matrix has a negative trace and a positive determinant. A sufficient condition for the trace to be negative is that the second-order conditions for profit maximization be met, since this means that each diagonal element is negative.

A sufficient condition for the determinant to be positive,

$$\frac{\partial^2 \pi_1(q_1^*, q_2^*)}{\partial q_1^2} \frac{\partial^2 \pi_2(q_1^*, q_2^*)}{\partial q_2^2} - \frac{\partial^2 \pi_1(q_1^*, q_2^*)}{\partial q_1 \partial q_2} \frac{\partial^2 \pi_2(q_1^*, q_2^*)}{\partial q_1 \partial q_2} > 0, \tag{2.24}$$

is that own-output effects on marginal profit be greater in magnitude than cross-output effects,

$$\left| \frac{\partial^2 \pi_i(q_1^*, q_2^*)}{\partial q_i^2} \right| > \left| \frac{\partial}{\partial q_j} \left[\frac{\partial \pi_i(q_1^*, q_2^*)}{\partial q_i} \right] \right|, \tag{2.25}$$

for $i, j = 1, 2$ and $j \neq i$. Thus the second-order conditions together with (2.25) are sufficient for equilibrium to be stable.

---

[22] For general discussions or applications of this methodology, see Samuelson (1947, p. 263, pp. 270–6), Chiang (3rd edn, 1984, pp. 641–5), Huang and Crooke (1997, pp. 586–99), and, in the context of oligopoly models, Dixit (1986).

2.6.2   Cournotian adjustment

Cournot's behavioral assumption was that each firm observes the output of the other and picks its own output to maximize its own profit. If firm 2's current output is q_2, firm 1's best-response output $\hat{q}_1(q_2)$ is defined implicitly by the first-order condition:

$$\frac{\partial \pi_1(\hat{q}_1, q_2)}{\partial q_1} = 0. \tag{2.26}$$

$\hat{q}_2(q_1)$ is determined in the same way.

Following Seade (1980b), if firms move toward their best-response functions with proportionality factors $k_1, k_2 > 0$, the adjustment equations are

$$\begin{pmatrix} \dfrac{dq_1}{dt} \\ \dfrac{dq_2}{dt} \end{pmatrix} = \begin{pmatrix} k_1 & 0 \\ 0 & k_2 \end{pmatrix} \begin{pmatrix} \hat{q}_1(q_2) - q_1 \\ \hat{q}_2(q_1) - q_2 \end{pmatrix}. \tag{2.27}$$

If a firm's profit-maximizing output is greater than its current output, it increases its output, at a rate that is proportional to the difference between current and profit-maximizing output. In this formulation, firms adjust output toward their best-response functions; in the previous formulation, firms adjust output toward equilibrium.

To linearize the adjustment equations around (q_1^*, q_2^*), note that

$$\hat{q}_1(q_2) - q_1 \approx \hat{q}_1(q_2^*) - q_1^* + \frac{\partial[\hat{q}_1(q_2) - q_1]}{\partial q_1}\bigg|_* (q_1 - q_1^*) + \frac{\partial[\hat{q}_1(q_2) - q_2]}{\partial q_2}\bigg|_* (q_2 - q_2^*)$$

$$= (-1)(q_1 - q_1^*) + \frac{d\hat{q}_1}{dq_2}\bigg|_* (q_2 - q_2^*), \tag{2.28}$$

where an asterisk indicates that the expression is evaluated at the equilibrium output pair.

The linearized adjustment equations are

$$\begin{pmatrix} \dfrac{dq_1}{dt} \\ \dfrac{dq_2}{dt} \end{pmatrix} \approx \begin{pmatrix} k_1 & 0 \\ 0 & k_2 \end{pmatrix} \begin{pmatrix} -1 & \dfrac{d\hat{q}_1}{dq_2}\bigg|_* \\ \dfrac{d\hat{q}_2}{dq_1}\bigg|_* & -1 \end{pmatrix} \begin{pmatrix} q_1 - q_1^* \\ q_2 - q_2^* \end{pmatrix}. \tag{2.29}$$

The trace of the central matrix on the right is negative. Stability also requires that the determinant of this matrix be positive:

$$\det \begin{pmatrix} -1 & \dfrac{d\hat{q}_1}{dq_2}\bigg|_* \\ \dfrac{d\hat{q}_2}{dq_1}\bigg|_* & -1 \end{pmatrix} = 1 - \left(\frac{d\hat{q}_1}{dq_2}\bigg|_*\right)\left(\frac{d\hat{q}_2}{dq_1}\bigg|_*\right) > 0. \tag{2.30}$$

A sufficient condition for (2.30) is that the slope of the best-response functions in the neighborhood of equilibrium be less than 1 in absolute value:

$$\left|\frac{d\hat{q}_1}{dq_2}\right|_* < 1, \qquad \left.\frac{d\hat{q}_2}{dq_1}\right|_* < 1. \tag{2.31}$$

Stability conditions expressed in terms of the slopes of best-response curves have been applied, for example, in the context of noncooperative research and development (d'Aspremont and Jacquemin, 1988; Henriques, 1990).

Using (2.10) to express (2.31) in terms of the second derivatives of the profit functions gives an alternative version of the stability condition (2.30):

$$1 - \left[-\frac{\partial^2\pi_1(\hat{q}_1, q_2)/\partial q_1 \partial q_2}{\partial^2\pi_1(\hat{q}_1, q_2)/\partial q_1^2}\right]_* \left[-\frac{\partial^2\pi_2(\hat{q}_1, q_2)/\partial q_1 \partial q_2}{\partial^2\pi_2(\hat{q}_1, q_2)/\partial q_2^2}\right]_* > 0. \tag{2.32}$$

The product of the second derivatives in the denominators is positive, which makes it possible to multiply through (2.32) by the denominators without changing the sense of the inequality. This converts (2.32) to (2.24). Thus the two approaches to stability analysis, although they involve different stories about out-of-equilibrium adjustment, lead to the same place as far as stability conditions are concerned.

2.7 COMPARATIVE STATICS: THE NUMBER OF FIRMS

We now examine the comparative static properties of the Cournot model as the number of firms increases.[23] Assume that there are n firms in the market, all with the same cost function.[24] Firm i's profit is

$$\pi_i = p(Q)q_i - c(q_i), \tag{2.33}$$

where Q is total output.

With Cournot behavior, the first- and second-order conditions for profit maximization are

$$\frac{\partial\pi_i}{\partial q_i} = p + q_i\frac{dp(Q)}{dQ} - \frac{dc(q_i)}{dq_i} = 0 \tag{2.34}$$

and

$$\frac{\partial^2\pi_i}{\partial q_i^2} = 2\frac{dp(Q)}{dQ} + q_i\frac{dp^2(Q)}{dQ^2} - \frac{d^2c(q_i)}{dq_i^2} < 0 \tag{2.35}$$

respectively (which generalize (2.4) and (2.5) from the case of 2 to n firms).

---

[23] This section follows Ruffin (1971).

[24] For a given number of firms, it is straightforward to deal with the case in which firms have different cost functions; see Problem 2.1 for the case of linear demand and constant marginal cost. For a discussion of limiting behavior, it is convenient to assume identical costs for all firms, which allows us to focus on the change in market performance as the number of firms increases without having to model the costs of entering firms.

In equilibrium, all firms will have the same output (q). Substitute $q_i = q$ in (2.34) to obtain a condensed first-order condition,

$$p(Q) + q\frac{dp(Q)}{dQ} - \frac{dc(q)}{dq} = 0, \tag{2.36}$$

where the relation between industry output and firm output is

$$Q - nq = 0. \tag{2.37}$$

Treating the number of firms as a continuous variable,[25] differentiate (2.36) and (2.37) with respect to n, to obtain the system of equations

$$\begin{pmatrix} \dfrac{dp(Q)}{dQ} + q\dfrac{d^2p(Q)}{dQ^2} & \dfrac{dp(Q)}{dQ} - \dfrac{d^2c(q)}{dq^2} \\[2mm] 1 & -n \end{pmatrix} \begin{pmatrix} \dfrac{dQ}{dn} \\[2mm] \dfrac{dq}{dn} \end{pmatrix} = \begin{pmatrix} 0 \\ q \end{pmatrix}. \tag{2.38}$$

The determinant of the matrix on the left in (2.38) is

$$DET = -n\left[\frac{dp(Q)}{dQ} + q\frac{d^2p(Q)}{dQ^2}\right] - \left[\frac{dp(Q)}{dQ} - \frac{d^2c(q)}{dq^2}\right]. \tag{2.39}$$

There are several ways to sign DET. The first term in brackets on the right in (2.39) is

$$\frac{dp(Q)}{dQ} + q\frac{d^2p(Q)}{dQ^2} = \left.\frac{\partial MR_i}{\partial Q_{-i}}\right|_*, \tag{2.40}$$

where $Q_{-i} = Q - q_i$ is the combined output of all firms except for i.

This is negative if, in equilibrium, firm i's marginal revenue falls as the output of all other firms rises, which is the Hahn–Novshek stability condition.

The second term in brackets on the right is negative,

$$\frac{dp(Q)}{dQ} - \frac{d^2c(q)}{dq^2} < 0, \tag{2.41}$$

if the inverse demand curve is downward-sloping ($dp(Q)/dQ < 0$) and marginal cost is nondecreasing ($d^2c(q)/dq^2 \geq 0$).

Hence, if the Hahn–Novshek condition is met, if the inverse demand curve is downward-sloping, and if marginal cost is nondecreasing, the determinant of the coefficient matrix on the left in (2.38) is positive.

---

[25] Seade (1980a, p. 482):

> if ξ is any dependent variable defined on the number of firms n, its change when one firm enters is $\Delta\xi = \int_n^{n+1} \xi'(v)\,dv$. It is clear that (sign $\Delta\xi$) = (sign $\xi'(v)$) whenever the latter sign does not change in the relevant range $(n, n+1)$ .... It is essentially this single-signedness assumption, which one can check, that underlies the common continuous treatment of discrete variables in problems of the present sort.

Alternatively, rewrite (2.39) as

$$-(n-1)\left[\frac{\mathrm{d}p(Q)}{\mathrm{d}Q}+q\frac{\mathrm{d}^2p(Q)}{\mathrm{d}Q^2}\right]-\left[2\frac{\mathrm{d}p(Q)}{\mathrm{d}Q}+q\frac{\mathrm{d}^2p(Q)}{\mathrm{d}Q^2}-\frac{\mathrm{d}^2c(q)}{\mathrm{d}q^2}\right]. \tag{2.42}$$

The Hahn–Novshek condition once again suffices to make the first term in brackets in (2.42) negative. The second term in brackets in (2.42) is the second-order condition for profit maximization. This alternative combination of conditions is also sufficient to make *DET* positive.

Solving (2.38) gives expressions for the comparative static derivatives:

$$\frac{\mathrm{d}Q}{\mathrm{d}n}=-\frac{q}{DET}\left[\frac{\mathrm{d}p(Q)}{\mathrm{d}Q}-\frac{\mathrm{d}^2c(q)}{\mathrm{d}q^2}\right]>0, \tag{2.43}$$

$$\frac{\mathrm{d}q}{\mathrm{d}n}=\frac{q}{DET}\left[\frac{\mathrm{d}p(Q)}{\mathrm{d}Q}+q\frac{\mathrm{d}^2p(Q)}{\mathrm{d}Q^2}\right]=\frac{q}{DET}\left.\frac{\partial MR_i}{\partial Q_{-i}}\right|_*<0, \tag{2.44}$$

using (2.40). If firm i's equilibrium marginal revenue falls as the output of all other firms rises, equilibrium output per firm falls as the number of firms increases.

Given otherwise good behavior on the part of cost and demand functions, conditions that are commonly assumed to obtain stability also ensure that output increases – market performance improves – as the number of firms increases.[26]

2.8 LIMITING BEHAVIOR

That market performance improves as the number of firms increases does not mean that market performance approaches that of perfect competition in the limit as the number of firms goes to infinity.[27]

To examine the issues involved, we consider an example due to Ruffin (1971). Let inverse demand function be linear,

$$p(Q)=a-bQ, \tag{2.45}$$

where Q is total output, and let the technology be described by a firm-level cubic cost function without fixed cost:

$$C(q)=cq-dq^2+eq^3. \tag{2.46}$$

Here, a, b, c, d, $e\geq0$. Assume also that $a-c>0$ and $d>b$; the reasons for these assumptions will be brought out below.

Figure 2.11(a) shows typical average and marginal cost curves for this example.

---

[26] See also Seade (1980a, p. 483), and see Frank and Quandt (1963, pp. 94–6) for a Cournot example in which conditions of the kind presented here fail and an increase in the number of firms worsens market performance.

[27] See also Amir and Lambson (2000).

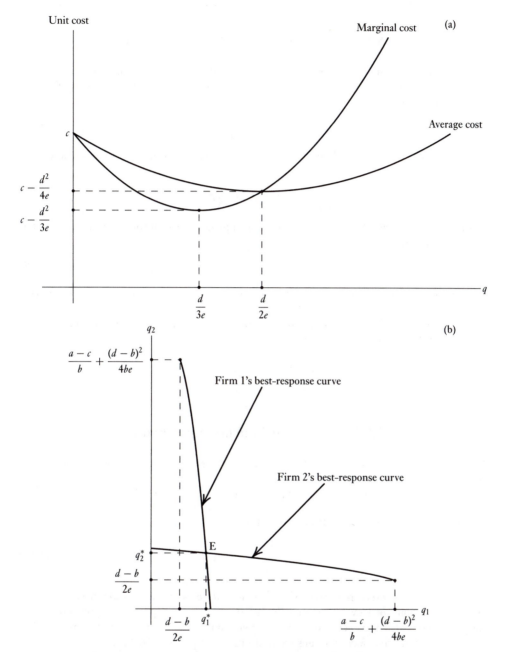

Figure 2.11 Ruffin duopoly example: $p = a - bQ$, $C(q) = cq - dq^2 + eq^3$. (a) Average and marginal cost curves, $C(q) = cq - dq^2 + eq^3$; (b) best-response curves.

2.8.1   Long-run competitive equilibrium

In long-run competitive equilibrium, firms act as price-takers, and the number of firms adjusts so that price is equal to marginal and average cost. Thus the long-run equilibrium price is (see figure 2.11(a))

$$p_c^{lr} = c - \frac{d^2}{4e}. \tag{2.47}$$

At this price, the quantity demanded is (using the equation of the inverse demand curve)

$$Q_c^{lr} = \frac{a - c}{b} + \frac{d^2}{4be}. \tag{2.48}$$

In long-run competitive equilibrium, each firm produces the output that makes marginal cost equal to price,

$$q_c^{lr} = \frac{d}{2e}, \tag{2.49}$$

and this is the output (sometimes called *minimum efficient scale* output) that minimizes average cost.

The long-run equilibrium number of firms makes economic profit per firm equal to zero. Under perfect competition, this is[28]

$$n_c^{lr} = \frac{Q_c^{lr}}{q_c^{lr}} = \left(\frac{a - c}{b} + \frac{d^2}{4be} \right) \frac{2e}{d} = \left(\frac{2e}{d} \right) \frac{a - c}{b} + \frac{d}{2b}. \tag{2.50}$$

2.8.2   Long-run Cournot equilibrium

Writing $Q_{-i} = Q - q_i$ for the combined output of all firms except firm i, firm i's profit is

$$\pi_i = p(Q)q_i - c(q_i) = [a - c + (d - b)q_i - eq_i^2 - bQ_{-i}]q_i. \tag{2.51}$$

From (2.51), marginal profit from zero output is

$$\left. \frac{\partial \pi_i}{\partial q_i} \right|_{q_i = 0} = a - c > 0. \tag{2.52}$$

a, the vertical-axis intercept of the inverse demand curve, is the reservation price, the value, from a social point of view, of the first (incremental) unit of output. c, marginal cost when output is zero, is the social cost of the first incremental unit of output. The assumption that $a - c > 0$ implies that society values the first unit of output more than the marginal cost of its cost of production. In the absence of fixed cost, this guarantees that it will be profitable for at least one firm to produce positive output.

---

[28] More precisely, the long-run equilibrium number of firms is the greatest integer less than or equal to the value given by (2.50).

The first-order condition to maximize (2.51), which is the equation of firm i's best-response function in implicit form, is

$$\frac{\partial \pi_i}{\partial q_i} = a - c + (d - b)q_i - eq_i^2 - bQ_{-i} + q_i(d - b - 2eq_i) = 0. \qquad (2.53)$$

It follows from (2.53) that, anywhere along its best-response function, and in particular in equilibrium, firm i's profit is

$$\pi_i = 2eq_i^2 \left(q_i - \frac{d - b}{2e} \right). \qquad (2.54)$$

Hence firm i's profit is zero if its equilibrium output is zero (given the structures of demand and of cost, this should be expected) or $(d - b)/2e$. The assumption that $d - b > 0$ ensures that this second zero-equilibrium-profit output is positive, and that there is a positive number of firms that will drive equilibrium firm profit to zero (this is the number of firms that makes equilibrium firm output equal to $(d - b)/2e$).

The second-order condition sufficient for (2.53) to identify a maximum is

$$\frac{\partial^2 \pi_i}{\partial q_i^2} = -6e \left(q_i - \frac{d - b}{3e} \right) < 0. \qquad (2.55)$$

The second-order condition is satisfied for $q_i > (d - b)/3e$. From (2.54), the equilibrium output at which firm i's profit goes to zero lies within the output range over which the second-order condition is satisfied.

The equation of firm i's first-order condition, (2.53), can be rewritten as

$$\left(q_1 - \frac{d - b}{3e} \right)^2 = \frac{b}{3e} \left[\frac{a - c}{b} + \frac{(d - b)^2}{3be} - Q_{-1} \right], \qquad (2.56)$$

showing that firm 1's best-response curve is a parabola.

Best-response curves for the two–firm case are shown in figure 2.11(b). If firm 2 produces nothing, firm 1 is a monopolist, and maximizes profit by producing its monopoly output. This is the horizontal-axis intercept of firm 1's best-response curve. As firm 2's output increases, firm 1's profit-maximizing output and profit fall. If firm 2's output is sufficiently great,

$$\frac{a - c}{b} + \frac{(d - b)^2}{4be},$$

firm 1's profit-maximizing output is $(d - b)/2e$, which by (2.54) yields firm 1 zero profit. For larger values of q_2, firm 1 shuts down; its best-response function shifts discontinuously from the parabola with equation (2.56) to the vertical axis (the line $q_1 = 0$).

In long-run equilibrium, profit per firm is zero. Long-run Cournot equilibrium output per firm is less than long-run output per firm under perfect competition:

$$q_{\text{Cour}}^{\text{lr}} = \frac{d - b}{2e} < \frac{d}{2e} = q_{\text{c}}^{\text{lr}}. \tag{2.57}$$

The long-run Cournot price is average cost for the long-run Cournot output, and therefore greater than price in long-run competitive equilibrium:

$$p_{\text{Cour}}^{\text{lr}} = c - \frac{d^2 - b^2}{4e} > c - \frac{d^2}{4e} = p_{\text{c}}^{\text{lr}}. \tag{2.58}$$

The profit-maximizing oligopolist operates on the downward-sloping segment of the average cost curve, and the number of firms adjusts so that the residual demand curve of any one firm is tangent to its average cost curve at its profit-maximizing output. Thus, in figure 2.11(a), long-run output per firm occurs where the slope of the average cost curve is $-b$, the slope of the residual inverse demand curve.

At the price $p_{\text{Cour}}^{\text{lr}}$ the quantity demanded is

$$Q_{\text{Cour}}^{\text{lr}} = \frac{a - c}{b} + \frac{d^2 - b^2}{4be}. \tag{2.59}$$

This is long-run Cournot equilibrium output.

By subtraction, Cournot long-run equilibrium output is less than long-run equilibrium output under perfect competition:

$$Q_{\text{c}}^{\text{lr}} - Q_{\text{Cour}}^{\text{lr}} = \frac{b}{4e} > 0. \tag{2.60}$$

The Cournot long-run equilibrium number of firms is[29]

$$n_{\text{Cour}}^{\text{lr}} = \frac{Q_{\text{Cour}}^{\text{lr}}}{q_{\text{Cour}}^{\text{lr}}} = \left(\frac{a - c}{b} + \frac{d^2 - b^2}{4be} \right) \frac{2e}{d - b} = \frac{2e}{d - b} \frac{a - c}{b} + \frac{d + b}{2b}. \tag{2.61}$$

By subtraction (ignoring integer problems), the long-run Cournot number of firms exceeds the long-run perfect competition number of firms:

$$n_{\text{Cour}}^{\text{lr}} - n_{\text{c}}^{\text{lr}} = 2e \frac{a - c}{d - b} + \tfrac{1}{2} > 0. \tag{2.62}$$

This is our first encounter with the general phenomenon of excess entry in long-run equilibrium in imperfectly competitive markets.

---

[29] Once again, in a strict sense the long-run equilibrium number of firms is the greatest integer less than or equal to the value given by (2.61).

2.8.3   Recapitulation

Firms exercise market power in Cournot oligopoly equilibrium. The economic profit that this creates for $n < n_{\text{Cour}}^{\text{lr}}$ attracts entrants until profit per firm is driven to zero. The resulting long-run Cournot equilibrium number of firms exceeds the number that would be socially optimal if firms acted as price-takers – inequality (2.62) – even though long-run Cournot equilibrium output falls short of long-run perfectly competitive equilibrium output – inequality (2.60).

The essential requirement for a Cournot oligopoly to converge to the perfectly competitive outcome as the number of firms becomes large is that there be no initial downward-sloping segment of the average cost curve – no economies of scale. For such technologies, the number of firms can go to infinity under either perfect competition or Cournot oligopoly. In the limit, each firm produces an infinitesimal output, with price equal to the minimum value of average cost, and total output equal to the quantity demanded at that price.

2.9   CONCLUSION

At the end of the Preface to the first edition of his *Principles*, Marshall (1920, p. xi) wrote that "Cournot's genius must give a new mental activity to everyone who passes through his hands." Marshall went on to advise against too great a reliance on the mathematical method,[30] but Cournot's methodology, as well as his substantive contributions, have overcome initial inattention and subsequent rejection to become the fundamental framework for the analysis of imperfectly competitive markets.

Classical oligopoly theorists explored and made more precise the conditions under which the results Cournot claimed for his oligopoly model hold. In chapter 3, we move on to early extensions of the Cournot model – conjectural variations and product differentiation. The first topic leads to a consideration of the relation between the classical and the game-theoretic versions of the Cournot model. The second leads to discussion of Bertrand's (1883) criticism of Cournot and to models of price-setting oligopoly.

PROBLEMS

2.1 Let a market have linear inverse demand curve with equation

$$p = a - bQ.$$

  (a) Find Cournot equilibrium price, output, and output per firm if the market is supplied by n firms, each with constant marginal and average cost c per unit.
  (b) Find Cournot equilibrium price, output, and output per firm if the constant marginal and average cost of firm i is c_i. (Without loss of generality, let $c_1 \leq c_2 \leq \cdots \leq c_n$ and (hint) write $\bar{c} = (1/n)\sum_1^n c_i$ for the industry-average value of unit cost.)

---

[30] "Yet it seems doubtful whether any one spends his time well in reading lengthy translations of economic doctrines into mathematics, that have not been made by himself."

2.2 (Stigler, 1940) In a duopoly market, let the equation of the inverse demand curve be

$$p(q_1 + q_2) = 85 - \tfrac{1}{20}(q_1 + q_2),$$

and let the cost functions of the two firms be

$$c_1(q_1) = 3000 + 9q_1 + \tfrac{1}{200}q_1^2$$

and

$$c_2(q_2) = 3500 + 8q_2 + \tfrac{1}{200}q_2^2$$

respectively.

   (a)   Find the equations of the best-response functions, identifying the levels of rival firm output at which each firm would shut down because its maximum profit would be negative if it produced positive output. Graph the best-response functions on the same diagram; indicate the Cournot equilibrium point.
   (b)   Find the Cournot equilibrium outputs by solving the equations of the best-response functions. What are the Cournot equilibrium price, consumer surplus, and net social welfare?

2.3 (Constant elasticity of demand) In a duopoly market, let the equation of the demand curve be

$$Q = ap^{-\varepsilon},$$

for $Q = q_1 + q_2$ and $a > 0$, $\varepsilon > 1$. Let average and marginal cost be $c > 0$.
   Discuss the shape of the best-response curves; find the equilibrium outputs.

2.4 (Stackelberg, 1934, p. 126) In a duopoly market, let the equation of the inverse demand curve be

$$p = 100e^{-(1/10)\sqrt{Q}},$$

for $Q = q_1 + q_2$. Let average and marginal cost be zero.
   Discuss the shape of the best-response curves; find the Cournot equilibrium outputs.

2.5 In a duopoly market, let the equation of the inverse demand curve be

$$p(Q) = \frac{a}{1 + bQ},$$

for $Q = q_1 + q_2$ and $a, b > 0$. Let average and marginal cost be c, with $0 \le c < a$.
   Discuss the shape of the best-response curves; find the Cournot equilibrium outputs.

CHAPTER THREE

FOUNDATIONS OF OLIGOPOLY THEORY II

Anything goes.

Cole Porter

3.1 INTRODUCTION

We begin this chapter with a game-theoretic reformulation of the Cournot model. What the game-theoretic version of the Cournot model has that the classical version does not is a precise specification of what firms (players) do, when they do it, and what they know while they are doing it. The game-theoretic version of the Cournot model leads to discussions of conjectural variations, consistent conjectures, and of the relation between Cournot and Nash equilibrium concepts.

A review of two common representative consumer models of product differentiation lays the foundation for consideration of the Cournot model with product differentiation, of Bertrand's (1883) criticism of Cournot, and of the models of price-setting oligopoly that follow in Bertrand's wake. The chapter concludes with a comparison of quantity-setting and price-setting oligopoly models and with discussions of the supply-function oligopoly model (which generalizes the Cournot and Bertrand models to conditions of uncertain demand), and of two-stage models of capacity-constrained price-setting oligopoly.

3.2 COURNOT DUOPOLY AS A STATIC GAME

In its game-theoretic incarnation,[1] the Cournot model is a simultaneous move, one-shot, noncooperative game. An extensive form for Cournot duopoly is shown in figure 3.1. Moving at decision node D_1, firm 1 picks its output q_1 from the strategy space $Q = [0, \bar{q}]$. $\bar{q}$ may be

---

[1] Following Daughety (1988, pp. 7–11). For other such formulations, see Friedman (1986, pp. 54–7), Rasmussen (1989, pp. 76–8), and Gibbons (1992, pp. 14–21).

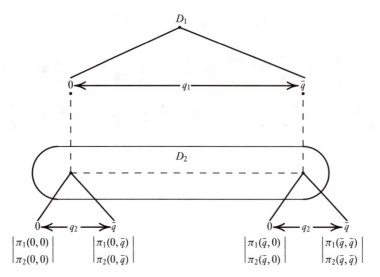

Figure 3.1 The extensive form of the Cournot game.

taken to be the smallest output level for which price along the inverse demand curve is zero. We assume that there is such an output level, and that it is finite.

Moving at information set D_2, and not knowing firm 1's output choice because the two firms move simultaneously, firm 2 also picks its output q_2 from the strategy space Q. Payoffs $\pi_1(q_1, q_2)$ and $\pi_2(q_1, q_2)$ are functions of the outputs chosen by both firms. The payoff vectors shown in figure 3.1 below the extremes of firm 2's information set bound the range of possible payoff vectors for all admissable output combinations.

The one-shot Cournot game can also be written in normal or strategic form as the triple $(N, [0, \bar{q}] \times [0, \bar{q}], \pi)$, where $N = (1, 2)$ is the set of players, $[0, \bar{q}] \times [0, \bar{q}]$ is the strategy space, and $\pi = (\pi_1, \pi_2)$ as the vector of payoff functions.

Each firm knows its own strategy set and the strategy set of its rival. Each firm knows that both firms move simultaneously, and knows that the other firm knows this, and so on. Each firm seeks to maximize its own profit and knows that the other firm does the same, and so on. The structure of the game is common knowledge.

Cournot equilibrium is defined as the Nash equilibrium of this one-shot game: (q_1^C, q_2^C) is an equilibrium if

$$\pi_1(q_1^C, q_2^C) \geq \pi_1(q_1, q_2^C) \,\forall\, q_1 \in Q,$$
$$\pi_2(q_1^C, q_2^C) \geq \pi_2(q_1^C, q_2) \,\forall\, q_2 \in Q. \tag{3.1}$$

Each firm's Nash equilibrium output maximizes its profit, given the equilibrium output of the other firm.

When the Cournot model is viewed as a one-shot game, the classical oligopoly literature contains what appears to be a mishmash of interpretative statements that either try to give the Cournot model a dynamic gloss or else criticize dynamic stories about the Cournot model. For example, each firm maximizes its own profit, taking the output of the other firm as given;

or, each firm assumes that the other does not react to what it does, although it bases its own output decisions on the output of the other. At heart, these are statements about dynamic behavior, and the common knowledge assumption rules them out in the context of a one-shot game.

From a game-theoretic perspective, figure 2.3 and the stability story that accompanies it are out of place in discussions of the Cournot model. A firm's Cournot equilibrium output maximizes the firm's profit, given the equilibrium output of the other firm. This definition has nothing to say about the output that a firm would choose if its rival were to produce some non-equilibrium output level; to address that question requires a dynamic model.

In a one-shot game, neither firm maximizes its profit taking the output of the other as given, because outputs are chosen simultaneously. Likewise, neither firm reacts to the choice of the other: firms select outputs with the same (complete and perfect) information, with the same (unlimited) computing ability, and they do so simultaneously. From the game-theoretic perspective (Johansen, 1982), in a one-shot game each firm analyzes what it knows about its own situation and also analyzes what it knows about the situation of the other firm (which is everything that the other firm knows) and picks its Nash–Cournot equilibrium output because it has fully analyzed the game and is able to work out the Nash equilibrium output level.

A similar viewpoint appears in Nash's dissertation, discussing the equilibrium of a one-shot game (1950, p. 23; quoted by Leonard, 1994, p. 502):

> By using the principles that a rational prediction should be unique, that the players should be able to deduce and make use of it, and that such knowledge on the part of each player of what to expect the others to do should not lead him to act out of conformity with the prediction, one is led to the concept of a solution defined before . . . . In this interpretation we need to assume the players know the full structure of the game in order to be able to deduce the prediction for themselves. It is quite strongly a rationalistic and idealizing interpretation.

Cournot equilibrium is defined as *the* Nash equilibrium of the one-shot Cournot game. Multiple equilibria raise problems for the Nash equilibrium concept when the Cournot model is treated as a one-shot noncooperative game (Johansen, 1982, p. 437):

> When the equilibrium is unique, all players solve the same problem, determining all actions, and they all reach the same result, thus predicting other players' actions correctly in the same operation as they determine their own actions. When there are several equilibria and they are not interchangeable, so that it matters which action is taken from among the equilibrium sets, then each player will be unable to predict the decisions of other players unless we introduce some further elements into the theory.

Classical oligopoly theorists criticized the Cournot model (as they conceived it) because its assumptions required firms to behave stupidly, myopically, to assume that rivals behave in one way while they themselves behave in another, to be unable to learn. It is possible to criticize the noncooperative game theory approach to modeling imperfectly competitive markets on opposite grounds, that it assumes players to have unrealistically complete knowledge and unrealistically sophisticated computational ability (Mailath, 1998, p. 1347):

> Noncooperative game theory, like neoclassical economics, is built on two heroic assumptions: *Maximization* – every economic agent is a rational decision maker with a clear understanding

of the world; and *consistency* – the agent's understanding, in particular, expectations, of other agents' behavior, is correct (i.e., the overall pattern of individual optimizing behavior forms a Nash equilibrium) . . . .

   A major challenge facing noncooperative game theorists today is that of providing a compelling justification for these two assumptions . . . . without such justification, the use of game theory in applications is problematic.

One such justification might be to argue that one would expect noncooperative equilibrium to describe the behavior of experienced or long-lived players.[2] Another (Myerson, 1999) is to argue that the rationality assumptions that underlie the Nash equilibrium concept are appropriate when the use of the model is to analyze the performance of social institutions. Other responses are to explicitly model learning or to develop explicitly dynamic models to describe dynamic behavior.

3.3   STATIC VERSUS DYNAMIC? (NASH VERSUS COURNOT?)

Underlying the question of what Cournot firms know and when they know it is a deeper question: is it appropriate to interpret Cournot's model as a static game? Perhaps not (Leonard, 1994, p. 505):

   What is important to note is that all understandings of the Cournot duopoly up to this assume that the analysis involves the passage of real time, each firm simultaneously reacting to the other until equilibrium is achieved. There is no suggestion that producers make alternate production decisions, with only one entrepreneur making a choice in any particular period: all that would come later. All. . . read Cournot as telling a story about how the two producers make simultaneous decisions, both moving in each period, and achieve equilibrium through time, to which they are compelled perpetually to return.

"Up to this" refers to the time of Nash's work on noncooperative equilibrium.
   Cournot's own words seem to refer to the passage of real time (1838; 1927, p. 79):

   Proprietor (1) can have no direct influence on the determination of D_2; all that he can do, when D_2 has been determined by proprietor (2), is to choose for D_1 the value which is best for him.

Firm 1 chooses output *when firm 2's output has been chosen*. This seems clearly to describe firm 1 making a decision after having observed firm 2's choice. There are other such passages throughout the classical literature (Hotelling, 1929, p. 43; Stackelberg, 1934, p. 70; Fellner,

---

[2] Something like this view is ascribed to Nash (Leonard, 1994, p. 503, fn. 23). In the words of Binmore (1996, p. xi):

   But, as Nash's thesis records, he saw other reasons for proposing his equilibrium notion than as a candidate for the rational solution of a game. He also recognized that interactive adjustment processes, in which boundedly rational agents observe the strategies played by their likely opponents over time, and gradually learn to adjust their own strategies to earn higher payoffs, will eventually converge to a Nash equilibrium – if they converge to anything at all.

1949, p. 57). Morgenstern (1948, p. 196) explicitly rejects the interpretation that adjustments to equilibrium are "merely events in the mind[s] of the duopolists."

It would, however, be just as imprecise to say that Cournot and the classical oligopolists worked with a (roughly formed) dynamic model as it would be to say that they worked with a static model. Classical oligopoly theorists simply did not distinguish clearly between static and dynamic models in the way in which that is done today.

3.4 CONJECTURAL VARIATIONS

An early classical generalization of the Cournot model was to explicitly model the beliefs of each firm about the conduct of the other. When the Cournot model is conceived of as a one-shot game, this generalization is misplaced, since it is a story about reactions told in a context within which reactions cannot occur. But it provides a widely used substitute for full-fledged dynamic modelling and a framework for empirical tests of static oligopoly models.

3.4.1 Conjectural derivatives

In the Cournot model, total revenue for (say) firm 1 is

$$TR_1(q_1, q_2) = p(q_1 + q_2)q_1, \tag{3.2}$$

and the assumption that firm 1 maximizes its own profit given the output of firm 2 enters when we calculate firm 1's marginal revenue as

$$MR_1 = \frac{\partial TR_1(q_1, q_2)}{\partial q_1} = p(q_1 + q_2) + q_1 \frac{\mathrm{d}p}{\mathrm{d}Q}. \tag{3.3}$$

By setting firm 1's marginal revenue equal to its marginal cost, we obtain the equation of firm 1's best-response function, equation (2.4) (in implicit form).

If q_2 is *not* treated as given when this exercise is carried out, then firm 1's marginal revenue becomes

$$MR_1 = \frac{\partial TR_1(q_1, q_2)}{\partial q_1} = p(q_1 + q_2) + q_1 \frac{\mathrm{d}p}{\mathrm{d}Q} \left(1 + \frac{\mathrm{d}q_2}{\mathrm{d}q_1}\right). \tag{3.4}$$

The *conjectural derivative* $\mathrm{d}q_2/\mathrm{d}q_1$ in (3.4) is the way firm 1 thinks firm 2's output changes as firm 1's output changes.

From the classical oligopoly theory point of view, it is natural to take the position that the specification of some value for the conjectural derivative is an essential element of the Cournot model (Bramness, 1979, p. 4):

it is important to remember that before some alternative assumptions about the conjectural derivative ... are chosen, nothing is "right", because the [oligopolists] have no defined behavior at all.

Following Bowley (1924, p. 38) or Hicks (1935), treat the conjectural derivative as a constant:[3]

$$\frac{dq_2}{dq_1} = \lambda_1. \tag{3.5}$$

$\lambda_1 = 0$ is the Cournot case: firm 1 believes that if it changes output, firm 2's output remains as it is.

A negative conjectural derivative means that firm 1 believes that if it restricts q_1, firm 2 will increase q_2. This reduces the marginal profitability of output restriction, compared with Cournot conjectures. A positive conjectural derivative means that firm 1 believes that if it restricts q_1, firm 2 will restrict q_2. This increases the marginal profitability of output restriction, compared with Cournot conjectures.

In the general conjectural derivative case, the first-order condition to maximize firm 1's profit is

$$p(q_1 + q_2) + q_1 \frac{dp}{dQ}(1 + \lambda_1) - \frac{dc_1(q_1)}{dq_1} \equiv 0. \tag{3.6}$$

Because the conjectural derivative appears in the first-order condition, it affects the location of the firm's best-response function, and therefore it affects equilibrium outputs.[4]

The first-order condition (3.6) can be rewritten as

$$\frac{p - c_1'(q_1)}{p} = -\frac{q_1}{Q}\left(\frac{Q}{p}\frac{dp}{dQ}\right)(1 + \lambda_1) = \frac{(1 + \lambda_1)s_1}{\varepsilon_{Qp}}, \tag{3.7}$$

where $c_1'(q_1) = dc_1(q_1)/dq_1$ is firm 1's marginal cost, $s_1 = q_1/Q$ is firm 1's market share, and ε_{Qp} is the market price elasticity of demand.

Equation (3.7) is a generalization of the Lerner (1934) index of monopoly power to duopoly. For simplicity, let the firms have identical cost functions and conjectures. Then, in symmetric equilibrium, each firm has a market share equal to one-half, and (3.7) becomes

$$\frac{p - c'(q)}{p} = \frac{(1 + \lambda)}{2\varepsilon_{Qp}}, \tag{3.8}$$

with all functions evaluated at equilibrium values.

The equilibrium price–marginal cost margin is zero (the competitive outcome) for $\lambda = -1$, and the inverse of the price–elasticity of demand (the monopoly outcome) for $\lambda = +1$. Symmetric Cournot duopoly encompasses the range of outcomes from perfect competition to monopoly as the conjectural derivative ranges from -1 to $+1$.

---

[3] More generally, one might wish to allow conjectures to vary with outputs or with market shares.

[4] Problem 3.1 asks you to examine the impact of conjectures on the location of best-response curves for the linear demand, constant marginal cost version of the Cournot model.

3.4.2   Conjectural elasticities

A second approach to modeling conjectures, due to Frisch (1933, p. 252), treats the elasticity implied by the conjectural derivative as a constant:

$$\alpha_1 = \frac{d \log q_2}{d \log q_1} = \frac{q_1}{q_2} \frac{dq_2}{dq_1}. \tag{3.9}$$

α_1 is the percentage change in firm 2's output that firm 1 expects in response to a 1 percent change in its own output.

If $\alpha_1 = 0$, we are back in the Cournot case: firm 1 expects that firm 2's output does not change as it maximizes its own profit. If $\alpha_1 = 1$, firm 1 expects that when it restricts output, firm 2 will make an equal percentage reduction in output. In other words, if $\alpha_1 = 1$, firm 1 expects firm 2 to act in a way that promotes output restriction. On the other hand, if $\alpha_1 = -1$, firm 1 expects that if it reduces output, firm 2 will expand output by an equal percentage amount, thus making attempts to restrict output less effective, all else equal.

With conjectural elasticities, the first-order condition to maximize firm 1's profit is

$$p(q_1 + q_2) + q_1 \frac{dp}{dQ} \left(1 + \frac{q_2}{q_1}\alpha_1\right) - \frac{dc_1(q_1)}{dq_1} = 0. \tag{3.10}$$

Once again, this yields a generalization of the Lerner index of monopoly power:

$$\frac{p - c_1'(q_1)}{p} = \frac{\alpha_1 + (1 - \alpha_1)s_1}{\varepsilon_{Qp}}. \tag{3.11}$$

As before, let firms have identical cost functions and conjectures. The symmetric duopoly equilibrium Lerner index is

$$\frac{p - c'(q)}{p} = \frac{\alpha + (1 - \alpha)\frac{1}{2}}{\varepsilon_{Qp}}. \tag{3.12}$$

If $\alpha = 1$ (matching conjectures), firm 1's price–cost margin is the inverse of the industry price elasticity of demand, the monopoly result. If $\alpha = 0$, there is the Cournot result, and for the lower limit (with two firms)[5] $\alpha = -1$, the price–cost margin is zero, the competitive outcome. With conjectural elasticities, as with conjectural derivatives, the set of possible duopoly equilibria spans the range from perfect competition to monopoly.

3.4.3   Consistent conjectural variations

The conjectural derivative is a parameter that measures what a firm believes is the relationship between its own output and the output of its rival. The rival's best-response function shows

---

[5] With n symmetric firms, the lower limit $\alpha = -1/(n - 1)$ makes price equal to marginal cost. The lower limit is -1 for two firms, $-\frac{1}{2}$ for three firms, and so on. This lower limit applies if there are no fixed costs. If there are fixed costs, price cannot fall to marginal cost in equilibrium; fixed costs imply a lower limit for α that is above $-1/(n - 1)$.

the actual relationship between a firm's output and the output of its rival. It is natural to try to impose the requirement that conjectured relations be consistent with the relations implied by the best-response functions.

Leontief 1

Leontief (1936), in a review of Stackelberg (1934), used a specific example to explore the consequences of imposing the requirement that actual and conjectured responses be the same. Consider a quantity-setting duopoly with inverse demand function

$$p = 6 - q_1 - q_2, \tag{3.13}$$

and let both firms have the same quadratic cost function,[6]

$$c(q_i) = \tfrac{1}{4}q_i^2, \tag{3.14}$$

for $i = 1, 2$.

Firm 1's payoff is

$$\pi_1 = (6 - q_1 - q_2)q_1 - \tfrac{1}{4}q_1^2 = (6 - \tfrac{5}{4}q_1 - q_2)q_1. \tag{3.15}$$

Allowing for a constant conjectural derivative, the first- and second-order conditions for firm 1's profit maximization are

$$\frac{\partial \pi_1}{\partial q_1} = 6 - \left(\tfrac{5}{2} + \lambda_1\right)q_1 - q_2 \equiv 0 \tag{3.16}$$

and

$$\frac{\partial^2 \pi_1}{\partial q_1^2} = -\left(\tfrac{5}{2} + \lambda_1\right) < 0 \tag{3.17}$$

respectively.

The equation of firm 1's best-response function is

$$q_1 = \frac{6 - q_2}{\tfrac{5}{2} + \lambda_1} \quad \Rightarrow \quad \frac{dq_1}{dq_2}\bigg|_{1\text{'s foc}} = -\frac{1}{\tfrac{5}{2} + \lambda_1}. \tag{3.18}$$

In the same way, the equation of firm 2's best-response function is

$$q_2 = \frac{6 - q_1}{\tfrac{5}{2} + \lambda_2} \quad \Rightarrow \quad \frac{dq_2}{dq_1}\bigg|_{2\text{'s foc}} = -\frac{1}{\tfrac{5}{2} + \lambda_2}. \tag{3.19}$$

The consistency requirement is that each firm's conjecture about its rival's response equal the slope of the rival's best-response curve; that is, that

$$\lambda_1 = \frac{dq_2}{dq_1}\bigg|_{2\text{'s foc}} = -\frac{1}{\tfrac{5}{2} + \lambda_2} \quad \text{and} \quad \lambda_2 = \frac{dq_1}{dq_2}\bigg|_{1\text{'s foc}} = -\frac{1}{\tfrac{5}{2} + \lambda_1}. \tag{3.20}$$

---

[6] Leontief includes a fixed cost equal to 1 in the cost function.

For general functional forms, the consistency conditions and the two first-order conditions form a system of four equations in four unknowns – two equilibrium outputs and two equilibrium conjectures. In this example, the consistency conditions form a stand-alone subsystem of equations. In addition, in this example we can limit our attention to symmetric solutions. Set $\lambda_1 = \lambda_2 = \lambda$ in (3.20) and rearrange terms to obtain the quadratic equation

$$\lambda^2 + \tfrac{5}{2}\lambda + 1 = 0, \tag{3.21}$$

with solutions

$$\lambda = -2, -\tfrac{1}{2}. \tag{3.22}$$

The solution $\lambda = -1/2$ satisfies the second-order condition for profit maximization, (3.17), while $\lambda = -2$ does not. $\lambda = -1/2$ is therefore the unique consistent conjecture for this example.

The general conjectural model encompasses all possible market performances by allowing conjectures to range from negative to positive values. The consistency requirement eliminates all but one of those values and identifies a single corresponding pair of consistent-conjectures equilibrium outputs.

Solving (3.18) and (3.19), the equations of the first-order conditions, gives symmetric equilibrium output as a function of conjectures:

$$q_1 = q_2 = \frac{12}{7 + 2\lambda}. \tag{3.23}$$

Equilibrium firm output with Cournot conjectures ($\lambda = 0$) is $q = 1\tfrac{5}{7}$. Equilibrium firm output with consistent conjectures is $q = 2$. Consistent conjectures therefore imply greater output and better equilibrium market performance than Cournot conjectures.

Leontief 2

The concept of consistent conjectural variations is considerably more slippery than this discussion suggests. To see this, examine a more general version of Leontief's example. Let the inverse demand function be

$$p = a - bQ, \tag{3.24}$$

for $Q = q_1 + q_2 + \cdots + q_n$, and let the cost function (the same for all firms) be

$$c(q) = dq^2. \tag{3.25}$$

Then, going through the same steps as for the numerical example leads to the consistent conjecture

$$\lambda = \frac{-(1 + \delta) + \sqrt{(1 + \delta)^2 - (n - 1)}}{n - 1}, \tag{3.26}$$

for $\delta = d/b$, the diseconomies of scale parameter normalized by the absolute value of the slope of the inverse demand curve.

In Leontief's example, $n = 2$, $\delta = 1/4$, the discriminant $(1 + \delta)^2 - (n - 1) = 9/16 > 0$ and λ has the real, negative value reported above: $\lambda = -1/2$. But for two or more firms, the discriminant is negative, so that no consistent conjectural variation exists. More generally, for these inverse demand and cost functions there is no consistent conjectural derivative unless $\delta = d/b$ exceeds a lower bound that rises with the number of firms:

$$\delta_{min} > \sqrt{n - 1} - 1. \tag{3.27}$$

There is no obvious reason to expect this condition to be met, and when it is not, there is no consistent-conjectures equilibrium.

Alternatively, if there are constant returns to scale, $d = \delta = 0$. Then the discriminant is nonnegative only for $n = 2$, and in this case the consistent conjecture is $\lambda = -1$.

Outside the context of this specific example, the result that $\lambda = -1/(n - 1)$ is a consistent conjecture holds under general conditions when marginal cost is constant (Perry, 1982, p. 201; Kamien and Schwartz, 1983, p. 201).[7] If $\lambda = -1$, a firm believes that if it restricts output one unit, its rivals will collectively expand output one unit, so that industry output will not change. Then (Kamien and Schwartz, 1983, p. 201):

> If each firm believes that it will have no impact on industry output, it will have none, and the industry will produce the competitive output.

Empirical tests generally reject the prediction that conjectures take the value that predicts competitive market performance. Holt (1985) rejects convergence to consistent conjectures in an experimental environment.

Conceptual difficulties

This is only the tip of the iceberg. The Leontief example illustrates what might be termed "computational difficulties" with the concept of consistent conjectures. In the 1980s, a large literature, beginning with Bresnahan (1981b), sought to sort these difficulties out, either by trying to identify conditions under which a consistent conjecture equilibrium of the kind discussed above exists or by redefining the notions of conjectures and of consistency (Daughety, 1985; Klemperer and Meyer, 1988) so that computational difficulties do not arise.[8]

Another school of thought rejects the whole conjectural approach. At the heart of this rejection is the fundamental difference between the way in which the Cournot model is viewed in classical oligopoly theory and the way in which it is viewed from a game-theoretic perspective. To paraphrase[9] Friedman (1983b, p. 107):

> Consider [a] model . . . where the two firms are assumed to make their [quantity] decisions simultaneously. It is not possible for q_2 to be a function of q_1, and it would be ridiculous for firm

---

[7] As pointed out in footnote 5, conjectures that make equilibrium price equal to marginal cost are not feasible if there are fixed costs.

[8] For a nice overview of this literature, see Lindh (1992).

[9] Friedman's remarks appear in a discussion of price-setting oligopoly; I have transposed them to the context of quantity-setting oligopoly.

1 to think that. Such a situation would imply that as firm 1 contemplated various [outputs] for itself, it would expect various possible q_2 according to the relation $q_2 = \phi_1(q_1)$. Hence, at the level of simultaneous decisions in a single-period model, conjectural variation is not meaningful.

In the one-shot game conception of the Cournot model, reactions cannot either take place or be anticipated; decisions are made simultaneously, the structure of the game is common knowledge, and there is no time over which reactions might occur.

Resolutions

Dockner (1992) (working with a differential game), Sabourian (1992), Lapham and Ware (1994, pp. 585–6), and Cabral (1995) (working with repeated games), embed a static Cournot model in a dynamic model and examine the conditions under which the outcome of the dynamic game is mimicked by the outcome of a static conjectural model. These approaches provide a formal justification for using the static conjectural variations model as a "short cut" (Sabourian, 1992, p. 236) to analyze inherently dynamic imperfectly competitive markets.[10]

3.5 THE COEFFICIENT OF COOPERATION

Edgeworth (1881, p. 53) introduced what has come to be known as the "coefficient of cooperation" approach.[11] The coefficient of cooperation model, which allows the analysis of partial joint profit maximization, relaxes the Cournot assumption that firms maximize their own profit and only their own profit.

Consider again a duopoly, and suppose that firm 1 maximizes the sum of its own profit and a fraction of firm 2's profit, or, equivalently, a weighted average of its own profit and the profit of all other firms:

$$G_1 = \pi_1 + \phi_1\pi_2 = (1 - \phi_1)\pi_1 + \phi_1(\pi_1 + \pi_2). \tag{3.28}$$

ϕ_1 is firm 1's coefficient of cooperation, and indexes the weight that firm 1 gives to other firms' profit when it takes its own decisions.

Such an objective function might be thought of as describing tacit or overt collusion.[12] Alternatively, it could be thought of as describing the behavior of a firm that owns a fraction ϕ_1 of its rival, so inheriting that share of their profits (Bresnahan and Salop, 1986; Reynolds and Snapp, 1986).

---

[10] As we will see in section 7.6, empirical implementations of this approach have been the subject of criticism.

[11] Edgeworth used the term "coefficient of effective sympathy"; "coefficient of cooperation" is due to Cyert and DeGroot (1973).

[12] "Tacit collusion" seems to be behavior that aims at or leads to outcomes in which firms jointly exercise market power, but does not constitute collusion in a legal sense.

Written in terms of its underlying components, firm 1's objective function is

$$G_1(q_1, q_2) = p(q_1 + q_2)q_1 - c_1(q_1) + \phi_1 \left[p(q_1 + q_2)q_2 - c_2(q_2) \right]. \tag{3.29}$$

With Cournot conjectures, the first-order condition to maximize G_1 is

$$\frac{\partial G_1(q_1, q_2)}{\partial q_1} = p(q_1 + q_2) + q_1 \frac{dp}{dQ} - \frac{dc_1(q_1)}{dq_1} + \phi_1 \frac{dp}{dQ} q_2 = 0. \tag{3.30}$$

With some manipulation, (3.30) can be rewritten as

$$\frac{p - c_1'(q_1)}{p} = \frac{\phi_1 + (1 - \phi_1)s_1}{\varepsilon_{Qp}}, \tag{3.31}$$

which has the same form as (3.11).

The conjectural elasticity model and the coefficient of cooperation model are therefore formally equivalent. We can model firms as maximizing their own profit and only their own profit, with beliefs about the elasticities with which rivals react to output decisions. We can model firms as maximizing a weighted average of their own profit and industry profit, holding Cournot conjectures about rivals' reactions to output decisions. Provided that the conjectural elasticities in the first approach have the same values as the coefficients of cooperation in the second, the models yield the same predictions for market performance.[13]

3.6 REPRESENTATIVE CONSUMER MODELS OF PRODUCT DIFFERENTIATION

Two linear models of aggregate demand for differentiated products are widely used in industrial economics. One is due to Bowley (1924) and the other to Shubik and Levitan (1980). Both generalize the linear inverse demand model

$$p = a - bQ. \tag{3.32}$$

The two models are similar but differ in one important respect. In the Bowley formulation, market size increases as the number of varieties increases. In the Shubik–Levitan formulation, market size is fixed as the number of varieties increases.

3.6.1 Bowley

Bowley (1924, p. 56) works with linear inverse demand functions that are equivalent to

$$p_1 = a - b(q_1 + \theta q_2), \qquad p_2 = a - b(\theta q_1 + q_2). \tag{3.33}$$

This specification is used by Spence (1976a) and Dixit (1979).

---

[13] For an empirical application of an equivalent formulation, see Kadiyali (1996).

Note that a and b are positive, and $0 \leq \theta \leq 1$. Negative values of θ would make the model one of demand for complementary goods. If $\theta = 0$, the two varieties are independent in demand. As θ approaches 1, the varieties become closer and closer substitutes, and they are perfect substitutes for $\theta = 1$.

Bowley derives the inverse demand functions from a representative consumer utility function of the form

$$U(q_1, q_2) = a(q_1 + q_2) - \tfrac{1}{2}b(q_1^2 + 2\theta q_1 q_2 + q_2^2) + m, \qquad (3.34)$$

where m represents all other goods and has a price normalized at $p_m = 1$.

It is possible to generalize (3.34) so that the reservation price (a) and slope parameter (b) are different for different varieties. In the interest of simplicity, these generalizations are not pursued here.

Economists distinguish two types of product differentiation, horizontal and vertical (Phlips and Thisse, 1982, p. 2):[14]

> Differentiation is said to be horizontal when . . . between two products the level of some characteristics is augmented while it is lowered for some others, as in the cases of different versions . . . of a car. [A consumer] will buy the "closest" product in terms of a certain distance. . . . Differentiation is called vertical when . . . between two products the level of all characteristics is augmented or lowered, as in the case of cars of different series. . . . There is unanimity to rank the products according to a certain order.

Although the Bowley model is a representative consumer model of horizontal product differentiation, it can be derived by aggregation from a standard individual consumer model of vertical product differentiation (which we will discuss in chapter 4).

The aggregation story is as follows (for details, see Problem 3.2). There are two varieties, 1 and 2, and two groups of consumers, A and B. Consumers in group A regard variety 1 as being of higher quality and variety 2 as being of lower quality. Consumers are uniformly distributed along an interval $[0, 1]$; the willingness of consumers in group A to pay for quality declines as consumer location moves from 0 toward 1. Consumers in group B have preferences of the same form as consumers in group A, but consumers in group B regard variety 2 as being of higher quality and variety 1 as being of lower quality. Producers cannot distinguish or price discriminate between consumers in the two groups. Aggregate demands in this model of vertical product differentiation have forms that can be transformed, by appropriate redefinition of parameters, into the aggregate demands of the Bowley model.

From this point of view, aggregate models of horizontal product differentiation describe market demand when different groups of consumers have distinct vertical preferences and suppliers cannot classify individuals according to preferences.

In the Bowley model, the overall size of the market increases with the number of varieties. This is easiest to see if $\theta = 0$: in that case, varieties are independent in demand, and adding an additional "variety" amounts to adding a completely new market with inverse demand function of form (3.32).

---

[14] We examine the distinction between horizontal and vertical differentiation at greater length in section 4.3.

By inverting the equations of the inverse demand functions, one obtains the equations of the demand functions implied by the Bowley model:

$$q_1 = \frac{(1 - \theta)a - p_1 + \theta p_2}{(1 - \theta^2)b}, \qquad q_2 = \frac{(1 - \theta)a - p_2 + \theta p_1}{(1 - \theta^2)b} \tag{3.35}$$

(and these expressions are valid provided that $\theta < 1$).

The equations of the demand functions (3.35) and the equations of the inverse demand functions (3.33) are all valid on the condition that all prices and quantities are nonnegative. These nonnegativity constraints come into play when we derive the firms' best-response functions.

It is instructive to rewrite the equations of the inverse demand functions in a way that facilitates later comparison with the Shubik and Levitan model. Let

$$\bar{p} = \tfrac{1}{2} (p_1 + p_2) \tag{3.36}$$

be average price. Then the equation of the demand function for variety 1 can be written

$$q_1 = \frac{(1 - \theta)(a - p_1) - 2\theta(p_1 - \bar{p})}{(1 - \theta^2)b}. \tag{3.37}$$

The quantity demanded of variety 1 is less as p_1 is higher and as p_1 is greater than average price.

With n firms rather than two, the equations of the inverse demand functions and demand functions in the Bowley model are

$$p_i = a - b(\theta q_1 + \theta q_2 + \cdots + q_i + \cdots + \theta q_2) \tag{3.38}$$

and the equations of the demand functions are

$$q_i = \frac{(1 - \theta)\, a - [1 + (n - 2)\theta]p_i + \theta \sum_{j \neq i} p_j}{b(1 - \theta)[1 + (n - 1)\theta]} \tag{3.39}$$

$$= \frac{(1 - \theta)(a - p_i) - n\theta(p_i - \bar{p})}{(1 - \theta^2)b} \tag{3.40}$$

(see Problem 3.3).

Expression (3.40) is not particularly convenient for the analysis of firm i's profit-maximizing decisions, because p_i is one element in average price $\bar{p}$. Equation (3.39) might be thought to provide an intuitive description of consumer behavior when the number of varieties is large, with consumers making decisions based on comparison of the difference between a variety's price and average price.

3.6.2 Shubik–Levitan

Shubik and Levitan (1980, p. 69) write linear duopoly demand functions for differentiated products of the form:

$$q_1 = \tfrac{1}{2}\left[\alpha - \beta\left(1 + \frac{\gamma}{2}\right)p_1 + \frac{\beta\gamma}{2}p_2\right], \qquad q_2 = \tfrac{1}{2}\left[\alpha + \frac{\beta\gamma}{2}p_1 - \beta\left(1 + \frac{\gamma}{2}\right)p_2\right].$$

(3.41)

The demand function for variety 1 can be rewritten as

$$q_1 = \tfrac{1}{2}\left\{\alpha - \beta\left[p_1 + \gamma(p_1 - \bar{p})\right]\right\}.$$

(3.42)

This can be interpreted in the same way as (3.37): the quantity demanded of variety 1 is less as p_1 is higher and as p_1 is greater than average price.

In the Shubik–Levitan model, it is the parameter γ that indexes the degree of product differentiation. If $\gamma = 0$, the demand function (3.41) becomes

$$q_1 = \tfrac{1}{2}(\alpha - \beta p_1).$$

(3.43)

The two varieties are then independent in demand, and each variety has its own demand function, along which the quantity demanded at any price is half the quantity that would be demanded if consumers were offered only a single variety.

Solve (3.42) for $p_1 - \bar{p}$, to obtain

$$p_1 - \bar{p} = \frac{1}{\gamma}\left[\frac{2q_1 - (\alpha - \beta p_1)}{\beta}\right].$$

(3.44)

Then as $\gamma \to \infty$, $p_1 \to \bar{p}$. The larger is γ, the less room there is for prices to differ. In the limit, products are standardized, and all varieties sell for the same price. As γ rises from 0, varieties become closer and closer substitutes.

These relationships can also be seen by examining the equations of the inverse demand functions for the Shubik–Levitan model. These are

$$p_1 = \frac{\alpha}{\beta} - \frac{1}{\beta}\frac{2+\gamma}{1+\gamma}\left(q_1 + \frac{\gamma}{2+\gamma}q_2\right)$$

(3.45)

and

$$p_2 = \frac{\alpha}{\beta} - \frac{1}{\beta}\frac{2+\gamma}{1+\gamma}\left(\frac{\gamma}{2+\gamma}q_1 + q_2\right)$$

(3.46)

respectively.

Rewrite (3.45) as

$$p_1 = \frac{\alpha}{\beta} - \frac{1}{\beta} \left(\frac{1+2/\gamma}{1+1/\gamma} q_1 + \frac{1}{1+2/\gamma} q_2 \right).$$ (3.47)

As $\gamma \to \infty$, the inverse demand function for variety 1 approaches

$$p_1 = \frac{\alpha}{\beta} - \frac{1}{\beta} (q_1 + q_2).$$ (3.48)

Once again, as $\gamma \to \infty$ the two varieties approach perfect substitutability.

In the n-firm version of the Shubik–Levitan model, the demand functions are

$$q_i = \frac{1}{n} \left[\alpha - \beta p_i - \beta \gamma (p_i - \bar{p}) \right]$$ (3.49)

$$= \frac{\beta}{n} \left[\frac{\alpha}{\beta} - \left(1 + \frac{n-1}{n} \gamma \right) p_i - \gamma \sum_{j \neq i}^{n} p_j \right],$$ (3.50)

with corresponding inverse demand functions

$$p_i = \frac{\alpha}{\beta} - \frac{1}{\beta} \frac{n+\gamma}{1+\gamma} \left(\frac{\gamma}{n+\gamma} q_1 + \frac{\gamma}{n+\gamma} q_2 + \cdots + q_i + \cdots + \frac{\gamma}{n+\gamma} q_n \right)$$ (3.51)

(see Problem 3.3).

Once again (solving (3.49) for $p_i - \bar{p}$), as $\gamma \to 0$ varieties become more and more independent in demand, and the demand function facing each variety approaches

$$q_i = \frac{1}{n} (\alpha - \beta p_i).$$ (3.52)

In the Shubik–Levitan model, in contrast to the Bowley model, market size is fixed as the number of varieties increases.[15]

Comparing (3.51) and (3.38), the two models are equivalent *for a fixed number of firms*: the relationship between the parameters is

$$a = \frac{\alpha}{\beta}, \qquad b = \frac{1}{\beta} \frac{n+\gamma}{1+\gamma}, \qquad \theta = \frac{\gamma}{n+\gamma}.$$ (3.53)

If parameters are chosen so that these relationships hold for a given n, the two models behave differently as the number of varieties increases. In the Bowley model, the maximum amount of consumers' surplus possible rises as the number of varieties rises. In the Shubik–Levitan model, it does not.

---

[15] One could examine a product differentiation model in which the demand facing a variety is a weighted average of demand in the Bowley model and demand in the Shubik–Levitan model. In such a model, market size would increase with the number of varieties, but less rapidly than in the Bowley model.

3.7 COURNOT WITH PRODUCT DIFFERENTIATION

Beginning with duopoly, let firms have identical constant marginal and average cost c per unit. With the Bowley linear inverse demand model of product differentiation,[16] firm 1's profit is

$$\pi_1 = [a - c - b(q_1 + \theta q_2)]q_1. \tag{3.54}$$

The first-order condition to maximize π_1 with respect to q_1 gives the equation of firm 1's quantity best-response function,

$$2q_1 + \theta q_2 = \frac{a - c}{b}. \tag{3.55}$$

In the same way, the equation of firm 2's quantity best-response function is

$$\theta q_1 + 2q_2 = \frac{a - c}{b}. \tag{3.56}$$

Segments of the curves traced out by (3.55) and (3.56) are shown in figure 3.2(b).[17] Consider firm 1's best-response curve. If $q_2 = 0$, firm 1 is a monopolist and maximizes its profit by producing the monopoly output. This is point A_1, the horizontal-axis intercept of firm 1's best-response function. As firm 2's output increases, firm 1's profit-maximizing output falls, moving up along the line with equation (3.55). At the same time, as firm 2's output increases, p_2 falls. When q_2 becomes sufficiently large, p_2 falls to zero (point B_1) and the price 2 nonnegativity constraint,

$$p_2 = a - b(\theta q_1 + q_2) \geq 0, \tag{3.57}$$

becomes binding. If q_2 increases beyond the level that makes $p_2 = 0$ along firm 1's first-order condition (3.55), firm 1's profit-maximizing output is constrained to move along the equality version of (3.57).[18] This continues through point C_1, where firm 2 is producing so much that firm 1's profit-maximizing output is zero.

In the same way, firm 2's best-response curve has two segments, one part given by (3.56) (point A_2 to point B_2) and one part given by the equality version of the price 1 nonnegativity constraint,

$$p_1 = a - b(q_1 + \theta q_2) \geq 0 \tag{3.58}$$

(point B_2 to point C_2).

---

[16] For the case of the Shubik–Levitan linear product differentiation model, see Problem 3.4.

[17] Figure 3.2 is valid if products are sufficiently differentiated, $\theta \leq (a - c)/a$. If varieties are sufficiently strong substitutes, $\theta > (a - c)/a$, firm 1's best-response output falls to zero for $q_2 = (a - c)/\theta b$, before p_2 falls to 0.

[18] Formally, one can set up firm 1's decision as a constrained maximization problem, with Kuhn–Tucker conditions giving the necessary first-order conditions.

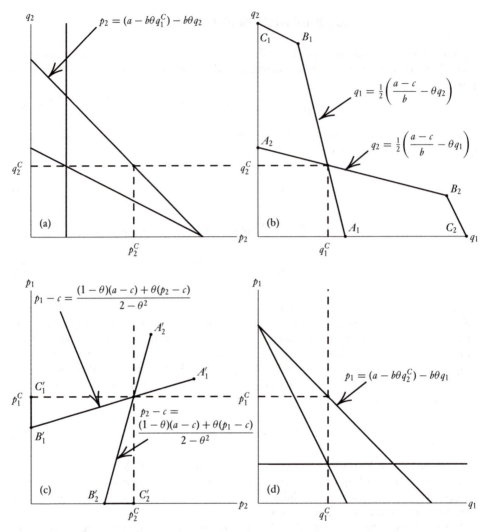

Figure 3.2 Quantity-setting duopoly equilibrium with product differentiation. (a) Firm 2's equilibrium demand curve; (b) quantity best-response curves; (c) price-space reflections of quantity best-response curves; (d) firm 1's equilibrium demand curve.

Noncooperative equilibrium outputs are found at the intersection of the curves defined by the first-order conditions; they are

$$q_1 = q_2 = q = \frac{1}{2+\theta} \frac{a-c}{b}. \tag{3.59}$$

Given the equilibrium outputs, we can find the Cournot equilibrium prices,

$$p_1 = p_2 = c + bq = c + \frac{1}{2+\theta}(a - c). \tag{3.60}$$

With equilibrium prices and outputs, we can find equilibrium profits. Substituting equilibrium outputs into the representative consumer welfare function (3.34) gives equilibrium consumer welfare.

The first-order conditions (3.55) and (3.56) give each firm's profit-maximizing output as a function of the output of the other firm. The equations of the demand curves (3.35) express outputs in terms of prices. Substituting the equations of the demand curves into the equations of the first-order conditions gives equations for the price-space reflections of the quantity best-response curves; these are

$$p_1 - c = \frac{(1 - \theta)(a - c) + \theta(p_2 - c)}{2 - \theta^2}, \qquad p_2 - c = \frac{(1 - \theta)(a - c) + \theta(p_1 - c)}{2 - \theta^2}. \tag{3.61}$$

The price-space reflections of the quantity best-response curves slope upward. They are shown in figure 3.2(c), where the points A'_1, B'_1, and C'_1 correspond to points A_1, B_1, and C_1 respectively, and similarly for firm 2.[19]

In Cournot equilibrium, each firm is maximizing its profit, given the equilibrium output of the other. This is shown by the intersections of the marginal revenue and marginal cost curves in figures 3.2(a) and 3.2(d).

In the n-firm case, Cournot equilibrium output per variety and price are

$$q_C = \frac{1}{2 + (n - 1)\theta} \frac{a - c}{b} \quad \text{and} \quad p_C = c + bq_C = c + \frac{1}{2 + (n - 1)\theta}(a - c) \tag{3.62}$$

respectively. When products are differentiated, as when products are standardized, equilibrium price falls as the number of varieties (firms) increases. Equilibrium price also falls as θ increases (that is, as products become more standardized). The Cournot model with product differentiation implies that a small number of firms and a high degree of product differentiation facilitate the exercise of market power.

3.8   BERTRAND WITH PRODUCT DIFFERENTIATION

Section 2.3 presents the classical understanding of Cournot's contribution. The validity of Cournot's work was generally rejected following an 1883 review by Bertrand, who viewed the assumption that firms would set price as obvious, and dismissed the modelling of quantity-setting firms as an inexplicable oversight (1883, p. 503; translation Friedman, 1988, p. 77):

> Such is the study... of the struggle between two proprietors who own mineral springs of the same quality and have no fear of other competition. It would be in their interest to join together in partnership or at least to fix a common price so as to get from the buyers the greatest common

---

[19] It is a numerical coincidence that, for the example used to draw figure 3.2, firm 1's price at point C'_1 is the same as the noncooperative Cournot equilibrium price. This is not true in general.

profit, but this solution is rejected. Cournot conjectures that one of the competitors will lower his price to attract buyers, and that the other, in order to bring them back, will lower his more. They will continue until each of them would no longer gain anything more by lowering his price. A peremptory objection arises: With this hypothesis a solution is impossible; the price reduction would have no limit. In fact, whatever jointly determined price were adopted, if only one of the competitors lowers his, he gains, disregarding all unimportant exceptions, all the sales, and he will double his sales if his competitor allows him to do so. If Cournot's formulas mask this result, it is because, through a peculiar oversight, he introduces under the names D and D' the quantities sold by the two competitors, and treating them as independent variables, he assumes that the one quantity happening to change through the will of one owner, the other would remain constant. The contrary is obviously true.

Besides raising the issue of price versus quantity as a decision variable, this brief but remarkable passage anticipates two other themes that have since occupied industrial economists: (i) entry must be blocked if incumbent firms are to exercise market power; (ii) if entry is blocked, incumbents have an incentive to collude.

Bertrand gives no special justification for the view that firms set prices rather than quantities.

Early work after Bertrand's review similarly regarded the modeling of quantity-setting firms as an obvious mistake, not calling for discussion (Fisher, 1898a, p. 126; Edgeworth, 1922). Although Bertrand's view held the field for more than 40 years, it did not much survive Chamberlin's (1929, p. 72) observation that neither the price-setting nor the quantity-setting specification can be held to be correct in an absolute sense:[20]

> [Bertrand's] conclusion seems hardly a refutation of Cournot, unless the converse be also granted, that it is in turn refuted by Cournot. The two complement, rather than oppose each other, each flowing from a particular assumption.

Equilibrium in the Bertrand model with a standardized product is quite different from equilibrium in the Cournot model. The Cournot model emphasizes the number of firms as the critical element in determining market performance. Bertrand's model predicts the same performance as in long-run equilibrium of a perfectly competitive market if as few as two producers supply a standardized product.

The qualitative nature of the predictions of the Cournot model are robust to the introduction of product differentiation. The same cannot be said of the Bertrand model.

The equations of the demand curves in the Bowley duopoly model are given by (3.35). With identical constant marginal cost c for both firms, firm 1's profit, as a function of the

---

[20] See also Hotelling (1929, p. 56):

> The difficulty as to whether prices or quantities should be used as independent variables can now be cleared up. This question has troubled many readers of Cournot. The answer is that either set of variables may be used; that the q's may be expressed in terms of the p's, and the p's in terms of the q's.

prices chosen by both firms, is[21]

$$\pi_1 = (p_1 - c)\frac{(1 - \theta)(a - c) - (p_1 - c) + \theta(p_2 - c)}{(1 - \theta^2)b}. \tag{3.63}$$

Note from (3.63) that with substitute products ($\theta > 0$) prices are strategic complements:

$$\frac{\partial^2 \pi_1}{\partial p_1 \partial p_2} = \frac{\theta}{(1 - \theta^2)b} > 0.$$

If firm 2 raises its price, firm 1's marginal profitability goes up. Thus (by analogy with (2.10) for the case of quantity-setting firms) price best-response functions slope upward for the case of linear demand and constant marginal cost.

The first-order condition to maximize (3.63) is

$$2(p_1 - c) - \theta(p_2 - c) = (1 - \theta)(a - c). \tag{3.64}$$

In the same way, the first-order condition to maximize firm 2's profit is

$$-\theta(p_1 - c) + 2(p_2 - c) = (1 - \theta)(a - c). \tag{3.65}$$

Provided that all prices and quantities are nonnegative, (3.64) and (3.65) are the equations of the firms' price best-response functions. Price best-response functions are indeed upward-sloping: as shown in figure 3.3(c), firm 1's profit-maximizing price rises as p_2 rises from 0 (point A_1).[22] As p_2 rises from 0 along firm 1's price best-response curve, p_1 rises and q_2 falls. When q_2 falls to zero, the constraint that q_2 be nonnegative becomes binding (point B_1). From that point onward, firm 1's profit-maximizing price rises along the $q_2 = 0$ constraint until it reaches the point at which firm 1's price equals its unconstrained monopoly price (point C_1). For higher values of p_2, since q_2 is zero, firm 1 simply charges its unconstrained monopoly price to maximize its profit; its best-response curve is horizontal from point C_1 rightward.

In the same way, firm 2's price best-response curve has three segments, one part given by (3.65) (point A_2 to point B_2), one part along the $q_1 = 0$ constraint (point B_2 to point C_2), and one part vertical from C_2 onward ($q_1 = 0$ and p_1 so high that firm 2 is able to set its unconstrained monopoly price).

Noncooperative equilibrium prices are found at the intersection of the curves defined by the first-order conditions; they are

$$p_1 = p_2 = c + \frac{1 - \theta}{2 - \theta}(a - c). \tag{3.66}$$

From the equilibrium prices follow equilibrium outputs and net social welfare.

---

[21] If marginal costs are constant for each firm (not necessarily identical across firms), then without loss of generality it is possible to express prices as deviations from marginal cost. When marginal costs are constant and identical across firms, it is often a convenient simplifying assumption to normalize the constant value of marginal cost to be zero.

[22] Figure 3.3 is valid if products are sufficiently differentiated, $\theta \leq (a - c)/a$. If varieties are sufficiently strong substitutes, $\theta > (a - c)/a$, firm 1's best-response price is c for $p_2 = [c - (1 - \theta)a]/\theta > 0$.

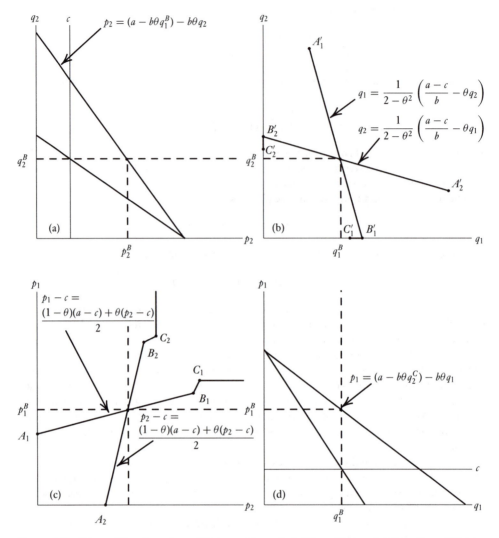

Figure 3.3 Price-setting duopoly equilibrium with product differentiation. (a) Firm 2's equilibrium demand curve; (b) quantity-space reflections of price best-response curves; (c) price best-response curves; (d) firm 1's equilibrium demand curve.

Substituting the equations of the demand curves (3.35) allows us to express the price best-response curves in terms of quantities. These are shown in figure 3.3(b), where the points A'_1, B'_1, and C'_1 correspond to points A_1, B_1, and C_1 respectively, and similarly for firm 2. The quantity-space reflections of the price best-response functions slope downward.

In Bertrand equilibrium with product differentiation, each firm is maximizing its profit, given the equilibrium price of the other. This is shown by the intersection of the marginal revenue and marginal cost curves in figures 3.3(a) and (d).

In the n-firm case, noncooperative equilibrium prices in the Bertrand model with the Bowley demand specification are

$$p_B = c + \frac{1-\theta}{2 + (n-3)\theta}(a - c). \tag{3.67}$$

Equilibrium outputs are

$$q_B = [1 + (n-2)\theta](p_B - c) = (1 - \theta)\frac{1 + (n-2)\theta}{2 + (n-3)\theta}(a - c). \tag{3.68}$$

For $0 \leq \theta \leq 1$, equilibrium prices fall, and equilibrium output per variety rises, as θ rises (as products become more standardized) and as n, the number of varieties, increases. Qualitatively, these are the same predictions yielded by the Cournot model with product differentiation.

Bertrand's criticism of Cournot was that if firms set prices rather than quantities, equilibrium price would equal marginal cost with as few as two suppliers. This conclusion is correct *if the product is homogeneous*, as can be seen by setting $\theta = 1$ in (3.67). If the varieties are differentiated (as is usually the case), the impacts of changes in the number of firms and in the degree of product differentiation affect market performance in the same general way, whether firms set prices or quantities.

3.9 PRICES VERSUS QUANTITIES

There are, however, systematic differences between structure–performance relationships in quantity-setting and price-setting oligopoly. These differences are important not only for understanding the determinants of performance in one-shot games, but also for understanding the determinants of performance in multistage games that include product market oligopoly as one component.[23]

Confining ourselves to duopoly, let a system of inverse demand curves for two varieties be derived from the constrained maximization of a well-behaved representative consumer utility function,

$$\max U(q_1, q_2) + m + \lambda(Y - m - p_1 q_1 - p_2 q_2), \tag{3.69}$$

where Y is income and m, representing all other goods, has price normalized at $p_m = 1$. The inverse demand functions,

$$p_1 = U_1(q_1, q_2), \qquad p_2 = U_2(q_1, q_2), \tag{3.70}$$

are the derivatives of the utility function. We then have downward-sloping inverse demand curves,

$$\frac{\partial p_i}{\partial q_i} = U_{ii} < 0, \tag{3.71}$$

---

[23] For examples of oligopoly models in which a firm chooses both its price and its quantity, see Levitan and Shubik (1978), Shubik and Levitan (1980), Davidson and Deneckere (1986), and Friedman (1988).

by declining marginal utility; equality of cross-price effects

$$\frac{\partial p_i}{\partial q_j} = U_{ij} = \frac{\partial p_j}{\partial q_i}; \tag{3.72}$$

and, from the second-order conditions,

$$U_{11} U_{22} > U_{12}^2. \tag{3.73}$$

A sufficient condition for condition (3.73) is that own-price effects be greater in magnitude than cross-price effects.

If firm 2 acts as a quantity-setter, then firm 1 maximizes profit along inverse demand function (3.70), which has slope

$$\left.\frac{\partial p_1}{\partial q_1}\right|_{\bar{q}_2} = U_{11}. \tag{3.74}$$

If, instead, firm 2 sets prices, firm 1 maximizes profit along the inverse demand function

$$p_1 = U_1[q_1, q_2(p_1, p_2)], \tag{3.75}$$

with slope[24]

$$\left.\frac{\partial p_1}{\partial q_1}\right|_{\bar{p}_2} = \frac{U_{11} U_{22} - U_{12}^2}{U_{22}}. \tag{3.76}$$

The ratio of the slope of firm 1's demand curve when firm 2 sets price to the slope of firm 1's demand curve when firm 2 sets quantity is

$$\left.\frac{\partial p_1}{\partial q_1}\right|_{\bar{p}_2} \Big/ \left.\frac{\partial p_1}{\partial q_1}\right|_{\bar{q}_2} = \frac{U_{11} U_{22} - U_{12}^2}{U_{11} U_{22}}. \tag{3.77}$$

The numerator and the denominator on the right are both positive (by (3.71) and (3.73)), and the numerator is less than the denominator, so that

$$0 < \left.\frac{\partial p_1}{\partial q_1}\right|_{\bar{p}_2} \Big/ \left.\frac{\partial p_1}{\partial q_1}\right|_{\bar{q}_2} < 1. \tag{3.78}$$

Since demand curves are downward-sloping, multiplying (3.78) through by $(\partial p_1/\partial q_1)|_{\bar{q}_2}$ reverses the direction of the inequalities and shows that firm 1 faces a flatter, more elastic demand if firm 2 sets price than if firm 2 sets quantity:

$$0 > \left.\frac{\partial p_1}{\partial q_1}\right|_{\bar{p}_2} > \left.\frac{\partial p_1}{\partial q_1}\right|_{\bar{q}_2}. \tag{3.79}$$

---

[24] Assume that the conditions of the implicit function theorem are met, and consider the system of equations (3.70) as implicitly defining $q_2(q_1, p_2)$ and $p_1(q_1, p_2)$; that is, $p_1(q_1, p_2) = U_1(q_1, q_2(q_1, p_2))$ and $p_2 = U_2(q_1, q_2(q_1, p_2))$. Differentiate these two equations with respect to q_1 to obtain $\partial p_1/\partial q_1 = U_{11} + U_{12}\partial q_2/\partial q_1$ and $0 = U_{12} + U_{22}\partial q_2/\partial q_1$, which together yield (3.76).

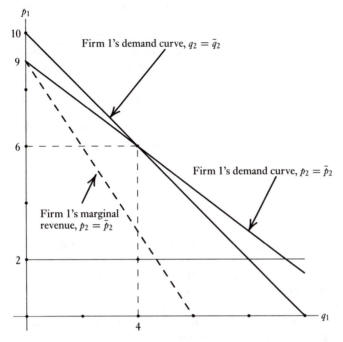

Figure 3.4 Demand curves, quantity versus price; Bowley specification. $a = 12$, $b = 1$, $c = 2$, $\theta = 1/2$.

This is illustrated in figure 3.4 for the Bowley product differentiation specification.[25] For the parameter values used in figure 3.4, $q_1 = 4$ maximizes firm 1's profit if firm 2 sets quantity and produces $q_2 = 4$ (these are the noncooperative outputs with quantity-setting firms). But if firm 2 sets price, firm 1 faces a more elastic demand curve, and its marginal revenue when it is producing four units of output exceeds its marginal cost. Facing a price-setting rival, firm 1 would maximize output by producing more than its Cournot equilibrium output level.

Firm 2 is in the same situation. If both firms set price, equilibrium outputs are greater, and prices and profits less, than if both firms set quantities.[26]

Many multistage models in industrial economics picture situations in which firms decide the level of some investment in an early (the first) period in hopes of profit to be earned in a later (the second) period. Research and development expenditures are one example. Generically in such models, the profit to be earned in the second period is less, and therefore firms' incentives to make the investment in the first period are less, if product–market competition is in terms of prices rather than quantities.

---

[25] In which case $(\partial p_1/\partial q_1)|_{\bar{p}_2} = -(1 - \theta^2)b$, $(\partial p_1/\partial q_1)|_{\bar{q}_2} = -b$.

[26] Okuguchi (1987, p. 134) derives this result under the assumptions that prices are strategic complements, and that the effect of an increase in own price on own-price marginal profitability outweighs the effect of an increase in own price on the sum of cross-price marginal profitabilities. See also Hathaway and Rickard (1979), Shubik and Levitan (1980, ch. 6), Vives (1984), Singh and Vives (1984), and Cheng (1985).

In the same way, it is common to model the long-run equilibrium number of firms in a market (in the absence of strategic entry-deterring behavior by incumbents) by supposing that the number of active firms adjusts until profit is zero. When profits are less, holding the number of firms constant, for price-setting than for quantity-setting behavior, the long-run equilibrium number of firms will be less in price-setting oligopoly than for quantity-setting oligopoly, all else equal.

Note (Cheng, p. 150) that a firm's choice variable has an impact on the behavior of its rival, because it affects the rival's demand curve. That firm 1 sets price improves equilibrium market performance because when firm 1 sets price, firm 2 faces a flatter demand curve, not because of any consequence that the setting of price by firm 1 has for firm 1. Note also that we can consider markets in which some firms set prices, while others set quantities (Problem 3.6).

3.10   SUPPLY FUNCTION OLIGOPOLY

There are reasons to be dissatisfied with the methodological approach of modeling firms as choosing either price or quantity to maximize own profit. The discussion of figure 3.4 suggests that there is no reason a firm should think of itself as setting either prices or quantities: what matters for the firm is what its rivals' choice variables are, because this fixes the location of the firm's demand curve. Given the location of the firm's demand curve, however, it will maximize profit by making its marginal revenue equal to its marginal cost, whether it sets price or quantity. Is it logically satisfactory to model a firm as believing that its rivals set price, when its own action is the same whether it is described as setting price or quantity?

Klemperer and Meyer (1989) put forward a model of oligopoly behavior in a market with uncertain demand, in which each firm specifies the output that it will put on the market, depending on the realized value of price. Each firm's choice of its price–output combination – its supply function – is made to maximize its own profit, given the supply functions chosen by other firms and the demand function or residual demand function that those choices imply.

The supply functions that are developed in this analysis are not supply functions in the conventional sense – firms are not price-takers. Use of the supply function approach to model firm behavior in imperfectly competitive markets requires that the firm be committed to its choice of supply function. In some cases, such commitment arises naturally, as when firms supply a government agency or a downstream firm and do so by submitting bids specifying legally binding quantities that they will supply at different price levels. For example, Green and Newbery (1992) use the supply-function oligopoly model to analyze the British electric power generation market, which fits this framework. More generally, Klemperer and Meyer argue that, under conditions of uncertainty (1989, p. 1243)

> Adjustment costs and the problems of organizational communication mean that decisions about the size and structure of the organization, the organization's values, and the decision rules to be followed by lower-level managers must be made in advance. These decisions implicitly determine a *supply function* that relates the quantity the firm will sell to the price the market will bear.

3.10.1 General

Let a duopoly market have a well-behaved ($D_p < 0$, $D_{pp} \leq 0$) demand function

$$Q(p, \varepsilon) = D(p) + \varepsilon, \tag{3.80}$$

where the random part of demand ε is distributed over the range $[\varepsilon_L, \varepsilon_U]$. Without loss of generality, assume that the expected value of ε is zero.

Define $e(Q, p)$ as the value of the random term that makes the quantity demanded equal to Q when price equals p:

$$e(Q, p) = Q - D(p). \tag{3.81}$$

Suppose also that both firms (1 and 2) have cost function $C(q)$, with nonnegative first and positive second derivatives.

A strategy for firm i is a function that maps price to output,[27]

$$q_i : [0, p) \to (0, \infty). \tag{3.82}$$

Firms choose supply functions simultaneously, before the value of ε is realized. The equilibrium sought is a Nash equilibrium in supply functions – each firm's supply function maximizes its expected profit, given the supply function chosen by the other firm. Equilibrium price and outputs must also clear the market:

$$D[p^*(\varepsilon)] = q_1[p^*(\varepsilon)] + q_2[p^*(\varepsilon)]. \tag{3.83}$$

If the set of expected profit-maximizing price–output combination points for firm i can be described by a supply function, that supply function will maximize firm i's profit for each value of ε; that is, it will solve

$$\max_p p[D(p) + \varepsilon - q_2(p)] - C[D(p) + \varepsilon - q_2(p)]. \tag{3.84}$$

The first-order condition to maximize (3.84) is

$$D(p) + \varepsilon - q_2(p) + \{p - C'[D(p) + \varepsilon - q_2(p)]\}[D_p(p) + \varepsilon - q_2'(p)] = 0, \tag{3.85}$$

and this can be rewritten as

$$q_1(p) + \{p - C'[q_1(p)]\}[D_p(p) + e(q_1(p) + q_2(p), p) - q_2'(p)] = 0. \tag{3.86}$$

Now impose symmetry of equilibrium supply functions and rearrange terms to obtain the differential equation that must be satisfied by the equilibrium supply functions:

$$q'(p) = \frac{q(p)}{p - C'[q(p)]} + D_p(p). \tag{3.87}$$

---

[27] To simplify derivations, Klemperer and Meyer (1989, p. 1250, fn. 12) allow firms the possibility of choosing negative outputs.

3.10.2   Linear demand, quadratic cost

Klemperer and Meyer (1989) provide general existence results and examine the properties of supply function equilibria for the general case. Here we consider the case of linear demand,

$$p = a - b(Q - \varepsilon), \qquad Q = \frac{a}{b} - \frac{1}{b}p + \varepsilon, \qquad (3.88)$$

with quadratic cost functions

$$C(q) = fq + gq^2, \qquad (3.89)$$

for $f \geq 0, g > 0$.

For this example, the differential equation (3.87) is

$$\frac{dq}{dp} = \frac{q}{(p-f) - 2gq} - \frac{1}{b}. \qquad (3.90)$$

Suppose that the solution to (3.90) takes the form

$$q(p - f) = K(p - f), \qquad (3.91)$$

where the value of the parameter K is to be determined.

Then substituting (3.91) into (3.90) gives

$$K(b, g) = \frac{\sqrt{g^2 + 2bg} - g}{2bg} > 0, \qquad (3.92)$$

the solution of a quadratic equation. Symmetric equilibrium supply functions are then linear in the excess of price over initial marginal cost ($C'(0) = f$):

$$q(p - f) = \frac{\sqrt{g^2 + 2bg} - g}{2bg}(p - f), \qquad (3.93)$$

or, written in inverse form,

$$p_S = f + \frac{2bg}{\sqrt{g^2 + 2bg} - g}q_S. \qquad (3.94)$$

$K(b, g)$ falls as b or g rise: the steeper the inverse demand curve or the more rapidly cost rises as output rises, the less is the quantity supplied at any price.

Given the equilibrium supply functions, the supply-function oligopoly equilibrium price is found at the intersection of the demand and supply curves. Having found the equilibrium price, it is straightforward to compute equilibrium quantities (Problem 3.8).

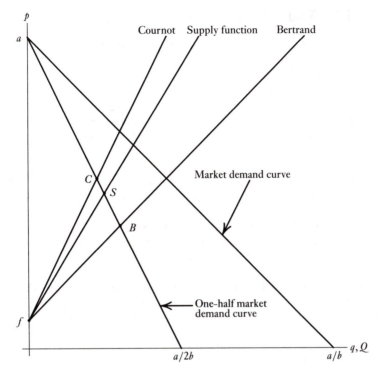

Figure 3.5 A comparison of Cournot, supply function, and Bertrand equilibria; $p = a - bQ$, $C(q) = fq + gq^2$.

The equilibrium supply function (3.94) can be compared with the "supply functions" implied by the Bertrand and the Cournot duopoly models. For Bertrand oligopoly with homogeneous products, equilibrium price equals marginal cost,

$$p_B = f + 2gq_B, \tag{3.95}$$

which is also linear but flatter than (3.94), as shown in figure 3.5.

The Cournot supply function is a version of the first-order condition to maximize firm profit (equivalently, it is a version of the equation of a firm's best-response function). Leaving calculations to Problem 3.8, the equation of the Cournot supply function is

$$p_C = f + (b + 2g)q_C. \tag{3.96}$$

The Cournot supply function is linear and steeper than (3.94), as shown in figure 3.5.

The Bertrand and Cournot supply functions are within the strategy space of the supply function duopoly model, but neither is an equilibrium outcome: with uncertainty, they do not maximize expected firm profit. Cournot behavior obliges firms to make all responses to changes in the level of demand by adjusting output; Bertrand behavior obliges firms to make all such responses by adjusting price. When firms have the possibility of making adjustments along both dimensions, they maximize their profit by doing so.

3.11   TWO-STAGE CAPACITY-CONSTRAINED COMPETITION

3.11.1   Rigid capacity constraints

Kreps and Scheinkman (1983) develop an extension of the Cournot and Bertrand duopoly models in which (1983, p. 327)

> *Capacities* are set in the first stage by the two producers. Demand is then determined by Bertrand-like price competition, and production takes place . . . subject to capacity constraints generated by the first-stage decisions.

Equilibrium in this two–stage game has firms selecting in the first stage capacities that are just sufficient to produce the Cournot equilibrium outputs, and producing those outputs in the second period.[28]

The Kreps and Scheinkman finding is frequently cited as providing a justification for use of the Cournot model, which is characterized as being differentially unsatisfactory compared with the Bertrand model (Maggi, 1996, p. 240):[29]

> If taken literally, the Cournot model assumes that firms dump their production on the market and that an auctioneer determines the price that clears the market. In most industries there is nothing that resembles an auctioneer, and firms use prices as a strategic variable.

This argument should not be pushed too far: it could also be applied to the standard model of perfectly competitive markets. It should also be kept in mind that the concept of capacity does not apply to many technologies. But the Kreps and Scheinkman model is of interest, leaving aside its roles as a justification for use of the Cournot model. The Kreps and Scheinkman model is a seminal example of analysis of rivalry in an imperfectly competitive market, in which outcomes depend critically on the sequence in which decisions are taken and on the way in which earlier decisions condition the payoffs associated with later decisions.

Kreps and Scheinkman assume that the product is homogeneous, and include in their model a rationing rule that determines the quantity demanded of a higher-price firm if the capacity chosen by a lower-price firm does not allow the lower-price firm to supply the entire quantity demanded of it at the lower price. Their results depend on the particular form of rationing rule that is used, as they suggest (Kreps and Scheinkman, 1983, p. 328) and as Davidson and Deneckere (1986) show formally.[30]

In this section, we discuss a version of the Kreps and Scheinkman model with differentiated products. Firms set capacities in the first stage of the game. In the second stage of the game,

---

[28] See also Osborne and Pitchik (1986); Hviid (1991) for an extension to include uncertain demand; and Madden (1998).

[29] The same point is made by Güth (1995, p. 245):

> Ever since the pioneering approach of Cournot (1838) markets with quantities as strategic variables have played a dominant role in economic theory. Without special institutions like auctioneers quantity competition is, however, hardly possible.

[30] See Coase (1935) for an early discussion of the modelling of demand when firms may turn customers away, and Dixon (1987, 1990) for comprehensive treatments.

firms noncooperatively set prices to maximize own profits, subject to capacity constraints and supplying the quantities demanded at the named prices. The Kreps and Scheinkman result holds in this version of the model.[31]

There is a sense in which the Kreps and Scheinkman result is intuitive. Let the cost of a unit of capacity be ρ and define the units in which capacity is measured so that one unit of capacity installed in the first stage allows a firm to produce one unit of output in the second stage (with cost per unit c of other inputs).

One would not expect firms to hold excess capacity in equilibrium. With the Bowley model of product differentiation, if there is no excess capacity in the second stage, then from (3.35) the quantities demanded in the second period satisfy

$$q_1 = \frac{(1 - \theta)a - p_1 + \theta p_2}{(1 - \theta^2)b} = k_1, \qquad q_2 = \frac{(1 - \theta)a - p_2 + \theta p_1}{(1 - \theta^2)b} = k_2. \qquad (3.97)$$

If the equations given by the second equals signs in (3.97) are inverted, one obtains (of course) the equations of the inverse demand curves, writing capacities in place of quantities:

$$p_1 = a - b(k_1 + \theta k_2), \qquad p_2 = a - b(\theta k_1 + k_2). \qquad (3.98)$$

Then in the first period firms select capacities noncooperatively to maximize

$$\pi_1 = [a - c - \rho - b(k_1 + \theta k_2)]k_1 \quad \text{and} \quad \pi_2 = [a - c - \rho - b(\theta k_1 + k_2)]k_2 \qquad (3.99)$$

respectively, where ρ is the unit cost of capacity.

But these payoff functions are functionally identical to the objective functions maximized by firms in the Cournot model with linear demand, Bowley product differentiation, and constant marginal and average cost. If firms noncooperatively select capacities to maximize own payoffs of the form (3.99), equilibrium capacities must be just sufficient to allow firms to produce the equilibrium outputs from the corresponding Cournot game. Except for the labels of the choice variables (capacities instead of outputs), if there is no excess capacity in the second stage then the objective functions in the first stage of the two-stage game and the objective functions in the Cournot game are the same. One therefore expects that the equilibrium outcomes in the two models will correspond.

A formal demonstration that this intuition is valid requires analyzing price best-response functions and second-stage equilibrium payoffs, and working back from these second-stage payoffs to express first-stage payoffs in terms of capacities. For many capacity choices, one firm or the other, or both, will have excess capacity in the equilibrium of the price-setting game. Such capacity choices will not be made in equilibrium, but their consequences must nonetheless be analyzed to show that they will not be chosen in equilibrium.

A firm's price best-response curve may have up to four segments, depending on the first-period capacity choice. If firm 1 has excess capacity in the second period, it selects its price to maximize

---

[31] See Furth and Kovenock (1993) for a Stackelberg leadership version of the Kreps–Scheinkman model that uses a variation of the Bowley product differentiation demand specification.

$$\pi_1 = (p_1 - c)\frac{(1 - \theta)a - p_1 + \theta p_2}{b(1 - \theta^2)} - \rho k_1. \tag{3.100}$$

Loosely, this case should occur if firm 2's price is low. The first-order condition to maximize (3.100) is the same as the first-order condition for the Bertrand model with Bowley product differentiation and marginal cost c. This first-order condition is the equation of *branch one* of firm 1's price best-response function.[32]

For higher values of p_2, the quantity demanded of firm 1 will rise. If firm 1's capacity constraint becomes binding in the second stage, (3.97) holds and is the equation of firm 1's price best-response function. Call this *branch two* of firm 1's price best-response function.

For still higher values of p_2, the quantity demanded of firm 2 falls to zero. At this point, firm 1 is constrained to set price along the $p_2 = 0$ line, which is *branch four* of firm 1's price best-response function. Finally, if firm 2 sets a very high price, firm 1 will set either the unconstrained monopoly price or the market-clearing price for its installed capacity, if that capacity does not allow it to produce the monopoly output. At this point, firm 1's second-stage best-response function becomes vertical (*branch five*).[33]

Figure 3.7(b) shows second-stage price best-response functions with branch one, branch two, and branch five segments.

Although a firm's second-stage price best-response function may have up to four segments, in second-stage equilibrium a firm is either on its branch one (excess capacity) or its branch two (capacity constrained). There are four possible second-stage equilibrium types. If both firms have low capacity levels, both are capacity constrained. If both firms have high capacity levels, neither firm is capacity constrained. If one firm has a high capacity level and the other a low capacity level, then the low–capacity firm is constrained in second-stage equilibrium. The corresponding regions of capacity space are defined in table 3.1 and shown in figure 3.6.

Having determined the second-stage equilibrium types that correspond to alternative capacity choices, one can compute a firm's second-stage payoff as a function of capacities and find the firm's best-response capacity function.[34]

The capacity functions are discontinuous, as shown in figure 3.7(a), but intersect in the $(b2, b2)$ region of capacity space, where both firms are capacity-constrained in the second stage. Best-response functions in this region of capacity space are functionally identical to

---

[32] The terminology *branch one*, *branch two*, and so on follows Maggi (1996). For an explanation of branch three, see section 3.11.2.

[33] In the formulation used here, if a price-setting firm is capacity constrained, its price adjusts so that the quantity demanded of it equals its capacity. This determines the residual demand curve facing the other firm as the residual demand curve of a Bertrand duopolist. Price best-response functions are continuous. Yin and Ng (1997, 2000) present an extension of the Kreps and Scheinkman model to differentiated products in which a firm assumes that the other firm's output is fixed if the other firm should be capacity constrained. In such cases, the first firm is maximizing profit along a Cournot residual demand curve. Schulz (2000) shows that price best-response functions can be discontinuous in the Yin and Ng formulation.

[34] Firm 1's payoff function needs to be analyzed separately for three vertical ranges of k_2. For $0 \leq k_2 \leq k^*_{B(c)}$, firm 1's payoff is that of $(b2, b2)$ equilibrium on the left, and of $(b1, b2)$ equilibrium on the right. For $k_D \leq k_2$ (where k_D is the $k_1 = 0$ intercept of firm 2's Bertrand best-response function translated into capacity space), firm 1's payoff is that of $(b2, b1)$ equilibrium on the left, and of $(b1, b1)$ equilibrium on the right. For both ranges, firm 1's payoff function has one local (and therefore global) maximum. For $k^*_{B(c)} \leq k_2 \leq k_D$, firm 1's payoff is (moving from left to right) that of $(b2, b2)$ equilibrium, of $(b2, b1)$ equilibrium, and that of $(b2, b2)$ equilibrium.

Table 3.1 First-stage equilibrium types by region of capacity space. $k^*_{B(c)} =$ capacity that is just sufficient to allow a firm to produce its Bertrand equilibrium output when both firms have marginal cost c; $k^{br}_{B(c)}(k) =$ capacity that just allows a firm to produce its Bertrand best-response output if marginal cost is c and the other firm produces output k

	Region of capacity space	Firm 1	Firm 2
$(b1, b1)$	$k_1 \geq k^*_{B(c)}, k_2 \geq k^*_{B(c)}$	Branch one	Branch one
$(b1, b2)$	$k_1 \geq k^{br}_{B(c)}(k_2), k_2 \leq k^*_{B(c)}$	Branch one	Branch two
$(b2, b1)$	$k_1 \leq k^*_{B(c)}, k_2 \geq k^{br}_{B(c)}(k_1)$	Branch two	Branch one
$(b2, b2)$	$k_1 \leq k^{br}_{B(c)}(k_2), k_2 \leq k^{br}_{B(c)}(k_1)$	Branch two	Branch two

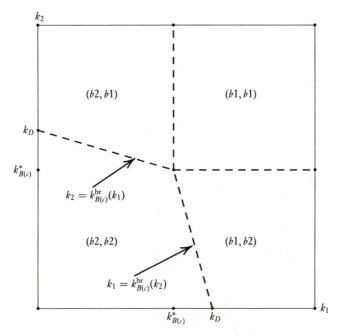

Figure 3.6 Segments of price best-response functions that intersect in equilibrium, capacity space; (bi, bj) indicates that in second-stage equilibrium, firm 1's branch i intersects with firm 2's branch j. $k^*_{B(c)} =$ capacity that is just sufficient to allow a firm to produce its Bertrand equilibrium output when both firms have marginal cost c; $k^{br}_{B(c)}(k) =$ capacity that just allows a firm to produce its Bertrand best-response output if marginal cost is c and the other firm produces output k.

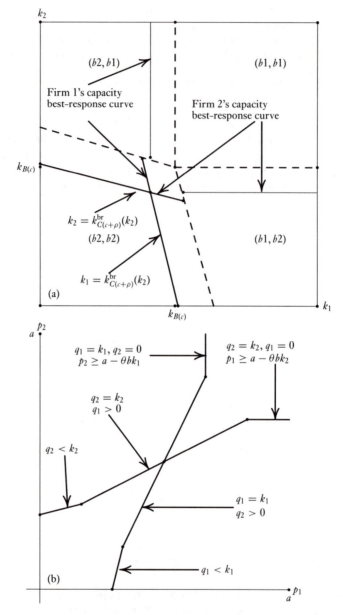

Figure 3.7 Two-stage capacity-constrained price-setting duopoly equilibrium. $k^{br}_{C(c+\rho)}(k) =$ capacity that just allows a firm to produce its Cournot best-response output if both firms have marginal cost $c + \rho$; $k^*_{B(c)} =$ capacity that is just sufficient to allow a firm to produce its Bertrand equilibrium output when both firms have marginal cost c. (a) Capacity best-response curves; (b) second-stage price best-response curves.

the Cournot best-response functions and therefore intersect at the capacity levels that just allow firms to produce the Cournot equilibrium outputs.[35]

3.11.2   Permeable capacity constraints

One might regard the specification of an inflexible capacity constraint as unduly restrictive. Güth (1995) and Maggi (1996) extend the Kreps and Scheinkman with product differentiation model to allow a firm to expand capacity in the second period, if necessary to meet demand, at a differentially higher cost compared to first-period installation.[36]

If the unit cost of adding capacity in the second period is $\rho + \delta > \rho$, firm 1's payoff when it adds such capacity is

$$
\pi_1 = (p_1 - c - \rho)k_1 + (p_1 - c - \rho - \delta)\left[\frac{(1-\theta)a - p_1 + \theta p_2}{b(1-\theta^2)} - k_1\right]. \tag{3.101}
$$

Branch three is the segment of a firm's price best-response function when it chooses to expand capacity to meet demand. The equation of branch three is the first-order condition to maximize (3.101).

Price best-response functions may have up to five segments, depending on capacity choices and the parameters of the model. In second-stage equilibrium a firm is either on its branch one, its branch two, or its branch three (capacity constrained). The are nine possible second-stage equilibrium types, in regions shown in figure 3.8.[37]

Figure 3.8 may be compared with figure 3.6. In the Güth–Maggi model, if firms select moderate or high capacity levels in the first period, equilibrium types are as in the Kreps and Scheinkman model. If a firm selects a low capacity level in the first period, in second-stage equilibrium it produces beyond capacity and is on branch three of its price best-response function.

Knowing the segment each firm is on in different regions of capacity space, it is possible to compute first-stage payoffs as a function of capacity choices.[38] There are three types of results.

Figure 3.9 shows equilibrium capacity and price best-response curves in the Güth–Maggi model when

$$
\delta \geq \delta^H = \frac{\theta^2}{2+\theta}(a - c - \rho). \tag{3.102}
$$

[35] Anderhub et al. (2000) report the results of experiments based on a model in which, like that of Maggi, firms can produce above capacity at a cost penalty. They find that pricing tends to be optimal, given capacities, and that capacities converge on levels above those of Cournot equilibrium.

[36] See also Friedman (1992). Boccard and Wauthy (1998) examine the robustness of the results of the Güth–Maggi results when firms are allowed to ration consumers.

[37] In figure 3.8, $k^*_{B(c+\rho+\delta,c)}$ is the first firm's equilibrium capacity if the first firm has unit cost $c + \rho + \delta$, the second firm has unit cost c, firms compete as Bertrand duopolists, and both firms hold just enough capacity to produce their equilibrium outputs. $k^*_{B(c,c+\rho+\delta)}$ is interpreted in a corresponding way. The discussion assumes that both firms have positive output, which implies some restrictions on the parameters of the model.

[38] In the Güth–Maggi model, firm 1's payoffs need to be analyzed over five distinct ranges of k_2. For two of these ranges, $k^*_{B(c+\rho+\delta,c)} \leq k_2 \leq k^*_{B(c+\rho+\delta)}$ and $k^*_{B(c)} \leq k_2 \leq k^*_{B(c,c+\rho+\delta)}$, the payoff function may have two local maxima, the payoffs at which must be compared to determine the global maximum.

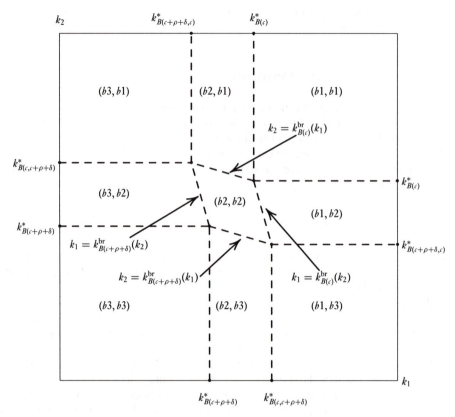

Figure 3.8 Equilibrium price best-response curve intersections, capacity space, Güth–Maggi model. $a = 12$, $b = c = \rho = 1$, $\theta = 1/2$, $\delta = 3/2$.

If $\delta = \delta^H$, Bertrand and Cournot equilibrium prices are the same when both firms have marginal cost $c + \rho + \delta^H$ under Bertrand oligopoly, or $c + \rho$ under Cournot oligopoly.[39] For $\delta \geq \delta^H$, capacity best-response curves in the neighborhood of equilibrium (figure 3.9(a)[40]) have the same functional form as the capacity best-response functions of the Kreps and Scheinkman model. These are the Cournot best-response functions, written in capacity space rather than output space. In second-stage equilibrium (figure 3.9(b)), firms are on segment two of their price best-response functions. For $\delta = \delta^H$, as in the Kreps and Scheinkman model, in equilibrium, in the first period firms select capacities that are just sufficient to produce Cournot equilibrium outputs; in the second period, they produce to capacity.

[39] The size of δ relative to δ^H is a factor determining the location of the global maximum of firm 1's payoff function when $k^*_{B(c+\rho+\delta)} \leq k_2 \leq k^*_{B(c,c+\rho+\delta)}$.
[40] Note that figures 3.9(a) and 3.10(a) are close-ups of the central region of capacity space.

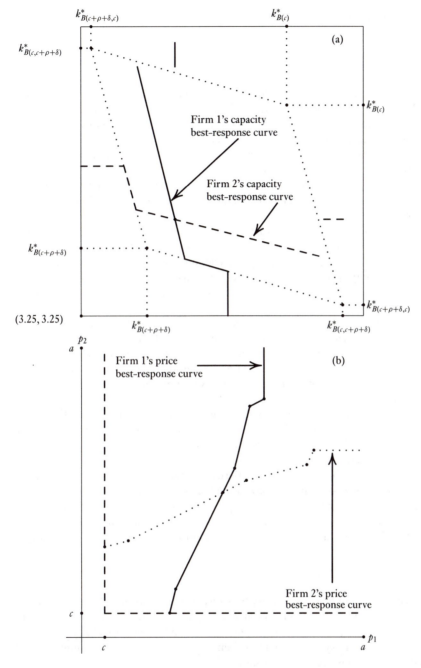

Figure 3.9 High-δ equilibrium, Güth–Maggi model. $a = 12$, $b = c = 1$, $\theta = 1/2$, $\delta = 3/2$. (a) Central region of capacity space; (b) equilibrium price best-response curves.

For intermediate values of δ,

$$\delta^L = \frac{\theta^2(1-\theta)}{4 - 2\theta - \theta^2}(a - c - \rho) \leq \delta \leq \delta^H \tag{3.103}$$

(figure 3.10(a)), firm 1's best-response capacity first rises to the lower boundary of the $(b2, b2)$ region.[41] This line shows firm 2's best-response output if firms compete as Bertrand duopolists, if both firms have marginal cost $c + \rho + \delta$, and if firm 1 produces output k_1. Moving left along this line, firm 1's best-response capacity reaches the point $(k^*_{B(c+\rho+\delta)}, k^*_{B(c+\rho+\delta)})$, where both firms hold the capacity needed to produce Bertrand equilibrium output when both firms have marginal cost $c + \rho + \delta$.

Since firms are identical and capacity best-response functions are symmetric, $(k^*_{B(c+\rho+\delta)}, k^*_{B(c+\rho+\delta)})$ is an equilibrium, and the symmetric equilibrium, for intermediate values of δ.

Firm 1's capacity best-response curve continues up the left boundary of the $(b2, b2)$ region.

Figure 3.10(b) below shows price best-response curves for the symmetric equilibrium capacities $(k^*_{B(c+\rho+\delta)}, k^*_{B(c+\rho+\delta)})$. The symmetric equilibrium is in both the $(b3, b3)$ and $(b2, b2)$ regions of capacity space, and the price best-response curves intersect at the juncture of the branch two and branch three segments of the firms' price. Firms do not hold excess capacity in symmetric equilibrium.

As shown in figure 3.10(a), firm 1's capacity best-response curve includes a small segment of the lower boundary of the $(b2, b2)$ region and all of the left boundary of the $(b2, b2)$ region. By symmetry, firm 2's capacity best-response curve includes a small segment of the left boundary of the $(b2, b2)$ region and all of the lower boundary of the $(b2, b2)$ region. For intermediate values of δ, there is an interval of asymmetric capacity equilibria in the neighborhood of $(k^*_{B(c+\rho+\delta)}, k^*_{B(c+\rho+\delta)})$.[42]

As δ declines within the range (3.103), the vertical segments of firm 1's capacity best-response curve shift to the left, while the horizontal segments of firm 2's capacity best-response curves shift downward. This movement continues until the lower vertical segment of firm 1's best-response curve coincides with the segment $k_1 = k^*_{B(c+\rho+\delta)}$ (the capacity just sufficient to allow a firm to produce its Bertrand equilibrium output when both firms have marginal cost $c + \rho + \delta$) and the upper vertical segment of firm 1's best-response curve coincides with the segment $k_1 = k^*_{B(c+\rho+\delta,c)}$ (the capacity just sufficient to allow firm 1 to produce its Bertrand equilibrium output when firm 1 has marginal cost $c + \rho + \delta$ and firm 2 has marginal cost c). Firm 2's capacity best-response curve moves in the same way. For low values of δ,

$$\delta \leq \delta^L, \tag{3.104}$$

the initial segment of firm 1's capacity best-response curve is the vertical line with equation $k_1 = k^*_{B(c+\rho+\delta)}$, the initial segment of firm 2's capacity best-response curve is the horizontal line $k_2 = k^*_{B(c+\rho+\delta)}$, and the best-response curves intersect only at $(k^*_{B(c+\rho+\delta)}, k^*_{B(c+\rho+\delta)})$; see figure 3.11. The symmetric equilibrium $(k^*_{B(c+\rho+\delta)}, k^*_{B(c+\rho+\delta)})$ is unique. Equilibrium capacity best-response curves are as shown in figure 3.10

---

[41] If $\delta^L \leq \delta$, then the global maximum of firm 1's $(b2, b3)$ payoff function occurs within region $(b2, b3)$.

[42] Maggi (1996, pp. 244–5) discusses asymmetric equilibria.

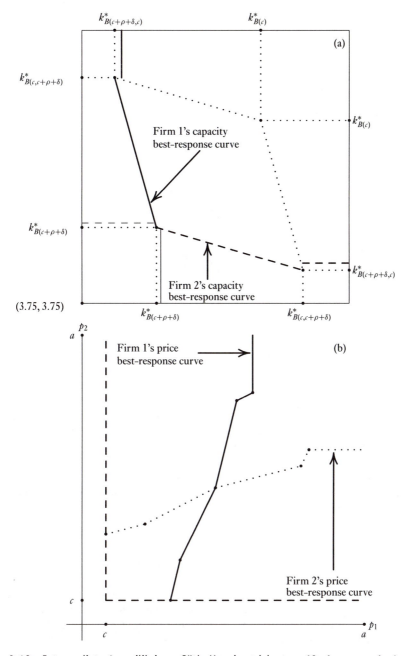

Figure 3.10 Intermediate-δ equilibrium, Güth–Maggi model. $a = 12$, $b = c = 1$, $\theta = 1/2$, $\delta = 1/2$. (a) Central region of capacity space; (b) equilibrium price best-response curves.

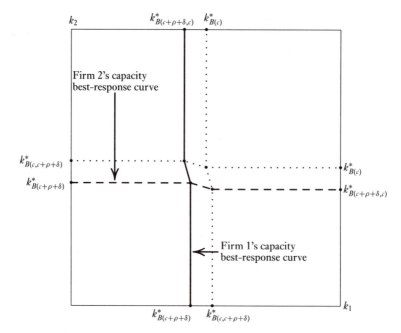

Figure 3.11 Capacity best-response curves, Güth–Maggi model, low-δ case. $a = 12$, $b = c = 1$, $\theta = \frac{1}{2}$, $\delta = \frac{1}{4}$.

Once again, these results are intuitive. It is never optimal for a firm to hold excess capacity. If δ is sufficiently high, then in the first stage firms are in a situation similar to that of the Kreps and Scheinkman model with marginal cost $c + \rho$, and their equilibrium behavior is the same as in that model. If δ is low, then in the second period firms are very nearly in the situation of Bertrand duopolists with marginal cost $c + \rho + \delta$; their equilibrium capacity choice is the capacity that just allows them to produce their Bertrand equilibrium output with this level of marginal cost.

3.12   CONCLUSION

The contemporary version of the Cournot model interprets it as a one-shot game, in which firms simultaneously act with complete and perfect knowledge and unlimited computing ability. Nash equilibrium in this one-shot game coincides with Cournot's result. Interpreting the Cournot model as a one-shot game, the equilibrium of the Cournot model is defined as the Nash equilibrium of the one-shot game.

Generalizations of the Cournot model allow for conjectures, for partial joint-profit-maximizing behavior, and for product differentiation. When products are differentiated, it is natural to consider models of the Bertrand type, in which firms set price rather than quantity. All else equal, models in which firms set price present firms with more elastic residual demand curves than models in which firms set quantity, yielding better equilibrium market performance.

In the presence of uncertainty, and if firms can commit in advance to schedules that relate the quantity supplied to price, equilibrium supply curves imply market behavior that is intermediate between Cournot and Bertrand outcomes.

The supply-function oligopoly model appeals informally to firm or market characteristics which imply that firms commit to supply schedules before an uncertain part of market demand is realized. A large class of multiperiod oligopoly models examine behavior when firms take some decisions in early periods, conditioning the nature of strategic interaction in later periods. The models of Kreps and Scheinkman and Güth–Maggi are examples, and we will meet others in chapter 8.

PROBLEMS

3.1 In a Cournot duopoly, let the inverse demand function be linear,

$$p = a - b(q_1 + q_2),$$

and let marginal and average cost per unit be a constant c.

(a) Graph best-response curves in the conjectural derivative model if firms hold identical conjectures $\lambda = -1, 0, +1$.
(b) Graph best-response curves in the conjectural elasticity model if firms hold identical conjectures $\alpha = -1, 0, +1$.

3.2 There are two varieties, 1 and 2. There are two groups of n consumers each, A and B, uniformly distributed over $[0, 1]$.

Consumers in group A regard variety 2 as being of higher quality than variety 2. A consumer in group A located at $i \in [0, 1]$ gets utility $e - fi - p_1$ from purchasing variety 1 and utility $g - i - p_2$ from purchasing variety 2, where $e > g, f > 1$.

Consumers in group B have preferences of the same functional forms as consumers of group A, but group B consumers regard variety 2 as being of higher quality than variety 1. Producers cannot price discriminate between members of the two groups.

Show that the equations of the demand curves and the inverse demand curves for the two varieties are

$$q_1 = \frac{n}{f - 1} [(f - 1)g - (1 + f)p_1 + 2p_2],$$

$$q_2 = \frac{n}{f - 1} [(f - 1)g + 2p_1 - (1 + f)p_2],$$

and

$$p_1 = g - \frac{1}{n}\frac{(1+f)q_1 + 2q_2}{3+f} = g - \frac{1}{n}\frac{1+f}{3+f}\left(q_1 + \frac{2}{1+f}q_2\right),$$

$$p_2 = g - \frac{1}{n}\frac{2q_1 + (1+f)q_2}{3+f} = g - \frac{1}{n}\frac{1+f}{3+f}\left(\frac{2}{1+f}q_1 + q_2\right),$$

respectively.

Compare the equations of the inverse demand curves with inverse demand curves from the Bowley model of product differentiation.

3.3 Derive (a) (3.39), the demand function for the Bowley linear model of product differentiation,

$$q_i = \frac{(1-\theta)a - [1 + (n-2)\theta]p_i + \theta \sum_{j\neq i}p_j}{b(1-\theta)[1 + (n-1)\theta]},$$

and (b) (3.51), the inverse demand function implied by the Shubik–Levitan linear model of product differentiation:

$$p_i = \frac{\alpha}{\beta} - \frac{1}{\beta}\frac{n+\gamma}{1+\gamma}\left(\frac{\gamma}{n+\gamma}q_1 + \frac{\gamma}{n+\gamma}q_2 + \cdots + q_i + \cdots + \frac{\gamma}{n+\gamma}q_n\right).$$

3.4 Find quantity-setting oligopoly equilibrium outputs and prices with the Shubik–Levitan linear model of product differentiation if firms have identical constant marginal and average cost c per unit.

3.5 Find price-setting oligopoly prices and outputs with the Bowley linear model of product differentiation if firms have identical constant marginal and average cost c per unit.

3.6 Find noncooperative equilibrium prices, quantities, and payoffs for a duopoly if demand follows the Bowley linear model of product differentiation, if firms have identical constant marginal and average cost c per unit, and if firm 1 sets quantity while firm 2 sets price.

3.7 For duopoly with the Bowley product differentiation specification and constant marginal cost c per unit for both firms:

(a) Find Cournot equilibrium prices and quantities if firms have symmetric conjectural quantity elasticities $\alpha = (q_i/q_j)(\partial q_j/\partial q_i)$, for $i, j = 1, 2$ and $j \neq i$.

(b) Find Bertrand equilibrium prices and quantities if firms have symmetric conjectural price elasticities $\beta = (p_i/p_j)(\partial p_j/\partial p_i)$, for $i, j = 1, 2$ and $j \neq i$.

(c) Show that the equilibrium prices and quantities from (a) and (b) are the same for

$$\beta = \frac{\alpha + \theta}{1 + \alpha\theta}.$$

3.8 Derive expressions for supply function duopoly price and output if the inverse demand function is

$$p = a - b(Q - \varepsilon)$$

and firms have the cost function

$$C(q) = fq + gq^2.$$

Compare these results with those for Cournot and Bertrand duopoly.

3.9 If the inverse demand function is

$$p = a - b(Q - \varepsilon)$$

and each firm has its own cost function

$$C_i(q) = f_i q + g_i q^2$$

for $i = 1, 2$, show that the equilibrium supply functions (written in inverse form) are

$$p = f + \frac{\sqrt{(b + g_1)(b + g_2)(bg_1 + g_2g_1 + bg_2)} - g_1(b + g_2)}{b(bg_1 + 2g_2g_1 + g_2b)} q_1$$

and

$$p = f + \frac{\sqrt{(b + g_1)(b + g_2)(bg_1 + g_2g_1 + bg_2)} - g_2(b + g_1)}{b(bg_1 + 2g_2g_1 + g_2b)} q_2.$$

3.10 If products are differentiated with inverse demand curves following the Bowley specification,

$$p_1 = a - b(q_1 + \theta q_2), \qquad p_2 = a - b(\theta q_1 + q_2)$$

for $i = 1, 2$, and firms have the same cost function,

$$C(q) = fq + gq^2,$$

show that the equilibrium supply functions (written in inverse form) are

$$p = f + \frac{\sqrt{g^2 + 2bg + (1 - \theta^2)b^2} - g}{b((1 - \theta^2)b + 2g)} q.$$

CHAPTER FOUR

FOUNDATIONS OF OLIGOPOLY THEORY III

Although the [mathematical] methods are elementary, their application is complicated.
Smithies (1941)

4.1 HOTELLING

The Bowley (1924) and Shubik–Levitan (1980) models are traditionally referred to as representative consumer models of product differentiation. It would be more precise to call them aggregate demand models. They model aggregate demand for differentiated products without exploring what kind of individual consumer behavior, and what distribution of individual consumers, would be required to produce the aggregate behavior that is assumed.

Despite notable antecedents,[1] it is Hotelling's (1929) analysis of spatial product differentiation that is the progenitor of the wide range of models of imperfectly competitive markets that derive the properties of aggregate demand from explicit assumptions about individual demand and the way in which individual demand is related to product characteristics.[2]

4.1.1 Setup

Hotelling saw the assumption that the product was standardized as the key to the stark difference between the results of the Cournot and Bertrand models. Standardization implies that all sales are made by the supplier with the lowest price, an implication which Hotelling thought to be unrealistic as a description of consumer behavior. He expected small price

---

[1] In particular, Launhardt (1885, 1993), on whose contribution see Dos Santos Ferreira and Thisse (1996). It is natural to speculate about a possible influence of chapter 13 of Abbott (1884) on Hotelling.

[2] We have seen (section 3.6.1) that the Bowley model of aggregate horizontal differentiation can be derived from a variation of the standard vertical differentiation model. It is in large measure because of the lessons of the Hotelling approach that the usefulness of such exercises is appreciated.

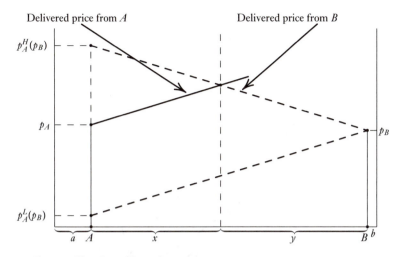

Figure 4.1 The Hotelling linear duopoly model: $l = 35$, $a = 4$, $b = 1$, $c = 1$.

differences to translate into small differences in sales (1929, p. 41):

> of all the purchasers of a commodity, some buy from one seller, some from another, in spite of moderate differences in price. If the purveyor of an article gradually increases his price while his rivals keep theirs fixed, the diminution in volume of his sales will in general take place continuously rather than in the abrupt way which has been tacitly assumed.

With his linear model, which has become one of the canonical models of product differentiation, Hotelling aimed (unsuccessfully, as it turns out) to provide a framework for the analysis of duopoly interactions within which the quantity demanded of an individual producer is a continuous function of the prices of all producers.

Figure 4.1 illustrates the linear duopoly model. Consumers, one per unit length and each purchasing one unit of the good, are uniformly distributed along a line of length l.

There are two firms. Firm A is located $a > 0$ units from the left end of the line and firm B is located $b > 0$ units from the right end of the line, with $a + b \leq l$ (that is, firm A is located to the left of firm B).

Firm A's mill price is p_A, and firm B's mill price is p_B. A consumer located x units away from the A mill pays delivered price $p_A + cx$ for one unit of the product purchased from A; a consumer located y units away from the B mill pays delivered price $p_B + cy$ for one unit of the product purchased from B.

The charge c per unit distance may be thought of as transportation cost in a literal sense. Alternatively,[3] each point on the line may be taken to identify an amount of some product characteristic – sweetness, for example – that varies in a continuous way. In this interpretation,

---

[3] This interpretation is given by Hotelling (1929, p. 55) and by Lerner and Singer (1937, p. 146, fn. 4); see also Lancaster (1980); Horstmann and Slivinski (1985); Neven (1986), and for a synthesis, Archibald et al. (1986, pp. 7–14). See Freeman and Dungay (1981) for a case study in which the transportation cost model is applied in a literal sense.

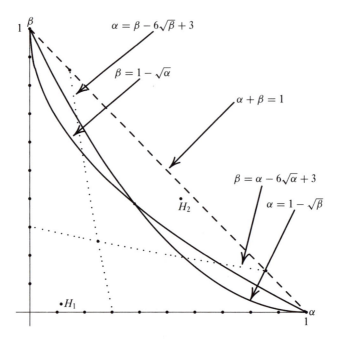

Figure 4.2 Regions in location space, Hotelling linear duopoly model: $\alpha = a/l$, $\beta = b/l$. H_1: $l = 35$, $a = 4$, $b = 1$. H_2: $l = 20$, $a = 11$, $b = 8$.

the point at which a consumer is located indicates that consumer's most preferred amount of the characteristic, while the location of a plant indicates the amount of the characteristic in the variety produced by the plant. Under this interpretation, cx represents the loss of utility of a consumer who takes a variety x units distant from his most preferred variety.

Each consumer buys one unit of the product from the plant that offers the lowest delivered price.

4.1.2   Locations with well-behaved best-response functions

Figure 4.1 is drawn for parameter values $l = 35$, $a = 4$, $b = 1$, $c = 1$ and with $p_B = 34$. The location pair (a, b) of figure 4.1 is shown as point H_1 in figure 4.2, on the axes of which distances from the ends of the line are measured as fractions of the length of the linear market. For the parameters of figure 4.1, firms are located relatively close to the ends of the market.

Since consumers buy from the firm offering the lowest delivered price, if firm A sets a price greater than B's delivered price at A's location,

$$p_A^H(p_B) = p_B + c(l - a - b), \tag{4.1}$$

all consumers will buy from firm B. If firm A sets a price less than

$$p_A^L(p_B) = p_B - c(l - a - b), \tag{4.2}$$

then A's delivered price at B's location is less than B's mill price, and all consumers will buy from firm A.[4]

Here $l - a - b$ is the distance between the two plants. Thus for prices that are sufficiently high or low, a small price change will cause all demand to shift from one supplier to another, and what "sufficiently high or low" means depends on the distance between the two plants.

But for intermediate prices,

$$p_A^L(p_B) \leq p_A \leq p_A^H(p_B), \tag{4.3}$$

the quantity demanded of firm A is a continuous function of the prices of both firms and the two firms both make sales in the central region of the market. There is then a consumer who faces the same delivered price from either firm,

$$p_A + cx = p_B + cy, \tag{4.4}$$

where x is the distance to plant A and y is the distance to plant B, and that consumer is indifferent between buying from A or B.

Solving the equal-delivered-price equation (4.4) and the length-of-market identity

$$a + x + y + b \equiv l, \tag{4.5}$$

we obtain

$$x = \tfrac{1}{2}\left(l - a - b + \frac{p_B - p_A}{c}\right). \tag{4.6}$$

The quantity demanded of firm A for p_A in the range (11.3) is then

$$q_A = a + x = \tfrac{1}{2}\left(l + a - b + \frac{p_B - p_A}{c}\right). \tag{4.7}$$

For locations of the kind shown in figure 4.1, A faces the demand function

$$q_A = \begin{cases} l, & p_A < p_A^L(p_B); \\ \tfrac{1}{2}\left(l + a - b + \frac{p_B - p_A}{c}\right), & p_A^L(p_B) \leq p_A \leq p_A^H(p_B); \\ 0, & p_A^H(p_B) < p_A. \end{cases} \tag{4.8}$$

A's demand function exhibits a double discontinuity. As p_A rises from below to $p_A^L(p_B)$, q_A falls from l to $l - b$. As p_A rises above $p_A^H(p_B)$, q_A falls from a to 0.

A's profit function is

$$\pi_A = \begin{cases} p_A l, & p_A < p_A^L(p_B); \\ \tfrac{1}{2}p_A\left(l + a - b + \frac{p_B - p_A}{c}\right), & p_A^L(p_B) \leq p_A \leq p_A^H(p_B); \\ 0, & p_A^H(p_B) < p_A. \end{cases} \tag{4.9}$$

---

[4] If $p_A^L(p_B) < 0$, which can occur if p_B is low, c large, and $l - a - b$ large (firms near the ends of the line), firm A cannot undercut firm B's mill price.

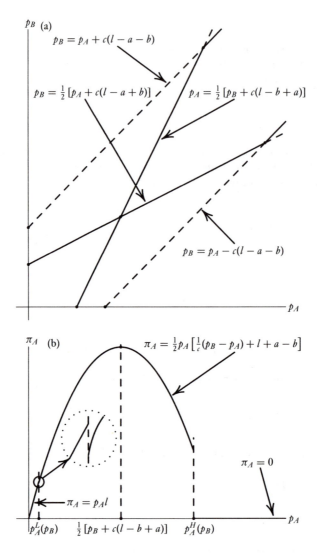

Figure 4.3 The Hotelling linear duopoly model: $l = 35$, $a = 4$, $b = 1$, $c = 1$. (a) Best-response curves; (b) firm A's profit curve, $p_B = 34$.

The profit function is illustrated in figure 4.3(b), for the parameters of figure 4.1 and with p_B set at its equilibrium value. For this example, firm A's best-response function has two segments.

For low and intermediate values of p_B, firm A's profit is maximized along the middle segment of its profit function. The corresponding first-order condition can be written as

$$p_A = \tfrac{1}{2}\left[p_B + c(l - b + a)\right]. \qquad (4.10)$$

For sufficiently high values of p_B, firm A's profit-maximizing strategy is to set

$$p_A = p_B - c(l - a - b) - \varepsilon, \tag{4.11}$$

for ε small, so that A just undercuts B's mill price and supplies the entire market.

For the parameter values of figures 4.1 and 4.3, both firms have best-response functions of the same type, and the best-response curves intersect at prices for which the two firms share the middle of the market (figure 4.3(a)). Solving the equations of the best-response functions, the Nash equilibrium prices and payoffs are

$$p_A^* = \left(l + \frac{a - b}{3}\right) c, \qquad \pi_A^* = \frac{1}{2c}\left(p_A^*\right)^2,$$

$$\tag{4.12}$$

$$p_B^* = \left(l + \frac{b - a}{3}\right) c, \qquad \pi_B^* = \frac{1}{2c}\left(p_B^*\right)^2.$$

From (4.12), π_A rises with a and π_B rises with b. If locations are now considered to be choice variables of the firms, the fact that a firm's payoff rises as it moves away from its end of the market suggests that A and B would wish to move toward the center of the market.[5] This led Hotelling (1929, p. 54) to formulate what (following Boulding, 1966) has come to be called the *Principle of Minimum Differentiation*:

> Buyers are confronted everywhere with an excessive sameness. When a new merchant or manufacturer sets up shop he must not produce something exactly like what is already on the market or he will risk a price war of the type discussed by Bertrand. . . . But there is an incentive to make the new product very much like the old, applying some slight change which will seem an improvement to as many buyers as possible without ever going far in this direction. . . [a] tendency to make only slight deviations in order to have for the new commodity as many buyers of the old as possible, to get. . . between one's competitors and a mass of customers.

Today, this analysis would be formalized as a two–stage static game. In the second stage, with locations given, firms noncooperatively set prices to maximize own profit. In the first stage, firms noncooperatively pick locations to maximize own profit, anticipating equilibrium payoffs in the second stage.

4.1.3   Locations with badly behaved best-response functions

However, the equilibrium prices and payoffs of (4.12) are not valid if a and/or b are too large.[6] For such location pairs, pure-strategy equilibrium prices are not well defined, making it impossible to calculate payoffs in the second, price-setting stage of the game. Lacking values for second-stage payoffs when firms are located too close together, it is impossible to analyze equilibrium behavior in the first, location-setting, stage of the game.

---

[5] Recall that we assume $a + b \leq l$. For analysis that relaxes this assumption, allowing firm A to locate to the right of firm B, in a model with quadratic transportation cost, see Bester et al. (1991).

[6] Vickrey (1964, pp. 323–34); d'Aspremont et al. (1979).

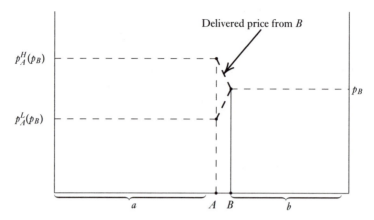

Figure 4.4   The Hotelling linear duopoly model: $l = 20$, $a = 11$, $b = 8$, $c = 1$; $p_B = \hat{p}_B = 3\frac{1}{9}$.

To see the issues involved, consider another example discussed by Hotelling (1929, p. 48, fn. 1): $l = 20$, $a = 11$, $b = 8$, $c = 1$. The linear market of this example is shown in figure 4.4. Firms' locations (point H_2 in figure 4.2) are relatively close to the center of the linear market.

Firm A's profit function (figure 4.5(b)) has three segments, given by (4.9). Firm A has the option of setting a price in the range $p_A^L(p_B) \leq p_A \leq p_A^H(p_B)$ and sharing the center of the market with firm B. But for close locations, sharing the center of the market is not firm A's most profitable option.

As shown in figure 4.5(b), for $p_A^L(p_B) \leq p_A < p_A^H(p_B)$ firm A's profit sharing the center of the market with B is strictly less than firm A's profit from slightly undercutting firm B's mill price (setting $p_A = p_B - c(l - a - b) - \varepsilon$ for some small ε) and supplying the whole market. For $p_A = p_A^H(p_B)$, firm A's payoff is the same if it undercuts B's mill price at B's location or if it matches B's delivered price at A's location ($p_A = p_B + c(l - a - b)$), supplying only its own hinterland.

There is a discontinuity in A's best-response function at $p_B = \hat{p}_B$ (figure 4.5(a)). The discontinuity price

$$\hat{p}_B = c \frac{l + a}{l - a}(l - a - b) \tag{4.13}$$

is the value for which A's profit supplying its hinterland ($[p_B + c(l - a - b)]\, a$) and its profit supplying the whole market ($[p_B - c(l - a - b)]\, l$) are the same.

For $p_B < \hat{p}_B$, firm A would need to set a very low price to capture the entire market; its most profitable choice is to match B's delivered price at A's location and sell a units to the customers located in its hinterland. For $p_B > \hat{p}_B$, it is most profitable for firm A to undercut B's mill price and supply the whole market.

There is a similar discontinuity in firm B's best-response function. For close locations, of the kind shown in figure 4.5(a), the best-response functions of the two firms do not intersect,

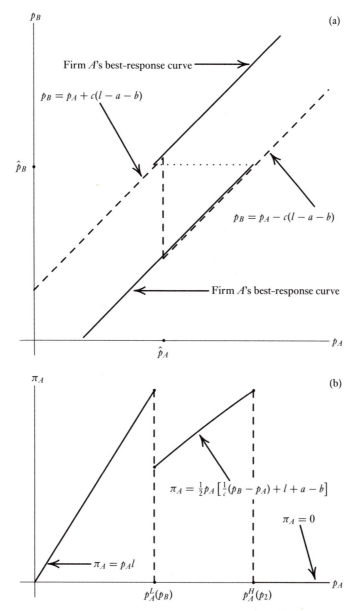

Figure 4.5 The Hotelling linear duopoly model: $l = 20$, $a = 11$, $b = 8$, $c = 1$. (a) Price best-response curves; (b) firm A's profit function, $p_B = \hat{p}_B = 3\frac{4}{9}$.

meaning that there is no pure-strategy equilibrium in prices. This result reflects the fact that for close locations payoff functions are not quasi-concave (figure 4.5(b)).[7]

4.1.4   Best-response functions

Anderson (1987) shows that, for the linear duopoly model, best-response functions have two types of configuration, depending on locations.

For $l - a \leq \sqrt{lb}$ or $\alpha \geq 1 - \sqrt{\beta}$, for $\alpha = a/l$, $\beta = b/l$, firm A's best-response function is

$$p_A(p_B) = \begin{cases} p_B + c(l - a - b), & p_B \leq \hat{p}_B; \\ p_B - c(l - a - b) - \varepsilon, & p_B > \hat{p}_B. \end{cases} \qquad (4.14)$$

There is a corresponding expression for firm B's best-response function when $\beta \geq 1 - \sqrt{\alpha}$.

For low p_B, firm A supplies only its hinterland; for high p_B, firm A supplies the whole market. This case applies when a and b are relatively large. The curves $\alpha = 1 - \sqrt{\beta}$ and $\beta = 1 - \sqrt{\alpha}$ are shown as solid lines in figure 4.2. Location pair H_2 lies above both curves, showing that for this case both firms have two-segment best-response curves of form (4.14).

For $l - a > \sqrt{lb}$ or $\alpha < 1 - \sqrt{\beta}$, firm A's best-response function is

$$p_A(p_B) = \begin{cases} p_B + c(l - a - b), & p_B < \tilde{p}_B; \\ \frac{1}{2}[p_B + c(l - b + a)], & \tilde{p}_B \leq p_B \leq \bar{p}_B; \\ p_B - c(l - a - b) - \varepsilon, & p_B > \bar{p}_B. \end{cases} \qquad (4.15)$$

There is a corresponding expression for firm B's best-response function when $\beta < 1 - \sqrt{\alpha}$.

In (4.15), $\tilde{p}_B = c(3a + b - l)$ is the value for which A's profit supplying only its hinterland and its profit sharing the center of the market with firm B are the same. $\bar{p}_B = c(3l + b - a) - 4\sqrt{lb}$ is the value for which A's profit sharing the center of the market and its profit supplying the whole market are the same.

For $\tilde{p}_B > 0$, the length of the middle price range in (4.15) is

$$\bar{p}_B - \tilde{p}_B = 4l\left(1 - \alpha - \sqrt{\beta}\right), \qquad (4.16)$$

and this is positive for $\alpha < 1 - \sqrt{\beta}$.

For low p_B, firm A supplies only its hinterland; for intermediate prices, it shares the center of the market with firm B and has best-response price (4.10); for high p_B, firm A supplies the whole market. This case applies when a and b are relatively small.

In figure 4.2, the location pair H_1 lies below the curves $\alpha = 1 - \sqrt{\beta}$ and $\beta = 1 - \sqrt{\alpha}$. For location H_1, a and b are sufficiently small so that $\tilde{p}_B < 0$, so that only the second and third segments of (4.15) occur.

---

[7] A function f on a convex set X is *concave* if $f[\alpha(x_1) + (1 - \alpha)x_2] \geq \alpha f(x_1) + (1 - \alpha)f(x_2)$, for $0 \leq \alpha \leq 1$ and $x_1, x_2 \in X$. Concavity implies continuity. f is *quasi-concave* if $f[\alpha(x_1) + (1 - \alpha)x_2] \geq \min[f(x_1), f(x_2)]$.

4.1.5 Existence of pure-strategy equilibrium prices

D'Aspremont et al. (1979) characterize the location pairs for which pure-strategy equilibrium prices exist. Such location pairs are of two types.

If firms are located at the same point ($a + b = l$), the usual Bertrand argument shows that $p_A^* = p_B^* = 0$ is a noncooperative equilibrium price pair.[8] Equilibrium payoffs are also zero.[9]

If firms have distinct locations ($a + b < l$), d'Aspremont et al. show that equilibrium prices must differ by less than transportation cost between the two firms:

$$\left| p_A^* - p_B^* \right| < c(l - a - b). \tag{4.17}$$

If prices do not satisfy (4.17), one or the other of the two firms could always increase its profit by altering its price, meaning that such prices could not be an equilibrium.

If prices satisfy (4.17), firms share the center of the market. Prices and payoffs are given by (4.12). For the payoffs of (4.12) to be globally optimal, they must be at least as great as the payoffs that firms would earn by undercutting the rival's mill price and supplying the whole market. The conditions for such undercutting not to be profitable are

$$\pi_A^* = \tfrac{1}{2} c \left(l + \frac{a - b}{3} \right)^2 \geq \left[p_B^* - c(l - a - b) - \varepsilon \right] l,$$

$$\pi_B^* = \tfrac{1}{2} c \left(l + \frac{b - a}{3} \right)^2 \geq \left[p_A^* - c(l - a - b) - \varepsilon \right] l, \tag{4.18}$$

for ε small.

Substituting in (4.18) from (4.12) to eliminate p_A^* and p_B^*, letting ε go to zero, and rearranging terms, pure-strategy equilibrium prices are well defined for locations that satisfy

$$\alpha \leq 3 + \beta - 6\sqrt{\beta}, \qquad \beta \leq 3 + \alpha - 6\sqrt{\alpha}, \tag{4.19}$$

and they are the prices given in (4.12).

The equality versions of (4.19) are shown as dotted lines in figure 4.2. Both inequalities are satisfied in a relatively small region of location space. Hotelling's first example (point H_1) lies within this region.

As d'Aspremont et al. point out, for symmetric location pairs, (4.19) reduces to

$$\alpha = \beta \leq \tfrac{1}{4}. \tag{4.20}$$

With symmetric locations, for pure-strategy equilibrium prices to exist, firms must be located in the outer quartiles of the linear market. The symmetric location pair for which pure-strategy equilibrium prices exist that is closest to the center of the market is $\alpha = \beta = \tfrac{1}{4}$, the location pair that minimizes transportation cost.

---

[8] Osborne and Pitchik (1987, fn. 4) note that consumers must have finite reservation prices for this equilibrium to be unique.

[9] This in itself suggests that firms would not in equilibrium choose to locate at the same point (d'Aspremont et al., 1983a).

4.1.6   Mixed-strategy equilibrium prices

Outside the region defined by (4.19), the Hotelling model does not have pure-strategy equilibrium prices. Osborne and Pitchik (1987) draw on a result of Dasgupta and Maskin (1986) to show that the price-setting stage of the Hotelling game always has a noncooperative equilibrium. They use numerical methods to characterize mixed-strategy equilibria for location pairs where pure-strategy price equilibria fail to exist.[10]

Using this approximate characterization of mixed-strategy price equilibria, they identify the pure-strategy equilibrium of the location stage of the Hotelling game at approximately $\alpha = \beta = 0.27$, just outside the region within which there are pure-strategy price equilibria.[11] Taking mixed-strategy equilibrium prices into account in the Hotelling model does not restore the Principle of Minimum Differentiation.

4.2   BEYOND HOTELLING

4.2.1   Reservation price

In the basic Hotelling model, demand is completely price-inelastic: each consumer takes one and only one unit of the good from the firm offering the lowest delivered price, no matter how high that price is. The inelasticity of demand contributes to the centralizing tendencies of the model.

When the payoff functions (4.12) apply, firm A increases its profit by moving toward firm B's location and reducing its delivered price to some consumers that would otherwise be supplied by firm B. By moving toward firm B's location, firm A increases its delivered price to consumers in its hinterland. Since demand is assumed to be completely price-inelastic, this increase in delivered price to its hinterland costs A nothing in terms of sales or profits: so long as firm A has the lowest delivered price in its hinterland, it supplies consumers located in that part of the line. If, in contrast, demand in the hinterland were sensitive to price, then moving toward firm B's location would reduce A's sales and profit in its hinterland, thus reducing the profitability of centralizing.

Lerner and Singer (1937) add a reservation price ρ to the demand side of the Hotelling model. The reservation price is an upper limit to the delivered price, above which individual demand falls discontinuously from one to zero.[12] The kinds of changes that this implies for the aggregate demand facing a firm are illustrated in figure 4.6.

For concreteness, consider the demand facing firm A. In figure 4.6, firm A's left-hand market extends d_A units, where the distance d_A makes firm A's delivered price equal to the reservation price:

$$p_A + cd_A = \rho \rightarrow d_A = \frac{\rho - p_A}{c}. \tag{4.21}$$

---

[10] Gal–Or (1982) also discusses mixed-strategy price equilibria of the Hotelling model.

[11] They also discuss mixed-strategy equilibrium locations.

[12] Neven (1986, p. 7) suggests that this specification describes demand for indivisible, durable differentiated commodities.

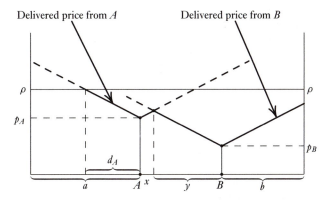

Figure 4.6 The Hotelling linear duopoly model with reservation price.

On its left, A sells either d_A units or a units, whichever is less. That is,

$$q_{AL} = \min(d_A, a). \tag{4.22}$$

A will supply its entire hinterland if it is located near the left end of the line (a small), if p_A is small relative to ρ, and if transportation cost c is low.

On its right, if firm A undercuts firm B's mill price, it can sell either a distance d_A from its mill or to the right end of the line, whichever is less. If firm A does not undercut firm B's mill price, it can sell either a distance d_A from its mill or until its delivered price equals B's delivered price, whichever is less.

For locations of the kind shown in figure 4.6, the quantity demanded of firm A is therefore

$$q_A = \begin{cases} \min(d_A, a) + \min(d_A, l - a), & p_A < p_A^L(p_B); \\[2mm] \min(d_A, a) \\ \quad + \min\left(d_A, \dfrac{p_B - p_A}{2c} + \dfrac{l - a - b}{2}\right), & p_A^L(p_B) \leq p_A \leq \min\left[\rho, p_A^H(p_B)\right]; \\[2mm] 0, & \min\left[\rho, p_A^H(p_B)\right] < p_A. \end{cases} \tag{4.23}$$

If the reservation price ρ is infinite, (4.23) reduces to (4.8), the expression for the demand facing firm A in the basic Hotelling model. For ρ sufficiently small, the reservation price becomes binding for some consumers and the resulting changes in demand affect firms' incentives to centralize, compared with the basic model.

Economides (1984) analyzes the two-stage game for finite reservation prices. He shows that low reservation prices reduce the incentives of firms to move toward the center and expand the set of locations for which pure-strategy equilibrium prices exist. For sufficiently low reservation prices, there are ranges of equilibrium locations toward either end of the line, with one firm located in each range, each firm acting as a monopolist toward the customers it supplies, and with some consumers in the center of the market left unserved. The critical factor in this formulation is cl/ρ, a normalized measure of the length of the market.[13]

Smithies (1941) examined a further modification of the specification of the demand side of the linear model by assuming that individual demand is negatively related to delivered price; see Problem 4.1.[14] Eaton (1972) assumes that demand at each point on the line is negatively related to price, also making the assumption of no mill-price undercutting, to which we now turn.

4.2.2   No mill-price undercutting

Early followers in Hotelling's wake seized upon the implication of the Nash equilibrium concept[15] that one firm could supply the entire market, driving its rival's sales to zero, by setting a price so that its delivered price at the rival's location undercuts the rival's mill price (Lerner and Singer, 1937, p. 168; Smithies, 1941; see also Eaton, 1972; Eaton and Lipsey, 1978; Novshek, 1980).

An alternative specification is to assume "no mill-price undercutting" conjectures, so that a firm in general sets its own price taking the price of the other firm as given, but expects the rival to match price cuts that would, if unmatched, drive the rival out of business.[16]

With this change, firm A's demand function (4.8) becomes

$$
q_A = \begin{cases}
l - b, & p_A < p_A^L(p_B); \\
\frac{1}{2}\left(l + a - b + \dfrac{p_B - p_A}{c}\right), & p_A^L(p_B) \leq p_A \leq p_A^H(p_B); \\
0, & p_A^H(p_B) < p_A.
\end{cases}
\qquad (4.24)
$$

Firm A may drive its own sales to zero if it sets a sufficiently high price (it would never choose to do so in equilibrium), but it expects firm B to react to avoid the same fate if A sets a very low price. For $p_A = p_A^L(p_B)$, firm A sells $q_A = l - b$. For $p_A < p_A^L(p_B)$, A expects firm B to match firm A's price, so that the quantity demanded of firm A remains $l - b$, rather than increasing to $q_A = l$.

In this alternative specification, A's profit function is continuous at $p_A = p_A^L(p_B)$. The portion of location space for which firms share the center of the line becomes much larger.[17] Within this sharing region, best-response functions have the form (4.10) and the tendency to minimize differentiation highlighted by Hotelling holds. Outside this region, there are multiple price equilibria, but one firm or the other will always earn greater profit by moving toward the location of the other.

---

[13] Hinloopen and van Marrewijk (1999) distinguish three cases: high reservation prices, in which Hotelling's results apply; low reservation prices, in which local monopolies of the kind identified by Economides emerge; and intermediate reservation prices, where locations imply intermediate differentiation levels.

[14] Following up on footnote 12, one might interpret the Smithies formulation as describing demand for divisible, nondurable differentiated goods (such as breakfast cereals or canned vegetables).

[15] Not, of course, identified as such at that time.

[16] It is possible to interpret Hotelling (1929, p. 48) as making this assumption (Archibald et al., 1986, p. 25). If so, he did not do so explicitly.

[17] In figure 4.2, the sharing region is defined by the inequalities $\alpha + 5\beta \leq 3$, $5\alpha + \beta \leq 3$; see Problem 4.2.

Novshek (1980) demonstrates that the possibility of mill-price undercutting means there is no pure-strategy equilibrium in prices and locations in the basic Hotelling model, and defends the use of no mill-price undercutting conjectures on the ground that it is the minimal departure from Nash conjectures that permits existence of pure-strategy equilibrium. But Gabszewicz and Thisse (1986, p. 164, fn. 1) show that pure-strategy price equilibrium can fail to exist even with no mill-price undercutting conjectures if transportation cost rises both linearly and quadratically in distance.

From (4.12), if firms locate at the center ($a = b = 1/2$), equilibrium prices are $p_A^* = p_B^* = cl$. With no mill-price undercutting conjectures, if firms are located at the same point, neither firm has an incentive to undercut the price of the other: the expected result would be to reduce revenue on sales that the price-cutter would make in any event at a higher price, without any increase in sales.

The discussion of conjectures in section 3.4 applies here. In a Nash equilibrium of a two-stage model, there is no mechanism for conjectures to be formed. The no mill-price undercutting literature can then be viewed as an *ad hoc* way of introducing dynamic considerations into a static model while avoiding the methodological baggage that a full-fledged dynamic analysis would entail.

Even if the use of a conjectural variation specification is considered acceptable on this basis, there remain deep conceptual problems with outcomes of the linear model that have firms located at the same point. When firms occupy distinct locations, an essential element of each firm's situation is that its two sides are different from the point of view of strategic interaction: to one side is its hinterland, to the other its rival. The essential logic of the linear model depends on being able to identify for each firm a hinterland, to which it is closer than its rival. Such identification is possible if and only if firms occupy distinct locations.[18]

If firms A and B were to locate at the same point in the equilibrium of the first-stage of a two-stage game, one might wish to appeal to a kind of virtual memory to identify firm A as having a hinterland on the left and firm B a hinterland on the right, carrying over the territories that would bear these labels when served from out-of-equilibrium locations. This does not seem satisfactory in a static model, in which such out-of-equilibrium locations would never be realized. Nor does it seems satisfactory to simply assume that two firms cannot occupy the same location (Eaton and Lipsey, 1975).

4.2.3 Quadratic transportation cost

Treating transportation cost as linear in distance is an obvious initial specification. But if transportation cost is thought of as a proxy for the disutility that arises from purchasing something other than the most preferred variety, it is plausible that unit "transportation cost" – disutility – rises more than proportionately with distance.

---

[18] Suppose that firm A is located just to the left, and firm B just to the right, and equidistant from, the $\frac{1}{4}$ point of the linear market. If the two firms charge the same price, firm A will supply 25 percent of the market and firm B will supply 75 percent of the market. These market shares will remain constant if the two firms charge the same price while approaching the $\frac{1}{4}$ point. But if both firms locate at the $\frac{1}{4}$ point, continuing to charge the same point, they are indistinguishable from the point of view of consumers, and each should supply half the market.

An alternative specification (d'Aspremont et al., 1979; Capozza and Van Order, 1982) is to let transportation cost be proportional to the square of distance. Keeping all other assumptions of the Hotelling model unchanged, firm A's delivered price at a distance x from its plant is then $p_A + cx^2$.

The marginal consumer – who has the same delivered price from A or B – is located x units from firm A, y units from firm B, with

$$p_A + cx^2 = p_B + cy^2. \tag{4.25}$$

The length-of-market identity (4.5) gives a second equation in x and y. Equations (4.5) and (4.25) can be solved for

$$x = \tfrac{1}{2}\left[l - a - b + \frac{p_B - p_A}{c(l - a - b)}\right]. \tag{4.26}$$

The quantity demanded of firm A is[19]

$$q_A = \begin{cases} l, & p_A < \tilde{p}_A^L(p_B); \\ \tfrac{1}{2}\left[l + a - b + \dfrac{p_B - p_A}{c(l - a - b)}\right], & \tilde{p}_A^L(p_B) \leq p_A \leq \tilde{p}_A^H(p_B); \\ 0, & \tilde{p}_A^H(p_B) < p_A; \end{cases} \tag{4.27}$$

for $\tilde{p}_A^L(p_B) = p_B - c\left[(l - a)^2 - b^2\right]$ and $\tilde{p}_A^H(p_B) = p_B + c\left[(l - b)^2 + a^2\right]$; the quantity demanded in the middle price range is $a + x$.

Taking locations as given, we can obtain price best-response curves in the usual way. Provided that q_A lies between 0 and l, firm A's profit is

$$\pi_A = \tfrac{1}{2}p_A\left[l + a - b + \frac{p_B - p_A}{c(l - a - b)}\right]. \tag{4.28}$$

π_A is maximized for

$$p_A = \tfrac{1}{2}\left\{p_B + c\left[(l - b)^2 - a^2\right]\right\}, \tag{4.29}$$

which is the equation of firm A's best-response function. For this price, firm A's payoff is

$$\pi_A = \frac{1}{2c(l - a - b)}p_A^2. \tag{4.30}$$

In the same way, the equation of firm B's best-response function is

$$p_B = \tfrac{1}{2}\left\{p_A + c\left[(l - a)^2 - b^2\right]\right\}. \tag{4.31}$$

Solving the equations of the best-response functions, noncooperative equilibrium prices are

$$\begin{pmatrix} p_A^* \\ p_B^* \end{pmatrix} = \frac{c}{3}(l - a - b)\begin{pmatrix} 3l + a - b \\ 3l + b - a \end{pmatrix}. \tag{4.32}$$

[19] If $p_A < \tilde{p}_A^L(p_B)$, $a + x > l$. If $p_A > \tilde{p}_A^H(p_B)$, $a + x < 0$.

Using (4.30), firm A's equilibrium profit is

$$\pi_A^* = \frac{c}{18}(l - a - b)(3l + a - b)^2, \tag{4.33}$$

and the derivative of π_A^* with respect to a is negative:

$$\frac{\partial \pi_A^*}{\partial a} = -\frac{c}{18}(l + 3a + b)(3l + a - b) < 0. \tag{4.34}$$

A corresponding result holds for firm B. With quadratic transportation cost, if firms select locations in the first stage of a two-stage game, anticipating equilibrium payoffs in the second (price-setting) stage, they will locate at the ends of the market. With quadratic transportation costs, the principle of minimum differentiation is replaced by the principle of maximum differentiation: to maximize profit, duopolists locate as far apart as possible.

Extensions

Gabszewicz and Thisse (1986) and Anderson (1988) examine a Hotelling linear model in which transportation cost includes both linear and quadratic terms: firm A's delivered price to a consumer x units away from mill A is $p_A + c_1 x + c_2 x^2$. So long as $c_1 > 0$, there are some locations for which pure-strategy equilibrium prices fail to exist. The degree of convexity of transportation cost emerges as critical for the properties of the model.

Friedman and Thisse (1993) examine a model with quadratic transportation cost in which two firms pick locations once and for all in a first stage and then repeatedly set price in an infinite sequence of periods. They find conditions under which noncooperative collusion supported by a trigger strategy[20] will make agglomeration in the center of the market an equilibrium outcome in the first stage.

Böckem (1994) analyzes a model in which each consumer takes at most one unit of the product, provided that delivered price is less than a reservation price that is uniformly distributed across consumers. Transportation cost is quadratic in distance. Pure-strategy equilibrium prices exist for all locations. Equilibrium locations are at the $\alpha = a/l = \beta = b/l = 0.272$ points on the line.[21]

Rath and Zhao (2001) present a model with downward-sloping linear demand at each point and quadratic transportation cost.[22] Pure-strategy equilibrium prices exist for every pair of locations. Writing ρ for the price-axis intercept of the inverse demand curve[23] and cx^2 for transportation cost over distance x, equilibrium locations depend on the ratio ρ^2/c. For ρ^2/c above a critical value, firms locate at the ends of the linear market. As ρ^2/c falls below the

---

[20] See chapter 10.

[21] Tantalizingly, these are (at least to two decimal places) the same equilibrium locations identified by Osborne and Pitchik (1987) for the original Hotelling model.

[22] When the quantity taken by each consumer is variable, one needs to specify whether "transportation" cost should be a function of distance alone or of distance and quantity. Rath and Zhao assume that transportation cost is a function of distance alone.

[23] Rath and Zhao assume that the slope of the demand curve is -1, so that the equation of the demand curve could be written $q = \rho - p$ or, equivalently, $p = \rho - q$.

critical value, firms locate toward the center of the line, approaching the center in the limit as ρ^2/c goes to zero.

4.2.4   Consumer heterogeneity

Anderson et al. (1992, ch. 9)[24] outline a model in which the linear market is the interval $[0, l]$, and a consumer located at z buying from firm i located at z_i has utility

$$V_i(z) = y - (p_i + c\,|z - z_i|) + a + \sigma\varepsilon_{iz}, \tag{4.35}$$

where y is the consumer's income, p_i is firm i's mill price, c is transportation cost, a is a quality index (taken to be the same for the products of all firms), $\sigma > 0$, and ε_{iz} is a well-behaved random variable with zero mean and variance equal to one.

The random term in (4.35) might be interpreted as a description of consumer behavior that is random in a literal sense – "animal spirits" at the micro-level. Alternatively, the random term might describe firms' uncertainty about consumer behavior: individual consumers behave in a deterministic way, but consumers differ in some dimensions that firms cannot observe. Consumer behavior then appears to firms to have a random element, and firms make their decisions accordingly.

It is the magnitude of σ that measures the degree of actual or perceived consumer heterogeneity. If $\sigma = 0$, utility is deterministic and the result is a variant of the standard spatial model.

For positive σ, there is always some probability that any consumer will buy from any firm. The demand facing an individual firm is therefore continuous in prices, in contrast to the basic Hotelling model.

The incentive for firms to disperse in the Hotelling model is the profit to be had by supplying consumers located toward the outer boundaries of the market. In the Hotelling model, by locating away from the center of the line a firm is able to supply one of the outer parts of the market with certainty. When consumer preferences are random, the expected gain from dispersing is less, compared to the deterministic demand case, because some consumers toward the edge of the market will patronize the other firm. Random preferences reduce the payoff to dispersal.

In alternative specifications, Anderson et al. (1992) outline conditions for firms to locate in the center of the line. A common element to these conditions is that σ must be sufficiently great. If firms are sufficiently uncertain about consumer preferences, the Principle of Minimum Differentiation is restored.

4.2.5   Beyond duopoly

Chamberlin (1933, p. 261) and Lerner and Singer (1937, section XI) argued that there would be no location equilibrium (in pure strategies, as we would now say) in a Hotelling linear model with three firms: for any candidate set of locations, either the middle firm would profit

---

[24] See also de Palma et al. (1985).

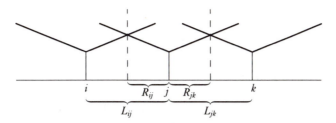

Figure 4.7 Three firms on a segment of an infinite linear market.

by leapfrogging toward one of the extremities (if pinned between relatively close rivals) or one of the extreme firms would profit by relocating in the middle (if relatively close to an endpoint).

Shaked (1982) derives the mixed strategy location equilibrium for the three-firm case. The probability that a firm locates in the first or last quartile of the line is zero, and the probability of a location between the $\frac{1}{4}$ and $\frac{3}{4}$ points of the line is uniformly distributed.[25]

To finesse endpoint problems, consider (as shown in figure 4.7) three firms (i, j, and k) on a segment of an infinite linear market. Firm j is located L_{ij} units to the right of firm i and L_{jk} units to the left of firm k. There is a fixed cost of production F and constant marginal production cost, which we normalize to be zero.

Suppose that demand is as in the Hotelling model. There is one customer per unit distance, and each customer purchases one unit of the product from the supplier that offers the lowest delivered price. Also, as in the Hotelling model, suppose that each firm sets a mill price. Transportation cost is c per unit distance, and firm j's delivered price to a consumer located x units distant is $p_j + cx$.

We now analyze firm j's short-run price decision. Firm j operates in two half-markets, stretching R_{ij} units to the left and R_{jk} units to the right. The quantity demanded of firm j is $R_{ij} + R_{jk}$, and firm j's profit is

$$\pi_j = p_j(R_{ij} + R_{jk}) - F. \tag{4.36}$$

The first-order condition for profit maximization with respect to price p_j is

$$p_j \left(\frac{\partial R_{ij}}{\partial p_j} + \frac{\partial R_{jk}}{\partial p_j} \right) + R_{ij} + R_{jk} = 0. \tag{4.37}$$

The half-market radii, R_{ij} and R_{jk}, are determined so that firm i's delivered price to the marginal consumer is the same as the delivered price of the adjacent supplier. R_{jk} thus satisfies

$$p_j + cR_{jk} = p_k + c(L_{jk} - R_{jk}), \tag{4.38}$$

leading to

$$R_{jk} = \frac{1}{2} \left(L_{jk} + \frac{p_k - p_j}{c} \right). \tag{4.39}$$

---

[25] See Collins and Sherstyuk (2000) for an experimental test of Shaked's results and de Palma et al. (1987) for an analysis of equilibrium locations with three firms on the Hotelling line with consumer heterogeneity.

In like manner,

$$R_{ij} = \tfrac{1}{2}\left(L_{ij} + \frac{p_i - p_j}{c}\right). \tag{4.40}$$

From (4.39) and (4.40), we obtain

$$\frac{\partial R_{jk}}{\partial p_j} = \frac{1}{2c}\left(\frac{\partial p_k}{\partial p_j} - 1\right), \qquad \frac{\partial R_{ij}}{\partial p_j} = \frac{1}{2c}\left(\frac{\partial p_i}{\partial p_j} - 1\right). \tag{4.41}$$

$\partial p_k / \partial p_j$ and $\partial p_i / \partial p_j$ are price conjectural variations. If we follow Hotelling and make Nash conjectures (as they would now be called), then[26]

$$\frac{\partial p_k}{\partial p_j} = \frac{\partial p_i}{\partial p_j} = 0 \tag{4.42}$$

and

$$\frac{\partial R_{jk}}{\partial p_j} = \frac{\partial R_{ij}}{\partial p_j} = -\frac{1}{2c}. \tag{4.43}$$

The intuition behind (4.43) is evident from figure 4.7. If firm j increases its price while its neighbors hold their prices fixed, the boundaries of firm j's market retreat toward firm j's location.

Substituting (4.43) in the first-order condition (4.37) gives

$$p_j = c(R_{ij} + R_{jk}). \tag{4.44}$$

Substituting from (4.39) and (4.40) into (4.44) and collecting terms, we obtain j's best-response price:

$$p_j^{br}(p_i, p_k) = \tfrac{1}{4}\left[c(L_{ij} + L_{jk}) + p_i + p_k\right]. \tag{4.45}$$

Best-response prices are higher, the higher is transportation cost, the greater the distance that separates a firm from its neighbors and the greater the prices charged by its neighbors.

To say something about equilibrium prices, we assume, as did Hotelling, that location can be changed without cost. We suppose further that firms enter until profit is driven to zero. We also rely on the fact that firms are identical and use the assumption of symmetry to simplify the analysis.

In symmetric equilibrium, all firms charge the same price p and operate over markets with identical radius R (so that $L = 2R$). The first-order condition for profit maximization (4.37)

---

[26] Two other types of conjecture have been prominently explored in the literature. Greenhut and Ohta (1973) assume that conjectures equal -1, implying relatively aggressive expected responses and leading to lower equilibrium prices than with Nash conjectures. Lösch (1938, 1944, 1954) assumes that conjectures equal $+1$, implying that firms believe that their market areas are independent of prices and would raise their price to infinity (under Hotelling's specification) or to the reservation price (following Lerner and Singer).

becomes

$$p = 2cR. \tag{4.46}$$

The condition that profit be zero in long-run equilibrium is

$$\pi = p(2R) - F = 0. \tag{4.47}$$

Combining (4.46) and (4.47) gives the Nash long-run equilibrium market radius:

$$R_{LR}^N = \frac{1}{2}\sqrt{\frac{F}{c}}. \tag{4.48}$$

The equilibrium quantity demanded per firm is $2R_{LR}^N$, and the symmetric Nash equilibrium price is

$$p_{LR}^N = \sqrt{cF}. \tag{4.49}$$

Efficiency and monopolistic competition

The model outlined here is one way to formalize Chamberlin's (1933) model of monopolistic competition: many small firms producing different varieties of a differentiated product, with all firms maximizing profit and entry taking place until profit is driven to zero.[27]

A principal result of the theory of monopolistic competition is that in long-run equilibrium firms produce at a level below that which minimizes long-run average cost. A lively literature (reviewed by Capozza and Van Order, 1982) debates the existence and interpretation of this effect: Does it occur? If so, is it a sign of the inefficiency of monopolistic competition as a form of market organization? Or is the increment in average cost over its minimum value simply the cost of variety?

We address here the former question – whether or not average cost is minimized. The question of social desirability of variety does not arise, since in this model products are differentiated only by location. All varieties of the product are equally satisfactory, and the socially optimal scheme is to minimize the firm–level average cost of production and delivery.

If a firm supplies a market of radius R, transportation cost is cR^2 (see figure 4.8). The cost of production and transportation is $F + cR^2$, and average cost is

$$AC = \frac{F + cR^2}{2R} = \frac{1}{2}\left(\frac{F}{R} + cR\right). \tag{4.50}$$

Average cost is minimized for

$$R^{op} = \sqrt{\frac{F}{c}}, \tag{4.51}$$

which is twice the Nash equilibrium market radius (compare with (4.48)).

Nash equilibrium in this spatial model is inefficient. There are too many producers, producers do not ship far enough, and average cost exceeds the socially optimal level.

---

[27] The leading nonspatial alternatives are Dixit and Stiglitz (1977) and Spence (1976b). Spence (1976a) uses the Bowley model of product differentiation to model monopolistic competition, and one might do the same with the Shubik and Levitan model.

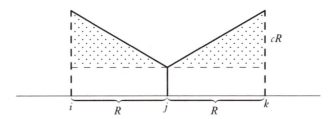

Figure 4.8 Transportation cost, market radius R: transportation cost = area of triangles = $2\left(\frac{1}{2}\right)R(cR) = cR^2$.

4.2.6   The circular road

The idea of joining the ends of Hotelling's line to form a one-dimensional space without endpoints is due to Chamberlin (1953).[28] He indicated frankly that this was a device for eliminating troublesome endpoint effects on location decisions in the Hotelling model, but argued that the circular road model was of independent interest (pp. 19–20):[29],[30]

> The ends may be got rid of by the expedient of bending them around and joining them, in other words by assuming a "circular street." This is of course only a symbol, but as a symbol it is probably more meaningful than a line with ends, since the idea of a "chain of substitutes" without sharp breaks and which therefore "defies subdivision" has become commonplace.

Subsequent researchers have been more cautious. Taken literally, the circular road model applies to departure times in markets for transportation services, where the circle is the 24-hour day, and little else.[31] But if what is measured along the line is some product characteristic that varies from low to high levels, joining the ends of the line will not do: consumers who prefer fuel-efficient vehicles are not near in characteristic space to consumers who prefer gas-guzzlers.[32]

---

[28] A publication that he described as a revision of a paper "prepared and almost completed in 1936."

[29] The reference to "a chain of substitutes without sharp breaks" seems closer to Robinson's (1933, p. 17) definition of an industry as firms producing a commodity bounded by a marked gap with its closest substitutes than to Chamberlin's own (1933, p. 103) discussion of chain linking of markets for differentiated products, in which each producer competes most intensely with rivals who are producing close substitutes. For a formalization of Chamberlin's (1933) concept, see Rothschild (1982).

[30] See von Ungern-Sternberg (1991) for a spatial model that is in some respects a generalization of the circular market model.

[31] Greenhut et al. (1987, ch. 17); Waterson (1989); Takahashi and de Palma (1993); Borenstein and Netz (1999).

[32] Salop (1979, p. 142) emphasizes the technical advantages of the circle model (the innovative aspects of Salop's model are due as much to explicit treatment of an outside good, with the implied reservation price, as to the use of a circular market). Archibald et al. (1986, p. 12) criticize the circle specification and argue that "we cannot in characteristics space avoid the problems associated with boundaries." See Takahashi and de Palma (1993) for an ingenious attempt to combine the line and circle models (introducing a toll to pass from one side to the other of a circular space).

With these qualifications in mind, if one assumes free entry and costless relocation, the circle model gives a straightforward expression for the equilibrium number of firms. Let the circumference of the circle be L, assume that figure 4.7 is a typical segment of the circular market and apply the analysis of section 4.2.5, so that equilibrium market radius per firm is $\frac{1}{2}\sqrt{F/c}$, (see (4.48)). Then the equilibrium number of firms is (the greatest integer less than or equal to)[33]

$$n_m = \frac{L}{2\left(\frac{1}{2}\right)\sqrt{F/c}} = L\sqrt{\frac{c}{F}}. \tag{4.52}$$

The assumption of costless relocation essentially assumes away the baby along with the bathwater. Much scope for strategic entry-deterring behavior and for long-term economic profit appears when relocation is taken to be costly.

4.2.7   Other extensions of the Hotelling model

Hotelling himself, and the generalizations of the Hotelling model that we have discussed, assumed mill pricing: a firm receives the same revenue from every customer, net of the cost of delivering to that consumer. Alternatively, firms might practice uniform pricing, so that all consumers pay the same delivered price, regardless of location. Under uniform pricing, a firm receives a different net price from consumers at different locations. Uniform pricing is therefore one type of price discrimination.

In a model that assumes downward-sloping demand at every point in a spatial market, firms might explicitly discriminate, setting a different delivered price at every point (Hoover, 1937; Holahan, 1975; Phlips, 1983; Hobbs, 1986; Greenhut et al., 1987; Coyte and Lindsey, 1988). Price discrimination is one aspect of basing-point pricing – for references to the large literature on which, see Thisse and Vives (1988) and Phlips (1993).

Once again following Hotelling, our discussion has been of price-setting firms in spatial markets. Anderson and Neven (1991) examine quantity-setting behavior in a linear market with linear demand at each point on the line. They assume that demand is sufficiently great so that all points on the market are served by both firms. There is a standard linear Cournot model at each point on the line, and in a two-stage game (locations chosen first) firms locate together at the center of the market as long as transportation costs increase more than proportionately to distance.[34]

Other contributions to the spatial literature include models with consumer search (Stahl, 1982; Gabszewicz and Garella, 1987); models with price-taking firms (Anderson and Engers, 1994); and models with multiproduct firms.

---

[33] See Chamberlin (1953, pp. 20–1), Anderson (1986), and Katz (1995).

[34] For discussions of Cournot competition in spatial models without price discrimination, see Hamilton et al. (1994), al-Nowaihi and Norman (1994), and Gupta et al. (1997). Such models have a tendency toward analytic intractability.

4.3 VERTICAL PRODUCT DIFFERENTIATION

The kind of differentiation that appears in the Hotelling model is said to be horizontal. This usage may well stem from the visual image of consumers (more precisely, consumers' most preferred product types) distributed along a line, but it has come to be a term of art describing a market in which different consumers regard different combinations of product characteristics as being first best, all else equal. When differentiation is horizontal, the ranking of product varieties is not unanimous.

In contrast, when product differentiation is vertical, all consumers rank products in the same way,[35] and quality differences move to center stage. Here too there is a natural visual image of varieties laid out along a vertical line, with higher-quality varieties above lower-quality varieties.[36]

The *term* vertical differentiation is due to Lancaster (1979, pp. 27–9), but the idea was in the air at the time of his writing. Early on, an active literature emphasized the differences between horizontal and vertical differentiation. Underlying common elements later came to the surface.

4.3.1 Monopoly

Mussa and Rosen's (1978) seminal model compares quality choice under monopoly and perfect competition. Denoting quality by χ, a simple version of their model is one in which individual consumers with net utility functions (utility net of price, that is) of the form

$$u(\theta, \chi) = v(\theta, \chi) - p(\chi) = \theta \chi - p(\chi) \tag{4.53}$$

are uniformly distributed on an interval $\theta_L \leq \theta \leq \theta_H$, with $\theta_L \geq 0$. Each consumer takes one unit of the quality product that yields the greatest net utility, provided that net utility is positive, and otherwise does not buy the good. θ is the marginal utility of quality.

In the Mussa and Rosen model, there is systematic quality downshifting under monopoly for all marginal utilities of quality except $\theta = \theta_H$. By raising the price of high-quality varieties above marginal cost, the monopolist creates an incentive for high-θ consumers to switch to a lower-quality variety. Put another way, the availability of lower-quality alternatives limits the ability of the monopoly supplier to extract economic profit from consumers with high marginal utility of quality. Systematically reducing lower levels of quality offered makes those alternatives less attractive and allows the monopolist to extract a higher level of economic profit from high-θ consumers.

Donnenfeld and White (1988) and Srinagesh and Bradburd (1989) show that the quality-downshifting result of the Mussa–Rosen models depends on the assumption that a change in quality affects total utility and marginal utility in the same way – in (4.53), as χ rises,

---

[35] See the discussion of vertical differentiation in section 3.6.1.

[36] As is all too often the case, this natural image turns out to be misleading: see Gabszewicz and Thisse (1986) and Problem 4.4 for a Hotelling-line model of vertical product differentiation.

$v(\theta, \chi) = \theta\chi$ rises and $\theta = v_\chi(\theta, \chi)$ does not fall. When this aspect of the specification is relaxed, monopoly quality distortion may be upward or downward.[37]

4.3.2 Oligopoly: consumers distributed by marginal utility of quality

In this section, we outline a duopoly version of the Mussa–Rosen model. There are two firms in the market: firm A produces a variety of quality χ_A, while firm B produces a variety of quality χ_B. Without loss of generality, let $\chi_A \leq \chi_B$.

We concentrate on a one-stage version of the model, taking qualities to be given, and investigate the nature of equilibrium prices. We will later discuss two-stage models, in which firms set prices in the second stage, taking qualities as given, and select qualities in the first stage, knowing how second-stage payoffs are related to qualities.[38]

In the most general version of the model, n consumers are uniformly distributed over the interval $[\theta_L, \theta_H]$ of parameter space. n turns out to be a scale factor that multiplies the quantities demanded but does not affect equilibrium prices. Without loss of generality, we normalize to $n = 1$.

It proves convenient to work with quality-adjusted prices,[39]

$$\theta_{\phi A} = \frac{p_A}{\chi_A}, \qquad \theta_{\phi B} = \frac{p_B}{\chi_B}. \tag{4.54}$$

A consumer with marginal utility of quality $\theta = \theta_{\phi A}$ would get zero net utility purchasing variety A at price p_A. Consumers with $\theta > \theta_{\phi A}$ would get positive net utility purchasing variety A at price p_A, and consumers with $\theta \leq \theta_{\phi A}$ would get negative net utility purchasing variety A at price p_A. If $\theta_{\phi A} < \theta_L$, then all consumers would get positive net utility by buying variety A at price p_A. $\theta_{\phi B}$ may be interpreted along similar lines.

Let θ_{AB} denote the marginal utility of quality of the consumer who receives the same net utility buying from A or B:

$$\theta_{AB}\chi_A - p_A = \theta_{AB}\chi_B - p_B, \tag{4.55}$$

from which

$$\theta_{AB} = \frac{p_B - p_A}{\chi_B - \chi_A} = \frac{\theta_{\phi B}\chi_B - \theta_{\phi A}\chi_A}{\chi_B - \chi_A}. \tag{4.56}$$

Consumers with $\theta < \theta_{AB}$ get greater net utility buying variety A; consumers with $\theta > \theta_{AB}$ get greater net utility buying variety B.

The equations of the demand functions facing the two firms in different regions of quality-adjusted price space are shown in figure 4.9(a). Consider, for example, the region on the left side of the graph defined by the inequalities $0 \leq \theta_{\phi A} \leq \theta_L$ and $\theta_L \leq \theta_{AB} \leq \theta_H$. Because

---

[37] See Neven (1986) for a discussion of the role of this assumption in oligopoly models.

[38] For references to the literature on minimum quality standards, see Ronnen (1991) and Scarpa (1998).

[39] These should be read "theta-null A" and "theta-null B," with apologies to A. E. van Vogt.

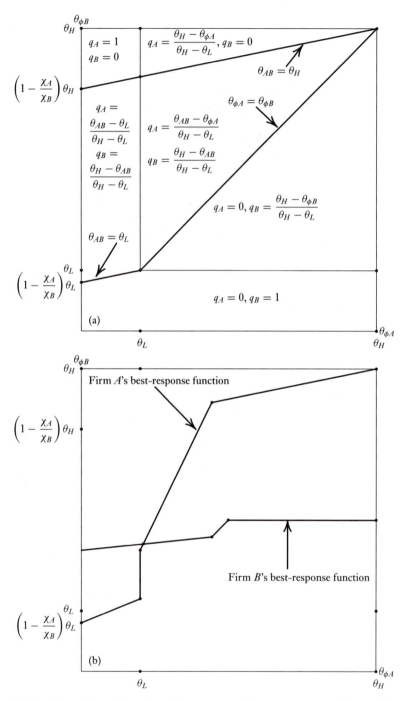

Figure 4.9 The Mussa–Rosen duopoly model: $\theta_L = \chi_A = 1$, $\theta_H = \chi_B = 5$. (a) Demands by regions of quality-adjusted price space; (b) best-response functions.

$\theta_{\phi A} \leq \theta_L$, consumers down to the bottom of the range of marginal utilities get positive net utility buying variety A at price p_A. Consumers in the interval $\theta_L \leq \theta_{AB}$ get greater net utility buying variety A than variety B; since we have normalized the number of consumers to be 1, the quantity demanded of firm A in this region is

$$q_A = \frac{\theta_{AB} - \theta_L}{\theta_H - \theta_L}. \tag{4.57}$$

Consumers in $\theta_{AB} \leq \theta_H$ get greater net utility buying from firm B than from firm A. The quantity demanded of firm B in this region is

$$q_A = \frac{\theta_H - \theta_{AB}}{\theta_H - \theta_L}. \tag{4.58}$$

Demand functions in the other regions may be derived by similar arguments.

Depending upon quality-adjusted prices, the market may be covered – all consumers buy a unit of the product – or uncovered – there is an interval of consumers at the bottom of the θ distribution who do not consume the product. Adding the quantities demanded of the two firms in a region in figure 4.9(a) shows whether or not the market is covered in that region – if the total quantity demanded is one the market is covered, otherwise not.

Given the demand curves, it is straightforward but tedious to find the firms' (quality-adjusted) price best-response functions, by examining each firm's payoff function for different ranges of values of the quality-adjusted price of the other firm.[40] In general, firms' payoff functions are not nicely behaved. It is often the case that a firm's payoff function for a given value of the rival's price has two local maxima, values of which must be explicitly compared to determine the global maximum.

Best-response functions for a particular set of parameter values are shown in figure 4.9(b). For these parameter values, the market is uncovered in equilibrium. Equilibrium quality-adjusted prices are $\theta_{\phi A} = 1\frac{1}{19}$ and $\theta_{\phi B} = 2\frac{2}{19}$,[41] and consumers with marginal utilities of quality in the interval $0 \leq \theta \leq \theta_{\phi A}$ do not buy the product.

Wauthy (1996) shows that, for $0 < \theta_H \leq 2\theta_L$, firm B supplies the entire market in equilibrium. As θ_H/θ_L rises, firm A's equilibrium output becomes positive with $\theta_{\phi A}$ first less than θ_L, then equal to θ_L, and finally greater than θ_L, so that the market is uncovered in equilibrium if θ_H/θ_L is sufficiently large.

Having determined payoffs in the price-setting stage of the game, it is possible to ask how firms' payoffs change with quality levels[42] and what equilibrium qualities would emerge from a two-stage game, with qualities selected in the first stage and payoffs that are the equilibrium values of the subsequent price-setting game. Wauthy (1996) assumes that quality choice is costless[43] and shows that for $\theta_H/\theta_L > 2$, in equilibrium one firm sets $\chi = \chi_H$ and the other firm a lower quality – exactly what quality depending on θ_H/θ_L. The market may be covered

[40] For example, firm A's payoff function must be examined separately on the intervals (A1) $0 \leq \theta_{\phi B} \leq (1 - \chi_A/\chi_B)\theta_L$, (A2) $(1 - \chi_A/\chi_B)\theta_L \leq \theta_{\phi B} \leq \theta_L$, (A3) $\theta_L \leq \theta_{\phi B} \leq (1 - \chi_A/\chi_B)\theta_H$, (A4) $(1 - \chi_A/\chi_B)\theta_H \leq \theta_{\phi B} \leq (1 - \chi_A/\chi_B)\theta_H + (\chi_A/\chi_B)\theta_L$, and (A5) $(1 - \chi_A/\chi_B)\theta_H + (\chi_A/\chi_B)\theta_L \leq \theta_{\phi B} \leq \theta_H$.

[41] So that $p_A = \chi_A\theta_{\phi A} = 1\frac{1}{19}$, $p_B = \chi_B\theta_{\phi B} = 10\frac{10}{19}$.

[42] For the parameter values of figure 4.9, each firm's payoff is increasing in the quality of its product.

[43] Motta (1993) examines alternative specifications of costly quality choice. He assumes that the market is uncovered in equilibrium.

or uncovered in the equilibrium of the two–stage game.[44] It is thus the degree of dispersion of consumer preferences that drives the nature of equilibrium in the two–stage version of the model.

4.3.3   Oligopoly: consumers distributed by income

Shaked and Sutton (1982) develop a model in which it is income distribution that determines the equilibrium number of quality levels supplied in a static model of a market for a differentiated product.[45] Firms have three decisions to make, which are taken sequentially. They first decide whether to enter, then (if they have entered) what quality to produce, and finally what price to charge, given quality. We work backward from the pricing decision, seeking a noncooperative equilibrium at each stage.

Demand

Consumers are uniformly distributed according to income t, which lies between a and b: $a \leq t \leq b$. The utility of a consumer with income t is

$$U(t, 0) = tu_0 \tag{4.59}$$

if the consumer does not purchase the good. u_0 is thus the marginal utility of income of a consumer who does not purchase the good.

Let there be n varieties in the market, and suppose that each consumer takes at most one unit of one variety. If a consumer with income t purchases variety k at price p_k, the consumer's utility is

$$U(t - p_k) = (t - p_k)u_k. \tag{4.60}$$

u_k is the marginal utility of income of a consumer who purchases variety k.

Without loss of generality, let products be ordered in terms of increasing marginal utility:

$$u_0 \leq u_1 \leq \cdots \leq u_n. \tag{4.61}$$

There is an income level t_1 such that a consumer with income level t_1 is indifferent between not purchasing any variety and purchasing variety 1 at price p_1. t_1 satisfies the relation

$$t_1 u_0 = (t_1 - p_1)u_1, \tag{4.62}$$

so that

$$t_1 = p_1 \frac{u_1}{u_1 - u_0} = p_1 C_1. \tag{4.63}$$

This serves to define $C_1 = u_1/(u_1 - u_0)$. $1/C_1$ is the increase in marginal utility going from variety 0 to variety 1, as a fraction of the marginal utility of variety 1.

---

[44] Constantatos and Perrakis (1997) examine the question of market coverage by a multi-variety incumbent facing the possibility of entry.
[45] See also Gabszewicz and Thisse (1979, 1980, 1982).

Similarly, a consumer with income level t_k is indifferent between purchasing variety k at price p_k and variety $k-1$ at price p_{k-1}, where t_k satisfies the relation

$$(t_k - p_k)u_k = (t_k - p_{k-1})u_{k-1}, \tag{4.64}$$

so that

$$t_k = \frac{u_k p_k - u_{k-1}p_{k-1}}{u_k - u_{k-1}} = p_k C_k - p_{k-1}(C_k - 1) \tag{4.65}$$

for

$$C_k \equiv \frac{u_k}{u_k - u_{k-1}} > 1, \qquad k = 1, 2, \ldots, n. \tag{4.66}$$

Now consider a consumer with income $t > t_1$. The consumer's utility from purchasing good 1 at price p_1 is $(t - p_1)u_1$. The consumer's utility from not purchasing at all is tu_0. The change in the consumer's utility from purchasing good 1 at price p_1 is therefore

$$(t - p_1)u_1 - tu_0 = (u_1 - u_0) > 0. \tag{4.67}$$

Hence consumers with income greater than t_1 prefer to buy good 1 at price p_1 rather than not to purchase at all.

Now consider a consumer with income $t > t_k$, for $k = 2, 3, \ldots, n$. Such a consumer's utility from purchasing good k at price p_k is $(t - p_k)u_k$, while utility from purchasing good $k-1$ at price p_{k-1} is $(t - p_{k-1})u_{k-1}$. The change in utility from purchasing good k at price p_k rather than good $k-1$ at price p_{k-1} is therefore

$$(t - p_k)u_k - (t - p_{k-1})u_{k-1} = (u_k - u_{k-1})(t - t_k) > 0. \tag{4.68}$$

Hence consumers with income t_2 prefer to buy good 2 at price p_2 rather than to buy good 1 at price p_1, and so on. From this, it follows that:

- If $t_1 \leq a$, all consumers purchase the product (the market is covered); firm 1's sales are $t_2 - a$, firm 2's sales are $t_3 - t_2$, and firm n's sales are $b - t_n$.
- If $t_1 > a$, consumers with incomes in the range (a, t_1) do not purchase the product (the market is uncovered); firm 1's sales are $t_2 - t_1$, firm 2's sales are $t_3 - t_2$, and firm n's sales are $b - t_n$.

Supply

For simplicity, we suppose that firms produce with constant marginal cost, and that there are no fixed costs. Without loss of generality, we may set marginal cost equal to zero. Then we have the following expressions for firms' profits and the first-order conditions for maximization of those profits:

$$\pi_1 = \begin{cases} p_1(t_2 - a), & \dfrac{\partial \pi_1}{\partial p_1} = t_2 - a - p_1(C_2 - 1) \equiv 0, \\ & \text{or} \\ p_1(t_2 - t_1), & \dfrac{\partial \pi_1}{\partial p_1} = t_2 - t_1 - p_1\left[(C_2 - 1) + C_1\right] \equiv 0; \end{cases} \tag{4.69}$$

$$\pi_k = p_k(t_{k+1} - t_k), \qquad \frac{\partial \pi_k}{\partial p_k} = t_{k+1} - t_k - p_k\left[(C_{k+1} - 1) + C_k\right] \equiv 0$$
$$(k = 2, 3, \ldots, n - 1); \tag{4.70}$$

$$\pi_n = p_n(b - t_n), \qquad \frac{\partial \pi_n}{\partial p_n} = b - t_n - p_n C_n. \tag{4.71}$$

We now work backward from firm n to determine conditions for the equilibrium number of firms in the market. From the definition of t_n (4.65), for $k = n$, we have

$$p_n C_n = t_n + p_{n-1}(C_n - 1). \tag{4.72}$$

Substituting (4.72) in the first-order condition from (4.71), we obtain

$$b - 2t_n = p_{n-1}(C_n - 1) > 0. \tag{4.73}$$

If firms n and $n - 1$ do not supply the entire market, (4.70) gives the first-order condition for firm $n - 1$:

$$t_n - t_{n-1} = p_{n-1}(C_n - 1) + p_{n-1}C_{n-1}. \tag{4.74}$$

But from the definition of t_{n-1}, we have

$$p_{n-1}C_{n-1} = t_{n-1} + p_{n-2}(C_{n-1} - 1). \tag{4.75}$$

Substituting (4.74) in (4.75) and rearranging terms gives

$$t_n - 2t_{n-1} = p_{n-1}(C_n - 1) + p_{n-2}(C_{n-1} - 1) > 0. \tag{4.76}$$

In addition, if firms n and $n - 1$ do not supply the entire market, $t_{n-1} > a$. Then we have $b > 2t_n$ and $t_n > 2t_{n-1}$, so $b > 4a$. If this condition is violated, so that $b \le 4a$, there is room for at most two firms in the market (with positive sales).

It is thus a condition on the range of incomes that determines the number of firms in the market. We know that $a < b$. If in addition $b \le 4a$, there will be at most two firms in the market.

Continuing in the same way, if firms n, $n - 1$, and $n - 2$ do not supply the entire market, it must be the case that $b > 8a$. Thus if $b \le 8a$, there is room for at most three firms in the market.

This conclusion depends on the assumption that there are no fixed costs. Fixed costs, if sufficiently large, would reduce the number of firms that could profitably operate in the market below the upper limit determined by the distribution of income.[46]

For simplicity, we confine ourselves in what follows to the case in which $b \leq 4a$, so that at most two firms have positive sales. But this is not an essential aspect of the model.

To characterize equilibrium prices, define a measure of relative quality

$$V = \frac{u_2 - u_0}{u_2 - u_1} = \frac{C_2 - 1}{C_1} + 1 > 1. \tag{4.77}$$

The first-order conditions for profit maximization become

$$t_2 = a + t_1(V - 1) \tag{4.78}$$

if $t_1 \leq a$,

$$t_2 = t_1(V + 1) \tag{4.79}$$

if $t_1 \geq a$, for firm 1, and

$$b - 2t_2 = t_1(V - 1) \tag{4.80}$$

for firm 2.

If $t_1 \leq a$, equilibrium values of t_1 and t_2 are found by solving (4.78) and (4.80) as a system of simultaneous equations. The results are

$$t_1 = \frac{b - 2a}{3(V - 1)}, \qquad t_2 = \frac{a + b}{3}. \tag{4.81}$$

The requirement that $t_1 \leq a$ is satisfied if

$$V \geq \frac{a + b}{3a}. \tag{4.82}$$

We refer to this as case I. Given solutions for the income ranges that define market boundaries, prices can be recovered from (4.62) and (4.64).

If $t_1 \geq a$, equilibrium values of t_1 and t_2 are found by solving (4.79) and (4.80) as a system of simultaneous equations. The results are

$$t_1 = \frac{b}{3V + 1}, \qquad t_2 = \frac{V + 1}{3V + 1}b. \tag{4.83}$$

The requirement that $t_1 \geq a$ is satisfied if

$$V \leq \frac{b - a}{3a}. \tag{4.84}$$

We refer to this as case III. Once again, given solutions for the income ranges that define market boundaries, prices can be recovered from (4.62) and (4.64).

---

[46] Indeed, if fixed cost is sufficiently great, it will not be profitable for any firm to supply a variety of the product.

From (4.82) and (4.84), if $(b - a)/3a \leq V \leq (b + a)/3a$, we are in an intermediate case for which $t_1 = a$, and t_2 is found by substituting in (4.80). In this case II,

$$t_1 = a, \qquad t_2 = \tfrac{1}{2}\left(\frac{a + 2b}{3}\right). \tag{4.85}$$

Because we restrict ourselves to the case $b \leq 4a$, we know that there are at most two firms with positive sales in the market. What we seek now are conditions for $b - t_2 > 0$, $t_2 - a > 0$, and $a \geq t_1$. If these inequalities are satisfied, both firms have positive sales and all customers purchase the product.

Derivation of the resulting conditions is mostly mechanical. The three conditions are always satisfied in case II, and never satisfied in case III. In case I, $t_2 - a = (b - 2a)/3$, and so $t_2 - a > 0$ if and only if $b > 2a$. The other two conditions are satisfied in case I. Henceforth, assume that $2a \leq b \leq 4a$, which imposes an additional restriction on the range of incomes. Then, in noncooperative equilibrium two firms have positive shares and supply all customers.

Equilibrium qualities

We now seek to characterize the equilibrium choice of qualities, given noncooperative equilibrium prices. Suppose that prices are determined as in case I. Then the firms' profits are

$$\pi_1(u_1, u_2) = p_1(t_2 - a) = \left(\frac{b - 2a}{3}\right)^2 \frac{u_2 - u_1}{u_1}, \tag{4.86}$$

$$\pi_2(u_1, u_2) = p_2(b - t_2) = \left(\frac{2a - b}{3}\right)^2 \frac{u_2 - u_1}{u_1}. \tag{4.87}$$

But (4.86) rises as u_1 falls, while (4.87) rises as u_2 rises. It follows that the first firm picks the lowest possible quality level, and the second firm picks the greatest possible quality level, consistent with being in case I. This result is similar to the principle of maximum differentiation that appears in spatial models with quadratic transportation cost.

If equilibrium falls in case II, firms' profits are affected by choice of quality as in case I.[47] In either case, firms have an incentive to pick different quality levels. In this type of equilibrium, both firms earn positive profit and the high-quality firm earns a larger profit than the low-quality firm.

The equilibrium number of firms

Shaked and Sutton show that the two-firm equilibrium described above is a noncooperative equilibrium for the game in which firms pick quality and then price. There are other equilibria with more than two firms, but then all firms earn zero profit.

[47] Although for case II it is tedious to sign $\partial \pi_2 / \partial u_2$; see Shaked and Sutton (1982) for details.

They also establish that, if there is an arbitrarily small cost of entry, in the only subgame-perfect equilibrium two firms enter, they produce products of different qualities, and they earn positive profit.

4.4 THE RELATION BETWEEN MODELS OF HORIZONTAL AND VERTICAL DIFFERENTIATION

The stories behind models of horizontal and of vertical differentiation are quite different. Yet it will not have escaped the reader that the ways in which the models work are similar. In the horizontal differentiation duopoly model, the demand facing firm A depends on the location of the consumer who is indifferent between buying from firm A and firm B. That location depends on the prices both firms charge and on transportation cost. In a vertical differentiation duopoly model, demand facing the firm producing a low-quality variety depends on the marginal utility of quality (Mussa–Rosen) or on the income (Shaked–Sutton) of the consumer who is indifferent between buying the low-quality and the high-quality varieties. Where that consumer is in parameter space depends on the prices that both firms charge and on the precise form of the individual utility functions.

Cremer and Thisse (1991), Neven (1986), Champsaur and Rochet (1989), and Anglin (1992) emphasize the close relationship between some classes of models of the two types of product differentiation.

For example, consider a version of the Hotelling model with quadratic cost, in which a consumer at location x on a unit interval $[0, 1]$ gets net utility

$$\tfrac{1}{2}x^2 - \tfrac{1}{2}(x - y_i)^2 \tag{4.88}$$

from consuming one unit of the product of a firm i located at y_i in the same interval, with reservation price $\tfrac{1}{2}x^2$ varying by location and transportation or disutility cost $-\tfrac{1}{2}(x - y_i)^2$. If marginal and average cost are assumed to be constant and normalized to be zero, (4.88) is also the maximum profit firm i could extract from a consumer at x.

Now consider a Mussa–Rosen model with marginal utilities of income θ distributed along a unit interval $[0, 1]$ and suppose that the cost of producing a product of quality χ_i, with $0 \le \chi_i \le 1$, is quadratic:

$$c(\chi_i) = \tfrac{1}{2}\chi_i^2. \tag{4.89}$$

Let the utility of a consumer with marginal utility of income θ be $\theta\chi$. The maximum economic profit that a firm producing a product of quality i could extract from a consumer with marginal utility of income θ is

$$\theta\chi_i - \tfrac{1}{2}\chi_i^2. \tag{4.90}$$

But

$$\theta\chi_i = \tfrac{1}{2}\chi_i^2 + \tfrac{1}{2}\theta^2 - \tfrac{1}{2}(\theta - \chi_i)^2, \tag{4.91}$$

so the maximum economic profit that a firm producing a product of quality χ_i could extract from a consumer with marginal utility of income θ can be written as

$$\tfrac{1}{2}\chi_i^2 + \tfrac{1}{2}\theta^2 - \tfrac{1}{2}(\theta - \chi_i)^2 - \tfrac{1}{2}\chi_i^2 = \tfrac{1}{2}\theta^2 - \tfrac{1}{2}(\theta - \chi_i)^2. \tag{4.92}$$

Figure 4.10   Linear vertical product differentiation duopoly.

Expression (4.92) has the same form as (4.88); if we rewrite $x = \theta$, $y_i = \chi_i$, the two are identical. If other aspects of the specification of the models are conformable (the distribution of consumer locations in the horizontal model corresponds to the distribution of marginal utilities of quality in the vertical model, for example), equilibrium outcomes in the horizontal model correspond to equilibrium outcomes in the vertical model.

4.5   CONCLUSION

Hotelling failed in the way Columbus failed. Columbus did not discover a westward sea route to India, and Hotelling did not demonstrate a tendency for firms to minimize differentiation. Columbus opened the way to new and different lands, and Hotelling's analytic apparatus, characterized as it is by particular attention to modeling the demands of individual consumers, opened the way to new and different approaches to analyzing performance in imperfectly competitive markets.

Hotelling pointed to discontinuities in demand as a key aspect in the Bertrand model of standardized-product oligopoly. Early critiques of the Hotelling linear model pointed to its own discontinuities in demand as key to the nonexistence of pure-strategy price equilibrium for some locations. We now highlight instead the lack of quasi-concavity of firms' payoff functions.

Models of quality differentiation emphasize the distribution of consumer preferences as the factor driving the equilibrium number of varieties and nature of market performance. Recent work has explored the relationship between models of horizontal and vertical product differentiation. While the distinction between the two types of differentiation retains intuitive appeal, underlying common elements between the two approaches are now recognized.

PROBLEMS

4.1 In the Hotelling linear duopoly model, analyze the demand facing firm A if the quantity demanded at any point on the line is

$$q = \max\left(0, s\rho - sp_D\right),$$

for delivered price p_D.

4.2 Analyze the Hotelling model with no mill-price undercutting conjectures.

4.3 Answer Problem 4.1 if firms maintain no mill-price undercutting conjectures.

4.4 Assume quadratic transportation cost. Maintaining all other assumptions of the Hotelling model but with $b > a > l$, find equilibrium prices for the case shown in figure 4.10.

CHAPTER FIVE

EARLY EMPIRICAL STUDIES OF STRUCTURE– CONDUCT–PERFORMANCE RELATIONSHIPS

Naturally I am biased in favor of economists learning theory; I would make them all learn theory; and then I would let the clever ones learn econometrics as an honor, and do empirical research as a treat.

After Winston Churchill (1930)

5.1 INTRODUCTION

We begin an extended discussion of empirical studies of the causes and effects of market performance. Dating from the seminal work of Joe S. Bain, such studies (at this writing) span something like half a century. It is not surprising, therefore, that the literature records a considerable evolution of techniques and emphasis. Nonetheless, it constitutes an organic, if contentious and disorderly, whole.[1] Chronologically, the literature falls into four overlapping phases:

1   1951–68: elementary statistical analysis of small cross-section samples of industry-level data, with subjective evaluation of many aspects of market structure.
2   1967–77: econometric analysis, primarily of large cross-section samples of industry-level data, with objective evaluation of most aspects of market structure and increasing attention to issues of specification; some use of large cross-sections of firm-level data.
3   1974–83: disenchantment with empirical work in general, and with large cross-sections of industry-level data in particular.
4   1982–present: empirical renaissance in industrial economics – increasing use of firm- and line-of-business-level data, of time series and pooled cross-section time series data; studies of price and of long-run rates of return; motivation of empirical models by formal theoretical models.

---

[1]   See Schmalensee (1990) and Bresnahan (1992, pp. 137–40) for surveys.

Like all classification schemes, this one imposes an artificial order on unruly data. There is considerable room for debate as regards the boundaries of the various periods.[2] They often differ more in terms of emphasis than in terms of hard-and-fast differences in methodology. But the general nature of the divisions seems clear.

We begin this chapter by considering early, descriptive, studies of structure–conduct–performance relationships – work falling in period 1 above, and critiques of these studies.

This is followed by a discussion of the initial econometric studies of structure–conduct–performance relations – work falling in period 2 above. When we consider the most important critiques of such studies, in chapter 6, we move into period 3. Such critiques have led to an increasingly formal motivation of empirical research in industrial economics, and to new directions in this research, in period 4. These are taken up in chapter 7.

5.2   BAIN AND THE CRITICS

A series of papers by Bain,[3] the arguments and evidence of which are summarized and extended by Bain (1956), remain the ancestors of much current empirical work in industrial economics.

Replications of this work, which obtained similar results, were carried out.[4] Other scholars alleged fundamental flaws in Bain's methodology, and argued that his results disappeared if these were corrected.[5]

5.2.1   Bain

Erecting the structure–conduct–performance framework

There was empirical work on subjects within the scope of industrial economics before Bain's contributions of the 1940s and 1950s. This work was more descriptive than analytic (Bain, 1949a, pp. 129–30):

> Business organization and behavior have been studied intensively ... since the early "merger movement," and even the earliest treatments were in general concerned with all of what we currently regard as the primary issues: (1) the structure, organization, and ownership of business; (2) the competitive behavior and price policies of enterprise – including motives, strategy, and tactics; (3) the price, output, and associated results of this behavior; and (4) the public policy issues raised by such structure, behavior, and results. ... Much of the work prior to 1930 ... featured simple description and superficial interpretation of financial organization, structural change, and competitive tactics, and ... emphasized the norms of law rather than economics.

---

[2] I have dated period 1 from Bain (1951), period 2 from Comanor and Wilson (1967), and period 3 from Goldschmid et al. (1974). Period (4) is harder to pin down, as it represents in some sense a return to period (2) with certain changes of emphasis. However, Bresnahan (1981a) and Porter (1983b) are typical of work that characterizes this period. For discussion, see Bresnahan and Schmalensee (1987).

[3] Bain (1949a,b, 1950, 1951). For a review of Bain's work, see Shepherd (1976). See also Meehan and Larner (1989).

[4] Among which, Schwartzman (1959) and Mann (1966, 1969).

[5] Among which, Brozen (1969a,b, 1971).

In it there was frequently a lack of close or extended analysis of price–output results, or of how observed market structure and competitive behavior affected the determination of prices and outputs . . . .

These limitations were especially apparent in the trust problem and marketing fields. They arose primarily from a general lack of rapport with the corresponding field of "economic theory," and this in turn stemmed from the "institutionalist" bias of writers, from their frequent lack of theoretical training, and from the inadequacy of contemporary price theory.

Entering the second half of the 20th century, therefore, empirical researchers in industrial economics sought a solid theoretical paradigm for their work. Those associated with the structure–conduct–performance school of industrial economics consciously rejected contemporary microeconomic theory as a basis for empirical research. They argued that microeconomic theory used concepts that could not be measured and proposed tests that could not be carried out (Bain, 1949a, pp. 158–9):[6]

"Degree of monopoly" classifications . . . like those advanced by Lerner and Rothschild, rest upon practically non-ascertainable sellers' demand curves and cannot be considered as objective or empirically applicable.

Today it seems natural to look at generalizations of the Lerner index such as (3.11),

$$\frac{p - c_i}{p} = \frac{\alpha_i + (1 - \alpha_i)s_i}{\varepsilon_{Qp}}, \qquad (5.1)$$

wave hands over the distinction between marginal and average cost, say "Treat α/ε_{Qp} and $(1 - \alpha_i)/\varepsilon_{Qp}$ as parameters to be estimated," and go out to confront the data. Bain and his contemporaries worked before the infection[7] of economics by mathematics and econometrics. What seems natural today was infeasible in the 1950s. Industrial economists of that period developed a less formal theoretical framework, one that emphasized measurable market and behavioral characteristics. The structure–conduct–performance approach that developed out of this search for an analytic paradigm amenable to empirical testing dominated industrial economics for a quarter of a century, and exerts considerable influence today. Current techniques, which demonstrate the progress of formal economic theory since the 1940s, in many cases reproduce the hypotheses advanced by the less formal and less mathematically rigorous structure–conduct–performance approach.

In retrospect, the basic form of the structure–conduct–performance framework can be described quite simply. The central hypothesis is that observable structural characteristics of a market determine the behavior of firms within that market, and that the behavior of firms within a market, given structural characteristics, determines measurable aspects of market performance.

The structure–conduct–performance framework developed much less neatly than this compact, backward-looking description might suggest. At most, an anticipation of a relation

[6] References are to Lerner (1934) and Rothschild (1942). For an earlier statement of the same position, see Mason (1939).

[7] If that is the appropriate term.

between structure, conduct, and performance appears in an early essay on the measurement of profit (Bain, 1941, p. 272):

> the direct statistical measurement either of the elasticity of demand or of marginal cost is in most cases next to impossible. ... One may proceed instead with a qualitative analysis of the characteristics of industrial markets (including numbers, degree of differentiation of the product, etc.) in order to find where monopoly power may be expected to exist and where (assuming profit maximization) it is exploited.

By 1949, structure as a determinant of the possibility of entry and the conduct of incumbents in the face of possible entry received more explicit attention. Limit price models of conduct by incumbent firms were elaborated to explain why collusive firms would hold price below the joint profit–maximizing level (Bain, 1949b, p. 448):

> But more striking is the evidence in some of these industries of prices held persistently over many years within a range where the industry demand curve is evidently inelastic, the corresponding marginal revenue thus being negative and necessarily below long-run marginal cost. This indicates a prolonged tendency ... to hold price well below the level which would maximize [joint profit], and apparently contradicts the basic *a priori* predictions of a theory of collusive pricing.

The essential thesis of the limit price model was (Bain, 1949b, p. 449) "that established sellers persistently ... forgo prices high enough to maximize the industry profit for fear of thereby attracting new entry to the industry and thus reducing the demands for their outputs and their own profits." Bain took the failure to maximize short-run joint profit as evidence that incumbents maximize the present discounted value of profit (Bain, 1951, p. 295, fn. 7): "price is enough lower to forestall entry and thus to maximize long-run profits of the established firms."

Bain did not suppose that entrants naively expected the pre-entry price to be maintained after entry (1949b, pp. 452–3):[8]

> At the extreme, it could even be argued that a potential entrant to an oligopoly should pay little regard to price or profit received by established firms, especially if he thought price was being held down in order to "bluff" him away from the industry. He should look at the industry demand, the current competitive or collusive conditions in the industry, the prospects for rivalry or collusion after his entry, the share of the market he expects to capture, and his projected costs of production. Paramount in his considerations, provided the industry demand under some conceivable arrangement could provide profits to an entrant, should be his appraisal of the sort of rivalry and the type of price policies he will encounter from the previously established seller(s) after he enters. In judging these determinants of his decision, current price or profit need play

[8] Compare with Friedman (1979, p. 237):

> after entry occurs, the established firm and the entrant are in a two person game whose structure and form are entirely independent of the pre-entry price policy of the established firm; hence, whose equilibria are independent of the pre-entry price policy of the established firm. If both participants are fully informed at the outset concerning the profit functions which would prevail after entry, then it is difficult to see the relevance of pre-entry prices to the plans of the entrant.

The naive version of the limit price model is properly associated with Modigliani's (1958) review of Sylos-Labini (1957) and Bain (1956).

no *direct* role, since the anticipated industry price *after entry* and the entrant's anticipated market share are the strategic considerations. And if he knows the industry demand with reasonable certainty and makes calculations concerning the conditions of rivalry after his entry . . . he might look entirely past any current price set by the established firm(s). He would then be immune to bluffing, and the established firm(s) could never discourage entry by lowering price and earning moderate profits.

This anticipates the essential logic of the credible threats literature and the game-theoretic notion of subgame perfection. Bain (1949b, p. 453) expected a potential entrant to regard current price "as an indicator both of the character of industry demand and of the probable character of rival policy after his entry."

The limit price model (Bain, 1949b, p. 463) "tracing the effects of a sort of oligopolistic interdependence between firms already in a concentrated industry and potential entrant firms," also anticipates the theory of contestable markets (Baumol et al., 1983, p. 494). Bain envisaged extensions that allowed for strategic investment in advertising and dynamic limit pricing (Bain, 1949b, pp. 463–4).

Shortly thereafter, Bain highlighted the elements of market structure and performance that later received principal attention (1950, p. 37):

I would suggest the following general signs of nonworkable competition . . . a profit rate averaging quasi-perpetually well above an established normal return on investment . . . scale of many firms seriously outside the optimal range; considerable chronic excess capacity . . . competitive selling costs exceeding a stated proportion of total cost; persistent lag in adoption of cost-reducing technical changes or persistent suppression of product changes which would advantage buyers.

He suggested their mostly likely determinants (1950, p. 38):

As the association of market structure to results is explored . . . a priori analysis would suggest attention not only to product differentiation . . . but also to . . . the number and size distribution of sellers and of buyers and the condition of entry to the market.

Bain elaborated a theoretical framework within which various elements of market structure determined firm conduct, and that structure and conduct together interacted to determine market performance. The major elements of market structure were buyer and seller size, product differentiation, and entry conditions. Within this framework, profitability, size of selling costs, and efficiency of scale were interpreted as an indices of market performance.

Testing the structure–conduct–performance framework

CONCENTRATION AND PROFITABILITY

In 1951, Bain published the first – but certainly not the last – empirical test of structure–conduct–performance relationships. He aimed to test two hypotheses (Bain, 1951, pp. 295–6):

(a) There is a systematic positive relationship between seller concentration and the probability of effective collusion.

and (1951, p. 295)

> (b) Average excess profit rates on sales should be higher with than without monopoly or effective oligopolistic collusion.

If both hypotheses hold, there ought to be a positive relationship between seller concentration and average profit rates on sales. This is a relationship that Bain expected to find in the long run, or on average. He expected short-run factors to introduce noise – statistical disturbances – to the long-run relationship.

On the way to testing the existence of this relationship, Bain confronted various issues of empirical specification. Many of these continue to be debated today:

1 How should industries be defined, for the analysis of structure–conduct–performance relationships?
2 How should the concentration of sales be measured, for the analysis of structure–conduct–performance relationships?
3 How should profitability be measured, for the analysis of structure–conduct–performance relationships?

INDUSTRY DEFINITION

To Bain, the theoretical basis for industry definition was demand substitutability (Bain, 1951, p. 298): "the industry appears to be primarily a concept of demand – it is a group of outputs that to all (or most) of the buyers of each are generally close substitutes for each other and distant substitutes for all other outputs."

Application of this standard in a literal sense would require estimates of the cross-price elasticity of demand for all products that were candidates for inclusion in an alleged industry. It would require a decision as to how high the cross-price elasticity of demand would have to be before products were included in the same industry. The former data are generally unavailable, and the latter question requires a judgment concerning which reasonable students might differ.

Bain's empirical specification was based on available data.[9] He began with 340 manufacturing industries defined for the 1935 US Census of Manufactures, and eliminated industries that seemed incompatible with the theoretical standard for one reason or another. He eliminated regional industries, since census data is reported on a national basis. He eliminated industries – like the three sugar industries – that were defined in terms of production techniques and seemed to exclude close substitutes in demand. He eliminated census industries like "Chemicals not elsewhere classified" on the ground that they were residual categories rather than industries composed of suppliers providing competing products (Bain, 1951, p. 302).

---

[9] For industry cross-sectional studies, economists tended to follow Bain and work with industry classifications devised by some government agency. Concerns about the suitability of such classifications (Shepherd, 2000, p. 249) have been a factor in the move to time-series studies of single industries and cross-section studies of firms within single industries. Perhaps the most active discussion of the methodology of industry definition arises in the context of the analysis of market power in antitrust cases; see Elzinga and Hogarty (1973, 1978), Boyer (1979, 1984), and the 1982 Merger Guidelines of the US Department of Justice.

SELLER CONCENTRATION

What is wanted in a measure of sales concentration is a summary index of the extent to which the largest few firms control supply. There are many ways to measure concentration (chapter 11).

The measure of market concentration that emerges most often from theoretical discussions is the Herfindahl index, the sum of squares of firms' market shares:

$$H = s_1^2 + s_2^2 + \cdots + s_n^2. \tag{5.2}$$

The most common measure of concentration in early empirical studies was an m-firm concentration ratio, the sum of the market shares of the m largest firms:

$$CRm = s_1 + s_2 + \cdots + s_m \tag{5.3}$$

(where s_i is the market share of firm i, there are n firms in the industry, and firms are numbered so that firm 1 has the largest market share, firm 2 has the second-largest market share, and so on).

Bain did not discuss the theoretical merits of alternative measures of concentration. He relied on the eight-firm concentration ratio, because it was available for most census industries. He excluded industries from the sample if concentration data were not available. He also excluded industries within which manufacturers appeared to be specialized in the production of different but competing products. For such industries, the industry-level concentration ratio would understate concentration at the product level (Bain, 1951, pp. 301–2, fn. 8).

MEASUREMENT OF PROFITABILITY

Bain preferred the rate of return on sales as a measure of profitability, but used the rate of return on stockholders' equity because it was easily available. To construct estimates of industry profitability, Bain began with data on firm profitability collected by the Securities and Exchange Commission (SEC) for the period 1936–40. He classified firms by industry, and eliminated industries for which profitability data existed for only one or two firms from the sample (Bain, 1951, p. 315). For remaining industries, he measured firm profitability as the ratio of yearly net profit after taxes to net worth, using raw data reported by the SEC. The firm average profit rate was the simple average of a firm's average profit rate for the five years 1936–40 inclusive. He computed the industry average profit rate by taking a weighted average of the profit rates of firms in an industry, using net worths as weights, and then taking an unweighted average of the industry annual average profit rates (Bain, 1951, pp. 310–1).

RESULTS

Bain's final sample consisted of 42 industries, with industry profit data computed from 335 firms (an average of just under eight firms per industry). Bain remarked that profit data for about half the industries were calculated by averaging the profitability of three, four, or five firms, and that the underlying SEC data source tended to overrepresent large firms at the expense of small firms. The concentration and profitability data analyzed by Bain

Table 5.1 Bain's 1936–40 sample; $CR8$ = eight-firm seller concentration ratio, 1935 (percent); π_{36-40} = profit/net worth, 1936–40 (percent)

	Census number		$CR8$	π_{35-36}
(1)	222	Asphalt/felt/linoleum floor coverings	100.0	9.0
(2)	1652	Cigarettes	99.4	14.4
(3)	1314	Typewriters and parts	99.3	15.8
(4)	108	Chewing gum	97.3	17.9
(5)	113	Corn syrup, sugar, oil, and starch	95.0	9.3
(6)	1408	Motor vehicles	94.2	16.3
(7)	803	Rubber tires and tubes	90.4	8.2
(8)	629	Rayon and allied products	90.2	12.1
(9)	1301	Agricultural implements	87.7	9.1
(10)	1022	Gypsum products	86.4	10.1
(11)	1123	Tin cans and other tinware	85.6	9.1
(12)	1636	Photographic apparatus and materials	84.9	12.9
(13)	1647	Tobacco, chewing and smoking	84.3	11.7
(14)	1405	Cars, railroad	84.0	2.8
(15)	1201	Aluminum products	83.7	9.7
(16)	631	Soap	83.1	15.2
(17)	1634	Pens, fountain, and so on	82.8	12.3
(18)	1218	Smelting and refining, zinc	82.2	4.7
(19)	1315	Washing machines	79.7	14.0
(20)	1401	Aircraft and parts	72.8	20.8
(21)	133	Liquors, distilled	71.4	14.2
(22)	1638	Roofing	68.2	7.4
(23)	201	Carpets and rugs	68.2	4.7
(24)	1112	Steel works and rolling mills	63.8	4.9
(25)	123	Meat packing	63.5	3.6
(26)	1102	Cast iron pipe	63.0	8.6
(27)	705	Petroleum refining	58.9	6.8
(28)	1126	Wire	54.0	7.5
(29)	115	Flavoring extracts	54.0	1.8
(30)	1608	Cigars	50.7	6.9
(31)	1104	Doors and shutters, metal	49.0	18.3
(32)	1325	Printers' machinery	47.4	2.2
(33)	1002	Cement	44.7	5.4
(34)	116	Flour	37.0	7.6
(35)	907	Leather	34.3	0.8
(36)	1117	Screw machine products	32.9	8.2
(37)	904	Boots and shoes	30.8	7.5
(38)	105	Canned fruits and vegetables	30.4	7.4
(39)	209	Rayon manufactures	27.1	8.4
(40)	408	Paper goods	23.7	12.4
(41)	112	Confectionery	19.9	16.0
(42)	311	Lumber and timber products	7.6	9.1

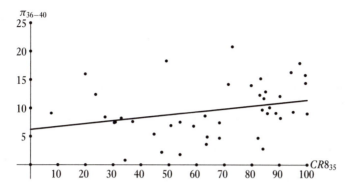

Figure 5.1 Bain's 1936–40 sample; $CR8$ = eight-firm seller concentration ratio, 1935 (percent); π_{36-40} = profit/net worth, 1936–40 (percent).

Table 5.2 Regression results, Bain's 1936–40 sample; dependent variable, industry-average profit/net worth (t-statistics in parentheses)

Equation	Intercept term	$CR8 \geq 70$ dummy	$CR\,8$	R^2
(1)	6.2190[a] (3.1186)		0.0521[c] (1.8406)	0.0781
(2)	7.4524[a] (7.9912)	4.3857[a] (3.3253)		0.2166
(3)	10.9898[a] (4.6821)	7.8325[a] (3.1693)	−0.0800[c] (1.6361)	0.2669

[a] Statistical significance at the 1 percent level.
[c] Statistical significance at the 10 percent level.

are reported in table 5.1, and illustrated in figure 5.1. Figure 5.1 reveals a modest positive relationship between concentration and profitability in Bain's sample.

We take advantage of modern computing firepower to carry out regression analyses not available to Bain in 1951. Table 5.2 reports the results of regressions of industry-average profitability in Bain's 1936 sample on the eight-firm concentration ratio, on a dummy variable that takes the value 1 if the eight-firm concentration ratio exceeds 70 and 0 otherwise, and on both explanatory variables.

Equation (1) in table 5.2 shows the estimated relationship between concentration and profitability when the relationship is assumed to be linear. The relationship is positive, but not very large or significant in a statistical sense. The range of profitability in Bain's sample is from 0.8 to 20.8 percent, while the range of concentration is from 7.6 to 100 percent. According to the regression results reported in equation (1), the estimated profitability in the lowest-profitability industry is 6.6 percent, while the estimated profitability in the highest-profitability industry is 11.4 percent, a difference of 4.8 percent. The linear specification explains a modest part of the variation in profitability.

As Bain notes, and as shown in equation (2) of table 5.2, considerably more explanatory power is obtained if one simply compares average profitability in industries with eight-firm concentration ratios greater than and less than 70 percent.

Average profitability in the low concentration industries is 7.5 percent, and average profitability in the high concentration industries is 11.8 percent. The difference in average profitability for the two groups is, in a statistical sense, quite significant. The explanatory power of equation (2), just more than one-fifth of total sample variation in the industry average rate of return on net worth, is substantially higher than that of equation (1).

A final specification combines the discrete (dummy variable) and linear specifications of the influence of concentration on profitability. The importance of the discrete change is confirmed: the estimated coefficient of the 70 percent concentration dummy variable is large and significant. The estimated coefficient of the continuous concentration variable is negative and modestly significant.

This finding is striking, because it is reminiscent of Chamberlin's argument that the recognition of oligopolistic interdependence, and the consequences of that recognition for market performance, would be discrete rather than continuous (Chamberlin, 1933, p. 48):[10]

> There is no gradual descent to a purely competitive price with increase of numbers, as in Cournot's solution. The break comes when the individual's influence upon price becomes so small that he neglects it . . . as soon as the sellers begin to neglect their direct influence upon the price, it will fall at once to the competitive level . . . regardless of their numbers.

The result that industry-average profitability is significantly higher, all else equal, when the eight-firm concentration ratio exceeds 70 percent ignores variations in profit among firms within an industry. Bain therefore examined the impact of market concentration on firm profitability (1951, pp. 317–21).

Bain omitted two extreme observations[11] from his sample of 335 firms, and compared the relationship between average firm profit rates and industry concentration when firms were split into nine groups by firm size. The group of smallest firms included firms with 1936 net worth of $50,000 or less. The group of largest firms included firms with 1936 net worth of $50 million or more. The impact of market concentration on firm profitability seemed confined to firms with 1936 net worth of at least $5 million (Bain, 1951, p. 320):

> If a tentative hypothesis were to be drawn from this showing, it would be that for firms with net worth greater than five million dollars, 1936–1940 profit rates were on the average significantly higher if the firm was a member of an industry where eight firms controlled 70 percent or more of value product; for firms with less than five million net worth, the average firm profit rate does not seem to have been significantly associated with industry concentration.

Leaving aside other qualifications that Bain attached to his results, his study seems to show a significantly higher industry-average profitability if the eight-firm industry concentration ratio is above 70 percent. This result seems to reflect greater profitability of large firms in concentrated industries, when size is measured by net worth.

[10] See White (1976) for a test of the critical concentration ratio hypothesis.
[11] Showing rates of return on net worth of -140 and -215 percent.

Bain concluded this study of structure–conduct–performance relations by noting the omission of relevant explanatory variables (1951, p. 320):

> we have been unable with available data to test for the relation of profit rates to certain potential determinants – especially other characteristics of market structure – which in theory seem likely to influence profits and also perhaps to be associated with industry concentration. The condition of entry to the industry is perhaps the most prominent of these.

Bain's next contribution to the development of the structure–conduct–performance framework was a test of the influence of entry conditions on profitability.

Concentration, entry conditions, and profitability

Seller concentration is an index of the extent to which incumbent firms are likely to face competition from within the market. The greater is seller concentration, the more likely are incumbents to recognize their mutual interdependence and the less likely are they to act as price-taking firms.

Entry conditions, on the other hand, determine the extent to which incumbent firms need to fear competition from potential entrants – competition from outside the market. The more costly it is to enter a market, the greater the profit that incumbents will be able to take without inducing entry. With *Barriers to New Competition* Bain (1956) affirmed the importance of entry conditions as a determinant of market performance. The hypotheses that he advanced were similar to those of his earlier empirical work: he argued that the rate of return on equity would rise as entry became more difficult, provided that concentration was sufficiently large to allow effective collusion. High concentration and difficult entry were expected to benefit mainly large firms (1956, p. 191):

> In regard to the appearance of the predicted association of the condition of entry to profit rates, it would be expected to be evident most definitely for the largest or dominant established firms in an industry, which will in general have the maximum aggregate advantage over potential entrants, and are most likely to be operating with minimal or close to minimal average costs. The profit rates of smaller firms, with inefficiently small plants or firm scales or with smaller product-differentiation advantages over entrants, might be expected to show a less certain or distinct relationship to a condition of entry calculated primarily with reference to the positions of the dominant firms.

Bain defined entry conditions in terms of the cost advantages that incumbents enjoyed, *vis-à-vis* entrants (1956, p. 10):

> the condition of entry to an industry...refers to advantages which established firms in an industry have over established entrant firms; it is evaluated in general by measures of the heights of entry inducing prices relative to defined competitive levels.

Bain emphasized economies of large scale, product differentiation, and absolute cost advantages of incumbent firms compared with entrants as determinants of the condition of entry.

Table 5.3 Bain's 1947–51 sample, study of entry conditions, concentration, and profitability, US manufacturing; $CR4$ = four-firm seller concentration ratio, 1947 (percent); profit rate = large firm rate of return on stockholders' equity (percent)

	Profit rate (%)	CR4 (%)
Very high entry barriers		
Automobiles	23.9	90
Cigarettes	12.6	90
Liquor	18.6	75
Typewriters	18.0	79
Fountain pens	21.8	57
Average	19.0	78
Substantial entry barriers		
Copper	14.6	92
Steel	11.2	45
Farm machines and tractors	13.4	36
Petroleum refining	12.9	37
Soap	15.8	79
Shoes[a]	13.4	28
Gypsum products	15.4	85
Metal containers	10.7	78
Average	13.4	60
Moderate-to-low entry barriers		
Canned fruit and vegetables	9.8	27
Cement	14.3	30
Flour	10.1	29
Meat packing	5.1	41
Rayon	18.0	78
Shoes[b]	11.0	28
Tires and tubes	12.7	77
Average	11.6	44

[a] Men's and specialties.
[b] Women's and low-priced men's.
Source: Bain, 1956, pp. 45, 192–3, 195

To test the relation between the condition of entry and market performance, Bain (1956) assembled a sample of 20 industries. He subjectively evaluated the condition of entry for each industry, analyzing the importance of scale economies, product differentiation, and absolute cost advantages of incumbents. He classified industries in three groups: those with moderate to low entry barriers, those with substantial entry barriers, and those with very high entry barriers. The distinguishing characteristic of the groups was the extent to which incumbents could raise price above cost without inducing entry (Bain, 1956, p. 170):

(1) . . . in the "very high" category, established firms might be able to elevate price 10 percent or more above minimal costs while forestalling entry;

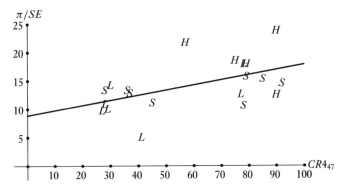

Figure 5.2 Bain's sample, study of entry conditions, concentration, and profitability, 1947–51, US manufacturing. L indicates moderate-to-low entry barriers; S indicates substantial entry barriers; H indicates very high entry barriers.

(2) . . . with "substantial" barriers, the corresponding percentage might range a bit above or below 7 percent;

(3) . . . in the "moderate to low" category the same percentage will probably not exceed 4, and will range down to around 1 percent . . .

Bain combined his subjective assessment of entry conditions with four-firm seller concentration ratios from the 1947 Census of Manufactures. He used SEC data to measure the rate of return on stockholders' equity for up to four large firms in each industry, and used the average of these large-firm rates as a profitability measure. The resulting sample is reported in table 5.3, and illustrated in figure 5.2.

It is evident from table 5.2 that average profitability and seller concentration are higher in the industries that Bain classified as having very high entry barriers. Concentration seems higher, on average, in the substantial entry barrier group than in the moderate-to-low entry barrier group, but profitability does not.

The scatter diagram of profit rate and concentration shown in figure 5.2 is consistent with this interpretation.

Table 5.4 reports some simple linear regressions for Bain's 1947–51 sample.[12] Equation (1) tests the relationship between profitability and a linear four-firm seller concentration ratio. The estimated coefficient of the concentration ratio is positive and statistically significant, and the equation explains a modest amount of the variance in profitability across industries. Equation (2) adds dummy variables identifying substantial (SB) and very high (VHB) entry barrier industries. The continuous concentration variable loses all explanatory power in the presence of the entry barrier dummies. Only the high-barrier dummy has a significant effect on profitability, and the explanatory power of the equation is about twice that of equation (1).

These results are confirmed by equation (3), which omits the substantial barrier dummy from the explanatory variables.

---

[12] For other regression analyses of Bain's sample, see Weiss (1971, p. 376). Scott (1991) presents an alternative explanation of Bain's results, that the concentration/barriers–profitability relationship found by Bain reflects contact of diversified firms in many markets.

Table 5.4 Regression results, Bain's 1947–51 sample; dependent variable, large-firm average profit/stockholders' equity (*t*-statistics in parentheses)

Equation	Intercept term	SB dummy	VHB dummy	CR4	CR4 ≥ 50 dummy	R^2
(1)	8.8801[a] (3.9582)			0.0895[a] (2.5505)		0.2655
(2)	9.7701[a] (4.7803)	1.2144 (0.6635)	6.0291[a] (2.6000)	0.0407 (1.1251)		0.5012
(3)	10.0257[a] (5.0791)		5.1913[a] (2.7141)	0.0481[c] (1.4239)		0.4875
(4)	11.3900[a] (11.4968)		4.0800[a] (2.0591)		2.5100[a] (2.0455)	0.5997

[a] Statistical significance at the 1 percent level.
[c] Statistical significance at the 10 percent level.

Considering equations (2) and (3), one would conclude that it is entry conditions – scale economies, product differentiation, and absolute cost advantages – that explain differences in industry profitability, and that market concentration has no significant effect, once differences in entry conditions are taken into account.

This conclusion is sensitive to the specification of the functional form through which concentration is assumed to affect profitability. Equation (4) reports a regression that includes the high-entry barrier dummy variable and a high-concentration dummy variable (four-firm seller concentration ratio at least 50 percent) as variables explaining differences in industry profit rates. Both variables have significant and positive coefficients. In terms of explanatory power, equation (4) is the most successful of those reported in table 5.4. In this sample, there appears to be an independent, if discontinuous, impact of market concentration on the average profitability of large firms, over and above the impact of entry conditions.

Bain himself expected an interactive effect of entry barriers and concentration on profitability (1956, p. 191):

> This predicted influence of the condition of entry on the size of price–cost margins and profits is clearly subject to the concomitant influence of the degree of seller concentration within the industry. Specifically, it is expected to be evidenced in a verifiable simple association of the condition of entry to profits mainly as far as seller concentration throughout is high enough to support effective collusion in industries with both high and medium entry barriers. ... we would anticipate some complex relationship of at least three variables – profit rate, degree of seller concentration, and condition of entry – of such a character that some net positive association of the barrier to entry and the profit rate would be apparent.

The evidence from Bain's sample seems to confirm this expectation.[13]

---

[13] Anderson and Rynning (1991) present evidence that is consistent with the interactive effect of concentration and barriers to entry on market performance.

5.2.2   Criticism

Brozen (1971; see also Brozen, 1970) criticized Bain (1951) on three counts. He argued that Bain's sample covered a disequilibrium time period, that Bain's selection of industries biased his results, and that Bain's use of large-firm profit rates led to a biased measure of profitability.

Disequilibrium

Brozen[14] noted that Bain formulated a hypothesis concerning the long-run equilibrium relationship between concentration and profitability (Bain, 1951, p. 309, quoted in part by Brozen, 1971, p. 352):

> Our hypothesis refers to profit results which should occur in long-run equilibrium, or the average over time for many cases so far as results on the average tend to approximate those of long-run equilibrium. So far as in individual cases demand and cost are not accurately anticipated or fully adjusted to – or so far as "risk" is miscalculated – profit differences will emerge among firms and industries which are explicable only as windfalls and not by our hypothesis. Thus we should expected our predicted relation to hold strictly only "plus or minus windfalls," which windfalls should tend largely to cancel out in group averages.

For this reason, among others, Bain used group averages as a measure of profitability. He expected high short-run profits of some firms to be canceled out, on average, by low short-run profits of other firms.

Brozen argued that postwar movements in the profitability of the industries in Bain's sample indicate that Bain's 1936–40 sample reflected a disequilibrium relationship between concentration and profitability (Brozen, 1971, pp. 352–3; footnote omitted):

> The average rate of return in the unconcentrated industries used in Bain's sample moved up from 2.1 percentage points below the 1936–1940 average for his total sample to only 0.5 percentage points below the 1953–1957 average for the total sample. The average rate of return in the concentrated industries in Bain's sample moved down from 2.2 percentage points above the total sample average to 0.6 percentage points above the total sample average. On the basis of this evidence . . . it becomes probable that the above average return for his concentrated group of industries is better explained as a disequilibrium phenomenon than as a consequence of oligopoly.

After a 16-year interval, the rate of return in Bain's concentrated industries moved down, toward the industry average, and the rate of return in Bain's unconcentrated industries moved up, toward the average. This, argued Brozen, suggests that the relationship uncovered by Bain was a disequilibrium one.

Brozen (1970, table 1) reports average 1953–7 rates of return for the 42 industries used by Bain (1951). A simple linear regression shows a significant positive relationship between

---

[14] See also Brozen (1969a,b) and Mann (1969).

1936–40 profitability and 1953–7 profitability:

$$\pi_{1953-57} = 8.5357 + 0.2686\,\pi_{1936-40}$$
$$(7.3560) \quad (2.4846) \tag{5.4}$$

(t-statistics in parentheses; $r^2 = 0.1337$). Thus *if* Bain's sample describes disequilibrium rates of return, roughly 25 percent of those disequilibrium rates, high or low, persisted 17 years later. That indicates a slow speed of adjustment of profit rates to long-run equilibrium.

Further, it should be noted that Brozen's study has one thing in common with that of Bain. Neither contains any independent test of the equilibrium or disequilibrium nature of the data. Bain averaged profit data over firms and years, and argued that the resulting figures could be used to represent long-run values, "plus or minus" random fluctuations. Brozen found movements in rates of return toward the mean, and concludes that the later data better represent long-run equilibrium values. It could be, as Brozen asserts, that the later data are closer to long-run equilibrium values. But it could just as well be that Brozen's data represent a short-run fluctuation from long-run values that are better approximated by Bain's data.[15]

Sample bias in industry selection

Bain (1951) used a sample of 42 industries from the 1935 US Census of Manufactures (out of a possible 340). As previously noted, Bain excluded industries from the sample on various grounds, including:

- concentration data were not available; the industry definition seemed inappropriate
- the industry was regional or local in nature, meaning that national concentration ratios would understate concentration in meaningfully defined markets
- the "industry" was really a residual category, rather than firms that competed in an economic sense
- profitability data were available for only one or two firms

Bain excluded 34 industries from his sample because he had information on the profitability of only one or two firms in each industry. Bain noted (1951, p. 315), as is acknowledged by Brozen (1971, p. 353), that the concentration–profitability relationship in this group of 34 industries was inconsistent with the relationship in the final sample of 42 industries. Brozen concludes (1971, p. 353; footnote omitted):

> This strongly suggests that the finding of a dichotomous relationship between concentration and profits was a consequence of the particular group of industries composing his sample.

Bain insisted on having information on the profitability of at least three firms in each industry as a way of averaging out short-run fluctuations in profitability. If Bain had included these 34 industries in his sample, he would have left himself open to the charge that whatever

---

[15] For a contemporary attempt to deal with this issue, see Winn and Leabo (1974). Mueller (1986) estimates long-run firm profit rates and investigates determinants of differences in such rates. We discuss Mueller's approach in section 7.9.

concentration–profitability relationship appeared in the enlarged sample was a disequilibrium phenomenon.

Brozen assembled concentration and profitability data for samples of 78 industries in 1939 (at least three firms in each industry) and 75 industries in 1940 (at least five firms in each industry). Comparing average rates of return in high-concentration (eight-firm seller concentration ratio above 70 percent) and low-concentration industries for these samples, Brozen (1971, table 2) finds essentially no difference.

The enlarged samples employed by Brozen are not without their problems, however. Comparison of Brozen's sample with a contemporaneous classification of industries by nature of geographic market (Schwartzman and Bodoff, 1971) shows that many of the industries in Brozen's enlarged samples are regional or local. National concentration ratios for such industries understate concentration in less-than-national markets. Use of such industries will tend to bias results against finding a concentration–profits relationship, if there is one.[16]

Brozen includes two sugar industries in his sample – beet sugar and cane sugar. It is widely accepted that these two Census "industries" comprise only a single industry in an economic sense. Brozen includes as industries in his samples several residual categories (for example, "Machinery, not elsewhere classified"). While Brozen is able to assemble larger samples than Bain, it is not obvious that results from those larger samples should be treated with greater confidence than results from Bain's samples.

Data bias from firm selection

Bain drew his profitability data from a report of the SEC. Leading firms in small industries might well not be large enough in an absolute sense to be listed on the stock exchange. Thus, Brozen observes, such industries would tend to be excluded from Bain's sample.

Brozen's other observation concerning the use of large-firm data is an anticipation of the "efficiency" critique later leveled at econometric studies of structure–conduct–performance relations. The gist of this argument (also made by Demsetz, 1973, 1974) is that any observed positive concentration-profitability relationship should be interpreted as reflecting the superior efficiency of large firms, not their exercise of market power (Brozen, 1971, p. 362):

> Suppose that the concentrated industries grew concentrated because large firms were more efficient, adaptive, and innovative or better able to cope with risks peculiar to their industries than small firms. Further, suppose that some of these industries were in a structural disequilibrium such that the number of small firms had not yet adjusted to this situation
>
> If such industries were short of long run output equilibrium, the larger firms would earn higher rates of returns than small firms and higher than long run equilibrium rates of return. . . . If these concentrated industries had not yet reached their new organizational pattern, the use only or mainly of large firms to measure returns would show the average return in the industry to be higher than it was.

If, as Brozen suggests, large more efficient firms and small less efficient firms coexist because the market is out of equilibrium (small firms unable to adopt cost-saving techniques or

---

[16] See Kania (1987) for econometric evidence on this point.

large firms unable to expand output to supply the entire market), then profitability differences indeed reflect the superior efficiency of large firms. But if large more efficient firms and small less efficient firms coexist because large firms have raised price and created an umbrella under which small, less efficient firms can survive, profitability differences reflect the exercise of market power. The mere existence of cost differences does not demonstrate that low–cost firms are not exercising market power.[17]

5.2.3 Summary

Bain's seminal work suggests that concentration and barriers to entry, together, serve to raise the profitability of large firms. Barriers to entry – economies of large scale, absolute capital requirements, and product differentiation – separate the firms within the market from potential entrants. A sufficiently high level of concentration triggers the awareness of oligopolistic interdependence that allows joint- and single-firm exercise of market power.

Brozen (1971) advanced three criticisms of Bain's empirical work. He suggested that Bain's results reflected disequilibrium relationships. By presenting data for a later period in which results similar to those of Bain did not hold, Brozen demonstrated that this might be the case. But Brozen does not demonstrate that his sample is any more likely to represent a situation of long-run equilibrium than Bain's sample.

Brozen suggests that Bain's selection of industries is biased. Brozen reports results for larger samples of industries. But the results obtained from these larger samples are contaminated by the use of regional and local industries and of "industries" that are in fact residual categories.

Brozen also suggests that Bain's rate of return data were biased because Bain estimated industry profitability as an average of the profitability of large firms. On this point, Brozen anticipated an important criticism of later econometric studies of structure–conduct–performance relations.

5.3 EARLY ECONOMETRIC WORK

Bain pioneered the use of cross-section industry-level samples in the empirical analysis of structure–conduct–performance relationships. The samples employed in these and subsequent studies were relatively small, which limited the number of independent explanatory variables that could be included in any single study. Economists soon turned to econometric analysis of larger samples as a way of exploring the determinants of market performance.[18]

The econometric analysis of cross-section data by industrial economists, despite important antecedents,[19] became a growth industry with the publication of studies by Comanor and Wilson (1967) and Collins and Preston (1969). These studies remain influential in their own right: when a prominent game theorist sought a characteristic example of empirical work in industrial economics, it was to one of them that he turned (Selten, 1988).

---

[17] See section 6.2.1 for further discussion.

[18] For a survey of the literature through 1973, see Weiss (1974); for later surveys, see Cubbin (1988) and Schmalensee (1989).

[19] For example, Weiss (1963), Stigler (1963, 1964), and Hall and Weiss (1967).

Further, they defined a research program for empirical industrial economics that was reported in the literature for at least a decade, as the robustness and sensitivity of the basic results were tested against various samples and specifications.

The Comanor–Wilson and Collins–Preston studies used industry-level data. Although Bain had also used primarily industry-level data, he analyzed firm-level data as well. The firm-level approach was taken up by Shepherd (1972). As a subject for tests of structure–conduct–performance relationships, firm-level studies were long the weak sister of industry-level work. Partly as a result of extensive criticism of industry-level studies in the 1970s, this is decidedly no longer the case.

5.3.1 Industry-level studies

Comanor and Wilson

Comanor and Wilson (1967; see also 1974) employed a sample of 41 Internal Revenue Service (IRS) minor industries, all consumer good industries, to analyze the simultaneous impact of advertising, market concentration, economies of scale, and other factors on industry profitability.[20] IRS data were the first extensively used source for industry-level advertising expenditures.[21]

Comanor and Wilson's hypotheses are essentially the same as those of Bain. They expected profitability, an index of market performance, to be higher, the greater is product differentiation, for three reasons (Comanor and Wilson, 1967, pp. 425–6):

1 Entrants will have to spend more on advertising, per unit of sales, than incumbents, since incumbents benefit from past advertising; this creates an absolute cost advantage for incumbents.
2 If firms must advertise at a minimum level to stay in the market and maintain market share – if there is a threshold effect – then there will be economies of scale in advertising, which will benefit larger incumbent firms.
3 An investment in product differentiation, like an investment in physical capital, carries with it an opportunity cost of financial capital, and capital markets are likely to impose higher costs on entrants than incumbents, given the greater likelihood that entrants will go bankrupt.

Comanor and Wilson regarded advertising by incumbents as an index of the extent of product differentiation. Thus there should be a positive relationship between advertising – an index of product differentiation – and profitability.

[20] The sample of 41 industries came to lead a life of its own; it was used, for example, by Boyer (1974) and Porter (1974). IRS minor industries are roughly at the three-digit Standard Industrial Classification level, somewhat more aggregated than the four-digit SIC industries more commonly used in cross-sectional studies. With such a sample, it is desirable to use concentration figures for three-digit industries that are weighted averages of concentration figures for component four-digit industries (Weiss, 1974, p. 195). For a comparison of profitability measures based on IRS minor industries and SIC data, see Liebowitz (1982).

[21] Information on advertising at what is more or less the four-digit industry level is reported in input–output tables for the United States, as first noted (I believe) by Ornstein (1977).

They acknowledged that advertising has structural and conduct aspects (1967, pp. 423–4):[22]

> past advertising outlays appear to be an important determinant of the extent of product differentiation. Differences in advertising, therefore, reflect both structural and behavioral differences between industries.

Comanor and Wilson's results generally show advertising and absolute capital requirements to be more important determinants of profitability than market concentration. Most of their equations show a statistically insignificant, and often negative, impact of market concentration on profitability. When they use an explanatory variable that is the product of a four-firm concentration ratio and a high barrier-to-entry dummy variable, the effect of concentration is significantly positive (Comanor and Wilson, 1974, p. 124, table 6.7, equation (1)):

$$\pi = \underset{(4.94)}{0.0398} + \underset{(1.79)}{0.254 ASR} + \underset{(1.60)}{0.00577 \log (ACR)}$$
$$+\underset{(2.68)}{0.0339 GR} + \underset{(1.07)}{0.0184 Local} + \underset{(2.03)}{0.000395(CR4)(HBD)} \tag{5.5}$$

$(R^2 = 0.57)$.

In (5.5), ASR is the ratio of spending on advertising to dollar of sales, ACR is an estimate of the absolute capital requirements for entry at minimum efficient scale, GR is the growth rate of industry sales between 1947 and 1957, and $Local$ is a dummy variable that takes the value 1 for local industries and 0 otherwise. $CR4$ is the four-firm seller concentration ratio and HBD is a dummy variable that takes the value 1 for high-barrier industries and 0 otherwise. The t-statistics are reported in parentheses under the estimated coefficients.

The estimates show positive effects of advertising and absolute capital requirements on profitability. Profit is greater, the more rapid the rate of growth of demand. National concentration ratios understate actual concentration when markets are local. The local industry dummy variable is included to control for this understatement. It should therefore have a positive coefficient, and this is the result, although the estimated coefficient is not statistically significant. Finally, in high-entry barrier industries, profitability rises with concentration.

This specification, and the results obtained by using it, are consistent with Bain's argument that the impact of concentration and entry conditions is interactive, and that concentration raises large-firm profit only if entry is costly enough to bar rivals from the market. An important aspect of Comanor and Wilson's results, generally borne out by later work, is that advertising intensity is a stronger and more significant determinant of profitability than market concentration. This highlights the role of single-firm exercise of market power over tacit collusion and the joint exercise of market power. A limitation of their work is that it was carried out at the three-digit industry level.

---

[22] This is one of the first hints of simultaneous relationships in the structure–conduct–performance literature. If advertising depends on behavioral differences between industries, then advertising is endogenous. Comanor and Wilson (1974, tables 7.3–7.8) report the results of regressions explaining differences in advertising–sales ratios across industries. Comanor and Wilson (1967, table 8) report equations explaining differences in concentration across industries. Implicitly at least, advertising, concentration, and profitability are treated as forming a simultaneous system.

Collins and Preston

Studies of market performance based on the Census of Manufactures use some variation of the census price–cost margin,

$$\frac{\text{value of shipments} - (\text{cost of materials} + \text{payroll})}{\text{value of shipments}}, \tag{5.6}$$

as a measure of profitability. The price–cost margin is a rate of return on sales, gross of the normal rate of return to capital. Write economic profit per unit of sales as

$$\frac{PQ - (wL + \lambda p^k K)}{PQ} = \frac{PQ - wL}{PQ} - \lambda \frac{p^k K}{PQ}, \tag{5.7}$$

where w is a vector of prices of variable inputs, L is a vector of variable inputs (so that wL is the cost of all variable factors), λ is the rental cost of capital services, $p^k K$ is the value of capital assets, p is output price, and Q is the quantity of output. Then the first term on the right-hand side in (5.7) corresponds to the census price–cost margin, and the second term is the normal rate of return on capital per value of sales.

It follows that if some economic model indicates that the rate of return on sales is a function of certain structural (S) and conduct (C) variables,

$$\frac{PQ - (wL + \lambda p^k K)}{PQ} = f(S, C), \tag{5.8}$$

there is a corresponding relationship involving the Census price–cost margin:

$$\frac{PQ - wL}{PQ} = f(S, C) + \lambda \frac{p^k K}{PQ}. \tag{5.9}$$

The Census price–cost margin can therefore be used to test structure–conduct–performance relationships, provided that one controls for differences across industries in the normal rate of return on capital. This allows computation of a measure of performance, using a uniform methodology, for samples covering a broad range of industries defined at a fairly disaggregate level.

This contrasts with the methodology of Bain (and of Comanor and Wilson), who preferred smaller samples for which the quality of data could be subjectively evaluated.[23]

Collins and Preston's basic hypothesis was that there would be a positive relationship between market concentration and price–cost margins (1969, pp. 271–2):

> Low levels of concentration – reflecting the presence of a substantial number of similar firms and, at least implicitly, the absence of substantial entry barriers – should be associated with price–cost relationships indicating "normal" profitability.
>
> Departures from competitive structural conditions (i.e., higher levels of concentration) should be associated with evidence of abnormal profitability.

[23] For a defense of the use of small samples, see Mann and Meehan (1969). For a critical discussion of the use of price–cost margins, see Liebowitz (1982).

Table 5.5 Regression results, Collins and Preston: for a sample of 417 1963 four-digit SIC industries and subsamples of producer (Prod) and consumer (Cons) good industries

Equation	Intercept	Geo	CR4	KSR	R^2
(1) (All)	19.54	-0.029^b	0.121^a	0.092	0.19
(2) (Prod)	19.48	-0.035^a	0.033^c	0.133	0.26
(3) (Cons)	17.36	-0.022	0.199^a	0.103	0.28
(4) (Cons, high–moderate differentiation)	20.05	-0.027	0.189^a	0.053	0.21
(5) (Cons, low differentiation)	14.69	-0.005	0.150^b	0.165	0.32

[a] Indicates statistical significance at the 1 percent level.
[b] Indicates statistical significance at the 5 percent level.
[c] Indicates statistical significance at the 10 percent level.
Source: Collins and Preston, 1969, table 4

Typical results for their entire sample are given in row (1) of table 5.5. The coefficient of the market concentration variable is positive and statistically significant. By this estimate, a difference of ten percentage points in the concentration ratio is associated, on average, with a difference of 1.21 percentage points in price–cost margins. For comparison, the average price–cost margin for this sample is 24.9 percent (Collins and Preston, 1969, p. 274).

"Geo" is a geographic dispersion index, intended to control for the use of national concentration figures when some markets are regional or local. It is measured so that the expected sign of the coefficient is negative. This is the case for the results in table 5.5, although significance is modest at best.

Collins and Preston split up their sample in various ways, to determine whether the overall relationship between concentration and price–cost margins was based on any particular part of the sample. Some of these results are also reported in table 5.5. The positive impact of concentration on margins is larger for consumer good industries than for producer good industries. Within consumer good industries, the impact of concentration on margins is greater in high-product-differentiation industries than in low-product-differentiation industries.

Collins and Preston examined changes in concentration between 1958 and 1963, and examined concentration–margin relations separately in subsamples composed of industries in which concentration was declining, stable, and increasing. The largest and most significant effects of concentration on profitability were found for consumer good industries where concentration was stable or increasing. The effect of concentration on price–cost margins was not significant for consumer good industries where concentration was decreasing.

Collins and Preston suggest that such industries are likely to be in disequilibrium, masking any underlying structural relationships. The effect of concentration on margins was not significant for any of the producer good industry subsamples.

Finally, Collins and Preston examined whether the effect of concentration on margins depended on firm size (1969, p. 280):

> We test here the hypothesis that the association between concentration and margins is stronger in those industries in which the largest firms had price–cost margin advantages over their stronger

Table 5.6 Regression results, Collins and Preston: for a sample of 142 1963 four-digit SIC consumer good industries

Equation	Intercept	Geo	CR4	KSR	R^2
Large-firm margins greater than small-firm margins					
(1) PCM/large	25.08	−0.032	0.190[a]	0.073	0.15
(2) PCM/small	21.26	−0.0395[c]	0.061	0.088	0.09
Large-firm margins less than small-firm margins					
(3) PCM/large	9.78	−0.020	0.091[c]	0.227[a]	0.29
(4) PCM/small	14.62	−0.029	0.047	0.217[a]	0.27

[a]Indicates statistical significance at the 1 percent level.
[c]Indicates statistical significance at the 10 percent level.
Source: Collins and Preston, 1969, table 7

rivals. Theory would suggest that when the largest firms possess distinct advantages, the potential competitive impact of the smaller firms would be reduced and the ability of leaders to pursue a shared-monopoly behavior pattern would therefore be enhanced.

Collins and Preston explicitly argued that this shared-monopoly behavior need not mean higher margins for small firms (1969, p. 280):

> Advantages of the largest firms, that would be reflected in wider price–cost margins, might arise from differences in either their cost or their demand conditions, as compared to those of smaller firms within their industries. If the smaller firms have higher costs, their ability to pursue aggressively competitive policies against the largest firms is substantially reduced. The largest firms will be able to gain higher profits from any given price common to both groups of firms; and they will be able to use additional expenditures (out of those profits) and the threat of price reductions as a means of disciplining the industry and expanding their market control.

Because of the later development of the literature, it is important to note that Collins and Preston did not assert or expect that concentration would result in higher price–cost margins for all firms but, rather, for large firms that enjoyed cost advantages over smaller firms. Such cost differences provide a barrier to competition between large firms and incumbent smaller firms, behind which large firms may be able to exercise market power.[24]

Their results, reproduced in table 5.6, show a large and significant impact of concentration on the price–cost margins of large firms when large firms have cost advantages over small firms (equation (1)). When small firms have a cost advantage over large firms (equation (3)), the impact of concentration on large-firm margins is smaller and less significant. In neither subsample does concentration have a significant effect on the price–cost margins of small firms.

---

[24] See the discussion of efficiency rents in section 6.2.1.

5.3.2   Firm-level studies

Early industry-level studies emphasized the characteristics of markets – concentration and entry conditions – as determinants of differences in economic profitability. Firm-level data are required to examine the impact of firm characteristics on profitability. One of the earliest efforts in this direction is due to Shepherd (1972).[25] A typical result is

$$\pi = 6.67 + \underset{(4.72)}{0.2123 MS} + \underset{(1.56)}{0.0273 CR4} - \underset{(1.54)}{0.2995 \log (assets)}$$
$$+ \underset{(1.54)}{0.2498 ASR} \tag{5.10}$$

$R^2 = 0.504$ (t-statistics are in parentheses).[26]

Here π is the firm average rate of return after taxes, as a percent of stockholders' equity for the period 1960–9. MS is market share and $CR4$ is the four-firm seller concentration ratio. The logarithm of firm assets is included to control for differences in firm size. ASR is the advertising–sales ratio. The regression is based on data for 231 firms.

Shepherd's results are typical of later studies in which market share and concentration appear as variables explaining profitability or price–cost margins. The coefficient of market share is substantially larger and more significant than the coefficient of market concentration. This suggests that the typical positive coefficient of market concentration in industry-level studies reflects mainly firm characteristics and firm-specific market power, not collusion or the joint exercise of market power.[27]

Shepherd finds a modestly significant negative effect of greater firm size on the rate of return, which he interprets as evidence of inefficiency of large-scale firms. The positive and significant effect that Shepherd finds for the advertising–sales ratio is consistent with the results of Comanor and Wilson.

Shepherd explores the impact of other factors, in regressions that are not reported here. He finds that firms with rapidly growing sales tend to be significantly more profitable.

---

[25] See also Hall and Weiss (1967), Kamerschen (1968), and Vernon and Nourse (1973).

[26] Shepherd uses a specification of explanatory variables that masks the t-statistic of the market share coefficient, although one can infer that the coefficient of market share is highly significant. Shepherd includes $CR4 - MS$ and MS as independent right-hand side variables. Results from such a regression are equivalent to treating $CR4$ and MS as right-hand side variables. See Smirlock et al. (1986).

[27] This argument holds exactly if market concentration is measured by the Herfindahl index, and can be expected to hold approximately otherwise. Let profitability be measured by a price–cost margin or rate of return on sales, and let the price–cost margin of firm i in industry j be

$$PCM_{ij} = \alpha MS_{ij} + \beta H_j + \cdots$$

where H_j is the Herfindahl index for industry j and other explanatory variables are left unspecified. Multiply each firm's margin equation by its own market share and add over all firms; the resulting industry price–cost margin equation is

$$PCM_j = (\alpha + \beta)H_j + \cdots$$

Thus the industry-level coefficient of the Herfindahl index is the sum of the firm-level share and Herfindahl index coefficients. See Martin and Ravenscraft (1982).

The coefficients of entry barrier dummy variables suggests that firms in high-barrier industries are significantly more profitable, all else equal. But the entry barrier effect is not as large as that of market share.

Shepherd also finds evidence that the size of the positive impact of market share on the rate of return declines as market share rises. When market share and the square of market share are both included as explanatory variables for the rate of return, the market share coefficient is consistently positive and significant, while the coefficient of the square of market share is negative and usually significant.

Shepherd's main result is that market share has a significant positive effect on firm profitability. As we shall see in chapter 7, this result is supported by recent work using firm and division-of-firm data.

5.4 SUMMARY

Early econometric studies of structure–conduct–performance relationships at the industry level show a typical pattern of results. When concentration alone is regressed against measures of profitability, there is a strong positive effect. When variables reflecting differences across industries in entry conditions are included as explanatory variables, the size and significance of the concentration coefficient is typically reduced. The impact of concentration on profitability appears strongest for differentiated consumer good industries, and weakest for producer good industries. Concentration appears to enhance the profitability of large firms rather than small firms, particularly if small firms operate at some cost disadvantage vis-à-vis large firms. This is consistent with the results of early firm-level studies, which show a significant positive effect of market share on profitability.[28]

---

[28] A large literature shows that the results of these basic studies are robust to the inclusion of a wide variety of additional explanatory variables; see, among others, Fisher and Hall (1969) and Bothwell and Keeler (1976) (risk); Brooks (1973), Lustgarten (1975), and McGucken and Chen (1976) (buyer concentration); Martin (1983a) (supplier concentration); Weiss (1966) and many others (union coverage); and Esposito and Esposito (1971) and many others (trade flows).

CHAPTER SIX

DEBATES OVER INTERPRETATION AND SPECIFICATION

The history of scholarship is a record of disagreements.
Charles Evans Hughes

6.1 INTRODUCTION

Econometric studies of structure–conduct–performance relations appeared from the 1960s onward. They flowered in the early and mid-1970s, and continue to appear. Scholarly discussion of the specification and interpretation of such studies occupied center stage in the late 1970s.

We review three parts of this literature. One involves the interpretation of industry-level studies of profitability or price–cost margins. Researchers working in the tradition of the Chicago school of industrial economics asserted that any observed positive association between rates of return and market concentration ought to be interpreted as reflecting the superior efficiency of large firms, not the exercise of market power. In this view, empirical tests of structure–conduct–performance relations are not specified in a way that distinguishes between the exercise of market power and superior efficiency.

A second debate concerns the specification of the dependent variable in empirical studies of market power. If one is to analyze profitability for market power, how should profitability be measured? Are there variables other than profitability that could be analyzed to determine the presence or absence of market power? Are there data problems that make it impossible to compute theoretically acceptable indices of market power?

A final debate involves an econometric question. If a simultaneous equations model of industrial structure, conduct, and performance fails to satisfy certain criteria, it is impossible to estimate some of the parameters of the system. The simultaneity literature asks whether or not this identification problem arises in structure–conduct–performance models.

6.2 MARKET POWER VERSUS EFFICIENCY

6.2.1 Theory

The market power versus efficiency argument is most prominently associated with Demsetz (1973, 1974).[1,2] The efficiency school argued that if large firms have higher profits in concentrated markets but small firms do not, a correlation between profitability and market concentration reflects the superior efficiency of large firms (Demsetz, 1973, p. 3):

> Profit does not arise because the firm creates "artificial scarcity" through a reduction in its output. Nor does it arise because of collusion. Superior performance can be attributed to the combination of great uncertainty plus luck or atypical insight by the management of a firm.

Demsetz employs "the parable of the taxi medallions"[3] to illustrate the efficiency argument. The parable describes a situation in which a taxi medallion is required to operate a taxi and the number of medallions is exogenously fixed below the long-run equilibrium free market level, although the number of medallions is sufficiently large that each taxi driver-firm acts as a price-taker. If medallions are valued at historical cost for accounting purposes, taxi drivers who happen to have inherited their medallions at a time when prices were low will earn high accounting profit. They do not earn a high economic profit, since the correct valuation of a taxi medallion from an economic point of view is its opportunity cost, the value for which it could be sold.

The lessons of the parable of the medallions do not carry over to imperfectly competitive markets in which scarcity is endogenous and the equilibrium number of firms sufficiently small that they do not act as price-takers.

To see this, consider figure 6.1, which depicts a market with linear inverse demand function

$$p = a - Q. \tag{6.1}$$

One of the firms that can supply this market is firm L; it has cost function

$$c(q_L) = F + c_L q_L. \tag{6.2}$$

All other firms have cost function

$$c(q_H) = F + c_H q_H, \tag{6.3}$$

where

$$c_L < c_H. \tag{6.4}$$

What the equilibrium number of firms is will depend on the assumed type of competition.[4] By appropriate specification of fixed cost F, we can make the maximum number of firms in

---

[1] The exchange between Mancke (1974) and Caves et al. (1977) on random effects is a precursor of the market power versus efficiency debate.

[2] But see Brozen (1969a,c, 1971).

[3] Also discussed by Dick and Lott (1990).

[4] That is, firm conduct is one determinant of market structure.

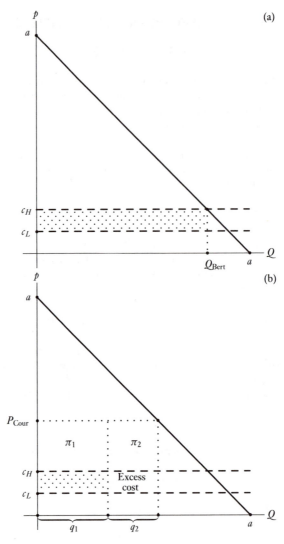

Figure 6.1 Market power and welfare losses with efficiency differentials; shaded areas are efficiency rents. (a) Price-taking behavior; (b) Cournot duopoly.

the market two. Henceforth assume this to be the case. We will thus speak of "firm L" and "firm H."

If firms are price-takers, the market is supplied only by firm L, at a price equal to the marginal cost of firm H (figure 6.1(a)). Firm L earns an accounting profit

$$(c_H - c_L)Q_{\text{Bert}} - F, \qquad\qquad (6.5)$$

where equilibrium output $Q_{\text{Bert}} = a - c_H$.

The first (positive) element of this accounting profit is an efficiency rent. The efficiency rent *per unit of output*, $c_H - c_L$, is known only after price-taking market equilibrium is reached. Rent is determined by price, not the other way around.[5]

If firms act as Cournot duopolists (figure 6.1(b)), both firms have positive equilibrium output. Compared with the price-taking case, there are three types of welfare changes.

Output falls, leading to a reduction in consumers' surplus.

Firm L's accounting profit rises, compared with the price-taking case. The change in firm L's accounting profit is the difference between the economic profit that it collects on the output that it does produce, $(p_{\text{Cour}} - c_H)q_L$, and the lost efficiency rent due to output restriction, $(c_H - c_L)(Q_{\text{Bert}} - q_L)$.

In Cournot equilibrium, firm H earns an economic profit. In addition to oligopolistic output restriction, there are two inefficiencies associated with the fact that firm H has positive output. The output that it does produce, q_H, is produced at an inefficiently high cost. Given that total output is $Q_{\text{Cour}} = q_L + q_H$, resources would be used more efficiently if all output were produced at cost c_L. In Cournot equilibrium, q_H units of output are produced at cost $c_H > c_L$ each.

In addition, society incurs a fixed cost F if firm H produces. The fixed cost F and the excess production cost $(c_H - c_L)q_H$ are social costs of oligopolistic output restriction: they are costs of the exercise of market power by firm L. The existence of a cost difference does not mean that the accounting profits of the low-cost firms are an efficiency rent. In an industry like that shown in figure 6.1(b), the presence of high-cost firms is a signal that low-cost firms exercise market power (Brozen, 1969c, p. 114):[6]

> Unfortunately, the umbrella held by a partial monopolist or an oligopoly conspiracy may shelter inefficient companies as well as efficient companies enjoying monopoly returns in the form of high accounting profits.

If low-cost firms restrict output, they exercise market power and create a niche for less efficient firms. In such cases, the presence of less efficient firms is a signal of the exercise of market power, not a demonstration of its absence. A positive concentration–profitability relationship for large firms and an insignificant concentration–profitability relationship for small firms is perfectly consistent with the exercise of market power by large firms.

6.2.2 Early empirical evidence

Demsetz' empirical tests of the efficiency hypothesis rest on the argument that the exercise of market power will raise the profit of all firms in concentrated industries (Demsetz, 1973, p. 5):

> A successful collusion is very likely to benefit the smaller firms, and this suggests that there should be a positive correlation between the rate of return earned by small firms and the degree to which the industry is concentrated. By the same token, if efficiency is associated with concentration, there should be a positive correlation between concentration and the difference between the rate

---

[5] Thus, firm L maximizes profit $\pi_L = (p - c_L)q_L - F$, not $\pi_L = [p - (c_H - c_L + c_L)]q_L - F$.

[6] Hazledine (1984) reports evidence of just such price umbrellas in Canadian manufacturing.

Table 6.1 Rates of return by size and concentration. The rate of return measure is weighted average profit plus interest/value of assets for firms in the size class, with weights given by the value of assets. R_1 refers to firms with less than $500,000 assets, R_2 to firms with at least $500,000 but less than $5 million assets, R_3 to firms with at least $5 million but less than $50 million assets, and R_4 to firms with over $50 million assets (in 1963); four-firm concentration ratios are for 1963

CR4	R_1	R_2	R_3	R_4	$\bar{R}$
10–20	7.3	9.5	10.6	8.0	8.8
20–30	4.4	8.6	9.9	10.6	8.4
30–40	5.1	9.0	9.4	11.7	8.8
40–50	4.8	9.5	11.2	9.4	8.7
50–60	0.9	9.6	10.8	12.2	8.4
Over 60	5.0	8.6	10.3	21.6	11.3

Source: Demsetz, 1973, table 2

of return earned by large firms and that earned by small firms; that is, large firms have become large because they are more efficient than other firms and are able to earn a higher rate of return than other firms.

As we have seen, Bain, Collins, and Preston explicitly argued that market concentration would increase the profits of large firms but not the profits of small firms. Their empirical results were generally consistent with this expectation. Thus the hypothesis that concentration and resulting (tacit or explicit) collusion raises the profit of small firms is not part of the market power interpretation of empirical studies.

In any event, Demsetz' argument incorrectly portrays efficiency differences and the exercise of market power as mutually exclusive alternatives. Furthermore, concentrating on collusion leaves aside the welfare consequences of the exercise of market power by single firms. If products are differentiated, a single firm will exercise market power whenever it maximizes profit. Empirical studies, from Comanor and Wilson onward, find that product differentiation has a significant positive effect on profitability and price–cost margins.

These results are consistent with the view that product differentiation allows single firms to exercise market power. The efficiency hypothesis is silent as regards this possibility.

Demsetz (1973) uses US Internal Revenue Service data to construct a breakdown of rates of return by firm size and industry concentration. Typical results are shown in table 6.1.[7] Demsetz interprets the market power-concentration hypothesis as predicting an increase in the rate of return of firms of all sizes as concentration rises. The results of table 6.1, in fact, show very little influence of concentration on the rate of return of firms of any size class.

This is not surprising. Leave aside the fact that the structure–conduct–performance framework predicts that concentration allows higher rates of return mainly for large firms. Another

[7] For other examples, see Demsetz (1973, table 1; 1974, table 8).

qualification, quite clear from Bain onward, is that concentration allows higher profitability *only* if barriers to entry impede potential competition or the actual competition of new entrants. Demsetz' rate of return breakdown makes no allowance for differences in entry conditions across industries.[8]

Weiss (1974), in an article that appears in the same volume as Demsetz (1974), surveys 46 empirical studies of structure–conduct–performance relations, from Bain (1951) onward, and reports an additional study of his own. Weiss's study, which is an econometric analysis that controls for the effect of differences across industries in capital intensity, advertising intensity, minimum efficient scale, the extent of sales going to final consumer demand, and inventory per dollar of sales, is characteristic of the state of the art at that time. It shows the typical result: a weakly significant positive effect of market concentration and a consistently significant positive effect of advertising intensity on price–cost margins.

Demsetz' methodology is much closer to that used by Bain (1951). As noted by Amato and Wilder (1988, p. 6),[9,10]

> Demsetz' original study can be criticized on the grounds that his empirical methods lacked rigor. Demsetz' conclusions are based upon descriptive classifications; his results cannot be subjected to the usual tests of statistical significance.

6.2.3   Later empirical evidence

Clarke, Davies, and Waterson

Clarke et al. (1984) estimate the conjectural elasticity parameter for each of 29 UK industries. They regress the estimated values of the conjectural elasticity parameter on the Herfindahl index of seller concentration and obtain the equation

$$\hat{\alpha}_j = 0.170 + 1.682 H_j \qquad (6.6)$$

(the *t*-statistic of the coefficient of H_j is 2.57). Interpreting the conjectural elasticity parameter as an index of collusion, they say that (Clarke et al., 1984, p. 448)

> at least part of the reason why concentration and industry profitability are correlated is that more concentrated industries tend to be more collusive.

---

[8] Demsetz (1974, table 9) presents partial correlation coefficients between concentration and rates of return, by size class, after taking account of the correlation between advertising–sales ratios and rates of return. This leaves the impact of differences across industries in minimum efficient scale, import–sales ratios, buyer–concentration ratios, and so on, unaccounted for.

[9] Amato and Wilder's work suggests that Demsetz' results depend on the way in which he aggregated data, and that his empirical results are not replicated using a less aggregated version of his own sample.

[10] Demsetz (1973) brings regression evidence to bear on the efficiency question. Critical coefficients lack statistical significance and the results are as consistent with Demsetz' characterization of structure–conduct–performance predictions as with efficiency hypotheses.

Substituting (6.6) into the expression for the industry-average price–cost margin (aggregate (3.11) to the industry level), they obtain

$$\left(\frac{p - \bar{c}}{p}\right)_j = \frac{\alpha + (1 - \alpha)H_j}{\varepsilon_{Qp}} = \frac{0.170 + 2.512H_j + 1.682H_j^2}{\varepsilon_{Qp}}. \tag{6.7}$$

The derivative of the expression on the right with respect to the Herfindahl index is positive for $H_j < 0.75$. All observations in the Clarke et al. sample are below this level. In their sample, therefore, industry price–cost margins rise with concentration. But increases in concentration from low levels bring a larger increase in margins than increases in concentration from high levels.

Martin

Martin (1988a) examines price–cost margins for subgroups of firms within SIC four-digit industries. The subgroups are the largest four firms, the fifth through eighth largest firms, and remaining smaller firms. For each group, he defines a relative productivity index RP: value added per worker for firms in the group as a fraction of industry average value added per worker. The larger is RP, all else equal, the more productive are firms in the group, compared with the industry average. If profit differences are a result of efficiency differences, group margins should rise as RP rises.

He also includes the combined market shares of the firms in the various groups as explanatory variables. $CR14$, the combined market shares of the four largest firms, is just the four-firm seller concentration ratio. $CR58$ is the combined market shares of the fifth through eighth firms, and $CR9P$ is the combined market share of remaining smaller firms.[11] If the market power hypothesis is correct, margins of all groups should rise as the share of the largest firms rises. But if large firms are more successful at exercising market power than small firms, then the impact of $CR14$ on $PCM58$ and $PCM9P$ should be smaller and less significant than its impact on $PCM14$. At the same time, competition from smaller firms should limit the exercise of market power by large firms. Margins of all groups should therefore fall as $CR58$ and $CR9P$ rise.

Martin's results (table 6.2) are consistent with the presence of cost differences. Efficiency is evidently a highly significant determinant of group price–cost margins. The accounting profit that low-cost firms earn when they raise price above the marginal cost of high-cost firms is an economic profit, reflecting the exercise of market power.

Once the influence of productivity differences is controlled for, there remains a positive effect of market concentration on price–cost margins. The share of the largest four firms has a large and significant positive effect on the margins of the largest four firms, a smaller and less significant positive effect on the margins of the fifth to the eighth firms, and a still smaller and less significant positive effect on the margins of smaller firms. Even if all the profit that the productivity variables pick up is an efficiency rent, the degree of market power is positively affected by seller concentration.

---

[11] Since the three share variables must add to unity, only two coefficients can be independently estimated. The coefficients of the three variables are constrained to sum to zero for the results reported in table 6.2. This is a costless normalization.

Table 6.2 Martin's regression results: for a sample of 185 1972 four-digit SIC industries. Own *RP* is value added per worker for firms in the group as a fraction of industry-average value added per worker; *CR*14 is the combined market share of the largest four firms, *CR*58 is the combined market share of the fifth through eighth largest firms, *CR*9P is the combined market share of remaining smaller firms. Coefficients of other explanatory variables are suppressed for compactness. *t*-statistics in parentheses

	Intercept	*Own RP*	*CR*14	*CR*58	*CR*9P
*PCM*14	−0.3160	0.2241	0.1933	−0.2071	0.0138
	(7.2196)	(7.6642)	(4.3292)	(2.6748)	(0.3795)
*PCM*58	−0.3239	0.2724	0.1062	−0.1561	0.0498
	(7.3858)	(11.8961)	(2.1205)	(1.8907)	(1.3597)
*PCM*9P	−0.2453	0.3507	0.0664	−0.0257	−0.0408
	(5.6336)	(9.9852)	(1.9177)	(0.4769)	(1.7823)

Source: Martin, 1988a

6.2.4 Summary

The efficiency hypothesis asserts that accounting profits of large low-cost firms in concentrated industries are economic rents. This argument has a weak theoretical foundation and little empirical support. Accounting profits are rents if they reflect exogenous capacity limitations. If accounting profits result from voluntary output restrictions, they are economic profit and result from the exercise of market power. In the latter case, the existence of cost differences among firms is a result of the exercise of market power by low-cost firms. The presence of high-cost firms should be expected if low-cost firms restrict output.

Empirical tests suggest the presence of cost differences among firms. Once such differences are controlled for, there is a residual positive effect of market concentration on profitability. This effect is consistent with the hypothesis that concentration of sales enhances the ability of firms to control prices.[12]

6.3 MEASUREMENT ISSUES IN THE DIAGNOSIS OF MARKET POWER

6.3.1 Early arguments

Bain carried out his empirical tests using a rate of return to stockholders' equity as a measure of profitability. It seems clear from his discussions (1951, pp. 294–7; 1956, pp. 190–2) that he

---

[12] See also Ravenscraft (1984). This is a simulation study based on an underlying model in which price rises with market concentration while cost falls as market share rises, provided that market share is less than minimum efficient scale share. This specification does not allow for the possibility that firm-specific market power may mean that price–cost margins rise with market share. For a theoretical discussion, see Harris (1988). Dickson (1991) models the relationship between unit cost and market concentration and obtains evidence supporting the efficiency hypothesis with a sample of Canadian data.

preferred the rate of return on sales, but used the rate of return on equity on the ground of data availability.

Others have preferred the rate of return on capital, on the ground that it is the marginal rate of return on capital that drives the movement of resources from one investment opportunity to another (Stigler, 1963, p. 54):

> There is no more important proposition in economic theory than that, under competition, the rate of return on investment tends toward equality in all industries. Entrepreneurs will seek to leave relatively unprofitable industries and enter relatively profitable industries. . . .

Hall and Weiss (1967, pp. 320–1) defend the rate of return on equity as a measure of profitability:

> We prefer the rate of return on equity to that on total capital . . . It is what managers acting in the owners' best interests would seek to maximize. We argue that capital structure is an element of input mix. Either profit maximization or sales maximization would require some optimal rate of borrowing, which differs from industry to industry. As a result, rates of return on assets should differ between industries, even in perfectly competitive long-run equilibrium, but rates of return on equity should tend to equality between industries.

Weiss (1974, pp. 198–9) makes a case for both the rate of return on sales and the Census of Manufactures' price–cost margin, provided that differences across industries in the capital–sales ratio are taken into account. He observes that since the price–cost margin is computed with data collected at the plant level, it avoids problems of data referring to firms that are diversified across industries. However, it includes certain kinds of expenses (central office expense, taxes) that one might wish to subtract from a measure of profitability.

6.3.2   Formal approaches

The choice of profitability measure can be subjected to formal analysis. This formal literature does not highlight any one measure of profitability as correct or best. Rather, the formal literature provides guidance concerning the specification of tests for market power changes using different measures of profitability.

Price–cost margins

Generalizations of Lerner's (1934) expression for a monopolist's price–cost margin arise naturally in models of quantity-setting oligopoly.[13] For a single firm in an oligopoly producing

---

[13] It seems likely that this will be the case in the context of any model in which firms are assumed to maximize profit or present-discounted value. See also Dansby and Willig (1979).

a homogeneous product, the price–marginal cost ratio is

$$\frac{p - MC_i}{p} = \frac{\alpha_i + (1 - \alpha_i)s_i}{\varepsilon_{Qp}}. \tag{6.8}$$

In (6.8), α_i is firm i's conjectural elasticity parameter, and s_i is its market share. MC_i is firm i's marginal cost.

For the moment, suppose that returns to scale are constant. Then marginal cost equals average cost, and the price–marginal cost margin is the same as the price–average cost margin. Average cost includes a normal rate of return on investment:

$$AC_i = \frac{wL_i + \lambda_i p^k K_i}{q_i}. \tag{6.9}$$

Substitute (6.9) into (6.8) and rearrange terms, to obtain

$$\frac{pq_i - wL_i}{pq_i} = \frac{\alpha_i + (1 - \alpha_i)s_i}{\varepsilon_{Qp}} + \lambda_i \frac{p^k K_i}{pq_i}. \tag{6.10}$$

The term on the left-hand side, the rate of return on sales gross of the cost of capital, corresponds to Collins and Preston's price–cost margin. The second term on the right is the product of the rental cost of capital services and the capital–sales ratio. Thus firm price–cost margins should rise with market share, with the firm's cost of capital, and with the firm's capital intensity.

Equation (6.10) could be estimated with firm-level data on revenue, costs other than capital costs, and capital intensity. An empirical specification corresponding to (6.10) is

$$PCM_i = a_0 + a_1 s_1 + a_2 \frac{p^k K_i}{pq_i} + \varepsilon_i, \tag{6.11}$$

where ε_i is a random error term. Estimates of a_0 and a_1 could be solved to provide estimates of α_i and ε_{Qp}.[14] In the context of the model underlying (6.10), the firm exercises market power if $a_0 + a_1 s_i$ is greater than zero in a statistical sense.

To obtain an expression for the industry price–cost margin, assume that the conjectural variations parameter α_i takes a common value α for all firms. Given this assumption, multiply (6.10) by s_i, for all i, and add over all firms. The result is

$$\frac{pQ - wL}{pQ} = \frac{\alpha + (1 - \alpha)H}{\varepsilon_{Qp}} + \bar{\lambda} \frac{p^k K}{pQ}, \tag{6.12}$$

where H is the Herfindahl index of market concentration, the sum of squares of the market shares of the firms in the industry. $\bar{\lambda}$ is a weighted average rental cost of capital,

$$\bar{\lambda} = \sum_i \lambda_i \left(\frac{K_i}{K} \right), \tag{6.13}$$

[14] Thus $\varepsilon_{Qp} = 1/(a_0 + a_1)$, $\alpha_i = a_0/(a_0 + a_1)$. Estimates of ε_{Qp} and α_i are nonlinear functions of the estimates of a_0 and a_1; standard errors for estimates of ε_{Qp} and α_i can be obtained using the parameter variance–covariance matrix. See Goldberger (1964, pp. 124–5).

with each firm's cost of capital given a weight equal to the firm's share of industry capital. Industry price–cost margins should rise with market concentration, with the industry-average cost of capital, and with the industry-average capital intensity.

Equation (6.10) can be generalized to cover the case in which returns to scale at the firm level are not constant (Neumann and Haid, 1985; Martin, 1988b). The neoclassical index of the nature of returns to scale is the function coefficient (Ferguson, 1969), the ratio of average cost to marginal cost:

$$FC_i = \frac{AC_i}{MC_i}. \tag{6.14}$$

If average cost is greater than marginal cost, then average cost falls as output increases, the function coefficient is greater than unity, and there are increasing returns to scale. If average cost is less than marginal cost, then average cost rises as output increases, the function coefficient is less than unity, and there are decreasing returns to scale. The borderline case, when average cost equals marginal cost and the function coefficient equals unity, is constant returns to scale.

Combining (6.8) and (6.14) gives

$$\frac{p - MC_i}{p} = 1 - \frac{1}{FC_i}\frac{AC_i}{p} = \frac{\alpha_i + (1 - \alpha_i)s_i}{\varepsilon_{Qp}}. \tag{6.15}$$

Solving (6.15) for AC_i/p yields and subtracting the result from 1 gives an expression for the price – average cost margin when returns to scale are not constant:

$$\frac{p - AC_i}{p} = 1 - FC_i + FC_i\frac{\alpha_i + (1 - \alpha_i)s_i}{\varepsilon_{Qp}}. \tag{6.16}$$

Finally, substituting (6.9) for AC_i in (6.16) yields an expression for the firm price–cost margin or gross rate of return on sales when returns to scale are not constant:

$$\frac{pq_i - wL_i}{pq_i} = 1 - FC_i + FC_i\frac{\alpha_i + (1 - \alpha_i)s_i}{\varepsilon_{Qp}} + \lambda_i\frac{p^k K_i}{pq_i}. \tag{6.17}$$

If there are constant returns to scale, $FC_i = 1$ and (6.17) reduces to (6.10). From (6.17), as before, the firm's price–cost margin should rise as market share rises, as the firm's rental cost of capital rises, and as the firm's capital intensity rises. Taking the derivative of (6.16) with respect to the function coefficient gives

$$\frac{\partial}{\partial FC_i}\left(\frac{p - AC_i}{p}\right) = \frac{\alpha_i + (1 - \alpha_i)s_i}{\varepsilon_{Qp}} - 1 = \frac{p - MC_i}{p} - 1 = -\frac{MC_i}{p} < 0. \tag{6.18}$$

Increases in the function coefficient – an increase in returns to scale – reduce the firm's profit-maximizing price–cost margin, all else equal. If returns to scale increase, a profit-maximizing firm increases output, since increases in output bring reductions in average cost. With a downward-sloping market or residual demand curve, increases in output mean a lower price. Price–cost margins fall, but the reduction in marginal cost is sufficient to bring an increase in the firm's profit.

Table 6.3 Market power statistics, US motor vehicle industry. t-statistics in parentheses

	$a_0 + a_1 MS$	Min. FC
American Motors	0.1653	0.90
	(5.9006)	
Chrysler	0.1492	0.98
	(2.6077)	
Ford	0.2521	0.83
	(7.2067)	
General Motors	0.3286	0.72
	(15.2722)	

Source: Martin, 1988b

Equation (6.17) can be tested by estimating an equation like (6.11) with firm-level data. In the context of this model the firm exercises market power if $[\alpha_i + (1 - \alpha_i)s_i]/\varepsilon_{Qp}$ is greater than zero in a statistical sense. Comparing (6.11) and (6.17), when returns to scale are not constant

$$a_0 + a_1 s_i = 1 - FC_i + FC_i \frac{\alpha_i + (1 - \alpha_i)s_i}{\varepsilon_{Qp}}, \qquad (6.19)$$

and so

$$\frac{\alpha_i + (1 - \alpha_i)s_i}{\varepsilon_{Qp}} = \frac{a_0 + a_1 s_i - (1 - FC_i)}{\varepsilon_{Qp}}. \qquad (6.20)$$

It follows that $[\alpha_i + (1 - \alpha_i)s_i]/\varepsilon_{Qp}$ is greater than zero if and only if

$$a_0 + a_1 s_i > 1 - FC_i. \qquad (6.21)$$

If returns to scale are not constant, one must be able to say something about the function coefficient to test for market power. For given estimates of a_0 and a_1, and a given market share, the inequality (6.21) is more likely to be satisfied, the greater are economies of scale (the larger is the function coefficient).

Martin (1988b) estimates a variation of (6.17) for four US motor vehicle producers, using quarterly data for 1973.1 through 1982.4.[15] Two sets of market power statistics are reproduced in table 6.3.

The first column in table 6.3 assumes that $FC = 1$ and evaluates the resulting market power statistic, $a_0 + a_1 s_i$, at the sample mean value of market share. If returns to scale are constant, then each of the firms represented in the sample exercised market power over the sample period.

[15] He also reports estimates for four US medical–surgical supply companies. The estimating equations control for the sale of bonds and shares of stock; see section 6.3.2.

The second column in table 6.3 looks at the test (6.21) in a different way, and asks how small the function coefficient can be – how great diseconomies of scale would need to be – before the market power statistic loses statistical significance at the 1 percent level.

If Chrysler operates with slightly decreasing returns to scale, the estimates would not indicate statistically significant market power. Increasing returns to scale, on the other hand, would provide additional support for a finding of market power.[16]

Price–cost margins and advertising expense

Bloch (1974, p. 268) concisely makes the case that profit rates should be adjusted to take account of investments, such as advertising, that create a long-lived but intangible asset (Bloch, 1974, p. 268):[17]

> Studies which demonstrate that advertising has a long-lasting effect on sales have been done by Nerlove and Waugh (1961), Telser (1962), Palda (1964), Lambin (1970), and Peles (1971). Yet, normal accounting practice is to treat advertising expenditures as a current expense in the calculation of reported profit and net worth. The assets on the balance sheet of firms exclude the value of undepreciated advertising expenditures, so that the reported net worth of firms is understated. Also, when firms have current expenditures on advertising which differ from the amount of depreciation of their advertising asset, the reported profit of the firm is misstated.

The kind of market which is envisaged is one in which current advertising contributes to a long-lived asset that affects demand. Consider, then, a monopolist[18] who faces a demand that is affected not only by price but also by the stock of goodwill:

$$Q^d(t) = Q[p(t), a(t)].$$ (6.22)

$a(t)$ is the stock of goodwill built up at time t. It depends on all past advertising according to the equivalent relations:

$$\frac{\mathrm{d}a}{\mathrm{d}t} = A(t) - \gamma a(t),$$ (6.23)

$$a(t) = \mathrm{e}^{-\gamma t} a(0) + \int_{\tau=0}^{t} \mathrm{e}^{-\gamma(t-\tau)} A(\tau) \,\mathrm{d}\tau.$$ (6.24)

Equation (6.23) specifies the rate of change of the stock of goodwill as the difference between current advertising $A(t)$ and depreciation of the stock of goodwill, which occurs at rate γ. Equation (6.24) is the integral of (6.23) from time 0 to time t. It gives the stock of goodwill at time t as the undepreciated portion of initial goodwill $a(0)$ plus the undepreciated portion of later additions to goodwill.

---

[16] An alternative approach clearly would be to estimate a cost or production function and obtain a direct estimate of the function coefficient.

[17] See also Weiss (1969), Siegfried and Weiss (1974), and Benston (1982, pp. 167–8; 1985, pp. 44–5). See section 9.4 for a discussion of the literature on the duration of advertising effects on demand.

[18] Extensions to oligopoly, using conjectural variations models, are straightforward and are omitted here.

Suppose that there were no expenditures that created intangible assets. Then the rate of return on capital would be (this can be obtained from (6.10))[19]

$$\frac{pQ - wL - \lambda p^k K}{p^k K}. \tag{6.25}$$

Here λ is the rental rate of capital services. For the moment, ignore all complications induced by financial markets and tax codes. Then, in a continuous-time model, λ is

$$\lambda = r + \delta - \frac{1}{p^k}\frac{\mathrm{d}p^k}{\mathrm{d}t}, \tag{6.26}$$

where δ is the rate of physical depreciation of capital.

The economic interpretation of λ is straightforward. If a firm invests €1 in physical capital, then it forgoes the interest income r that it might have earned by leaving the Euro in the bank. This forgone interest income is the opportunity cost of investing in physical capital. δ is the rate of physical depreciation of capital: at each instant, δ percent of capital stock wears out. The value of this lost capital is also part of the rental cost of capital services. Finally, $(1/p^k)(\mathrm{d}p^k/\mathrm{d}t)$ is the instantaneous rate of change in the value of a unit of capital. It should be subtracted from the rental cost of a unit of capital services – if capital becomes more valuable over time, it is cheaper to use capital.

Bloch's argument is that if investments in advertising create an intangible asset, then when profitability is measured that intangible asset should be treated like the physical assets of the firm. The rate of return on capital would then be

$$\frac{pQ - wL - \lambda p^k K - \lambda^a p^A a}{p^k K + p^A a}, \tag{6.27}$$

where λ^a is the rental cost of goodwill:

$$\lambda^a = r + \gamma - \frac{1}{p^A}\frac{\mathrm{d}p^A}{\mathrm{d}t}. \tag{6.28}$$

If this argument were correct, a rate of return like (6.25), or an empirical equivalent derived from it, would misstate economic profitability on two grounds. It does not include the rental cost of goodwill in the numerator, and it does not include the capitalized value of goodwill in the denominator.

Now consider formally the problem of a monopolist maximizing the present-discounted value of cash flow with demand (6.22), where the stock of goodwill is defined by (6.23). Cash

---

[19] This comes from a continuous-time dynamic model in which the firm hires labor at wage rate $w(t)$ and invests in physical capital at purchase price p^k per unit, where capital depreciates at rate δ.

flow at time t is

$$[p(t) - c]Q[p(t), a(t)] - p^A(t)A(t). \tag{6.29}$$

The present-discounted value of the firm's cash flow is

$$PDV = \int_{t=0}^{\infty} e^{-rt} \left\{ [p(t) - c]Q[p(t), a(t)] - p^A \left[\frac{da}{dt} + \gamma A(t) \right] \right\} dt, \tag{6.30}$$

where (6.23) has been used to eliminate $A(t)$ in (6.30).

The monopolist maximizing (6.30) has two choice variables, the functions $p(t)$ and $a(t)$ (or equivalently, $A(t)$). The first-order conditions for the maximization of (6.30) are given by the Euler conditions of the calculus of variations.[20] The first-order condition for advertising is

$$e^{-rt} \left\{ [p(t) - c] \frac{\partial Q}{\partial a} - \gamma p^A \right\} + \frac{d}{dt} \left[e^{-rt} p^A(t) \right] = 0. \tag{6.31}$$

Integrating from time t to ∞, (6.31) becomes

$$p^A(t) = \int_{\tau=t}^{\infty} e^{-(r+\gamma)(\tau-t)} [p(\tau) - c] \frac{\partial Q}{\partial a} d\tau. \tag{6.32}$$

To maximize the present-discounted value of cash flow, the monopolist should purchase advertising until the marginal cost of advertising $-p^A$ – equals the present-discounted value of instantaneous marginal profit, over all future time, that results from a current increment to advertising. Future revenue from current advertising is discounted at rate $r + \gamma$. r is the opportunity cost of funds invested in goodwill; γ is the rate at which goodwill depreciates.

Of interest for the present discussion, however, is the first-order condition for price which, upon some rearrangement, can be written as

$$\frac{p - c}{p} = \frac{1}{\varepsilon_{Qp}}. \tag{6.33}$$

This is the Lerner index of monopoly power. Average cost c covers wage and capital cost but not advertising cost, which appears separately in (6.29).

Substituting (6.9) into (6.33) and rearranging terms, we obtain

$$\frac{pQ - wL}{pQ} = \frac{1}{\varepsilon_{Qp}} + \lambda \frac{p^k K}{pQ}. \tag{6.34}$$

Thus even if a monopolist engages in advertising that creates an intangible asset, the gross rate of return on sales can be analyzed for the exercise (or not) of monopoly power. To convert

---

[20] If one seeks to maximize

$$\int_{t_1}^{t_2} I \left[x(t), \frac{dx(t)}{dt}, t \right] dt$$

the Euler (first-order) condition for maximization is

$$I_1 - \frac{d}{dt}(I_2) \equiv 0.$$

(6.34) to a rate of return on capital, multiply both sides by the ratio of sales to capital. The result is

$$\frac{pQ - wL}{p^k K} = \frac{1}{\varepsilon_{Qp}} \frac{p^k K}{pQ} + \lambda. \tag{6.35}$$

To analyze a gross rate of return on capital as an index of monopoly power, the rate of return should be defined with respect to the stock of capital that enters the production function. It should be expected that the rate of return to capital, so defined, will rise with the turnover rate $pQ/p^k K$. But the rental cost of goodwill is not subtracted from revenue in the numerator on the left-hand side of (6.35), and the capitalized value of goodwill is not added to the value of physical capital in the denominator. Expression (6.27) is not the appropriate form of the dependent variable.

Overhead costs

The early 1980s saw the development of databases that contained structural information on costs and revenues at the business segment or line-of-business level.[21] Major corporations are typically diversified across several industries, and hold assets and incur costs – overhead costs, corporate management costs – that are not directly traceable to operations in any particular line of business. The argument is sometimes made that the presence of common assets makes the definition of profit at the line-of-business level impossible (Benston, 1985, p. 47; see also Benston, 1982, pp. 194–204):

> When company-wide costs do not vary as a consequence of individual outputs or outputs aggregated by lines of business, any allocation method is arbitrary, and profit by product line cannot be determined.

This argument is incorrect. It is straightforward to show that corporate overhead costs of the kind discussed here should not be allocated to the line-of-business level when profitability is analyzed to diagnose the presence or absence of market power. Since they should not be allocated to the line-of-business level, the argument that there is no theoretically correct way to make such an allocation is without force.

Consider a firm with two divisions, each operating in a different market. The profit of the firm is

$$\pi = [p_1(Q_1) - c_1(X)] q_1 - F_1(X) + [p_2(Q_2) - c_2(X)] q_2 - F_2(X) - p^X X. \tag{6.36}$$

Here subscripts denote divisions. Q_i is total output in market i, and q_i is the firm's output in market i. c_i is marginal and average variable cost for division i. F_i is fixed cost for division i. X is the quantity of a corporate-level input, which may be thought of as management or

---

[21] One example is the PIMS (*Profit Impact of Market Strategy*) database; see Buzzell and Gale (1987). Another was produced by the Federal Trade Commission's Line of Business Program; see Martin (1983b), Ravenscraft (1983), and Ravenscraft and Wagner (1991) for descriptions. Scherer et al. (1987) give further references.

strategic planning. Greater use of X reduces costs, but at a decreasing rate, so that

$$c_1'(X)q_1 + F_1'(X) + c_2'(X)q_2 + F_2'(X) < 0, \tag{6.37}$$

$$c_1''(X)q_1 + F_1''(X) + c_2''(X)q_2 + F_2''(X) > 0. \tag{6.38}$$

This model can be made formally dynamic by having current purchases of X contribute to the stock of a corporate asset x and having the corporation maximize the present-discounted value of cash flow. Similar qualitative results are obtained with the simpler static model.

Suppose that the firm picks q_1, q_2, and X to maximize profit. There are three first-order conditions:

$$p_1 - c_1 + q_1 \frac{\mathrm{d}p_1}{\mathrm{d}Q_1} \frac{\mathrm{d}Q_1}{\mathrm{d}q_1} = 0, \qquad p_2 - c_2 + q_2 \frac{\mathrm{d}p_2}{\mathrm{d}Q_2} \frac{\mathrm{d}Q_2}{\mathrm{d}q_2} = 0, \tag{6.39}$$

$$p^X = - \left[c_1'(X)q_1 + F_1'(X) + c_2'(X)q_2 + F_2'(X) \right]. \tag{6.40}$$

Equation (6.40) indicates that the firm should purchase the overhead input until the marginal cost of the overhead input equals the marginal reduction in cost resulting from its use. Equations (6.39) become line-of-business price–cost margin equations:

$$\frac{p_1 - c_1}{p_1} = \frac{\alpha_1 + (1 - \alpha_1)s_1}{\varepsilon_1}, \qquad \frac{p_2 - c_2}{p_2} = \frac{\alpha_2 + (1 - \alpha_2)s_2}{\varepsilon_2}. \tag{6.41}$$

ε_i is the price elasticity of demand in market i. From (6.41), corporate overhead costs, costs that are fixed with respect to line-of-business output, should not be allocated to the line-of-business level before line-of-business profit is calculated. For the diagnosis of market power, therefore, line-of-business profit should be measured gross of corporate overhead costs. In the usual way (using the line-of-business equivalent of (6.9)), we obtain, for division 1,

$$\frac{p_1 q_1 - w L_1}{p_1 q_1} = \frac{\alpha_1 + (1 - \alpha_1)s_1}{\varepsilon_1} + \lambda \frac{p^k K_1}{p_1 q_1} \tag{6.42}$$

or, equivalently,

$$\frac{p_1 q_1 - w L_1}{p^k K_1} = \frac{\alpha_1 + (1 - \alpha_1)s_1}{\varepsilon_1} \frac{p_1 q_1}{p^k K_1} + \lambda. \tag{6.43}$$

Corporate overhead costs are not allocated to the divisional level when testing for market power. K_1 is the capital stock of division 1. Thus if one wishes to analyze a rate of return on capital (6.43) for the exercise of market power at the line-of-business level, corporate overhead capital assets are not allocated from the firm level to the line-of-business level.

Equation (6.36) is a firm-level profit function for the case in which all corporate costs are of the pure overhead type. Suppose that some corporate costs are related to line-of-business output (and suppose, for simplicity, that the relationship is linear); then (6.36) becomes

$$\pi = [p_1(Q_1) - c_1(X)]q_1 - F_1(X) + [p_2(Q_2) - c_2(X)]q_2$$
$$- F_2(X) - p^X(\kappa_1 q_1 + \kappa_2 q_2 + X). \tag{6.44}$$

The corresponding first-order condition for the output of (say) division 1 can be rewritten as

$$\frac{p_1 - c_1 - p^X \kappa_1}{p_1} = \frac{\alpha_1 + (1 - \alpha_1)s_1}{\varepsilon_1}. \tag{6.45}$$

Thus marginal corporate costs that can be traced to line-of-business output should be subtracted from line-of-business profit for the diagnosis of market power. In a similar way, corporate capital assets the possession of which can be traced to line-of-business operations should be added to line-of-business capital stock when measuring the capital intensity of line-of-business operations.

Taxes

Nothing is certain except death and taxes. Leaving aside the economics of religion, the former is beyond our province. Here we examine the way in which a tax system affects the measurement of profitability for the diagnosis of market power.

To establish a frame of reference, begin by assuming that there is no tax system. Let δ be the rate of physical depreciation of capital. A firm inherits a capital stock $(1 - \delta)K_0$ from the past, and purchases capital I_1 at the start of the period. The firm hires labor at wage w_1; the wage is paid at the end of the period. Output q_1 is sold at price $p_1(Q_1)$, where Q_1 is industry output, at the end of the period, and the firm passes a capital stock $(1 - \delta)K_1$ on to the next period.

At the start of the period, the present-discounted value of the firm's cash flow is[22]

$$PDV = -p_1^k I_1 + \frac{p_1 q_1 - w_1 L_1 + (1 - \delta)p_2^k K_1}{1 + r^*}, \tag{6.46}$$

where r^* is the rate of return on a safe asset, $1 + r^*$ is the factor used to discount future income, and investment is the difference between current and inherited capital stock:

$$I_1 = K_1 - (1 - \delta)K_0. \tag{6.47}$$

---

[22] Capital inherited from the past is valued at its opportunity cost, p_1^k per unit; capital passed on to the future is valued at the purchase price of capital at the start of the following period, p_2^k. Modeling a firm that maximizes (6.46) is equivalent to having the firm maximize the present-discounted value of cash flow over all future time,

$$PDV = -p_1^k I_1 + \sum_{t=1}^{\infty} \frac{p_t q_t - w_t L_t - p_{t+1}^k I_{t+1}}{(1 + r^*)^t},$$

where $I_t = K_t - (1 - \delta)K_{t-1}$. Equation (6.46) is used for simplicity.

A little manipulation shows that (6.46) can be rewritten

$$PDV = (1 - \delta)p_1^k K_0 + \frac{p_1 q_1 - w_1 L_1 - \lambda_1 p_1^k K_1}{1 + r^*}, \tag{6.48}$$

where λ_1, the rental cost of capital services, is

$$\lambda_1 = r^* + \delta - (1 - \delta)\frac{p_2^k - p_1^k}{p_1^k}. \tag{6.49}$$

The firm picks L_1 and K_1 to maximize (6.48). First-order conditions are

$$\frac{\partial p_1 q_1}{\partial q_1} MP_L = w_1, \tag{6.50}$$

$$\frac{\partial p_1 q_1}{\partial q_1} MP_K = \lambda_1, \tag{6.51}$$

where MP_L is the marginal product of labor and MP_K is the marginal product of capital. Multiply (6.50) by L_1, multiply (6.51) by K_1, and add; the result is

$$(L_1 MP_L + K_1 MP_K)\frac{\partial p_1 q_1}{\partial q_1} = w_1 L_1 + \lambda_1 p_1^k K_1. \tag{6.52}$$

In a conjectural elasticity model,

$$\frac{\partial p_1 q_1}{\partial q_1} = p_1 + q_1 \frac{\mathrm{d}p_1}{\mathrm{d}Q_1}\frac{\partial Q_1}{\partial q_1} = p_1 \left[1 - \frac{\alpha_1 + (1 - \alpha_1)s_1}{\varepsilon_{Qp}} \right]. \tag{6.53}$$

Substitute (6.53) and one expression for the function coefficient,

$$FC = \frac{K_1(MP_K) + L_1(MP_L)}{q_1}, \tag{6.54}$$

into (6.52) and rearrange terms. The result is identical in form to (6.17):

$$\frac{pq_i - wL_i}{pq_i} = 1 - FC_i + FC_i\frac{\alpha_i + (1 - \alpha_i)s_i}{\varepsilon_{Qp}} + \lambda_i\frac{p^k K_i}{pq_i}. \tag{6.55}$$

Now suppose that at the end of the period the firm is obliged to pay a tax bill:

$$T = t\left(p_1 q_1 - w_1 L_1 - D_0 - dp_1^k I_1\right) - cp_1^k I_1. \tag{6.56}$$

t is the tax rate. D_0 is the amount of depreciation allowed, for tax purposes, on capital inherited from the past. D_0 has no particular relationship with δ, the rate of physical depreciation of capital. d is the rate of depreciation allowed for tax purposes on beginning-of-period investment. d, like D_0, has no relation with δ. c is the rate at which tax credits are granted for new investments.

The present-discounted value of the firm's cash flow is

$$PDV = -p_1^k I_1 + \frac{p_1 q_1 - w_1 L_1 + (1 - \delta)p_2^k K_1 - T}{1 + r^*}. \tag{6.57}$$

After a certain rearrangement of terms, (6.57) becomes

$$PDV = (1 - \delta)p_1^k K_0 + \frac{(1 - t)(p_1 q_1 - w_1 L_1) + (1 - \delta)\lambda_{1t}p_1^k K_0 - (1 - t)\lambda_{1t}p_1^k I_1}{1 + r^*}, \tag{6.58}$$

where

$$\lambda_{1t} = \frac{1}{1 - t}\left[r^* + \delta - (c + td) - (1 - \delta)\frac{p_2^k - p_1^k}{p_1^k}\right] \tag{6.59}$$

is the rental rate of capital services as altered by the tax system.

Purchase of an additional unit of capital brings a marginal reduction in taxes, $c + td$. This is subtracted from the rental cost of capital. Then the whole rental cost is scaled up by $1/(1 - t)$. This reflects the fact that a fraction t of the value of the marginal product of capital is given up in taxes.

With a tax payment, the firm picks L_1 and I_1 to maximize (6.58). The resulting first-order conditions are identical in form to (6.50) and (6.51), substituting λ_{1t} for λ_1 in (6.51). Proceeding step by step, one can derive an expression like (6.55), again substituting λ_{1t} for λ_1. As before, one can estimate an equation like (6.11) with firm-level data. The test for the exercise of market power is (6.21). The effect of a tax system on the analysis of market power is to alter the definition of the rental cost of capital services.

Stock and bond markets

Economists have sometimes used measures of profitability such as profit plus interest payments as a fraction of the value of assets or profit as a fraction of stockholder's equity as dependent variables in structure–conduct–performance studies.[23] Here we show that formal models of firms that borrow funds and sell shares of stock yield tests for market power that are generalizations of the Lerner index of market power.

BOND MARKETS

We make minor alterations in the one-period model of the firm without taxes (the model in which the firm maximizes (6.46)) to allow for the financing of investment by the sale of bonds. As before, the firm inherits some capital from the past, invests additional capital, sells output and pays workers at the end of the period, and passes capital on to the next period. Now, however, the firm finances investment by borrowing. It borrows by selling B bonds,

---

[23] This section follows Martin (1988b, 1989).

each for €1. Enough bonds must be sold to pay for investment in new capital:

$$B_1 = p_1^k I_1 = p_1^k [K_1 - (1 - \delta)K_0].$$ (6.60)

For each bond sold at the start of the period, the firm promises to pay $€(1 + r_1)$ at the end of the period. r_1 is the rate of interest that the firm agrees to pay on its bonds. r_1 exceeds r^*, the rate of return on a safe asset, to compensate lenders for the risk of bankruptcy.

The firm's end-of-period return is uncertain. The realized present-discounted sell-off value of the firm is

$$PDS = \frac{p_1 q_1 - w_1 L_1 - (1 + r_1)B_1 + (1 - \delta)p_2^k K_1 + \psi}{1 + r^*},$$ (6.61)

where ψ is the uncertain element in the firm's end-of-period return. Suppose that ψ lies in the range $[\psi_L, \psi_U]$. It can be thought of as an uncertain element in the firm's fixed cost.

The firm is bankrupt if it is unable to redeem its borrowings and make its interest payments at the end of the period. If PDS is negative, the firm is unable to redeem its bonds at the end of the period, even if it sells all its remaining capital. So if PDS is negative, the firm is bankrupt.

In the event of bankruptcy, owners of the firm receive nothing, the assets of the firm are sold off, and a partial payment is made to bondholders. There is a critical value of ψ, ψ^*, that makes $PDS = 0$:

$$\psi^* = (1 + r_1)B_1 - (p_1 q_1 - w_1 L_1) - (1 - \delta)p_2^k K_1$$
$$= (r_1 - r^*)B_1 - (p_1 q_1 - w_1 L_1 - \lambda_1 p_1^k K_1) - (1 + r^*)(1 - \delta)p_1^k K_0.$$ (6.62)

If $\psi < \psi^*$, the firm is bankrupt. Otherwise, operations continue into the following period.

We expect r_1 to rise as B_1 rises. The more bonds are sold, the greater the end-of-period repayment that must be made to avoid bankruptcy and, therefore, the more likely it is that the firm will go bankrupt, all else equal. The more bonds are sold, the greater the interest premium lenders demand before they will loan funds to the firm. However, r_1 should fall as q_1 rises. In the usual case, greater output means that greater use of both labor and capital. A greater end-of-period capital stock means that the firm could raise more funds by the sale of capital, if necessary, to redeem its bonds.

Let $f(\psi)$ be the owners' density function for the random variable ψ. For simplicity, assume that $f(\psi)$ is continuous and defined over the range $[\psi_L, \psi_U]$.

Define

$$\pi_< = \int_{\psi_L}^{\psi^*} f(\psi)\,d\psi, \qquad \pi_> = \int_{\psi^*}^{\psi_U} f(\psi)\,d\psi, \qquad E_> = \int_{\psi^*}^{\psi_U} \psi f(\psi)\,d\psi.$$ (6.63)

$\pi_<$ is the owners' assessment of the probability that the firm goes bankrupt. $\pi_> = 1 - \pi_<$ is the owners' assessment of the probability that the firm does not go bankrupt. $E_>$ is the owners' expected value of ψ, given that the firm does not go bankrupt.

We suppose that the owners of the firm pick L_1, K_1, and B_1 to maximize their own expected return, which is

$$B_1 - (1 - \delta)p_1^k K_0 - p_1^k I_1 + \frac{[p_1 q_1 - w_1 L_1 - (1 + r_1)B_1 + (1 - \delta)p_2^k K_1]\pi_> + E_>}{1 + r^*}. \quad (6.64)$$

In (6.64), B_1 is the beginning-of-period inflow of cash from the sale of bonds. $(1 - \delta)p_1^k K_0$ is an opportunity cost to the owners of the firm: rather than liquidating the firm and taking the value of its assets elsewhere, they leave that investment with the firm. $p_1^k I_1$ is spending on new capital at the beginning of the period (and by assumption $B_1 = p_1^k I_1$, so the first and third terms cancel out).

The beginning-of-period cash flows take place whether or not the firm is bankrupt at the end of the period. The final fraction in (6.64) is the present-discounted value of the owners' expected end-of-period return, which owners receive only if the firm does not go bankrupt. Thus the final term in (6.64) includes the probability term $\pi_>$ and the expected return term $E_>$.

Expression (6.64) can be rewritten

$$-(1 - \delta)p_1^k K_0 \pi_< + \frac{[p_1 q_1 - w_1 L_1 - \lambda_1 p_1^k K_1 - (r_1 - r^*)B_1]\pi_> + E_>}{1 + r^*}. \quad (6.65)$$

The owners' problem is to maximize (6.65) subject to the investment financing constraint (6.60). Derivation of the first-order conditions for this constrained optimization problem is left to Problem 6.2. The first-order conditions imply a gross rate of return on sales equation

$$\frac{p_1 q_1 - w_1 L_1}{p_1 q_1} = 1 - FC_1 + FC_1 \frac{\alpha_1 + (1 - \alpha_1)s_1}{\varepsilon_{Qp}} + FC_1 \varepsilon_{r_1 q_1} \frac{r_1 B_1}{p_1 q_1} + \lambda_B \frac{p^k K_1}{p_1 q_1}. \quad (6.66)$$

This may be compared with (6.17) or (6.55).

The fourth term on the right is the ratio of interest payments to sales. It has as coefficient the product of the function coefficient and the elasticity of interest payments with respect to output, $\varepsilon_{r_1 q_1}$. The latter should be negative if, as argued above, greater output means lower interest rates, all else equal.

The final term on the right in (6.66) is the capital–sales ratio. When the firm raises capital by borrowing, the rental rate of capital services depends on the firm's marginal cost of capital, not the rate of return on a safe asset:

$$\lambda_B = r_B + \delta - (1 - \delta)\frac{p_2^k - p_1^k}{p_1^k}, \quad (6.67)$$

where

$$r_B = r_1 + B_1 \frac{\partial r_1}{\partial B_1} = (1 + \varepsilon_{r_1 q_1})r_1. \quad (6.68)$$

$\varepsilon_{r_1 q_1}$ is the elasticity of the firm's interest rate, r_1, with respect to the number of bonds sold. When the firm sells an additional bond, the increase in its interest bill is the interest it pays on that bond plus the marginal increase in interest payments on all other bonds.

If the price–cost margin of a firm that finances investment by sale of bonds is to be analyzed for the exercise, or not, of market power, the ratio of interest rate payments to sales should be included as an explanatory variable in empirical tests.

STOCK MARKETS

Now suppose that the firm can sell stock as well as bonds. Like the sale of bonds, the sale of stock brings in funds at the start of the period. But the sale of stock does not entail end-of-period interest payments. Rather, it means that beginning of period stockholders give up part of their ownership of the firm.

If we extend the model of section 6.3.2 by allowing the firm to sell S_N shares of stock at the beginning of the period, at price m_1 per share, so that investment is financed by the sale of stocks and bonds, with constant returns to scale we obtain a gross rate of return on sales equation

$$\frac{p_1 q_1 - w_1 L_1}{p_1 q_1} = \frac{\alpha_1 + (1 - \alpha_1)s_1}{\varepsilon_{Qp}} + \varepsilon_{r_1 q_1} \frac{r_1 B_1}{p_1 q_1} - (1 + r_{SB})\varepsilon_{m_1 q_1} \frac{m_1 S_N}{p_1 q_1} + \lambda_B \frac{p^k K_1}{p_1 q_1}, \quad (6.69)$$

where the firm's marginal cost of capital is

$$r_{SB} = \frac{1}{1 + S_N \partial m_1 / \partial B_1} \left(r_1 + B_1 \frac{\partial r_1}{\partial B_1} - S_N \frac{\partial m_1}{\partial B_1} \right) \quad (6.70)$$

and its marginal rental rate of capital services is

$$\lambda_{SB} = r_{SB} + \delta - (1 - \delta)\frac{p_2^k - p_1^k}{p_1^k}. \quad (6.71)$$

The first two terms in parentheses on the right-hand side of (6.70) are the marginal bond rate from the model of the previous section. The sale of additional bonds, which increases the likelihood of bankruptcy, lowers the price of new shares of stock (m_1). The third term in parentheses on the right is the marginal reduction in receipts from the sale of stock as a result of the sale of bonds.

If the price–cost margin of a firm that firm finances investment by sale of stocks and bonds is to be analyzed for the exercise, or not, of market power, the ratio of interest rate payments to sales and the ratio of revenue raised by the share of stock should be included as explanatory variables in empirical tests.

An estimating equation for analysis of the exercise, or not, of market power, motivated by (6.69) is

$$\frac{p_1 q_1 - w_1 L_1}{p_1 q_1} = a_0 + a_1 s_1 + a_2 \frac{r_1 B_1}{p_1 q_1} + a_3 \frac{m_1 S_N}{p_1 q_1} + a_4 \frac{p^k K_1}{p_1 q_1} + \varepsilon, \quad (6.72)$$

where ε is a random error term.

There is nothing that compels use of about the gross rate of return on sales as a dependent variable. One could obtain a corresponding specification using the rate of return on capital by multiplying both sides of (6.72) by the ratio of sales to capital. One could obtain a corresponding specification using the rate of return to the stock market value of the firm by multiplying both sides of (6.72) by the ratio of sales to the stock market value of the firm $m_1(S_E + S_N)$. Provided that appropriate corrections were made for heteroskedasticity in each case, conclusions about the presence or absence of market power would be independent of the choice of independent variable.

From the estimate of an equation like (6.72), one can obtain an estimate of $a_0 + a_1 s_1$, which is an estimate of $[\alpha_1 + (1 - \alpha_1)s_1]/\varepsilon_Q p$. If this is zero, then marginal revenue equals price, and the firm does not exercise market power. If the estimate is greater than zero, in a statistical sense, then marginal revenue is less than price, and within the context of this model the firm can be said to exercise market power.[24]

Equations such as (6.72) could be aggregated to the industry level. To maintain tractability, this would require the strong assumptions that the values of the function coefficient and the various financial market elasticities were the same for all firms in the industry. With regard to the financial market elasticities, in particular, such assumptions are not plausible: lenders and investors are likely to believe that the risk of bankruptcy is different for different firms, and this means different marginal interest rates and share prices for different firms.

Even stronger assumptions would be required to justify estimating aggregated versions of the rate of return equations developed here against cross-section industry samples. Extensions of the Lerner index of market power to include nonconstant returns to scale and financial markets are most compatible with the analysis of time series firm-level data.

Tobin's q ratio

James Tobin defined q as the ratio of the stock market value of a firm to the replacement cost of its assets.[25] His purpose was to analyze the investment decision of the firm, and to pursue the macroeconomic implications thereof. If q were greater than 1, he argued, the firm would have an incentive to invest, since the value of capital to the firm would exceed the purchase price of capital.

Industrial economists have pursued the use of q as an index of market power, arguing that q will exceed 1 for firms that exercise market power, as investors bid up the stock market value of the firm to reflect the present discounted value of future economic profits (Lindenberg and Ross, 1981, p. 2).

At the same time, q may exceed 1 for a price-taking firm that earns economic rents, because it possesses unique, efficiency-producing, assets. Thus q, like accounting profit, is open to the efficiency argument. Investors may place a high value on a firm, relative to the cost of its physical assets, because they anticipate that the firm will earn economic profits in the future. Investors may place a high value on a firm, relative to the cost of its physical assets, because

[24] For estimates with firm-level data, see Martin (1988b).

[25] For a discussion of measurement issues relating to the q ratio, see Klock et al. (1991). Criticisms of the use of accounting data, discussed below, apply to the q ratio as well as to accounting rates of return. Accounting values for a firm's capital stock are unlikely to correspond to the economic value of a firm's capital stock. But it is possible to recompute the replacement value of a firm's capital stock. See, for example, the appendix to Lustgarten and Thomadakis (1987).

Table 6.4 The correlation between economic and accounting values, Tobin's q and the rate of return on capital

Experiment	q	r
1	0.79	0.65
2	0.78	0.62
3	0.73	0.56
4	0.73	0.53
5	0.77	0.66
6	0.70	0.53
7	0.77	0.66
8	0.84	0.69
9	0.81	0.72
10	0.75	0.51

Source: McFarland, 1988, table 2

they anticipate that it will persistently collect efficiency rents. Knowing that IBM has a q ratio of 4.21 (Lindenberg and Ross's estimate) does not tell us why IBM has a q of 4.21.[26]

Salinger (1984) argues that q, a measure of long-run market power, should be preferred to profitability measures. Public policy intervention against the exercise of market power provides the greatest benefits where the problem would persist over the long run. He also argues that q is less subject to measurement error than accounting measures of profitability.

McFarland (1988) investigates this question with a simulation analysis. He constructs ten samples, each consisting of a large number of firms that make investment decisions and accounting choices in various ways. For each sample, he computes the true and accounting values of q and of the rate of return on capital.

Table 6.4 reports the correlation coefficients between the correct and the accounting values for the ten samples. As he comments (McFarland, 1988, p. 618),

> Accounting estimates of both q and the rate of return are fairly highly correlated with the true values. Estimates of q perform substantially better in this regard than estimates of the rate of return.

Shepherd (1986) compares q and the rate of return on stockholders' equity, using a relatively standard specification, against a sample of 117 large US corporations (table 6.5). Within his sample, the correlation between q and the rate of return is 0.65.

---

[26] Smirlock et al. (1984) attempt to finesse this problem by assuming that a significant positive correlation between market share and q reflects efficiency, while a significant positive correlation between concentration and q reflects market power. Shepherd (1986) points out that the traditional position of industrial economics is that a positive impact of market share on market power can reflect firm-specific market power. Smirlock et al. (1986) argue the need for a firmer theoretical foundation before a relation between market share and market power can be assumed. This would seem to suggest the need for a firmer theoretical foundation before such an assumption can be ruled out. See also Spiller (1985), whose work suggests that risk and market power affect q in the same way, and Heywood (1987) and Stevens (1990), who provide evidence contrary to the assumption that a positive relationship between market share and market power must reflect efficiency rather than firm-specific market power.

Table 6.5 A comparison of q and the rate of return on stockholders' equity. t-statistics in parentheses

	Intercept	MS	CR4	log($ASSET$)	ASR	GR	R^2
Π	7.69	0.20	0.04	−0.56	0.26	0.51	0.573
	(3.21)	(6.27)	(1.55)	(1.79)	(3.98)	(2.09)	
q	1.09	0.06	0.01	−0.19	0.09	0.27	0.558
	(1.42)	(5.64)	(0.79)	(1.94)	(4.09)	(3.48)	

Source: Shepherd, 1986, table 1

Shepherd's results using the rate of return are similar to the usual results with firm-level data: a highly significant positive coefficient for market share and advertising; a modestly significant positive coefficient for market concentration. When q is used as a dependent variable instead of the rate of return, the coefficient of market concentration becomes insignificant; the coefficient of the growth rate of sales increases in significance.

Shepherd's results, together with those of McFarland, suggest that q and profitability measures should be regarded as complements rather than substitutes. Both contain information about market power, and there is no compelling reason to think that either type of measure dominates the other.

The Panzar–Rosse statistic

Let us return once again to a static model of a firm without taxes or financial markets. The firm maximizes

$$\pi = pq_1 - w_1L_1 - \lambda_1 p_1^k K_1 = R(L_1, K_1) - C(L_1, K_1; w_1, \lambda_1),\qquad(6.73)$$

where R is the revenue function and C the cost function.

Write

$$R^*(w_1, \lambda_1) \equiv R[L_1^*(w_1, \lambda_1), K_1^*(w_1, \lambda_1)]\qquad(6.74)$$

for the reduced-form revenue function, where L_1^* and K_1^* are the profit-maximizing input levels.

Panzar and Rosse (1987) define

$$\varphi \equiv \frac{w_1}{R^*}\frac{\partial R^*}{\partial w_1} + \frac{\lambda_1}{R^*}\frac{\partial R^*}{\partial \lambda_1}\qquad(6.75)$$

and show that:

- for monopoly, $\varphi < 0$
- in equilibrium in a symmetric monopolistically competitive industry, $\varphi < 1$
- in long-run competitive equilibrium, $\varphi = 1$

By estimating a reduced form revenue function, the Panzar–Rosse statistic φ could be estimated, and one could test whether any of these restrictions were satisfied. One could also work out restrictions implied by other structure or conduct assumptions.

Shaffer (1982; see also 1983) shows that

$$\varphi = 1 - \varepsilon_{qp},\tag{6.76}$$

where ε_{qp} is the (absolute value of) the price elasticity of demand facing a single firm.

We can also write the Lerner index for a single firm as

$$L_i = \frac{1}{\varepsilon_{qp}},\tag{6.77}$$

allowing us to obtain a relation between the Panzar–Rosse statistic and the Lerner index:

$$\varphi_i = 1 - \frac{1}{L_i}.\tag{6.78}$$

Furthermore, if we write the Lerner index in terms of conjectural elasticities,

$$L_i = \frac{\alpha_i + (1 - \alpha_i)}{\varepsilon_{Qp}},\tag{6.79}$$

and substitute in (6.78), we obtain a conjectural variation version of the Panzar–Rosse statistic.

6.3.3   The use of accounting data

Industrial economists have long fretted over the quality of empirical indices of market power.[27] Sometimes this discussion has focused on the way in which available data ought to be corrected or adjusted before use (see, for example, Weiss, 1974). In other cases, it has involved comparisons of one measure with another (Ornstein, 1975; Liebowitz, 1982). Two contributions to this debate are quite pessimistic. One asserts that it is impossible for economists to use available data, no matter how it is adjusted. Another asserts that available measures of profitability should not be used because they are poor proxies for one particular measure, which is the only correct way to measure the rate of return.

Accounting data

Benston argues that accounting data cannot be used by economists because the interpretation of accounting data requires idiosyncratic knowledge about the environment that produces the

---

[27] For references to the literature discussed here, see Edwards et al. (1987) and the *Journal of Accounting and Public Policy* 7(7) (1988).

data. His position is that since economists lack this knowledge their analyses of accounting data are necessarily flawed (Benston, 1982, pp. 161–2) (see also Benston, 1987, p. 219):[28]

> The economic concepts of assets, liabilities, income and expense necessarily are subjectively determined. Accounting, however, is concerned primarily with recording data to meet the requirements and peculiarities of specific business organization and managers. Their familiarity with the business and the accounting system allows them to use the numbers effectively. But, for others who are not in this position, the internal accounting numbers generated by an enterprise's accounting system often provide measures that can be very inaccurate and misleading.

If this argument were correct, the consequences would be severe indeed. It would mean that industrial economists could not carry out empirical research. It would mean that macroeconomists could not carry out empirical research. It would mean that a wide spectrum of government publications describing economic activity ought to be discontinued, since they are based on what is, originally, accounting data. It would mean that policy decisions affecting all fields of the economy would have to be based entirely on theory, since testing of theory against real-world data would be impossible.

Economists in a wide variety of disciplines continue to carry out empirical research. By revealed preference, this suggests that the argument that accounting data can be interpreted only by those intimately familiar with the environment in which the data were generated has not been generally accepted. In short (Horowitz, 1984, p. 493),[29]

> While only God can make a tree, only accountants can make the data upon which economists are forced to rely in their antitrust analyses. Given that constraint and the resulting data imperfections, all that the economist can be expected to do is to use those data to tell a story as to what has taken place in a market over time and to provide the most cogent economic explanation for that history.

The internal rate of return

The internal rate of return (IRR) of an investment project is (Fisher and McGowan, 1983, p. 82) "that discount rate that equates the present value of its expected net revenue stream to its initial outlay." Suppose that an investment produces income Y_t per period but requires expenditure I_t per period over a lifetime of n periods. The internal rate of return of the investment is the interest rate ρ that satisfies

$$Y_1 - I_1 + \frac{Y_1 - I_1}{1 + \rho} + \cdots + \frac{Y_n - I_n}{(1 + \rho)^n} = 0. \qquad (6.80)$$

---

[28] The sense in which the economic concepts of assets, liabilities, income, and expense are subjectively determined is not obvious. Calculation of the gross rate of return on sales requires information on revenue from sales and the cost of variable factors of production; calculation of the capital–sales ratio requires information on revenue from sales and on the replacement cost of capital assets that enter the production function. Accounting versions of these variables may not match the corresponding economic concepts, but the economic concepts are objective in nature. Verma (1990) suggests that the results of econometric tests for market power are largely robust to alternative accounting techniques.

[29] Footnote omitted; the quote is from a comment on Fisher and McGowan (1983).

Table 6.6   A comparison of internal rate of return and
present-discounted value rankings of two investment projects

| | Net cash flow by period | | | | IRR (%) | PDV |
	1	2	3	4		
Project 1	−100	102	14.4	8.64	20	11.12
Project 2	−100	5.75	13.225	129.27	15	13.28

Source: Edwards et al., 1987, p. 17

Equation (6.80) is an nth degree polynomial, with n solutions, some of which may be multiple. Sometimes there will be a unique positive solution to (6.80) and sometimes not. Assume, however, that (6.80) defines a unique internal rate of return. Then an investment project yields an economic profit if the internal rate of return exceeds the cost of capital to the firm considering the project. In such cases, the present-discounted value of the project, using the firm's cost of capital, is positive.

The internal rate of return does not, however, provide a ranking of investment projects, which should be compared according to their present value when discounted at the firm's cost of capital. For example, table 6.6 compares the internal rate of return and the present-discounted value of two projects if the cost of capital is 10 percent. Project 1 has a larger internal rate of return than project 2. But project 2 has a greater present-discounted value than project 1 if the firm's cost of capital is 10 percent. From the point of view of investors, therefore, project 2 would be preferred to project 1.[30]

Accountants and economists have long investigated the relationship, if any, between accounting rates of return (usually the rate of return on capital) and the internal rate of return (Bain, 1941; Harcourt, 1965; Salamon, 1970; Solomon, 1970; Stauffer, 1971; Kay, 1976; and others). The consensus result is that the rate of return on capital is the same as the internal rate of return only under special circumstances.[31] Although the techniques of this literature have moved far beyond his, the general conclusion is very much that of Bain (1941, p. 292):

> Although we are thus forced to abandon the usual accounting profit rate as a measure of monopoly, it would be unfortunate to abandon with it all accounting income and asset data. As unadjusted accounting rates are unreliable for our purposes, so a proper scheme of adjustment of accounting data may provide an apparent measure of monopoly profits.

Fisher and McGowan (1983) examine the same issue and reach a rather more pessimistic conclusion.[32] They begin with the argument that (1983, p. 82)

---

[30] See also Fisher and McGowan (1983, fn. 5).

[31] For example (Kay, 1976, p. 449), if the rate of return on capital is constant over the life of a project, then the rate of return on capital and the internal rate of return are the same.

[32] See also Fisher (1984, 1987) and van Breda (1984), Horowitz (1984), Long and Ravenscraft (1984), and Martin (1984c). Domowitz et al. (1986, fn. 6) seem to imply that the Census of Manufactures price–cost margin is somehow immune to criticisms leveled at accounting data. But Census of Manufactures data are themselves derived from accounting data, and the price–cost margin is in principle a rate of return on sales, of the kind discussed by Fisher (1987).

it is clear that it is the [internal] rate of return that is equalized within an industry in long-run industry competitive equilibrium and (after adjustment for risk) equalized everywhere in a competitive economy in long-run equilibrium. It is the [internal] rate of return (after risk adjustment) above the cost of capital that promotes expansion under competition and is produced by output restriction under monopoly. Thus, the [internal] rate of return is the only correct measure of the profit rate for the purposes of economic analysis. Accounting rates of return are useful only insofar as they yield information as to [internal] rates of return.

In a series of numerical examples, they show that the after-tax rate of return on capital can vary substantially depending on accounting assumptions about depreciation, and in any event is a poor proxy for the internal rate of return. Having argued that accounting rates of return are useful only to the extent that they convey information about the internal rate of return, and having shown that accounting rates of return often convey little information about the internal rate of return, they conclude (1983, p. 91) that "examination of absolute or relative accounting rates of return to draw conclusions about monopoly profits is a totally misleading enterprise."

This conclusion depends on the premise that accounting rates of return are of interest only to the extent that they convey information about the internal rate of return. But the arguments that Fisher and McGowan advance in favor of the internal rate of return as a measure of economic profitability apply equally well to the rate of return on capital. Indeed, Fisher and McGowan's arguments in favor of the internal rate of return as the appropriate measure of payoff or profitability are strikingly similar to Stigler's (1963) argument (quoted above) in favor of the rate of return on assets as the appropriate measure of profitability. The rate of return on capital is equalized within an industry in long-run competitive equilibrium. After risk adjustment, the rate of return on capital is equalized everywhere in a competitive economy in long-run equilibrium. A risk-adjusted rate of return on capital above the cost of capital promotes expansion under competition and is produced by output restriction if firms exercise market power.

Others have argued that the internal rate of return is ill-suited to the analysis of market power, on the ground that the internal rate of return of a firm depends on its income and expenses over its entire lifetime, while what competition policy and financial analysis call for is evidence on the firm's performance over specific and much more limited time periods (Edwards et al., 1987, p. 33).

Nor do the Fisher–McGowan arguments give any clues as to the specific form of tests for market power using the internal rate of return.[33] In this sense, the use of the internal rate of return as an index of market power represents a step backward from the use of measures derived from formal oligopoly models.

---

[33] Thus the form of empirical tests of the internal rate of return has tended to be "Is the IRR higher when market share (market concentration) (substitute the variable of your choice) is higher." Increasingly, the question of interest is thought to be "Is the observed value of the IRR higher than would be expected in the Nash equilibrium of a one-shot game?" The nature of the test to answer this question is not specified in the literature. (The same comment applies to Tobin's q ratio.)

Besides lacking any formal link with the analysis of market power, the internal rate of return suffers the disadvantage that it cannot be reliably measured. Bosch (1989) estimates the internal rate of return for a sample of 1013 large industrial firms. Estimation requires strong assumptions; as he notes (1989, p. 236),[34]

> The overwhelming advantage of the accounting rate of return over a given period is that it is a single, easy to calculate number. The internal rate of return is clearly much more difficult and sometimes impossible to evaluate. The main reason is the lack of a definite closing period and lack of data.

Fisher argues (1991, p. 224) that his

> work proves some underlying theorems showing that the generalization in question (accounting rate of return equals [the internal rate of return]) is true under extremely restrictive circumstances.

This description suggests a fundamental misunderstanding. The basic question is not whether some or any accounting rates of return equal the internal rate of return. Given that the internal rate of return can be measured only with great difficulty and that we lack models which tell us how the internal rate of return could be analyzed to see whether or not it signals the exercise of market power, it is not even clear why this question is interesting. The basic question is how accounting rates of return should be analyzed to see whether or not they signal the exercise of market power. The Fisher and Fisher–McGowan arguments do not address this issue.

6.3.4   Summary

Empirical tests of the determinants of market power employ a variety of profitability measures based on accounting data and combining stock market data with accounting data. Formal analysis can indicate the way in which tests of such data should be specified. An advantage of the formal approach to specifying tests of market power is that the underlying theoretical model indicates the form of the test. A limitation is that explanatory variables cover only factors that are included in the formal model.

The empirical analogs of theoretical measures of profitability are subject to shortcomings, and ordinarily require some adjustment. The general nature of empirical results is not sensitive to the choice of profitability measure. The proposition that empirical testing of theoretical models is impossible is not widely accepted. Nor is the position that the internal rate of return is the only measure of profitability suitable for economic analysis.

---

[34] The number of assumptions made by Shinnar et al. (1989) to reach their estimates of the internal rate of return is also impressive.

6.4 IDENTIFICATION

The identification problem is an econometric one.[35] If some endogenous variables in a system of structural equations are functions of other endogenous variables in the system, and the equations fail to satisfy certain conditions, it will be impossible to estimate the coefficients of some or all equations in the system. Structure–conduct–performance models involve substantial simultaneous determination. The research question raised in the simultaneity literature is: if we specify what we believe to be a correctly formulated structure–conduct–performance model, can the parameters of the system be estimated? Are they identified? If the coefficients of the system can be estimated, which elements of the specification are critical for identification?

Here we review what might be termed a "generic" simultaneous model from the mid-1970s, and show that all equations in the system are identified. We pinpoint and comment on the aspects of the specification that are critical to identification. In final comments, we deal with more general issues of the specification of simultaneous systems and related practical issues of estimation.

6.4.1 A three-equation system

Equations (6.81), (6.82), and (6.83) are a three-equation simultaneous system explaining price–cost margins, four-firm concentration ratios, and advertising–sales ratios as functions of a variety of exogenous and predetermined variables. By and large, the specification of the three equations is consistent with typical single-equation empirical models used in industry cross-section studies of the mid-1970s:[36]

$$PCM = \alpha_2 ASR + \alpha_3 CR4 + a_0 + a_1 REG + a_2 CDSR + a_3 IMSR$$
$$+ a_4 BCR + a_5 GR + a_6 MES + a_7 CDR + a_8 KSR, \tag{6.81}$$

$$ASR = \beta_1 PCM + \beta_2 CR4 + b_3 CR4^2 + b_0 + b_2 CDSR$$
$$+ b_3 IMSR + b_4 BCR + b_5 GR + b_9 DUR, \tag{6.82}$$

$$CR4 = \gamma_2 ASR + g_0 + g_1 REG + g_5 GR + g_6 MES$$
$$+ g_7 CDR + g_{10} PCM_{-1} + g_{11} CR_{-1}. \tag{6.83}$$

[35] For a general treatment of the identification problem, consult any econometrics textbook. Peltzman (1969) contains a section headed "The identification problem." His discussion, however, concerns problems associated with the omission of relevant explanatory variables, not with identification. The same is true of Phillips (1976, pp. 246–8). For discussions of identification in the context of New Empirical Industrial Organization models, see section 7.4.

[36] Martin (1979). Influential theoretical discussions of the specification of such systems, particularly the price–cost margin equation, include Cowling (1976), Cowling and Waterson (1976), Clarke and Davies (1982), Dickson (1982), Sawyer (1982), and Martin (1984a). Interesting but more empirical papers are those of Geroski (1981, 1982), Cooley (1982), and Gisser (1991).

The profitability equation

Some of the explanatory variables in the profitability equation measure differences across industries in entry conditions. These include the advertising–sales ratio (ASR), minimum efficient scale as a fraction of industry output (MES), and the cost–disadvantage ratio (CDR). Following Comanor and Wilson (1967), ASR is regarded as an index of product differentiation. MES tells how large an entrant would have to be, relative to the market, to operate efficiently. CDR is a measure of the productivity of small firms relative to large firms. It is measured so that larger values of CDR mean that small firms are nearer in productivity to large firms. Thus the larger CDR is, the smaller is the cost disadvantage of small incumbent or entrant firms *vis-à-vis* large incumbent firms, and the lower, all else equal, should be the price–cost margin (PCM).[37]

Other variables on the right-hand side of the profitability equation control for differences across industries in demand conditions – in the price elasticity of demand. They are the fraction of sales going to final consumer demand ($CDSR$), the import–sales ratio ($IMSR$), the buyer–concentration ratio (BCR), and the growth rate of industry sales (GR).

The greater are sales going to final consumer demand, the more susceptible should be the product be to differentiation. This suggests a positive impact of $CDSR$ on price–cost margins.

Price–cost margins are computed for domestic producers only. The greater are sales by importers, the more elastic is the residual demand facing domestic producers, and the lower should be price–cost margins, all else equal. Use of the import–sales ratio as an explanatory variable should also control for the measurement of seller concentration in terms of domestic suppliers only. This also suggests that $IMSR$ will have a negative coefficient in the PCM equation.

The greater is the fraction of industry sales going to the largest four customers (BCR), the greater the bargaining power such customers have, and the more credibly they can threaten entry themselves. Higher values of BCR should reduce PCM.

The capital–sales ratio (KSR) is an explanatory variable in the PCM equation to control for the normal rate of return on capital. The four-firm concentration ratio appears on the right-hand side to test whether or not margins are higher in concentrated industries. The regional industry dummy variable (REG) is included to control for the fact that concentration ratios calculated with reference to a national market understate concentration in regional or local markets.

The advertising equation

The Dorfman–Steiner condition[38] suggests that the advertising–sales ratio will be greater, the greater the price–cost margin and the greater the elasticity of demand with respect to advertising. Thus the price–cost margin and demand variables appear on the right-hand side in the ASR equation specified in (6.82).

Comanor and Wilson (1974, p. 141) also suggest that advertising will be less where consumers are able to acquire information about a product from direct personal experience. This

---

[37] For further discussion, see Caves et al. (1975).
[38] See section 9.1.

argument justifies inclusion of a durable goods dummy variable (DUR) on the right-hand side in the ASR equation.

The final explanatory variables in the ASR equation are the four-firm seller concentration ratio and the square of the four-firm seller concentration ratio. These appear to test the hypothesis that advertising rises with concentration as concentration rises from low levels, but falls as concentration rises from intermediate levels. If concentration is sufficiently low, firms should be price-takers. For price-taking firms, the advertising elasticity of demand is zero, since a price-taking firm can sell all it wants at the market price but nothing at a price even slightly above the market price. Thus the advertising–sales ratio should be low in unconcentrated markets.

As concentration rises, firms recognize their mutual interdependence, realize that there is a demand curve for their variety, and that its location can be affected by sales efforts. Moving from low to intermediate concentration levels, advertising intensity should rise as the perceived elasticity of demand with respect to advertising rises. In fact, in the intermediate concentration range, increasing recognition of oligopolistic interdependence may divert rivalry from output or price to advertising and other types of sales efforts, and advertising per dollar of sales may exceed the joint-profit-maximizing level. But as concentration reaches high levels, oligopolistic coordination should extend to sales efforts as well as price. Advertising intensity should therefore fall as concentration rises from intermediate to high levels (Greer, 1971; Cable, 1972; Sutton, 1974). These arguments predict a positive coefficient for the linear concentration term, and a negative coefficient for the quadratic concentration term, in the ASR equation.

The concentration equation

The concentration equation[39] assumes a lagged adjustment of concentration to a long-run level determined by entry conditions:

$$CR - CR_{-1} = \lambda[CR^*(ASR, CDS, GR, MES, CDR) - CR_{-1}]. \qquad (6.84)$$

CR^* is the long-run level of concentration. The subscript -1 denotes the value of a variable one period in the past. λ is a speed-of-adjustment parameter: the larger the move the concentration ratio makes toward the long-run level in a single period. On rearrangement, (6.84) becomes

$$CR = \lambda CR^*(ASR, CDS, GR, MES, CDR) + (1 - \lambda)CR_{-1}. \qquad (6.85)$$

Current concentration is a weighted average of past concentration and the long-run concentration level. The greater is λ, the greater the weight given CR^* in any period and the more rapid convergence to the long-run level. For simplicity, suppose that CR^* is a linear function of its arguments.[40]

---

[39] For another approach to modeling concentration, one which has not been taken up by the literature, see Grossack (1965, 1972).

[40] Use of a specification like (6.85) in a cross-section sample implies that the speed of adjustment is the same in all industries. This is implausible. The greater past profitability is, the more rapidly should new firms come into the

The final explanatory variable in the concentration equation is the regional industry dummy variable. As with the profitability equation, this controls for the use of national concentration ratios. It should have a negative coefficient.

6.4.2 Identification of the three-equation system

In the three-equation system model (6.81), (6.82) and (6.83), KSR appears only in the profitability equation, DUR and $CR4^2$ appear only in the advertising-intensity equation, and lagged values of PCM and $CR4$ appear only in the concentration equation. This means that all equations are identified.[41]

Nonidentification is a problem that arises when endogenous variables are simultaneously determined – when endogenous variables are explanatory variables in other equations in the system. Identification is therefore a question about real-world relationships among endogenous variables. But it is a question that can only be addressed in the context of specific models of real-world relationships. It follows that identification can only be determined conditional on the specification of the system of equations to be estimated. In a fundamental sense, the decision to treat certain variables as endogenous in a limited system of equations does not carry with it the assumption that all other variables in the system are exogenous. It carries with it the assumption that the specification of equations explaining additional endogenous variables in a larger system will not upset the identification of equations in the more limited system.[42,43]

6.4.3 Summary

Identification is a statistical problem; it arises when a model indicates a substantial amount of simultaneous causality among endogenous variables. In much of econometrics, identification comes easily (Theil, 1971, p. 450):

> structural equations are usually overidentified except when the system is small . . . . The reason is that the number . . . of predetermined variables tends to increase with the number of equations,

market. The rate of adjustment ought also to be more rapid, for any value of past profitability, the lower barriers to entry are. In other words, λ should itself be a function of structural variables. Geroski et al. (1987) specify and estimate a model in which λ varies from industry to industry.

[41] Schmalensee (1989, p. 955) objects to treating KSR as exogenous. If firms minimize cost and there are constant returns to scale in relevant ranges of output, KSR is determined by the technology. Formally, identification can be analyzed by examining the rank of the submatrix of the coefficient matrix formed, for each endogenous variable, by the columns that have coefficient zero in the equation of that variable. The nature of the rank condition for the concentration equation is complicated by the presence of the quadratic term in concentration in the ASR equation. See Fisher (1966, pp. 127–51).

[42] See also Friedman and Schwartz (1991, pp. 41–2): "In our view, exogeneity is not an invariant statistical characteristic of variables. Everything depends on the purpose. In economic analysis, it may be appropriate to regard a variable as exogenous for some purposes and endogenous for others."

[43] Baker and Bresnahan (1988, p. 293) argue that a beer brewing firm's capacity, which is plainly endogenous in the strict sense, can be treated as exogenous in the short run "since capacity is altered infrequently and in large increments." By this sort of argument, it is probably valid to treat seller concentration as exogenous in industry cross-section profitability studies. The slow estimated adjustment of seller concentration to long-run levels is consistent with this conclusion.

whereas the number . . . of unknown parameters in any particular equation is typically three or four and usually at most six or seven.

The need to verify parameter identification in models of industrial structure, conduct, and performance reflects the fact that such models typically have a relatively small number of dependent variables, with a large number of parameters to be estimated. On balance, it seems unlikely that lack of identification prevents the estimation of the relationships that have most interested industrial economists.

6.5 FIRM EFFECTS VERSUS INDUSTRY EFFECTS

Although the bulk of structure–conduct–performance school took the industry as the unit of observation, it was recognized early on that market power was as much a phenomenon of firms as of industries (Lerner, 1934, p. 160, fn. 2):

> Monopoly is essentially a property of *firms* and by a monopolistic industry is meant nothing more than an industry in which *firms* have downward sloping demand curves . . . If the demand curve for the whole industry is horizontal, the industry is in a competitive condition, but that is only because in this case every firm in the industry must also have a horizontal demand curve . . . .

In an oblique sort of way, the debate over firm versus industry effects on profitability was part and parcel of the market power versus efficiency debate. The Chicago School tended to identify "the monopoly problem" as one of collusion: if firms do not collude, then rivalry among incumbents will ensure good market performance. Part of this argument was the view that anything that allowed a single firm to persistently hold price above marginal cost was, by definition, a rent-generating asset that was not treated in an economically correct way by accounting conventions.

If one accepts that differences in firm-level price–cost margins must reflect differences in efficiency across firms, then it makes sense to investigate only whether or not there are important industry-level influences on market power. If one considers that firm-specific market power is a possibility, firm effects and industry effects are both of interest.

6.5.1 Schmalensee

Schmalensee (1985) distinguishes three schools of thought concerning the determinants of profitability. First (1985, pp. 341–2):

> In the *classical* tradition, following Joe Bain (1951, 1956), industrial economists treated the industry or market as the unit of study. Differences among firms were assumed transitory or unimportant, unless based on scale economies, which were generally found to be insubstantial. Equilibrium industry profitability was generally assumed to be primarily determined by the ability of established firms to restrict rivalry among themselves and the protection afforded them by barriers to entry. A central hypothesis in virtually all classical work was that increases in seller concentration tend to raise industrywide profits by facilitating collusion.

As we have seen, Bain (1951, pp. 323–4), expected concentration to affect the profitability of firms with net worth greater than 5 million; Bain (1956, p. 191), expected entry barriers to affect the profitability of large and dominant firms. Collins and Preston (1969, p. 280) explicitly distinguished the abilities of large and small firms to exercise market power, and carried out statistical tests which they interpreted as indicating greater exercise of market power for large firms. The mainstream did not treat industries as homogenous units.

The efficiency school, however, described the mainstream as holding this view (Demsetz, 1973, p. 4):

> The classic portrayal of the inefficiency produced by concentration through the exercise of monopoly power is that of a group of firms cooperating somehow to restrict entry and prevent rivalrous price behavior. Successfully pursued, this policy results in a product price and rate of return in excess of that which would have prevailed in the absence of collusion. However, if all firms are able to produce at the same cost, then the rate of return to successfully colluding firms would be independent of the particular sizes adopted by these firms to achieve low cost.

The emphasis on collusion glides past the possible single-firm exercise of market power, although by the time of Demsetz' writing there was substantial evidence that product differentiation created just such a possibility. Mainstream investigations of a price umbrella held by large firms over less efficient smaller firms indicates that the key qualification, "if all firms are able to produce at the same cost," was rejected by mainstream industrial economics.

This efficiency school is the second noted by Schmalensee (1985, p. 342; footnote omitted):

> An anticlassical, *revisionist* view of industrial economics has emerged in the last decade. In the simplest model consistent with this view, all markets are (at least approximately) competitive, and scale economies are absent (or negligible). The key assumption is that within at least some industries there are persistent efficiency differences among sellers. Because more efficient enterprises tend both to grow at the expense of their rivals and to be more profitable, these differences tend to induce a positive intra-industry correlation between share and profitability even in the absence of scale economies.

The third approach singled out by Schmalensee was (1985, pp. 342–3)

> *managerial.* . . . Business schools and management consultants exist because it is widely believed that some firms are better managed than others and that one can learn important management skills that are not industry specific.

Estimation

Schmalensee (1985, p. 345) uses FTC line-of-business data to estimate the relation

$$r_{ij} = \mu + \alpha_i + \beta_j + \gamma MS_{ij} + \varepsilon_{ij}. \tag{6.86}$$

for a sample of 1775 observations on the operations of 456 firms in 261 industries (defined at roughly the three- and four-digit Standard Industrial Classification level) for 1975.

In (6.86), r_{ij} is the gross rate of return on assets for firm i in industry j. μ is a constant term. α_i takes the same value for all divisions of firm i, and β_j takes the same value for all

Table 6.7   Variations in explanatory power by
model, Schmalensee sample

Combination of variables	$\bar{R}^2$
Firm	0.0106
Industry	0.1884
Share	0.0017
Firm and share	0.0134
Industry and share	0.1946
Firm and industry	0.1644
Firm and industry and share	0.1702

Source: Schmalensee, 1985, figure 1

divisions operating in industry j. MS_{ij} = firm i's market share in industry j, and ε_{ij} is a random error term.

He writes (1985, p. 344)

> An extreme classicist . . . would expect the β's to differ substantially with $\alpha_i = \gamma = 0$ for all i.

Thus the classical hypothesis as formulated by Schmalensee has firm effects and market share effects absent ($\alpha_i = \gamma = 0$), while divisional rates of return differ from industry to industry.

Also

> An extreme revisionist would presumably expect a large γ with all the α's and β's near zero *if* the r_{ij} were observations on *equilibrium* rates of return.

Thus market share effects are identified with efficiency, while firm and industry effects are absent. Finally,

> an extreme managerial position might be that variations in the α's should be much more important in equilibrium than those in the β's or in the γMS_{ij} terms.

Table 6.7 shows the essential portion of Schmalensee's results. When firm dummy variables, industry dummy variables, and market shares are used as alternative explanatory variables, the adjusted R^2 is far greater with industry dummy variables than with the other two. When the groups of variables are entered in pairs, explanatory power with firm and share variables is negligible. When all three types of variables are included, explanatory power is slightly less than with industry dummy variables alone.

On the basis of these and other results, Schmalensee (1985, p. 349) concludes that firm effects do not exist. He also infers that industry effects exist and account for 75 percent of the variance in industry rates of return, and that market share effects exist but explain a negligible portion of the variance in line-of-business rates of return.

One of Schmalensee's conclusions is that (1985, p. 349):

> The finding that industry effects are important supports the classical focus on industry-level analysis as against the revisionist tendency to downplay industry differences.

While this may be so, the fixed-effects analysis does not encourage the study of cross-sections of industry data. If the bulk of the explanatory power of (6.86) lies with industry dummy variables, that implies the differences in performance are due to differences across industries that cannot otherwise be characterized. If anything, this calls for study of single industries.

6.5.2   Scott and Pascoe

Scott and Pascoe (1986) analyzed the impact of including firm and industry dummy variables on the estimated coefficients of structural variables. Suppose that the true structural model of line-of-business profitability is

$$p = \begin{pmatrix} R & S & T \end{pmatrix} \begin{pmatrix} b_R \\ b_S \\ b_T \end{pmatrix} + e, \tag{6.87}$$

where p is a $1 \times m$ column vector of observations of line-of-business profitability, R is an $m \times F$ matrix of observations of industry-specific explanatory variables, S is an $m \times G$ matrix of observations of firm-specific explanatory variables, T is an $m \times H$ matrix of observations of other explanatory variables, and e is a vector of errors that are assumed to have all desirable properties.

Now suppose that A is an $m \times I$ matrix, the columns of which are dummy variables that form a basis for R; and D is an $m \times N$ matrix, the columns of which are dummy variables that form a basis for S.

Then (6.87) can be rewritten

$$p = \begin{pmatrix} AW_A & DW_D & T \end{pmatrix} \begin{pmatrix} b_R \\ b_S \\ b_T \end{pmatrix} + e = \begin{pmatrix} A & D & T \end{pmatrix} \begin{pmatrix} W_A b_R \\ W_B b_S \\ b_T \end{pmatrix} + e, \tag{6.88}$$

where W_A is an $I \times F$ weighting matrix that generates the observations R from the basis A, W_B is an $N \times G$ weighting matrix that generates the observations S from the basis D, and I_H is an $H \times H$ identity matrix.

Scott and Pascoe then note that if the dummy variable specification (6.88) is estimated, the dummy variables under some circumstances inherit the explanatory power of the industry and firm explanatory variables in the true model (6.87) (1986, p. 285):

> if the true model did not include the set of vectors $T, \ldots$ the regression of the variable p on A and D, less one dummy variable or with an intercept and less one firm and one industry dummy variable, would provide the explanatory power $\ldots$ of the true model $\ldots$. The explanatory power

of the estimated model with dummy variables is based on the fact that the dummy variable model actually fitted has explanatory power equivalent to a true model . . . .

Scott and Pascoe's results for a traditional specification are

$$p = 0.035 + 0.18ko + 0.16CR4 + 0.40MES + 0.092GR$$
$$\quad\quad (1.9) \quad\quad (6.9) \quad\quad (3.0) \quad\quad (11.0)$$

$$\quad - 0.085IMSR - 0.000032DISP - 0.088DIV - 0.019LEV$$
$$\quad\quad (2.0) \quad\quad\quad\quad (5.0) \quad\quad\quad\quad (4.7) \quad\quad\quad (4.7)$$

$$\quad - 0.27CR4 * LBKSR + 0.14MS + 0.20LBASR, \quad\quad R^2 = 0.13$$
$$\quad\quad\quad (14) \quad\quad\quad\quad\quad (3.7)$$
$$\tag{6.89}$$

Industry variables are on the first two lines,[44] firm variables on the third line,[45] and line-of-business variables on the last line.[46]

The estimated effect of changes in market concentration on profitability is positive for low levels of capital intensity, negative for high levels of capital intensity:

$$\frac{\partial p}{\partial CR4} = 0.16 - 0.27LBKSR. \tag{6.90}$$

Scott and Pascoe generate a range of results, alternatively replacing industry-specific variables by a set of industry-effect dummy variables and firm-specific variables by a set of firm-effect dummy variables. These estimates imply that firm effects and industry effects are both important. They also find that the impact of line-of-business variables interacts in important ways with firm and industry variables.[47]

6.5.3   Kessides 1

Kessides (1989) subjects Schmalensee's sample to diagnostic tests, identifies 55 of the 1,775 observations as extreme outliers, and reruns Schmalensee's analysis deleting these observations. As Kessides interprets his results (1989, p. 4):

> once the influential outliers are excluded from the sample, firm effects become both statistically significant and quantitatively important. Indeed, all the tests of the null hypothesis of no firm

---

[44] ko is a measure of the cost of capital, $CR4$ is an adjusted four-firm seller concentration ratio, MES is minimum efficient plant as a fraction of industry output, GR is the 1976 value of shipments divided by 1972 value of shipments, $IMSR$ is the import–sales ratio, and $DISP$ is the radius from plant within which 80% of plant shipments were made.

[45] DIV is the sum of squares of the share of the firm's sales in different industries; LEV is the firm's debt–equity ratio.

[46] $LBKSR$ is the line-of-business capital–sales ratio, MS is market share, and $LBASR$ is the line-of-business advertising–sales ratio.

[47] These findings are consistent with those of Rumelt (1991), who carries out an analysis similar to that of Schmalensee, with a sample covering four years rather than one, and finds evidence of important line-of-business effects.

effects signal rejection at P-levels below .01 percent. In addition, a comparison of the adjusted R^2s indicates that firm effects add between 8 and 11 percent to variance explained. We also note that industry effects remain quantitatively important accounting for 19 and 24 percent of the sample variance of r while market share effects continue to account for a negligible fraction (between .3 and 1 percent) of the variance of business unit rates of return.

6.5.4   Kessides 2

On the basis of a theoretical model that is interesting in its own right, Kessides (1990b) specifies the following equation for line-of-business profitability:

$$r_{ij} = \beta_j + \eta_i + (\theta_j - 1)\tilde{s}_{ij} + \varepsilon_{ij}, \tag{6.91}$$

where PC_{ij} is the price–cost margin of firm i in industry j, $r_{ij} = \ln(1 - PC_{ij})$, βj is an industry effects cost parameter, s_{ij} is the market share of firm i in industry j, and $\tilde{s}_{ij} = \ln s_{ij}$.

His estimates show that firm, industry, and market share effects are all significant and large. They also suggest that the market share-margin relationship interacts with industry characteristics, so it differs from industry to industry. This is consistent with the results of Scott and Pascoe (1986).

6.5.5   Amel and Froeb

Amel and Froeb (1991) provide a different perspective on the firm and/or industry effects debate, with a time-series data set on bank operations in regional geographic markets in Texas. They test for firm and industry effects, controlling for the impacts of market share and market concentration and find (Amel and Froeb, 1991, pp. 329–30):

(i) During the recession in the Texas banking industry, firm effects are large and significant.
(ii) Prior to the recession, firm effects and market effects are much smaller, though statistically significant.
(iii) Market share effects are very small.
(iv) Market concentration effects are very small.

They interpret the finding of large firm effects in recession as supporting what Schmalensee calls the managerial approach.

6.5.6   Roberts and Supina

Roberts and Supina (1996, 1997) are able to analyze plant-level data collected for the preparation of the US Census of Manufactures. The Census plant data classifies products at the very disaggregated, seven-digit level.

In Roberts and Supina (1996), they analyze average prices, marginal costs, and markups[48] by plant for six homogeneous products: gasoline, cans, corrugated boxes, concrete, bread, and coffee.

Concrete and gasoline show no systematic relation between marginal cost and size. For corrugated boxes and tin cans, marginal cost falls as size increases until a plant is about 10% larger than the smallest plant, a result that recalls the common finding of L-shaped cost curves. For coffee and bread, marginal cost declines with size throughout the plant size range.

Prices decline with plant size for five of the six products examined. The exception is gasoline, for which no particular price-plant size relation emerges.

Not surprisingly, given the results for price and marginal cost, there is also no systematic relation between plant size and the markup ratio for gasoline. For cans, corrugated boxes and concrete the markup declines significantly as plant increases throughout size distribution. Roberts and Supina attribute this result to the location of larger plants in larger, more competitive geographic markets. For bread and coffee, markups increase significantly with plant size – marginal cost declines more rapidly than price as plant size rises.[49]

Roberts and Supina (1997) analyze plant size – performance relationships over time for 13 relatively homogeneous products. They find significant persistence of plant location in the distributions of performance. High-price plants tend to remain high-price plants; low-price plants tend to remain low-price plants, and so on. For 11 of the 13 products, larger plants tend to have lower prices.

Roberts and Supina's results suggest the existence of persistent plant-level effects, and by implication the existence of firm-level effects as well.

6.5.7   McGahan

McGahan (1999) uses the Compustat® database to construct a sample covering 4,947 US corporations over the 14 years 1974–77. In addition to industry effects and firms effects, she allows for macroeconomic influences by way of "year effects" and for the impact of diversification through a "corporate focus effect" that measures the extent to which a firm operates in related industries. She uses three alternative performance measures, Tobin's q ratio, the gross accounting rate of return on assets, and a constructed rate of return on the replacement value of assets.

In the analysis of Tobin's q ratio, years effects are small and corporate focus effects nonexistent. Industry and firm effects are both important, and firm effects are more important than industry effects. Results for the two other performance measures are similar; firm effects appear to be more important when performance is measured by accounting profitability than by Tobin's q ratio.

---

[48] They measure the markup ratio as the natural logarithm of the ratio of price to marginal cost.

[49] That is, not all cost reductions are passed on to consumers.

6.5.8   Mueller and Raunig

Mueller and Raunig (1999) use the techniques of the persistence-of-profits literature
(section 7.9) to divide US four-digit SIC industries into two groups, those in which
firm profit rates tend to converge to the same level (*homogeneous industries*) and the
others (*heterogenous industries*). They then estimate a conventional industry-level structure–
conduct–performance profitability equation (of the kind discussed in section 6.4.1) for
subsamples of homogeneous and heterogeneous industries.

First, they estimate the equation for industry-average profit rates constructed from the
profit rates of the firms used to analyze convergence of profit rates. The profitability equation performs reasonably well for the homogeneous-industry subsample, and badly for
heterogeneous industries.[50]

They obtain similar results when they estimate the profitability equation using US Census
of Manufactures price–cost margins as a dependent variable. They again obtain similar results
when industry-level variables are used to explain firm-level profitability rates. Industry-level
variables explain 20 percent of the variance in firm profit rates for firms in homogeneous
industries, versus 11 percent for heterogeneous industries.

Mueller and Raunig's results indicate that both firm and industry effects need to be taken
into account to understand performance in heterogeneous industries. Industry effects alone
may be sufficient to understand performance in homogeneous industries.

6.5.9   Overall

On balance, this literature suggests that market, firm and line-of-business characteristics
jointly determine firm and market performance. Firm and industry effects both matter.
Recent contributions to this literature have compared results with accounting data and with
other performance measures and found the results to be robust.

6.6   Conclusion

Empirical studies of profitability and market power – particularly cross-section studies using
industry data – came under severe attack in the mid-1970s. By and large, these criticisms do
not stand up to close examination, and there is a renewed willingness to use accounting data
in the analysis of firm and market performance.

The logical foundation of the efficiency critique of cross-section studies is very nearly
tautological – if there is persistent accounting profit over time, it must be a rent to some
scarce, possibly intangible, asset. If it were not, new firms would enter and compete it away.
But if accounting profit is a rent, it is not economic profit.

---

[50] See also Bloch (1994) for an analysis that suggests the importance of sample selection for S–C–P empirical
studies.

Nor is empirical evidence to support the efficiency interpretation particularly compelling. There is evidence that there are persistent cost differences among firms in the same industry, but this does not mean that lower-cost firms fail to exercise market power.

The most telling criticisms of industry-level cross-section studies come from applications of formal oligopoly models to structure–conduct–performance relations. Such models suggest that market power is much more a firm-specific than an industry-specific phenomenon and that a firm's price–cost margin depends on its own conjectures, its own market share, its own cost of capital, and its own financial structure. These formal models suggest the redirection of empirical studies for market power from the industry and the cross-section to the firm and the time series, and that has been a major trend in empirical research in industrial economics.[51]

PROBLEMS

6.1 (Differential efficiency) Let the market demand function be

$$p = 10 - Q,$$

and suppose that the market is potentially supplied by two firms, firm L (marginal cost $c_L = 1$ and firm H (marginal cost $c_H = 2$). Each firm must cover a fixed cost $F > 0$ if it has positive output.

Compare net social welfare if the firms act as price-takers with net social welfare if the firms act as Cournot duopolists.

6.2 Considering the model of a firm that raises funds for investment by the sale of bonds, suppose that K_1, L_1, and B_1 are chosen to maximize

$$M = -(1 - \delta)p_1^k K_0 \pi_<$$
$$+ \frac{\left[p_1 q_1 - w_1 L_1 - \lambda_1 p_1^k K_1 - (r_1 - r^*)B_1\right]\pi_> + E_>}{1 + r^*}$$
$$+ \gamma \left[B_1 + (1 - \delta)p_1^k K_0 - p_1^k K_1\right],$$

where γ the Lagrangian multiplier associated with the constraint (6.60). Write out the first-order conditions for B_1, K_1, and L_1. Derive (6.66).

6.3 Considering the model of a firm that raises funds for investment by the sale of stock and bonds, suppose that K_1, L_1, and B_1 and S_N are chosen to maximize

$$M = -\frac{S_E}{S_E + S_N}(1 - \delta)p_1^k K_0 + \frac{S_E}{S_E + S_N}\Bigg\{ -(1 - \delta)p_1^k K_0 \pi_<$$
$$+ \frac{\left[p_1 q_1 - w_1 L_1 - \lambda_1 p_1^k K_1 + (1 + r^*)m_1 S_N - (r_1 - r^*)B_1\right]\pi_> + E_>}{1 + r^*}\Bigg\}$$
$$+ \gamma \left[B_1 + m S_N + (1 - \delta)p_1^k K_0 - p_1^k K_1\right].$$

Write out the first-order conditions for B_1, S_N, K_1, and L_1.

[51] Even here, there is an alternative. If conjectures, for example, are related in a regular way to various aspects of market structure, conjectural variation models can be estimated with cross-section samples. See Clarke et al. (1984) and Brack (1987).

CHAPTER SEVEN

EMPIRICAL STUDIES OF MARKET PERFORMANCE

Many a beautiful theory has been thwarted by an ugly fact.
Aldous Huxley

7.1 INTRODUCTION

The multiplication and specialization of theoretical models of imperfectly competitive markets has been matched by the development of a whole menu of empirical techniques for testing those theories. Industrial economists have estimated structure–conduct–performance models using panel data, conjectural models using accounting data, structural equations from oligopoly models using sales and output data alone, and event studies using stock-market data, and have analyzed industry-level productivity changes to estimate price–cost margins in attempts to shed new light on the evidence about the determinants of market performance from small-sample and large-sample industry cross-section studies. Studies using these various techniques generally yield consistent results.

7.2 CONJECTURES

As we have seen (section 3.4), the conjectural variations approach developed as an early generalization of the Cournot model and is now viewed as a way to measure the outcome of dynamic interactions in what is otherwise a static model. The conjectural elasticity model is equivalent to the coefficient of cooperation or partial collusion model.

7.2.1 Iwata

Iwata (1974) estimates (3.7), a conjectural derivative generalization of the Lerner index:

$$\frac{p - c_1'(q_i)}{p} = \frac{(1 + \lambda_i)s_i}{\varepsilon_{Qp}}. \tag{7.1}$$

Table 7.1 Market power and conjectural variations,
Iwata Japanese flat glass study: Asahi Glass Co. Ltd

	Window glass		Polished plate glass	
	PCM	λ	PCM	λ
1965.I	0.606	0.267	0.484	−0.188
1965.II	0.610	0.203	0.446	−0.241

Source: Iwata, 1974, tables I and II

$\lambda_i = \mathrm{d}(Q - q_i)/\mathrm{d}q_i$ is the response that firm i expects from all other firms per unit change in its own output. s_i is firm i's market share.

Rearranging (7.1), we obtain an expression for the conjectural derivative:

$$\lambda_i = \left(1 - \frac{c_i}{p}\right) \frac{\varepsilon_{Qp}}{s_i} - 1. \tag{7.2}$$

Iwata estimates constant elasticity demand curves for the two products, assuming the quantity demanded to be a function of real price and aggregate demand shift variables. He treats labor[1] and capital as fixed inputs in the short run and estimates variable costs for other inputs (silica, soda-ash, electricity, and others) assuming a fixed-coefficient technology, so that short-run marginal cost is a constant. Given the estimates of ε_{Qp} and c_i, (7.2) yields an estimate of λ_i, the conjecture that makes the firm's observed behavior consistent with profit-maximizing behavior.

Iwata estimates conjectural derivatives and price–cost margins semiannually for the period 1956–65. The estimates for 1965 for one of the two firms and the two product markets considered by Iwata are reproduced in table 7.1. Estimates of the conjectural derivative are slightly positive for window glass and slightly negative for polished plate glass. Over the whole time period, estimated conjectures exhibit considerable instability. For the whole time period and for both product markets, the estimated degree of market power is relatively stable, although declining over time. In a statistical sense, it is not possible to reject the hypothesis of Cournot behavior for this industry. The relatively large values of the price–cost margin are consistent with what one would expect for a Cournot triopoly.

7.2.2 Appelbaum

Appelbaum (1982; see also 1979) takes a similar approach, using industry-level data. He assumes that the product is homogeneous and that the conjectural elasticity is the same for all firms, and aggregates firm-level optimality conditions to the industry level. The

[1] Although cracks have appeared in the Japanese lifetime employment system, Iwata's analysis covers the period 1956–65.

Table 7.2   Market power and conjectural elasticities, Appelbaum industry study. Conjectural elasticity is estimated elasticity of industry output with respect to the output of a single firm; the Lerner index is an industry-average index of market power; estimates evaluated at the sample mean; *t*-statistics in parentheses

Industry	Rubber	Textile	Electrical machinery	Tobacco
Conjectural elasticity Θ	0.0186 (1.065)	0.0368 (0.739)	0.2001 (3.678)	0.4019 (3.052)
Lerner index	0.0559 (1.417)	0.0671 (2.457)	0.1960 (6.998)	0.6508 (10.949)

Source: Appelbaum, 1982, table 3

assumption that the product is homogeneous will be inappropriate for many industries, and may well be so for two of the industries studied by Appelbaum, electrical machinery and tobacco.

For each of the industries that he studies, Appelbaum estimates a constant elasticity demand function, a system of factor share equations (based on a generalized Leontief technology), and an aggregate profit-maximization condition.

He parameterizes conjectures as the conjectured elasticity of industry output with respect to own output. $Q = q_i + Q_{-i}$ implies that

$$\Theta = \frac{\mathrm{d}Q}{\mathrm{d}q_i} = 1 + \frac{\mathrm{d}Q_{-i}}{\mathrm{d}q_i} = 1 + \lambda_i, \tag{7.3}$$

where λ_i is the conjectured change in the output of all other firms with respect to firm output (as in (3.7) or (7.1)).

The competitive conjecture, in Appelbaum's formulation, is zero (a competitive firm believes that it can sell as much or as little as it wishes without altering industry price, and by implication that it can sell as much or as little as it wishes without altering industry output). The Cournot conjecture equals the firm's market share.

The results yield estimates of the price elasticity of demand, the conjectural elasticity of industry output with respect to a change in the output of a single firm, and the industry-average Lerner index of market power.

Typical results are shown in table 7.2. Observations are annual for the period 1947–71. Appelbaum estimates a separate Lerner index and conjectural elasticity for each year. He allows the conjectural elasticity to vary from year to year with input prices.

The conjectural elasticities for the rubber and textile industries are essentially zero. This is consistent with price-taking behavior: if firms believe that industry output does not change when their own output changes, then they believe that price is invariant to changes in their own output.

The Lerner index for the rubber industry is not significantly different from zero. The Lerner index for the textile industry is significantly different from zero, but relatively small.

Table 7.3 Estimated conjectural derivatives, Roberts' study. Firms are
rank ordered by size (firm 1 is the largest firm and firm 52 is the smallest
firm). t_1 is the t-statistic under the null hypothesis that the true value of the
conjectural derivative is 0. t_2 is the t-statistic under the null hypothesis that
the true value of the conjectural derivative is -1

Firm	1	2	3	4	14	52
λ	−0.967	−0.959	−0.961	−0.966	−0.933	−1.365
t_1	193.40	68.50	35.81	31.16	9.52	2.26
t_2	6.60	2.93	1.44	1.10	0.68	0.61

Source: Roberts, 1984, table 1

For the two remaining industries, electrical machinery and tobacco, conjectural elasticities
and Lerner indices are both significantly different from zero. In the context of this model,
it seems clear that the electrical machinery and tobacco industries are oligopolies in which
firms, on average, succeed in exercising market power.

7.2.3   Roberts

Roberts (1984) is a nice example of the use of estimates of conjectural variations to test
hypotheses about firm conduct in oligopolistic markets. In his theoretical model, he expresses
the firm's marginal revenue in terms of its market share and the conjectural derivative it
holds about the way changes in its own output affect the combined output of all other firms.
Results from duality theory lead to expressions for input demands and profit-maximizing
output supply in terms of the parameters of the profit function, for which Roberts assumes
a modified generalized Leontief functional form.

This demand–supply model yields equations that Roberts estimates for a sample of 52
firms in the US coffee roasting industry. He estimates conjectural derivatives for six so-called
benchmark firms (including the largest and the smallest firm) directly, and parametrizes the
conjectural derivative for each of the remaining 46 firms as a function of the conjectures
estimated for the immediate larger and immediate smaller benchmark firms.

One of the critical values of the conjectural derivative is -1. If a firm makes decisions on
the assumption that rivals reduce output as it expands output, then it expects total output
and hence price to remain unchanged as it changes output: that is, it acts as a price-taker.
The estimated conjectural derivatives, reported in table 7.3, are in fact tantalizingly close to
-1. For the two largest firms, however, the estimated conjectural derivatives are significantly
different from -1 (see the row labeled t_2 in table 7.3). According to these estimates, the
largest firms expect industry output to increase slightly if they expand their own output.
Conjectural derivatives for the four remaining firms are not significantly different from -1,
which is consistent with price-taking behavior. It is not possible to reject the hypothesis that
all firms except the top two act as price-takers.

Roberts reports the results of a series of tests of market conduct. Estimated conjectural derivatives are inconsistent with the hypotheses that the largest firm acts as a dominant firm facing a competitive fringe, that the two largest firms jointly act as a dominant cartel facing a competitive fringe, and that all firms act as Cournot oligopolists. As Roberts notes, the latter result is not surprising, given that behavior of the third and smaller firms is consistent with price-taking behavior. It would be interesting to test the hypothesis that the two largest firms act as Cournot firms along the residual demand curve obtained by subtracting the supply of the price-taking fringe from the market demand curve.[2]

7.2.4   Spiller and Favaro

Spiller and Favaro (1984) estimate a conjectural elasticity model of the Uruguayan banking sector. Their work illustrates the way in which conjectural models can be used to test for structural change.[3]

They work with a homogeneous good oligopoly model, and assume that the output elasticity expected by firm i from firm j is a linear function of firm i's market share:

$$\frac{q_i}{q_j}\frac{\partial q_j}{\partial q_i} = \alpha_{ji} + \delta_{ji}s_i, \tag{7.4}$$

where $s_i = q_i/Q$ is firm i's market share. Using (7.4), straightforward manipulations of firm i's first-order condition for profit maximization yield the price–cost margin equation:

$$\frac{p - c_i}{p} = \frac{s_i + \sum_{j \neq i} s_j \alpha_{ji} + s_i \sum_{j \neq i} \delta_{ji} s_j}{\varepsilon_{Qp}}. \tag{7.5}$$

Suppose that an industry is divided into a dominant group and a fringe. It is reasonable to suppose that a firm in the dominant group expects other firms in the dominant group to react aggressively if it expands output. A dominant firm would expect fringe firms to react to an output expansion by reducing their own output. Output expansion by a dominant firm should lower price, all else equal, and this should lead to an output reduction by fringe firms. These arguments imply the following restrictions on dominant firm conjectures:

$$\alpha_{DD} + \delta_{DD}s_i > 0, \qquad \alpha_{FD} + \delta_{FD}s_i < 0. \tag{7.6}$$

Fringe firms might expect some aggressive response by dominant firms to their own output expansion. They should expect little if any reaction from other fringe firms. These arguments lead to

$$\alpha_{DF} + \delta_{DF}s_i > 0, \qquad \alpha_{FF} + \delta_{FF}s_i \approx 0 \tag{7.7}$$

as restrictions on fringe firm conjectures.

---

[2] Roberts (1984, p. 374, fn. 10) discusses testing the Stackelberg leadership model, according to which fringe firms follow the Cournot behavioral assumption.
[3] See Kadiyali (1996) and Steen and Salvanes (1999) for other such studies.

Table 7.4 Estimated conjectures, Uruguayan banking. s_i
assumed equal to 0.1 for large firms, 0.015 for small firms;
t-statistics in parentheses

Large firms			
Before June 1978:			
$\alpha_{DD} + \delta_{DD}s_i$	$= 1.67$	$-3.64s_i$	$= 1.31$
	(1.74)	(1.60)	
$\alpha_{FD} + \delta_{FD}s_i$	$= 0.04$	$-4.65s_i$	$= -0.43$
	(0.08)	(6.23)	
After June 1978:			
$\alpha_{DD} + \delta_{DD}s_i$	$= 1.35$	$-5.83s_i$	$= 0.77$
$\alpha_{FD} + \delta_{FD}s_i$	$= -0.30$	$-1.42s_i$	$= -0.44$
Small firms			
Before June 1978:			
$\alpha_{DF} + \delta_{DF}s_i$	$= 0.30$	$-11.65s_i$	$= 0.13$
	(1.47)	(1.73)	
$\alpha_{FD} + \delta_{FD}s_i$	$= -0.31$	$+14.39s_i$	$= -0.09$
	(0.76)	(1.14)	
After June 1978:			
$\alpha_{DF} + \delta_{DF}s_i$	$= 0.04$	$-1.53s_i$	$= 0.02$
$\alpha_{FD} + \delta_{FD}s_i$	$= 0.10$	$-2.47s_i$	$= 0.06$

Source: Spiller and Favaro, 1984

If it is assumed that conjectures are identical within groups, the Lerner index equation (7.5) can be aggregated to a system of two group weighted–average price–cost margin equations, one for the dominant group and one for the fringe. Estimates of these weighted equations can be used to test whether or not the restrictions (7.6) and (7.7) are satisfied.

If it is assumed that all firms hold identical conjectures, then (7.5) can be aggregated to a single-industry weighted-average price–cost margin equation. This equation is interesting in its own right. It generalizes the conjectural elasticity model to include the sum of cubes of market shares, a measure of skewness in the size distribution of firms, as an explanatory variable:

$$\frac{p - wmc}{p} = \frac{\alpha + (1 - \delta - \alpha)H + \delta \sum_{i=1}^{n} s_i^3}{\varepsilon_{Qp}}. \tag{7.8}$$

Spiller and Favaro's empirical tests, however, lead to rejection of the hypothesis that all firms hold identical conjectures. Their group estimates are reproduced in table 7.4. Conjectural parameters are allowed to differ before and after June 1978. Before June 1978, regulation imposed effective barriers to entry. These barriers were abolished in the later period, and a substantial amount of entry occurred.

Estimated conjectures for the period of blocked entry fit the pattern (7.6) quite nicely. $\alpha_{DD} + \delta_{DD}s_i$, for example, the large-firm conjecture of large-firm reactions, is positive provided that the firm has a market share less than 45 percent. Entry reduced this value,

Table 7.5 Aluminum demand and scrap supply equations. Coefficients of a number of exogenous variables, including a time trend, are omitted; t-statistics in parentheses

Primary demand	$\log Q_A =$	-1.62	$-2.08 \log P_A$	$+1.25 \log P_S + \cdots$
		(0.24)	(2.74)	(2.40)
Scrap demand	$\log Q_S =$	-3.73	$+0.77 \log P_A$	$-0.73 \log P_S + \cdots$
		(0.67)	(0.54)	(1.24)
Scrap supply	$\log Q_S =$	0.74	$+1.62 \log P_S$	
		(0.86)	(2.22)	

Source: Suslow, 1986, table 2

although it remains positive unless the firm has a market share of 23 percent or more. The small-firm reaction conjectured by large firms is negative before and after the regulatory change.[4] Small-firm conjectures are essentially equal to zero before and after the regulatory change. Small firms appear to act as a Cournot fringe in an industry with a dominant group of firms that is conscious of oligopolistic interdependence.

7.2.5 Suslow

Suslow (1986) studies the US aluminum market over the period 1923–40. Alcoa, the Aluminum Company of America, was the sole US producer of primary aluminum. It faced some competition from producers of secondary or recycled aluminum, which supplied on average about 20% of the market.

The underlying theoretical model treats Alcoa as a dominant firm that maximizes profit along a residual demand curve. Suslow estimates a system of equations composed of: (a) a demand function for primary aluminum; (b) a demand function for scrap aluminum; (c) a supply function for scrap aluminum; and (d) a short-run marginal cost function for Alcoa. The short-run plant-level cost function assumes constant returns to scale, up to a capacity limit; aggregation of the plant-level cost function to the firm-level is made to depend on the extent of excess capacity. As shown in table 7.5, the estimating equations treat primary and scrap aluminum as differentiated products: the price of each variety enters the demand function of the other.

Solving the scrap aluminum demand and supply equations in table 7.5 yields a semi-reduced form equation that explains variations in scrap price P_S as a function of Alcoa's price P_A:

$$-3.73 + 0.77 \log P_A - 0.73 \log P_S + \cdots = 0.74 + 1.62 \log P_S + \cdots \qquad (7.9)$$

---

[4] Using the parameter variance–covariance matrix, it would be possible to calculate t-statistics for all the estimates that appear in table 7.4.

or

$$\log P_S = 1.90 + 0.33 \log P_A + \cdots \qquad (7.10)$$

Then from the demand equation for primary aluminum and (7.10) we obtain an estimate of the elasticity of residual demand facing Alcoa:

$$\varepsilon_{Q_A, P_A} = \frac{d \log Q_A}{d \log P_A} = \frac{\partial \log Q_A}{\partial \log P_A} + \frac{d \log Q_A}{d \log P_S} \frac{\partial \log P_S}{\partial \log P_A}$$

$$= -2.08 + (1.25)(0.33) = -1.67. \qquad (7.11)$$

The inverse of this elasticity, $1/1.67 = 0.59$, is Alcoa's estimated Lerner index of market power during this time period.

To interpret this result, it is useful to examine the price coefficients in the two demand equations reported by Suslow. In the scrap aluminum demand equation, the coefficients of $\log P_A$ and $\log P_S$ are essentially identical, but differing in sign. Primary aluminum is a very good substitute for scrap aluminum; an increase in P_A or a reduction in P_S of equal magnitude affect the demand for scrap aluminum in the same way. But in the primary aluminum demand equation, the coefficient of P_S is only about 60 percent of the magnitude of the coefficient of P_A. Scrap aluminum is not a good substitute for primary aluminum. It is the imperfect substitutability of scrap aluminum for primary aluminum that allowed Alcoa to exercise a substantial amount of market power (Suslow, 1986, p. 399):

> before 1940, even when accounting for the contemporaneous impact of the recycling sector, Alcoa had sufficient market power to have a Lerner index of approximately 60%. The source of Alcoa's market power was not so much inelastic fringe supply as it was less than perfect substitutability with the fringe's product.

This is an example of firm-specific market power based in product differentiation.

7.2.6 Breakfast cereal 1: Liang

The US breakfast cereal industry is highly concentrated, with extensive product differentiation. Liang (1989) estimates linear demand functions and price reaction functions for 12 pairs of competing brands in the US breakfast cereal industry, which between them account for 52% of breakfast industry sales.

Typical results – for Kellogg's Corn Flakes and Post Toasties – are reproduced in table 7.6. The quantity demanded of each brand is negatively affected by own price and positively affected by the price of the rival brand. This is the expected result. Price reaction curves are upward-sloping.

Estimation of each demand function/reaction function pair produces an estimate of the firm's conjectured rival price elasticity. It is possible to compare the conjectural elasticity with zero (the value that corresponds to Bertrand behavior) and with the actual price elasticity (a test of the consistency of conjectures).

Estimated conjectures show that firms expect a substantial degree of matching of price changes. Bertrand behavior is rejected, in a statistically significant sense, for 11 brands.

Table 7.6 Corn flake demand and conjecture estimates. Elasticities are evaluated at the sample mean. All coefficients except the Post cross-price elasticity are significant at the 5 percent level

	Price reaction functions		Demand functions	
	Rival price elasticity	Conjectural elasticity	Own-price elasticity	Cross-price elasticity
Kellogg	0.69	0.63	−1.53	1.48
Post	0.72	0.94	−3.24	2.79

Source: Liang, 1989

Estimated conjectural elasticities are generally different from the consistent conjectures (estimated by imposing an additional constraint during estimation). It is only for the corn flake brands, for which results are given in table 7.6, that the consistency hypothesis cannot be rejected.

Liang's results (like those of Suslow (1986) for the aluminum industry) highlight the importance of product differentiation for market performance (Liang, 1989, p. 48):

> The estimated conjectural variations and the price reaction function elasticities show that the degree of price interdependence varies widely across the brand pairs. In general, the estimated price conjectural variations support the allegation that prices in the breakfast cereal industry are noncompetitively high. Further, anticipated pricing behavior depends on whether the competing brand is a close demand substitute. If a brand was found to have a close demand substitute, the hypothesis of collusive pricing could not be rejected. On the other hand, pricing behavior for brands that were sufficiently differentiated from its close demand substitutes were found to be priced independently.

7.3 TIME SERIES

7.3.1 Domowitz, Hubbard, and Petersen 1

Domowitz et al. (1986) analyze a cross-section time series sample of 284 US manufacturing industries for the 24 year period 1958–81. Statistics describing the relation between concentration and price–cost margins are reproduced in table 7.7.[5]

The price–cost margin is a rate of return on sales computed from US census data. The average price–cost margin rises with concentration for a given time period. Across time periods, the average price–cost margin rose for all industries and for industries with four-firm seller concentration ratios of 60 percent or less. For industries in the two high-concentration

---

[5] See Domowitz et al. (1986, table 1) for separate breakdowns for consumer good and producer good industries.

Table 7.7 Price–cost margins by concentration quintile over time, for a sample of 284 US four-digit SIC manufacturing industries. σ, standard deviation; the number in parentheses gives number of observations in each category

	Concentration range						
	0–100 (284)	0–20 (64)	21–40 (92)	41–60 (72)	61–80 (41)	81–100 (15)	σ
1958–65	0.244	0.213	0.232	0.242	0.284	0.348	0.058
1966–73	0.267	0.242	0.254	0.263	0.305	0.358	0.051
1974–81	0.273	0.256	0.269	0.269	0.294	0.332	0.033

Source: Domowitz et al., 1986, p. 4

quintiles, price–cost margins rose from the first time-period to the second, and fell from the second to the third. Price–cost margins narrowed over time: the standard deviation fell from 0.058 over 1958–65 to 0.033 over 1974–81.

Domowitz et al. begin with a basic price–cost margin equation, explaining price–cost margins as a function of the four-firm seller concentration ratio ($CR4$) and the capital–sales ratio (KSR) (1986, p. 5):

> As a starting point, we consider an approach similar to that taken by Collins and Preston (1969), who regressed the price-cost margin on the four-firm concentration ratio, the capital-sales ratio, and a measure of geographic dispersion by using data for 417 industries from the 1958 and 1963 *Census of Manufactures*.

They estimate an identical specification for each of the 24 years in their sample. Results for 1963 and 1981 are

$$PCM_{63} = \underset{(15.818)}{0.174} + \underset{(5.087)}{0.117 CR4} + \underset{(4.444)}{0.080 KSR}, \qquad R^2 = 0.18 \tag{7.12}$$

and

$$PCM_{81} = \underset{(19.000)}{0.247} + \underset{(1.808)}{0.047 CR4} + \underset{(0.808)}{0.021 KSR}, \qquad R^2 = 0.01 \tag{7.13}$$

respectively (*t*-statistics in parentheses). 1963 is the year for which the regression produced the largest $CR4$ coefficient. 1981 (the final year in the sample) is the year for which the regression produced the smallest coefficient.

Broadly speaking, the estimated coefficient of $CR4$ falls in size and statistical significance as regression samples move forward in time. The estimated coefficient of KSR also falls in size and significance moving forward in time. The latter result is particularly disquieting, since the coefficient of the capital–sales ratio is an estimate of the normal rate of return on capital. At the start of the sample period, the estimating equation yields statistically significant coefficients and has reasonable (by cross-section standards) explanatory power.

Table 7.8   Pooled price–cost margin equations, 1958–81: t-statistics in parentheses; for ASR, null hypothesis is that true value of the coefficient is 1

	Constant	*CR4*	*KSR*	*ASR*	R^2
All industries	0.193	0.055	0.075	1.180	0.26
	(96.5)	(11.0)	(18.75)	(5.625)	
Producer good industries	0.205	0.037	0.074	0.794	0.14
	(68.3)	(6.2)	(18.5)	(3.96)	
Consumer good industries	0.169	0.109	0.037	1.454	0.49
	(42.3)	(12.1)	(2.9)	(10.32)	

Source: Domowitz et al., 1986, p. 7

By the end of the sample period, based on year-by-year estimates, the explanatory power of the estimating specification has fallen away to nothing.

One clear implication of these results is that the specification of the estimating equation is incomplete: it includes no variables (minimum efficient scale, for example) that control for differences across industries in entry conditions.

Table 7.8 shows the coefficients obtained from pooled time-series cross-section regressions that include the advertising–sales ratio (ASR) as an explanatory variable. This variable is taken from the IRS *Sourcebook of Statistics of Income*, which uses an industry classification scheme that is more aggregated than the four-digit SIC level.

The results in table 7.8 are similar to typical results from cross-section studies, in that advertising has a larger and more significant coefficient for consumer good industries than for producer good industries, and the model performs better for consumer good industries than for producer good industries.

In view of the changes in coefficient estimates reported between (7.12) and (7.13), it is natural to investigate the extent to which estimated structure–conduct–performance relationships vary with industry-specific and macroeconomic demand conditions. To test the influence of macroeconomic demand conditions on industry-level price–cost margins, Domowitz et al. add the percentage change in industry demand, GR, and the national unemployment rate, U, as explanatory variables. They interact these demand variables with the concentration ratio and the capital–sales ratio, so that the estimating equation is nonlinear. They also add the advertising–sales ratio (ASR) as an explanatory variable. One of the equations they estimate is

$$
\begin{aligned}
PCM = & +0.146CR4 & +0.058KSR & +0.046ASR \\
& (10.429) & (2.231) & (0.500) \\
& +0.004GR & +1.123U & +0.038(CR4)(GR) \\
& (0.267) & (3.899) & (1.462) \\
& -0.859(CR4)(U) & +0.009(KSR)(GR) & -1.711(KSR)(U), \\
& (4.594) & (0.333) & (4.766) & \qquad (7.14)
\end{aligned}
$$

where intercept terms are allowed to vary from industry to industry and t-statistics are in parentheses. Because the specification is interactive, the partial derivatives implied by (7.14) vary from point to point in the sample. For market concentration,

$$\frac{\partial PCM}{\partial CR4} = 0.146 + 0.038GR - 0.859U. \tag{7.15}$$

The impact of $CR4$ on the industry price–cost margin is larger, the greater the growth rate of industry demand. It is also larger, the lower the national unemployment rate is. The derivatives that bear on the impact of demand conditions on price–cost margins are

$$\frac{\partial PCM}{\partial GR} = 0.004 + 0.038CR4 + 0.009KSR \tag{7.16}$$

and

$$\frac{\partial PCM}{\partial U} = 1.123 - 0.859CR4 - 1.711KSR. \tag{7.17}$$

When evaluated at the sample mean values of $CR4$ and KSR, these are 0.022 and -0.01 respectively.[6] On average, therefore, greater industry demand (greater GR) and greater aggregate demand (lower U) increase margins. These effects are greater, the greater is market concentration and the greater is industry capital intensity. The aggregate demand derivative, (7.17), is particularly intriguing. If the capital–sales ratio takes its sample mean value, (7.17) is

$$\frac{\partial PCM}{\partial U} = 0.300 - 0.859CR4, \tag{7.18}$$

which is positive for $CR4 \leq 0.349$ (or 34.9 percent, which is almost exactly the sample mean for $CR4$). In low-concentration industries, price–cost margins move countercyclically, with greater aggregate demand (lower U) meaning lower margins. In high-concentration industries, margins tend to move procyclically: reduced aggregate demand means higher unemployment and lower margins, all else equal. Since it is in low-concentration industries that price–cost margins move countercyclically, these results do not support market power explanations of the business cycle.

In additional regressions, Domowitz et al. add linear ($IMSR$) and interactive ($IMSR \times CR4$) terms in the import–sales ratio as explanatory variables to their estimating equation. The results, although not without anomalies, suggest that the increasingly poor performance of the cross-section specification (7.12) over time reflects increasing import penetration of the US economy over the sample period.

---

[6] This implies that the mean values for the sample are $CR4 = 0.3596$ and $KSR = 0.4816$. It would be interesting to have t-statistics for the values of the derivatives evaluated at the sample mean. The parameter variance–covariance matrix is required to calculate these t-statistics.

7.3.2 Domowitz, Hubbard, and Petersen 2

Domowitz et al. (1987) is motivated as a test of competing microeconomic models from the macroeconomics literature (p. 379):

> In the model of Green and Porter [1984], demand shifts are imperfectly observed by oligopolists and output does not vary as long as price remains above the trigger price. Since all adjustments occur through price unless a reversion occurs, prices and price–cost margins should be pro-cyclical with the possibility of occasional very sharp price declines. In contrast, Rotemberg and Saloner [1986] assume that demand shifts are perfectly observable and versions of their model predict that price–cost margins should be countercyclical.

The distinction between procyclical and countercyclical price movements is potentially vital for macroeconomic adjustment: in particular, if prices move countercyclically, resisting downward movement in recessions, then the burden of adjustment will fall on output and through output on employment.

In the Green–Porter model, noncooperative collusion is enforced by a trigger strategy. If price falls, (which may result either from weak overall demand or from an illicit expansion of output by some firm), firms expand output (reduce price) for a certain number of periods to maintain incentives for output restriction during the other phases of the game.[7] This implies that price will fall when demand is low, all else equal.

In the Rotemberg and Saloner (1986) model, in contrast, demand shifts are observable. When demand is low, the payoff to cheating on the tacitly collusive arrangement is less, hence cheating is less likely to occur. Price cuts are then less likely during recessions, all else equal.

Domowitz et al. begin with a conjectural derivative Lerner index:

$$\frac{p - c_i'}{p} = \frac{s_i(1 + \lambda_i)}{\varepsilon_{Qp}}. \tag{7.19}$$

Assuming constant returns to scale and aggregating to the industry level yields

$$\frac{p - \bar{c}}{p} = \frac{\sum_i s_i^2(1 + \lambda_i)}{\varepsilon_{Qp}}, \tag{7.20}$$

where $\bar{c}$ is weighted-average average cost.

Domowitz et al. single out a 57-industry subset of their full sample. About this subsample they say (pp. 385–7; footnotes omitted):

> The common characteristics of these industries are (i) they are "producer-good" industries; (ii) they have been recognized as Census industries at least since 1958; (iii) they have four-firm concentration ratios above 0.50 in 1972; and (iv) they are not listed as "miscellaneous" or "not elsewhere classified". The object of (i)–(iv) was to select mature, homogeneous-goods oligopolies operating in well defined markets.

---

[7] In equilibrium, defection does not in fact occur; see chapter 10.

There is at least one reason to have reservations about this sample: most cross-section studies, as well as the cross-section time-series results of Domowitz et al. (1986), suggest that the explanatory power of the structure–conduct–performance specification is much stronger in consumer good industries than in producer good industries.

The equation they estimate is

$$PCM_{it} = \beta_0 + \beta_1 CR4_{it} + \beta_2 KSR_{it} + \beta_3 ASR_{it} + \beta_4 CU_t + \varepsilon_{it}, \qquad (7.21)$$

where CU is a measure of capacity utilization in manufacturing. Ordinary least-squares results for the whole sample are

$$\begin{aligned}
PCM = \ & 0.107 + 0.110 CR4 + 0.030 KSR \\
& (0.017) \quad (0.0005) \qquad (0.002) \\
& \qquad\quad + \ 1.064 ASR + 0.096 CU \\
& \qquad\qquad\ (0.031) \qquad (0.021)
\end{aligned} \qquad (7.22)$$

(standard errors in parentheses).[8] The estimated coefficients of CU are positive: margins tend to be higher, all else equal, when the strength of the economy puts pressure on capacity.

7.3.3 Final remark

The movement from cross-section data to panel data – tracking a cross section over time – expands the range of questions empirical researchers can address. But if panel data consists of observations on industries, they are open to all the criticisms that were laid at the feet of traditional cross-section work from the 1970s.[9] Researchers who reject these criticisms will welcome the use of panel data. Those who hold that it is impossible to analyze the relationship between accounting rates of return and market power, that all accounting profits are really economic rents, that accounting profit does not control for investment in intangible assets, and that in any event simultaneity problems make it impossible to estimate structure–conduct–performance relationships will reject the results of the industry-level panel data literature, just as they have rejected the results of the industry cross-section literature.

7.4 AVOIDING COST DATA I: NEIO

In reaction to the assault on accounting data,[10] industrial economists sought approaches to the analysis of price–cost margins that avoided the need to analyze cost data. One such

---

[8] The implied t-statistic for the coefficient of concentration in that all-industries sample is 220. If the reported standard error is not a typographical error, this is a cause for concern.

[9] There is also that point that certain explanatory variables that are found to be important in cross-section work will not be available for panel samples.

[10] See Bresnahan (1987, p. 460):

Column 9 shows the accounting profits of the five largest operating automobile companies. The obvious, through wrong, inference is that there was a decrease in automobile competition in 1955. The technology of automobile manufacturing is characterized by large fixed costs: plant costs and product development

approach, due to Bresnahan (1982) and Lau (1982), is the root of what has come to be known as the *New Empirical Industrial Organization* (NEIO) literature.[11] The other, due to Hall (1986, 1988) developed out of the macroeconomics literature and has only recently been applied to data sets that seem suitable from the point of view of industrial economics.

Suppose, for simplicity, that the product of an oligopoly market is homogeneous. Then the profit-maximization problem of a single firm is to

$$\max_{q_i} p(Q)q_i - c_i(q_i), \tag{7.23}$$

where $Q = q_i + Q_{-i}$ is industry output, q_i the output of firm i, and Q_{-i} the output of all other firms. The first-order condition for profit maximization is

$$p + \Theta_i q_i \frac{dp}{dQ} = c_i'(q_i), \tag{7.24}$$

where $\Theta_i = dQ/dq_i$ is firm i's conjectured change in industry output as its own output changes. In terms of the conjectural derivative model (section 3.4.1 and (3.5)), $\Theta_i = 1 + \lambda_i$. This way of formalizing conjectures is used, for example, by Appelbaum (see (7.3)).

Equation (7.24) is not a supply function; supply functions are defined only if the industry is perfectly competitive. It can be thought of as a supply relation, however. If (7.24) can be estimated, then one can seek to explain the implied price–cost margins $p - c_i'$.

Following Steen and Salvanes (1999), suppose that inverse demand and marginal cost are both linear. Let inverse demand be

$$Q = \alpha_0 + \alpha_p p + \alpha_Z Z + \alpha_{pZ} PZ + \varepsilon, \tag{7.25}$$

where Z is a variable that affects demand and ε is an error term. Let marginal cost be

$$c'(Q) = \beta_0 + \beta_Q Q + \beta_W W, \tag{7.26}$$

where W is a variable that affects marginal cost.[12]

Substituting (7.26) in (7.24), adding an error term η, and rearranging terms slightly gives a version of the supply relation that can be estimated simultaneously with the inverse demand function (7.25):

$$P = \beta_0 + \beta_Q Q + \beta_W W - \Theta_i \frac{Q}{\alpha_p + \alpha_{pZ} Z} + \eta. \tag{7.27}$$

---

costs are joint costs of production in many years. Standard accounting practice spreads these costs out smoothly over many years. As a result there is no stable time-series relationship between accounting profit and price–cost margins in the economic sense.

The modeling approach taken in sections 6.3.2 and 6.3.2 suggests ways to analyze accounting data despite the standard practices in question (specifically, in this case, rather than analyzing accounting measures of profit, to use the underlying data to compute a price–cost margin or gross rate of return on sales, with accounting depreciation rules seen as affecting the rental rate of capital services).

[11] In addition to the studies discussed below, see Baker and Bresnahan (1988) and also Sumner (1981), the latter being in some sense an anticipation of the NEIO approach. See Schroeter et al. (2000) for an extension of the NEIO approach to bilateral oligopoly.

[12] Z and W can be made to be vectors without changing the argument.

Bresnahan (1982) and Lau (1982) show that the conjectural parameter Θ_i is identified so long as the true value of the interaction coefficient α_{pZ} in the inverse demand equation is not equal to zero. Informally, for $\alpha_{pZ} \neq 0$, the variable Q in (7.25) and the ratio $Q/(\alpha_p + \alpha_{pZ}Z)$ in (7.27) move in different ways and their respective coefficients can be estimated. If the true value of α_{pZ} is zero, what could be estimated in (7.27) is the coefficient of Q, the sum $\beta_Q + (\Theta_i/\alpha_p)$, which would not permit recovery of β_Q or Θ_i.[13]

The New Empirical Industrial Organization framework has been and continues to be widely used, although it is also the subject of recent criticism (section 7.6).

7.4.1   The automobile industry

Bresnahan 1

The demand side of the Bresnahan (1981a; see also 1980) model of the automobile market[14] is one of vertical product differentiation. A consumer at location v along the interval $[0, V_{max}]$ has utility function

$$U(x, Y, v) = \begin{cases} Y + vx & \text{if an automobile is purchased,} \\ V(Y, v) & \text{if not,} \end{cases} \tag{7.28}$$

where Y is income not spent on automobiles, x is the quality of the automobile purchased, v is the consumer's marginal utility of automobile quality. Bresnahan assumes that consumers are distributed uniformly over the interval $[0, V_{max}]$ with density δ, a parameter to be estimated.

The demand for each variety can be computed as in section 4.3. For an automobile model i of intermediate quality, this involves finding the consumers who are indifferent between variety i and varieties $i-1, i+1$ (where varieties are ordered in terms of quality, leading to

$$q_i = \delta \left(\frac{P_{i+1} - P_i}{x_{i+1} - x_i} - \frac{P_i - P_{i-1}}{x_i - x_{i-1}} \right), \tag{7.29}$$

so that the demand for an automobile model of intermediate quality depends on the prices and qualities of its two immediately neighboring varieties.

Making specific arguments that need not detain us here, Bresnahan derives similar expressions for the demand facing the highest- and lowest-quality varieties.

Bresnahan assumes a firm-level cost function with fixed cost that depends on the number and qualities of models produced and constant marginal cost per variety (with the level of marginal cost depending on quality):

$$C(X_k, Q_k, n_k) = A(n_k, X_k) + \sum_{j \in \mathcal{J}_k} \mu e^{x_j} q_j, \tag{7.30}$$

---

[13] Formally, identification needs to be checked using the conditions for nonlinear systems given in Fisher (1966).

[14] The automobile industry is a favorite proving ground for empirical analysis of imperfect competition. In addition to the studies mentioned here, see Berry et al. (1995) and Goldberg (1995).

where n_k is the number of car models sold by firm k, x_j is the quality of variety j, q_j is the quantity produced of variety j, X_k and Q_k are vectors corresponding to x_j and q_j, and $\mathcal{J}_k$ is the set of indices of varieties produced by firm k.[15]

Having specified the demand and cost sides of the model, the profit-maximization problem and the implied supply behavior is in principle straightforward, although complicated and not without interest in its own right. This interest lies in the way a firm's profit-maximization problem is affected by the relations among the qualities of the models it produces. If a firm produces models that are adjacent in quality space, then it internalizes the cross-model impact of price changes on the quantities demanded of those varieties. If a firm produces models that are insulated one from another by the models of other firms, a firm's pricing decisions for different models are independent. For details, see Bresnahan (1981a, pp. 208–9).

Bresnahan transforms the theoretical model estimation by adding stochastic error terms to the reduced-form equations for prices and quantities and by assuming that product quality is a stochastic function of observable product characteristics:

$$x_i^* = \sqrt{\beta_0 + \sum \beta_j z_{ij}} + \varepsilon_{xi}, \qquad (7.31)$$

where the z_{ij}s measure product characteristics, the β_js are parameters to be estimated, and the square root formulation implies decreasing quality returns to product attributes.

Estimation itself is messy: assuming all error terms are normal and assuming desirable independence properties allows one to write down the maximum likelihood function. This must be estimated iteratively; for further discussion, see Bresnahan (1980, 1981a).

Bresnahan estimates the model separately for 1977 and 1978. Prices are wholesale prices. The characteristics that are used as determinants of product quality are length, weight, the number of cylinders, horsepower, fuel usage (gallons per mile), and dummy variables for models with a hardtop or a hatchback.[16] The data requirements to estimate the model are prices, quantities, and product characteristics.

Table 7.9 shows estimated prices, margins, and Lerner indices for different classes of vehicles. It is apparent that margins are higher for higher-quality models.

The model also yields estimates of welfare effects. These include producers' surplus and the conventional deadweight welfare loss, as some consumers who would purchase automobiles if price were equal to marginal cost leave the market. There is also a welfare loss due to quality downshifting, as consumers in the market shift from higher-quality vehicles that they would prefer if price were equal to marginal cost to lower-quality vehicles. Bresnahan's estimates, shown in table 7.10, suggest the importance of quality downshifting.

---

[15] If firm 1 produces models 2 and 4, then

$$C(X_1, Q_1, 2) = A(2, X_1) + \mu(e^{x_2} q_2 + e^{x_4} q_4),$$

with $X_1 = (x_2, x_4)$, $Q_1 = (q_2, q_4)$, and μ a parameter to be estimated.

[16] Models are defined in terms of characteristics, not the name under which the vehicle was sold to the public. It is not clear that this is appropriate, but the spatial model breaks down if two models have identical characteristics (some denominators in the expressions for demand go to zero). An alternative approach would be to use dummy variables to distinguish models with identical characteristics.

Table 7.9 Estimated prices, margins, and Lerner indices

	P	P − mc	L
Subcompacts	3775	231	0.0612
Compacts	4270	361	0.0845
Intermediates	4804	573	0.1193
Large	6717	1442	0.2147

Source: Bresnahan, 1981a

Table 7.10 Estimated welfare effects

	1977	*1978*
Revenue	39.9	42.8
Producers' surplus	4.11	4.36
Consumer's loss	7.23	7.68
Deadweight	0.71	0.82
Quality downshifting	6.52	6.86
Net welfare loss	3.12	3.32

Source: Bresnahan, 1981a

Bresnahan 2

The year 1955 stands out for the US automobile industry. In the absence of obvious changes in the characteristics of the demand side of the market, the quantity sold was substantially higher in 1955 than in 1954 or 1956. Bresnahan (1987) adapts the model of Bresnahan (1981a) to compare the explanatory power of assumed collusive (joint-profit-maximizing) and Nash behavior, year by year, for the US auto industry in the mid-1950s. Nash behavior has superior explanatory power for 1955. Bresnahan concludes (1987, pp. 478–9):

> The 1955 auto model year had three anomalous features: price fell during a macroeconomic expansion, quantity increased well out of proportion to experience, and the share of the basic transportation segment in total auto sales increased. The hypothesis that tacit collusion among the automakers broke down in 1955 explains these anomalies.

It is interesting to speculate what might have been behind such a breakdown in tacit collusion. Ward mentions (1995, p. 110) the removal of government controls on production, (p. 132) a race between Ford and Chevrolet for the largest market share, and (pp. 187–8) a structural increase in consumer use of credit to finance auto purchases. The latter factor may indicate a possible misspecification of the demand side of the Bresnahan model.

Feenstra and Levinsohn

Feenstra and Levinsohn (1995) specify a demand model assuming that individual consumer utility depends on a vector of characteristics, not a single quality level. They assume that utility is quadratic in characteristics, and that consumers (more precisely, consumers' most preferred combinations of characteristics) are uniformly distributed in characteristics space. Each automobile model supplies the region of characteristics space where it delivers consumers the greatest net utility. Because utility is defined over multiple characteristics, each model will potentially have several neighbors, rather than just one neighbor of higher quality and one of lower quality.

Marginal cost for any given model is assumed to be constant, and a linear function of characteristics. Feenstra and Levinsohn assume profit maximization, allowing for the fact that firms produce many varieties and for the fact that some firms may set prices while others set quantities.[17]

Product characteristics are taken as given. Thus what is being modeled is the second stage of a two-stage game, with product characteristics being selected in the first stage. The first-order conditions for profit maximization are used to obtain expressions for equilibrium prices. These equations are estimated by numerical methods.

The sample is for the 82 new car models sold in the US in 1987 that had sales of at least 500 vehicles. Models are defined in terms of characteristics, not the names under which the vehicles were marketed. The characteristics are weight, horsepower, a European vehicle dummy variable, interacted with weight and with horsepower, and a reliability rating from a consumer magazine. The characteristics used are those of the basic model and prices is the list prices of the basic model.

Feenstra and Levinsohn make estimates using alternative behavioral assumptions. The specification that yields the lowest sum of squared residuals assumes that all European firms except Volkswagen set quantity, while Volkswagen, US, and Japanese firms set price.

Their estimates imply that the average new car model had 5.9 neighbors in characteristics space. Their price and implied Lerner index estimates are shown in figure 7.1. It is evident that the Lerner index rises with price.[18]

7.4.2   Breakfast cereal 2: Nevo

Nevo (2001) specifies a discrete choice demand model for the ready-to-eat breakfast cereal market. Assuming constant marginal costs for each brand, he estimates brand-specific price–cost margins taking differences in brand characteristics and in demographic characteristics across 65 regional markets.

Nevo estimates price–cost margins for three alternative supply-side structures: single-firm ownership of each breakfast cereal brand, the observed pattern of brand ownership by firms, and joint ownership of the 25 brands in the sample.

---

[17] Voluntary export restraints might impose quantity-setting behavior on non-US suppliers.
[18] These results recall Henry Ford II's terse response when asked why Ford Motor Company did not develop models for the mini-car segment of the market: "Mini cars – mini profits."

Lerner index

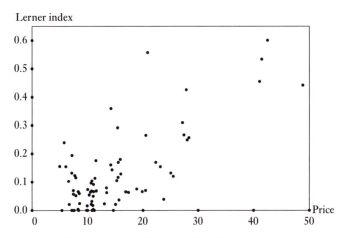

Figure 7.1 Estimated prices and Lerner indices, mixed Nash behavior, Feenstra and Levinsohn study. Prices measured in thousands of 1987 dollars. *Source*: Feenstra and Levinsohn, table 6.

Table 7.11 Median estimated margins, ready-to-eat cereal industry

Single-product firms	35.2%
Observed brand ownership	40.1%
Joint ownership, 25 brands	64.7%
Estimated margins from accounting data	46.0%

Source: Nevo, 2001

He reports similar results from alternative demand specifications. Typical margins estimates are shown in table 7.11. For comparison purposes, he reports as well accounting estimates of the price–cost margin. The supply-side estimates that come closest to matching the accounting figures are those based on the assumption of noncooperative one-shot game behavior by the observed pattern of multiproduct firms. This aspect of Nevo's results differ from those of Liang (although both emphasize the role of product differentiation as a determinant of performance).

7.5   AVOIDING COST DATA II: THE SOLOW RESIDUAL

7.5.1   Solow

Solow (1957) sought to obtain a measure of the rate of technical progress. Begin with an aggregate production function of the form

$$Q = A(t)F(K, L). \tag{7.32}$$

Take a logarithmic derivative with respect to time to get an expression for the time rate of change of output:

$$\frac{\dot{Q}}{Q} = \frac{\dot{A}}{A} + \frac{F_K}{F}\dot{K} + \frac{F_L}{F}\dot{L} = \frac{\dot{A}}{A} + A\frac{F_K}{Q}\dot{K} + A\frac{F_L}{Q}\dot{L}. \tag{7.33}$$

Assume that input markets are competitive, so that factors of production are paid the values of their marginal products. Factor shares of total output are

$$\alpha_L = \frac{L}{Q}Q_L = A\frac{L}{Q}F_L, \qquad \alpha_K = \frac{K}{Q}Q_K = A\frac{K}{Q}F_K. \tag{7.34}$$

Substituting (7.34) in (7.33) gives

$$\frac{\dot{Q}}{Q} = \frac{\dot{A}}{A} + \alpha_K\frac{\dot{K}}{K} + \alpha_L\frac{\dot{L}}{L}. \tag{7.35}$$

Now also assume constant returns to scale, so that F is first-degree homogeneous. Then write output per unit of labor input as

$$q = \frac{Q}{L} = A(t)\frac{F(K,L)}{L} = A(t)F\left(\frac{K}{L},1\right) = A(t)f(k). \tag{7.36}$$

Once again, take a logarithmic time derivative:

$$\frac{\dot{q}}{q} = \frac{\dot{A}}{A} + \frac{k}{f}\frac{df}{dk}\left(\frac{\dot{k}}{k}\right). \tag{7.37}$$

Now rewrite α_K in condensed form as

$$\alpha_K = \frac{K}{F(K,L)}F_K(K,L) = \frac{K/L}{[F(K,L)/L]}F_K\left(\frac{K}{L},1\right) = \frac{k}{f(k)}\frac{df}{dk}. \tag{7.38}$$

(since the production function is homogeneous of degree one, the derivatives of the production function are homogeneous of degree zero).

Hence (7.37) becomes

$$\frac{\dot{q}}{q} = \frac{\dot{A}}{A} + \alpha_K\frac{\dot{k}}{k}. \tag{7.39}$$

With time series data on Q/L, K/L, and α_K, one can obtain a measure of $\dot{A}/A$, the rate of change of output that cannot be traced to changes in input levels – the rate of change of technological progress.

7.5.2   Hall 1

Hall (1986) looked to imperfectly competitive markets to explain why markets might remain away from full-employment equilibrium for long periods of time (1986, pp. 287–8):

> Consider a competitive firm with a well-defined level of capacity (capacity is the level of output where the marginal cost curve turns upward and becomes nearly vertical). Such a firm is unlikely to be satisfied with producing less than its capacity output . . . . marginal cost is low when output is below capacity . . . . there is substantial incremental profit to be made by putting more output on the market. The competitor never fears that added output will spoil the market, for the absence of that concern is the definition of competition. Hence, output rises to capacity . . . .
>
> In the world described by my empirical findings, the incentive to keep output at capacity is nowhere near as strong. A business faced with disappointing sales in a recession hesitates to push more output on the market, because the market will absorb it only at a lower price . . . .
>
> . . . It is true, of course, that recessions bring large reductions in profit for most businesses. However, they cannot recover profit by cutting price and raising volume. A minimum conclusion from my research, then, is that the incentives are weak for those business actions that would restore full employment.

The model

Hall (1986, p. 288) uses a short-run concept of marginal cost:

> I define marginal cost as the derivative of the cost function with respect to output, holding the capital stock constant.

Hall's measure of marginal cost is:

$$c = w \frac{\Delta N}{\Delta Q - \theta Q}, \tag{7.40}$$

where w is the hourly wage rate, N is the number of hours of labour input, Q is the quantity of output, and θ is the rate of technical progress. $\Delta Q - \theta Q$ is the incremental output that would have been produced by labor input ΔN in the absence of technical progress.

Except for a few industries, and working on the most disaggregated level, the output measure that would be available would be in value terms, not physical quantities. This is not a trivial problem when one wishes to deal with imperfect competition. In (7.40), Q is really pq, where q, is a physical output measure; ΔQ is really $p\Delta q + q\Delta p$; and p, Δp will be affected by both the level of and changes in market power.

Further, implicit in (7.40) is the awkward use of intertemporal data to measure an atemporal concept. Marginal cost is the increase in (minimum) cost to produce slightly more output *at a given time*. The Δs in (7.40) refer to observed changes from one time period to another; it is for this reason that the productivity correction appears in the denominator on the right.

Now assume that technical progress varies randomly around a trend rate of change:

$$\theta_t = \theta + u_t, \tag{7.41}$$

and assume also that u_t is uncorrelated with the business cycle.

Hall rationalizes this specification based on two maintained hypotheses (1986, p. 290):

> First, the ups and downs of the economy . . . do not cause year-to-year changes in productivity. On-the-job learning by doing or research and development stimulated by a vibrant economy does not yield immediate improvements in productivity. The effects are spread over sufficiently many years that the correlation of u_t with the business cycle is negligible. Second, fluctuations in productivity growth do not themselves cause the business cycle.

As Hall notes, the latter assumption is in direct contradiction to the assumptions that underlie real business cycle models.

The first assumption is open to question. The work of Schmookler (1966, 1972) and Scherer (1982) suggests that R&D efforts respond fairly directly to demand fluctuations, which in turn suggests that the technological progress resulting from R&D is affected by movements over the business cycle.

Hall also says (1986, p. 290)

> Another assumption I make is that a firm's markup ratio – the ratio of price to marginal cost – can be reasonably approximated as a constant over time . . . . the outcome of the decision process by which a firm chooses its marginal cost and, possibly, its price is such that the ratio of the two is approximately constant.

Take first the case of monopoly and constant marginal cost. The Lerner index (first-order condition for profit maximization) can be rewritten

$$\mu = \frac{p}{c} = 1 \Big/ \left(1 - \frac{1}{\varepsilon}\right). \tag{7.42}$$

It follows that for the markup μ to be a constant, under monopoly, would require a constant price elasticity of demand (as one would expect; see also Hall, p. 316).

In conjectural variations quantity-setting oligopoly, and making the strong assumption that firms hold identical conjectures, the corresponding expression is

$$\mu = \frac{p}{c} = 1 \Big/ \left(1 - \frac{\alpha + (1 - \alpha)H}{\varepsilon}\right). \tag{7.43}$$

To believe that oligopoly markups can be treated as constant over the business cycle, one must believe that market concentration is roughly constant over the business cycle and that conjectures are roughly constant over the business cycle.

The first assumption is plausible: all empirical evidence is that seller concentration changes very slowly relative to other industry-level variables that are usually thought of as endogenous.

The second assumption is not plausible: in fact, the basis of the literature that disputes whether price wars are more likely during booms or recessions is that conjectures do change over the business cycle (although the contributors to that literature differ in their opinions about the way in which conjectures change).

In the first paragraph of his paper, Hall says (1986, p. 285):

> Students of industrial organization have not generally exploited cyclical movements in their research; they have concentrated almost entirely on cross-sectional analysis. One of my goals

in this paper is to look at some standard issues in industrial organization through time series variation in individual industries as it is associated with the aggregate business cycle.

The remarks about cross-sectional analysis were correct at the time of Hall's writing. But an essential question for industrial economists is how margins vary over the course of the business cycle. By assuming that markups are constant over the business cycle, Hall forecloses investigation of this issue.

But suspending disbelief and substituting (7.40) and (7.41) into a slightly rearranged version of the definition of the markup (7.43) gives

$$\frac{p}{\mu} = c = w \frac{\Delta N}{\Delta Q - (\theta + u)Q}, \tag{7.44}$$

$$\frac{\Delta Q}{Q} = \mu \frac{wN}{pQ} \frac{\Delta N}{N} + \theta + u. \tag{7.45}$$

Writing $\Delta q = \Delta Q / Q$ and $\Delta n = \Delta N / N$ for proportional rates of change and $\alpha = wN/pQ$ for labor's share of income, (7.45) becomes the estimating equation

$$\Delta q = \mu \alpha \Delta n + \theta + u. \tag{7.46}$$

Results

Hall estimates the value of μ that makes the residual u uncorrelated with the rate of growth of real GNP, Δy, which is used as an instrumental variable for $\alpha \Delta n$. He uses annual data on 48 mainly two–digit SIC industries over the period 1949–78. Hall's discussion of his sample (pp. 296–7) does not confront the issue of whether or not it makes sense to use "industry" categories at this level of aggregation.

Hall estimates markup ratios greater than or equal to 2 for seven industries, from 1.6 to 1.8 for 16 industries, and below 1 for six. Estimates for the remaining industries are statistically imprecise.[19] High estimated markups are taken to support the idea that imperfectly competitive markets explain why firms do not maintain output near capacity during recessions.

Hall appeals to the Chamberlinian theory of monopolistic competition to reconcile large estimates of market power with received small observations of (accounting) profit. It seems doubtful that monopolistic competition is an appropriate model for producer good industries, where product differentiation is usually thought to be much less important than in consumer good industries.[20]

---

[19] See Hubbard (1986, p. 332) for a comparison of Hall's estimates with figures from the US Census of Manufactures.

[20] A student of industrial economics would at this point raise the possibility that economic profits are devoted to strategic behavior that aims to maintain positions of market power (Posner, 1975). The closest Hall comes to this possibility is (1986, pp. 300–1):

> The basic finding is that profit is nowhere near as high as it would be under full exploitation of market power with constant returns. My interpretation is that firms face setup costs, advertising costs, or fixed costs that absorb a good part of the latent monopoly profit.

Discussion

The initial reaction of the student of industrial economics is that Hall's markup estimates are meaningless: the "industries" that he examines are too aggregated to represent industries in any reasonable economic sense. A perhaps more constructive reaction is that before the worth of Hall's estimates can be assessed, what is called for is a model of the impact of data aggregation on tests of the kind that Hall carries out. Such an effort would be useful for more traditional tests for the presence of market power as well, since four-digit industry data are also aggregations of economically meaningful industries. A simulation approach might be useful.

Assuming that satisfactory data could be obtained, and also that econometric problems could be dealt with, the assumption that the markup is fixed over the business cycle is not plausible, and with industry-level data, one would wish to integrate the model with an appropriate oligopoly model.

From a methodological point of view, the pertinent question is whether the margin estimates produced by the Hall approach are in some sense more reliable than margin estimates based on official data (for the US, the Census of Manufactures) or on accounting data. An advantage of the Hall margins is that the process by which they are estimated also gives an estimate of the precision with which they are estimated. But the Hall approach requires a sufficiently large number of assumptions that it does not seem obvious that it can be taken to dominate more familiar sources for margin figures.

7.5.3   Hall 2

Hall (1988) is an extension of Hall (1986). In this case, Hall assumes that labor is purchased on a competitive labor market at wage w and that capital stock is chosen (not necessarily optimally) before output decisions are made.

Hall states (1988, p. 925) – and this is in contrast to Hall (1986) – that he does not assume constancy of the markup ratio over time. He does produce an estimate of a constant markup parameter, however.

Hall (1988) also allows for changes in the capital stock. In place of (7.40) we now have marginal cost given by

$$c = \frac{w\Delta N + r\Delta K}{\Delta Q - \theta Q}, \tag{7.47}$$

so that

$$\frac{\Delta Q}{Q} = \frac{wN}{cQ}\frac{\Delta N}{N} + \frac{rK}{cQ}\frac{\Delta K}{K} + \theta. \tag{7.48}$$

Concerning (7.47), Hall (1988, p. 926) says:

> The change in cost in the numerator now includes a term $r\Delta K$, which is the cost of the change in the capital stock ΔK, evaluated at the actual service cost of the new capital, r. Alternatively, if the firm is not in equilibrium with respect to its use of capital, r is the shadow value of capital. In any case, r is not the rate of profit calculated as a residual.

Concerning (7.48), Hall says:[21]

> this relation is not directly usable because the shadow value of capital, r, is not generally observed.

Since Hall (1988) takes the position that r cannot be observed, he proceeds to get rid of it:[22]

> Under constant returns to scale, however, it is possible to eliminate c from equation [(7.48)]. With constant returns to scale, the two shares wN/cQ and rK/cQ are competitive factor shares; that is, they sum to one.

Then, substituting

$$\frac{rK}{cQ} = 1 - \frac{wN}{cQ} \tag{7.49}$$

in (7.48) gives

$$\frac{\Delta Q}{Q} - \frac{\Delta K}{K} = \mu \alpha_L \left(\frac{\Delta N}{N} - \frac{\Delta K}{K} \right) + \theta. \tag{7.50}$$

Hall rewrites this in a way that is essentially the same as (7.46), but allows for time dependence:

$$\Delta q_t = \mu_t \alpha_t \Delta n_t + \theta_t. \tag{7.51}$$

Now treat θ as a constant plus a random term:

$$\Delta q_t = \mu_t \alpha_t \Delta n_t + \theta + u_t. \tag{7.52}$$

Then the Solow residual is

$$\Delta q_t - \alpha_t \Delta n_t = (\mu_t - 1)\alpha_t \Delta n_t + \theta + u_t. \tag{7.53}$$

If an instrumental variable Δz that is uncorrelated with u is used in estimation to approximate $\alpha_t \Delta n_t$, the Solow residual is correlated with the instrument unless $\mu_t = 1$:

$$\text{cov}\,(\Delta q_t - \alpha_t \Delta n_t, \Delta z_t) = \text{cov}[(\mu_t - 1)\alpha_t \Delta n_t, \Delta z_t]. \tag{7.54}$$

Hall (1988, p. 929) writes:

> The proposed test rests on the simple proposition that, to the extent that the firm is non-competitive, its measured productivity will be associated with an exogenous instrument. When productivity rises along with employment in response to an outside force, it is a sign that the firm is not competitive.

---

[21] Hall (1986, pp. 302–4) computes time series for the rental cost of capital.
[22] Hall writes x for marginal cost; I have substituted c.

Value-added

Let Q^* be output, and let

$$Q = p^*Q^* - vM \tag{7.55}$$

be value-added. Then, from

$$c = \frac{w\Delta N + v\Delta M + r\Delta K}{\Delta Q^* - \theta Q^*}, \tag{7.56}$$

one can obtain a generalization of the Solow residual equation (7.53):

$$\Delta q^* - (\alpha^*\Delta n + \gamma^*\Delta m) = (\mu^* - 1)(\alpha^*\Delta n + \gamma^*\Delta m) + \theta^*. \tag{7.57}$$

The rate of growth of the ratio of real value-added to the capital stock is

$$\Delta q = \frac{\Delta(Q/K)}{Q/K} = \frac{p^*\Delta(Q^*/K) - v\Delta(M/K)}{(p^*Q^*/K) - (vM/K)} = \frac{\Delta q^* - \gamma^*\Delta m}{1 - \gamma^*}. \tag{7.58}$$

Hence

$$\Delta q^* = (1 - \gamma^*)\Delta q + \gamma^*\Delta m; \tag{7.59}$$

and substituting in (7.57) to eliminate Δq^* gives the estimating equation

$$\Delta q - \alpha\Delta n = (\mu^* - 1)\left(\alpha\Delta n + \frac{\gamma^*}{1 - \gamma^*}\Delta m\right) + \theta. \tag{7.60}$$

Estimation

Hall (1988, p. 932) writes:

> The instrumental variables for the test should cause important movements in employment and output but be uncorrelated with the random fluctuations in productivity growth. Such exogenous variables could operate through product demand or through factor supplies. Lack of correlation with the random element of productivity growth involves two considerations: First, the instrument must not cause movements in productivity, and, second, it must not respond to random variations in productivity growth.

The instruments that Hall examines are military spending, world oil prices, and the political party of the president. He uses annual data on seven one-digit industries and 26 two-digit industries over the period 1953–84. He does not discuss the possibility that the industry categories are not satisfactory.

Estimated markup ratios for the seven one-digit industries range from 1.864 to 3.791. Results for two–digit industries are all over the map, from -139.478 to 36.313.[23]

---

[23] Waldmann (1991) shows that the way some of the value-added series used by Hall are constructed makes them unsuitable for Hall's purposes.

7.5.4   Norrbin

Norrbin (1993) reestimates (7.57) using an extended version of Hall's data set that uses a measure of the value of output in place of value-added as an output measure. His results vary depending on alternative estimation techniques, but in general show smaller estimated markups than Hall and in most cases markups not significantly different from one.

7.5.5   Domowitz, Hubbard, and Petersen 3

Domowitz et al. (1988) derive a Solow residual equation that explicitly allows for materials use and imperfect competition (the degree of which is measured by the Lerner index). Like Hall, they assume that the productivity shock is not affected by aggregate fluctuations. As instrumental variables, they use current and lagged GNP growth, current and lagged rate of growth of real military purchases, and the rate of growth of the relative price of imports. They also allow for fixed industry effects.

Comparing their margin estimates with those from Census of Manufactures data, they write (Domowitz et al., 1988, pp. 58–9):

> The two methodologies should yield roughly the same estimates as long as the marginal product of production workers is not too different from their average product. In fact, the two procedures do generate roughly similar estimates of price–cost margins. The new methodology generates an average margin of 0.359 while the average [Census] margin . . . is 0.359. The correlation coefficient . . . is 0.773.

They also estimate a version of the Solow residual equation assuming that the Lerner index varies with seller concentration and the percentage of unionized workers in the industry. They find a positive impact of seller concentration and a negative impact of unionization on margins. As is usual for this type of study, the estimated impact of seller concentration is larger and more significant for consumer good industries than for producer good industries.

They also estimate a version of the Solow residual equation in which the Lerner index varies with industry capacity utilization. The results indicate that margins are procyclical overall, rising during booms. This is what one would expect, based on a large number of studies of price–cost margins that include the growth rate of sales as an explanatory variable. They also find that margins in concentrated durable good industries are countercyclical.

7.5.6   Roeger

Roeger (1995) uses duality theory to develop Solow-residual estimates of the markup ratio based on the cost function rather than the production function.[24] The least aggregated

---

[24] See Roeger (1996) and Oliveira Martins et al. (1996) for other applications.

industries examined by Roeger are at the two–digit level. He does not discuss whether or not this is appropriate. As he describes his results (1995, p. 325):

> imperfect competition explains more than 90 percent of the difference between the primal and dual productivity measures with generally significant markups. The generally excellent fit of these equations suggests that imperfect competition might be the cause of this discrepancy. In this respect, my results support Hall's initial claim that prices exceed marginal cost in U.S. manufacturing. . . . My results suggest substantially lower markups.

7.5.7   Klette

Klette (1999) extends Hall's approach to allow for variable returns to scale, and tests the extended model against plant-level data taken covering Norwegian manufacturing from 1980 to 1990. The results suggest that 7 of the 13 industries for which the model appears to be well specified have small (ratio of price to marginal cost about 1.05) and statistically significant degrees of market power. Markups are not different from one for the remaining industries. The null hypothesis of constant returns to scale cannot be rejected for any of the industries studied.

7.5.8   Reprise

The Solow residual literature was developed by macroeconomists. It presents some innovative techniques, and to the extent that its results should be taken seriously, they seem to confirm the findings of industrial economists. The level of aggregation at which the techniques have been applied relegates most empirical applications to the category of finger exercises.

In contrast to Solow residual analysis, largely at the two-digit industry level, industrial economists increasingly question the use of four-digit industry samples (Shepherd, 2000, p. 249), and turn to micro-level data for single industries. Klette (1999) shows that Solow residual analysis can be applied to micro-level data, and for industrial economics at least this is no doubt the way forward for Solow residual analysis.

7.6   VALIDITY CHECKS

Early conjectural models (Iwata, 1974; Appelbaum, 1979, 1982; Roberts, 1984) estimated both the demand and the supply sides of the model. The second, NEIO, wave of conjectural models, anxious to avoid use of accounting cost data, specified models within the context of which it is possible to estimate price–cost margins without using cost data. This methodology is now itself the subject of investigation.

Genesove and Mullin (1998a) are able to measure the marginal cost of refined sugar directly, relying on the fact that there is a fixed-coefficient input–output relationship between raw sugar and refined sugar and good information about other costs. They estimate four alternative specifications of the demand function and combine these estimates with the direct measure of marginal cost to obtain direct measures of the industry average elasticity-adjusted Lerner index:

$$\frac{P - c'_i}{P}\varepsilon = (1 + \lambda_i)s_i. \tag{7.61}$$

The alternative measures are similar. For linear demand the result is 0.107, the value for a Cournot oligopoly with ten equally sized firms.

Point estimates of the same parameter using demand-side information only are lower, at about 0.0375. They present reasons for thinking that this estimate is biased downward, and indicate that they reject estimates consistent with Cournot behavior by nine or fewer firms. They conclude that use of direct cost information can improve estimates of structural models.

Corts (1999) applies the NEIO methodology to simulation data generated by a model of tacit collusion supported by trigger pricing (chapter 10). The resulting estimated conduct parameter is inaccurate, and Corts shows that such inaccuracy will be present unless the average and marginal response of margins to shifts in demand are the same.

Hyde and Perloff (1995) anticipate Corts' approach.[25] They carry out a comparative simulation analysis of three methods of measuring market power: the NEIO conjectural estimation, the Panzar–Rosse statistic, and Hall's method.[26] They find that the NEIO estimates work well if the assumed specification matches that used to generate the data, but not otherwise. The Hall method tends to underestimate markups when the simulated market is imperfectly competitive. The results that they report for the Panzar–Rosse statistic are mixed.[27]

7.7   EVENT STUDIES

7.7.1   Mullin et al.

The event-study methodology[28] seeks to draw conclusions about the market power and efficiency aspects of a discrete change in a market by analyzing the impact of the change on the stock market value of affected firms. The event study approach could in principle be applied to any well-defined change that affects the value of some types of firms differently, depending on whether the changes improves or worsens market performance. For example,

---

[25] See also the comments by Boyer (1996) and Cairns (1996). The former advocates the use of reduced-form estimation, the latter favors some return to the use of accounting data.

[26] Hyde and Perloff also attempt to apply the three approaches to three Standard Industrial Classification four-digit industries, with limited success.

[27] As Hyde and Perloff remark (1995, p. 477):

It is not obvious how to conduct a "fair" test of the Panzar–Rosse approach. If one estimates the true structural model, then the Panzar–Rosse test has the properties that they show analytically. On the other hand, if one estimates the true structural model there is no need to conduct their test as one has an estimate of the actual market structure.

[28] See Eckbo (1983), Stillman (1983), and Eckbo and Wier (1985).

consider the possible impacts of a merger:

- if a merger makes it easier for all firms in the industry to tacitly collude, then the merger should increase the value of the firms involved and also the value of other firms in the industry
- if a merger increases the efficiency of the firms involved, then the merger will increase their value and reduce the value of their rivals

It follows that by examining the impact of a merger on the stock-market value of firms in the industry, one can get an indication whether the merger was perceived by financial markets as improving market performance or worsening market performance.

Requirements for the use of this approach are that there be sharp, well-defined events, that one can be reasonably certain that information about events has not leaked out in advance, and that financial markets are well enough developed so that one can be confident of having satisfactory measures of the value of firms being studied.

Mullin et al. (1995) note also that a merger would affect the profitability of customers:

- a merger that increases efficiency will increase the value of the customers of the post-merger firm
- a merger that increases market power will decrease the value of the customers of the post-merger firm

They examine the impact of the formation of the United States Steel Corporation and steps in the US government antitrust challenge to the merger on the values of steel producers and of railway firms, major publicly traded purchasers of steel in this period.

The equations that are estimated are based on the capital asset pricing model. They are

$$R_{it} - R_{ft} = \alpha_i + \beta_i(R_{mt} - R_{ft}) + \sum \delta_{is} D_{st} + \varepsilon_{it}, \qquad (7.62)$$

where R_{it} is the rate of return from holding common stock in firm i in week t, R_{mt} is the rate of return on the market portfolio[29] at time t, R_{ft} is the rate of return on a risk-free asset at time t, and D_{st} is a dummy variable with value 1 if an event occurs in week s.

The model is estimated using weekly data covering the period January 8, 1910 – April 4, 1910 for all independent steel producers and street railways traded on the New York stock exchange. They examine 13 distinct events that occurred along the course of the landmark antitrust case. Results for the impact of major events in the antitrust case on the stock price of railroads suggest that breaking up US Steel would have improved market performance, lowering steel prices and left railroads better off.

---

[29] The 50 stocks in the *New York Times* index.

Table 7.12 Cotterill retail food price equations

Intercept	CR4	MS	MS/CR4	IND	SF	$(SF)^2$	R^2
93.277	0.167			1.196	−0.381	0.0127	0.411
	(2.70)			(1.16)	(0.95)	(0.86)	
109.169		0.061		2.128	−0.821	0.0274	0.547
		(4.19)		(2.28)	(2.37)	(2.13)	
99.36	0.089		0.052	1.952	−0.678	0.0226	0.564
	(1.49)		(3.02)	(2.07)	(1.85)	(1.69)	

Dependent variable, price index; $CR4$ = four-firm index of supermarket seller concentration; MS = market share; IND = dummy variable with value one for an independent supermarket, 0 for member of a supermarket chain; SF = thousands of square feet of selling area; other variables with insignificant coefficients not reported here; t-statistics in parentheses.
Source: Cotterill, 1986

7.8 PRICE VERSUS RATE OF RETURN

Part of the empirical renaissance is the analysis of the determinants of price rather than the rate of return. In part, this line of research is a natural consequence of the shift in interest from cross-section work to studies of single industries.

In part, it is motivated by a desire to carry out tests of structure–conduct–performance relationships that are less vulnerable to the criticisms leveled at empirical studies of the determinants of profitability.[30]

7.8.1 Retail prices

Food 1

Cotterill (1986) estimates equations explaining differences across supermarkets in an index of food prices in 18 local geographic markets in Vermont. His work makes clear that the industry price study shares some of the advantages of the industry profitability or price–cost margin study, in that it is possible to tailor the specification of the estimating equations to control for very particular aspects of market structure. As shown in table 7.12, Cotterill includes variables measuring floor space and indicating whether or not a supermarket is part of a chain as explanatory variables.[31]

---

[30] Weiss (1989); see also Weiss (1985). In addition to the studies discussed below, see Geithman et al. (1981).

[31] Newmark (1990) examines the relation between the retail price of a basket of grocery items and market concentration for a sample of 14 US cities. He finds a negative impact of market concentration on price. It is not clear whether or not Newmark mixes data from supermarkets and grocery stores.

From the first equation in table 7.12, if a four-firm seller concentration ratio is used as an index of market structure, it has a significant positive coefficient.[32] So does market share, if it is used as an index of market structure. These results are qualitatively the same as those of profitability studies that use firm-level data.

The really interesting question is what results are obtained if market concentration and market share both appear as explanatory variables. Unfortunately, Cotterill does not report results for an equation including both the four-firm seller concentration ratio and market share. However, he reports what is very nearly the same specification using the four-firm seller concentration ratio as a concentration index.

The third equation in table 7.12 includes both $CR4$ and market share divided by $CR4$ as explanatory variables. Since $CR4 = 100$ in 14 of the 18 local markets studied by Cotterill, $MS/CR4$ is very close to $MS/100$. In the third equation, the coefficient of $CR4$ is positive but statistically insignificant. $MS/CR4$ has a significant positive coefficient.

These results are similar to those of profitability studies that include seller concentration and market share as explanatory variables. Overall, Cotterill's results suggest that retail supermarkets in concentrated markets are able to exercise some market power, and that this result is more related to firm-specific market power than to tacit collusion.

Food 2

Marion (1989) discusses the work of Marion et al. (1979a,b). Price data are for a basket of 94 grocery products. Observations are for 36 firms in 32 US Standard Metropolitan Statistical Areas. Marion et al. explore a number of specifications relating market concentration and market share to price, always controlling for various firm and market characteristics. A typical result is

$$P = 90.16 + 24.730HERF + 9.968MS + \cdots, \qquad R^2 = 0.61$$
$$(10.748) \qquad (5.112) \qquad\qquad\qquad\qquad (7.63)$$

(where the numbers in parentheses are t-statistics).

Market share, MS, has a significant positive effect on price. This is evidence of firm-specific market power. Over and above this effect, prices are significantly higher in concentrated markets, which is consistent with the joint exercise of market power in oligopoly.

Gasoline

Marvel (1989) reports a number of analyses of the retail price of gasoline. For a sample referring to 22 US cities, the equation explaining the average minimum price of regular gasoline over the period 1964–71 is

$$P = 0.186 + 807HERF + \cdots$$
$$(7.36) \qquad (4.84) \qquad\qquad\qquad\qquad (7.64)$$

---

[32] Substantially more significant estimates are obtained if a Herfindahl index is used in place of $CR4$ as a concentration measure.

Table 7.13 Coefficients of
number-of-bidder dummy variables, US
Offshore Oil Auctions, 1954–71; t-statistics in
parentheses

Bidders	Coefficient	t-statistic
1	−3.03	(17.82)
2	−2.46	(13.67)
3	−1.99	(9.95)
4	−1.63	(8.15)
5	−1.16	(5.52)
6	−0.95	(4.32)
7	−0.87	(3.95)
8	−0.42	(1.75)
9	−0.53	(2.30)
10	−0.20	(0.83)
11	−0.09	(0.35)

Source: Brannman et al., 1987, table 1

(where t-statistics are in parentheses and variables not reported here control for differences in market structure). Market concentration therefore has a significant positive impact on minimum price. The impact of concentration on maximum prices is less significant than in (7.64), but remains positive. The impact of concentration on the price of premium gasoline is qualitatively similar to the impact of concentration on the price of regular gasoline.

Auctions

Auctions are an especially favorable subject for the analysis of concentration–price relationships. Many of the measurement issues that arise elsewhere in empirical industrial economics do not arise when auction prices are the dependent variable. Prices are measured exactly, the number of bidders is known with certainty, and the number of bidders is an appropriate measure of market concentration.

Brannman et al. (1987) analyze the relationship between the number of bidders and the winning price for bond, oil, and timber auctions.[33] For each of six data sets, they estimate a regression explaining the winning bid as a function of dummy variables that take the value 1 as the number of bidders passes from 1 to 11 and other variables designed to control for product and market characteristics. The coefficient of the dummy variable D_i measures the difference between the winning bid if there are i bidders and the winning bid if there are 12 or more bidders.

Typical results for auctions for offshore oil leases over the period 1954–71 are reproduced in table 7.13. Winning bids with 10 or 11 bidders do not differ significantly from winning

[33] See also Hansen (1985).

bids if there are 12 or more bidders. Coefficients of other dummy variables are significantly negative. Winning bids with one to nine bidders are significantly less than winning bids if there are 12 or more bidders. Similar results are found for the other auctions examined by Brannman et al. (1987). In auction markets, buyers pay lower prices the fewer the number of buyers.

Fulton fish market

Graddy (1995) analyzes the price of whiting at the Fulton fish market. The market appears to have all the characteristics of a perfectly competitive market except one, complete and perfect information (Graddy, 1995, p. 77): "Although it is quite easy because of the centralized location for a buyer to ask different sellers for a price, sellers are discreet when naming a price. A particular price is for a particular customer."

Graddy finds evidence of systematic price discrimination: buyers of Asian ethnicity pay about 7 percent less than white buyers, all else equal. She also estimates a conjectural derivative parameter. Point estimates suggest some joint exercise of market power, but the estimate is imprecise. Neither the assumption of perfect competition nor the assumption of joint profit maximization can be rejected (although the prior finding that price discrimination takes place is sufficient to rule out perfect competition).

7.8.2   Reservations

Econometric studies of structure–conduct–price relationships are a valuable addition to industrial economists' collection of evidence on structure–conduct–performance relationships. They avoid the efficiency criticism leveled by Demsetz at studies of profitability and price–cost margins. But otherwise it seems doubtful that structure–conduct–price studies rest on a firmer theoretical or empirical foundation than structure–conduct–profitability studies.

Theory

Empirical models of structure–conduct–price relations tend to be specified using the same sort of seat-of-the-pants model justifications that characterize 1970s cross-section profitability studies. This does not mean that the specifications are incorrect. It does mean that they have failed to take advantage of the advances in modeling market performance since that time. This is surprising, since every model of profitability implies a model of price, and vice versa.

Suppose that, on the basis of some economic model, one has a price–cost margin equation

$$\frac{p - c}{p} = f(x), \tag{7.65}$$

where x is a vector of explanatory variables. The model may come from the structure–conduct–performance framework, from a formal oligopoly model, or from a model tailored to a specific industry.

In any event, the price–cost margin equation (7.65) implies a price equation

$$p = \frac{c}{1 - f(x)}. \tag{7.66}$$

It is evident that there is a one-to-one mapping between price models and price–cost margin models. Similar mappings can be worked out if one starts with a model of the rate of return on assets or any of the other common measures of profitability. In principle, if one has a model of profitability, one also has a model of price.

Empirical

As noted above, one of the advantages of auction data is that prices of specific products are measured exactly. In many other price studies, what is tested is often a price index or the total price of a representative basket of goods. Results are therefore dependent on the way in which the price index is calculated or the composition of the basket of goods. It is not obvious that measurement problems in price studies are less serious than measurement problems in profitability studies.

7.9 THE PERSISTENCE OF PROFITS

Various strands of the empirical structure–conduct–performance literature suggest the need for explicitly dynamic models of firm and industry profitability. One such strand is Brozen's (1971) criticism of Bain (1951, 1956) on the ground that the profitability observed in Bain's samples was a short-run disequilibrium phenomenon. There is no explicit demonstration, however, that the sample used by Brozen is any more or less in long-run equilibrium than the samples used by Bain. Indeed, the static models used by Bain and Brozen are not really suited to address the equilibrium versus disequilibrium question.

Another such strand is the argument, going back to Bain (1956) and recently re-emphasized by Baumol et al. (1982), that market performance depends in an essential way on the importance of potential entry. The problem this raises for econometric work is that potential entry is an unobservable variable. Indeed, the discussion of actual entry in chapter 11 reveals that most entry is short and unsuccessful. This suggests that even actual entry, of the kind that affects the performance of incumbents, is an unobservable variable.

To deal with these issues, and following Mueller (1977, 1986), a cottage industry of sorts[34] has used a simple autoregressive model[35]

$$\pi_{it} = \alpha_i + \lambda_i \pi_{i,t-1} + \mu_{it} \tag{7.67}$$

[34] See Pakes (1987), Geroski and Mueller (1990), and Geroski (1990). See also Waring (1996).

[35] Geroski and Mueller (1990, p. 189); see also Mueller (1986, p. 13). This is the same sort of lagged adjustment model that is commonly used to model industrial concentration; see section 6.4.1.

Table 7.14   Average long-run profit and speed-of-adjustment parameters, Mueller (1986) sample. Subsample 1 is the 100 firms with the highest average 1950–2 profit rates, subsample 2 the 100 firms with the next highest average 1950–2 profit rates, and so on

	1	2	3	4	5	6
π_{ip}	0.305	0.115	0.005	−0.102	−0.154	−0.189
λ_i	0.566	0.469	0.514	0.483	0.469	0.454

Source: Mueller, 1986, table 2.2

to examine the intertemporal and implied long-run behavior of profitability. In some studies, π_{it} is the profit of firm i in period t. In others, t is the deviation of the profit of firm i in period t from some measure of average profitability. λ_i is a speed-of-adjustment parameter, which lies between 0 and 1. The closer λ_i is to one, the more rapidly firm i's profits converge to their long-run level. μ_{it} is a random error term.

The long-run profitability level (alternatively, the long-run deviation of firm profitability from average profitability) implied by (7.67) is

$$\pi_{ip} = \frac{\alpha_i}{1 - \lambda_i}. \tag{7.68}$$

7.9.1   The United States

Mueller

Mueller (1986) estimates a version of (7.67) for each of 600 firms that were among the 1000 largest US manufacturing companies in 1950 and/or 1972 and for which a complete set of annual data was available for the period 1950–72 inclusive.[36] He measures profitability as profit after taxes plus interest payments divided by the value of assets. He estimates (7.67) for fractional deviations of firm profitability from average profitability. A positive estimate of π_{ip} therefore implies a long-run rate of return on assets persistently above average. A negative estimate of π_{ip} implies a long-run rate of return on assets persistently below average.

A summary of results, reported for firms ranked according to the 1950–2 profitability, appears in table 7.14. This summary suggests persistent profitability differences across firms. The 100 most profitable firms in 1950–2 have estimated long-run profitability levels some 30 percent above the average for the whole sample. The 100 least profitable firms in 1950–2 have estimated long-run profitability rates nearly 20 per cent below the average for the whole sample. Average estimates of π_{ip} fall with average initial profitability.[37]

---

[36] See also Connolly and Schwartz (1985), Glick and Ehrbar (1990), Coate (1991), and Keating (1991).
[37] On the stability of profitability of subsamples, see Schohl (1990).

The average estimates of λ are all around 0.5. By repeated substitution from (7.67), we obtain

$$\pi_{i,t+\tau} = (1 - \lambda_i^{t+\tau})\pi_{ip} + \lambda_i^{t+1}\pi_{i,t-1}. \tag{7.69}$$

An estimated value of $\lambda = 0.5$ implies fairly rapid convergence of profits to long-run levels. For $\lambda = 0.5$, the coefficient of $\pi_{i,t-1}$ in the expression for $\pi_{i,t+4}$ is only $\frac{1}{32}$. This is a much more rapid convergence to long-run levels than has been found for seller concentration. The claim that cross-sectional studies pick up mainly short-run variations in profitability around a competitive long-run level appears to be unfounded.

Coate

Using a time series cross-section sample of observations on 48 US four-digit SIC industries for the period 1958–82, Coate (1989) estimates the following lagged adjustment price–cost margin equation:[38]

$$PCM = \cdots + \underset{(3.11)}{0.0250GR} + \underset{(2.24)}{0.0369CR4} + \underset{(37.5)}{0.766PCM_{-1}}, \qquad \bar{R}^2 = 0.9268 \tag{7.70}$$

(where intercept terms differ from industry to industry, GR is the growth rate of industry output, and t-statistics are in parentheses).

Market concentration and industry growth both have the expected significant positive effects. Convergence to long-run profitability levels is again estimated to be rapid, although not as rapid as implied by the firm-level estimates. With annual data, the coefficient of PCM_{-1} in the equation for PCM_{+4} is $(0.766)^5 = 0.26$.

7.9.2   France, West Germany, and the United Kingdom

Geroski and Jacquemin

Geroski and Jacquemin (1988) estimate a version of (7.67) in deviation form,[39]

$$\pi_t - \bar{\pi}_t = \alpha_0 + \alpha_1\bar{\pi}_t + \lambda_1 (\pi_{t-1} - \bar{\pi}_{t-1}) + \mu_t, \tag{7.71}$$

for firms in three European Community member states.[40] π_t is firm profit in period t and $\bar{\pi}_t$ is average profit in period t.

---

[38] The coefficient of lagged PCM is smaller for consumer good industries (0.636) than for producer good industries (0.786). The coefficient of GR is negative and insignificant for consumer good industries, 0.357 and significant for producer good industries. The coefficient of $CR4$ is positive and significant in industries where $CR4$ is increasing or decreasing, but statistically insignificant where $CR4$ is stable. See Coate (1989) for details.

[39] Geroski and Jacquemin test for second- and third-order lags in profit adjustment. For most firms, evidence suggested a first-order lagged adjustment process, and it is these estimates that we discuss.

[40] For additional evidence on the UK, see Cubbin and Geroski (1987). See also Odagiri and Yamawaki (1986) (Japan) and Contini (1989) (Italy).

Table 7.15   Average persistence of profits results for France, Germany, and the UK

	α_0	α_1	λ_1	π_{LR}
France	−0.022	0.021	0.459	0.022
Germany	0.009	−0.089	0.461	0.110
UK	0.188	−0.930	0.520	0.219

Source: Geroski and Jacquemin, 1988

If $\alpha_1 \neq 0$ in (7.71), the deviation of firms' profitability from the average varies over the business cycle. Setting $\pi_t - \bar{\pi}_t$ equal to $\pi_{t-1} - \bar{\pi}_{t-1}$ in (7.71) gives the implied long-run level of profitability:

$$\pi_{LR} = \frac{\alpha_0 + (1 - \lambda + \alpha_1)\bar{\pi}_{LR}}{1 - \lambda}. \tag{7.72}$$

Average estimates for 55 French, 28 West German, and 51 UK firms are reproduced in table 7.15. Values of α_0 for most UK firms were significantly different from zero. Values of α_1 were significantly different from zero for only one-third of the French firms and 10 percent of the German firms. Similarly, estimates of α_1 were significantly different from zero for all UK firms, for one-third of the French firms, and for 20 percent of the German firms. Evidence for persistent divergences of firm profitability from the average is much stronger for the UK than for France or Germany.

Estimates of the long-run level of profitability point in the same direction. These estimates are larger for the UK than for either France or Germany.

Estimated values of the speed-of-adjustment parameter λ are somewhat less than $\frac{1}{2}$ for France and Germany, and somewhat more than $\frac{1}{2}$ for the UK. As with Mueller's US sample, adjustment to long-run levels is fairly rapid. Apparently, adjustment is less rapid for the UK than for the other two countries. Geroski and Jacquemin report that for many German and French companies the estimated value of λ was not significantly different from zero. This implies adjustment to equilibrium within one year.

Geroski and Jacquemin also report regressions explaining differences in 98 estimated values of α_0 and λ_1 as a function of various firm and market characteristics. α_0 is significantly larger, all else equal, for UK firms and the larger the share of exports in a firm's sales. These factors therefore tend to raise the firm's long-run profitability level. The speed-of-adjustment parameter λ_1 is larger (adjustment is slower) for UK firms, for more specialized firms, and for firms that operate in less concentrated industries.

Goddard and Wilson

Goddard and Wilson (1999) analyze the persistence of profits for a sample of 335 UK firms over the period 1972–91. Their results suggest that the methodology of previous studies tends to underestimate λ_1 and the rate of convergence of profit to the long-run equilibrium rate. The average estimate of λ_1 for their sample is 0.59. They also reject the hypothesis that profit rates of different firms converge to the same level: there are persistent profit differences across the firms in their sample.

7.10 NOT THE LAST WORD

The danger that industrial economists will rely on any one methodology for the empirical analysis of market power seems behind us. There is now a range of diverse methodologies to investigate market performance: studies of single markets using accounting cost data, studies of single markets using output and revenue data, the analysis of time-series data, studies of the determinants of price, event studies, fully dynamic models, and others. No one of these is immune from criticism. Broadly speaking, these diverse methodologies yield consistent results, tending to support the hypotheses advanced by the structure–conduct–performance school.

CHAPTER EIGHT

STRATEGIC BEHAVIOR: INVESTMENT IN ENTRY DETERRENCE

Our analysis of strategic behavior leads us to the conjecture ... that the market equilibrium will converge on the extreme that yields the largest profits that sitting firms can earn without attracting entry.

Archibald, Eaton, and Lipsey (1986, p. 5)

8.1 INTRODUCTION

Strategic behavior is the investment of resources to affect the choices that are open to rivals. There is scope for strategic behavior only in oligopoly.

In monopoly, there is a single supplier and entry is impossible. A monopolist has no rivals, actual or potential, and need not contemplate strategic behavior.

A firm in a perfectly competitive market has no need to take account of rivals or rivals' behavior, but for a different reason. A firm in a perfectly competitive market is a price-taker. Nothing rivals do can deny a firm in a perfectly competitive industry the opportunity to sell all it wants at the market price; no investment a firm in a perfectly competitive industry makes can gain a firm the opportunity to sell at anything other than the market price. There is no scope for strategic behavior in a perfectly competitive market, because there is no payoff to strategic behavior.

In oligopoly, there are few enough suppliers so that the profits of each firm depend on the actions of all firms, and some or all firms are aware of this mutual interdependence. In this context, oligopoly includes the cases of a single incumbent firm facing the possibility of entry, and the analysis of strategic behavior includes cases in which an incumbent firm makes some costly investment in order to deter future entry. Strategies examined in the literature have included output expansion (limit pricing), predatory pricing, brand proliferation, advertising, technology choice, research and development, and others.[1]

---

[1] For surveys, see Vickers (1985), Encaoua et al. (1986), Gilbert (1986, 1989), Neven (1989), and Ordover and Saloner (1989).

Another avenue for strategic behavior arises if consumers incur costs when they switch suppliers. In such markets, an incumbent firm may find it profitable to expand sales, tying customers to its brand of the product and leaving fewer customers available for potential entrants. The strategic behavior literature also examines the possibility that incumbents may deter entry by forcing higher costs on rivals, rather than accepting higher costs themselves.

8.2 EXCESS CAPACITY

The modern literature on the strategic use of excess capacity begins with Spence (1977), who extends the basic model of quantity-setting oligopoly to include an additional decision variable: capacity, an upper limit on output that rivals believe will be fully utilized in the event of entry. Dixit (1980) alters the specification of the Spence model in two fundamental ways, and explores the consequences of imposing the requirement that the threat to utilize capacity be credible, in this altered model.

8.2.1 Excess capacity committed to use in the event of entry

Spence (1977) develops a model in which technology requires that capacity be installed in advance of production. Once installed, capacity imposes an absolute upper limit on output (a specification later adopted by Kreps and Scheinkman, 1983). A single incumbent firm, the sole supplier of its market, is able to install capacity before potential entrants make their entry decision. Potential entrants believe that if entry occurs the incumbent will fully utilize the installed capacity. Spence investigates the conditions under which the incumbent precludes entry by installing capacity that is not used except in the event of entry.

A linear version of Spence's cost function is

$$C(q) = F + rk + cq. \tag{8.1}$$

F is fixed costs (other than capital costs). r is the unit rental cost of capital services, k is capacity, and c is the unit variable (and marginal) cost of factors other than capital. Capacity is measured in the same units as output, so that one unit of capacity allows the production of one unit of output. Production is subject to the constraint $q \leq k$: output cannot exceed installed capacity.[2]

Because the incumbent installs capacity in advance, the cost of capacity is a fixed cost for the incumbent. The marginal cost of the incumbent is c per unit, over the output range $0 \leq q \leq k$. We rule out strategic behavior by the entrant by assumption. If entry occurs, the

---

[2] Let the technology be described by a Stone–Geary modification of a fixed coefficient production function:

$$q = \min\left(\frac{K - \bar{K}}{a_K}, \frac{L - \bar{L}}{a_L}\right).$$

Cost minimization implies use of the input levels $K = \bar{K} + a_K q$ and $L = \bar{L} + a_L q$. Substitution in the expression for cost, $C(q) = wL + rK$, gives a cost function of form (8.1), with $F = w\bar{L} + r\bar{K}$, $c = wa_L + ra_K$. If capital is measured so that $a_K = 1$, then output cannot exceed $k = K - \bar{K}$.

entrant installs capacity sufficient for its chosen output.[3] The marginal cost of the potential entrant, therefore, is $c + r$ per unit.

Now consider the decision of a firm considering entry to a market with the linear inverse demand function

$$p = a - b(q_1 + q_2). \tag{8.2}$$

The subscript 1 denotes the incumbent firm and the subscript 2 denotes the potential entrant.

The incumbent has capacity k. The potential entrant believes that this capacity will be fully used in the post-entry market. Under these circumstances, the profit-maximizing potential entrant selects q_2 to maximize its expected post-entry profit,

$$\Pi_2 = [p - (c + r)] q_2 - F = b (S_{c+r} - k - q_2) q_2 - F, \tag{8.3}$$

if it produces at all (where $S_{c+r} = [a - (c + r)]/b$ is the quantity that would be demanded if price were $c + r$). The potential entrant produces positive output only if the resulting profit is positive.

Maximization of (8.3) gives the equation of the entrant's best-response function,

$$q_2 = \tfrac{1}{2} (S_{c+r} - k), \tag{8.4}$$

provided that the entrant's expected profit at this output is positive. Otherwise, the profit-maximizing output is $q_2 = 0$. Note that it is firm 1's capacity (k) that appears in the entrant's best-response function, because the entrant expects that if entry occurs the incumbent will expand output to capacity.

With best-response function (8.4), the entrant's expected post-entry profit is

$$\Pi_2 = \frac{b}{4} (S_{c+r} - k)^2 - F. \tag{8.5}$$

The entrant expects lower profit, the greater the incumbent's pre-entry capacity, k. Setting $\Pi_2 = 0$ in (8.5) and solving for k gives an expression for the entry-deterring level of capacity:

$$\bar{k} = S_{c+r} - 2\sqrt{\frac{F}{b}}. \tag{8.6}$$

The incumbent maximizes profit subject to two constraints. The first constraint is imposed by the technology: production cannot exceed capacity. The second constraint is strategic: capacity must be at least enough to deter entry. Formally, the incumbent's constrained

---

[3] If the cost of capacity is sunk, one can conceive of strategic investment by an entrant, creating conditions by a large initial investment that rule out some strategies, in equilibrium, by the incumbent. In situations involving entry by a large multiproduct firm in a niche market, such behavior may be plausible. For models in which an entrant picks capacity strategically, see Ware (1984), Saloner (1985), Arvan (1986), and Bagwell and Ramey (1996).

optimization problem is to

$$\max_{q_1, k} (p - c)q_1 - rk - F \qquad \text{such that } q_1 \le k, k_1 \ge \bar{k}. \tag{8.7}$$

Necessary conditions for the solution to this problem are the Kuhn–Tucker conditions to maximize the Lagrangian

$$\mathcal{L} = b(S_c - q_1)q_1 - rk - F + \lambda(k - q_1) + \mu(k - \bar{k}), \tag{8.8}$$

with respect to capacity k and output q_1, where λ and μ are Lagrangian multipliers, and $S_c = (a - c)/b$ is the quantity that would be demanded if price were equal to c.
$\mu = -\partial \mathcal{L}/\partial \bar{k}$ is the shadow cost to the firm, in terms of lost profit, of deterring entry – the reduction in profit from a small increase in $\bar{k}$. $\lambda = \partial \mathcal{L}/\partial k - \mu$ is the shadow cost of capacity, over and above the shadow cost of deterring entry.

The Kuhn–Tucker conditions that characterize the solution to the incumbent's constrained optimization problem are as follows:

$$\frac{\partial \mathcal{L}}{\partial q_1} = b(S_2 - 2q_1) - \lambda \equiv 0 \qquad \Longleftrightarrow \qquad q_1 = \tfrac{1}{2}\left(S_c - \frac{\lambda}{b}\right); \tag{8.9}$$

$$\frac{\partial \mathcal{L}}{\partial k} = -r + \lambda + \mu \equiv 0 \qquad \Longleftrightarrow \qquad r = \lambda + \mu; \tag{8.10}$$

$$\frac{\partial \mathcal{L}}{\partial \lambda} = k - q_1 \ge 0, \qquad \lambda(k - q_1) \equiv 0, \qquad \lambda \ge 0; \tag{8.11}$$

$$\frac{\partial \mathcal{L}}{\partial \mu} = k - \bar{k} \ge 0, \qquad \mu(k - \bar{k}) \equiv 0, \qquad \mu \ge 0. \tag{8.12}$$

The solution defined by conditions (8.9)–(8.12) falls into one of three cases, depending on the size of fixed costs. We begin with the case in which F is quite large, and work out the way the solution changes as F becomes smaller.

Case 1: blocked entry, no excess capacity

If F is sufficiently large, the incumbent does not need to maintain excess capacity to deter entry. If unconstrained monopoly output requires a capacity sufficient to deter entry, then there is no effective threat of entry. Formally, if the incumbent maintains no excess capacity, its marginal cost is $c + r$. A monopolist with marginal cost $c + r$ produces an output $q_1 = S_{c+r}/2$. If capacity $k = q_1 = S_{c+r}/2 \ge \bar{k}$, the incumbent is able to produce monopoly output without attracting entry. If the profit-maximizing capacity level k is greater than or equal to $\bar{k}$, then (8.12) implies $\mu = 0$. If $\mu = 0$, then (8.10) implies $\lambda = r$. If $\lambda = r$, then (8.9) implies that $q_1 = S_{c+r}/2$.

There is an implied consistency condition that must be met for the solution to fall in case 1: installed capacity $k = q_1$ must be greater than or equal to $\bar{k}$, the entry-deterring capacity level. Using $q_1 = S_{c+r}/2$ and $\bar{k} = S_{c+r} - 2\sqrt{F/b}$, the consistency condition is

$$F \geq \frac{b}{16}S_{c+r}^2. \tag{8.13}$$

If F satisfies (8.13), the incumbent's optimal strategy is in case 1. For example, take $a = 10$ and $b = c = r = 1$. Then the inverse demand function is $p = 10 - (q_1 + q_2)$, and $S_{c+r} = 8$. Entry is blocked – the incumbent's profit-maximizing strategy lies in case 1 – provided that $F \geq 4$.

Case 2: entry deterred, no excess capacity

The entry-deterring capacity level $\bar{k}$ rises as F falls. If F falls below the level given by the right-hand side of (8.13), fixed cost is insufficient to deter entry if the incumbent produces the monopoly output. There are then two ways to deter entry. The incumbent could expand output above the unconstrained profit-maximizing level; the cost of expanding output is lost profit. Alternatively, the incumbent could maintain excess capacity, at a cost of r per unit. For modest expansions of output above the monopoly level, lost profit is less than the cost of excess capacity, and for values of F that are just below $bS_{c+r}^2/16$, the incumbent prefers to deter entry by expanding output. In this intermediate case, $k = \bar{k} = q_1$. Substitute $\lambda = r - \mu$ from (8.10) into (8.9) to eliminate λ and express q_1 in terms of μ; then use the definition of $\bar{k}$, equation (8.6), to express the condition $\bar{k} = q_1$ as

$$S_{c+r} - 2\sqrt{\frac{F}{b}} = \frac{1}{2}\left(S_{c+r} + \frac{\mu}{b}\right). \tag{8.14}$$

Solve (8.14) for the value of μ, the shadow cost of maintaining capacity sufficient to deter entry when there is no excess capacity:

$$\mu = bS_{c+r} - 4\sqrt{bF}. \tag{8.15}$$

For consistency, the value of μ given by (8.15) must be nonnegative (this is part of (8.12)). But in case 2, $F < b(S_{c+r}/4)^2$. This is sufficient to make the value of μ given by (8.15) positive.

Using (8.15) and (8.10), we obtain the value of λ, the shadow cost of capacity:

$$\lambda = 2r - bS_c + 4\sqrt{bF}. \tag{8.16}$$

From (8.11), another consistency condition for case 2 is that $\lambda \geq 0$. This provides a lower limit for F in case 2, while (8.13) provides an upper limit. Using (8.14), (8.16), and (8.11), the incumbent's optimal strategy is in case 2 as long as

$$\frac{b}{16}\left(S_{c+r} - \frac{r}{b}\right)^2 \leq F \leq \frac{b}{16}S_{c+r}^2. \tag{8.17}$$

If F is so small that the right-hand inequality in (8.17) is violated, the incumbent's constrained profit-maximizing choice falls out of case 2. For the example used to illustrate case 1 ($a = 10, b = c = r = 1$), $S_{c+r} - (r/b) = 7$, and the incumbent's profit-maximizing strategy is in case 2 for F in the range $3\frac{1}{16} \leq F < 4$.

Case 3: entry deterred with excess capacity

In case 2, the incumbent deters entry by expanding output and capacity together. The cost to the incumbent of deterring entry is the revenue lost as output expands and price falls. If the incumbent maintains excess capacity, the cost of deterring entry comes from the increase in average cost because fixed cost per unit of output, which includes the cost of idle capacity, increases. If F is sufficiently small, it becomes profitable for the incumbent to deter entry by maintaining some excess capacity, as well as through the expansion of output.

In case 3, $k = \bar{k} > q_1$; the firm maintains some excess capacity. By (8.11), $k > q_1$ means $\lambda = 0$. If $\lambda = 0$, (8.10) implies $\mu = r$. The cost to the firm of deterring entry is r per unit of excess capacity – this is the cost to the firm of maintaining the marginal unit of capacity that deters entry. Given that the firm maintains excess capacity, the shadow cost of capacity (λ) to the firm is zero. Thus in case 3 $\lambda = 0$ and $\mu = r$. Then (8.9) implies that $q_1 = S_c/2$, unconstrained monopoly output with marginal cost c, which is less than $k = \bar{k} = S_{c+r} - 2\sqrt{F/b}$.

In a limit quantity model, the incumbent must produce $q_1 = S_{c+r} - 2\sqrt{F/b}$ to deter entry. The resulting price would be $p_{\text{limit}} = c + r + \sqrt{bF}$. In case 3, price is $p_{\text{excap}} = c + bS_c/2$. It follows that if the incumbent deters entry by maintaining excess capacity, price is higher than the limit price. The difference in price is directly proportional to the amount of excess capacity:

$$p_{\text{excap}} - p_{\text{limit}} = b(\bar{k} - S_c/2). \tag{8.18}$$

8.2.2 Credible threats

Spence

A potential entrant might well regard the threat to expand output to capacity as empty if the incumbent would find it unprofitable to carry out the threat. Thus we should investigate whether it would be profitable, in the model, for an incumbent to expand output in the event of entry. Suppose that fixed costs are so small,

$$F \leq \frac{b}{16}\left(S_{c+r} - \frac{r}{b}\right)^2, \tag{8.19}$$

that the incumbent's entry deterrence strategy requires it to carry excess capacity. Suppose further that the incumbent installs the entry-deterring capacity level, $\bar{k} = S_{c+r} - 2\sqrt{F/b}$ (see (8.6)), but that the entrant comes in anyway.

In terms of figure 8.1, the incumbent finds itself at decision node D_3. It has threatened to expand output to capacity if entry occurs. If this threat is carried out, the entrant will earn a zero profit. From the equation of its best-response function, (8.4), the entrant's output would be $q_2 = \sqrt{F/b}$. Price would be

$$p_{\text{TH}} = c + r + \sqrt{bF}, \tag{8.20}$$

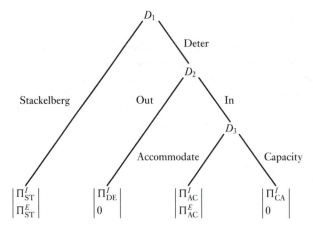

Figure 8.1 A game tree for the Spence entry deterrence game. ST denotes Stackelberg leadership payoffs; DE denotes deterrence payoffs; AC denotes accommodation payoffs; CA denotes capacity output payoffs.

and the incumbent's profit, at this price and producing at capacity $\bar{k}$, is

$$\Pi^I_{\text{TH}} = (r + \sqrt{bF})\bar{k} - r\bar{k} - F. \tag{8.21}$$

Knowing that the incumbent is a profit-maximizer, the entrant will expect the incumbent to carry out the threat to expand output to capacity only if it makes a greater profit by carrying out the threat than by accommodating entry.

To evaluate whether or not the incumbent would prefer to carry out the threat to expand output to capacity, we must specify the nature of post-entry competition. Many choices are possible. An obvious benchmark is to suppose that the incumbent acts as a Stackelberg leader in the post-entry market. The incumbent must have all the information that is usually assumed to be in the possession of the Stackelberg leader, since it is able to compute the entry-deterring capacity level. The incumbent is assumed to move first, by its choice of capacity, just as the Stackelberg leader is assumed to move first, by its choice of output.

The incumbent's marginal cost is c per unit; the entrant's marginal cost is $c + r$ per unit. Using the equation of the entrant's best-response curve, we find the equation of the residual demand curve facing the incumbent:

$$p = c + r + \tfrac{1}{2}S_{c+r} - \tfrac{1}{2}bq_1. \tag{8.22}$$

With marginal cost c per unit, the incumbent's profit-maximizing output and profit are

$$q^I_{\text{AC}} = \tfrac{1}{2}S_{c+r} + \frac{r}{b} \tag{8.23}$$

and

$$\Pi^I_{\text{AC}} = \frac{b}{2}\left(\tfrac{1}{2}S_{c+r} + \frac{r}{b}\right)^2 - r\bar{k} - F \tag{8.24}$$

respectively. Π^I_{AC} is always positive if the solution falls in case 3.

The incumbent finds it most profitable to accommodate entry if

$$\Pi_{AC}^I - \Pi_{TH}^I = 2b \left(\tfrac{1}{2} S_{c+r} - \tfrac{1}{2} \frac{r}{b} - \sqrt{\frac{F}{b}} \right)^2 \geq 0, \qquad (8.25)$$

a condition which is always met. For the range of fixed costs over which entry could be deterred by maintaining excess capacity in the Spence model, the Spence capacity leader would prefer not to deter entry if placed in the position of having to decide whether or not to do so.[4] In the Spence model, the threat to deter entry is not credible.

Since the Spence capacity leader would earn a greater profit by acting as a Stackelberg quantity leader than by expanding output to the entry-deterring capacity level if entry should occur, we ought to suspect that it would earn a still greater profit by not choosing to carry excess capacity in the first place if it had as an alternative the possibility of simply acting as a Stackelberg quantity leader from the beginning. This turns out to be the case; see Problem 8.2.

Dixit

Dixit (1980) alters the assumption that capacity is inflexible upward in the short run. Output cannot exceed capacity, but capacity can be expanded at will. Capacity does not impose an upper bound on output.

In addition, in the Dixit model the potential entrant is assumed to know that if entry occurs the incumbent will hold output constant (the Cournot behavioral assumption). Since the incumbent moves first, this allows the Dixit incumbent to act as a Stackelberg quantity leader.

In the Spence model, the entry decision depends on whether or not the entrant will make a profit if the incumbent expands output to capacity. In contrast, in the Dixit model, the entry decision depends on whether or not the potential entrant would make a profit in Cournot duopoly equilibrium.

Dixit's analysis lends itself to a graphical exposition (figure 8.2). For the entrant, marginal cost is $c + r$ per unit. Where the entrant's profit is positive, the entrant's best-response curve is a straight line connecting $(0, S_{c+r}/2)$ on the vertical axis with $(S_{c+r}, 0)$ on the horizontal axis.

Moving down the entrant's best-response curve from the vertical axis, the incumbent's output rises, the entrant's output falls, total output rises, and price falls. Since price falls and the entrant's output falls moving down the best-response curve, the entrant's profit also falls moving down the best-response curve. When the incumbent's output is so large that the entrant's profit is zero, the entrant's best-response output falls discontinuously to zero: the entrant remains only potential, staying out of the market.

---

[4] If the post-entry regime is Cournot duopoly, there is a range of fixed cost over which it is most profitable for the incumbent to expand output to capacity and deter entry.

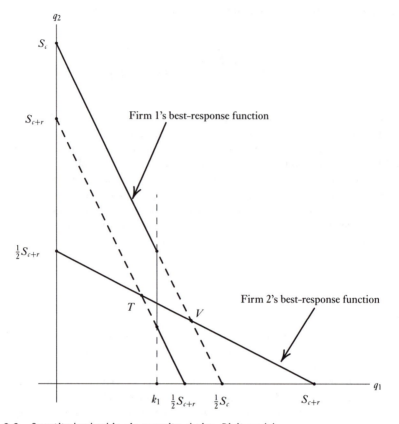

Figure 8.2 Quantity leadership via capacity choice, Dixit model.

The incumbent's best-response curve thus has two segments, depending on the size of installed capacity. With installed capacity k_1, the incumbent's cost function is

$$C(q_1) = \begin{cases} F + rk_1 + cq_1 & q_1 \leq k_1, \\ F + (r + c)q_1 & q_1 > k_1. \end{cases} \tag{8.26}$$

For output q_1 less than or equal to k_1, the incumbent's capital cost is fixed. Variable and marginal cost are both c per unit. Over this output range, the incumbent's best-response curve coincides with the straight line connecting $(0, S_c)$ on the vertical axis and $(S_c/2, 0)$ on the horizontal axis.[5]

To produce above installed capacity, the incumbent would need to expand capacity, at marginal cost r per unit. For $q_1 > k_1$, marginal cost is $c + r$ per unit. In this output range,

---

[5] To be precise, the incumbent would shut down for an output level $q_2 < S_c$. For q_2 above this level, the incumbent would not be able to cover its fixed costs.

the incumbent's best-response curve coincides with the straight line connecting $(0, S_{c+r})$ on the vertical axis and $(S_{c+r}/2, 0)$ on the horizontal axis.[6]

Thus there is a discontinuity in the incumbent's best-response function, at output level $q_1 = k_1$. The discontinuity reflects the fact that the incumbent's marginal cost is c per unit for $q_1 < k_1$ and $c + r$ for $q_1 > k_1$. By choice of k_1, the incumbent can determine the location of the discontinuity in its best-response curve. Within limits, it can determine the intersection of the two best-response curves. By choice of k_1, the incumbent can place the post-entry equilibrium anywhere along the segment TV of the entrant's best-response curve (figure 8.2). Over this range, by choice of capacity, the incumbent is able to act as a Stackelberg quantity leader.

The entrant's profit,

$$\Pi_2 = \frac{b}{4}(S_{c+r} - q_1)^2 - F, \tag{8.27}$$

falls as the post-entry equilibrium moves from T to V. Possible outcomes depend on the size of fixed costs, which determines whether or not the incumbent can drive the entrant's post-entry profit to zero.

CASE 1: BLOCKED ENTRY

Point T in figure 8.2 represents the Cournot duopoly equilibrium when both firms have marginal cost $c + r$ per unit. At point T, $q_1 = q_2 = S_{c+r}/3$. Substituting in (8.27), the entrant's profit at T is

$$\Pi_2(T) = \frac{b}{9}S_{c+r}^2 - F. \tag{8.28}$$

If F is so large that $\Pi_2(T) < 0$, the entrant will lose money anywhere along line segment TV. In this case entry is blocked; the incumbent has no need to maintain excess capacity to preclude entry.

In section 8.2.2 we used the parameters $a = 10$, $b = c = r = 1$ to illustrate the Spence model. For these values, entry is blocked in the Dixit model if $F \geq 7\frac{1}{9}$. Observe that F must be much larger to preclude entry in the Dixit model than in the Spence model. For entry to be blocked in the Dixit model, F must be so large that a Cournot duopolist would not earn a profit with the incumbent supplying one-third of the market. For entry to be blocked in the Spence model, F need only be large enough so that the post-entry price, with the incumbent producing the limit output $\bar{k}$, will not exceed the entrant's average cost.

CASE 2: ENTRY DETERRENCE POSSIBLE

Point V in figure 8.2 represents Cournot equilibrium if the incumbent has marginal cost c per unit, while the entrant has marginal cost $c + r$ per unit. At V, $q_1 = S_{c+r}/3 + 2r/3b$.

---

[6] In the Güth–Maggi model of section 3.11.2, capacity costs more if installed later in the game. In the Dixit model, the cost of a unit of capacity is the same at all stages of the game. In the Dixit model, a strategic effect arises because the cost of capacity that is installed early is fixed at the time the entrant makes its decision, while the cost of capacity that is installed later is variable.

Substituting in (8.27), the entrant's profit at V is

$$\Pi_2(V) = \frac{b}{9}\left(S_{c+r} - \frac{r}{b}\right)^2 - F. \tag{8.29}$$

Using (8.28) and (8.29), we find that if fixed cost F lies in the range

$$\frac{b}{9}\left(S_{c+r} - \frac{r}{b}\right)^2 \leq F \leq \frac{b}{9}S_{c+r}^2, \tag{8.30}$$

the entrant will make a positive profit at T but a loss at V. For the parameters $a = 10$, $b = c = r = 1$, case 2 of the Dixit model occurs for $5\frac{4}{9} \leq F \leq 7\frac{1}{9}$. The entrant's profit is positive at T, falls as q_1 rises, and is negative at V. It follows that in case 2, there is a value of q_1 which just drives Π_2 to zero.

If the incumbent produces this level of output, the entrant is at the shutdown point on its best-response curve. Case 2 of the Dixit model occurs when the shutdown point on the entrant's best-response curve lies between points T and V. By setting capacity k_1 so that the vertical segment in the incumbent's best-response curve crosses the entrant's best-response curve at this point of discontinuity, the incumbent can deter entry.[7]

Although the incumbent has the option of deterring entry, it may prefer not to exercise it. The incumbent will select the strategy – entry-limitation or quantity leadership – which yields it the greatest profit.

If the incumbent chooses to deter entry, it will have no need to maintain excess capacity. If the incumbent allows entry, it acts as a quantity leader and by its choice of capacity places equilibrium at the point along TV that yields it the greatest profit. Again, it will have no need to maintain excess capacity.[8]

CASE 3: ENTRY LIMITATION IMPOSSIBLE

The entrant's Cournot duopoly profit at V is positive if

$$F < \frac{b}{9}\left(S_{c+r} - \frac{r}{b}\right)^2. \tag{8.31}$$

For fixed cost in this range, the incumbent cannot preclude entry. The incumbent can act as a Stackelberg quantity leader and position the equilibrium at the point on TV that yields it the greatest profit. Whatever point is chosen, the incumbent has no incentive to carry excess capacity, which would be costly without deterring entry.

---

[7] Let $a = 10$, $b = c = r = 1$, and $F = 6$. Then the incumbent's output at T is $2\frac{2}{3}$, the incumbent's output at V is $3\frac{1}{3}$, and the incumbent could deter entry by setting capacity and output equal to $8 - 2\sqrt{6} \approx 3.1$.

[8] Bulow et al. (1985a) show that this result depends on Dixit's demand specification, which implies that one firm's marginal revenue falls as the other firm's output rises. If this assumption is not met, as for example when there is a constant price elasticity of demand, it may be optimal for the incumbent to hold excess capacity even in the Dixit model.

Extensions

The Spence (1977) and Dixit (1980) models are essentially static, although it is possible to draw dynamic inferences from them by investigating results if the basic model (game) is repeated over and over again.[9] A more deliberately dynamic approach to the issue of investment and entry takes off from Spence (1979), who supposes that firms invest subject to constraints on the rate at which the capital stock can be expanded. In this model, firms invest as quickly as possible to reach the unconstrained optimal capital level. An incumbent firm, knowing the investment strategy of an entrant, can act as a "capital-leader," inducing the entrant to select the target level of capital that is most profitable for the incumbent. This is comparable with Stackelberg quantity leadership in a conventional quantity-setting oligopoly model. Fudenberg and Tirole (1983) extend Spence (1979).

These models generally focus on strategic competition between a single incumbent or dominant firm and a single entrant. Additional issues arise if the pre-entry market structure is oligopoly.

Eaton and Ware (1987) examine entry in oligopoly with perfect information. In their model's equilibrium, firms do not hold excess capacity. Entry occurs so long as the marginal entrant can make a profit in post-entry Cournot equilibrium. This is a form of noncooperative limit pricing.

Waldman (1987) examines entry-deterring investment by an oligopoly when incumbents cannot collude and the precise entry-deterring level of investment is uncertain. He shows that uncertainty may lead the oligopoly to invest less to deter entry than would a single incumbent. Each oligopolist takes a marginal "free ride" on the entry-deterring investment of others, reducing the equilibrium level of investment in entry deterrence compared with the collusive or single-incumbent case.[10] But this is not a necessary result. Waldman presents an alternative model in which uncertainty does not lead to a lower investment in deterrence.

Von Ungern-Sternberg (1988b) points out that entry deterrence need not be an incumbent's only motive for holding excess capacity. Excess capacity deters entry, if at all, because it constitutes a commitment to stay in the industry in the face of entry. If an incumbent firm engages in long-term relationships with vertically related firms, then excess capacity can serve as a signal that the incumbent intends to remain in the industry. The benefit of holding excess capacity, in this case, is the reduction in transaction costs in dealings with vertically related firms, not the deterrence of entry. Similarly, Saloner (1985) shows that a dominant firm may hold excess capacity to induce incumbent rivals to reduce output.

Malueg and Schwartz (1991) model entry deterrence when the market is growing and it is possible for entrants to come in at an initially small scale. They show that when such "toehold" entry is possible it is not, in general, optimal for an incumbent to deter all entry. It is often privately profitable for an incumbent to let some firms into the market, and the expected reactions of those firms to later entry acts as a deterrent to later entry.

[9] For other extensions of the Dixit model, see Schmalensee (1981); Spulber (1981) (an explicitly dynamic model in which the incumbent acts as a Stackelberg quantity leader); Perrakis and Warskett (1983, 1986); Kirman and Masson (1986) (who model entrants' expectations concerning incumbents' post-entry actions); and Bonanno (1988) (who adds two types of uncertainty to a modification of the Dixit model).

[10] For other discussions of free riding and deterrence when there is more than one incumbent firm, see Bernheim (1984) and Gilbert and Vives (1986).

8.2.3   Evidence

Masson and Shaanan (1986) estimate (for a sample of 26 industries) a three-equation system of equations explaining excess capacity, price–cost margins, and the market share of new entrants in terms of various structural and behavioral variables. They find that excess capacity has a modestly significant positive effect on price–cost margins, which is consistent with the hypothesis that excess capacity deters entry and allows the exercise of market power. They also find that excess capacity reduces the market share of new entrants. Results from the equation that seeks to explain the magnitude of excess capacity are inconclusive: although the equation as a whole has a high degree of explanatory power,[11] only the coefficient of the durable-good industry dummy variable is significant (and positive). Masson and Shaanan interpret their results as showing support of limit pricing, with excess capacity increasing the limit price.

Ghemawat and Caves (1986) use the PIMS line-of-business database in another test of the hypothesis that maintenance of excess capacity deters entry. They argue that entry deterrence through maintenance of excess capacity will result in a lower rate of return on investment, all else being equal.[12] They find a frequent result of studies of profitability using line-of-business data: the rate of return on investment falls as capital intensity rises. This result is consistent with the excess capacity, entry deterrence hypothesis, but one suspects that other forces (which economists have yet to analyze successfully) are at work as well.

Gilbert and Lieberman (1987) study capacity investment with a cross-section time-series sample of 24 oligopolistic chemical product markets from the late 1950s or early 1960s through 1982. They use a logit model to estimate the probability that a firm will expand capacity. The probability of expansion is taken to depend on capacity utilization, the growth rate of product sales, the firm's share of industry capacity, the change in the firm's share of industry capacity, and the rate at which rivals are expanding capacity.

A consistent theme of their results is that small firms behave differently from large firms (size being measured by market share). Small firms invest in a way that follows changes in market share, while large firms invest in a way that tends to keep market share constant. Small firms tend to invest when other firms in the industry are investing (which Gilbert and Lieberman call a "bandwagon" effect). Large firms (with market shares greater than 30 percent) invest less when other firms invest more. Thus investment can preempt or deter investment by large firms but not by small firms. Since large firms tend to invest in a way that maintains market share, however, deterrence is likely to be a short-run rather than a long-run phenomenon.

Lieberman (1987b) examines the investment response of incumbent firms to actual entry using a sample of 39 chemical product industries that is related to the sample of Gilbert and Lieberman (1987). His evidence does not suggest that incumbents held excess capacity in advance of entry (see also Lieberman, 1987a). But he finds evidence of post-entry coordination of investment by incumbents in concentrated industries. Incumbents tended to cut back

---

[11]   For a cross-section sample: $R^2 = 0.56$.

[12]   Crudely: the rate of return on investment is profit divided by the value of capital. If profit rises with excess capacity but in less than a one-to-one ratio, the rate of return on investment falls as excess capacity rises. On the other hand, if profit rises more than proportionately to increases in capacity, the rate of return on investment will rise with capacity.

on investment when an incumbent built a new plant, but accelerated investment if an entrant built a new plant.

Paraskevopoulos and Pitelis (1995) examine the role of capacity expansion for a sample of European chemical industries. Like Gilbert and Lieberman, they find evidence of a bandwagon effect. They also find that announcements of investment projects are used to coordinate the expansion of capacity, and that large firms act to preempt the investment by small firms.

On balance, these empirical studies provide support for the hypothesis that investment in capacity can be used to influence investment decisions of rivals. This may deter or delay rival investment, and allow incumbents to condition market structure in a way that allows the exercise of market power. At the same time, empirical evidence makes clear that the investment decision is a complicated one. Strategic motives are likely to be part of the investment story, but they are not all of it.

8.3   SWITCHING COSTS

The act of consumption often involves an investment in product-specific knowledge. Once one has learned how food is laid out in a particular local grocery store, it is easier and more efficient to shop there than to explore some other local grocery store. Once one has learned how to use a particular word processor, it requires less effort to upgrade to later generations of the same word processor than to switch to some other word processor.[13] This kind of product-specific knowledge creates a cost, to the consumer, of switching from one brand to another.[14]

Such consumer switching costs may arise in other ways – cumulative loyalty discounts, for example, or a frequent flyer plan. Rental contracts may impose a penalty if a product is returned early, but reduce or waive the penalty if the rental unit is replaced by another variety of the same producer.[15]

Demand for such products can be modeled by supposing that there is a switching cost s per unit that must be paid by new consumers of any particular variety. All varieties are identical, except for switching costs. That is, all products are functionally identical, but a consumer must expend some resources to learn how to use a new variety.

Suppose also that producers are unable to price discriminate. If demand is linear and a firm supplies only experienced consumers, it receives the price given by the inverse market demand function as

$$p = a - bQ. \tag{8.32}$$

But if the marginal units of a firm's product are sold to new consumers, price must fall short of the value given by (8.32) by the amount of the switching cost. If an experienced consumer will pay €10 per unit of output, and a new customer must expend resources with

---

[13] For this argument to hold, later software generations must be backward compatible. Switching costs tend not only to tie consumers to consumption of a particular product – the one they have learned how to use – they also tie firms to production of a particular product – the one that their consumers have learned how to use. See Farrell and Shapiro (1988).

[14] See Klemperer (1987), Caminal and Matutes (1990), and Shy (2001).

[15] See *U.S. v. United Shoe Machinery Corporation* 110 F. Supp. 295 (1953).

an opportunity cost of €1 to consume a product, then a new consumer will pay only €9 per unit of the product. If price discrimination is impossible and there are new consumers, the equation of the inverse demand curve is

$$p = a - s - bQ. \tag{8.33}$$

8.3.1 A monopolist with switching costs

Suppose that a market operates for two periods and is supplied by a single firm that is protected from entry. The firm acts to maximize the present-discounted value of its profit over both periods,

$$G_1 = \Pi_{11} + \frac{1}{1+r}\Pi_{12}, \tag{8.34}$$

where Π_{11} is the firm's first-period profit and Π_{12} is the firm's second-period profit.

In the first period, all of firm 1's customers are new. Consequently, the equation of the first-period inverse demand curve is given by (8.33), and

$$\Pi_{11} = (a - c - s - bq_{11})q_{11} = b(S_{c+s} - q_{11})q_{11}, \tag{8.35}$$

where $S_{c+s} = (a - c - c)/b$ is the quantity that would be demanded if price were equal to $s + c$.

The form of the firm's second-period profit function depends on the relation between second-period output and first-period output:

$$\Pi_{12} = \begin{cases} (a - c - bq_{12})q_{12} = b(S_c - q_{12})q_{12} & q_{12} \leq q_{11}, \\ (a - c - s - bq_{12})q_{12} = b(S_{c+s} - q_{12})q_{12} & q_{12} > q_{11}. \end{cases} \tag{8.36}$$

If all the monopolist's second-period customers consume the product in the first period, the upper expression gives the monopolist's second-period profit. But if the monopolist has some second-period customers who consume the product for the first time, the monopolist's second-period profit is given by the lower expression.

Because such consumers have an opportunity cost s per unit of the good consumed, they will pay s less per unit than an experienced consumer. If price discrimination is impossible, then all consumers benefit from the lower price that the monopolist must offer to attract new consumers.

Suppose first that the firm produces more in period 2 than in period 1: $q_{12} > q_{11}$. Then the objective function maximized by the firm is

$$G_1 = b(S_{c+s} - q_{11})q_{11} + \frac{b}{1+r}(S_{c+s} - q_{22})q_{22}. \tag{8.37}$$

A firm maximizing (8.37) selects $q_{12} = q_{11} = S_{c+s}/2$. But this contradicts the initial premise that $q_{12} > q_{11}$. Thus the monopolist maximizing profit over both periods must pick $q_{12} \leq q_{11}$.

Formally, the firm's problem can be described as maximization of the Lagrangian

$$\mathcal{L} = b(S_{c+s} - q_{11})q_{11} + \frac{b}{1+r}(S_c - q_{12})q_{12} + \lambda(q_{11} - q_{12}). \qquad (8.38)$$

λ is the Lagrangian multiplier associated with the constraint $q_{11} \geq q_{12}$, and the expression for second-period profit reflects the fact that if $q_{11} \geq q_{12}$ then all second-period consumers are experienced and no second-period consumers pay switching costs.

The first-order conditions for maximization of (8.38) are as follows:

$$\frac{\partial \mathcal{L}}{\partial q_{11}} = b(S_{c+s} - 2q_{11}) + \lambda \equiv 0; \qquad (8.39)$$

$$\frac{\partial \mathcal{L}}{\partial q_{12}} = \frac{b}{1+r}(S_c - 2q_{12}) - \lambda \equiv 0; \qquad (8.40)$$

$$\frac{\partial \mathcal{L}}{\partial \lambda} = q_{11} - q_{12} \geq 0, \qquad \lambda(q_{11} - q_{12}) \equiv 0, \qquad \lambda \geq 0, \qquad (8.41)$$

Suppose first that the firm produces strictly more in the first period than in the second: $q_{11} > q_{12}$. Then (8.41) implies $\lambda = 0$. If $\lambda = 0$, (8.39) and (8.40) imply $q_{11} = S_{c+s}/2$ and $q_{12} = S_c/2$, respectively. But this means that $q_{11} < q_{12}$, a contradiction. Hence the first-order conditions require that $q_{11} = q_{12}$. Given $q_{11} = q_{12}$, (8.39) and (8.40) imply that[16]

$$q_{11} = q_{12} = \tfrac{1}{2}\left(S_{c+s} + \frac{1}{2+r}\frac{s}{b}\right). \qquad (8.42)$$

By comparison, a monopolist myopically maximizing single-period profit would produce $q_m = S_{c+s}/2$. With switching costs and a two-period horizon, the firm finds it profitable to produce somewhat more than single-period monopoly output in the first period. In the second period, the additional customers are bound to the firm by switching costs, with the result that in the second period the firm operates on a more profitable demand curve, one that is higher by the amount of switching costs. In the second period, the firm is able to sell its product to the same customers at a higher price because they need not pay an additional set of switching costs.

8.3.2   Entry deterrence with switching costs

Now suppose that the incumbent faces the possibility of entry, by a single firm, in the second period. If the potential entrant comes into the market, it must cover a fixed and sunk cost of entry, F. Any customers attracted by the entrant in the second period will pay switching costs. Thus the potential entrant's profit function is

$$\Pi_{22} = [a - c - s - b(q_{12} + q_{22})]q_{22} - F = b(S_{c+s} - q_{12} - q_{22})q_{22} - F. \qquad (8.43)$$

Suppose also that if the potential entrant comes into the market it acts as a Cournot quantity-setting firm, and that this is known to the incumbent. Maximization of (8.43) gives

---

[16] It follows that $\lambda = s/(1+r)$.

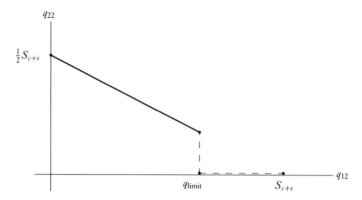

Figure 8.3 A potential entrant's best-response function, switching costs and fixed and sunk entry costs.

the equation of the entrant's best-response function,

$$q_{22} = \tfrac{1}{2}(S_{c+s} - q_{12}),$$ (8.44)

which shows the entrant's output, provided that the resulting profit is positive. Substituting (8.44) into (8.43) and setting the resulting expression for Π_{22} equal to zero, we find that, if firm 1 produces

$$q_{\text{limit}} = S_{c+s} - 2\sqrt{\frac{F}{b}} = S_c - \frac{s}{b} - 2\sqrt{\frac{F}{b}}$$ (8.45)

or more in the second period, the entrant will be unable to earn a positive profit, and entry will not occur.

From (8.45), the limit quantity is smaller, the greater is fixed cost and the greater are switching costs. The entrant's best-response curve is shown in figure 8.3. An increase in fixed cost shifts the shutdown point on the entrant's best-response curve to the left. An increase in switching cost has the same effect, and also lowers the best-response curve.

We proceed by analogy with the model of entry deterrence. What output will the incumbent select if it maximizes the present-discounted value of profit subject to the constraint that second-period output be at least large enough to deter entry?

Two cases are possible. The incumbent may produce more in the second period than in the first, maximizing profit subject to the constraint that second-period output is large enough to deter entry. In this case, the incumbent's optimization problem is described by the Lagrangian

$$\mathcal{L} = b(S_{c+s} - q_{11})q_{11} + \frac{b}{1+r}(S_{c+s} - q_{12})q_{12} + \mu(q_{12} - q_{\text{limit}}),$$ (8.46)

where μ is the Lagrangian multiplier associated with the entry limitation constraint.

The first-order conditions for maximization of (8.46) are as follows:

$$\frac{\partial \mathcal{L}}{\partial q_{11}} = b(S_{c+s} - 2q_{11}) \equiv 0; \tag{8.47}$$

$$\frac{\partial \mathcal{L}}{\partial q_{12}} = \frac{b}{1+r}(S_{c+s} - 2q_{12}) + \mu \equiv 0; \tag{8.48}$$

$$\frac{\partial \mathcal{L}}{\partial \mu} = q_{12} - q_{\text{limit}} \geq 0, \qquad \mu(q_{12} - q_{\text{limit}}) \equiv 0, \qquad \mu \geq 0. \tag{8.49}$$

If $q_{12} > q_{\text{limit}}$, (8.49) implies $\mu = 0$. Then in turn (8.47) and (8.48) imply that $q_{12} = q_{\text{limit}} = S_c + s/2$, a contradiction. Thus if the incumbent is to sell more in the second period than in the first, it must be the case that $q_{12} = q_{\text{limit}}$.

Thus $q_{12} = q_{\text{limit}}$ and hence, from (8.47), $q_{11} = S_{c+s}/2$. The requirement that $q_{12} = q_{\text{limit}} > q_{11} = S_{c+s}/2$ implies that

$$S_{c+s} > 4\sqrt{\frac{F}{b}}, \tag{8.50}$$

which is a consistency condition for the solution to require greater output in the second period than in the first.[17]

Alternatively, the incumbent's output in the second period may be less than or equal to the incumbent's output in the first period. Then the incumbent's constrained profit-maximization problem is described by the Lagrangian

$$\mathcal{L} = b(S_{c+s} - q_{11})q_{11} + \frac{b}{1+r}(S_c - q_{12})q_{12} + \lambda(q_{11} - q_{12}) + \mu(q_{12} - q_{\text{limit}}), \tag{8.51}$$

where λ is the Lagrangian multiplier associated with the constraint $q_{11} \geq q_{12}$ and μ is the Lagrangian multiplier associated with the entry limitation constraint.

The first-order conditions to maximize (8.51) are as follows:

$$\frac{\partial \mathcal{L}}{\partial q_{11}} = b(S_{c+s} - 2q_{11}) + \lambda \equiv 0; \tag{8.52}$$

$$\frac{\partial \mathcal{L}}{\partial q_{12}} = \frac{b}{1+r}(S_c - 2q_{12}) - \lambda + \mu \equiv 0; \tag{8.53}$$

$$\frac{\partial \mathcal{L}}{\partial \lambda} = q_{11} - q_{12} \geq 0, \qquad \lambda(q_{11} - q_{12}) \equiv 0, \qquad \lambda \geq 0; \tag{8.54}$$

$$\frac{\partial \mathcal{L}}{\partial \mu} = q_{12} - q_{\text{limit}} \geq 0, \qquad \mu(q_{12} - q_{\text{limit}}) \equiv 0, \qquad \mu \geq 0. \tag{8.55}$$

The solution falls into one of two possible cases. Suppose first that $q_{12} > q_{\text{limit}}$. Then (8.55) implies that $\mu = 0$. If $\mu = 0$, then (8.52) and (8.53) imply that $\lambda \neq 0$. If $\lambda \neq 0$, (8.54)

---

[17] An additional consistency condition is that $\mu = b(S_{c+s} - 4\sqrt{F/b}/(1+r) \geq 0$, but this is satisfied if (8.50) is satisfied.

implies that $q_{11} = q_{12}$. Then (8.52) and (8.53) can be solved for

$$q_{11} = q_{12} = \tfrac{1}{2}\left(S_{c+s} + \frac{1}{2+r}\frac{s}{b}\right) \tag{8.56}$$

(compare with (8.42)). If the output that would be produced by a monopolist not threatened by entry exceeds the quantity needed to preclude entry, then entry is blocked.[18]

The other possible solution has $q_{11} = q_{12} = q_{\text{limit}}$. Then (8.52) and (8.53) give the values of the Lagrangian multipliers,

$$\lambda = b\left(2q_{\text{limit}} - S_{c+s}\right), \tag{8.57}$$

$$\mu = \lambda - \frac{b}{1+r}(S_c - 2q_{\text{limit}}). \tag{8.58}$$

Consistency conditions for the solution to fall in this category are that λ and μ be positive. With some manipulation, one can show that μ is positive whenever the output given by (8.56) is less than the limit output, and that λ is positive whenever μ is positive.

There remains the question of comparing the incumbent's profit under the two entry-excluding solutions (that is, expanding output to q_{limit} or setting $q_{11} = q_{12}$) and contrasting the incumbent's profit by excluding entry with the incumbent's profit if it allows entry. Problem 8.6 gives you the opportunity to explore this question if the post-entry market is a Cournot quantity-setting duopoly.

8.4   RAISING RIVALS' COSTS

Entry-deterring strategies of the kind we have studied have a common characteristic that is, at least from the point of view of the deterring firm, very much to be regretted. They require the incumbent to make a short-run sacrifice of profit as a way of discouraging entry. The incumbent may sacrifice profit by carrying excess capacity, by expanding output and lowering price, or by marketing and product design programs that create switching costs. The payoff from such strategies is increased future profitability. But the incumbent would naturally prefer to have its rivals sacrifice profit rather than make the sacrifice itself.

It may be possible to arrange this if the incumbent can engage in behavior that increases rivals' costs. Increases in rivals' marginal costs, generally, cause them to reduce output. For the incumbent, the result is a higher price or a greater output, or some combination of the two. The incumbent is better off if it can shift the sacrifice of profit to rivals.[19]

Costs of firms in the same industry are often linked. This may occur formally, as when industry-wide negotiations set a common wage rate to be paid by all firms in the industry. If an incumbent firm employs more capital-intensive techniques than rivals do, it can force differentially higher costs on rivals by agreeing to pay higher wages (Williamson, 1968a).

---

[18] The consistency condition for this to be the solution, that $q_{11} > q_{\text{limit}}$, becomes $F > b(S_{c+[(3+r)/(2+r)]s}/4)^2$, using the notation $S_x = (a - x)/b$.

[19] See Salop and Scheffman (1983, 1987); Krattenmaker and Salop (1986); for a critical view, Brennan (1988); and for an earlier version, Lydall (1955).

Linkage of costs may occur through relationships with vertically related stages of the production process. If an incumbent dominant firm integrates forward from production into distribution, it can foreclose rivals from retail outputs through ownership or exclusive dealing contracts. Rivals will need to integrate forward themselves to ensure access to the downstream market. Over a large range of output (throughput), the cost of the distribution system is fixed. If the output of rivals is less than that of the incumbent dominant firm, their cost per unit increases more than the average cost of the incumbent firm. Again, rivals' costs increase differentially.

Similarly, if an incumbent firm invests more in high-quality deposits of an essential raw material input than it needs for its own production, it suffers some increase in average cost (greater fixed cost per unit of output). But if this forces rivals to exploit lower-quality reserves, their unit cost rises as well. If rivals' average cost rises more per unit than the incumbent's average cost, such a strategy is profitable for the incumbent. To show this, consider a market with demand

$$p = a - b(Q_D + Q_F) \qquad \text{or} \qquad Q_D + Q_F = \frac{a}{b} - \frac{1}{b}p, \tag{8.59}$$

where Q_D is the output of the dominant firm and Q_F is the output of a fringe of competitive, price-taking, firms. The fringe supply equation is

$$p = e + fQ_F \qquad \text{or} \qquad Q_F = \begin{cases} \dfrac{1}{f}(p - e) & p \geq e, \\ 0 & p \leq e. \end{cases} \tag{8.60}$$

If $p \leq e$, the fringe shuts down, and the incumbent firm operates on the market demand function. For $p \geq e$, the incumbent operates on a residual demand function

$$Q_D = \frac{a}{b} - \frac{1}{f}(p - e) - \frac{1}{b}p \tag{8.61}$$

that is the difference between market demand and fringe supply.

A profit-maximizing incumbent picks an output that equates marginal revenue along the residual demand curve to marginal cost c. Dominant firm output determines price, again along the residual demand curve. The fringe of competitive suppliers takes this price as given (each fringe firm picks an output that equates marginal cost to price) and produces the output given by the fringe supply curve (for details, see Problem 8.7).

Now suppose that, if the incumbent accepts an increase in its own marginal cost and average cost from c to $c + \alpha$, the supply curve of the fringe shifts upward to

$$p = e + (1 + \rho_1)\alpha - \rho_2\alpha^2 + fQ_F, \tag{8.62}$$

where $\rho_1, \rho_2 > 0$.

The quadratic specification in (8.62) has two essential characteristics. First, $\rho_1 > 0$: if the incumbent suffers a cost increase, fringe firms suffer a greater cost increase. That is, the price fringe firms must receive before they will bring a given quantity to market increases more than dominant firm marginal cost.

Second, there are decreasing returns to entry deterrence via cost increases: $\rho_2 > 0$. There is a level of α beyond which the ability of the incumbent to inflict cost increases on the fringe declines. If this were not the case, and cost raising were profitable at all, it would be profitable for the incumbent to raise cost sufficiently to drive fringe output to zero.

The effect of increasing cost in this way is to shift the fringe supply curve, and the residual demand curve, upward. But the incumbent's marginal cost shifts up as well. One can show (Problem 8.7) that the profit-maximizing value of α is

$$\alpha = \frac{f}{2\rho_2} \left(\frac{\rho_2}{f} - \frac{1}{b} \right). \tag{8.63}$$

The optimal value of α is positive if and only if the initial investment in raising rivals' cost raises the residual demand curve more than the incumbent's marginal cost.[20] If this condition is met, the cost-raising strategy increases the dominant firm's output and reduces fringe output. The cost-raising strategy increases price and the dominant firm's profit.

The increase in price also means a reduction in consumers' surplus: consumers are injured by the cost-raising strategy. The reduction in output means that there is an increase in dead-weight welfare loss relative to the original cost of production c. The increase in production cost due to the use of the cost-raising strategy is an additional welfare loss: more resources are used to produce the reduced output than would be necessary in the absence of the cost-raising strategy.

8.5   PREDATORY PRICING

Predatory pricing is a strategy in which a dominant firm cuts price below rivals' average cost, even if this means accepting short-run losses, to drive rivals from the market. Once rivals leave the market, the incumbent raises price and collects sufficient economic profit to make the present-discounted return from predatory pricing positive. A variation is that a dominant firm cuts price as a way of encouraging rivals to compete less vigorously, without necessarily driving them from the market.[21]

Non-game-theoretic models of predatory pricing (McGee, 1958, 1980; Bork, 1978; Easterbrook, 1981) are essentially static, although they are used to make inferences about dynamic relationships. They suggest that predatory pricing is unlikely to occur.

One such argument relies on the perfect functioning of financial capital markets. If the successful predator can collect profits after driving rivals from the market, then it will be profitable to be in the market after predation is successful. Capital markets should then be willing to loan money to the targets of predation, so that they can survive and share in economic profits. But if the targets of predation can survive, there will be no economic profits. Thus predation must fail; if it must fail, it will not occur.

---

[20] This is a specific case of a general result due to Salop and Scheffman (1987, Proposition 1).

[21] For general references, see Kamien (1987) and Milgrom (1987). We emphasize models of entry deterrence by a single incumbent or dominant firm. For discussions of entry deterrence under oligopoly, see Sherman and Willett (1967), Goldberg and Moirao (1973), Gilbert and Vives (1986), Harrington (1987b), Bucklin et al. (1989), and Lipman (1990). We do not discuss the large literature in which economists offer advice to policy-makers on the diagnosis of predatory behavior; see, for example, Schmalensee (1979), Rosenbaum (1987), and Ordover and Saloner (1989). Theoretically oriented contributions to this literature include Romano and Berg (1985), Easley et al. (1985), and Schwartz (1989).

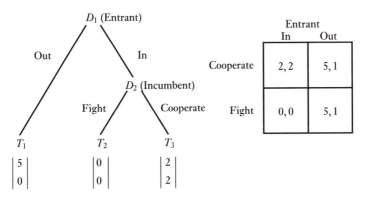

Figure 8.4 A game tree and payoff matrix for one stage of the chain store game.

Alternatively, it is sometimes argued, if capital markets will not loan money to targets of predation, then consumers ought to be willing to pay higher prices to the targets of predation, since it is consumers who will be worse off in the long run if predation succeeds. Again, predation will be unable to succeed, and if it is unable to succeed, it will not occur.[22]

These arguments go through only if capital markets are perfect or if consumers have complete information and are perfectly rational. Game-theoretic analyses of predatory behavior suggest that static models miss essential aspects of predation. Unless information is complete and reasoning power unlimited, a dominant firm that engages in predatory behavior in one market and time period can create an asset – reputation – that will allow it to extract profit in other markets and time periods.

8.5.1 The chain store paradox

Selten (1978) offers a stylized game that makes clear the stringent informational requirements needed to rule out predation as an equilibrium phenomenon. A dominant firm – the incumbent – operates a chain of stores in 20 separate local markets. In each market, one after another, it faces the prospect of entry by a single rival. A game tree and payoff matrix for one such stage game are shown in figure 8.4. Each entrant earns a payoff that is determined in a single market. The incumbent's overall payoff is the sum of its payoffs in the 20 markets.

In each market, the entrant's choices are to enter or to stay out of the market. If the entrant stays out, it earns €1 (the return from the best alternative investment); the incumbent earns €5. If the entrant comes in, then the incumbent must decide whether to cooperate with the entrant (both earn a return of €2) or to fight entry (both earn a zero return). A cooperative incumbent restricts output and shares the market; an aggressive incumbent expands output, even at the cost of lost profit.

[22] Porter (1983c) shows that this argument may fail on its own assumptions if future losses of consumers' surplus are discounted.

Selten contrasts two possible strategies for the incumbent. The deterrence strategy relies on the fact that if an entrant believes that the incumbent will react aggressively, then the entrant is better off staying out of the market. On this argument, the best strategy for the incumbent is to announce an intention to react aggressively to entry. If entry occurs, it is likely to be early on, and the incumbent will have to sacrifice its own profit by carrying out the threat to deter entry. But if later potential entrants are convinced that the incumbent is serious about the threat to react aggressively to entry, the incumbent will come out ahead.

Selten notes that deterrence will not work in the final market. An aggressive reaction in the final period would mean a loss for the incumbent without the prospect of any later gain; thus the threat of an aggressive reaction in the final market would be an empty one. A sufficiently clever firm considering entry into the next-to-last market could make a *backward induction* argument, and conclude that if a payoff-maximizing incumbent would have nothing to gain by reacting aggressively in the final period, then it would have nothing to gain by reacting aggressively in the next-to-last period either.

Suppose that an incumbent firm reacts aggressively to entry in the first three markets, and no entry occurs again until the final three. Realizing the game is up, or nearly so, the incumbent accommodates entry in the final three markets. Its payoff is €76 (3 multiplied by 0 plus 14 multiplied by 5 plus 3 multiplied by 2).

The backward induction argument pushes the reasoning that the incumbent could not credibly threaten to react aggressively to entry in the final period to its logical conclusion. If the incumbent could not credibly threaten to deter entry in the final period, then it would have nothing to gain from reacting aggressively to entry in the next-to-last period. But in this case, it would have nothing to gain from reacting aggressively to entry in period 18, and so on back to period 1. No entrant would ever believe a threat to react aggressively; the only subgame-perfect equilibrium has each entrant enter in each stage and the incumbent accommodate entry in each stage: the incumbent's payoff is €40.

Selten concludes his discussion (1978/88, pp. 38–9):[23]

> only the induction theory is game theoretically correct. Logically, the induction argument cannot be restricted to the last periods of the game. There is no way to avoid the conclusion that it applies to all periods of the game.
>
> Nevertheless the deterrence theory is much more convincing. If I had to play the game in the role of [the incumbent], I would follow the deterrence theory. I would be very surprised if it failed to work. From my discussions with friends and colleagues, I get the impression that most people share this inclination. . . . My experience suggests that mathematically trained persons recognize the logical validity of the induction argument, but they refuse to accept it as a guide to practical behavior.
>
> It seems to be safe to conjecture that even in a situation where all players know that all players understand the induction argument very well, [the incumbent] will adopt a deterrence policy and the other players will expect him to do so.
>
> The fact that the logical inescapability of the induction theory fails to destroy the plausibility of the deterrence theory is a serious phenomenon which merits the name of a paradox.

---

[23] Experimental evidence seems to confirm Selten's expectation; see Jung et al. (1994).

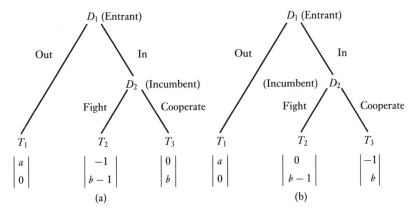

Figure 8.5 Possible game trees for one stage of the Kreps and Wilson entry game. (a) Weak incumbent; (b) strong incumbent ($a > 0$; $0 < b < 1$).

8.5.2   Resolutions of the chain store paradox

The chain store paradox is that the logically impeccable subgame-perfect equilibrium of the chain store game is implausible as a description of real-world behavior. The implied research agenda is to identify assumptions of the chain store game that, if relaxed, admit more plausible solutions.

Kreps and Wilson – imperfect information

Kreps and Wilson (1982) introduce imperfect information into the chain store game. They show that deterrence may emerge as an equilibrium strategy if it is possible that the incumbent earns a greater payoff by fighting than cooperating, and entrants are uncertain about the incumbent's payoffs.[24]

Game trees for a single stage of the Kreps and Wilson extension of the chain store game are shown in figure 8.5. The entrant earns zero if it stays out, loses money if it comes in and the incumbent fights ($b - 1 < 0$), and makes a profit ($b > 0$) if it comes in and the incumbent cooperates. If the potential entrant stays out, the incumbent's payoff is $a > 1$.

But the entrant is uncertain about the incumbent's payoffs in the event of entry. There are two possibilities. If the incumbent is weak, it earns more by cooperating than by fighting entry. Payoffs for the weak incumbent are shown in figure 8.5(a). If this game tree held for every stage of the game, and entrants knew that it held for every stage of the game, the backward induction argument would apply, and equilibrium would require the incumbent to cooperate with entry in every period.

But payoffs might be as shown in figure 8.5(b). Here, the incumbent breaks even by fighting, but loses money by cooperating. If these are the incumbent's payoffs, it will fight entry.

---

[24] Yang (1996) presents a model in which it is the cost types of the entrants that is uncertain.

Kreps and Wilson index time backward, so the incumbent plays against entrant N, entrant $N - 1, \ldots$, entrant 2, and entrant 1, in that order. Each entrant maximizes its payoff in its stage of the game. The incumbent maximizes the sum of its payoffs over all stages.

Call p_n the probability that entrant n assigns to the possibility that it faces a strong incumbent. The game begins with $p_N = \delta$ and p_n is updated whenever the incumbent's actions provide additional information. The rule for updating beliefs forms part of the sequential equilibrium. Each entrant's equilibrium strategy maximizes its payoff, given beliefs and the incumbent's strategy; the incumbent's strategy maximizes its payoff, given beliefs and the entrants' strategies.

Kreps and Wilson outline a sequential equilibrium in which early potential entrants will stay out of the market against a weak incumbent, and there is some probability that a weak incumbent will fight entry, at least until near the end of the game.

In this sequential equilibrium, beliefs are defined as follows:

1 $p_N = \delta$;
2 if there has been no entry up to period n, $p_n = \delta$;
3 if between periods N and n there has been an instance of unfought entry, $p_n = 0$;
4 if every instance of entry has been fought, and the most recent instance of entry was in period k, $p_n = \max(b^{k-1}, \delta)$.

This implies that if $p_{n+1} > 0$ and there is entry in period $n + 1$, and the incumbent fights, then $p_n = \max(b^n, p_{n+1})$.

A strong incumbent always fights entry. A weak incumbent's strategy is:

1 to fight if $n > 1$ and $p_n \geq b^{n-1}$;
2 to fight with probability $[(1 - b^{n-1})p_n]/[(1 - p_n)b^{n-1}]$ and otherwise cooperate, if $n > 1$ and $p_n < b^{n-1}$;
3 to cooperate in the final period ($n = 1$).

Each potential entrant

1 stays out if $p_n > b^n$;
2 stays out with probability $1/a$ if $p_n = b^n$;
3 enters if $p_n < b^n$.

It is useful to illustrate the implications of this equilibrium for the case of a weak monopolist. Table 8.1 shows the course of a game played out according to this strategy if $\delta = \frac{1}{10}$, $b = \frac{1}{2}$, and $N \geq 4$.[25]

The game begins in period N with $p_N = \delta = \frac{1}{10}$. The potential entrant comes in if $\frac{1}{10} < (\frac{1}{2})^N$. Since N is at least 4, this condition is not met, $\frac{1}{10} > (\frac{1}{2})^N$, and the entrant stays out. If entry were to occur in the first period, the incumbent would fight if there were at least five periods (if $N \geq 5$, then $\frac{1}{10} > (\frac{1}{2})^{N-1}$).

---

[25] Table 8.1 is based on figure 3 of Kreps and Wilson (1982).

Table 8.1 The sequential equilibrium path of the Kreps and Wilson entry deterrence game; $\delta = \frac{1}{10}, b = \frac{1}{2}$

Period	p_n	Entrant: enter if	Weak incumbent: fight if
N	$\delta = \frac{1}{10}$	$\delta < \left(\frac{1}{2}\right)^N$	$\frac{1}{10} \geq \left(\frac{1}{2}\right)^{N-1}$, else with probability $\dfrac{1 - (\frac{1}{2})^{N-1}}{1 - (\frac{1}{10})} \dfrac{\frac{1}{10}}{(\frac{1}{2})^{N-1}}$
$N-1$	$\frac{1}{10}$	$\frac{1}{10} < \left(\frac{1}{2}\right)^N$	$\frac{1}{10} \geq \left(\frac{1}{2}\right)^{N-2}$, else with probability $\dfrac{1 - (\frac{1}{2})^{N-2}}{1 - (\frac{1}{10})} \dfrac{\frac{1}{10}}{(\frac{1}{2})^{N-2}}$
$\vdots$	$\vdots$	$\vdots$	$\vdots$
4	$\frac{1}{10}$	$\frac{1}{10} < \frac{1}{16}$	$\frac{1}{10} \geq \frac{1}{8}$, else with probability $\frac{7}{9}$
3	$\frac{1}{10}$	$\frac{1}{10} < \frac{1}{8}$	$\frac{1}{10} \geq \frac{1}{4}$, else with probability $\frac{1}{3}$
Scenario 1 – cooperate in period 3			
2	0	$0 < \frac{1}{4}$	$0 \geq \frac{1}{2}$, else with probability 0
1	0	$0 < \frac{1}{2}$	Do not fight
Scenario 2 – fight in periods 3 and 2			
2	$b^2 = \frac{1}{4}$	$\frac{1}{4} < \frac{1}{4}$, else with probability $1 - \frac{1}{a}$	$\frac{1}{8} \geq \frac{1}{4}$, else with probability $\frac{1}{3}$
1	$b = \frac{1}{2}$	$\frac{1}{2} < \frac{1}{2}$, else with probability $1 - \frac{1}{a}$	Do not fight

As entry does not occur in period N, entrants do not change the probability that they assign to the possibility that the incumbent is strong; $p_{N-1} = p_N = \delta$. In period $N - 1$, entrants stay out provided that $\delta = \frac{1}{10} \geq (\frac{1}{2})^{N-1}$.

Potential entrants continue to stay out through period 4. Through period 5, the incumbent would fight any instance of entry. In period 4, the incumbent would fight entry with probability $\frac{7}{9}$ and cooperate with probability $\frac{2}{9}$. The equilibrium strategy for the entrant, however, is to stay out in period 4.

Going into period 3, entrants have acquired no new information about the incumbent, and $p_3 = \delta = \frac{1}{10}$. The equilibrium strategy for the period 3 potential entrant is to come into the market, since $p^3 = \frac{1}{10} < (\frac{1}{2})^3 = \frac{1}{8}$. The incumbent responds by fighting with probability $\frac{1}{3}$ and otherwise cooperating.

Table 8.1 shows two possible scenarios for the endgame. If the incumbent cooperates in period 3, $p_2 = p_1 = 0$: after one incident of uncontested entry, potential entrants believe the incumbent is weak. Since $p_2 = p_1 = 0$, the potential entrants for periods 2 and 1 come into the market. Having conceded entry in period 3, the incumbent does not fight entry in period 2. The incumbent in any event does not fight entry in the final period (period 1), since to do so would involve an avoidable loss.

If the incumbent fights in period 3, then p_n rises from $\frac{1}{10}$ to $\frac{1}{4}$ (since $p_2 = \max[(\frac{1}{2})^2, \frac{1}{10}]$). The period 2 potential entrant comes into the market with probability $1/a$, and stays out otherwise. The incumbent fights with probability $\frac{1}{3}$. Suppose that the period 2 entrant comes in and the incumbent fights. Then p_1 rises to $\frac{1}{2}$ (since $p_1 = \max[(\frac{1}{2})^1, \frac{1}{10}]$). The period 1 entrant comes into the market, and the incumbent cooperates.

It remains to show that these strategies and beliefs constitute a sequential equilibrium. Consider first the rationality of beliefs. If no entry occurs, nothing is learned about the incumbent, so beliefs, whatever they are, are simply carried forward. In particular, $p_n = \delta$ until the first instance of entry occurs. If $p_n \geq b^{n-1}$, the incumbent's equilibrium strategy calls for it to fight entry. If the incumbent acts accordingly, there is no new information, and beliefs should simply be carried forward. If $p_n = 0$, the incumbent is expected to cooperate with entry. Again, if the incumbent acts accordingly there is no new information, and beliefs should simply be carried forward.

The remaining cases to verify occur when $0 < p_n < b^{n-1}$. In this case, the incumbent may cooperate or it may fight. It will cooperate only if it is weak, so entrants should thereafter believe $p_{n-1} = 0$, and this is what the equilibrium requires. If the incumbent fights, sequential equilibrium beliefs should be updated according to Bayes' rule; then

$$p_{n-1} = \Pr(\text{incumbent strong} \mid \text{incumbent fights})$$

$$= \frac{\Pr(\text{incumbent strong and fights})}{\Pr(\text{incumbent fights})}$$

$$= \frac{\Pr(\text{fights} \mid \text{strong}) \times \Pr(\text{strong})}{\Pr(\text{fights} \mid \text{strong}) \times \Pr(\text{strong}) + \Pr(\text{fights} \mid \text{weak}) \times \Pr(\text{weak})}$$

$$= \frac{(1)p_n}{(1)p_n + [(1 - b^{n-1})p_n/(1 - p_n)b^{n-1}](1 - p_n)} = b^{n-1}. \tag{8.64}$$

The rule for updating beliefs in this case is that $p_n = \max(b^{n-1}, p_n)$. This amounts to requiring that fighting never worsens an incumbent's reputation. Since in this case we have $p_n < b^{n-1}$, when the incumbent is playing randomly the rule for updating probabilities will always give $p_{n-1} = \max(b^{n-1}, p_n) = b^{n-1}$, as required by (8.64).

Now consider entrants' strategies. If $p_n \geq b^{n-1}$, the incumbent is supposed to fight entry; the entrant's best-response is to stay out, and this is what the equilibrium strategy requires. Now suppose instead that $p_n < b^{n-1}$. Then the entrant's expected payoff from entry is

$$(b - 1)\Pr\binom{\text{Incumbent}}{\text{strong}} + (b - 1)\Pr\binom{\text{Incumbent weak and}}{\text{incumbent fights}} + b\Pr\binom{\text{Incumbent weak and}}{\text{incumbent cooperates}}$$

$$= (b - 1)p_n + \left\{(b - 1)\frac{(1 - b^{n-1})p_n}{(1 - p_n)b^{n-1}} + b\left[1 - \frac{(1 - b^{n-1})p_n}{(1 - p_n)b^{n-1}}\right]\right\}(1 - p_n)$$

$$= \frac{b^n - p_n}{b^{n-1}}. \tag{8.65}$$

To maximize expected return, the entrant should come in if $p_n < b^n$ and stay out if $p_n > b^n$. This is what the equilibrium requires. If $p_n = b^n$, the entrant is indifferent between coming in and staying out. Staying out with a probability $1/a$ will do as well as any other mixed strategy.

We now verify that the incumbent will be willing to follow its part of the suggested strategy, given that entrants follow their strategy. A strong incumbent is supposed to fight all entry. If entry occurs in the final period, the strong incumbent will be better off fighting, since fighting yields a zero return while cooperation yields a negative return. If entry occurs before the final period, cooperation would involve a loss in the period of entry and (since p_n would be set equal to zero) would induce entry in every future period. The strong incumbent will therefore be better off fighting, since fighting will allow a zero return and reduce future entry.

A weak incumbent would suffer a needless loss by fighting entry in the final period (period 1). Hence a weak incumbent will prefer to cooperate, as the strategy requires, in the final period.

Now suppose that we are in the next-to-last period, period 2. If $p_2 = 0$, the rule for updating expectations means $p_1 = 0$ as well. Thus if $p_2 = 0$, entry will surely occur in period 1. If entry will surely occur in period 1, then a weak incumbent cannot possibly profit by fighting in period 2; it will therefore prefer to follow the equilibrium strategy, which requires it to cooperate with entry if $p_2 = 0$.

We therefore consider the case $p_2 > 0$. If entry occurs and the entrant is following the equilibrium strategy, $p_2 \leq b^2$. But since $b < 1$, we have $p_2 \leq b^2 < b$. Suppose that entry occurs. Let the weak incumbent fight with probability f_2, and cooperate with probability $1-f_2$. If the incumbent fights entry, then the rule for updating beliefs implies $p_1 = \max(b, p_2) = b$. Thus if the weak incumbent fights in period 2, the equilibrium strategy requires the period 1 potential entrant to stay out with probability $1/a$ and enter with probability $1 - (1/a)$.

Given this behavior of the period 1 potential entrant, the weak incumbent's expected return from fighting in period 2 is

$$0(1 - f_2) + \left[-1 + a\left(\frac{1}{a}\right) + 0\left(1 - \frac{1}{a}\right)\right]f_2 = 0. \qquad (8.66)$$

But if the weak incumbent will break even for an arbitrary probability f_2 of fighting, it will break even for $f_2 = [(1 - b)/(1 - p_2)](p_2/b)$, as required by the equilibrium strategy. Thus if the game reaches period 2 with $p_2 > 0$, a weak incumbent will be willing to follow the equilibrium strategy.

From this point, the argument works backward in time, but the logic is much the same.

Suppose that we are in period 3. If $p_3 = 0$, entry will surely occur in periods 2 and 1. Thus if $p_3 = 0$ a weak incumbent is best off following the equilibrium strategy.

If $p_3 > 0$ and entry occurs, the entrant's strategy implies $p_3 \leq b^3$. Since $b < 1$, we then have $p_3 < b^2$. It follows that if the incumbent fights in period 3, then $p_2 = \max(b^2, p_3) = b^2$. If this is the case, then in period 2 the entrant will stay out with probability $1/a$ and enter with probability $1 - (1/a)$.

Suppose that the weak incumbent fights in period 3 with probability f_3. Its expected return is

$$0(1 - f_3) + \left[-1 + a\left(\frac{1}{a}\right) + \left(\begin{array}{c}\text{Expected return if}\\\text{entry in period 2}\end{array}\right)\left(1 - \frac{1}{a}\right)\right]f_3. \qquad (8.67)$$

But from our discussion of period 2, we know that the weak incumbent's expected return if entry occurs in period 2 is zero. Substituting in (8.67), the weak incumbent breaks even fighting with probability f_3. But if the weak incumbent breaks even fighting with arbitrary probability, it will break even fighting with probability $f_3 = [(1 - b^2)/(1 - p_3)](p_3/b^2)$, as required by the equilibrium strategy. Thus if the weak incumbent reaches period 3 with $p_3 > 0$, it will be willing to follow the equilibrium strategy.

In the same way, one can work backward, period by period, and verify that the weak incumbent will be willing to follow the equilibrium strategy.

Observe the round-robin nature of the argument that determines the probabilities of sequential equilibrium actions if players follow mixed strategies. When an entrant is playing randomly it stays out with probability $1/a$, because that is the probability that will make the weak incumbent's expected return to fighting zero, so that the weak incumbent will be willing to play randomly. When the weak incumbent is playing randomly, the probability that it will fight is $(1 - b^{n-1})p_n/(1 - p_n)b^{n-1}$, because that will give the entrant's expected payoff the same sign as $b^n - p_n$, and in particular make the entrant willing to play randomly if $b^n = p_n$.

Kreps and Wilson resolve the chain store paradox by taking account of entrants' uncertainty concerning the incumbent's conduct. Early in the game, a weak incumbent will fight to convince entrants that it is strong. Knowing this, early potential entrants stay out of the market.

Toward the end of the game, even a weak incumbent may fight entry (if it has always fought entry before). Only late entrants "try the water," and a weak incumbent will randomize against entry. Along some equilibrium paths, entrants will stay out even against a weak incumbent.

Milgrom and Roberts – imperfect information

Milgrom and Roberts (1982b) also explore the consequences of imperfect information for the chain store paradox.[26] The Milgrom and Roberts entry game has one incumbent and N potential entrants. The incumbent's payoff if it fights entry is negative ($\alpha_0 < 0$), and the incumbent knows α_0. Entrants do not know α_0. Entrant n earns payoff β_n if it stays out. This payoff may be positive or negative ($-\infty < \beta_n < 1$), but it is never as large as the entrant's payoff if the incumbent cooperates (1). An entrant knows its payoff if it stays out, but the incumbent does not. The Milgrom–Roberts entry game thus includes two-sided uncertainty about rivals' payoffs.

Entrants believe that the game tree is most likely to be the one shown in figure 8.6(a). If the game follows this pattern, each entrant, from period N to period 1, decides whether or not to enter. If the entrant comes in, the incumbent decides to fight or to cooperate, and stage payoffs are as indicated. But entrants are not completely certain that figure 8.6(a) shows the correct game tree.

Entrants think there is a small possibility that the correct game tree is the one shown in figure 8.6(b), so that the incumbent always fights entry, and a small possibility that the game tree is the one shown in figure 8.6(c), so that the incumbent never fights entry.

The incumbent, on the other hand, knows the correct game tree. Observe that in the Milgrom–Roberts entry game, the incumbent is always worse off if it fights: $\alpha_0 < 0$. If the backward induction argument of the chain store game unravels in the Milgrom–Roberts entry game, it is not because entrants think the incumbent might collect a greater payoff by

---

[26] See Rosenthal (1981) for an anticipation of the Milgrom–Roberts approach.

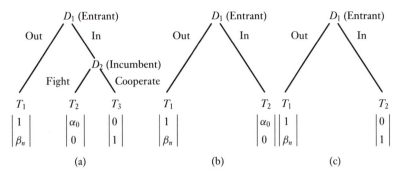

Figure 8.6 Possible game trees for one stage of the Milgrom and Roberts entry game ($-\infty < \alpha_0 < 0$; $-\infty < \beta_n < 1$). (a) Generic; (b) crazy; (c) wimp.

fighting than by cooperating. It is because entrants are not quite sure what game they are playing.

As the game begins (period N), the probabilities entrants assign to the different game trees are

$$\text{Pr (Generic)} = \frac{1}{1 + \varepsilon + \delta}, \qquad \text{Pr (Crazy)} = \frac{\varepsilon}{1 + \varepsilon + \delta},$$

$$\text{Pr (Wimp)} = \frac{\delta}{1 + \varepsilon + \delta}. \tag{8.68}$$

ε and δ assumed to be small, so that entrants begin the game thinking that it is unlikely that the incumbent is either crazy or a wimp.

Milgrom and Roberts outline a sequential equilibrium in which probabilities of entry and of fighting in response to entry are defined consistently with actions. The equilibrium has some features in common with the sequential equilibrium of the Kreps and Wilson entry game. In particular, if a generic incumbent fails to fight entry, entry occurs and the incumbent cooperates in every subsequent period.

Near the beginning of the game, in sequential equilibrium, if the incumbent has fought entry in the past and it suffers a new incident of entry, it will fight if α_0 is sufficiently close to zero. In other words, if entrants attach positive probability to the possibility that the incumbent will fight, the incumbent will fight if the cost of fighting is not too great. By so doing, it will reinforce entrants' belief that it will fight entry. Near the end of the game, however, the expected payoff from fighting – future entry deterrence – falls below the short-run cost, and the generic incumbent will cooperate in the event of entry.

Entrant n will come in if the expected return from entry, using beliefs that are sequentially consistent with strategies, is greater than β_n, the return from staying out. The most likely entrants are those with poor alternatives.

In the Milgrom and Roberts entry deterrence game, potential entrants stay out of the market because they are not quite sure what kind of incumbent they are playing against. If there is a small chance that an incumbent will fight no matter what, then potential entrant will rationally stay out until near the end of the game.

Financial market constraints

Benoit (1984) models a multiperiod entry game. Each stage game involves the incumbent and one potential entrant.

The complete information version of the game begins with a potential entrant deciding whether or not to come into the market. If the entrant stays out, the incumbent is a monopolist. If the entrant comes in, the incumbent decides whether to fight or to cooperate. After the incumbent makes its decision, the entrant decides to stay in the market or exits forever. If the entrant stays in the market, the game moves on to the next period and the sequence of decisions is repeated with another potential entrant.

Fighting commits the incumbent to some profit-reducing action (say, an output expansion). The entrant is financially constrained: its resources will allow it to fight for at most N periods. Benoit uses a backward induction argument to obtain a "reverse chain store paradox" result for the complete information game: the incumbent is always able to deter entry.

Like the chain store paradox, this result depends critically on the assumption of complete information. Benoit outlines an incomplete information version of the game in which the incumbent may be unable to deter entry. The incomplete information entry game is reminiscent of the Milgrom and Roberts (1982b) model of predation.

In the Milgrom and Roberts entry game, the entrant is not quite sure what kind of incumbent it faces: there is a small chance that the incumbent is crazy and will fight entry in all circumstances; there is a small chance that the incumbent is a wimp and will cooperate with the entrant in all circumstances. In the incomplete information version of the Benoit entry game, the incumbent is not quite sure what kind of entrant it faces. There is a small chance that once it comes in the entrant will stay in for N periods no matter what the incumbent does.

Sequential equilibrium in this version of the Benoit model can involve price wars, and the price wars may end with exit or with cooperation. In Kreps–Wilson–Milgrom–Roberts type models, predation occurs because the incumbent invests in reputation to discourage future entrants. In the Benoit model, predation occurs because the incumbent thinks it may be able to drive the entrant from the market.

It remains to explain why an entrant might be subject to financial constraints. As noted above, one of the standard arguments as to why predatory pricing cannot occur relies on perfect capital markets. But there is every reason to think that real-world capital markets are imperfect, and imperfect in a way that creates a role for precisely the kind of reputation studied in Kreps–Wilson–Milgrom–Roberts models of predation.

Real-world firms fund investment, in part, by raising funds on financial markets. But the possibility of bankruptcy induces lenders to charge a risk premium. Established firms have a history of borrowing, a reputation, that allows financial markets to assess the odds that they will go bankrupt. Potential entrants have no such reputation. Even though some potential entrants are in very little danger of going bankrupt, lenders will be unable to know this with certainty – they will be unable to distinguish good risks from bad. Entrants, as a class, will pay a higher risk premium than incumbents (Williamson, 1974; Martinelli, 1997). Not only that, but an entrant's risk premium will be higher, the greater the perceived risk of bankruptcy. An incumbent firm can influence this perceived risk by engaging in an occasional episode of predation.

8.6   LIMIT PRICING

8.6.1   Imperfect information

Milgrom and Roberts (1982a) develop models of the entry in which some equilibria resemble
Bain's (1949b) limit pricing model.[27]

There is one incumbent and one potential entrant.[28] Each operates with constant marginal
cost. The incumbent knows its own marginal cost, which is either low ($\underline{c}_2$) or high ($\bar{c}_2$). The
potential entrant knows that the incumbent's cost is either low or high, but does not know
which. The potential entrant knows that

$$\Pr(c_1 = \underline{c}_1) = 1 - u, \qquad \Pr(c_1 = \bar{c}_1) = u, \tag{8.69}$$

and the incumbent knows that the potential entrant knows this.[29]

The potential entrant likewise has constant marginal cost, with one of two possible values:
low ($\underline{c}_2$) or high ($\bar{c}_2$). The potential entrant knows its own marginal cost. The incumbent
knows that the potential entrant's marginal cost is either $\underline{c}_2$ or $\bar{c}_2$, but it does not know which.
The incumbent knows that

$$\Pr(c_2 = \underline{c}_2) = 1 - v, \qquad \Pr(c_2 = \bar{c}_2) = v, \tag{8.70}$$

and the potential entrant knows that the incumbent knows this.

The game takes place over two periods. In period 1 the incumbent (firm 1) decides what
to produce, knowing its own marginal cost but not the marginal cost of the potential entrant.
The potential entrant (firm 2) observes the incumbent's period 1 output and decides whether
or not to enter (knowing its own costs but not the marginal cost of the incumbent). If the
potential entrant stays out, the incumbent is a monopolist in period 2. If the potential entrant
comes into the market, it must cover a fixed cost of entry F; each firm learns the other's costs;
and the second-period market is a Cournot quantity-setting duopoly.

The incumbent's payoff is the sum of its payoffs in the two periods. The potential entrant's
payoff is zero if it stays out or its second-period Cournot duopoly profit if it comes in.

A pure strategy for the incumbent is a function s that gives the incumbent's first-period
output as a function of its unit cost ($\underline{c}_1$ or $\bar{c}_1$). A pure strategy for the potential entrant is a
function t that gives the entrant's decision (In, 1; or Out, 0) as a function of its own cost and
the first-period output of the incumbent.

Define an equilibrium as a pair of strategies, (s^*, t^*) and conjectures, $(\bar{s}, \bar{t})$, such that:

1   s^* maximizes the incumbent's payoff, given its beliefs $\bar{t}$ concerning the potential
     entrant's strategy;

---

[27] See section 5.2.1; see also Arvan (1986, pp. 113–7).

[28] See Bagwell and Ramey (1991) and Martin (1995) for extensions to oligopoly.

[29] The model incorporates uncertainty about rival's costs. But when the demand curve and the cost function are
linear, marginal cost enters payoff functions only through the market size parameter $S = (a - c)/b$. It follows that
the model could be reinterpreted as reflecting uncertainty about the true value of a, the price-axis intercept of the
inverse demand curve. For such a model, see Roberts (1986). For models that allow costs to vary over a range of
possible values, see Milgrom and Roberts (1982a, pp. 451–5) and Roberts (1987, pp. 160–5).

Table 8.2   Payoffs for the linear Milgrom–Roberts limit price model. Inverse demand curve $p = 10 - Q$; incumbent's marginal cost is either $\frac{1}{2}$ or 2; potential entrant's marginal cost is either $\frac{3}{2}$ or 2; fixed entry cost F. $\pi_2^C(\frac{1}{2}, \frac{3}{2})$ indicates firm 1's Cournot payoff if both firms have low cost, and so on

---

Incumbent's first-period profit:

$$\pi_1\left(\tfrac{1}{2}, q_1\right) = \left(\tfrac{19}{2} - q_1\right)q_1 \qquad \text{or} \qquad \pi_1(2, q_1) = (8 - q_1)q_1$$

Incumbent's monopoly profit:

$$\pi_1^m\left(\tfrac{1}{2}\right) = \left(\tfrac{19}{4}\right)^2 \qquad \text{or} \qquad \pi_1^m(2) = (4)^2$$

Second-period Cournot oligopoly profits:

$$\pi_1^C\left(\tfrac{1}{2}, \tfrac{3}{2}\right) = \tfrac{49}{4} \qquad\qquad \pi_2^C\left(\tfrac{1}{2}, \tfrac{3}{2}\right) = \tfrac{25}{4} - F$$

$$\pi_1^C\left(\tfrac{1}{2}, 2\right) = \tfrac{121}{9} \qquad\qquad \pi_2^C\left(\tfrac{1}{2}, 2\right) = \tfrac{169}{36} - F$$

$$\pi_1^C\left(2, \tfrac{3}{2}\right) = \tfrac{25}{4} \qquad\qquad \pi_2^C\left(2, \tfrac{3}{2}\right) = 9 - F$$

$$\pi_1^C(2, 2) = \tfrac{64}{9} \qquad\qquad \pi_2^C(2, 2) = \tfrac{64}{9} - F$$

---

2   t^* maximizes the potential entrant's payoff, given its beliefs concerning the incumbent's strategy;

3   $(s^*, t^*) = (\bar{s}, \bar{t})$: beliefs are correct.

It is convenient to retreat to a specific example. Let the demand function and cost values be

$$p = 10 - Q, \qquad \underline{c}_1 = \tfrac{1}{2}, \qquad \bar{c}_1 = 2, \qquad \underline{c}_2 = \tfrac{3}{2}, \qquad \bar{c}_2 = 2. \qquad (8.71)$$

If the entrant comes in, the second-period market is thus a Cournot oligopoly with linear demand and (at least in three out of four cases) cost differences. Table 8.2 shows various single-period payoffs for the second period.

Equilibria for this game fall into two categories. In a pooling equilibrium, a low-cost and a high-cost incumbent produce the same first-period output. Since correct beliefs are built into the definition of an equilibrium, the potential entrant will know that first-period output in pooling equilibrium is independent of the incumbent's cost. Consequently, in pooling equilibrium, the potential entrant will not be able to infer the incumbent's cost by looking at first-period output, and the potential entrant will understand this.

In contrast, in a separating equilibrium, the incumbent's strategy calls for different first-period output depending on whether the incumbent's costs are high or low. In a separating equilibrium, the potential entrant is able to infer the incumbent's marginal cost by observing first-period output.

Pooling equilibrium

The potential entrant knows its own fixed cost. Since it gains no information by observing the incumbent's first-period output, the potential entrant comes in if it expects a positive profit. From table 8.2, the entrant's expected profit is

$$(1 - u)\left(\tfrac{25}{4} - F\right) + u(9 - F) = \tfrac{25}{4} + \tfrac{11}{4}u - F \tag{8.72}$$

if it has low cost and

$$(1 - u)\left(\tfrac{169}{36} - F\right) + u\left(\tfrac{64}{9} - F\right) = \tfrac{169}{36} + \tfrac{29}{12}u - F \tag{8.73}$$

if it has high cost.

For a given entry cost F, entry is more likely to be profitable the greater is u (the probability that the incumbent has high marginal cost). For a given value of u, entry is more likely to be profitable the lower is F. If F is very low, high-cost and low-cost entrants will come into the market. For intermediate values of F, low-cost entrants will come in while high-cost entrants stay out. If F is very high, even low-cost entrants will stay out of the market.

Let entry cost take an intermediate value, $F = 7$. Then a low-cost entrant would come into the market ((8.72) will be positive) but a high-cost entrant would stay out ((8.73) will be negative), provided that[30]

$$\tfrac{3}{11} < u < \tfrac{83}{87}. \tag{8.74}$$

Suppose that u lies in this range. What this means is that in a pooling equilibrium low-cost entrants will come into the market and high-cost entrants will stay out. Thus the probability of entry is $1 - v$, the probability that the entrant has low cost.

We shall look for pooling equilibria of the form

$$s^*(\underline{c}_1) = s^*(\bar{c}_1) = q^m(\underline{c}_1), \tag{8.75}$$

$$t^*(\underline{c}_2, q_1) = IN, \tag{8.76}$$

$$t^*(\bar{c}_2, q_1) = \begin{cases} IN & q_1 < q^m(\underline{c}_1), \\ OUT & q_1 \geq q^m(\underline{c}_1). \end{cases} \tag{8.77}$$

The low-cost incumbent produces its unconstrained monopoly output, $q^m(\underline{c}_1)$. The high-cost incumbent mimics a low-cost incumbent, producing more than its unconstrained profit-maximizing output ($q^m(\underline{c}_1) > q^m(\bar{c}_1)$). A low-cost potential entrant always enters the market. A high-cost potential entrant comes in if it observes that the incumbent produces less than $q^m(\underline{c}_1)$.

Suppose that the incumbent follows the strategy s^*. Then the entrant gains no information from observing first-period output. For the example of table 8.2, with fixed cost of entry $F = 7$, the optimal response of the entrant is to come in if it has low cost and stay out if it

---

[30] For general values of F, u must fall in the range

$$\tfrac{4}{11}F - \tfrac{25}{11} < u < \tfrac{12}{29}F - \tfrac{169}{87}.$$

has high cost, provided that u lies in the range given by (8.74). But this is what the proposed strategy requires; hence the proposed strategy is optimal for entrants, given s^*.

Now suppose that potential entrants follow the strategy t^*. Is s^* a profit-maximizing response for the incumbent? If the incumbent has low cost and it produces more than $q^m(\underline{c}_1)$, it will reduce its first-period profit without inducing any change in the second period (a low-cost entrant will come in anyway; a high-cost entrant will stay out for $q_1 = q^m(\underline{c}_1)$, and it will stay out for $q_1 > q^m(\underline{c}_1)$. On the other hand, if a low-cost incumbent produces less than $q^m(\underline{c}_1)$, it will reduce first-period profit and induce entry by a high-cost potential entrant, reducing its (expected) second-period payoff. Hence, given t^*, a low-cost incumbent maximizes its payoff by following s^*.

s^* calls for the high-cost incumbent to produce more than its unconstrained profit-maximizing output, but also to produce where its profit declines as its output rises. So if a high-cost incumbent produces more than $q^m(\underline{c}_1)$, its first-period payoff will fall, and its second-period payoff will not change. Thus a high-cost incumbent has no incentive to produce more than $q^m(\underline{c}_1)$.

Production of any output less than $q^m(\underline{c}_1)$ has the same consequences for entry in the second period. Thus if a high-cost incumbent were to produce less than $q^m(\underline{c}_1)$, it would choose to produce $q^m(\bar{c}_1)$, which at least will maximize its payoff in the first period.

The high-cost incumbent's expected payoff from following strategy s^* is

$$[8 - q^m(\underline{c}_1)]\, q^m(\underline{c}_1) + \pi^m(\bar{c}_1)v + \pi^C(\bar{c}_1, \underline{c}_2)(1 - v)$$
$$= \left(8 - \tfrac{19}{4}\right) \tfrac{19}{4} + 16v + \tfrac{25}{4}(1 - v)$$
$$= \tfrac{247}{16} + 16v + \tfrac{25}{4}(1 - v). \tag{8.78}$$

On the other hand, the high-cost incumbent's expected payoff from producing $q^m(\bar{c}_1)$ in the first period is

$$\pi^m(\bar{c}_1) + \pi^C(\bar{c}_1, \underline{c}_2)(1 - v) + \pi^C(\bar{c}_1, \bar{c}_2)v$$
$$= 16 + \tfrac{64}{9}v + \tfrac{25}{4}(1 - v). \tag{8.79}$$

For (8.75)–(8.77) to be an equilibrium, (8.78) cannot be less than (8.79); that is,

$$\tfrac{247}{16} + 16v + \tfrac{25}{4}(1 - v) \geq 16 + \tfrac{64}{9}v + \tfrac{25}{4}(1 - v), \tag{8.80}$$

or, equivalently,

$$v \geq \tfrac{81}{1280} = 0.0633. \tag{8.81}$$

Hence for this example, (8.75)–(8.77) is a pooling equilibrium strategy provided that (8.74) and (8.81) hold.

The pooling equilibrium strategy does not limit entry of a low-cost incumbent. A high-cost incumbent, however, by producing the monopoly output of a low-cost incumbent, can induce a high-cost potential entrant to stay out of the market. The high-cost entrant stays out of the market even though it would earn a profit in Cournot quantity-setting equilibrium.

Separating equilibrium

We seek separating equilibria of the form

$$s^*(\underline{c}_1) = q_L > q^m(\underline{c}_1), \tag{8.82}$$

$$s^*(\bar{c}_1) = q^m(\bar{c}_1), \tag{8.83}$$

$$t^*(c_2, q_1) = \begin{cases} IN, & q_1 < q_L, \\ OUT, & q_1 \geq q_L. \end{cases} \tag{8.84}$$

In equilibria of this type, the low-cost incumbent produces a limit output q_L that exceeds its unconstrained monopoly output. We shall determine the range within which q_L must lie. The high-cost incumbent produces its unconstrained monopoly output. Potential entrants of either type enter if they observe first-period output less than q_L, and stay out otherwise.

Consider first the strategy of the potential entrant. Given entry costs $F = 7$, a potential entrant of either type would prefer to stay out against a low-cost incumbent, since it would suffer a loss in the post-entry market. This is what t^* requires: if the potential entrant observes output q_L, it correctly infers that the incumbent has low cost, and it stays out of the market.

On the other hand, a potential entrant of either type would prefer to come into the market against a high-cost incumbent – it would earn a positive profit in the second period. Again, this is what t^* requires: if the potential entrant observes the incumbent producing the monopoly output of a high-cost incumbent, it correctly infers that the incumbent has high cost and it comes into the market. Thus the strategy t^* is optimal for the potential entrant, given s^*.

If a high-cost incumbent follows (8.83), entry occurs in the second period. Entry is by a low-cost firm with probability $1 - v$ and by a high-cost firm with probability v; the high-cost incumbent's expected return from following (8.83) is

$$\pi^m(\bar{c}_1) + (1 - v)\pi^C(\bar{c}_1, \underline{c}_2) + v\pi^C(\bar{c}_1, \bar{c}_2)$$
$$= 16 + (1 - v)\tfrac{25}{4} + v\tfrac{64}{9} = 16 + \tfrac{25}{4} + \tfrac{31}{36}v. \tag{8.85}$$

For (8.82)–(8.84) to be an equilibrium, the high-cost incumbent must prefer not to deviate, which will be the case if

$$16 + \tfrac{25}{4} + \tfrac{31}{36}v > (8 - q_L)q_L + 16 \tag{8.86}$$

or (rearranging terms and completing the square) if

$$(q_L - 4)^2 > \tfrac{39}{4} - \tfrac{31}{36}v. \tag{8.87}$$

Thus, if[31]

$$q_L > 4 + \sqrt{\tfrac{39}{4} - \tfrac{31}{36}v}, \tag{8.88}$$

the high-cost incumbent will prefer to follow its part of the separating strategy. Exactly what the lower limit is for q_L depends on v. For $v = 0$, $q_L > 7.12$ will serve. Positive values of v will allow smaller values of q_L to sustain separating equilibria.

The low-cost incumbent's payoff from following the equilibrium strategy is

$$\left(\tfrac{19}{2} - q_L\right) q_L + \pi^m(\underline{c}_1) = \left(\tfrac{19}{2} - q_L\right) q_L + \left(\tfrac{19}{4}\right)^2. \tag{8.89}$$

The low-cost incumbent has no incentive to deviate from the separating equilibrium strategy by producing more than q_L. To do so would reduce the low-cost incumbent's first-period profit without altering its second-period profit (entrants stay out if $q_1 = q_L$ and entrants stay out if $q_1 > q_L$). Producing any output less than q_L will induce entry. It follows that if the low-cost incumbent deviates from the separating equilibrium strategy by producing less than q_L, it will produce its unconstrained monopoly output in the first period, which will maximize its first-period profit. The low-cost incumbent's expected return from producing less than q_L is

$$\pi^m(\underline{c}_1) + v\pi^C(\underline{c}_1, \bar{c}_2) + (1 - v)\pi^C(\underline{c}_1, \underline{c}_2)$$
$$= \left(\tfrac{19}{4}\right)^2 + \tfrac{121}{9}v + \tfrac{49}{4}(1 - v) = \left(\tfrac{19}{4}\right)^2 + \tfrac{49}{4} + \tfrac{43}{36}v. \tag{8.90}$$

For the low-cost incumbent to be willing to follow the separating equilibrium strategy, q_L and v must be such that

$$\left(\tfrac{19}{2} - q_L\right) q_L + \left(\tfrac{19}{4}\right)^2 > \left(\tfrac{19}{4}\right)^2 + \tfrac{49}{4} + \tfrac{43}{36}v. \tag{8.91}$$

Rearranging terms and completing the square, the low-cost incumbent's payoff from the separating equilibrium strategy will exceed the payoff from deviating if

$$\left(q_L - \tfrac{19}{4}\right)^2 < \tfrac{165}{16} - \tfrac{43}{36}v \tag{8.92}$$

or if

$$\tfrac{19}{4} - \sqrt{\tfrac{165}{16} - \tfrac{43}{36}v} < q_L < \tfrac{19}{4} + \sqrt{\tfrac{165}{16} - \tfrac{43}{36}v}. \tag{8.93}$$

The lower limit in (8.88) is greater than the lower limit in (8.93). Combining (8.88) and (8.93), values of q_L that satisfy

$$4 + \sqrt{\tfrac{39}{4} - \tfrac{31}{36}v} < q_L < \tfrac{19}{4} + \sqrt{\tfrac{165}{16} - \tfrac{43}{36}v} \tag{8.94}$$

will sustain separating equilibria with which low-cost and high-cost incumbents will willingly comply. The exact bounds of this range depend on v. For $v = 0$, any q_L between 7.12 and

---

[31] The high-cost incumbent will also prefer to follow the separating strategy if

$$4 - \sqrt{\tfrac{39}{4} - \tfrac{31}{36}v} \geq q_L.$$

Separating equilibria of this kind are ruled out by (8.82), which requires q_L to exceed the low-cost incumbent's monopoly output.

7.96 will serve as the limit output in a separating equilibrium. Greater values of v reduce both the upper and the lower bounds of (8.94).

Observe that for separating equilibria of the type (8.82)–(8.84), entry occurs exactly when it would if the potential entrant knew the incumbent's cost. However, to obtain this result, the separating equilibrium strategy requires the low-cost incumbent to expand output above the unconstrained joint-profit-maximizing level. A low-cost incumbent is able to deter entry that would not occur under complete and perfect information by accepting reduced first-period profit.

8.6.2   Predation, limit pricing, and merger

One of the arguments that predation will never occur is based on the view that, if ever predation were profitable, it would always be dominated by some even more profitable alternative.

Instead of driving a rival from the market by engaging in a long, risky, and costly price war, an incumbent could simply buy the rival. Although this alternative strategy is costly, it is neither long nor risky. It has the further advantage of allowing the incumbent to begin acting as a monopolist right away, rather than at the end of the price war (McGee, 1958, pp. 139–40).[32]

Competition policy might prevent a dominant incumbent from acquiring an entrant or potential entrant (Posner, 1979, p. 939). However, competition policy is enforced with varying degrees of enthusiasm over time and space, and often contains an escape clause for failing firms. Predation, if successful, might qualify an entrant as a failing firm. Thus predation for merger is an interesting topic.

Predation without later entry

Saloner (1987) models two incumbent firms that compete over three periods. In the first period, the two firms compete as Cournot quantity-setters. Firm 1 knows firm 2's constant marginal cost. Firm 2 does not know firm 1's constant marginal cost, which takes one of two values, low ($\underline{c}_1$) or high ($\bar{c}_1$). At the end of the first period, firm 2 may revise its beliefs about firm 1's costs. In period 2, firm 1 makes a once-and-for-all offer to purchase firm 2. Firm 2 either accepts or rejects the offer. If firm 2 rejects the offer, the firms compete in the third period as Cournot duopolists. In the first version of the model, there is no possibility of entry in the third period. Thus if the merger takes place, firm 1 is a monopolist in period 3.

The amount firm 1 would be willing to offer to buy firm 2 and the amount firm 2 will be willing to accept both depend on the profit firm 2 expects to make in the third period if the merger does not take place. Thus we need to analyze the third-period Cournot market, even though if the merger takes place the third-period Cournot market never materializes.

Let u be the probability that firm 2 assigns, at the start of the third period, to the possibility that firm 1 has high cost. With linear inverse demand $p = a - bQ$, if the merger does not

---

[32] For a case study, see Burns (1986). For a model of strategic behavior by the entrant in anticipation of merger, see Rasmusen (1988).

take place, firm 2's expected third-period profit is

$$(1 - u)[a - c_2 - b(\underline{q}_1 + q_2)]q_2 + u[a - c_2 - b(\bar{q}_1 + q_2)]q_2$$
$$= b(S_2 - q_{1u} - q_2) q_2, \tag{8.95}$$

where $S_2 = (a - c_2)/b$ is the quantity that would be demanded if price were equal to c_2, $\underline{q}_1$ is the output of a low-cost firm 1 and $\bar{q}_1$ is the output of a high-cost firm 1, and $q_{1u} = (1 - u)\underline{q}_1 + u\bar{q}_1$ is firm 1's expected output.[33]

Maximization of (8.95) gives the equation of firm 2's best-response function, showing its profit-maximizing output as a function of firm 1's expected output:

$$q_2 = \tfrac{1}{2}\{S_2 - [(1 - u)\underline{q}_1 + u\bar{q}_1]\} = \tfrac{1}{2}(S_2 - q_{1u}). \tag{8.96}$$

The behavior of a high-cost firm 1 and a low-cost firm 1 in the third period can be described by the appropriate best-response function:

$$\underline{q}_1 = \tfrac{1}{2}(\underline{S}_1 - q_2) \qquad \text{or} \qquad \bar{q}_1 = \tfrac{1}{2}(\bar{S}_1 - q_2), \tag{8.97}$$

where $\underline{S}_1 = (a - \underline{c}_1)/b$ and $\bar{S}_1 = (a - \bar{c}_1)/b$.

Equations (8.96)–(8.97) form a system of three equations in three unknowns; they can be solved for the Cournot equilibrium outputs:

$$\underline{q}_1 = \tfrac{1}{3}\left(S_{1u} + \frac{c_2 - c_{1u}}{b}\right) + \tfrac{1}{2}u\frac{\bar{c}_1 - \underline{c}_1}{b}, \tag{8.98}$$

$$\bar{q}_1 = \tfrac{1}{3}\left(S_{1u} + \frac{c_2 - c_{1u}}{b}\right) - \tfrac{1}{2}u\frac{\bar{c}_1 - \underline{c}_1}{b}, \tag{8.99}$$

$$q_2 = \tfrac{1}{3}\left(S_{1u} - 2\frac{c_2 - c_{1u}}{b}\right), \tag{8.100}$$

where $c_{1u} = (1 - u)\underline{c}_1 + u\bar{c}_1$ and $S_{1u} = (a - c_{1u})/b$.

Given the equilibrium outputs, the demand function implies that price will be either

$$\underline{p} = c_{1u} + \tfrac{1}{3}b\left(S_{1u} + \frac{c_2 - c_{1u}}{b}\right) - \tfrac{1}{2}u(\bar{c}_1 - \underline{c}_1) \tag{8.101}$$

if firm 1 is a low-cost firm or

$$\bar{p} = c_{1u} + \tfrac{1}{3}b\left(S_{1u} + \frac{c_2 - c_{1u}}{b}\right) + \tfrac{1}{2}(1 - u)(\bar{c}_1 - \underline{c}_1) \tag{8.102}$$

if firm 1 is a high-cost firm.

---

[33] q_{10} is thus firm 1's expected output if firm 2 is certain that firm 1 is a low-cost firm, and q_{11} is firm 1's expected output if firm 2 is certain that firm 1 is a high-cost firm.

Firm 2's expected profit in the final period is therefore

$$\Pi_{2u} = \tfrac{1}{9}b\left(S_2 - \frac{c_2 - c_{1u}}{b}\right)^2.$$

(8.103)

Π_{2u} rises as u rises. The greater is u, the more likely it is that firm 1 has high cost and the smaller the cost difference term, $(c_2 - c_{1u})/b$, that is subtracted away in (8.103).

To acquire firm 2, firm 1 must offer at least Π_{2u}: firm 2 would accept no less, since that is its expected return from refusing the purchase offer. On the other hand, firm 1 would never offer more than Π_{20}, firm 2's expected profit in the third period if firm 2 is certain that firm 1 is a high-cost firm.

Saloner shows that high-cost and low-cost firms will make the same offer in equilibrium. Making reasonable restrictions on firm 2's beliefs, the equilibrium offer is Π_{2u}, firm 2's expected profit if the third period Cournot market occurs. By accepting such an offer, firm 2 does as well as it could by remaining in the market. Thus if there is no possibility of third period entry, firm 1 in equilibrium always makes an offer that firm 2 is willing to accept: the merger always takes place.

SEPARATING EQUILIBRIA

We now examine behavior in the first-period Cournot market. Let r be the probability that firm 2 assigns, at the start of the first period, to the possibility that firm 1 has high cost. A separating equilibrium will involve firm 2 and a high-cost firm 1 producing period 1 output along their best-response functions:[34]

$$q_2 = \tfrac{1}{2}(S_2 - q_{1r}),$$

(8.104)

where $q_{1r} = (1 - r)\underline{q}_1 + r\bar{q}_1$, and

$$\bar{q}_1 = \tfrac{1}{2}(\bar{S}_1 - q_2).$$

(8.105)

A low-cost firm, on the other hand, must produce enough so that a high-cost firm would not profit by mimicking a low-cost firm. If a high-cost firm copies a low-cost firm, its return is (ignoring discounting)

$$[a - \bar{c}_1 - b(\underline{q}_1 + q_2)]\underline{q}_1 - \Pi_{20} + \Pi^m(\bar{c}_1).$$

(8.106)

The first term is the high-cost firm's payoff in the first period, producing the same output as a low-cost firm. The second term is the cost of purchasing firm 2, paying what a low-cost firm would pay. The third term is the high-cost firm's third-period monopoly profit.

---

[34] In addition to the separating and pooling equilibria discussed here, there are mixed-strategy equilibria that combine elements of equilibria of the first two types. See Saloner (1987) for a discussion.

If the high-cost firm does not mimic the low-cost firm, then its return is

$$[a - \bar{c}_1 - b(\bar{q}_1 + q_2)]\bar{q}_1 - \Pi_{21} + \Pi^m(\bar{c}_1). \tag{8.107}$$

In separating equilibrium, q_1 must be large enough so that (8.107) is greater than or equal to (8.106). With some manipulation, this condition becomes

$$[\bar{S}_1 - (\bar{q}_1 + q_2)]\bar{q}_1 - [\bar{S}_1 - (\underline{q}_1 + q_2)]\underline{q}_1 \geq \frac{R}{b}, \tag{8.108}$$

where

$$R = \Pi_{21} - \Pi_{20} \tag{8.109}$$

is a high-cost firm's reward for convincing firm 2 that it is a low-cost firm: the difference between the purchase prices for a high-cost and a low-cost firm.

A low-cost firm must produce at least enough output to satisfy (8.108). It would never produce more than enough; to do so would reduce first-period profit without changing any of the other characteristics of equilibrium. Thus, in separating equilibrium, (8.108) must hold as an equality.

Equations (8.104), (8.105), and the equality version of (8.108) are then a system of three equations in three unknowns that define the first-period separating equilibrium. In separating equilibrium, the first-period outputs are

$$\underline{q}_1 = \tfrac{1}{3}\left(\bar{S}_1 + \frac{c_2 - \bar{c}_1}{b}\right) + \frac{4 - r}{3}\sqrt{\frac{R}{b}}, \tag{8.110}$$

$$\bar{q}_1 = \tfrac{1}{3}\left(\bar{S}_1 + \frac{c_2 - \bar{c}_1}{b}\right) + \frac{1 - r}{3}\sqrt{\frac{R}{b}}, \tag{8.111}$$

$$q_2 = \tfrac{1}{3}\left(\bar{S}_1 - 2\frac{c_2 - \bar{c}_1}{b}\right) - \frac{2(1 - r)}{3}\sqrt{\frac{R}{b}}. \tag{8.112}$$

The first term on the right in (8.110) is the low-cost firm's equilibrium output in Cournot quantity-setting equilibrium with cost differences, if each firm knows the other's costs. The second term is the extra output that the low-cost firm produces so that a high-cost firm would not care to copy it.

The second term increases with R: the greater the benefit from being thought of as a low-cost firm, the more a low-cost firm will have to produce to make copying irrational.

The high-cost firm 1 also produces more, in equilibrium, than it would in a complete information Cournot game. Firm 2 reacts to firm 1's expected output along its best-response function, so that the expansion of output by a low-cost firm 1 induces a reduction in output by firm 2. This reduction in output by firm 2 induces an increase in output by a high-cost firm 1.

POOLING EQUILIBRIA

There are also pooling equilibria, with first-period best-response functions

$$\underline{q}_1 = \bar{q}_1 = \tfrac{1}{2}\left(\underline{S}_1 - q_2\right), \qquad q_2 = \tfrac{1}{2}(S_2 - \underline{q}_1). \tag{8.113}$$

Here, firm 2 and the low-cost firm 1 simply produce along their respective best-response functions. The high-cost firm 1 mimics a low-cost incumbent.

There are two side-conditions that must be met for pooling equilibria to be possible. A high-cost firm 1 must prefer mimicking a low-cost incumbent and purchasing firm 2 at the price Π_{2r} to producing along its best-response function, revealing its type, and purchasing firm 2 at price Π_{21}.

By construction, a high-cost firm 1 will not mimic a low-cost firm 1 if the low-cost firm 1 produces its separating equilibrium output (this is condition (8.108)). For the pooling equilibrium to hold, therefore, a low-cost firm 1 must prefer pooling and purchasing firm 2 at price Π_{2r} to producing following a separating strategy, revealing its type, and purchasing firm 2 at price Π_{20}.

Predation with possible later entry

Saloner considers a variation of the above model in which entry may occur in the third period, after the offer to merge has been accepted or rejected. The entrant is assumed to have lower costs than firm 2. This means that firm 1's duopoly profits are greater against firm 2 than against the entrant.

At the same time, entry is assumed to require that the entrant sink entry costs that are sufficiently great so that it will only come in against a high-cost firm 1. Against a low-cost firm 1, or firm 1 and firm 2, the entrant would lose money and would prefer to stay out of the market.

In the first version of the model, the low-cost firm 1's incentive to expand output is to improve the terms of the merger. A low-cost firm 1 will have an additional incentive to expand output in the first period if entry is possible in the third: output expansion signals to the third-period entrant that firm 1 is likely to have low cost. This version of the model combines predation and limit pricing. There is a separating equilibrium for this altered model in which firm 1 expands first-period output, deters entry, and carries out the merger on favorable terms.

There are also pooling equilibria in which a high-cost firm 1 can deter entry and carry out a takeover by mimicking a low-cost firm 1. In other words, if rivals are uncertain about a dominant firm's costs, the dominant firm can simultaneously prey against fringe incumbents and discourage entry.

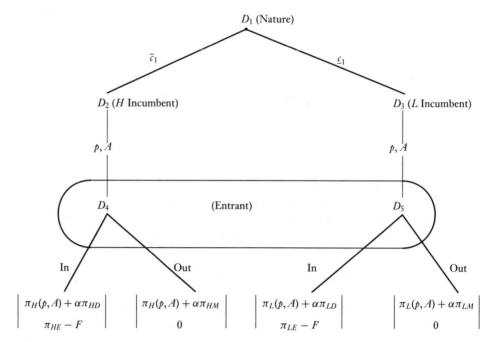

Figure 8.7 The extensive form of the Bagwell–Ramey limit advertising model. Subscripts H and L denote high- and low-cost incumbents, respectively; subscripts D and M denote second-period duopoly and monopoly, respectively; $F > 0 =$ fixed entry cost; α is the factor used to discount second-period income.

8.7 Advertising and Limit Pricing

8.7.1 Uncertainty about an incumbent's cost

Bagwell and Ramey (1988) present an entry game in which the incumbent can signal with advertising as well as price. The entrant is uncertain about the incumbent's average cost, but knows that it is either high ($\bar{c}_1$) or low ($\underline{c}_1$). The entrant observes the incumbent's first-period price and decides whether or not to enter in the second period. Entry is profitable only if the incumbent has high costs.

The formal structure of the model is shown in figure 8.7. At the first decision node, nature determines the incumbent's costs. These are revealed to the incumbent, but not to the potential entrant. Following nature's move, the incumbent sets its first-period price and advertising. Having observed the incumbent's first-period actions, the entrant decides whether or not to come into the market. If the entrant stays out, the incumbent earns a monopoly return in the second period. If the entrant comes in, the second-period market is a duopoly. Whatever the nature of the duopoly, we assume that the entrant's duopoly returns are such that the entrant earns more than enough to cover its entry costs F if the incumbent has high cost, but not if the incumbent has low cost:

$$\pi_{LE} - F < 0 < \pi_{HE} - F. \tag{8.114}$$

In separating equilibria, a low-cost incumbent selects values of price and advertising that a high-cost incumbent would not mimic.[35] In a separating equilibrium, the entrant is able to infer the incumbent's cost, and it comes into the market if the incumbent has high unit cost.

Since a high-cost incumbent cannot preclude entry, its profit-maximizing choices in the first period are the monopoly price and advertising: p_{HM} and A_{HM}.

In separating equilibrium, a low-cost incumbent's first-period choices, p_{LS} and A_{LS}, are subject to two constraints. First, they must be such that a high-cost incumbent would not care to imitate them. p_{LS} and A_{LS} must therefore satisfy

$$\pi_H(p_{LS}, A_{LS}) + \alpha \pi_H(p_{HM}, A_{HM}) \leq \pi_H(p_{HM}, A_{HM}) + \alpha \pi_{HD}. \tag{8.115}$$

The left-hand side of (8.115) is a high-cost incumbent's return if it mimics a low-cost firm in the first period and makes its monopoly choices in the second period. The right-hand side of (8.115) is a high-cost incumbent's return if it makes its monopoly choices in the first period and collects its duopoly profit in the second period. From (8.115), the no-mimicry constraint is that p_{LS} and A_{LS} satisfy the inequality

$$\pi_H(p_{LS}, A_{LS}) \leq (1 - \alpha)\pi_H(p_{HM}, A_{HM}) + \alpha \pi_{HD} \equiv \bar{\pi}_H. \tag{8.116}$$

At the same time, the separating equilibrium choices p_{LS} and A_{LS} must offer the low-cost incumbent a greater return than it would get by making its monopoly choices in the first period and collecting its duopoly profit in the second period. Otherwise, the low-cost incumbent is not willing to separate. Hence p_{LS} and A_{LS} must also satisfy

$$\pi_L(p_{LS}, A_{LS}) + \alpha \pi_L(p_{LM}, A_{LM}) \geq \pi_L(p_{LM}, A_{LM}) + \alpha \pi_{LD} \tag{8.117}$$

or

$$\pi_L(p_{LS}, A_{LS}) \geq (1 - \alpha)\pi_L(p_{LM}, A_{LM}) + \alpha \pi_{LD} \equiv \underline{\pi}_L. \tag{8.118}$$

Any (p, A) combination that satisfies (8.116) and (8.118) is a separating equilibrium. If any such points exist,[36] there typically are many of them. Impose the additional condition that the entrant expects that a low-cost incumbent will pick the (p, A) combination that maximizes the incumbent's return, while satisfying (8.116) and (8.118). This allows us to rule out dominated (p, A) combinations – (p, A) pairs that satisfy (8.116) and (8.118) but do not maximize the return of a low-cost incumbent. If an entrant saw such combinations, it would conclude that the incumbent had high cost, and come into the market.

Entry is blocked if the low-cost incumbent's profit-maximizing choices (p_{LM}, A_{LM}) satisfy both constraints. For the example of figure 8.8, (p, A) combinations that lie in the shaded

[35] Pooling equilibria are possible; see Bagwell and Ramey (1988).
[36] See Bagwell and Ramey (1988, Theorem 3) for a sufficient condition for the existence of equilibrium.

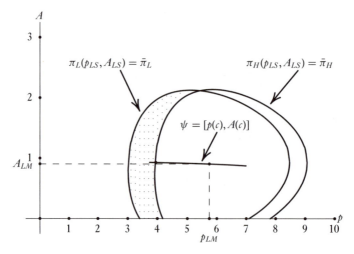

Figure 8.8   Separating equilibrium conditions, Bagwell–Ramey limit advertising model; the shaded area satisfies both the no-mimicry and the willingness-to-separate conditions.

region satisfy both constraints.[37] For such cases, the low-cost incumbent can simply maximize profit and the entrant recognizes that the incumbent has low cost and stays out of the market. If, as in figure 8.8, (p_{LM}, A_{LM}) does not satisfy (8.116), then a high-cost incumbent would find it profitable to mimic a profit-maximizing low-cost incumbent, and a low-cost incumbent is obliged to engage in signaling behavior to reveal that its costs are low.

To analyze the nature of the signaling behavior, consider the curve with equation $\psi = [p(c), A(c)]$ that traces out the monopoly profit-maximizing combinations of price and advertising for different values of marginal cost c.[38] As marginal cost rises, the profit-maximizing price rises and the profit-maximizing advertising level falls. Bagwell and Ramey show that if a low-cost incumbent must engage in signaling behavior to reveal that its costs are low, the constrained profit-maximizing (p, A) combination occurs where the incumbent selects a $[p(c), A(c)]$ combination that just satisfies the constraint $\bar{\pi}_H(p, A) = \bar{\pi}_H$, which is the boundary of the region that satisfies (8.116). This result has a natural interpretation: if a low-cost firm must give up profit to signal that it has low cost, it picks a (p, A) combination that would maximize profit if its unit costs were even lower than they are. Price is lower, and spending on advertising greater, than would be the case if signaling did not occur. For the parameter values used to draw figure 8.8, the separation is effected primarily by distorting price downward, and only slightly by distorting advertising upward.

---

[37] Figure 8.8 is drawn for monopoly inverse demand function $p = 10 + 2A - A^2 - q$ and duopoly inverse demand functions $p_1 = 10 + 2A_1 - A_1^2 - q_1 - 0.5q_2$, $p_2 = 10 + 2A_2 - A_2^2 - 0.5q_1 - q_2$. For simplicity in analyzing the second-stage duopoly, I assume that own advertising affects only own demand. $\underline{c}_1 = \frac{1}{2}$, $\bar{c}_1 = c_2 = 2$, and the price of a unit of advertising is 1. This specification generalizes the Milgrom and Roberts limit-pricing example (8.71) to include advertising.

[38] That is, $p(c)$ and $A(c)$ solve $\max_{p,A} (p - c)q(p, A) - p^A A$.

Table 8.3 The animal farm typology of incentives for strategic investment

	Investment makes incumbent:	
	Tough	*Soft*
Strategic substitutes	A: top dog	A: lean and hungry
	D: top dog	D: lean and hungry
Strategic complements	A: puppy dog	A: fat cat
	D: top dog	D: lean and hungry

Source: Fudenberg and Tirole, 1984

8.7.2 Extensions

It is often the case that models of oligopoly with uncertainty about cost and models of oligopoly with uncertainty about demand yield symmetric results, in the sense that both kinds of uncertainty translate into uncertainty about the number of units that would be demanded if price were equal to marginal cost.

Bagwell and Ramey (1996) obtain results of this kind when they extend their work to consider price and advertising decisions when an entrant is uncertain about the location of the demand curve. They show that if an incumbent wishes to signal that market size is small, it picks values of price and advertising that would be profit-maximizing for an even smaller market. If an incumbent wishes to signal that market size is large, it picks values of price and advertising that would be profit-maximizing for an even larger market.

8.8 ANIMAL FARM

Fudenberg and Tirole's (1984) "animal" taxonomy takes off from the fact that a first-moving firm's incentives are different depending on whether it seeks to deter or to accommodate entry.[39] If an incumbent firm invests – in capacity, in advertising, in R&D – to deter entry, then it aims to reduce the entrant's expected post-entry profit (below sunk entry cost). If the incumbent invests with a view to accommodating entry, it seeks to maximize its own expected payoff (cost of investment plus second-period payoff).

The incentives facing the incumbent depend not only on whether the second-stage regime is entry or accommodation[40] but also on the nature of strategic relationships in the post-entry market, as summarized in table 8.3.

Greater capacity reduces the incumbent's marginal cost. If the second-period market is one of strategic substitutes,[41] greater capacity shifts the incumbent's best-response function

---

[39] Lapham and Ware (1994) extend Fudenberg and Tirole's analysis to Markov games.
[40] The incumbent will prefer the option that yields it the greater payoff.
[41] As, for example, with homogeneous products, linear demand, constant marginal cost, and quantity-setting firms.

outward, making it a tougher competitor. The entrant's equilibrium output is less, which is the profitable outcome for the incumbent whether it seeks to deter or to accommodate entry. The incumbent's incentive is to overinvest in capacity and act as a "top dog."

If, in contrast, the second-period market is one of strategic complements,[42] overinvestment in capacity would lower marginal cost, shift the incumbent's best-response function in the direction of lower prices, and reduce the entrant's equilibrium price. The accommodating incumbent's incentive is to underinvest in capacity, acting like a "puppy dog" and raising the entrant's equilibrium second-period price.

In the same way, if first-period investment makes the incumbent a softer competitor and the second-period is one of strategic complements, the incumbent's first-period incentive is to overinvest, acting as a "fat cat" and evoking a softer equilibrium action from the entrant in the second period. If first-period investment makes the incumbent a softer competitor and the incumbent seeks to deter entry, it should underinvest, making itself a more formidable rival in the second period and reducing the entrant's expected second-period profit.

Slade (1995) examines strategic impacts of price and advertising in the market for saltine crackers in Williamsport, Pennsylvania. She finds that prices are strategic complements and advertising strategic substitutes. Her results indicate that when dynamic considerations are taken into account, incumbents advertise at higher levels, following top-dog strategies, but also set higher prices, following puppy-dog strategies.

Kadiyali (1996) finds that before Fuji's entry into the US photographic film industry, Kodak followed a low-price, high-advertising strategy to deter entry. In the event, entry occurred, after which it appears that Fuji and Kodak settled on a joint strategy of high advertising and low prices (but above Nash levels) to deter further entry.

Röller and Sickles (2000) estimate a two-stage (capacity-setting followed by price-setting) model of the European passenger airline industry. They find that the marginal impact of additional capacity on marginal cost is negative, which makes puppy-dog behavior optimal in the second stage of the game (in which firms' decision variables, prices, are strategic complements).

8.9 CONCLUSION

Profit-maximizing firms engage in entry-deterring investments to the extent that the marginal benefit of such investments (the profit that flows from reduced future competition) exceeds their current cost.

Investment in excess capacity is one such strategy. Whether or not investment in excess capacity constitutes a credible threat depends critically on what potential entrants think the post-entry regime will be, on whether or not there are economies of scale, and (if not) on the size of minimum output relative to the market. Whether incumbents find investment in excess capacity profitable depends on the certainty with which such investment will deter entry and perhaps on the possibility of free-riding by other incumbents. Empirical studies

---

[42] As, for example, with Bowley product differentiation, linear demand, constant marginal cost, and price-setting firms.

provide more support for the idea that incumbents use investment as a way of responding to entry than as a device for precluding entry.

If consumers incur costs in switching suppliers, then incumbents may strategically expand output, as a way of attracting consumers and making entry more difficult. This involves some sacrifice of short-run profit, a strategic investment in a customer base. It is costly to carry excess capacity or to make other strategic investments to deter entry. If incumbents can raise the costs of actual or potential rivals while suffering smaller cost increases themselves, they will generally find it profitable to do so.

Imperfect information is an essential aspect of real-world markets. Models of markets operating under conditions of imperfect information show that a dominant firm may find it worthwhile to engage in predation to create and maintain a reputation as a firm that will fight entry or as a low-cost firm. Such strategies may be unprofitable in the particular market in which they are carried out, but by discouraging entry in other markets they can be optimal, for the dominant firm, from an overall point of view.

Signaling models of limit pricing are based on the observation that a low-cost incumbent has an incentive to select a first-period price that would be unprofitable for a high-cost incumbent, thus signaling that it has low costs and preserving its monopoly.

PROBLEMS

8.1 (Stackelberg quantity leadership) Let the inverse demand function of a market supplied by two firms be

$$p = a - b(q_1 + q_2).$$

Both firms have cost function

$$c(q) = cq + F.$$

Firm 2, the follower, acts as a Cournot quantity-setter. Firm 1 knows this.
Find equilibrium outputs, price, and payoffs.
See Dowrick (1986), Hamilton and Slutsky (1990), and Daughety (1990).
8.2 Show that in the game beginning from decision node D_1 of figure 8.1, the incumbent's equilibrium choice is to act as a Stackelberg quantity leader.
8.3 Let the inverse demand function be

$$p = a - b(q_1 + q_2).$$

Suppose that the potential entrant can produce with cost function

$$c(q_2) = cq_2 + F.$$

The incumbent's long-run cost function exhibits constant average and marginal cost c per unit. But the incumbent's short-run cost exceeds the long-run cost by a factor that depends on short-run deviations of output from capacity k:

$$c(q_1) = cq_1 + d(q_1 - k)^2,$$

where $d > 0$ measures the extent to which cost rises if output differs from capacity.

Suppose that the entrant believes that the incumbent will expand output to capacity if entry occurs. What capacity level must the incumbent maintain to make the entrant's expected profit equal to zero? What output will the incumbent produce if it maintains this entry-precluding level of capacity?

Compare with Wenders (1971); for a similar approach, with careful attention to micro foundations, Dixon (1986); and Lapham and Ware (1994, p. 581).

8.4 Suppose that a price-setting incumbent firm operates with inverse demand function

$$p_1 = a - b(q_1 + \theta q_2)$$

and that if a price-setting entrant comes into the market it operates with the inverse demand function

$$p_2 = a - b(\theta q_i + q_2).$$

If the cost function is

$$C(q) = F + rk + cq,$$

if capacity must be installed in advance of production, and if the entrant believes that the incumbent will expand output to capacity, what is the entrant's best-response function? (You may ignore the boundary conditions imposed by the requirement that quantities be non-negative.) What level of capacity must the incumbent choose to drive the entrant's expected profit to zero?

8.5 Suppose that there are two technologies available to serve a market, the α technology and the β technology. The cost functions of the two technologies are

$$c_\alpha(q) = c_\alpha q + F_\alpha \quad \text{and} \quad c_\beta(q) = c_\beta q + F_\beta,$$

where

$$F_\beta > F_\alpha \quad \text{and} \quad c_\beta < c_\alpha.$$

That is, the α technology has low fixed cost but high marginal cost, while the β has high fixed cost but low marginal cost.

The product is homogeneous and the equation of the market inverse demand curve is

$$p = a - bQ.$$

(a) For what range of output is the α technology preferred?
(b) Assume that equilibrium outputs occur in the range for which the α technology has the lowest average cost. Suppose that up to three firms may enter a market, and that if more than one firm is in the market they compete as Cournot quantity-setting oligopolists.

In what circumstances will the first firm enter and choose the α technology, the second firm enter and choose the β technology, and the third firm decline to enter?

See McLean and Riordan (1989).

8.6 In the model of dominant firm behavior with switching costs discussed in the text, suppose that both firms know that if the entrant comes into the market second-period rivalry will be as in a Cournot quantity-setting duopoly. What is the incumbent's best-response curve? What is the range of possible equilibria, and what first-period output would the incumbent choose to maximize the present-discounted value of its profit?

8.7 Given (8.59) and (8.60), show that the equation of the incumbent's residual demand curve is

$$p = c + \frac{1}{1/b + 1/f}\left[S + \frac{1}{f}(e - c) - Q_D\right],$$

where $S = (a - c)/b$.

(a) Calculate dominant firm and fringe output, dominant firm profit, the price–cost margin, and deadweight welfare loss.
(b) Verify that the incumbent's profit-maximizing value of α is as given by (8.63). Compare the higher-cost equilibrium with the initial values.

8.8 Consider a duopoly of quantity-setting firms. The market demand function is

$$p = a - b(q_1 + q_2).$$

The dominant firm's marginal cost (c_1) is less than the rival's marginal cost (c_2). If the incumbent accepts an increase in marginal cost to $c_1 + \alpha$, the rival's marginal cost rises to

$$c_2 + (1 + \rho_1)\alpha - \rho_2\alpha^2,$$

with $\rho_1, \rho_2 > 0$.

Under what circumstances, if any, will the dominant firm set a positive value for α? Explain your answer.

CHAPTER NINE

ADVERTISING

He that toots not his own horn, the same shall not be tooted.

John L. Lewis

9.1 THE DORFMAN–STEINER CONDITION AND GENERALIZATIONS

To the extent that advertising provides information, a firm that advertises is selling a joint product – the physical product plus information – for a single price. If information and the physical product are complementary goods, then the quantity demanded of the physical good, at any price, is greater, the greater the amount of advertising. In such cases, a firm's advertising is a shift parameter that moves the demand curve for the firm's product, much as the price of gasoline is a shift parameter that moves the demand curve for automobiles. An important difference is that a firm determines the extent to which its product is advertised, while automobile manufacturers do not determine the price of gasoline.

Even if the role of advertising as a source of information is minimal, it can be a source of product differentiation (Kaldor, 1950–1, p. 14):

> Advertising is a method of differentiating, in the eyes of the consumer, the products of one firm from those of its competitors; it is a method, therefore, of reducing the scope and effectiveness of price-competition by attaching a strong element of "goodwill" to each firm.

By engaging in advertising, a firm can control, at least to some extent, the degree to which its product is differentiated from the products of rivals. Again, advertising acts to shift a firm's demand curve.

9.1.1   Advertising by a monopolist in a static model

We begin with a static model of advertising by a monopolist when the effect of advertising is to shift the demand curve. Suppose that a firm sets price p and advertising A to maximize profit

$$\pi = (p - c)Q(p, A) - F - p^A A, \tag{9.1}$$

where $Q_p(p, A) < 0$, $Q_A(p, A) > 0$, and p^A is the price of a unit of advertising.[1] Advertising moves the demand curve away from the origin.

The first-order condition for price, on some manipulation, can be written as

$$\frac{p - c}{p} = \frac{1}{\varepsilon_{Qp}}, \tag{9.2}$$

which is just the Lerner index of monopoly power. The monopoly supplier of a product that can be advertised maximizes profit by setting the price–cost margin equal to the inverse of the price elasticity of demand. When the product can be advertised, however, the price elasticity of demand depends on the level of advertising.

The first-order condition for advertising,[2] which has come to be known as the Dorfman–Steiner condition,

$$\frac{p^A A}{pQ} = \frac{p - c}{p} \varepsilon_{QA}, \tag{9.3}$$

shows that a profit-maximizing firm selects an advertising–sales ratio that is the product of the price–cost margin and the elasticity of demand with respect to advertising (ε_{QA}).

As (9.3) makes clear, advertising is a phenomenon associated with imperfectly competitive markets. In a competitive market, output is chosen to make marginal cost equal to price, and the profit-maximizing advertising–sales ratio is zero. A firm in a competitive market can sell all it wants at the market price and nothing at a higher price, whether it advertises or not.[3]

If a firm exercises some market power, it spends more on advertising, per unit of sales revenue, the greater is economic profit on the marginal unit of sales, all else equal. The

---

[1] Assume also that the usual second-order conditions, in particular $Q_{AA} < 0$, hold.

[2] See Dorfman and Steiner (1954), Cable (1972), and Schmalensee (1972). Substituting from (9.2), (9.3) can be rewritten

$$\frac{p^A A}{pQ} = \frac{\varepsilon_{QA}}{\varepsilon_{Qp}}.$$

An equivalent form is that the advertising–sales ratio should equal the elasticity of price with respect to advertising:

$$\frac{p^A A}{pQ} = \varepsilon_{pA}.$$

[3] Note that the "competitive markets" of Stegeman (1991) lack complete and perfect information, one of the standard assumptions of the perfectly competitive model. See Butters (1977) and Stahl (1994); and for an analysis of a real-world market that appears to approximately satisfy the usual assumption of a competitive market with the exception of complete and perfect information, see Graddy's (1995) analysis of the Fulton fish market (discussed in section 7.8.1).

greater the profit associated with an extra unit of output, the more the firm is willing to spend on advertising to induce consumers to buy an extra unit of output.

A firm also spends more on advertising, per unit of sales revenue, the greater the effect of advertising on sales. Even a firm that exercises market power will not advertise if advertising does not affect demand.

9.1.2   Advertising by a monopolist in a dynamic model

It may be objected that an essential element of the impact of advertising on demand is intertemporal. Current advertising affects current demand, but current advertising also affects future demand. No doubt, the effect of current advertising on future demand is less than the effect of current advertising on current demand. But the effect of current advertising on future demand is not zero, which means that a static model leaves aside a potentially important aspect of reality.[4]

The kind of market that is envisaged is one in which current advertising contributes to a long-lived asset – we can call it goodwill – that affects future demand. Consider, then, a monopolist facing a demand function that is affected not only by price but also by the stock of accumulated goodwill:[5]

$$Q_t = Q(p_t, a_t). \tag{9.4}$$

a_t is the stock of goodwill built up at the start of period t. The relationship between advertising and goodwill is

$$a_t = A_t + (1 - \gamma)a_{t-1} = \sum_{\tau=0}^{t}(1 - \gamma)^{t-\tau}A_\tau + (1 - \gamma)^{t+1}a_{-1}, \tag{9.5}$$

where γ is the per-period depreciation of goodwill.

The stock of goodwill at the start of period t is the amount of current advertising, A_t, which is an addition to the stock of goodwill, plus the undepreciated portion of goodwill inherited from the past.

The monopolist's cash flow in period t is

$$(p_t - c)Q(p_t, a_t) - p_t^A A_t, \tag{9.6}$$

and the present-discounted value of cash flow over all future time is

$$V = \sum_{t=0}^{\infty}(1 + r)^{-t}\left\{(p_t - c)Q(p_t, a_t) - p_t^A\left[a_t - (1 - \gamma)a_{t-1}\right]\right\}, \tag{9.7}$$

where we use (9.5) to eliminate A_t in (9.7).

---

[4] See section 9.4.

[5] A continuous-time version of this model appears in section 6.3.2.

The monopolist maximizing (9.7) has two choice variables per period, p_t and a_t (or, equivalently, A_t). The first-order condition for p_t is the Lerner index

$$\frac{p_t - c}{p_t} = \frac{1}{\varepsilon_{Qp,t}}.$$ (9.8)

The first-order condition for the period-t stock of goodwill is

$$p_t^A = (p_t - c)\frac{\partial Q_t}{\partial a_t} + \frac{1 - \gamma}{1 + r}p_{t+1}^A.$$ (9.9)

Substituting recursively forward in (9.9) from time t to ∞, we obtain

$$p_t^A = \sum_{\tau=0}^{\infty}\left(\frac{1 - \gamma}{1 + r}\right)^{\tau}(p_{t+\tau} - c)\frac{\partial Q_{t+\tau}}{\partial a_{t+\tau}}.$$ (9.10)

To maximize the present-discounted value of cash flow, the monopolist should purchase advertising until the marginal cost of current advertising – p_t^A – equals the present-discounted value of marginal profit, over all future time, that results from a current increment to advertising. This is the dynamic generalization of the Dorfman–Steiner condition for a monopolist supplier.

9.1.3 Advertising in oligopoly

Now suppose that n firms operate in a market for a differentiated product.[6] The inverse demand function for variety i in period t is

$$p_{it} = f(q_{it} + \theta Q_{-it}, a_{it} + \phi a_{-it}).$$ (9.11)

q_{it} is the output of firm i in period t, and Q_{-it} is the combined output of all other firms in period t. θ is a product differentiation parameter, interpreted as in the Bowley linear product differentiation model.

a_{it} is the stock of goodwill enjoyed by firm i in period t. It is determined by current and past advertising according to a relation of the form (9.5). a_{-it} is the combined period-t goodwill of all firms other than firm i. ϕ is an advertising interaction parameter. If $0 < \phi < 1$, advertising is cooperative in the sense that advertising by any firm shifts the demand curves for all varieties away from the origin, although a firm's advertising has a greater positive effect on its own demand than on rivals' demands. If $\phi = 1$, advertising is perfectly cooperative: advertising by any firm has an equal effect on the demand curves for all varieties. If $\phi = 0$, demand for any one firm's variety is not affected by the advertising of other firms. For $\phi < 0$, the interactive effect of advertising is predatory: a firm's advertising shifts its own demand curve away from the origin but shifts rivals' demand curves toward the origin.[7]

---

[6] See Cubbin (1983) and Friedman (1983a).

[7] The terminology is due to Friedman (1983a, pp. 466–7). See Gasmi and Vuong (1991) for an application; see also Gasmi, Laffont, and Vuong (1992).

The present-discounted value of firm i's cash flow is

$$V_i = \sum_{t=0}^{\infty} (1+r)^{-t} \{(p_{it} - c)q_{it} - p_t^A [a_{it} - (1-\gamma)a_{i,t-1}]\}. \tag{9.12}$$

The first-order condition for p_{it} can be written

$$\frac{p_{it} - c}{p_{it}} = \frac{s_{it}}{\varepsilon_{Qp,t}}, \tag{9.13}$$

where

$$s_{it} = \frac{q_{it}}{Q_{it}} = \frac{q_{it}}{q_{it} + \theta Q_{-it}} \tag{9.14}$$

is firm i's effective market share, measured to take account of product differentiation,[8] and

$$\varepsilon_{Qp,t} = -\frac{p_{it}}{Q_{it}} \frac{\partial Q_{it}}{\partial p_{it}} \tag{9.15}$$

is the price elasticity of demand in variety i's market. Firm i's degree of market power rises as its market share rises and as the price elasticity of demand for its variety falls. Advertising is one of the arguments that determines $\varepsilon_{Qp,t}$.

The first-order condition for advertising is

$$p_t^A = \frac{\partial p_{it}}{\partial a_{it}} q_{it} + \frac{1-\gamma}{1+r} p_{t+1}^A, \tag{9.16}$$

and substituting recursively forward from time t to ∞ gives

$$p_t^A = \sum_{\tau=0}^{\infty} \left(\frac{1-\gamma}{1+r}\right)^{\tau} \frac{\partial p_{i,t+\tau}}{\partial a_{i,t+\tau}} q_{i,t+\tau}. \tag{9.17}$$

The first-order condition for advertising is that a firm should purchase advertising in period t until the price of advertising in period t equals the present-discounted value of the revenue generated by a marginal increase in goodwill in all future periods.[9]

9.2 ADVERTISING AS A SIGNAL OF QUALITY

9.2.1 Search goods versus experience goods

If advertising provides information, it makes sense to think of advertising as a parameter that shifts the demand curve. Advertisements for goods with characteristics that can be concisely

---

[8] Multiplying Q_{-it} by θ converts the number of units of output of other varieties, which are imperfect substitutes for variety i, into an equivalent number of perfectly substitutable units. $Q_{it} = q_i + \theta Q_{-it}$ is total output in variety i's market, measured in units of output of variety i.

[9] In general, the comparative static effects of changes in θ and ϕ on the equilibrium values of p_{it} and a_{it} are indeterminate. See Problems 9.1 and 9.2.

described in an objective way – personal computers, for example, or jewelry – often contain detailed information about the product. For such search goods, it is practical to acquire information in advance of consumption, and advertisements provide such information.

But there are other types of goods that must be consumed before their qualities can be appreciated. It does little good to be told the number of calories per serving and the kind of sweetener in a soft drink if what one is interested in is whether or not it tastes good; the soft drink must be purchased and tasted. Detailed information about the kind of fabric used to make a pair of blue jeans is of little use if what one is interested in is whether or not the jeans are comfortable; the jeans must be purchased and worn. When a consumer tries such an experience good for the first time, he or she is taking a chance – the good might turn out to be unsatisfactory, and there is no way to tell in advance of purchase. Correspondingly, advertisements for experience goods rarely contain much in the way of information.

Nelson (1970, 1974) suggests that for experience goods the function of advertising is nothing more or less than to inform the consumer that the good is advertised. Producers of high-quality experience goods, he argues, are able to afford to spend more on advertising because first-time consumers are more likely to be satisfied, and make repeat purchases, than would be the case if the product were of low quality. For experience goods, therefore, advertising is a signal of product quality, not a source of information.

9.2.2 Quality signaling via price and advertising

Milgrom and Roberts (1986) offer a signaling model of advertising of a new experience good.[10] Quality is modeled very simply: either the good is satisfactory, or it is not. If the good is of low quality, the probability that it is satisfactory is L. If the good is of high quality, the probability that it is satisfactory is H. $0 < L < H < 1$. Consumers can ascertain the quality of the good only by purchasing it and consuming it.

When the product is introduced, the firm sets an initial price and level of advertising. Let $\pi(p, H, H)$ denote the payoff – before advertising expense – of a firm selling a high-quality product that consumers believe is a high-quality product at price p, and let p_{HH} be the price that maximizes this payoff. Let $\pi(p, L, H)$ denote the payoff of a firm selling a low-quality product that consumers believe is a high-quality product, maximized by price p_{LH}, and so on.

Consumers are willing to pay more for a product they believe to be of high quality because such a product is more likely to be satisfactory. This creates an incentive for a firm producing a low-quality good to imitate a firm producing a high-quality good. A firm producing a high-quality good, therefore, has an interest in setting an initial price–advertising combination that would be unprofitable for a firm producing a low-quality good. Observing such a combination, consumers conclude that the product is of high quality and are willing to pay more for it than would otherwise be the case.

If a high-quality firm picks a price–advertising combination (p, A) and by so doing convinces consumers that it is offering a high-quality product, its payoff is $\pi(p, H, H) - p^A A$. If it does not advertise and consumers incorrectly believe it is producing a low-quality product, the best payoff it can obtain is $\pi(p_{HL}, H, L)$. A firm producing a high-quality product is

[10] See also Schmalensee (1978a), von Ungern–Sternberg and von Weizsäcker (1981), Kihlstrom and Riordan (1984), and Doyle (1989).

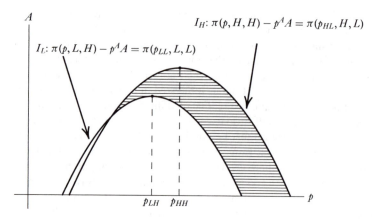

Figure 9.1 Regions of separating equilibria, Milgrom–Roberts advertising signaling model.

willing to advertise, therefore, only if there are (p, A) combinations such that

$$\pi(p, H, H) - p^A A \geq \pi(p_{HL}, H, L). \tag{9.18}$$

If a firm producing a low-quality product imitates a firm producing a high-quality product, its payoff is $\pi(p, L, H) - p^A A$. If such a firm does not advertise, revealing its product to be one of low quality, and maximizes its resulting payoff, its return is $\pi(p_{LL}, L, L)$. A firm producing a low-quality product prefers to reveal itself as such, therefore, if

$$\pi(p_{LL}, L, L) \geq \pi(p, L, H) - p^A A. \tag{9.19}$$

Combining (9.18) and (9.19), there are separating equilibria – (p, A) combinations open to a firm producing a high-quality product that a firm producing a low-quality product does not care to imitate – if and only if

$$\pi(p, H, H) - \pi(p_{HL}, H, L) \geq p^A A \geq \pi(p, L, H) - \pi(p_{LL}, L, L). \tag{9.20}$$

The implied restrictions on payoff functions are illustrated in figure 9.1, which shows one isoprofit curve for each type of firm. The isoprofit curve I_H, defined by the equality version of (9.18), shows price–advertising combinations that allow a firm producing a high-quality product which consumers believe is a high-quality product to earn just as much as it would by letting consumers believe it was producing a low-quality product and maximizing profit. Holding p constant, lower levels of advertising mean a greater net payoff. Isoprofit curves below I_H, therefore, mean greater profit for the firm producing a high-quality product. Such a firm prefers to operate below I_H and as close to the price axis as possible, while maintaining a price–advertising combination that consumers would not expect to see from a firm producing a low-quality product.

The isoprofit curve I_L, defined by the equality version of (9.19), shows price–advertising combinations that yield a copycat firm producing a low-quality product the same payoff that it would collect by setting advertising equal to zero, revealing its product to be of low quality, and maximizing profit. If a firm producing a high-quality product were to select a price–advertising combination below I_L, a firm producing a low-quality product would find imitation profitable. To reveal itself as the producer of a high-quality product, therefore, a firm would have to restrict itself to (p, A) combinations on or above I_L.

(p, A) combinations anywhere in the shaded region offer a firm producing a high-quality product a greater profit than it could get by keeping the nature of its product hidden, but offer a firm producing a low-quality product a lower profit than it could obtain by setting advertising equal to zero and revealing itself as the producer of a low-quality product. Points in the shaded region, if such points exist, allow consumers to distinguish between high-quality and low-quality products.

If the set of points satisfying (9.20) is nonempty, separating equilibria exist. Assuming this condition to be met, we expect a firm producing a high-quality product to maximize its profit, subject to the constraint that it reveal the quality of its product. In terms of figure 9.1, a firm producing a high-quality product would prefer to operate either on I_L or on the segment where the shaded region runs along the price axis.

Formally, the constrained optimization problem of a firm producing a high-quality product is

$$\max_{p, A \geq 0} \pi(p, H, H) - p^A A \qquad \text{such that } \pi(p_{LL}, L, L) \geq \pi(p, L, H) - p^A A. \tag{9.21}$$

It is possible that the solution to this problem involves $A = 0$. If $A > 0$, however, the separating equilibrium must occur where the constraint holds with equality. In terms of figure 9.1, if $A > 0$, the equilibrium (p, A) combination lies on I_L. If the firm producing a high-quality product were to pick a (p, A) combination lying above I_L, it could always increase its payoff by reducing A slightly and moving toward I_L.

This observation allows us to rewrite the constrained optimization problem (9.21) and characterize the kind of isoprofit curves that lead to the use of advertising as a signal. If $A > 0$, the constraint in (9.21) holds exactly, and so

$$p^A A = \pi(p, L, H) - \pi(p_{LL}, L, L). \tag{9.22}$$

Using (9.22) to eliminate A in (9.21), if $A > 0$ the constrained optimization problem of a firm producing a high-quality product can be written

$$\max_{p \geq 0} \pi(p, H, H) - \pi(p, L, H) \qquad \text{such that } \pi(p, L, H) - \pi(p_{LL}, L, L) \geq 0. \tag{9.23}$$

Now rewrite the maximand in (9.23) as

$$\pi(p, H, H) - p^A A - [\pi(p, L, H) - p^A A]. \tag{9.24}$$

For different values of m, $\pi(p, H, H) - p^A A = m$ is the equation of an isoprofit curve for a firm producing a high-quality product that is believed to be producing a high-quality product – a curve like I_H in figure 9.1. For different values of n, $\pi(p, L, H) - p^A A = n$ is the equation of an isoprofit curve for a firm producing a low-quality product that is believed to be producing a high-quality product – a curve like I_L in figure 9.1. When (9.23) is maximized

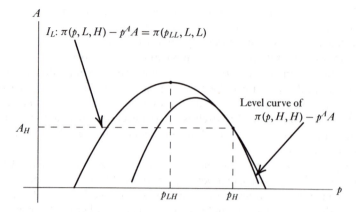

Figure 9.2   Advertising signals in the Milgrom–Roberts model.

with respect to p,[11] the resulting first-order condition is $\partial\pi(p,H,H)/\partial p = \partial\pi(p,L,H)/\partial p$, which means that equilibrium occurs where two isoprofit curves – one for each type of firm – are tangent. If equilibrium occurs at such a point, as in figure 9.2, then advertising is used as a signal of product quality.

Figure 9.2 is drawn so that, in the signaling equilibrium, $A > 0$ and $p > p_{LH}$. A little experimentation demonstrates that it is possible to illustrate separating equilibria with $A > 0$ but $p < p_{LH}$. Signaling equilibria, therefore, may involve no advertising at all, or a combination of some advertising with a price that is either higher or lower than the price a firm producing a high-quality product would choose if it did not use advertising to signal the quality of its product.[12]

9.2.3   An example

Here we sketch out the analysis of a linear model which may, for some parameter values, have signaling equilibria.[13] It is a two-period model. In the first period a firm introduces a new product. If consumers were certain that the good was satisfactory, the inverse demand function for the product would be

$$p = a - bq. \tag{9.25}$$

But consumers are not certain that the good is satisfactory. In advance of consumption, they know only that the good is of either high quality or low quality, where, recall, quality is interpreted as the probability that the good is satisfactory.

---

[11] There is a Lagrangian multiplier associated with the constraint that A be positive. However, since we restrict ourselves to cases in which A is positive, the value of this Lagrangian multiplier is zero.

[12] For further discussion of conditions to guarantee the existence of a separating equilibrium, and to rule out the existence of pooling equilibria, see Milgrom and Roberts (1986).

[13] This section is based on Milgrom and Roberts (1986, pp. 814–9).

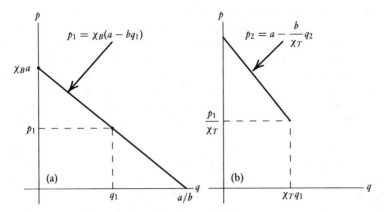

Figure 9.3 Demand curves, linear advertising signal example (χ_B, expected first-period quality; χ_T, true quality). (a) First period; (b) second period.

If the marginal consumer will pay $a - bq$ for one unit of a good that is known to be satisfactory, then the marginal consumer will pay $\chi(a - bq)$ for one unit of a good believed to be satisfactory with probability χ. Thus the first period inverse demand function is either

$$p = H(a - bq) \qquad \text{or} \qquad p = L(a - bq), \tag{9.26}$$

depending on whether consumers believe $\chi = H$ or $\chi = L$. The corresponding demand functions are

$$q = \frac{1}{b}\left(a - \frac{p}{H}\right) \qquad \text{or} \qquad q = \frac{1}{b}\left(a - \frac{p}{L}\right) \tag{9.27}$$

respectively.

For simplicity, suppose that only consumers who purchase the good in the first period can purchase the good in the second period. Once they get to the second period, such consumers know the actual quality of the good, based on their consumption experience. If the good is of true quality χ_T, then a fraction $1 - \chi_T$ of first-period consumers realize that the product is, for them, unsatisfactory, and drop out of the market.

Because a fraction $1 - \chi_T$ of first-period purchasers drop out of the market, the equation of the second-period demand curve is

$$q_2 = \chi_T \frac{a - p_2}{b} \tag{9.28}$$

over the price range $p_1/\chi_T \leq p_2 \leq a$ or, in inverse form,

$$p_2 = a - \frac{b}{\chi_T} q_2, \tag{9.29}$$

over the output range $0 \leq q_2 \leq \chi_T q_1$. First- and second-period demand curves are shown in figure 9.3.

To find conditions for a separating equilibrium, we must analyze the behavior of four types of firms: a firm that is producing a high-quality product, and is believed in the first period to be producing a high-quality product; a firm that is producing a high-quality product, but is believed in the first period to be producing a low-quality product; a firm that is producing a low-quality product, but is believed in the first period to be producing a high-quality product; and a firm that is producing a low-quality product, and is believed in the first period to be producing a low-quality product. No matter which case we consider, in the second-period there are two possibilities. It may be that the monopoly price along the second-period demand curve is greater than p_1/χ_T. In this case, any payoff-maximizing strategy must have the firm select the second-period monopoly price. Alternatively, it may be that the best price–quantity combination the firm can get in the second period is at the kink in its second-period demand curve. In this second case, any payoff-maximizing strategy must have the firm select price $p_2 = p_1/\chi_T$ and quantity $q_2 = \chi_T q_1$ in the second period.

For each type of firm, both alternatives are possible, depending on the values of H, L, and the other parameters of the model. For simplicity, we assume here that all firms prefer to operate at the kink in their second-period demand curve. From Problem 9.4, the payoffs of interest are

$$\pi(p_1, H, H) = \frac{1+\alpha}{Hb}\left(p_1 - \frac{1+\alpha H}{1+\alpha}c_H\right)(Ha - p_1), \tag{9.30}$$

$$\pi(p_{LL}, L, L) = \frac{(1+\alpha)L}{4b}\left[a - \frac{1+\alpha L}{(1+\alpha)L}c_L\right]^2, \tag{9.31}$$

$$\pi(p_1, L, H) = \frac{H+\alpha L}{H^2 b}\left[p_1 - \frac{H(1+\alpha L)}{H+\alpha L}c_L\right](Ha - p_1). \tag{9.32}$$

The constrained optimization problem of a firm producing a high-quality product that wishes to maximize profit while selecting a (q, A) combination that would not be imitated by a firm producing a low-quality product is found by solving the Kuhn–Tucker conditions obtained from the Lagrangian

$$\mathcal{L} = \pi(p_1, H, H) - p^A A + \lambda\left[\pi(p_{LL}, L, L) - \pi(p_1, L, H) + p^A A\right]. \tag{9.33}$$

The Kuhn–Tucker conditions are as follows:

$$\frac{\partial \mathcal{L}}{\partial p} = \frac{1+\alpha}{Hb}\left(Ha + \frac{1+\alpha H}{1+\alpha}c_H - 2p_1\right)$$
$$-\lambda\frac{1+\alpha}{H^2 b}\left[Ha + \frac{H(1+\alpha L)}{H+\alpha L}c_L - 2p_1\right] \equiv 0; \tag{9.34}$$

$$\frac{\partial \mathcal{L}}{\partial A} = -p^A + \lambda p_A \geq 0, \qquad Ap_A(\lambda - 1) \equiv 0, \qquad A \geq 0; \tag{9.35}$$

$$\frac{\partial \mathcal{L}}{\partial \lambda} = \pi(p_{LL}, L, L) - \pi(p_1, L, H) + p^A A \geq 0; \tag{9.36}$$

$$\lambda\frac{\partial \mathcal{L}}{\partial \lambda} \equiv 0, \qquad \lambda \geq 0. \tag{9.37}$$

What we wish to obtain are conditions under which there is a solution to this constrained optimization problem with $A > 0$. Such a solution is a separating equilibrium provided that the constrained optimum payoff exceeds $\pi(p_{HL}, H, L)$.

Assume, therefore, that $A > 0$. Then (9.35) implies that the shadow cost $\lambda = 1$. The first-order condition for first-period price, (9.34), can then be solved for

$$p_1 = \tfrac{1}{2}H\left[a + \frac{(1 + \alpha H)c_H - (1 + \alpha L)c_L}{\alpha(H - L)}\right]. \tag{9.38}$$

If $\lambda = 1$, (9.37) implies that the signaling constraint must hold with equality. It can then be solved for the constrained profit-maximizing level of advertising, which satisfies

$$p^A A = \frac{H + \alpha L}{H^2 b}\left[p_1 - \frac{H(1 + \alpha)}{H + \alpha L}c_L\right](Ha - p_1) - \frac{1 + \alpha}{4Lb}\left(La - \frac{1 + \alpha L}{1 + \alpha}c_L\right)^2. \tag{9.39}$$

Substituting (9.38) in (9.39) to eliminate p_1, we obtain an expression for constrained equilibrium advertising. We began working out this solution by assuming that $A > 0$. A consistency condition for signaling equilibrium, therefore, is that the value for A implied by (9.39) be positive. Depending on the specific parameter values, this consistency condition may or may not be met. If it is not, the only possible signaling equilibrium has $A = 0$.[14]

Assuming that the value for A implied by (9.39) is positive, we are not done yet. For the solutions implied by the Kuhn–Tucker conditions to yield a signaling equilibrium, constrained optimum profit must exceed $\pi(p_{HL}, H, L)$. If it does not, the only equilibria are pooling equilibria, in which firms producing a high-quality product do not advertise and consumers are unable to infer the quality of a product in advance of consumption.

9.2.4 Extension

The Milgrom–Roberts model provides a theoretical rationale for the advertising of new experience goods. As they themselves note (Milgrom and Roberts, 1986, p. 800) it "says little about advertising for established brands." While it can explain uninformative advertising of a new product, it does not address the continuing uninformative advertising of products with which the vast majority of consumers have some experience (Coca Cola, for example).

In the Milgrom and Roberts model, consumption fully reveals whether or not the product is satisfactory. Horstmann and MacDonald (1994) outline a model in which a consumer may find a product to be satisfactory at one time, unsatisfactory at another time. "Higher quality" means that a product is more likely to be satisfactory, but satisfaction is not guaranteed, even after having had consumption experience. In this model, there is an equilibrium in which a high-quality variety is advertised after introduction, and sold at a high price to consumers who have had satisfactory experience with the variety. In contrast to the Milgrom and Roberts model, there are no separating equilibria when a product is first put on the market.

---

[14] For this solution, (9.34) is solved for $\lambda > 0$. If $\lambda > 0$, (9.35) implies $A = 0$ and (9.37) implies that the signaling constraint is binding with equality; it can be solved for p_1.

9.3 WELFARE CONSEQUENCES OF ADVERTISING

The analysis of the welfare consequences of advertising and other sales efforts raises complex issues. Advertising is typically associated with greater output, which is usually thought of as welfare-improving. But advertising is also often associated with higher prices or price–cost margins, which are usually thought of as welfare-reducing. Furthermore, if advertising that shifts demand curves shifts the individual utility functions from which demand curves are derived, it also shifts the standard according to which welfare judgments are made.

9.3.1 Advertising that shifts demand curves

Suppose[15] that the aggregate welfare function is

$$U(y, a, A) = y + u(q, A). \tag{9.40}$$

q is the quantity of an advertised good that is produced by a monopolist.[16] A is the quantity of advertising, a shift parameter in the utility function.[17] y is the quantity consumed of all other goods.

The price of y is normalized at 1. Production of the advertised good entails a fixed cost F and a constant marginal cost c per unit of output. Advertising is supplied at constant marginal and average cost p^A. The total resource endowment of the economy is e. The social budget constraint is that the value of inputs used to produce q plus the value of all other goods equal available resources,

$$y + F + cq + p^A A = e. \tag{9.41}$$

At the same time, the constraint facing consumers is that spending on consumption goods not exceed income:[18]

$$y + pq = e. \tag{9.42}$$

From the social welfare function (9.40) and the consumer budget constraint (9.42),[19] the inverse demand function for the advertised good is

$$p = u_1(q, A), \tag{9.43}$$

where the subscript 1 indicates a partial derivative with respect to the first argument. To each value of A corresponds a different inverse demand function for the advertised good.

---

[15] This section follows Dixit and Norman (1978).

[16] For extensions to oligopoly and monopolistic competition, see Dixit and Norman (1978). See also Shapiro (1980) and Dixit and Norman (1980).

[17] It is also possible to interpret (9.40) as describing advertising that yields utility in its own right. See Fisher and McGowan (1979) and Dixit and Norman (1980).

[18] Note the implication of (9.41) and (9.42) that in equilibrium $(p - c)q - F = p_A A$: in equilibrium, the excess of revenue over production cost is just sufficient to cover spending on advertising.

[19] The constrained optimization problem is formalized by the Lagrangian $\mathcal{L} = y + u(q, A) + \lambda(e - y - pq)$.

A monopolist producer of the advertised good selects q and A to maximize his private payoff:

$$\pi(q,A) = [p(q,A) - c]q - F - p^A A. \tag{9.44}$$

The profit-maximizing values q^* and A^* are the solutions to the first-order conditions

$$\frac{\partial \pi(q^*, A^*)}{\partial q} \equiv 0, \qquad \frac{\partial \pi(q^*, A^*)}{\partial A} \equiv 0. \tag{9.45}$$

These can be manipulated to yield the Lerner index and the Dorfman–Steiner condition.

Suppose for the moment that advertising is fixed at an arbitrary level. Then (9.45) can be solved for $q^*(A)$, the profit-maximizing output level, given A. Of course, $q^*(A^*) = q^*$. Using (9.40)–(9.42) and (9.44), a combination $[y, q^*(A), A]$ yields social welfare

$$
\begin{aligned}
W[q^*(A), A] &= U[y, q^*(A), A] \\
&= y + u[q^*(A), A] \\
&= u[q^*(A), A] - cq^*(A) - F - p^A A + e \\
&= u[q^*(A), A] - p[q^*(A), A]q^*(A) + \pi[q^*(A), A] + e. \tag{9.46}
\end{aligned}
$$

Every change in advertising shifts the welfare function. To avoid such shifts while we are evaluating the impact of changes in the level of advertising, fix A in $u[q^*(A^*), A]$ at an arbitrary level $\bar{A}$. Then, for a combination $[y, q^*(A), A]$, we have welfare

$$W[q^*(A), \bar{A}] = u[q^*(A), \bar{A}] - p[q^*(A), A]q^*(A) + \pi[q^*(A), A] + e, \tag{9.47}$$

using the welfare function that corresponds to advertising level $\bar{A}$.

Differentiate (9.47) with respect to advertising (but keep the second argument in $u[q^*(A), \bar{A}]$ fixed at $\bar{A}$, so that the welfare function does not shift):[20]

$$
\begin{aligned}
\frac{\partial W[q^*(A), \bar{A}]}{\partial A} &= \left\{ u_1[q^*(A), \bar{A}] - p \right\} \frac{dq^*(A)}{dA} \\
&\quad - q^*(A)\frac{dp[q^*(A), A]}{dA} + \frac{\partial \pi[q^*(A), A]}{\partial A}. \tag{9.48}
\end{aligned}
$$

Equation (9.48) gives the effect of a small change in advertising on welfare, measured according to advertising level $\bar{A}$, when a monopolist supplier maximizes profit, given the level of advertising.

Now let $A = \bar{A} = A^*$ in (9.48). Since $\bar{A} = A^*$, (9.43) tells us that $u_1[q^*(A), \bar{A}] = u_1[q^*(A), A^*] = p$, and the first term on the right in (9.48) drops out. At the same time, if $A = A^*$, (9.45) tells us that the final term on the right in (9.48) is zero. We are left with

$$\frac{\partial W(q^*, A^*)}{\partial A} = -q\frac{dp}{dA}, \tag{9.49}$$

[20] In principle, there is a term $(\partial\pi/\partial q)dq/dA$ on the right. However, the assumption of profit maximization implies that $\partial\pi/\partial q = 0$.

which is negative if the effect of advertising is to increase price. Thus, if advertising increases price, a reduction in advertising by a monopolist increases social welfare, and vice versa.

Note that

$$\frac{\mathrm{d}p\,[q^*(A), A]}{\mathrm{d}A} = p_1 \frac{\mathrm{d}q^*}{\mathrm{d}A} + p_2, \tag{9.50}$$

where subscripts denote partial derivatives. We expect p_2 and $\mathrm{d}q^*/\mathrm{d}A$ to be positive, while p_1 is negative. Thus, in principle, the net effect of advertising on price can be positive or negative.

Kaul and Wittink (1995) survey empirical studies of the impact of advertising on price. They distinguish between price advertising, which informs consumers about product price and availability, and nonprice advertising, "geared toward brand positioning and the communication of unique brand characteristics," but without price information. These categories seem similar to the distinction made in the economics literature between informative and persuasive advertising.

Their distillation of the results of these studies is that higher levels of price advertising, the main form of advertising by local retailers, tend to increase the price elasticity of demand and lower prices. Equation (9.49) implies that such advertising is welfare-enhancing.[21]

Kaul and Wittink also conclude that nonprice advertising, the main form of national advertising by manufacturers, tends to lower the price elasticity of demand. To the extent that this leads to higher prices (the expected result in imperfectly competitive markets), (9.49) implies that such advertising is welfare-reducing.[22,23]

9.4 THE DURATION OF ADVERTISING EFFECTS

Clarke (1976) surveys 69 published studies of the effect of advertising on demand, with a view to drawing conclusions about the duration of advertising effects. One indication of the survey is that the estimated duration of advertising effects on demand rises with the length of time interval between observations: studies with annual data tend to produce estimates indicating a longer effect of advertising on demand than studies with monthly data, for example. Taking this into account, he suggests that the studies surveyed indicate (1976, p. 355)

> that 90% of the cumulative effect of advertising on sales of mature, frequently purchased, low-priced products occurs within 3 to 9 months of the advertisement.

---

[21] Milyo and Waldfogel (1999) examine the responses of prices to advertising following a change in the legal regime controlling liquor advertising in Rhode Island. They find that some price decreases occur, that price responses to advertising differ across firms and products and that the dispersion of prices across stores was not changed by the change in regime.

[22] Tremblay and Tremblay (1995) find a price-increasing effect of national advertising in the beer industry.

[23] As Kaul and Wittink note (pp. 157–8), the two different types of advertising will affect not only the level of the consumer price – marginal cost margin, but also the division of that margin between manufacturer and distributor.

Leone (1995) analyzes the studies surveyed by Clarke and others, taking the time interval effect into account, and finds a typical 90 percent duration interval of between six and nine months.[24],[25]

Caves et al. (1991) note that producers of patented pharmaceuticals reduced sales efforts two years before patent expiration, anticipating that entry would reduce the return to advertising. As they note, this suggests the durability of sales efforts aimed at prescribers (and also that the effect of the advertising is to increase the market as a whole, not just the variety originally subject to patent protection).

In section 8.8 we discussed Slade's (1995) study of the pricing and advertising of saltine crackers in a local retail market. She examines the duration of advertising effects by testing the statistical significance of lagged advertising on demand and finds that advertising effects exist, but persist for a brief period (1995, p. 448):

> the principal impact of an advertising campaign is felt in the three weeks surrounding the campaign. One reason for the high decay rate of product awareness is that consumers switch to rival brands when they are advertised. Brand loyalty therefore erodes quickly and must be reinforced.

The balance of empirical evidence suggests that the impact of advertising on demand is brief, although there is considerable variation across products.

9.5 THE ADVERTISING RESPONSE TO ENTRY

Cubbin and Domberger (1988) examine incumbents' responses to entry. They assemble a time-series sample of observations on 42 firms operating in 16 UK industries. They estimate time-trend equations that allow for post-entry changes in either the slope or the intercept of advertising expenditures of incumbent firms. They find a mixture of positive, insignificant, and negative responses, with positive responses for 16 of 42 incumbent firms. Their results for the cigarette industry, in which two incumbents responded to entry by decreasing advertising expenditures and one by increasing advertising expenditures, are shown in table 9.1.

Cubbin and Domberger then estimate a probit model to examine whether or not firm and market characteristics can explain differences in the estimated advertising response to entry.

This portion of their results suggests that dominant firms in static markets are more likely to use advertising to respond to entry. Having controlled for dominance, market share has no significant impact on the likelihood of an advertising response. Nor did the fact that a firm was owned by a US-based parent affect the likelihood of an advertising response.

---

[24] He suggests that if the researcher can choose the length of time between observations, the interval should be the average interval between purchases. If data is available only for longer intervals, he outlines estimation techniques that allow for this temporal aggregation.

[25] Roberts and Samuelson (1988) estimate long-term effects of cigarette advertising on demand. See also Gallet (1999), who finds that demand for cigarettes in the US market fell following the 1971 ban on radio and TV advertising of cigarettes, and that market power (assessed in a New Empirical Industrial Organization framework) increased following the ban.

Table 9.1   Advertising and entry: UK cigarette firms'
advertising spending (in pounds sterling) response to
entry: t-statistics in parentheses; D is a dummy variable
with value 0 before entry and 1 after entry

Gallaher	$A = 1,955,046 \quad - 407,485D \quad + 469,901t$
	$\quad\quad\quad (2.84) \quad\quad\quad (0.35) \quad\quad\quad (3.04)$
Rothmans	$A = 2,547,195 \quad + 3,235,967D \quad - 26,646t$
	$\quad\quad\quad (3.49) \quad\quad\quad (2.63) \quad\quad\quad (0.16)$
Imperial	$A = 1,772,731 \quad - 763,728D \quad + 1,107,848t$
	$\quad\quad\quad (0.72) \quad\quad\quad (0.19) \quad\quad\quad (2.01)$

Source: Cubbin and Domberger, 1988

These results suggest that it is rational for entrants to examine pre-entry market structure for clues about the likely nature of the post-entry market. Entry is likely to evoke a hostile response if the market is static and there is a dominant firm.

Thomas (1999) studies the price, advertising, and new brand interactions among incumbents and of incumbents to entrants in the US breakfast cereal industry. He finds that incumbents accommodate one another on price but respond aggressively to rival incumbent advertising. Entry, particularly large-scale entry, is likely to be met by lower prices.[26]

9.6   CONCLUSION

If advertising shifts preferences or provides information about product quality, firms have an incentive to advertise if they have some market power. If the effect of advertising is to raise price, then such advertising is excessive from a social point of view. Empirical evidence suggests that advertising that informs about prices may lead to lower prices, while persuasive advertising may lead to higher prices.

Firms may also advertise for strategic reasons. If advertising shifts demand curves, firms may advertise to discourage entry or to retaliate against entry. If advertising does not shift demand curves, new experience goods may be advertised as a signal of product quality.

Empirical evidence also suggests that advertising does affect demand, and that for most products such effects last for months rather than years.

PROBLEMS

9.1 Let the inverse demand function be (9.11). If a single firm maximizes (9.12), derive expressions for the partial derivatives of q_{it} and a_{it} with respect to θ and ϕ.

---

[26] These results are consistent with those of Slade (1995); see section 8.8.

9.2 Answer Problem 9.1 if the inverse demand function is

$$p_{it} = \alpha + u(a_{it} + \phi a_{-it}) - v(a_{it} + \phi a_{-it})^2 - \beta(q_{it} + \theta Q_{-it}).$$

9.3 (Cubbin, 1981) Let inverse demand functions be

$$p_i = a + \alpha(A_i + \phi A_j) - b(q_i + \theta q_j),$$

where $i, j = 1, 2$ and $\phi < 0$. Assume that the marginal and average cost of production is a constant, c; and that the cost of advertising is

$$c(A_i) = A_i + dA_i^2.$$

   (a)   If firm 1 is an incumbent monopolist, what are the profit-maximizing levels of output and advertising?

   (b)   Analyze the shape of the incumbent's isoprofit curves.

   (c)   If the incumbent knows that a potential entrant maximizes profit taking q_1 and A_1 as given, what levels of q_1 and A_1 deter entry? Under what circumstances would the incumbent find it profitable to deter entry?

9.4 Derive the prices and payoffs of the Milgrom and Roberts linear advertising signaling model (section 9.2.3).

CHAPTER TEN

COLLUSION AND NONCOOPERATIVE COLLUSION

Tomorrow, tomorrow . . . you're only a day away.

Annie

10.1 INTRODUCTION

Adam Smith's (1937, p. 128) remark that

> People of the same trade seldom meet together, even for merriment and diversion, but the conversation ends in a conspiracy against the public, or in some contrivance to raise prices . . .

demonstrates economists' long-standing interest in collusion.

This interest has developed in two distinct directions, as the word "collusion" has taken on different meanings in the economics and the legal literatures. It is primarily *noncooperative collusion* that has occupied economists. Noncooperative collusion is a joint restriction of output in which each individual firm independently and willingly engages.

Exactly what constitutes collusion in a legal sense differs from one legal regime to another, but an essential element is typically that the actions of individual firms be jointly arrived at – that is, not independently arrived at. Noncooperative collusion, therefore, is not collusion.[1]

The economic literature has focused on the analysis of strategies that will sustain non-cooperative collusion and the extent to which such strategies will allow firms to approach the monopoly outcome. We discuss such strategies, as well as the literature on facilitating practices and empirical evidence on tacit and overt collusion.

---

[1] For US antitrust, see Hay (2000, pp. 119, 128). For EU competition policy, see *Re Wood Pulp Cartel* [1993] 4 CMLR 407. See also Cooper (1986, fn. 12, p. 380), Baker (1993), and Martin (1993b).

10.2   NONCOOPERATIVE COLLUSION IN A STATIC MODEL

If agreements to restrict output cannot be enforced at law, then joint output restriction is internally stable only if every firm in the restricting group earns a greater profit by restricting output than by switching to Nash behavior ("joining the fringe"), taking into account the way other firms would adjust their behavior after its defection. If there are firms outside the restricting group, then restriction is externally stable if every firm in the fringe earns a greater profit by staying in the fringe than by joining the restrictive group, taking into account the way other firms would adjust their behavior after its move.[2]

We can derive conditions for internal and external stability in a standard model of quantity-setting oligopoly. Let N firms produce a homogeneous product and let the inverse demand function be linear:

$$p = a - bQ. \tag{10.1}$$

Each firm produces with constant average and marginal cost,

$$c(q) = cq. \tag{10.2}$$

F of the N firms form a fringe. Each firm in the fringe acts as a Cournot quantity-setting oligopolist – it maximizes its own profit, taking the output of other firms as given. The remaining K firms restrict output and maximize joint profit, taking fringe behavior into account.

Each fringe firm selects output along a best-response curve with equation

$$q_j = \tfrac{1}{2}(S - Q_K - Q_{F-j}), \tag{10.3}$$

where $S = (a - c)/b$, Q_K is the total output of the restrictive group and Q_{F-j} is the combined output of all fringe firms except firm j. But in equilibrium, all fringe firms produce the same output. Equilibrium fringe firm output and fringe output are therefore

$$q_f = \frac{S - Q_K}{F + 1} \quad \text{and} \quad Q_F = F\frac{S - Q_K}{F + 1}. \tag{10.4}$$

Substituting (10.4) into (10.1), the residual demand function facing the restrictive group is

$$p = c + \frac{b}{F + 1}(S - Q_K). \tag{10.5}$$

Given this residual demand function, the profit-maximizing per firm and total output of the restrictive group are

$$q_k = \frac{1}{K}\left(\tfrac{1}{2}S\right) \quad \text{and} \quad Q_K = \tfrac{1}{2}S. \tag{10.6}$$

---

[2] See Selten (1973). This section follows Martin (1990) and Shaffer (1995), and examines the case in which firms in the fringe maximize own profit à la Cournot. The original contribution to this literature is d'Aspremont et al. (1983b). For models of cartel stability with a price-taking fringe, see Donsimoni (1985), d'Aspremont and Gabszewicz (1986), Donsimoni et al. (1986), and Problem 10.2 (although one may wonder if it is plausible to ascribe price-taking behavior to firms with the knowledge about the market that fringe firms in this type of model are typically assumed to have).

If it faces a fringe of Cournot firms, a group of output-restricting firms maximizes its return by producing the output that would be produced by a Stackelberg quantity leader.[3]

Substituting (10.6) into (10.4) and (10.5) gives the fringe firm output and the equilibrium price

$$q_f = \frac{1}{F+1}\left(\tfrac{1}{2}S\right), \qquad p = c + \frac{1}{F+1}\left(\tfrac{1}{2}bS\right). \tag{10.7}$$

Profits per firm of firms inside and outside the restrictive group are

$$\pi_k(F,K) = \frac{b}{K(F+1)}\left(\tfrac{1}{2}S\right)^2 \quad \text{and} \quad \pi_f(F) = \frac{b}{(F+1)^2}\left(\tfrac{1}{2}S\right)^2 \tag{10.8}$$

respectively.

If all firms restrict output, we need only consider the condition for internal stability. Output restriction by all firms is stable if each firm earns at least as much by restricting output as it would earn by defecting and forming a fringe,

$$\pi_k(0,N) \geq \pi_f(1) \tag{10.9}$$

or, using (10.8), if

$$N \leq 4. \tag{10.10}$$

Output restriction by all firms is stable if there are four or fewer firms supplying the market. If five or more firms supply the market and restrict output, each firm's share of monopoly profit is so small that the most profitable course for a single firm is to defect and act as an independent Cournot firm.

If the number of fringe firms is positive, the conditions for internal and external stability can be rewritten

$$F + 1 + \frac{1}{F} \leq K \leq F + 3 + \frac{1}{F+1}, \tag{10.11}$$

where the first inequality is necessary and sufficient for internal stability and the second inequality is necessary and sufficient for external stability. Since K and F are integers, (10.11) implies that if there are F firms in the fringe, output restriction is stable only if output restriction is by groups of $F + 2$ or $F + 3$ firms.

If fringe firms act as Cournot oligopolists, output restriction is stable if there are enough firms in the fringe so that fringe firm profit is not too great; otherwise, a firm restricting output will find it profitable to join to the fringe. At the same time, there must be enough firms restricting output so that fringe firms do not find it profitable to join the output-restricting group.

If fringe firms take account of the effect that their output decisions have on price, then partial stable output-restricting groups are a possibility. In such cases, the presence of a fringe does not suggest that the restrictive group will eventually break down. The presence of a Cournot fringe only slightly smaller than the restrictive group has the effect of making output restriction stable.

---

[3] Lofaro (1999) shows that payoffs of individual firms are greater if all firms restrict output to a level that exceeds the monopoly level than if a core maximizes its joint profit acting as a Stackelberg leader with a fringe of Cournot firms.

Table 10.1   Notation, stage game of repeated game

S_i	Strategy set, player i
$S = (S_1, S_2, \ldots, S_n)$	Strategy set
$\pi_i(S)$	Payoff, player i
$\Pi = (\pi_1, \pi_2, \ldots, \pi_n)$	Payoff vector
$G = (S, \Pi)$	Stage game

10.3   NONCOOPERATIVE COLLUSION IN REPEATED GAMES

Static models omit an essential element of the cost of defecting from an output-restricting equilibrium – the profit that is lost once rivals realize that the agreement is being violated. Once rivals realize that output is greater than it should be, in equilibrium, it is implausible to expect that they will continue to produce their cartel outputs. Once the equilibrium breaks down, all firms (including the firm which initiates output expansion) suffer lost profits. Whether or not output restriction is stable in a dynamic sense depends on whether or not for a single firm the present value of lost future profit exceeds the present value of short-run gains from output expansion. But this tradeoff cannot, by its inherently intertemporal nature, be analyzed in a static model.[4]

10.3.1   The stage game

It is natural to think of a dynamic oligopoly game as a sequence of discrete time periods, within each of which rivalry takes place according to the rules of some static game. The resulting supergame is built up from repeated plays of the component single-period stage games. If the same static game is played in each period, the supergame is a repeated game.

Notation is summarized in table 10.1. If S_i is the range of outputs open to firm i, the stage game is Cournot quantity-setting oligopoly. If S_i is the set of prices open to firm i and products are differentiated, then the stage game is Bertrand price-setting oligopoly with product differentiation.

A strategy vector $s^* \in S$ is a noncooperative equilibrium if each element of s^* maximizes the corresponding player's payoff, taking the other elements of s^* as given. Formally, s^* is a noncooperative equilibrium if

$$\pi_i\left(s^*\right) = \max_{s_i \in S_i} \pi_i\left(s_1^*, \ldots, s_{i-1}^*, s_i, s_i^*, \ldots, s_n^*\right), \qquad i = 1, 2, \ldots, n. \qquad (10.12)$$

Friedman (1971, section II) gives a proof of the existence of a noncooperative equilibrium for such a stage game by generalizing the notion of a best-response function. For each player

---

[4] See Mohr (1988) for an argument that the literature discussed here depends on particular and implausible assumptions about behavior at different times during a repeated game. The implication that Mohr draws, that cooperative equilibria sustained by noncooperative behavior should be abandoned, seems too strong. His argument does emphasize the distinction between models of equilibrium and disequilibrium dynamics.

i, define a best reply mapping that matches each element s of the strategy space S with a subset $r_i(s)$ of player i's strategy space S_i. $r_i(s)$ is the set of all elements of S_i that maximize player i's payoff, taking all except the ith element of s as given:

$$r_i(s) = [t_i | t_i \in S_i$$

$$\text{and } \pi_i\left(s_1^*, \ldots, s_{i-1}^*, t_i, s_i^*, \ldots, s_n^*\right) = \max_{s_i \in S_i} \pi_i\left(s_1^*, \ldots, s_{i-1}^*, s_i, s_i^*, \ldots, s_n^*\right)].$$

$$(10.13)$$

The relation r_i maps S into S_i. It follows that $(r_1, r_2, \ldots, r_n)$ maps S into S. Friedman shows that under certain assumptions Kakutani's fixed point theorem can be applied to the vector $(r_1, r_2, \ldots, r_n)$.[5] This guarantees the existence of a point $s \in S$ that r maps into itself:

$$[r_1(s), r_2(s), \ldots, r_n(s)] = s. \qquad (10.14)$$

Any point s_{Nash} that satisfies (10.14) is a Nash equilibrium for the stage game: each player maximizes its own payoff, taking the payoff of other players as given.

10.3.2   The infinite supergame

Suppose that a game is repeated T times, and that player i seeks to maximize the present-discounted value of the stage game payoffs:

$$\sum_{t=1}^{T} \alpha^t \pi_i(S_t), \qquad (10.15)$$

where S_t is the vector of strategies of the n players in period t and $\alpha < 1$ is the factor used to discount future income.[6] The T-period supergame is then described by the vector $G^T = (S, \Pi, \alpha, T)$.

In this T-period game, a pure strategy for player i is a T-element vector σ_i. The first element of σ_i, $\sigma_i(1)$, is an element of S_i, and gives player i's move in the first period. The second element of σ_i, $\sigma_i(2)$, is a function mapping S to S_i. $\sigma_i(2)$ gives player i's move in the second period as a function of the moves of all players in the first period. The third element of σ_i, $\sigma_i(3)$, is a function mapping S^2 (the Cartesian product of S and itself) to S_i. $\sigma_i(3)$ gives player i's move in the third period as a function of the moves of all players in the first two periods. In like manner, $\sigma_i(t)$ is a function mapping S^{t-1} to S_i, and gives player i's move in period t as a function of all previous moves of all players.

With this notation, the elements of player i's strategy σ_i are

$$\sigma_i(1) \in S_i, \qquad \sigma_i(t): S^{t-1} \to S_i, \quad t = 1, 2, \ldots, T. \qquad (10.16)$$

---

[5] For a discussion of the conditions, see Friedman (1971, pp. 1–3; 1986, pp. 34–42). For a discussion of fixed point theorems, see Border (1985). This method of proof is nonconstructive: it shows that equilibrium points exist, but does not identify them.

[6] If the interest rate is r, then $\alpha = 1/(1 + r)$.

The action taken by player i in period t is the realized value of the function $\sigma_i(t)$: $\sigma_i(t)(S^{t-1}) = a_{it}$. Thus player i's action in period t depends on the choices of all players in all previous periods.

$\sigma = (\sigma_1, \sigma_2, \ldots, \sigma_n)$ is a strategy vector for the t-period game. A noncooperative equilibrium for the supergame is defined in the usual way. σ is a noncooperative equilibrium for $G^T = (S, \Pi, \alpha, T)$ if, for all i, element i of σ maximizes player i's payoff, taking all other elements of σ as given.

Now consider an infinitely repeated supergame: $T = \infty$. Let σ_{Nash} be the strategy vector if all players play their stage-game Nash equilibrium actions period by period. For σ_{Nash}, the supergame is simply a repetition of the stage game, period after period.

If all other players play their Nash equilibrium strategy in every period, the best that a single player can do is play his or her Nash equilibrium strategy in each period. Playing the Nash strategy from the stage game in every period is thus a noncooperative equilibrium for the supergame. The interesting question from the point of view of game theory is whether there are equilibrium strategies for the supergame that yield players a greater payoff than simply repeating the stage game equilibrium strategy, over and over. If such strategies exist, the interesting question from the point of view of industrial economics is how they are affected by changes in market structure or firm conduct.

10.3.3 Trigger strategies: the grim reaper

Consider any stage-game strategy s_{ncc} that yields each player at least as great a single-period payoff as the Nash strategy. If all firms have the same constant marginal and average cost, the joint-payoff-maximizing strategy is one example of such a strategy. There will ordinarily be many others. Following Friedman (1971),[7,8] define a trigger strategy for the supergame as follows:

1   each player begins by playing his or her part of s_{ncc} and continues to do so, as long as all other players do the same;
2   revert to s_{Nash} in the period following any defection from s_{ncc}, and continue to play s_{Nash} forever after.

Formally, the trigger strategy is defined as

$$\sigma_i(1) = s_{i,\text{ncc}},$$

$$\sigma_i(t) = \begin{cases} s_{i,\text{ncc}} & \text{if } \sigma_j(\chi) = s_{j,\text{ncc}}, \ j \neq i; \chi = 1, \ldots, t-1; t = 2, 3, \ldots, \\ s_{i,\text{Nash}} & \text{otherwise.} \end{cases} \quad (10.17)$$

Whether or not a player prefers to produce his or her part of s_{ncc} depends on a comparison of the payoff from defecting and the payoff from adhering to the s_{ncc} strategy. If defection

---

[7]   An anticipatory discussion is Luce and Raiffa (1957, pp. 97–102). See also Radner (1980) and Friedman and Samuelson (1990).
[8]   For discussions of noncooperative collusion in finite repeated games, see Friedman (1985; 1986, pp. 94–103), Benoit and Krishna (1985), and Harrington (1987a).

has not yet taken place, payoff streams following defection or adherence in period t are the same as payoff streams following defection or adherence in period 1. It follows that we need only consider the incentive to defect in the initial period.

Beginning from period 1, let $\pi_{i,\text{ncc}}$ be player i's per-period profit if all firms adhere to the restrictive strategy, let $\pi_{i,\text{defect}}$ be firm i's best-response one-period profit if it defects from the trigger strategy, and let $\pi_{i,\text{Nash}}$ be firm i's per-period profit if all firms play the Cournot strategy. Assume that

$$\pi_{i,\text{Nash}} < \pi_{i,\text{ncc}} < \pi_{i,\text{defect}}. \tag{10.18}$$

The right-hand inequality means that, from the point of view of single-period payoffs, it is profitable to defect from the s_{ncc} strategy. The left-hand inequality means that, from the point of view of single-period payoffs, reversion to the Nash strategy is costly compared with adhering to the s_{ncc} strategy. Such inequalities hold, for example, if the stage game is Cournot n-firm quantity-setting oligopoly with a linear demand function and marginal cost constant and identical across firms, and the s_{ncc} strategy is to have each firm produce a fraction $1/n$ of the joint-profit-maximizing output.

Firm i's payoff if it adheres to the noncooperative collusion strategy is

$$PDV_{i,\text{ncc}} = \alpha\pi_{i,\text{ncc}} + \alpha^2\pi_{i,\text{ncc}} + \cdots = \frac{\alpha}{1-\alpha}\pi_{i,\text{ncc}}. \tag{10.19}$$

Firm i's payoff if it cheats for one period and triggers retaliation thereafter is

$$PDV_{i,\text{defect}} = \alpha\pi_{i,\text{defect}} + \alpha^2\pi_{i,\text{Nash}} + \alpha^3\pi_{i,\text{Nash}} + \cdots$$

$$= \alpha\pi_{i,\text{defect}} + \frac{\alpha^2}{1-\alpha}\pi_{i,\text{Nash}}. \tag{10.20}$$

For the trigger strategy to be a noncooperative equilibrium, the payoff from adhering to the trigger strategy must be at least as great as the payoff from defection. Using (10.19) and (10.20), $PDV_{i,\text{ncc}} \geq PDV_{i,\text{defect}}$ if

$$\alpha \geq \frac{\pi_{i,\text{defect}} - \pi_{i,\text{ncc}}}{\pi_{i,\text{defect}} - \pi_{i,\text{Nash}}}, \tag{10.21}$$

or, using $\alpha = 1/(1+r)$ to express the same condition in terms of the interest rate, $PDV_{i,\text{ncc}} \geq PDV_{i,\text{defect}}$ if

$$\frac{1}{r} \geq \frac{\pi_{i,\text{defect}} - \pi_{i,\text{ncc}}}{\pi_{i,\text{ncc}} - \pi_{i,\text{Nash}}}. \tag{10.22}$$

Equation (10.22) is always satisfied if r is sufficiently close to zero. Equivalently, (10.21) is always satisfied if α is sufficiently close to one.

If the equivalent conditions (10.21) and (10.22) are satisfied, the trigger strategy is a subgame perfect noncooperative equilibrium. Suppose first that all firms have produced the restrictive output from period 1 through period $t - 1$. Then, from period t onward, firm i faces the alternative income streams (10.19) and (10.20). If (10.21)/(10.22) are satisfied, firm i's expected payoff from restricting output in period t is at least as great as its expected payoff from defecting.

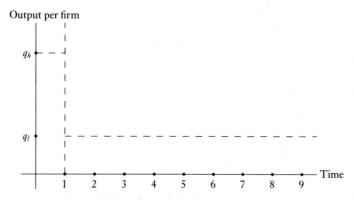

Figure 10.1 The firm output path, stick-and-carrot strategy.

In contrast, suppose that some firm defected from the trigger strategy in a period before period t. Then, when firm i arrives at period t it finds all other firms playing their stage-game Nash equilibrium strategies. The Nash strategy is a best response if all other firms play their Nash strategies, so the best that firm i can do is play its own stage-game Nash strategy. This is what the trigger strategy calls for. In other words, the strategy (10.17) defines a perfect equilibrium from any period onward, no matter what the history of the game. This is the defining characteristic of subgame perfection.

The result is that the trigger strategy (10.17) sustains output paths that allow each player to earn more than the Cournot payoff. This is an example of the Folk Theorem, which holds that noncooperative behavior can sustain any strategy producing individual payoffs that exceed stage-game Nash equilibrium payoffs if the interest rate is small enough (if the discount factor is close enough to one). The result is called the Folk Theorem because its precise authorship is uncertain, although it seems to have been known since the late 1950s (Aumann, 1987, p. 468). Much later work extends the reach of the Folk Theorem to a variety of imperfect information environments (Fudenberg and Maskin, 1986, 1990; Fudenberg et al., 1989; Fudenberg and Levine, 1990).

10.3.4   The stick-and-carrot strategy

A trigger strategy sustains cooperative behavior by a severe threat: if any player defects from the cooperative path, all players forgo collusive returns forever to punish the defector. The resulting strategy vector is a subgame perfect equilibrium. But it is natural to investigate the structure of strategies that are less grim than trigger strategies.

To this end, call an output path symmetric if all firms produce the same output in any one period. The unique firm output level may differ from period to period. Say also that an output path has two phases if in any period firms produce either one or the other of two values. Abreu (1986) shows that there is a symmetric, two-phase output path that sustains collusive outcomes for an n-firm oligopoly of identical quantity-setting firms.[9]

---

[9] See also Abreu et al. (1986) and Farrell and Maskin (1989). Häckner (1996) uses a spatial model.

The output path, shown in figure 10.1, has a stick-and-carrot pattern. It begins with a single period of high per-firm output q_h and low per-firm profit, followed by a switch to low per-firm output q_l and high per-firm profit. q_h and q_l are determined so that the two–phase output path is a subgame perfect equilibrium.

For the output pair (q_h, q_l) to define a subgame perfect equilibrium strategy, firms must prefer to produce q_h whenever the strategy calls for them to do so, and firms must prefer to produce q_l whenever the strategy calls for them to do so. These sustainability conditions yield a pair of two equations in two unknowns that determine q_h and q_l.

Let $\pi(q)$ be the per-firm profit if all firms produce q and let $\pi^*(q)$ be the best-response profit of a single firm if all other firms produce q. Suppose that the stick-and-carrot strategy calls for firms to produce q_h. This happens in the first period and in any period immediately following an episode of defection.

If a single firm (say, firm 1), adheres to the strategy, it will expect to earn $\pi(q_h)$ for one period and $\pi(q_l)$ in each subsequent period. Its payoff is

$$PDV_{\text{adhere},h} = \alpha\pi(q_h) + \alpha^2\pi(q_l) + \alpha^3\pi(q_l) + \cdots$$

$$= \alpha\pi(q_h) + \frac{\alpha^2}{1-\alpha}\pi(q_l). \tag{10.23}$$

If firm 1 prefers to defect when all other firms produce q_h, it will earn $\pi^*(q_h)$ in the first period. It will expect all other firms to produce q_h in the following period, as called for by the stick-and-carrot policy. Thus, if it prefers to defect when all other firms produce q_h, it will defect again. Its expected return is

$$PDV_{\text{defect},h} = \alpha\pi^*(q_h) + \alpha^2\pi^*(q_h) + \alpha^3\pi^*(q_h) + \cdots$$

$$= \frac{\alpha}{1-\alpha}\pi^*(q_h). \tag{10.24}$$

Firm 1 will prefer to adhere to the stick-and-carrot output path in the first period if adherence is at least as profitable as defection; that is, if

$$PDV_{\text{adhere},h} \geq PDV_{\text{defect},h}. \tag{10.25}$$

The larger is q_h, the smaller is $PDV_{\text{defect},h}$, but the smaller also is the income stream that faithful output-restricting firms would collect while inflicting punishment on a defector. The most profitable strategy for each individual firm in the output-restricting core is to make q_h just large enough so that (10.25) holds with equality.

Imposing equality in (10.25) and rearranging terms, the condition for sustainability in a high-output period becomes

$$\alpha = \frac{\pi^*(q_h) - \pi(q_h)}{\pi(q_l) - \pi(q_h)}, \tag{10.26}$$

the equation that determines $q_h(\alpha, q_l)$.

Now consider a period in which the stick-and-carrot strategy calls for all firms to produce q_l. If firm 1 adheres to the strategy, it earns $\pi(q_l)$ in the current period and, expecting mutual adherence, anticipates earning $\pi(q_l)$ in every future period. Its expected payoff is

$$PDV_{\text{adhere},l} = \frac{\alpha}{1-\alpha}\pi(q_l). \tag{10.27}$$

If firm 1 defects whenever all other firms produce q_l, it will earn its best-response profit $\pi^*(q_l)$ in the defection period. In the following period, all other firms will produce q_h. Provided that (10.26) holds, firm 1 prefers not to defect and will earn $\pi(q_h)$. Then, two periods after defection, all other firms will produce q_l, and firm 1 will defect. Firm 1's output therefore alternates between its defection output and q_h; its payoff is

$$\begin{aligned} PDV_{\text{defect},l} &= \alpha\pi^*(q_l) + \alpha^2\pi(q_h) + \alpha^3\pi^*(q_l) + \alpha^4\pi(q_h) + \cdots \\ &= \frac{\alpha}{1-\alpha^2}\left[\pi^*(q_l) + \alpha\pi(q_h)\right]. \end{aligned} \tag{10.28}$$

Firm 1 prefers to adhere to the stick-and-carrot strategy if

$$PDV_{\text{adhere},l} \geq PDV_{\text{defect},l}$$

$$\alpha \geq \frac{\pi^*(q_l) - \pi(q_l)}{\pi(q_l) - \pi(q_h)} \equiv \alpha_l. \tag{10.29}$$

Any discount rate greater than or equal to α_l makes it rational for a firm to produce q_l, if that is what the stick-and-carrot strategy calls for. The smaller is q_l, the more attractive is defection, since smaller values of q_l leave the defector with a residual demand curve farther from the origin. But, for sustainability, q_l cannot be so small that (10.29) is violated.

There are two possibilities. Let $q_l = q_m$, each firm's share of monopoly output, and solve (10.26) for q_h. If the resulting values satisfy (10.29), then the oligopoly can maximize joint profit using a stick-and-carrot strategy.

Alternatively, $q_l = q_m$ and the value of q_h that solves (10.26) may violate (10.29). In this case, the oligopoly cannot maximize joint profit using a stick-and-carrot strategy. Let (10.29) hold with equality. Equations (10.26) and (10.29) must then be solved as a system of simultaneous equations, giving the value for q_l closest to q_m that can be sustained using a stick-and-carrot strategy. Because (10.29) holds, firms' profit when producing q_l is the highest profit that can be sustained using a two-phase stick-and-carrot strategy. Because (10.26) holds, q_h inflicts the smallest possible damage on loyal firms, consistent with q_l. Punishment under the stick-and-carrot strategy is more severe than under a trigger strategy, but punishment is followed by a resumption of tacitly collusive output restriction.

10.3.5   Demons and repentance

Abreu's stick-and-carrot strategy is less grim than Friedman's trigger strategy, but it still requires that adhering firms punish themselves in order to punish the defector. It is attractive to consider strategies under which punishment wounds the defector more than it wounds other firms.

Repentance

Segerstrom (1988) outlines conditions under which it is a subgame perfect equilibrium strategy for a firm that defects from a noncooperatively collusive output pattern by expanding output to reduce output for a certain number of subsequent periods, while loyal firms respond optimally to the cheater's reduced output by expanding output. After the period of penitence is completed, all firms restrict output once again.

Demons

Friedman's trigger strategy, Abreu's stick-and-carrot strategies, and Segerstrom's repentance strategies all support noncooperatively collusive behavior if discount rates are sufficiently close to unity (if interest rates are sufficiently close to zero). But then (Segerstrom, 1988, p. 34):[10]

> It is important to remember . . . that in equilibrium, cheating never occurs when the players are adopting any of these strategies. The punishment threats are never carried out and the players' repeated game payoffs are the same regardless of which strategies they are using. Thus the question naturally arises, just as long as the punishment is sufficiently harsh to deter the crime, what difference does it make how cheaters are punished?

If players are completely rational and strategies like the ones discussed here are followed, then noncooperative collusion never breaks down. This is inconsistent with observed behavior in oligopolistic industries. Segerstrom extends his repentance model to explain occasional breakdowns in noncooperative collusion by supposing that there is a small probability ε that a player will maximize one-period profit rather than follow an equilibrium noncooperatively collusion strategy. Such a player is said to be possessed by an ε-demon. Redefining payoffs in expected value terms, trigger strategies, stick-and-carrot strategies, and repentance strategies will all sustain noncooperative collusion. Segerstrom outlines conditions under which the repentance strategy offers a greater expected return than reversion to Nash–Cournot output and stick-and-carrot strategies if ε is sufficiently small.

---

[10] See also Rees (1985).

Rational defection

Segerstrom models defection from tacitly collusive subgame perfect equilibrium in terms of occasional irrational behavior. Slade (1990) models such defection as a rational response to firms' uncertainty about the level of demand and about rivals' costs. If demand is uncertain and firms know their own cost but not rivals' costs, it is possible to define a subgame-perfect equilibrium strategy based on expected values of demand and cost. But it may nonetheless be profitable for firms sometimes to defect from such equilibria, on the basis of the relationship between realized demand and actual cost.

10.3.6   Structure, conduct, and the stability of noncooperative collusion

Whether or not noncooperative output restriction is stable depends on the present-discounted value of the return from adhering to the strategy and the present-discounted value of the return from defection. Both depend on the discount rate, on market structure, and on firm conduct, as specified by the strategy used to implement noncooperative collusion. Here, we examine the way in which the stability conditions – (10.21)/(10.22) for a trigger strategy, (10.26)/(10.29) for a stick-and-carrot strategy – are affected by changes in the number of firms, by whether or not firms set price or quantity, and by changes in the degree of product differentiation.[11]

Concentration

TRIGGER STRATEGY

For simplicity, consider the case in which firms are symmetric, so that concentration is inversely related to the number of firms. Examine an n-firm oligopoly with linear inverse demand function $p = a - bQ$ in which all firms enjoy the same constant marginal cost, c per unit.

If n firms settle on an output q per firm that is below the Nash equilibrium level of a one-shot game, then

$$\pi_{i,\text{ncc}} = b(S - nq)q, \qquad \pi_{i,\text{defect}} = \frac{b}{4}[S - (n-1)q]^2, \qquad (10.30)$$

for $S = (a - c)/b$.

We know (Problem 2.1(a)) that for this model Cournot profit per firm is

$$\pi_{i,\text{Cournot}} = \left(\frac{S}{n+1}\right)^2. \qquad (10.31)$$

---

[11] See also Harrington (1989, 1991).

From (10.30),

$$\frac{\pi_{i,\text{defect}} - \pi_{i,\text{ncc}}}{b} = \tfrac{1}{4}[S - (n+1)q]^2. \tag{10.32}$$

Equations (10.30) and (10.31) give

$$\frac{\pi_{i,\text{defect}} - \pi_{i,\text{Nash}}}{b} = \frac{n-1}{4(n+1)^2}[S - (n+1)q][(n+3)S - (n^2-1)q]. \tag{10.33}$$

Using (10.32) and (10.33), the condition for the trigger strategy to sustain equilibrium, (10.21), is

$$\alpha \geq \tfrac{1}{4}\frac{[S - (n+1)q]^2}{[S - (n+1)q][(n+3)S - (n^2-1)q]}\frac{4(n+1)^2}{n-1}, \tag{10.34}$$

which can be rewritten

$$q \geq \left[\frac{(n+1)^2 - (n-1)(n+3)\alpha}{(n+1)^2 - (n-1)^2\alpha}\right]\frac{S}{n+1} \equiv q_{ts}. \tag{10.35}$$

If $q_{ts} \leq S/2n$, noncooperative collusion can sustain joint-profit maximization. The condition for $q_{ts} \leq S/2n$ is

$$\alpha \geq \frac{(n+1)^2}{(n+1)^2 + 4n} \qquad \text{or, equivalently,} \qquad r \leq \frac{4n}{(n+1)^2} \equiv r_{ts}. \tag{10.36}$$

r_{ts} is the upper limit on the range of interest rates over which a trigger strategy is able to sustain noncooperative joint profit maximization. r_{ts} falls as the number of firms rises:

$$\frac{\partial r_{ts}}{\partial n} = -\frac{4(n-1)}{(n+1)^3} < 0. \tag{10.37}$$

As concentration increases – as n falls – the range of interest rates over which a trigger strategy will sustain noncooperative joint-profit maximization increases.

STICK–AND–CARROT STRATEGY

Now suppose that firms use a stick-and-carrot strategy to sustain noncooperative collusion. To begin with, let stability conditions (10.26) and (10.29) hold with equality. This is the case if the stick-and-carrot strategy does not support joint-profit maximization. Then, from

$$\alpha = \frac{\pi^*(q_h) - \pi(q_h)}{\pi(q_l) - \pi(q_h)} = \frac{\pi^*(q_l) - \pi(q_l)}{\pi(q_l) - \pi(q_h)}, \tag{10.38}$$

we have

$$\pi^*(q_h) - \pi(q_h) = \pi^*(q_l) - \pi(q_l). \tag{10.39}$$

Evaluating (10.39) gives

$$\left(q_h - \frac{S}{n+1}\right)^2 = \left(q_l - \frac{S}{n+1}\right)^2. \tag{10.40}$$

Equation (10.40) has two roots. One is $q_h = q_l$, which we can discard. The other is

$$q_h - \frac{S}{n+1} = -\left(q_l - \frac{S}{n+1}\right). \tag{10.41}$$

Thus if the stick-and-carrot strategy will not sustain joint-profit maximization, then stick output q_h is as much above Cournot output as carrot output q_l is below Cournot output. From (10.38), the remaining equation that defines q_h and q_l is

$$\alpha\left[\pi(q_l) - \pi(q_h)\right] = \pi^*(q_h) - \pi(q_h). \tag{10.42}$$

When evaluated in terms of the underlying parameters of the model, (10.42) becomes

$$\alpha(q_h - q_l)\left[n(q_h + q_l) - S\right] = \tfrac{1}{4}(n+1)^2\left(q_h - \frac{S}{n+1}\right)^2. \tag{10.43}$$

Equations (10.41) and (10.43) can be solved for

$$q_h = \left[1 + 8\alpha\frac{n-1}{(n+1)^2}\right]\frac{S}{n+1}, \qquad q_l = \left[1 - 8\alpha\frac{n-1}{(n+1)^2}\right]\frac{S}{n+1}. \tag{10.44}$$

If $q_l > q_m$, (10.44) gives the stick-and-carrot output pair that will sustain the closest possible approach to joint profit maximization, given the discount factor α. $q_l > q_m$ if

$$\alpha < \frac{(n+1)^2}{16n}. \tag{10.45}$$

On the other hand, if

$$\alpha \geq \frac{(n+1)^2}{16n} \qquad \text{or, equivalently,} \qquad r \leq \frac{16n}{(n+1)^2} - 1 \equiv r_{sc}, \tag{10.46}$$

then the stick-and-carrot strategy will sustain joint-profit maximization as a noncooperative equilibrium. In this case, $q_l = q_m$ and q_h is found by solving (10.43) with $q_l = q_m$.

Comparing (10.36) and (10.46), a stick-and-carrot strategy sustains joint-profit maximization if

$$r \leq r_{sc} = 4r_{ts} - 1. \tag{10.47}$$

Note that $r_{sc} < r_{ts}$ if $r_{ts} < 1/3$. If the trigger strategy is effective over a narrow range of interest rates, it is effective over a greater range of interest rates than the stick-and-carrot strategy. Further, r_{sc} and r_{ts} are positively related. Changes in n affect r_{sc} and r_{ts} in the same way. From (10.37), a decrease in n increases the range of interest rates over which a stick-and-carrot strategy will sustain noncooperative joint-profit maximization.

Fringe size and cartel stability in supergames

In a repeated game, noncooperative collusion is stable if it is supported by a subgame-perfect equilibrium strategy. We examine here the impact of fringe size on the stability of collusion in supergames when collusion is supported by a trigger strategy or by a stick-and-carrot strategy.

Even in a repeated game, external stability is the appropriate condition for firms in a Cournot fringe. Fringe firms maximize their own return, given the output of other firms. If subgame perfection induces core firms to restrict output, and firms in the fringe find it profitable to remain in the fringe, then no firm will wish to defect from its role and noncooperative collusion by the core will be stable.

TRIGGER STRATEGY

K core firms noncooperatively restrict output in a market with an F-firm Cournot fringe. The market operates for an infinite number of periods. Each firm in the core seeks to maximize the present-discounted value of its profit. A trigger strategy for firms in the output-restricting core is:

1   to produce $q_k = S/2K$ in the first period; after the first period, to play q_k if all core firms played q_k in the previous period;
2   to revert to $q_{\text{Cournot}} = S/(K + F + 1)$ in any period following defection from q_k, and continue to play q_{Cournot} thereafter.

Fringe firms act as Cournot quantity-setters. A fringe firm produces $q_f = S/[2(F + 1)]$ if output restriction has not broken down and q_{Cournot} if core firms have reverted to Cournot behavior. In each case, a fringe firm maximizes its own payoff, given the outputs of other firms.

A trigger strategy supports noncooperative collusion if the present-discounted value of the income stream from adhering to the strategy is at least as great as the present-discounted value of the income stream from defection. For the case at hand, output-restricting firms prefer to adhere to the trigger strategy if

$$\frac{1}{r} \geq \frac{\pi_{\text{defect}} - \pi_k}{\pi_k - \pi_{\text{Cournot}}}, \tag{10.48}$$

where r is the interest rate used to discount future income. π_k is given by (10.8).

If all firms play q_{Cournot}, each firm earns a profit

$$\pi_{\text{Cournot}} = b \left(\frac{S}{K + F + 1} \right)^2. \tag{10.49}$$

It remains to determine a core firm's one-period profit if it defects from the trigger strategy. If $K - 1$ firms in the core each produce q_k and F fringe firms each produce q_f, a single core firm faces the residual demand function

$$p = c + \frac{K+F+1}{K(F+1)} \left(\tfrac{1}{2}bS\right) - bq_1. \tag{10.50}$$

The defecting firm's profit-maximizing output and maximum profit are

$$q_{\text{defect}} = \frac{K+F+1}{K(F+1)} \left(\frac{S}{4}\right) \quad \text{and} \quad \pi_{\text{defect}} = b\left[\frac{K+F+1}{K(F+1)} \left(\frac{S}{4}\right)\right]^2 \tag{10.51}$$

respectively.

Substituting the various expressions for profit into (10.48) and simplifying, the trigger strategy outlined above sustains noncooperative joint-profit maximization by a core of K firms if[12]

$$\frac{1}{r} \geq \frac{(K+F+1)^2}{4K(F+1)}. \tag{10.52}$$

For notational simplicity, let $z = (K+F+1)^2/K(F+1)$. Then

$$\frac{\partial z}{\partial F} = -\frac{K^2 - (F+1)^2}{K(F+1)^2} < 0, \qquad \frac{\partial z}{\partial K} = \frac{K^2 - (F+1)^2}{K^2(F+1)} > 0, \tag{10.53}$$

$$\left.\frac{\partial z}{\partial F}\right|_{N=\bar{N}} = -\frac{(K+F+1)\left[K^2 - (F+1)^2\right]}{K^2(F+1)^2} < 0, \tag{10.54}$$

where $N = K + F$ and the signs of the derivatives depend on the assumption that the condition for external stability, (10.11), is met.

The derivatives (10.53)–(10.54) show that if fringe firms act as Cournot quantity-setters and the external stability condition is met, an increase in fringe size or an increase in fringe size holding the number of firms in the industry constant increases the upper limit of the range of interest rates over which the trigger strategy is a subgame-perfect equilibrium for cartel joint profit maximization. An increase in the number of firms restricting output has the opposite effect.

STICK–AND–CARROT STRATEGY

For a stick-and-carrot strategy, the conditions for stability are that adherence be at least as profitable as defection when $q = q_h$ and when $q = q_l$. If output is q_h, this condition is (10.26). If all firms produce q_l, the stability condition is (10.29).

If (10.29) is satisfied when all firms in the output-restricting core produce the joint-profit-maximizing output $q_k = S/2K$, then q_h is determined by solving (10.26) with $q_l = q_k$. If (10.29) is violated when $q_l = q_k$, then q_l and q_h are determined by solving the equality versions of (10.26) and (10.29) as a system of simultaneous equations.

---

[12] If (10.52) is violated, use of a trigger strategy allows a group of output-restricting firms to increase profit compared with Cournot behavior, but not to maximize joint profit.

Begin with the case in which $q_l > q_k$. If (10.26) and (10.29) hold with equality, then

$$\frac{\pi^*(q_h) - \pi(q_h)}{b} = \frac{\pi^*(q_l) - \pi(q_l)}{b}. \tag{10.55}$$

In the model considered here, this is

$$\left(q_h - \frac{S}{N+1}\right)^2 = \left(q_l - \frac{S}{N+1}\right)^2 \tag{10.56}$$

for $N = K + F$ and $S = (a - c)/b$.

Equation (10.56) has two roots. This first is $q_h = q_l$, which can be discarded. The second is

$$q_l + q_h = \frac{2S}{N+1}. \tag{10.57}$$

The other equation needed to solve for q_l and q_h, also from (10.26), is

$$\alpha \frac{\pi(q_l) - \pi(q_h)}{b} = \frac{\pi^*(q_h) - \pi(q_h)}{b}. \tag{10.58}$$

Evaluating the various expressions for profit, (10.58) becomes

$$\alpha \frac{K}{F+1}(q_h - q_l)\left(q_h + q_l - \frac{S}{K}\right) = \frac{(N+1)^2}{4(F+1)^2}\left(q_h - \frac{S}{N+1}\right)^2. \tag{10.59}$$

Solving (10.57) and (10.58) gives

$$q_l = \left\{1 - 8\alpha\frac{[K - (F+1)]}{(N+1)^2}\right\}\frac{S}{N+1}, \tag{10.60}$$

$$q_h = \left\{1 + 8\alpha\frac{[K - (F+1)]}{(N+1)^2}\right\}\frac{S}{N+1}. \tag{10.61}$$

These solutions are valid so long as $q_l > q_k = S/2K$, and from (10.60), this condition is met if

$$\frac{(N+1)^2}{K(F+1)} > 16\alpha. \tag{10.62}$$

If $q_l > S/2K$, use of a stick-and-carrot strategy allows an output-restricting core group of firms to increase profit compared with Cournot behavior, but not to maximize joint profit.

On the other hand, a stick-and-carrot strategy is a subgame-perfect equilibrium strategy for the maximization of joint profit of the core group if

$$\alpha \geq \frac{1}{16}\frac{(N+1)^2}{K(F+1)}. \tag{10.63}$$

In this case, q_h is found by solving the system of equations (10.59) and $q_l = S/2K$.

Comparing (10.52) and (10.63), and recalling that $\alpha = 1/(1+r)$, it is evident that changes in K and F affect the range of interest rates over which a partial cartel is able to sustain partial joint-profit maximization in the same way using a stock-and-carrot strategy and using a trigger strategy.

We conclude that if fringe firms act as Cournot quantity-setters and the external stability condition is met, an increase in fringe size or an increase in fringe size holding the number of firms in the industry constant increases the upper limit on the range of interest rates over which a stick-and-carrot strategy is a subgame-perfect equilibrium for cartel joint-profit maximization. An increase in the number of firms restricting output has the opposite effect.[13]

Prices versus quantities

We now turn to the Bowley linear product differentiation model of section 3.6.1 and ask whether noncooperative collusion sustained by trigger strategies is more likely to be stable in this model when firms set prices or when firms set quantities.[14]

The inverse demand function variety i is

$$p_i = a - \left(q_i + \theta \sum_{j \neq i} q_j \right).$$

(10.64)

Recall that if $\theta = 0$ products are completely differentiated, while if $\theta = 1$, products are homogeneous. We know from section 3.7 (see equations (3.62)) that in noncooperative quantity-setting equilibrium a single firm's payoff is

$$\pi_{q,\text{Cournot}} = \left[\frac{a - c}{2 + (n - 1)\theta} \right]^2.$$

(10.65)

If firms maximize joint profit, each firm's single-period payoff is (whether firms set price or quantity)

$$\pi_{j\pi m} = \frac{1}{4} \frac{(a - c)^2}{1 + (n - 1)\theta}.$$

(10.66)

A trigger strategy that threatens reversion to Cournot quantity-setting equilibrium outputs can sustain a strategy in which each firm produces its share of monopoly output if the interest rate is sufficiently low. To make this precise, we need to determine a firm's payoff if it defects from a joint-profit-maximizing strategy.

---

[13] Clyde and Reitzes (1998) analyze legal collusion in the ocean shipping industry, and find some evidence that cartel (conference) activity seems to raise profit of firms in and outside the cartel. This result is consistent with the model of collusion in repeated games with a fringe presented here.

[14] See Rothschild (1995) for a model in which the choice between price and quantity as a strategic variable is endogenous, and different strategic variables may be chosen in different parts of the game.

A defecting firm will select an output along its quantity-setting best-response curve. The resulting profit is

$$\pi_{q,\text{defect}} = \left[\frac{2 + (n-1)\theta}{1 + (n-1)\theta} \left(\frac{a-c}{4} \right) \right]^2. \tag{10.67}$$

Substituting from (10.65), (10.66), and (10.67) into the stability condition (10.22), and simplifying somewhat, we find that a trigger strategy threatening reversion to Cournot quantity-setting equilibrium supports joint-profit maximization if

$$\frac{1}{r} \geq \frac{1}{4} \frac{[2 + (n-1)\theta]^2}{1 + (n-1)\theta}. \tag{10.68}$$

If, in an otherwise identical market, firms set prices, one firm's single-period payoff is

$$\pi_{p,\text{Bertrand}} = (1 - \theta) \frac{1 + (n-2)\theta}{1 + (n-1)\theta} \left[\frac{a-c}{2 + (n-3)\theta} \right]^2. \tag{10.69}$$

If a single firm defects from a joint-profit-maximizing equilibrium, its payoff is[15]

$$\pi_{p,\text{defect}} = \frac{1}{(1 - \theta)} \frac{[2 + (n-3)\theta]^2}{[1 + (n-1)\theta][1 + (n-2)\theta]} \left(\frac{a-c}{4} \right)^2. \tag{10.70}$$

Substituting (10.66), (10.69), and (10.70) into the stability condition (10.22), a trigger strategy that threatens reversion to Bertrand noncooperative equilibrium supports joint-profit maximization if

$$\frac{1}{r} \geq \frac{1}{4} \frac{1}{1 - \theta} \frac{[2 + (n-3)\theta]^2}{1 + (n-2)\theta}. \tag{10.71}$$

The right-hand side of (10.71) is greater than the right-hand side of (10.68).[16] This means that there is a range of interest rates, defined by

$$4(1 - \theta) \frac{1 + (n-2)\theta}{[2 + (n-3)\theta]^2} < r \leq 4 \frac{1 + (n-1)\theta}{[2 + (n-1)\theta]^2}, \tag{10.72}$$

for which noncooperative collusion is sustainable by a trigger strategy in a quantity-setting market but not in a price-setting market. In this sense, as well as that of section 3.9, one finds that price-setting markets are "more competitive" than quantity-setting markets: all else equal, the interest rate used to discount future income must be lower to sustain noncooperative collusion in price-setting markets than in quantity-setting markets.

---

[15] Equation (10.70) gives the defecting firm's payoff if other firms produce positive output in the defection period.

[16] By subtraction, this holds for $n = 2$. A bit of algebra shows that the derivative of the difference with respect to n is positive.

Product differentiation

Inequality (10.68) gives the sustainability condition for noncooperative collusion in quantity-setting oligopoly with product differentiation. The derivative of the fraction on the right in (10.68) with respect to θ is

$$\frac{\theta}{4}[2 + (n-1)\theta]\left[\frac{n-1}{1 + (n-1)\theta}\right]^2 > 0. \tag{10.73}$$

As product differentiation increases, θ falls, and the right-hand side of (10.68) becomes smaller. It follows that, for a given interest rate and a given number of quantity-setting firms, noncooperative collusion is more likely to be stable – inequality (10.68) is more likely to be satisfied – the greater the degree of product differentiation.

Inequality (10.71) gives the sustainability condition for noncooperative collusion in price-setting oligopoly with product differentiation. The derivative of the fraction on the right in (10.71) with respect to θ is

$$[2 + (n-3)\theta]\frac{\theta}{4}\left\{\frac{n-1}{(1-\theta)[1 + (n-2)\theta]}\right\}^2 > 0. \tag{10.74}$$

Once again, increases in product differentiation – decreases in θ – make it more likely that noncooperative collusion will be stable.

Product differentiation reduces the incremental profit to be gained by departing from a joint-profit maximizing configuration because product differentiation insulates rivals' markets and reduces the extent to which a single firm can lure rivals' customers into its own market.[17]

---

[17] See Deneckere (1983, 1984), Majerus (1988), and Albæk and Lambertini (1998). Wernerfelt (1989) examines product differentiation and collusion when reversion is to an Abreu stick-and-carrot strategy. Davidson (1984) notes that small tariffs may stabilize and large tariffs destabilize tacit collusion; Messerlin (1990) notes that antidumping legislation may stabilize tacit collusion by protected domestic firms. Ross (1992) uses both the Bowley model and a spatial model to examine the impact of product differentiation on the stability of tacit collusion. Cheng (1991) and Häckner (1996) also employ spatial models. Symeonidis (1999a) examines conditions for tacit collusion when products are vertically differentiated. Gul (1987) and Ausubel and Deneckere (1987) examine conditions for noncooperative collusion when oligopolists produce durable goods. Maksimovic (1988) examines the impact of firms' financial capital structure on the stability of noncooperative collusion. Von Ungern–Sternberg (1988a) discusses collusion in auctions. Feinberg (1989) examines the impact of imports on the stability of collusion. Martin (1996) shows that existence of an R&D joint venture facilitates tacit collusion by the parent firms. Rothschild (1999) looks at the impact of cost differences on the stability of tacit collusion, on which see also Schmalensee (1987b) and Verboven (1997). Martin (1998) examines the impact of competition policy on the stability of noncooperative collusion. Tyagi (1999) examines the impact of the curvature of the demand curve on the product differentiation – collusion relationship.

10.4 PRICE WARS

10.4.1 Imperfect information and noncooperative collusion

To this point, we have considered models of noncooperative collusion which have a common characteristic: if one firm defects from an output-restricting strategy, other firms know it and are able to retaliate. But firms are typically unable to monitor rivals' output levels with precision. They often find themselves in the position of inferring whether or not defection has taken place on the basis of fluctuations of some observable variable, such as own sales or price. A model of trigger-price strategies when defection must be inferred includes a class of noncooperative equilibrium strategies that produces periodic reversions from collusive pricing, as a result of demand fluctuations, even if defection does not occur.[18]

Consider an n-firm quantity-setting oligopoly supplying a standardized product, demand for which is uncertain. Let the inverse demand function in period t have equation

$$p_t = \mu_t(a - bQ_t), \tag{10.75}$$

where μ_t is a random scale factor that shifts demand from period to period. Values of μ_t in different periods are independently and identically distributed, with expected value 1, density function $f(\mu)$ and cumulative distribution function $F(\mu)$. Firms observe p_t, but not μ_t; each firm knows its own output but is unable to observe rivals' outputs.

Because demand has a random element, noncooperative equilibrium must be defined in terms of expected values. A strategy vector $\sigma = (\sigma_1, \sigma_2, \ldots, \sigma_n)$ is a noncooperative equilibrium if σ_i maximizes the expected value of firm i, taking all other elements of σ as given.

For simplicity, suppose that firms are symmetric. Let the tacit collusion output per firm be q_χ, and let q_{NC} be noncooperative equilibrium output per firm from the stage game. For a trigger price $\bar{p}$ and number of periods ω, define period t as

$$
\begin{array}{ll}
1 & \text{normal if } \begin{cases} t = 0, \text{ or} \\ t - 1 \text{ was normal and } p_{t-1} \geq \bar{p}, \text{ or} \\ t - (\omega + 1) \text{ was normal and } p_{t-(\omega+1)} < \bar{p}; \end{cases} \\
2 & \text{reversionary if it is not normal.}
\end{array}
$$

The initial period is normal. After the initial period, a period is normal if the previous period was normal and price does not fall below the trigger price or if $\omega + 1$ periods have passed since the most recent normal period in which price fell below the trigger price. If a period is not normal, it is reversionary. A sequence of ω reversionary periods follows a normal period in which price falls below the trigger price.

---

[18] See Porter (1983a), Green and Porter (1984), and, for a seminal contribution, Stigler (1964). See also Dobson and Sinclair (1990).

Now let firm i's output be defined by the rule

$$q_{it} = \begin{cases} q_\chi & \text{if period } t \text{ is normal,} \\ q_{NC} & \text{if period } t \text{ is reversionary.} \end{cases} \tag{10.76}$$

In a normal period, each firm produces its share of the tacit collusion output. If price falls below the trigger price in a normal period, a sequence of ω reversionary periods follows, and during reversionary periods each firm produces its stage game noncooperative output.

To characterize equilibrium strategies, we need to describe the value of the firm. As all other firms produce q_{NC} in reversionary periods, the best that firm i can do is produce q_{NC} in a reversionary period. It follows that q_χ must be selected so that firm i prefers not to defect from the trigger strategy.

Suppose that firm i produces r units of output in normal periods, while all other firms together produce $(n-1)q_\chi$. Price is

$$p_t = \mu_t \left\{ a - b[r + (n-1)q_\chi] \right\} \tag{10.77}$$

and the probability that p_t is less than the trigger price $\bar{p}$ is

$$
\begin{aligned}
\Pr(p < \bar{p}) &= \Pr\left(\mu_t \left\{ a - b[r + (n-1)q_\chi] \right\} < \bar{p}\right) \\
&= \Pr\left(\mu_t < \frac{\bar{p}}{a - b[r + (n-1)q_\chi]}\right) = \Pr\left[\mu_t < \mu(r, q_\chi)\right] \\
&= \int_{\mu=\mu_{\min}}^{\mu(r, q_\chi)} f(\mu)\, d\mu = F[\mu(r, q_\chi)],
\end{aligned}
\tag{10.78}
$$

where $\mu(r, q_\chi)$ is the critical value of μ. For $\mu < \mu(r, q_\chi)$, the realized price is less than the trigger price, and a reversionary episode begins. Increases in either r or q_χ increase $\mu(r, q_\chi)$: the greater is the tacit collusion output per firm or the greater is a defector's output, the farther the inverse demand curve must be from the origin to hold price above the trigger level.

If firm i produces output r, while other firms each produce q_χ, firm i's expected profit is

$$E_\mu[\pi(r, q_\chi)] = b\left\{ S - [r + (n-1)q_\chi] \right\} r, \tag{10.79}$$

where $S = (a-c)/b$. On the other hand, during a reversionary episode firm i's profit is simply its Cournot equilibrium profit

$$E_\mu[\pi(q_{NC})] = b\left(\frac{S}{n+1}\right)^2. \tag{10.80}$$

Firm i's expected value, $V(r, q_\chi)$, is the present-discounted value of its future income stream. By producing output r, firm i collects $E_\mu[\pi(r, q_\chi)]$ in the current period. Future income depends on whether or not the current price falls below the trigger price $\bar{p}$. If price stays above $\bar{p}$, the expected value of the firm's income stream, discounted back to the initial period, is $\alpha V(r, q_\chi)$, where α is the discount factor. If price falls below $\bar{p}$, the firm passes through a reversionary episode. In this case, the expected value of the firm's income stream from one period in the future, discounted back to the initial period, is

$$\left(\alpha + \alpha^2 + \cdots + \alpha^\omega\right) E_\mu[\pi(q_{NC})] + \alpha^{\omega+1} V(r, q_\chi)$$

$$= \frac{\alpha}{1-\alpha}(1 - \alpha^\omega)E_\mu[\pi(q_{NC})] + \alpha^{\omega+1} V(r, q_\chi), \qquad (10.81)$$

where the first term is the present value of income during the reversionary period and the second term is the present value of income thereafter.

The expected present-discounted value of the firm is the sum of these income streams, weighted by the corresponding probabilities:

$$V(r, q_\chi) = E_\mu[\pi(q_{NC})] + \alpha V(r, q_\chi) \Pr(p \geq \bar{p})$$

$$+ \left\{\frac{\alpha}{1-\alpha}(1 - \alpha^\omega)E_\mu[\pi(q_{NC})] + \alpha^{\omega+1} V(r, q_\chi)\right\} \Pr(p < \bar{p}), \qquad (10.82)$$

Using (10.78) to evaluate the probability that output r triggers a reversionary episode and collecting terms in (10.82), we find the expected present-discounted value of a firm that produces output r during normal periods, while other firms produce q_χ each:

$$V(r, q_\chi) = \frac{E_\mu[\pi(q_{NC})]}{1-\alpha} + \frac{E_\mu[\pi(r, q_\chi)] - E_\mu[\pi(q_{NC})]}{1 - \alpha + \alpha(1 - \alpha^\omega)F[\mu(r, q_\chi)]}. \qquad (10.83)$$

The first term on the right is the expected present-discounted value of a firm in Cournot quantity-setting equilibrium. The second term on the right is the additional income collected by a firm producing r during normal periods while all other firms produce q_χ, discounted over time and allowing for the probability of reversionary episodes.

A defecting firm picks the value of r that maximizes $V(r, q_\chi)$, taking the output of all other firms as given. The first-order condition $\partial V(r, q_\chi)/\partial r = 0$ defines the profit-maximizing value of r as a function of q_χ.[19]

A defector's profit-maximizing output falls as q_χ rises, for two reasons. The greater is the output of all other firms, the closer to the origin is the residual demand curve facing the defector and the smaller the single-period profit-maximizing output. Further, the greater is q_χ, the more likely that price will fall below the trigger price $\bar{p}$, initiating a reversionary episode. When q_χ is larger, a defector will hold down output to reduce the probability of triggering a sequence of periods of Cournot behavior.

Since firms are symmetric, the problem of noncooperative collusion can be described as that of maximizing the return of a single firm subject to the constraint that firms willingly

[19] The first-order condition is complicated by the fact that r appears in the limit of the integral that defines $F[\mu(r, q_\chi)]$.

adhere to the equilibrium strategy:

$$\max V(q_\chi, q_\chi) \qquad \text{such that } V(q_\chi, q_\chi) \geq V\left[r(q_\chi), q_\chi\right], \qquad (10.84)$$

or, in Lagrangian form,

$$\max_{q_\chi} \mathcal{L} = V(q_\chi, q_\chi) + \lambda \left\{ V(q_\chi, q_\chi) - V\left[r(q_\chi), q_\chi\right] \right\}. \qquad (10.85)$$

The first-order conditions for this constrained maximization problem are as follows:[20]

$$\frac{\partial \mathcal{L}}{\partial q_\chi} = \frac{dV(q_\chi, q_\chi)}{dq_\chi} + \lambda \left\{ \frac{dV(q_\chi, q_\chi)}{dq_\chi} - \frac{\partial V\left[r(q_\chi), q_\chi\right]}{\partial q_\chi} \right\} \equiv 0, \qquad (10.86)$$

$$\frac{\partial \mathcal{L}}{\partial \lambda} = V(q_\chi, q_\chi) - V\left[r(q_\chi), q_\chi\right] \geq 0,$$

$$\lambda \left\{ V(q_\chi, q_\chi) - V\left[r(q_\chi), q_\chi\right] \right\} \equiv 0, \qquad (10.87)$$

$$\lambda \geq 0.$$

The solution falls in one of two cases. If $V(q_\chi, q_\chi) - V\left[r(q_\chi), q_\chi\right] \geq 0$ when $q_\chi = q_m$, the per-firm joint-profit maximizing output, $\lambda = 0$ and (10.86) reduces to the first-order condition for unconstrained joint-profit maximization.

Alternatively, it may be that a single firm would defect if others produced their share of joint-profit-maximizing output. Then λ, the shadow value of firm value lost to ensure the sustainability of collusive behavior, is positive, and (10.87) yields

$$V(q_\chi, q_\chi) - V\left[r(q_\chi), q_\chi\right] = 0 \qquad (10.88)$$

as the equation to be solved to determine q_χ. Solution of (10.88) gives the value of q_χ that makes the expected payoff from collusion as large as possible without making the temptation to defect so great that noncooperative collusion breaks down. In the second case, output is expanded above the joint-profit-maximizing level, to discourage defection.

Explicit solution of (10.85) requires a specification of the distribution of μ. Further, (10.85) is only a limited version of the noncooperative collusion problem. In principle, the trigger price $\bar{p}$ and the length ω of the reversionary period could be chosen to maximize firms' payoffs. These points are pursued by Porter (1983a). His results suggest that collusive behavior will in general involve producing more than the single-period joint-profit-maximizing output level.

Whether or not firms are able to maximize expected joint profit, there is a noncooperative equilibrium which includes periodic reversions to Cournot pricing. Such reversions do not signal a breakdown in tacit collusion: rather, they are an essential element of noncooperative behavior which makes defection unprofitable, in an expected value sense (Porter, 1983b, pp. 301–2):

> In equilibrium, firms maximize expected discounted profits by producing at collusive output levels, so that any price wars which are observed should occur after unexpected drops in demand,

[20] The term $\partial[r(q_\chi), q_\chi]/\partial r$ in (10.86) drops out by application of the envelope theorem. Since a defector chooses r to maximize V, taking q_χ as given, the value of this derivative is zero.

rather than after actual cheating by member firms. Thus price wars can be the occasional equilibrium output of a dynamic noncooperative game.

The Joint Executive Committee

Porter (1983b) analyzes the pricing behavior of a 19th-century US railroad cartel, the Joint Executive Committee (JEC) (1983b, p. 302):

> The JEC was a cartel which controlled eastbound freight shipments from Chicago to the Atlantic seaboard in the 1880s. It was formed in April 1879 by an agreement of the railroads involved in the market. The firms involved publicly acknowledged this agreement, as it preceded the passage of the Sherman Act...
>   The internal enforcement mechanism adopted by the JEC was a variant of a trigger price strategy.... there were several instances in which the cartel thought that cheating had occurred, cut prices for a time, and then returned to the collusive price.

The econometric model is motivated by the Green and Porter (1984) model of noncooperative collusion under demand uncertainty, but is not specific to that model (1983b, p. 302):

> ... there will be periodic switches or reversions between the Cournot and collusive output levels when such a noncooperative equilibrium exists. These reversions serve to identify periods of collusive behavior in a simultaneous equation switching regressions model. There is no explicit test of whether this sort of enforcement mechanism is employed. Instead, the econometric model is designed to test whether significant switches in supplier behavior occurred, and to identify the periods in which they took place.

Porter builds an industry supply equation from a model of firm behavior that is a simplified version of the conjectural elasticity/coefficient of cooperation models of chapter 3. Suppose that firm i's price–cost margin in period t is

$$\frac{P_t - MC_i(q_{it})}{P_t} = \frac{\phi_{it}}{\varepsilon_{Qp}}. \tag{10.89}$$

Depending on the value of ϕ_{it}, (10.89) covers a range of possible outcomes. $\phi_{it} = 0$ is the equilibrium outcome of Bertrand competition with standardized products: price equals marginal cost. $\phi_{it} = 1$ gives the joint-profit maximizing result: price–cost margin equal to the inverse of the price elasticity of demand. $\phi_{it} = s_{it}$, firm i's market share, gives the Cournot quantity-setting equilibrium price–cost margin.

Now suppose that firm i's cost function is

$$c_i(q_{it}) = a_i q_{it}^\delta + F_i. \tag{10.90}$$

a_i and fixed costs F_i vary from firm to firm. The diseconomies of scale parameter, $\delta > 1$, is the same for all firms.

Substituting marginal cost from (10.90) into the price–cost margin equation (10.89) gives the price–supply relationship for firm i:

$$P_t \left(1 + \frac{\phi_{it}}{\varepsilon_{Qp}}\right) = \delta a_i q_{it}^{\delta-1}. \tag{10.91}$$

Now suppose that the collusion parameter takes a common value for all firms in a single period: $\phi_{it} = \phi_t$ for all i. Then market share is determined by relative cost efficiency,

$$s_{it} = \frac{a_i^{1/(1-\delta)}}{\sum_{j=1}^{n} a_j^{1/(1-\delta)}}, \tag{10.92}$$

independent of the value of the collusion parameter ϕ_t.[21] In this case, multiplying (10.91) by s_i and adding over all i gives an industry aggregate supply relationship

$$P_t \left(1 + \frac{\phi_t}{\varepsilon_{Qp}}\right) = DQ_t^{\delta-1}, \tag{10.93}$$

where

$$D = a_1 s_{1t}^{\delta} + a_2 s_{2t}^{\delta} + \cdots + a_n s_{nt}^{\delta} \tag{10.94}$$

is an aggregate cost parameter and Q is total output.

Once again, the collusion parameter ϕ_t, now common to all firms, determines the nature of equilibrium in period t. $\phi_t = 0$ corresponds to Bertrand equilibrium, $\phi_t = 1$ corresponds to joint-profit maximization, and $\phi_t = H$, the Herfindahl index of market concentration, corresponds to Cournot equilibrium.

Taking logarithms on both sides of (10.93) gives a supply-side price–output relationship that is linear in logarithms,[22]

$$\log P_t = \log D - \log \left(1 + \frac{\phi_t}{\varepsilon_{Qp}}\right) + (\delta - 1) \log Q_t. \tag{10.95}$$

By analogy with the Green–Porter model of collusion under demand uncertainty, suppose that ϕ_t takes one of two values. During normal periods, $\phi_t = \phi > 0$. The closer is ϕ to 1, the closer the industry comes to joint-profit maximization during normal periods. During reversionary periods, $\phi_t = 0$, firms engage in Bertrand behavior and pick outputs that make marginal cost equal to price.

---

[21] Divide both sides of (10.91) by $Q^{\delta-1}$, where Q is total output. This yields $n - 1$ equations in the n market shares, namely

$$a_1 s_{1t}^{\delta-1} = a_2 s_{2t}^{\delta-1} = \cdots = a_n s_{nt}^{\delta-1}.$$

The nth equation is the identity that market shares sum to unity. Solution of these n equations yields (10.92).

[22] As with the Klemperer and Meyer (1989) supply function oligopoly model (section 3.10), (10.95) is not a supply function in the conventional sense: firms are not price-takers.

An estimating equation that captures the range of possible outcomes is

$$\log P_t = \beta_0 + \beta_1 I_t + \beta_2 \log q_t + U_t, \tag{10.96}$$

where $\beta_0 = \log D$, I_t is a dummy variable that takes the value 1 in normal periods and 0 otherwise, and $\beta_2 = \delta - 1$. An estimate of β_1 is an estimate of $\log[1 + (\phi/\varepsilon_{Qp})]$, and can be used to recover an estimate of ϕ.

It will not ordinarily be known *a priori* whether or not a period is normal, but use of a switching regimes technique permits one to infer this from the data. Porter estimates an equation like (10.96), generalized to include dummy variables that control for changes in industry structure during the sample period. The supply equation is estimated simultaneously with a demand equation. The results are that (Porter, 1983b, pp. 309–10):

> the value of $[\phi]$ implied by the estimates ... is 0.336. This is roughly consistent with Cournot behavior in cooperative periods. The finding of approximately Cournot behavior is by itself of no special significance. What matters is that cooperative period prices exceed those implied by competitive price setting, but are less than those consistent with static joint-profit maximizing ...

Porter's results also suggest that reversionary episodes, when they occurred, lasted for about ten weeks. Reversionary periods seemed to occur more frequently as the number of firms in the industry increased.

These results certainly support the argument that market performance in oligopoly will be inefficient compared with a competitive market. Despite his statement to the contrary, Porter's finding that market performance was approximately Cournot during cooperative periods has one significant implication. It does not support the occurrence of noncooperative collusion, which would require a finding that price exceeded the Cournot level during normal periods.

Ellison (1994) reexamines Porter's data set, allowing for serial correlation in the error term of the supply equation and testing for several possible indicators (other than low price) that might trigger price wars. His estimate of ϕ is 0.85, indicating a much closer approach to joint-profit maximization during collusive periods. He also presents a variety of evidence that is suggestive of at least some price-cutting by cartel members, contrary to the predictions of supergame models of noncooperative collusion.

10.4.2   Price wars during booms

A profit-maximizing, price-taking firm will produce a positive output if price is above the minimum value of average variable cost. Where fixed cost is a large portion of total cost, the lowest price at which firms find it (marginally) profitable to produce is far below the lowest price at which firms break even. For this reason, the folklore of industrial economics most often cites industries in which fixed cost looms large in discussions of price wars. Railroads are one example; cement is another. The expectation is that price wars break out in such industries when demand is slack, when the best price that a defecting firm can get is below the price at which it breaks even.

This presumption is consistent with the Porter–Green model of price wars, in which a sufficiently large slump pulls price below the trigger level, beginning a reversionary period.

The logic that underlies the two stories is different, however. In the traditional story, a sufficient fall in demand induces firms to defect from noncooperatively collusive behavior. No defection actually occurs in the Porter–Green model. Rather, a sufficient fall in demand induces firms to expand output and accept a lower price as a way of making defection irrational.

Rotemberg and Saloner (1986) argue that the results of the Porter–Green model, and indeed the traditional industrial economics argument, are sensitive to assumptions about the timing of information.[23]

Suppose that inverse demand is random, as for example

$$p_t = a + \varepsilon_t - bQ_t, \qquad (10.97)$$

where ε_t is a random, additive, disturbance term. For simplicity, assume that the expected value of ε_t is zero and that realized values of ε_t in different time periods are independently and identically distributed.

We can work out a noncooperatively collusive strategy for the supergame, along the lines of the Porter–Green model. The strategy has each firm produce its portion of the smallest sustainable joint output based on the expected value of ε_t (that is, zero), and calls for reversion to Cournot behavior if price falls below some trigger level.

Now alter the specifications of the Porter–Green model by assuming that:

1 firms know the realized value of ε_t before they set output;
2 a potential defector assumes other firms will adhere to their noncooperatively collusive outputs.

A defector believes that loyal firms will produce their collusive outputs, which are based on the expected value of ε_t: zero. But a defector, maximizing profit along a residual demand curve defined by those collusive outputs, knows the actual value of ε_t.

This re-specification is sufficient to create the possibility of price wars during booms. The expected lost income during a reversionary period is sufficient to defer cheating when ε_t takes its expected value. But the return to cheating is determined by the actual value of ε_t. If ε_t is sufficiently large, the actual return to cheating will outweigh the expected punishment, and cheating will occur (see Problem 10.4).

In markets of this kind, noncooperative collusion will be upset by episodes of actual defection. Price wars occur during booms, not slumps. They are triggered by actual defection, not by slack demand that cannot be distinguished from defection.

Re-specification of two elements of this model would reduce, but not eliminate, the incentive to defect during booms. First, it seems odd that all firms know the realized value of ε_t before they set their outputs, but the potential defector makes his decision assuming that other firms will maintain an output set by taking $\varepsilon = 0$. If the defector can set an output based on the realized value of ε, why should not loyal firms behave in the same way? This would be the case, for example, if oligopolists agreed on market shares rather than output

---

[23] Rotemberg and Saloner present price-setting and quantity-setting versions of their model. The price-setting version assumes standardized products, and that a defecting firm can capture essentially the entire market by a small price cut (Rotemberg and Saloner, 1986, p. 393). The logic behind their argument seems likely to carry through to a price-setting model with product differentiation. See Bagwell and Ramey (1997) for extensions.

levels. If loyal firms expand their quota outputs when ε is large, the residual portion of market demand left over for the defector, and the incentive to defect, will be reduced.

Second, what drives this result is the dependence of actual profit on the realized value of ε_t – on actual demand – while the punishment is based on the expected value of ε_t – zero. But booms are cyclic phenomena. If demand is high in the current quarter, so that the temptation to cheat is great, demand is likely to be high in the following quarter as well. But if demand is high in the following periods, punishment will be more severe as well. Realized values of ε in successive periods are likely to be positively correlated, and this will reduce the incentive to cheat.

Each re-specification will reduce the incentive to defect from a noncooperatively collusive strategy; neither will eliminate it. Price wars during booms may therefore be a realistic phenomenon if quantity-setting firms know the level of demand before they make their output decisions.

Empirical evidence

Rotemberg and Saloner present an econometric analysis of the real price of cement that seems to support their theoretical analysis. With yearly US data from 1947 to 1981, they regress a real price index for cement (the ratio of the price index for cement to the price index for construction materials) against the rate of growth of gross national product, and estimate the relationship[24]

$$\frac{\Delta P_{\text{cement}}}{P_{\text{cement}}} = 0.037 - 0.0876 \frac{\Delta GNP}{GNP} \qquad (10.98)$$
$$\phantom{\frac{\Delta P_{\text{cement}}}{P_{\text{cement}}} = } (4.635) \quad (5.879)$$

(where $\Delta x / x$ indicates the percentage change in the variable x).

They conclude (Rotemberg and Saloner, 1986, p. 399):

> A one percent increase in the rate of growth of GNP leads to a 0.5–1.0 percent fall in the price of cement. ... More casually, the price of cement relative to the index of construction prices rose in the recession year 1954, while it fell in the boom year 1955. Similarly, it rose during the recession year 1958 and fell in 1959. These results show uniformly that the price of cement has a tendency to move countercyclically ....

Rosenbaum (1986) carried out an analysis of cement prices, controlling for two industry characteristics not explicitly allowed for by Rotemberg and Saloner. The first is the regional nature of the cement industry (Rosenbaum, 1986, pp. 3–4):

> Portland cement is a homogeneous producer good. Given its low ratio of value to weight, portland cement is shipped only limited distances. In 1977, 82.5 percent of all shipments were less than 200 miles; 94.5 percent were less than 300 miles. This means the United States is effectively broken into several independent regional markets.

---

[24] t-statistics are in parentheses. The estimate is corrected for serial correlation of the error terms.

The second industry characteristic is the possible impact of capacity limitations (1986, pp. 5–6):

> Following Rotemberg and Saloner's theory, changes in real cement prices should be negatively related to changes in construction activity. This relationship is motivated by the assumption that any potential deviating firm can increase its sales by cheating on the collusive market equilibrium. If firms are constrained by capacity, however, this assumption is invalid. When all capacity is being utilized, firms essentially cannot expand output and, therefore, have no motive to deviate from the collusive equilibrium. When all capacity is utilized, the unconstrained monopoly profit rate becomes sustainable even when demand is increasing. Indeed, under these conditions, prices may even *rise* in a boom.

Rosenbaum constructs a cross-section time-series sample covering 25 regional US markets[25] for the period 1972–77. He reports a regression explaining a regional version of the same price index as that used by Rotemberg and Saloner in terms of the percentage change in construction activity, the product of the capacity utilization rate and the percentage change in construction activity, and the regional market Herfindahl index. His results are

$$\frac{\Delta P_{cement}}{P_{cement}} = \underset{(3.48)}{1.81} - \underset{(3.90)}{0.078}\frac{\Delta CA}{CA} + \underset{(1.65)}{0.86 CU}\frac{\Delta CA}{CA} + \underset{(3.00)}{0.21}\frac{\Delta Herf}{Herf} , \qquad (10.99)$$

where CA is an index of construction activity, CU is an index of capacity utilization, measured from 0 to 1, and $Herf$ is the Herfindahl index of market concentration.

These results suggest that excess capacity is a necessary condition for price wars during booms. The partial effect of an increase in the percentage change in construction activity implied by (10.99) is

$$\frac{\partial(\Delta P/P)}{\partial(\Delta CA/CA)} = -0.78 + 0.86 CU. \qquad (10.100)$$

The direct effect of a one percentage point increase in $\Delta CA/CA$ is thus to lower $\Delta P/P$ by 0.78 percentage points. This is as predicted by the model of price wars during booms. But the second term on the right in (10.100) shows that the total effect on $\Delta P/P$ of an increase in $\Delta CA/CA$ depends on CU, the extent of capacity utilization. If capacity utilization is low, the net effect of an increase in the rate of growth of construction activity on the rate of change of prices will be negative.

On the other hand, if capacity utilization is near 1 (greater than $0.78/0.86 = 0.91$), then the net impact of an increase in $\Delta CA/CA$ is to raise $\Delta P/P$. It seems unlikely that the net effect is statistically significant when CU is near 1.[26] Whether the net effect is positive or zero, in a statistical sense, is immaterial: it would have to be negative to support the hypothesis of price wars during booms. On this evidence, price wars during booms are likely to occur only if the boom starts from a situation of excess capacity. While this evidence is consistent with the model of price wars during booms, it is also consistent with the traditional industrial

---

[25] Each market is a major metropolitan area and all Portland cement plants within a radius of 200 miles.

[26] Calculating a standard error for the sum on the right in (10.100) requires the covariance of the estimates -0.78 and 0.86 from the parameter variance–covariance matrix, which Rosenbaum does not report.

economics analysis which suggests that it is the presence of excess capacity that triggers price wars.

10.4.3   Price wars and switching costs

In some markets, a consumer who switches suppliers or purchases a product for the first time bears a switching cost s over and above the purchase price (section 8.3). Entry into such a market results in a period of lower prices, followed by a period of higher prices, a time path of prices that looks very much like a price war.

One expects entry to result in lower prices because entry will typically result in an increase in output. This is the case, for example, if entry transforms a monopoly into a Cournot quantity-setting duopoly. When there are switching costs, an entrant produces even more output than in the Cournot case to attract customers who are later "locked in" by switching costs.

After securing a customer base, an entrant restricts output to exploit the limited monopoly that switching costs give it over its own customers. Output restriction by the entrant permits the original incumbents to restrict their own output. The eventual equilibrium price is lower than the pre-entry price, but higher than the price during the entry period.[27]

10.4.4   Demand shocks

Slade (1989) shows that price wars may emerge as an optimal response to infrequent random shifts in demand. We begin with the certainty version of Slade's model. For a price-setting duopoly with and Bowley product differentiation, linear inverse demand curves are

$$p_1 = a - b(q_1 + \theta q_2), \qquad p_2 = a - b(\theta q_1 + q_2), \tag{10.101}$$

for $0 \leq \theta < 1$.

The corresponding demand curves are

$$q_1 = \frac{(1 - \theta)(a - c) - (p_1 - c) + \theta(p_2 - c)}{b(1 - \theta^2)}, \tag{10.102}$$

$$q_2 = \frac{(1 - \theta)(a - c) + \theta(p_1 - c) - (p_2 - c)}{b(1 - \theta^2)}, \tag{10.103}$$

where c is marginal cost.

The one-period payoff of a single firm (say, firm 1) is

$$(p_1 - c)\frac{(1 - \theta)(a - c) - (p_1 - c) + \theta(p_2 - c)}{b(1 - \theta^2)}. \tag{10.104}$$

For a supergame composed of infinite repetitions of the single-period game, suppose that each firm seeks to maximize the present-discounted value of its payoffs, using strategies of

---

[27]   See Gallini and Karp (1989) and Klemperer (1989).

the form

$$p_{10} = p_R,$$

$$p_{it} = Rp_{j,t-1} + (1 - R)p_R, \qquad j \neq i, \quad t = 1, 2, \ldots,$$

(10.105)

where p_{it} is firm i's price in period t, $0 \leq R \leq 1$, and p_R will be determined shortly.

After the initial period, the best-response function specified in (10.105) determines each firm's current price as a weighted average of the long-run equilibrium price and its rival's price from the previous period. If best-response functions take this form, then each firm knows that if it defects from the price p_R, its rival will alter price in the same direction, one period later, but to a smaller extent. Built into the best-response function (10.105), therefore, is a kind of tit-for-tat behavior pattern: defection is met by retaliation in kind.

We now consider the circumstances under which it is optimal for a single firm to follow a strategy of this form, if the other firm does. If firm 2 follows a strategy of the form (10.105) firm 1's optimization problem is to select $p_{10}, p_{11}, \ldots$ to maximize

$$G_1 = (p_{10} - c) \left[\frac{(1 - \theta)(a - c) - (p_{10} - c) + \theta(p_R - c)}{b(1 - \theta^2)} \right] + \sum_{t=1}^{\infty} \alpha^t (p_{it} - c)$$

$$\times \left[\frac{(1 - \theta)(a - c) - (p_{it} - c) + \theta \left[R(p_{i,t-1} - c) + (1 - R)(p_R - c) \right]}{b(1 - \theta^2)} \right]. \quad (10.106)$$

The first-order conditions for $p_{10}, p_{11}, \ldots$ give the equations

$$(1 - \theta)(a - c) - 2(p_{10} - c) + \theta \left[(p_R - c) + \alpha R(p_{11} - c) \right] = 0, \quad (10.107)$$

$$(1 - \theta)(a - c) - 2(p_{10} - c)$$
$$+ \theta \left[(1 - R)(p_R - c) + p_{10} - c + \theta \alpha R(p_{12} - c) \right] = 0, \quad (10.108)$$

and so on.

Because firm 2's best-response function appears in firm 1's payoff function, the first-order conditions form a system of difference equations: the first-order condition for p_{10} depends partly on p_{11}, the first-order condition for p_{11} depends on p_{10} and p_{12}, and so on. If we substitute $p_{1t} = p_R$ for all t in (10.107) and (10.108) and solve, we obtain

$$p_R - c = \frac{(1 - \theta)(a - c)}{2 - \theta(1 + \alpha R)}. \quad (10.109)$$

The joint-profit-maximizing price is

$$p_{j\pi m} - c = \tfrac{1}{2}(a - c). \quad (10.110)$$

From (10.109) and (10.110), we then have

$$p_{j\pi m} - p_R = \theta \frac{1 - \alpha R}{2[2 - \theta(1 + \alpha R]} > 0, \quad (10.111)$$

since α and R both lie between 0 and 1. Thus strategies of the form (10.105) will not generally support joint-profit maximization.

Provided that firms use the value p_R given by (10.109), strategies of the form (10.105) are noncooperative equilibria. If one firm follows (10.105), the other maximizes its payoff by following (10.105).[28]

A model that produces price wars is obtained by generalizing this model to include infrequent changes in the structure of demand. Let the vector of parameters of the demand function (see (10.101)) in period t be

$$v_t = (a_t, b_t, \theta_t), \tag{10.112}$$

and let the relation between these parameters from one period to the next be

$$v_t = v_{t-1} + \eta_t, \tag{10.113}$$

where η_t is a vector of random disturbances

$$\eta_t = \omega_t(\varepsilon_{1t}, \varepsilon_{2t}, \varepsilon_{3t}). \tag{10.114}$$

Make the usual assumptions about the disturbances: ε_i is a normal random variable, with zero mean and variance σ_i^2, and the disturbances are independently distributed.

ω is a random variable which takes one of two values:

$$\Pr(\omega_t = 1) = \lambda, \qquad \Pr(\omega_t = 0) = 1 - \lambda, \tag{10.115}$$

where λ is small. Thus in most periods, $\omega_t = 0$, and there is no change in the structure of demand. Infrequently, $\omega_t = 1$ and the demand curve shifts.

If a demand shock occurs, firms will suddenly find that the quantity demanded at the price p_R has changed. This will reveal to firms that a demand shock has taken place, but it will not tell them the new values of (a_t, b_t, θ_t).[29]

To work out the new parameters of the demand curves, firms need to change price. If they change price in lockstep, both charging some price p, (10.102) and (10.103) show that the common quantity demanded is

$$q = \frac{a - p}{b(1 + \theta)}.$$

It follows that if the two firms change price together, they will collect information about the new values of a and $b(1 + \theta)$, but they will not be able to infer the new values of b and θ. Firms must charge different prices in the post-shock period to get the information they need to locate the new demand curves.

---

[28] Strategies of the form (10.105) are not, in general, subgame perfect. Slade shows, however, that if α is sufficiently close to 1, payoffs from following strategies of the form (10.105) differ from subgame-perfect payoffs by an arbitrarily small amount.

[29] It would be possible to combine the kind of demand uncertainty modeled by Slade with the kind of demand uncertainty modeled by Green and Porter. Then demand in each period would have a random element, and the parameters of the demand curve would change from time to time. In such a model, price wars would occur occasionally "by mistake," when firms incorrectly interpreted a fluctuation in demand for a change in the structure of demand.

Slade shows that:

1 The best response to price changes has both firms change price in the same direction: either both above the new value of p_R or both below the new value of p_R.
2 If one firm prices above the new value of p_R and one firm prices below the new value of p_R, the firm with the lower price has a greater expected return.

Rather than risk being stuck as the high-priced firm, both firms have an incentive to price low during the post-shock period. For this reason, post-shock experimentation with different prices is likely to take the form of a price war.

Slade outlines optimal rules for forming expectations about the new parameters of the demand function, and shows that if λ is sufficiently small – if demand shocks do not occur too often – firms that follow these rules will converge to the new equilibrium. Once firms have collected enough information to trace out the new demand curves, they will be able to raise price to the new value of p_R.[30] Thus (Slade, 1989, pp. 302–3):

> In the event that a price war does occur, the price-war dynamics produced by the model are very similar to the stylized facts in many markets where price wars are observed. First, prices can be stable over long periods of time; when a war starts, however, there is substantial price movement. Second, during the war, behavior resembles tit-for-tat. And finally, the war comes to a natural end when the learning process is over.

10.5 CONSCIOUS PARALLELISM

Simultaneous price changes are a hallmark of concentrated oligopoly. In some jurisdictions, such "consciously parallel" price movements have been taken as evidence of collusion.[31] MacLeod (1985) models the emergence of parallel price changes as rule-of-thumb behavior leading to noncooperatively collusive outcomes.

Consider an n-firm price-setting oligopoly, in which each firm produces one variety of a differentiated product and selects a price strategy to maximize the present-discounted value of profit over all future time. We know from our discussion of trigger and other strategies that there is a wide variety of equilibria that offer firms a payoff greater than they would get from simply repeating the stage game noncooperative equilibrium price period after period. This leaves open the question which of these equilibria will emerge, given noncooperative behavior.

Let $P = (p_1, p_2, \ldots, p_n)$ be a vector of equilibrium prices. Suppose that if firm i announces a price Δp_i, other firms react according to rules

$$\Delta p_j = r_{ij}(P, \Delta p_i), \qquad j \neq i. \tag{10.116}$$

---

[30] It is necessary to reformulate both the definition of equilibrium and the structure of the best-response strategy to allow for uncertainty. See Slade (1989) for details.

[31] In US antitrust law, see *American Tobacco Co.* et al. v. *United States* 328 US 781 (1946) but also *Theatre Enterprises, Inc.* v. *Paramount Film Distributing Corp.* et al. 346 US 537 (1953). For the European Community, see *ICI and others* v. *EC Commission* Cases 48-57/69 [1972] ECR 619 [1972] CMLR 557.

MacLeod imposes three conditions on the response functions r_{ij}:

1   they are continuous and continuously differentiable;
2   real responses are invariant to any change in the scale in which prices are measured:

$$r_{ij}(\alpha P, \alpha \Delta p_i) = \alpha r_{ij}(P, \Delta p_i) \qquad \text{for all } i,j \text{ and for all } \alpha > 0; \qquad (10.117)$$

3   response functions are independent of the order in which firms are labeled.

MacLeod shows that the unique set of response functions which satisfy these axioms requires firms to match price changes,

$$r_{ij}(P, \Delta p_i) = \Delta p_i. \qquad (10.118)$$

He embeds response functions of this kind in an announcement game in which firms change prices at the start of each period but are able to announce their intentions for the following period in advance. A strategy for the announcement game specifies the announcement that a firm j should make in response to an announced price change Δp_i by some other firm i. One such strategy is the conscious parallelism strategy:

1   match a price increase if it would be profitable to do so and all other firms match;
2   otherwise hold price constant (or retract an unmatched announcement);
3   match a price decrease;
4   if any other firms fail to follow 1–3, announce a return to single-period noncooperative equilibrium prices.

Noncooperative equilibrium for the announcement game is defined in the usual way. An announcement strategy is an equilibrium if following the strategy maximizes each firm's single-period profit, assuming other firms follow the strategy. MacLeod derives conditions to characterize price vectors from which the conscious parallelism strategy is an equilibrium for the announcement game. Given other assumptions, a vector of price announcements is an equilibrium for the announcement game if and only if it is unprofitable for a single firm unilaterally to increase its own price.

Given the conscious parallelism strategy for the announcement game, a price vector is an equilibrium for the market game if any proposed price change is not matched (and is therefore rescinded). Under MacLeod's assumptions, there is a single equilibrium price vector for the market game. It can be found, beginning from the noncooperative equilibrium for the stage game, by increasing prices in lockstep so long as the parallel increases raise the stage-game profit of all firms. Price increases stop at the level from which it is unprofitable for some firm to follow further increases. The conscious parallelism strategy for the announcement game requires firms to hold prices constant once a single firm fails to follow an announced increase.

MacLeod's model shows (1985, p. 40):

> that if the preconditions for collusion exist . . . then firms may . . . achieve a degree of collusion via price signaling. The role played by conscious parallelism, that is, an exact matching of announced price changes, was to act as an easily identifiable social convention that ensured firms had correct

expectations with respect to their competitors' actions. It thus serves as a plausible . . . means for an industry to achieve a collusive outcome.

Harstad et al. (1998) examine the impact of announcements and parallel price changes on outcomes in an experimental market. They find that allowing an announcement phase before prices are set results in prices above the Nash equilibrium level of a one-shot game, as does compelling experimental subjects to either match an announced price change exactly or nor change their announced price at all. Experience with the price-matching strategy also tends to increase prices. Prices do not rise to the conscious parallelism equilibrium or joint-profit-maximizing levels.

10.6 FACILITATING PRACTICES

The problem of stability of tacit or overt collusion arises because of an intertemporal inconsistency in the incentives facing individual firms. When no firms have restricted output, it is profitable for all firms to do so. If all firms have restricted output, it is profitable for each individual firm to restrict output a bit less than expected. Facilitating practices reduce the profit of defecting from an output-restricting equilibrium, thus enhancing the stability of noncooperative collusion.[32]

10.6.1 Most favored customer clauses

Salop (1986) notes that a most-favored customer clause, which commits a firm to offer to all customers a low price that is offered to any customer, eliminates selective price-cutting from a firm's range of options, ensuring (as in the standard calculation of marginal revenue) that revenue given up on *all* sales that might have been made at a higher price must be set against revenue from incremental sales that will be made only at a lower price, and therefore raising the cost of defecting from a tacitly collusive equilibrium.

On a different level, if all consumers are informed of a price cut, the probability that rivals will learn about the price cut, and retaliate, increases. Thus a most favored customer clause reduces the profit to be had by deviating from output restriction and also reduces the interval before rivals react to such a defection. Both effects should reduce incentives to deviate from a tacit collusion equilibrium.[33]

Cooper (1986) presents a two-stage model of retroactive most favored customer clauses. The market is one of two price-setting firms and a differentiated product. In the first stage,

[32] Bernheim and Whinston (1985) analyze use of a common sales agency as a facilitating device. Salop (1986) discusses the policy of advance notices of price changes as a facilitating device (on which, see Holt and Scheffman (1987). Such advance notice is typically part of basing-point pricing systems, and was required by public policy in the early years of the European Coal and Steel Community. More generally, see Albæk et al. (1997) on the impact of a public policy of price transparency on market performance (proposals for a price transparency policy were seriously put forward for the US wholesale beef market during the 1999–2000 presidential campaign). Policies employed in the depression-era United States under the National Industrial Recovery Act seem also to have served as facilitating practices; see Baker (1989) and Krepps (1999).

[33] See also Belton (1987) and Holt and Scheffman (1987).

each firm decides noncooperatively whether or not to adopt a most favored customer clause. In the second stage, which consists of two periods, firms noncooperatively set prices.

The logic behind the result that at least one firm will adopt a retroactive most favored customer clause is straightforward (Cooper, 1986, pp. 380–1): a most favored customer clause allows a firm to commit to a minimum price in the second period. Under the assumptions of the model, firms' prices are strategic complements, so if one firm commits to a higher minimum price, the optimal response of the other firm is to increase its price. The payoffs of both firms increase.[34]

Besanko and Lyon (1993) present a two-stage model in which firms decide whether or not to adopt a contemporaneous most favored customer clause in the first period and engage in price competition in the second period.[35] Depending on the parameters of the model, equilibrium may have none, some, or all of the firms adopting a most favored customer clause. Average price rises if a firm noncooperatively adopts a most favored customer clause. The welfare effects are ambiguous on both the demand side (products are differentiated and a price increase may cause some consumers to switch to another variety) and the supply side (output may shift from high-cost to low-cost producers).

Neither Cooper nor Besanko and Lyon formalize the impact of most favored customer clauses on the conditions for tacit collusion in a repeated game.[36]

10.6.2   Price-matching

With a price-matching policy, a firm commits to matching (and sometimes beating) a legitimate lower price of a competitor – "We will not be undercut." As noted by Salop (1986), price-matching policies have two effects that reduce incentives to defect from an output-restriction equilibrium. First, they create an incentive for consumers to inform rivals that price-cutting has taken place.[37] Second, on the expectation that price cuts would be matched, they reduce the gain from price-cutting to a proportionate share of the increase in total sales, eliminating any business-stealing effect.

Logan and Lutter (1989) use a two-stage duopoly model to examine the impact of price-matching policies in a two-stage game.[38] In the first stage, firms noncooperatively decide whether or not to adopt a price-matching policy. In the second stage, firms noncooperatively compete in prices. In the symmetric-firm case, the unique equilibrium is for both firms to adopt price-matching and to set the monopoly price in the second period. If firms have

---

[34] See also Neilson and Winter (1993), whose work suggests that in the context of Cooper's model, one should not expect both firms to adopt most favored customer clauses.

[35] They do not, therefore, examine the impact of contemporaneous most favored customer clauses on conditions for noncooperative collusion in a repeated game.

[36] Schnitzer (1994) analyzes most favored customer clauses in a finitely repeated market for a durable good.

[37] A consumer who makes him- or herself a conduit of information will bear some transaction costs, but perhaps also save any costs of switching suppliers. A sufficiently farsighted consumer might also work out that if the consequences of tattling about a secret price cut would be to make secret price cuts unprofitable, it would be better not to tattle. Nonetheless, human nature being what it is, it seems likely that the effect would occur.

[38] See also Doyle (1988), Corts (1997), and Kaplan (2001).

different cost functions, then in the absence of side payments there is no unique most-preferred second-period price. Depending on the magnitude of the cost difference, both, one, or no firms may adopt price-matching.[39]

10.7 EMPIRICAL STUDIES OF COLLUSION

10.7.1 Evidence from enforcement of competition law

The enforcement of competition policy generates samples that can be studied to analyze industry characteristics that favor the attempts to collude and influence the success or failure of such attempts.

In this vein, Hay and Kelley (1974) describe US criminal cases under Section 1 of the Sherman Act in the period 1963–73 that went to trial and were won by the government or that were settled by pleas of "no contest."[40]

Their sample gives comfort to the idea that fewness of numbers on the supply side of the market facilitates collusion. Seventy-nine per cent of the cases involved conspiracies of ten firms or less; seven of the eight cases that involved 15 or more firms also involved a trade association. Many of the cases involved a subset of firms, suggesting the relevance of models of a collusive core and a noncollusive fringe. They summarize their results (Hay and Kelley, 1974, pp. 26–7):

> ... conspiracy among competitors may arise in any number of situations but it is most likely to occur and endure when numbers are small, concentration is high and the product is homogeneous.

Hay and Kelley's results speak to the impact of market structure on collusion. Symeonidis (2000) draws inferences about the reverse chain of causality from the passage of the UK Restrictive Trade Practices Act of 1956,[41] a discrete-change toughening of UK competition policy toward collusion. The shift in competition policy caused the break-up of formal and informal collusive agreements in a wide range of UK industries, and was followed by increases in seller concentration in many of those industries. The implication is that collusion without the ability to block entry attracts more (and possibly less efficient) firms into the industry than would otherwise operate. The impact of collusion shows up in a excess number of firms in the market, not in economic profit of incumbents.

Symeonidis (1999b) reports the results of a probit analysis of groups that registered agreements under the UK Restrictive Trade Practices Act of 1956. His sample covers 151 four-digit industries, 71 of which were homes to registered restrictive agreements, and 80 not. His results suggest that capital intensity and moderate rates of industry sales growth favor the formation of restrictive agreements, while intensive advertising does not. There are traces of an inverted-U impact of seller concentration (measured by a five-firm concentration ratio)

---

[39] On the impact of cost differences on output restriction more generally, see Schmalensee (1987b).

[40] A layperson's explanation of a no-contest plea is that the defendant says "I didn't do it, and I promise never to do it again."

[41] Background on the Act is given in Symeonidis (1998, 1999b, 2000).

and the likelihood of existence of a restrictive agreement, but on balance the estimated coefficients are not statistically significant.

10.7.2   Case studies

Retail gasoline

Slade (1987) estimates demand curves and price best-response functions for a local Canadian retail gasoline market. The data set covers a three-month price war in 1983.

Slade divides retail gasoline stations into two groups, majors and independents. For each firm, she estimates a linear equation explaining the firm's price as a function of current and lagged weighted-average price of its own group and of the other group. The best-response functions implied by these estimates can be compared with Bertrand–Nash and single-period best-response functions. The implied industry profit can be compared with profit under Bertrand–Nash, single-period best response, and constrained joint-profit-maximizing profit.[42]

Generally, estimated responses exceed single-period best-reply responses, which in turn exceed the Bertrand–Nash response (zero). Independents and majors both respond more to price changes by independents than to price changes by majors. Fringe firms are punished more than majors for a price change of equal size.

The ranking of profits is:

Joint profit maximization	1,032,010
Estimated	419,948
One-period best response	303,011
Bertrand–Nash	277,628

As Slade concludes (1987, p. 513),

> Through repeated play, therefore, stations do better than they would if they played the noncooperative game only once. Profit, however, is far short of monopoly profit.

Slade's results suggest caution as regards the possibility of joint-profit maximization via noncooperative collusion. The market that she analyzes is one that seems as close to ideal, from the point of view of noncooperative collusion, as can be expected. In a local retail gasoline market, price changes are observed almost immediately. The technology is standardized and cost differences are small. There is product differentiation, but the degree of product differentiation from supplier to supplier is not subject to rapid changes. The threat of punishment allows a better profit than single-period noncooperative behavior, and a better profit than single-period best-response behavior. The threat of punishment, in this market, does not allow firms to approach constrained joint-profit maximization.

---

[42] That is, joint profit is maximized subject to the constraint that each group earn at least as much as it would in Bertrand–Nash equilibrium.

Salt

Rees (1993) discusses the UK salt market. Two domestic firms have a combined market share of 97 percent. The product is homogeneous, although one firm enjoys cost advantages over the other. Price is the strategic variable. The two firms operate under capacity constraints, but each has considerable excess capacity. Entry is effectively blocked. A trade association openly administered a collusive agreement until the 1956 passage of the Restrictive Practices Act. Parallel pricing continued after the formal agreement was abandoned, and market shares were approximately stable. In the early 1980s, the rates of return on capital of the two firms ranged from 24 to 53 percent, substantially above the rate of return on capital for large UK industrial firms. Rees points out that the observed market performance does not confirm the predictions of the Bertrand model of price-setting duopoly with homogeneous products. Rather, it seems likely that excess capacity and the ability to threaten output increases allowed firms to maintain effective collusion. Profits, nonetheless, were far from the joint-profit-maximizing level.

Sugar

Genesove and Mullin (1998b, 1999) discuss the role of an industry trade association, the Sugar Institute, in fostering effective collusion in the US sugar industry of the early 20th century. The Sugar Institute apparently did not fix price directly, but managed a variety of practices that had the effect of greatly increasing the transparency of prices and made it more difficult to make secret price cuts. Sugar Institute practices facilitated the detection of defection. There is evidence of retaliation when price cuts became apparent, but the relation was not as severe as that assumed in mainstream models: price cuts were matched, but there was no reversion to one-shot Nash conduct.[43]

10.8 CONCLUSION

Static models of collusion are limited by their inability to treat the possibility of retaliation following defection. If firms place sufficient weight on future income (if discount rates are sufficiently low), a variety of retaliation schemes will support noncooperative collusion and allow firms to maximize joint profit or expected joint profit.

Empirical evidence from natural and experimental markets suggests that profit in non-cooperative oligopoly can exceed the single-period noncooperative level, without reaching joint-profit maximization. There is some evidence that retaliation schemes of the kind modeled in the theoretical literature occur in practice, although not so severe as assumed in theoretical treatments. An important element in real-world collusion is the creation of an environment that facilitates detection of cheating.

---

[43] Levinstein (1997) reports similar findings for the bromine industry. Symeonidis (2000, p. 87) writes that "the administration of collusive agreements was one of the primary functions of British industrial trade associations in the 1950s."

PROBLEMS

10.1 Show that a single firm can profit by defecting from a joint-profit-maximizing cartel in an n-firm price-setting oligopoly with product differentiation. Assume that inverse demand functions and demand functions follow the Bowley model of product differentiation:

$$p_i = a - b(\theta q_1 + \theta q_2 + \cdots + q_i + \cdots + \theta q_2),$$

$$q_i = \frac{(1-\theta)a - [1 + (n-2)\theta]p_i + \theta \sum_{j \neq i} p_j}{b(1-\theta)[1 + (n-1)\theta]},$$

constant marginal cost, identical for all firms, and no fixed cost.

10.2 Adopt the linear demand function (10.1), and let each firm operate with the quadratic cost function

$$c(q_i) = cq_i + dq_i^2,$$

where $d > 0$ is a diseconomies-of-scale parameter. Let there be N firms, K of which form a cartel. The remaining F firms form a price-taking fringe. The K cartel members maximize joint profit, given cartel behavior. What restrictions on K and F are required for internal cartel stability? What restrictions on K and F are required for external cartel stability?

10.3 Suppose that the demand function is as in the Bowley model of product differentiation, firms produce under conditions of constant returns to scale, and firms set prices rather than quantities.

    (a)   For what values of α will a trigger strategy sustain noncooperative joint-profit maximization? For what values of α will a stick-and-carrot strategy sustain noncooperative joint-profit maximization?

    (b)   How do the limits on these values change as product differentiation increases?

10.4 Let the inverse demand function be

$$p_t = a + \varepsilon_t - bQ_t$$

and the firm cost function

$$c(q_i) = cq_i + dq_i^2.$$

In an n-firm quantity-setting oligopoly, show that a single firm's one-period payoff from defecting from a joint-profit-maximizing collusive equilibrium rises as ε_t rises.

CHAPTER ELEVEN
MARKET STRUCTURE, ENTRY, AND EXIT

Abandon all hope, ye who enter.

Dante Alighieri

11.1 INTRODUCTION

The analysis of the determinants of market structure is central to the study of market performance under oligopoly. We begin with a discussion of the measurement of the concentration of sales among firms in an industry. Seller concentration is perhaps the most prominent aspect of market structure, and an appreciation of the limitations of the most commonly used summary measures of seller concentration is necessary to understand empirical work in industrial economics.

We introduce the analysis of the determination of market structure by reviewing the role of the concept of entry barriers in the structure–conduct–performance paradigm. This provides a necessary background to the study of contemporary analyses of the determination of market structure, which differ in emphasis from the structure–conduct–performance approach. We conclude with a discussion of the recent flowering of theoretical and empirical work on entry and exit.

11.2 THE MEASUREMENT OF SELLER CONCENTRATION

For an industry producing a homogeneous product, the concentration of sales is completely described by the cumulative distribution of sales or, equivalently, of market shares.

But a description of the complete size distribution of firms in an industry is unwieldy and often not well suited for description or analysis. It is also often unavailable, a characteristic that it shares with other ways of describing market structure.

For descriptive and analytic purposes, it is useful to have a summary index that condenses the size distribution of firms in an industry to a single number. Inevitably, use of a one-dimensional index to represent a multidimensional phenomenon means a loss of information. To be useful, the index should be a number that can be calculated, or at least approximated, from available data. Several such indices have been proposed; two have been widely used.[1]

11.2.1 Algebraic properties

We maintain the convention that there are n firms in the industry, ordered according to market share: firm 1 is the largest firm, firm 2 the second largest, and so on. Using s to denote market shares, this means that $s_1 \geq s_2 \geq \cdots \geq s_n$.

The Herfindahl index

The Herfindahl index is the sum of squares of market shares of firms in the industry:[2]

$$H = s_1^2 + s_2^2 + \cdots + s_n^2. \tag{11.1}$$

If all n firms are the same size, $H = 1/n$. The lower limit of the Herfindahl index is zero, as the number of equally sized firms goes to infinity. If a single firm supplies the entire market, $H = 1$. Greater values of the Herfindahl index indicate greater concentration of sales.

The inverse of the Herfindahl index, $1/H$, is a numbers equivalent, and a convenient way to summarize the concentration of sales. It indicates the number of equally sized firms that would produce a given value of the Herfindahl index.[3]

The variance of market shares in an industry satisfies

$$n\sigma^2 = \sum_{i=1}^{n} \left(\frac{1}{n} - s_i \right)^2 = H - \frac{1}{n}, \tag{11.2}$$

so that

$$H = \frac{1}{n} + n\sigma^2. \tag{11.3}$$

Thus the Herfindahl index increases as the number of firms falls and as the variance of market shares increases. The Herfindahl index combines information about both the number and the size distribution of firms.

---

[1] See Stigler (1968a), Adelman (1969), Davies (1979), Encaoua and Jacquemin (1980), or Geroski (1983). For a discussion from a statistical point of view, see Hart (1975).

[2] For discussion of the properties of the Herfindahl index, see Weinstock (1982, 1984) or Kwoka (1985). On the origin of the index, see Herfindahl (1950) and Hirschman (1964).

[3] The numbers equivalent property is noted by Stigler (1968a) and Adelman (1969). m/CRm is a numbers equivalent based on the m-firm concentration ratio. See Blackorby et al. (1982) for an analysis of the measurement of concentration in terms of numbers equivalents.

The seller concentration ratio

The m-firm seller concentration ratio[4] is the combined market share of the largest m firms in the industry,

$$CRm = s_1 + s_2 + \cdots + s_m. \tag{11.4}$$

The number of firms included in the concentration is usually determined by the government agency that collects and reports the data, not from underlying principles.

If all firms are the same size, the m-firm concentration ratio is m/n. The lower limit of the concentration ratio is zero, as the number of equally sized firms goes to infinity. The upper limit, if m or fewer firms supply the entire market, is 1.

The relation between the concentration ratio and the Herfindahl index

Sleuwaegen and Dehandschutter (1986) show that, for a given m-firm concentration ratio, the Herfindahl index must lie between

$$H_{\min} = \frac{(CRm)^2}{m} \quad \text{and} \quad H_{\max} = \begin{cases} (CRm)^2 & CRm \geq 1/m, \\ CRm/m & CRm \leq 1/m. \end{cases} \tag{11.5}$$

It follows that, for $CRm \geq 1/m$,

$$H_{\max} - H_{\min} = \frac{m-1}{m}(CRm)^2, \tag{11.6}$$

which rises with the square of CRm. It is unlikely, therefore, that the relationship between the Herfindahl index and the concentration ratio will be even approximately linear. Nonlinearities will be more important, the closer the concentration ratio is to 1.

11.2.2 Market share, market concentration, and market performance

It is the relation of concentration to market performance that is of primary interest. We therefore ask what measures of market concentration, if any, emerge from standard models of market performance.

---

[4] From time to time, one meets the buyer concentration ratio (the combined market share of the largest four customers purchasing from firms in an industry) and the supplier concentration ratio (the combined market share of the largest four firms selling inputs to firms in an industry). See Lustgarten (1975) and Martin (1983a). From seller concentration ratios for different values of m, one can derive the so-called marginal concentration ratio. The difference between $CR4$ and $CR8$, for example, is the market share of the fifth to the eighth largest firms. See Miller (1967), Collins and Preston (1969), or Martin (1988a).

Let firm i's profit be[5]

$$p_i(Q)q_i - c(q_i), \tag{11.7}$$

where $p(Q)$ is the market inverse demand curve and $Q = q_1 + \cdots + q_n$ is total output. The first-order condition for maximization of (11.7) is

$$p + q_i p' \left(1 + \frac{dQ_{-i}}{dq_i}\right) = c_i', \tag{11.8}$$

where Q_{-i} is the combined output of all firms except firm i. If firm i treats the conjectural derivative,[6] $\lambda_i = dQ_{-i}/dq_i$, as a constant, we obtain the firm-specific Lerner index,

$$L_i = \frac{p - c_i'}{p} = \frac{(1 + \lambda_i)s_i}{\varepsilon_{Qp}}, \tag{11.9}$$

from (11.8), where $\varepsilon_{Qp} = (q_i/Q_{-i})\, dQ_{-i}/dq_i$ is the industry price elasticity of demand.

The firm's degree of market power depends on firm characteristics (the firm's market share, the firm's expectations about the conduct of rivals) and industry characteristics (the price elasticity of demand).

If all firms have the same conjectural derivative ($\lambda_i = \lambda$ for all i) and we take a weighted average of the firm-specific indices of market power, using market shares as weights, we obtain an industry-average Lerner index:

$$L = \frac{(1 + \lambda)H}{\varepsilon_{Qp}}. \tag{11.10}$$

If we run through the same exercise on the assumptions that firm i treats the conjectural elasticity (section 3.4.2), $\alpha_i = (q_i/Q_{-1})\, dQ_{-i}/dq_i$, as a constant and that $\alpha_i = \alpha$ for all i, we obtain firm-specific and industry Lerner indices

$$L_i = \frac{\alpha_i + (1 - \alpha_i)s_i}{\varepsilon_{Qp}}, \qquad L_i = \frac{\alpha + (1 - \alpha)H}{\varepsilon_{Qp}}. \tag{11.11}$$

If firms independently maximize profit, maintaining conjectures about rivals' reactions, structural relationships emerge between market share and firm market power and between the Herfindahl index and industry average market power.[7] For this reason, and because the Herfindahl index combines information about the number and the size distribution of firms, it is usually regarded as the preferred measure of market concentration (see, for example, Schmalensee, 1977).[8]

---

[5] See Cowling and Waterson (1976), Dickson (1979, 1981), and Clarke and Davies (1982).

[6] See section 3.4.1, and recall the interpretation of conjectures in section 3.4.3 as a device for representing dynamic interactions in static models.

[7] The Herfindahl index also arises in Stigler's (1964) model of collusion in oligopoly (but see McKinnon, 1966; Dansby and Willig, 1979; Encaoua and Jacquemin, 1980).

[8] See Saving (1970) for a model of a dominant group of the m largest firms which produces the m-firm seller concentration ratio as the natural measure of seller concentration.

Differentiated products

If firms maintain conjectural derivatives and products are differentiated as in the Bowley representative consumer model, one obtains a Lerner index of firm-level market power of the same form as (8.3), measuring firm i's market share with reference to what Geroski (1983) calls the effective output of variety i, $q_i + \theta Q_{-i}$, so that firm i's effective market share is $s_i(\theta) = q_i/(q_i + \theta Q_{-i})$ (see (9.14)). The same sort of result holds if firms maintain conjectural elasticities. These firm-level expressions can be aggregated to the industry level. When products are differentiated, however, the ability to hold price above marginal cost seems more a firm than an industry characteristic.

Structural indicators of market power

Structural indicators of market concentration are often used as proxy indicators of the presence/absence/likelihood of market power. The models presented here suggest that structural indicators are imperfect signals of market power.

If products are differentiated, market power is more likely to be a firm-specific than an industry-specific phenomenon. Measures of market concentration, while useful, are no more important than measures of the extent of product differentiation. If products are standardized, firm conduct – which has been modeled here in terms of conjectures about rivals' behavior – is as important for market performance as market share or market concentration.

11.2.3   Empirical evidence

Vanlommel et al. (1977) compare 1970 values of the Herfindahl index and the four-firm seller concentration ratio (as well as a number of other concentration measures) for a sample of 119 Belgian industries. The sample correlation coefficient between the Herfindahl index and the four-firm seller concentration ratio is 0.80. This is a typical result.

Kwoka (1981) points out that, from an econometric point of view, a high correlation between two variables does not mean that they will have similar correlations with a third variable (in this context, for example, the degree of market power). Using an otherwise identical set of explanatory variables, he examines the performance of ten alternative concentration measures ($CR1$–$CR10$) in an equation explaining price–cost margins for a sample of 314 1972 US manufacturing industries.[9] The strongest results, in terms of explanatory power and statistical significance, are obtained for $CR2$, the combined market share of the two largest firms. The estimated coefficient of $CR2$ is a good deal more significant than the estimated coefficient of $CR4$, by all odds the most common concentration measure in market structure–profitability studies.

In a later study with the same sample, Kwoka (1985) compares $CR2$, $CR4$, and H. As shown in table 11.1, the three variables are highly correlated. A scatter diagram showing $(CR4, H)$

---

[9]   See also Kwoka (1979).

Table 11.1   Correlation coefficients, three
concentration measures; for a sample of 314 1972 US
manufacturing industries

	CR2	CR4	H
CR2	1.000	0.976	0.961
CR4		1.000	0.976
H			1.000

Source: Kwoka, 1985, table 3

Table 11.2   A comparison of three concentration
measures in a price–cost margin regression, for a sample
of 314 1972 US manufacturing industries; t-statistics in
parentheses

		R^2	$\bar{R}^2$
(1)	$PCM = 0.2088 + 0.0853 CR2$		0.175
(2)	$PCM = 0.2094 + 0.0515 CR4$	0.184	
(3)	$PCM = 0.2180 + 0.1511 H$	0.186	

Source: Kwoka, 1981, table 2; 1985, table 5

pairs exhibits exactly the kind of relationship predicted by Sleuwaegen and Dehandschutter (1986).

Kwoka (1985) uses the three concentration measures as explanatory variables in regression equations with specification identical to those of Kwoka (1981). Leaving aside all other explanatory variables, the intercept terms and coefficients of the concentration measures are shown in table 11.2. CR2 has the most significant coefficient, followed by H, while CR4 has the least significant coefficient. The explanatory power of the three specifications is very much the same.

In another comparison, Sleuwaegen and Dehandschutter (1986) test the Herfindahl index and four-, eight-, and 20-firm concentrations in regressions explaining the rate of return on sales (price–cost margin) for a sample of 1958 US industries. Their estimated intercept terms and concentration coefficients are shown in table 11.3.

Some of their results are consistent with those of Kwoka. Of the three concentration ratios, CR4 has the most significant estimated coefficient, followed by CR8, while CR20 has a coefficient that is negative and statistically insignificant. But the Herfindahl index has a more significant coefficient than any of the concentration ratios, and the equation which uses the Herfindahl index as a concentration measure has the highest degree of explanatory power.

In addition, if H and CR4 are both included as explanatory variables, the coefficient of H is only slightly different (larger) from that reported in table 11.3 (although much less significant), while the coefficient of CR4 is negative and statistically insignificant. The results of Sleuwaegen and Dehandschutter lend rather more support to the use of H as a measure of concentration than those of Kwoka.

Table 11.3   A comparison of four concentration measures in a price–cost margin regression, for a sample of 1958 US manufacturing industries; t-statistics in parentheses

		R^2
(1)	$\Pi/R = -0.139 + 0.208CR4$ (1.475) (3.546)	0.432
(2)	$\Pi/R = -0.166 + 0.194CR8$ (1.574) (3.153)	0.400
(3)	$\Pi/R = 0.170 - 0.077CR20$ (1.386) (1.232)	0.209
(4)	$\Pi/R = -0.062 + 0.519H$ (0.786) (4.062)	0.480

Source: Sleuwaegen and Dehandschutter, 1986, table I

11.2.4   Entry barriers

Bain defined entry conditions in terms of the cost advantages of incumbents over entrants (1956, p. 10):

> the condition of entry to an industry ... refers to advantages which established firms in an industry have over established entrant firms; it is evaluated in general by measures of the heights of entry inducing prices relative to defined competitive levels.

This way of thinking about entry conditions is rooted in limit-price models of oligopoly. The more difficult it is to enter a market, the more incumbents can raise price above the competitive level without inducing entry. The difference between the competitive price and the entry-inducing price reflects unit costs that are borne by an entrant but not by an incumbent.

Bain emphasized economies of large scale, product differentiation, and absolute cost advantages of incumbent firms compared with entrants as the main determinants of entry conditions (1956, pp. 15–6).

Economies of scale

If output from a minimum efficient scale plant – a plant large enough so that average cost takes its minimum value – is a significant part of the quantity demanded at a competitive price, entrants face a distasteful choice. They can come into the market at large scale, which would certainly attract the attention and possibly the retaliation of incumbents. Or they can come into the market at small scale, and operate at a cost disadvantage compared with large firms.

Economies of scale arise if average cost falls as output rises, and may simply be a characteristic of the technology. Economies of scale also arise if large firms are able to bargain with suppliers and obtain inputs at lower cost than small firms.[10] Similarly, economies of firm scale arise if advertising and other sales efforts are more effective when carried out at large scale (whether or not this is the case is an empirical question).[11]

If economies of scale are measured by the function coefficient, greater economies of scale mean lower price–cost margins, all else equal (see (6.18)).

Product differentiation

Bain saw three possible sources for product differentiation advantages of large firms. Buyers might have strong preferences for established brands and for the products of firms with established reputations. Entrants could not expect to duplicate the brand preferences or reputational advantages of incumbents immediately, and would have to spend more than incumbents, per unit of output, to reach the final consumer. Patents might give incumbents legal monopolies over the use of favored products, which would make duplication by entrants either impossible or possible only on terms of licenses dictated by incumbents. Established firms might control access to major wholesale and retail outlets, implying higher per-unit distribution costs for incumbents.

Absolute cost advantages

Incumbents enjoy an absolute cost advantage over entrants if patents or secrets gave them control over state-of-the-art production processes. Incumbents might control access to higher-quality or lower-cost input suppliers. If, as seems likely, the possibility of bankruptcy is greater for entrants than for incumbents, then financial markets can be expected to impose a higher cost of capital on entrants than incumbents. The resulting absolute cost advantage will be greater, the more capital-intensive is the production process.

11.2.5   Critics

Stigler

Stigler restricts the term "barriers to entry" to differentially higher costs faced by entrants but not by incumbents (1968b, p. 67):

> A barrier to entry may be defined as a cost of producing (at some or every rate of output) which must be borne by a firm which seeks to enter an industry but is not borne by firms already in the industry.

[10] This is possible only if supplying industries are imperfectly competitive. If supplying industries supply inputs at marginal cost, there is nothing to bargain for.

[11] Or if price schedules of the advertising industry are such that the unit cost of advertising falls as the scale of advertising rises. For conflicting views, see Brozen (1974), Clarke (1976), Brown (1978), Arndt and Simon (1983), and Boyer and Lancaster (1986).

Economies of scale do not constitute a barrier to entry in the Stigler sense if entrants and incumbents have access to the same cost curve. Entrants could simply enter the market, produce at the same output level as the largest incumbent, and enjoy costs as low as those of incumbents.

High absolute capital requirements of operating at minimum efficient scale are a barrier to entry in the Stigler sense only if entrants face a systematically higher cost of capital than incumbents do. There is good reason to expect that this is the case. Financial markets systematically lack the ability to distinguish entrants who are likely to be successful from entrants who are likely to fail, while established firms' reputations make it possible to assess the probability that they will go bankrupt. Consequently, entrants face a systematically higher cost of capital than incumbents.[12]

In like manner, product differentiation is a barrier to entry in the sense only if it is costlier for an entrant than for an incumbent to generate a given amount of differentiation. If the current degree of differentiation enjoyed by incumbents depends in part on past design, advertising, and sales efforts, the cost of such activity constitutes a barrier to entry. But if current differentiation depends only on current expenditures on design, advertising, and sales efforts, and entrants can purchase such activities on the same terms as incumbents can, such expenditures do not constitute a barrier to entry.

Von Weizsäcker

Von Weizsäcker (1980a,b) extends Stigler's approach to include welfare effects in the definition of barriers to entry. Barriers to entry are of policy concern only if they lead to a suboptimal reallocation of resources. But resource allocation is a welfare concept; therefore von Weizsäcker puts forward the following refinement of Stigler's definition of entry barriers (1980a, p. 400):

> a barrier to entry is a cost of producing which must be borne by a firm which seeks to enter an industry but is not borne by firms already in the industry and which implies a distortion in the allocation of resources from a social point of view.

In the interest of objective analysis, it might have been useful if Bain had used the term "cost of entry" rather than the implicitly value-laden term "barriers to entry." But a cost of entry is a cost of entry whether it is or is not borne by incumbents and whether its consequences are to raise or lower welfare.[13] It is preferable to analyze costs of entry as such, and if it is their welfare consequences that of interest, to analyze their welfare consequences, but not to confuse what at a fundamental level are two distinct concepts.

---

[12] This is the Akerlof (1970) lemons argument applied to financial markets. See Williamson (1974), but also Stigler (1967).

[13] Nor is it clear that the welfare consequences of a particular type of cost of operating in a market can be assessed without reference to the market characteristics: welfare consequences depend on all factors that affect equilibrium (for example, whether choice variables are strategic substitutes or strategic complements), and may be positive in one case, negative in others.

11.3 ENTRY CONDITIONS AND MARKET STRUCTURE

11.3.1 Fixed cost and economies of scale

Von Weizsäcker (1980a,b) shows that the long-run Cournot equilibrium number of firms may exceed the socially optimal number of firms.[14]

Demand and supply

Suppose that n Cournot quantity-setting firms supply a market with linear inverse demand curve

$$p = a - bQ. \tag{11.12}$$

Let each firm produce with a quadratic cost function

$$C(q) = F + cq + dq^2. \tag{11.13}$$

We assume $d > 0$, which implies that marginal cost exceeds average variable cost and that for sufficiently large output levels there are diseconomies of scale.

The average-cost minimizing level of output for this cost function (the output for which marginal cost equals average cost) is

$$q_{MES} = \sqrt{\frac{F}{d}}. \tag{11.14}$$

Write

$$MES = \frac{q_{MES}}{S} = b\frac{\sqrt{F/d}}{a - c} \tag{11.15}$$

for minimum efficient scale as a fraction of market size $S = (a - c)/b$ (the quantity demanded if price equals the minimum value of marginal cost).

Short-run equilibrium

We begin with a short-run equilibrium in which the number of firms is exogenously fixed. With n firms, Cournot equilibrium output per firm is

$$q = \frac{S}{n + 1 + 2\delta}, \tag{11.16}$$

where $\delta = d/b$. Total output and price are

$$Q = \frac{nS}{n + 1 + 2\delta}, \qquad p = c + \frac{1 + 2\delta}{n + 1 + 2\delta}(a - c) \tag{11.17}$$

respectively. These reduce to the constant returns to scale results if we set $\delta = 0$.

[14] See also Martin (1984b), Mankiw and Whinston (1986), and Suzumura and Kiyono (1987).

In n-firm equilibrium, each firm earns a profit

$$\pi_{\text{Cour}}^{\text{SR}} = b(1 + \delta) \left(\frac{S}{n + 1 + 2\delta} \right)^2 - F.$$ (11.18)

Long-run equilibrium

To this point, what we have is a standard Cournot model, distinguished if at all by the fact that returns to scale are not constant. If we now assume that the number of firms n adjusts until each firm earns zero profit, we obtain a long-run Cournot model that has much in common with Chamberlin's 1933 model of monopolistic competition. Each firm maximizes profit along a residual demand curve, assuming that other firms hold output constant. The number of firms adjusts so that maximum profit is zero. In long-run equilibrium, each firm produces somewhat less than the output that will minimize average cost.[15]

If we set $\pi_{\text{Cour}}^{\text{SR}}$ in (11.18) equal to zero and solve for n, we obtain an expression for the long-run equilibrium number of plants:

$$n_{\text{Cour}}^{\text{LR}} = \frac{S}{\sqrt{F/(b+d)}} - (1 + 2\delta) = \frac{1}{MES} \sqrt{1 + \frac{1}{\delta}} - (1 + 2\delta).$$ (11.19)

The long-run number of plants is greater, the smaller is fixed cost or, equivalently, the smaller is minimum efficient scale output as a fraction of industry size.

If we substitute from (11.19) into (11.18), we obtain expressions for long-run equilibrium Cournot price and output with linear demand and quadratic cost function:

$$p_{\text{Cour}}^{\text{LR}} = c + (b + 2d) \sqrt{\frac{F}{b+d}}, \qquad Q_{\text{Cour}}^{\text{LR}} = S - (1 + 2\delta) \sqrt{\frac{F}{b+d}}.$$ (11.20)

Welfare

Gross social welfare (before allowing for the cost of production) is the area under the demand curve from zero to Q units of output,

$$GSW = aQ - \tfrac{1}{2}bQ^2.$$ (11.21)

In Cournot equilibrium, all plants produce the same output. Since all plants have the same cost function, it is also socially optimal for all plants to produce the same output level.[16] It

---

[15] In the Chamberlinian model of monopolistic competition, products are differentiated. In the model considered here, products are standardized, but the same type of results occur if the number of firms adjusts until profit is zero in a model of quantity-setting firms with differentiated products.

[16] Otherwise, it would be possible to obtain the same total output at lower cost by shifting output from plants with high marginal cost to plants with low marginal cost.

follows that we can write a social cost function for Q units of output produced by n plants as

$$c(Q, n) = nc(q) = n(F + cq + dq^2) = nF + cQ + \frac{d}{n}Q^2. \tag{11.22}$$

Subtracting $c(Q, n)$ from GSW, we obtain an expression for net social welfare when there are diseconomies of scale:

$$NSW = (a - c)Q - b\left(\frac{n + 2\delta}{2n}\right)Q^2 - nF. \tag{11.23}$$

Substituting from (11.16) and (11.17) into (11.23) shows that net social welfare in long-run Cournot equilibrium is just consumers' surplus:

$$NSW_{\text{Cour}}^{\text{LR}} = \tfrac{1}{2}b\left(Q_{\text{Cour}}^{\text{LR}}\right)^2 \tag{11.24}$$

(since in the long run the number of firms adjusts so that profit per firm and therefore total profit is zero).

The optimal regime

Differentiating (11.23) with respect to Q and solving the resulting first-order condition, we obtain an expression for socially optimal output, given the number of firms:

$$Q(n) = \frac{n}{n + 2\delta}S. \tag{11.25}$$

Substituting from (11.25) into (11.23) gives an expression for net social welfare as a function of the number of firms, if output is set according to (11.25) and divided equally among firms:

$$NSW = \tfrac{1}{2}n\frac{bS^2}{n + 2\delta} - nF. \tag{11.26}$$

Setting the derivative of (11.26) with respect to n equal to zero and solving for n yields an expression for the socially optimal number of plants:

$$n_{\text{op}} = \frac{S}{\sqrt{F/d}} - 2\delta = \frac{1}{MES} - 2\delta. \tag{11.27}$$

Substituting from (11.27) into (11.25), we find the socially optimal output:

$$Q_{\text{op}} = S - \frac{2}{b}\sqrt{dF}. \tag{11.28}$$

If we return to the demand curve (11.12), we find that if the optimal output were placed on the market, the market-clearing price would be

$$p = c + 2\sqrt{dF}. \tag{11.29}$$

But this is the minimum level of average cost, the long-run equilibrium price if firms act as price-takers. In such a competitive regime, each plant produces an output that makes marginal cost equal to average cost, and makes average cost a minimum.

Using (11.27) and (11.26), we find net social welfare with price-taking behavior:

$$NSW_{op} = \tfrac{1}{2}b(Q_{op})^2.$$ (11.30)

Comparison

NUMBER OF FIRMS

By subtraction, from (11.19) and (11.27) we find the difference between the Cournot equilibrium and the optimal number of firms:

$$n_{Cour}^{LR} - n_{op} = \frac{1}{MES}\left[\sqrt{1 + \frac{1}{\delta}} - 1\right] - 1.$$ (11.31)

If *MES* is small, the first term on the right in (11.31) is large, and the market equilibrium number of firms will exceed the socially optimal number of firms.[17]

If $MES = 1$, so that an efficiently sized firm would supply 100 percent of the market, (11.31) becomes

$$n_{Cour}^{LR} - n_{op} = \sqrt{1 + \frac{1}{\delta}} - 2.$$ (11.32)

This is positive for $\delta < 1/3$, negative for $\delta > 1/3$, and has lower limit (as δ goes to infinity) -1. In this model, the market number of firms can range from one less than the optimal number of firms to many more than the optimal number of firms.

The possibility that the market equilibrium number of firms is less than the socially optimal number of firms arises from the presence of diseconomies of scale. Suppose, in contrast, that $d < 0$, so that the cost function (11.13) has economies of scale at all output levels. Then the socially optimal number of plants is one – by consolidating all output in a single plant, average cost is made as low as possible. But the market equilibrium number of plants will never be less than one, and in general will exceed one.[18]

The tendency toward excessive entry in Cournot equilibrium is due to what Mankiw and Whinston (1986) call the "business stealing" effect. There is a business stealing effect if equilibrium output per firm falls as the number of firms rises. In such markets, the profit-maximizing entry decisions of individual firms fail to take account of the externality – lost profit – that entry imposes on incumbent firms. The result is an equilibrium number of firms that is excessive from a social point of view.

WELFARE

Although the market equilibrium number of firms is likely to exceed the socially optimal number of firms, it will not in general be desirable to restrict the number of firms unless

---

[17] Von Weizsäcker (1980a, p. 404) uses an example in which $b = 1$, $a - c = 10$, $F = 5$, and $d = 1/40$, so that $n_{op} = 0.65$ and $n_{Cour}^{LR} = 3.47$. The nearest integer values are $n_{op} = 1$ and $n_{Cour}^{LR} = 3$. But for this example, $MES = \sqrt{2}$. That is, minimum efficient scale is 142 percent of the quantity that would be demanded if price were equal to c.

[18] See Martin (1984b) and Mankiw and Whinston (1986).

output per firm can also be regulated. For example, in the absence of diseconomies of scale, the socially optimal number of firms is one. But a single unregulated firm will act as a monopolist, and market performance is worse under monopoly than in oligopoly.

We might ask, therefore, what the optimal number of firms is, given that incumbent firms behave as Cournot oligopolists. Substituting n-firm Cournot equilibrium output from (11.17) into (11.23) yields an expression for net social welfare in Cournot equilibrium as a function of the number of firms:

$$NSW^n_{\text{Cour}} = n \left[\frac{n + 2(1 + \delta)}{2(n + 1 + 2\delta)^2} bS^2 - F \right]. \tag{11.33}$$

Maximizing NSW^n_{Cour} with respect to n, we find

$$n^{\text{op}}_{\text{Cour}} = \frac{1}{MES} \sqrt{1 + \frac{1}{\delta}} - (1 + 2\delta) = n^{\text{LR}}_{\text{Cour}} \tag{11.34}$$

(compare with (11.19)). Hence if Cournot firms are allowed to make their own output decisions once they are in the market, it is optimal to allow entry to continue until firm profit is driven to zero.

Alternatively, we can consider the welfare consequences of fixed costs directly. Using (11.24) and (11.30), we can define an index of relative market performance that is the ratio of Cournot equilibrium to optimal net social welfare:

$$RNSW = \sqrt{\frac{NSW^{\text{LR}}_{\text{Cour}}}{NSW_{\text{op}}}} = \frac{Q^{\text{LR}}_{\text{Cour}}}{Q_{\text{op}}} = \frac{S - (1 + 2\delta)\sqrt{F/(b + d)}}{S - (2/b)\sqrt{dF}}. \tag{11.35}$$

Evaluating the derivative of $RNSW$ with respect to F, we find that $\partial RNSW / \partial F < 0$: increases in fixed cost, all else equal, worsen market performance. This result holds even if the number of firms exceeds the socially optimal level and increases in fixed cost reduce the market equilibrium number of firms.

Is fixed cost a barrier to entry?

Recall that von Weizsäcker defines an entry barrier as a cost of production that must be borne by a firm seeking to enter an industry, but need not be borne by firms already in the industry, and which implies a distortion in the allocation of resources from a social point of view. In this model, fixed costs create a welfare distortion, even though the market equilibrium number of firms is (generally) greater than the optimal number of firms. But fixed costs must be borne by entrants and incumbents alike. They do not, therefore, qualify as a barrier to entry under von Weizsäcker's definition.

Is sunk cost a barrier to entry?

Von Weizsäcker remarks that (1980a, p. 401)

> The difference between incumbent firms and entrants is that incumbent firms own plant and equipment specific to this industry and thereby are committed to continue operations in this industry, whereas this is not the case for a potential entrant. It is thus not just simple economies of scale which may cause a barrier to entry, but rather economies of scale in combination with irreversible capital commitments.

This is an anticipation of the notion of sunk costs, costs that must be paid by an operating firm and which cannot be recovered if a firm leaves the market.[19] To pursue the implications of sunk cost for market structure, consider a variation of the von Weizsäcker model.[20] The linear inverse demand curve is given by (11.12). There are fixed costs and constant marginal cost:

$$c(q) = F + cq \tag{11.36}$$

(there are no diseconomies of scale). A fraction s of fixed costs is sunk: if a firm enters, it pays what amounts to an entry fee of sF. If, after entry, it produces a positive output, it pays an additional fixed cost $(1 - s)F$.

Let n Cournot firms supply the market. Equilibrium firm output, industry output, and price are

$$q = \frac{S}{n+1}, \qquad Q = \frac{nS}{n+1}, \qquad p = c + \frac{a-c}{n+1} \tag{11.37}$$

(where $S = (a - c)/b$). It follows that gross profit per firm – profit before taking account of fixed cost – is

$$G\pi(n) = b\left(\frac{S}{n+1}\right)^2. \tag{11.38}$$

If the number of firms adjusts so that gross profit just equals fixed cost, we obtain an upper limit on the number of firms in the market with Cournot behavior:

$$n_{\max} = \frac{S}{\sqrt{F/b}} - 1. \tag{11.39}$$

Now suppose that the number of firms is strictly less than $n_{\max}$ and that an $(n + 1)$th firm considers entering the market, expecting the first n firms to continue producing the outputs given by (11.37). From the equation of its best-response curve, the output of the $(n + 1)$th

---

[19] Sunk costs, therefore, ought really to be analyzed with a dynamic model. The formulation given here is a way to shoehorn a dynamic concept into a static model.
[20] This section follows Vickers (1989); see also Lambson (1991).

firm is

$$q_{n+1} = \tfrac{1}{2}(S - Q) = \tfrac{1}{2}\frac{S}{n+1}. \tag{11.40}$$

If such a firm enters and produces the output given by (11.40), price falls to

$$p = c + \tfrac{1}{2}\frac{bS}{n+1} \tag{11.41}$$

and the entrant's gross profit will be

$$g\pi(n+1) = \tfrac{1}{4}b\left(\frac{S}{n+1}\right)^2 = \tfrac{1}{4}G\pi(n). \tag{11.42}$$

If the $(n+1)$th firm enters but does not produce, it loses the sunk "entry fee" sF. Such a firm, having entered, would select a zero output if the gross profit given by (11.42) were insufficient to cover the remaining, nonsunk, portion of fixed cost. That is, an $(n+1)$th firm, having entered, would not produce if

$$g\pi(n+1) \leq (1-s)F, \tag{11.43}$$

or if

$$n \geq \frac{1}{\sqrt{1-s}}\frac{n_{max}+1}{2} - 1. \tag{11.44}$$

The lower limit on the equilibrium number of firms is obtained if the inequality in (11.44) holds with equality:

$$n_{min} = \frac{1}{\sqrt{1-s}}\frac{n_{max}+1}{2} - 1. \tag{11.45}$$

If the number of incumbent firms lies between n_{min} and n_{max}, it is credible that they will produce the outputs given by (11.37), because those are their most profitable outputs if the $(n+1)$th firm produces nothing. And if the incumbent firms produce the outputs given by (11.37), the profit-maximizing strategy for an $(n+1)$th firm that has entered is to produce nothing. But a dominating strategy for the $(n+1)$th firm, given that the n incumbent firms produce the outputs given by (11.37), is to stay out of the market. Thus any n that lies between n_{min} and n_{max} is an equilibrium number of firms. Entry can be deterred, short of n_{max}, if incumbent firms maintain outputs that make it impossible for an entrant to cover the nonsunk portion of fixed cost. This is, in fact, a subgame-perfect equilibrium strategy in a two-stage game, for which the entry decision is taken in the first stage and the production decision is taken in the second stage.

Observe from (11.45) that if $s = \tfrac{3}{4}$, $n_{min} = n_{max}$. If three-quarters or more of fixed costs are sunk, entry cannot be deterred short of the usual Cournot equilibrium number of firms. When s is this large, the residual (nonsunk) portion of fixed cost is so small that $g\pi(n+1) > (1-s)F$ even if incumbents produce their n-firm Cournot equilibrium outputs.

11.3.2   Market structure with industry-specific assets

Some inputs may be used to produce a wide variety of products. Office space, typewriters, filing cabinets, and secretarial staff might be inputs in a life insurance company, a real estate office, or a university. Other inputs are quite specific to particular industries. A gifted computer programmer is far more productive working in Silicon Valley than elsewhere; a successful writer of mystery novels will do less well with light romance. When industry-specific assets are required for production, ownership of such assets is a fundamental determinant of market structure and performance.[21]

11.3.3   The model

A total of n quantity-setting firms with Cournot expectations supply a homogeneous product to an industry with inverse demand curve $p = p(Q)$. Firm i operates with cost function

$$c^i(q_i, k_i), \tag{11.46}$$

where q_i is the output of firm i and k_i is firm i's stock of an industry-specific asset that is essential for production. We assume that the cross-derivative $c^i_{qk} = \partial^2 c^i(q_i, k_i)/\partial q_i \partial k_i$ is negative: having more of the specific asset lowers the firm's marginal cost. Similar notation will be used for other derivatives of the cost function.

Firm i's profit is

$$\pi_i = p(Q)q_i - c^i(q_i, k_i). \tag{11.47}$$

Net social welfare is

$$NSW(q_1, \ldots, q_n; k_1, \ldots, k_n) = \int_{z=0}^{Q} p(z)\,\mathrm{d}z - \sum_{i=1}^{n} c^i(q_i, k_i), \tag{11.48}$$

where the integral gives the area under the demand curve for total output Q and the summation gives the cost of production.

11.3.4   Arbitrary changes in capital stocks

We now investigate the impact of arbitrary changes in capital endowments on Cournot equilibrium. This exercise is a building block for what comes later.

The first-order condition for maximization of (11.47) with respect to q_i, taking k_i as given, is

$$p(Q) + q_i p'(Q) - c^i_q(q_i, k_i) = 0, \tag{11.49}$$

where p' is the slope of the inverse demand curve. Implicitly (writing $Q = q_i + Q_{-i}$), this defines firm i's best-response function.

---

[21] See Farrell and Shapiro (1990b).

Taking the total differential of (11.49) and collecting terms in dq_i yields

$$dq_i = -\mu_i\, dQ + \chi_i\, dk_i, \tag{11.50}$$

where

$$\mu_i = \frac{p' + q_i p''}{c_{qq}^i - p'}, \qquad \chi_i = -\frac{c_{qk}^i}{c_{qq}^i - p'}. \tag{11.51}$$

The second term in (11.50) is the part of firm i's output change that is a direct response to changes in its own capital endowment. χ_i depends on the extent to which having more of the asset reduces firm i's marginal cost and on the way a change in q_i affects firm i's price – marginal cost margin.

The first term in (11.50) captures firm 1's response to rivals' output changes. This can be seen by rewriting (11.50) in terms of firm i's best-response function. Differentiating (11.49) with respect to Q_{-i}, the slope of firm i's best-response function is

$$R_i = \frac{\partial q_i}{\partial Q_{-i}} = -\frac{p' + q_i p''}{2p' + q_i p'' - c_{qq}^i} < 0. \tag{11.52}$$

Then the coefficient of dQ in (11.50) can be rewritten

$$\mu_i = -\frac{R_i}{1 + R_i}. \tag{11.53}$$

Substituting (11.53) and $Q = q_i + Q_{-i}$ into (11.50) and rearranging terms gives

$$dq_i = R_i\, dQ_{-i} + (1 + R_i)\chi_i\, dk_i. \tag{11.54}$$

The first term on the right-hand side in (11.54) is the part of firm i's output response that is its reaction to rival's output changes.

If we add (11.54) over all i and collect terms in dQ, we obtain

$$dQ = \frac{\chi_1\, dk_1 + \chi_2\, dk_2 + \cdots + \chi_n\, dk_n}{1 + \mu}, \tag{11.55}$$

where $\mu = \mu_1 + \mu_2 + \cdots + \mu_n$. This can be substituted back into (11.50) to obtain a final expression for the change in firm i's output as a result of an arbitrary set of changes in asset endowments.

Now turning to firm i's profit, we take the total differential of (11.47) to obtain

$$d\pi_i = (p - c_q^i)\, dq_i + q_i p'(Q) - c_k^i\, dk_i - \rho_i\, dk_i, \tag{11.56}$$

where ρ_i is the cost to firm i per unit of the specific asset. But from the first-order condition (11.49) we have $p(Q) - c_q^i = q_i p'(Q)$, so that (11.56) can be rewritten

$$d\pi_i = q_i p'\, dQ_{-i} - c_k^i\, dk_i - \rho_i\, dk_i. \tag{11.57}$$

The first term on the right-hand side is the change in firm i's revenue as all other firms change output. The second term on the right is the direct cost saving to firm i from having more of the specific asset. The third term on the right is the cost of the increment in the specific asset.

11.3.5   Investment by a single firm

We now explore the consequences of a small increase in the stock of the specific asset by a single firm. Let $dk_1 > 0$, $dk_2 = \cdots = dk_n = 0$. From (11.55),

$$\frac{dQ}{dk_1} = \frac{\chi_1}{1 + \mu} > 0. \tag{11.58}$$

Investment by a single firm leads to an output increase.
From (11.50),

$$\frac{dq_i}{dk_1} = -\mu_i \frac{dQ}{dk_1} = -\mu_i \frac{\chi_i}{1 + \mu} < 0, \qquad i \neq 1; \tag{11.59}$$

$$\frac{dq_1}{dk_1} = \chi_1 - \mu_1 \frac{dQ}{dk_1} = \chi_1 \left(1 - \frac{\mu_1}{1 + \mu}\right) > 0. \tag{11.60}$$

Investment by firm 1 results in an equilibrium output increase for firm 1, with equilibrium output decreases for all other firms.

Substituting from (11.59) and (11.60) into (11.57) gives the effect of investment by firm 1 on its own profit:

$$\frac{d\pi_1}{dk_1} = -p'(Q)\chi_1 \left(\frac{\mu - \mu_1}{1 + \mu}\right) q_1 - c_k^1 - \rho_1. \tag{11.61}$$

The first term is positive, and is firm 1's incremental profit as rivals reduce output. The second term is the direct reduction in cost from having a little more of the specific asset. The third term is the unit cost of the specific asset. We expect investment to take place only if (11.61) is greater than or equal to zero.

We now turn to the welfare consequences of investment by a single firm. Differentiating (11.49) with respect to k_1 (and allowing for the cost of the additional capital) gives

$$\frac{dNSW}{dk_1} = p(Q)\frac{dQ}{dk_1} - \sum_{i=1}^{n} c_q^i \frac{dq_i}{dk_1} - c_k^1 - \rho_1. \tag{11.62}$$

Now, substituting for the various output changes from (11.58), (11.59) and (11.60), we obtain

$$\frac{dNSW}{dk_1} = \frac{\chi_1}{1 + \mu} \left[p(Q) + c_q^i \mu_i - (1 + \mu)c_q^1\right] - c_k^1 - \rho_1. \tag{11.63}$$

Finally, use of the first-order condition (11.49) to eliminate terms in c_q^i yields

$$\frac{dNSW}{dk_1} = -p'(Q)\frac{\chi_1}{1 + \mu} \left[(1 + \mu)q_1 - \sum_{i=1}^{n} \mu_i q_i\right] - c_k^1 - \rho_1. \tag{11.64}$$

The first term on the right-hand side in (11.64) is the marginal net welfare effect of the output changes induced by firm 1's investment. The second term is the marginal cost saving resulting from the investment, and the third term is the marginal cost of the investment.

The first term on the right in (11.64) can be either positive or negative, which means that it is possible for investment to either raise or lower welfare. Substituting the definition of μ, the expression in square brackets in the first term is positive if

$$q_1 > \sum_{i=2}^{n} \mu_i(q_i - q_1).$$
(11.65)

This condition is certainly met if firm 1 is the largest firm, since in that case the term on the left is positive and the term on the right is negative. Then, if the investment is privately profitable before allowing for output changes (that is if $-c_k^1 - \rho_1 \geq 0$), the investment increases net social welfare.

But if q_1 is sufficiently small, the condition in (11.65) fails and the first term on the right in (11.64) is negative. Even if the last two terms on the right in (11.64) are positive, the net welfare effect of the investment may be negative.

Investment causes output to increase, which tends to improve welfare. Investment reduces the cost of the investing firm, which tends to improve welfare. But investment also induces a reallocation of output from rivals to the investing firm. If the investing firm is a large low-cost firm, this output reallocation effect tends to improve social welfare. But if the investing firm is a small high-cost firm, the output reallocation effect reduces social welfare. If the output reallocation is negative and large enough in magnitude, the overall welfare change from investment may be negative.

Equations (11.61) and (11.64) yield

$$\frac{d\pi_1}{dk_1} - \frac{dNSW}{dk_1} = -p'(Q)\frac{\chi_1}{1+\mu}\left(\sum_{i=2}^{n} \mu_i q_i - q_1\right).$$
(11.66)

It follows that, if q_1 is sufficiently small, the private profitability of investment exceeds the welfare gains from investment. Small firms have a systematic incentive to overinvest in the industry-specific asset, from a welfare point of view.

To conclude this section, consider the impact of a marginal investment by firm 1 on the Herfindahl index. From (11.1), we obtain

$$\frac{dH}{dk_1} = 2\sum_{i=1}^{n} s_i\frac{ds_i}{dk_1}.$$
(11.67)

But from the definition of market share, $s_i = q_i/Q$,

$$\frac{ds_i}{dk_1} = \frac{1}{Q^2}\left(Q\frac{dq_i}{dk_1} - q_i\frac{dQ}{dk_1}\right).$$
(11.68)

Substituting from (11.59) and (11.60) to eliminate terms that reflect marginal changes in the output of single firms gives

$$\frac{ds_i}{dk_1} = -\frac{\mu_i + s_i}{Q}\frac{dQ}{dk_1}, \qquad i \neq 1;$$
(11.69)

$$\frac{ds_1}{dk_1} = \frac{1}{Q}\left[\chi_1 - (\mu_1 + s_1)\frac{dQ}{dk_1}\right].$$
(11.70)

Substituting from (11.69) and (11.70) into (11.67),

$$\frac{dH}{dk_1} = \frac{2}{Q}\frac{dQ}{dk_1}\left[s_1(1+\mu) - \sum_{i=1}^{n} s_i(s_i + \mu)\right]. \tag{11.71}$$

Investment increases the Herfindahl index if the expression in brackets on the right is positive, and this is the case if and only if

$$\sum_{i=1}^{n} (s_1 - s_i)(s_i + \mu_i) > 0. \tag{11.72}$$

Investment increases the Herfindahl index if undertaken by the largest firm, and decreases the Herfindahl index if undertaken by the smallest firm. Between these two extreme cases, the impact of investment on market concentration is ambiguous.

Observe that investment by the largest firm in the industry will increase market concentration, but this is also the instance in which there is the best chance that investment will improve net social welfare. Similarly, investment by the smallest firm will reduce market concentration but is also most likely to reduce net social welfare.

11.3.6 Asset sales between incumbents

In the age of regulated mergers and leveraged buyouts, it is increasingly common for one incumbent to sell assets to another. Such sales can be fitted into the model outlined above by setting $dk_1 = dk = -dk_2 > 0$ and $dk_3 = \cdots = dk_n = 0$, so that firm 2 makes a marginal sale of the asset to firm 1.

From (11.55),

$$\frac{dQ}{dk} = \frac{\chi_1 - \chi_2}{1 + \mu}. \tag{11.73}$$

Consulting (11.50), an asset sale by one incumbent to another results in a net output increase if the output of the purchasing firm is more responsive to changes in the stock of the specific asset than the output of the selling firm.

In the general case, it is difficult to say much about the relative size of χ_1 and χ_2. If the inverse demand curve is linear and the cost function is quadratic one can show (Problem 11.2) that

$$\chi_i = \frac{p - c}{b}\frac{2\delta}{(k_i + 2\delta)^2}, \tag{11.74}$$

where all terms on the right-hand side are positive. For this example, since χ_i is larger for smaller firms, a capital sale raises output if and only if the firm buying the capital is smaller than the firm selling the capital.

The effects of an output sale on profit, welfare, and market concentration can all be derived in ways analogous to the derivations for the case of investment by a single firm. These are left as an exercise; details can be found in Farrell and Shapiro (1990b). As one would expect, asset sales by a small firm to a large firm increase market concentration. Such sales also offer the greatest likelihood of a welfare improvement, since they lead to an output expansion by a low-cost firm and an output contraction by a high-cost firm.

11.4   PRODUCT DIFFERENTIATION AS A BARRIER TO ENTRY

Bagwell (1990) presents a highly stylized model in which imperfect information about product quality may have the effect of precluding entry by firms producing high-quality products.[22]

11.4.1   The model

Varieties of the product may be of high quality (H) or low quality (L). There is one incumbent, and it is common knowledge that its product is of low quality. There is one potential entrant, and the entrant knows the quality of its own variety. The product is an experience good and so it is not possible to know the quality of the entrant's variety until it is purchased. Before observing prices, there is a probability r ($0 < r < 1$), common to the incumbent and the single consumer, that the entrant's variety is of high quality.

There is a single consumer, who buys 1 unit of the product from the incumbent, or buys 1 unit of the product from the entrant, or does not buy the product. If the consumer purchases, his utility function is

$$V(q,p) = U(q) - p, \tag{11.75}$$

where q is either H or L, $U(H) > U(L) > 0$, and p is the price paid for the product. If the consumer does not purchase, utility is zero. Marginal costs are constant, with $c(H) > c(L) > 0$. High-quality varieties are more desirable after allowing for production cost: $U(H) - c(H) > U(L) - c(L)$.

There are no fixed or sunk costs that must be paid upon entry; the entrant uses the same technology as the incumbent.

11.4.2   Strategies and payoffs

The consumer's strategy is a function $v(r, p_i, p_e)$ of the prior probability that the entrant's variety is of high quality and the incumbent's and entrant's prices. The function v takes one of three values: buy from the incumbent, buy from the entrant, or do not buy.

The consumer's beliefs about the quality of the entrant's product are updated after observing the entrant's price.[23] The consumer's beliefs are described by a function $b(r, p_e)$ that gives the posterior or post-observation probability that the entrant's product is of high quality as a function of the prior probability and the entrant's price.

---

[22] See Farrell (1986) for a related model.

[23] The incumbent and the consumer have the same prior probability r that the entrant's product is of high quality. Consequently, the incumbent's price p_i conveys no information that could be used by the consumer to reassess its estimate of the quality of the entrant's product.

The incumbent's strategy $p_i(r)$ gives its price as a function of the prior probability r. The entrant's strategy $p_e(r, q)$ gives its price as a function of the prior probability r and the quality of its variety.

Payoffs are $\pi^H(p_i, p_e)$, $\pi^L(p_i, p_e)$, and $\pi^i(p_i, p_e)$ for a high-quality entrant, a low-quality entrant, and the incumbent, respectively.

11.4.3   Sequential equilibrium

Definition

For (v, b, p_e, p_i) to be an equilibrium:

1   v must specify the action that yields the largest of the expected utilities

$$[V(L, p_i), bV(H, p_e) + (1 - b)V(L, p_e), 0]$$

that result from buying from the incumbent, buying from the entrant, and not buying;

2   the incumbent's price $p_i(r)$ must maximize its expected payoff

$$r\pi^i[p_i, p_e(H)] + (1 - r)\pi^i[p_i, p_e(L)];$$

3   $p_e(r, H)$ must maximize

$$\pi^H[p_i(r, H), p_e(r)]$$

and $p_e(r, L)$ must maximize

$$\pi^L[p_i(r, L), p_e(r)];$$

4   equilibrium beliefs must be consistent with Bayes' rule:
    (a) if $p_e(r, H) \neq p_e(r, L)$, then $b[r, p_e(r, H)] = 1$, $b[r, p_e(r, L)] = 0$;
    (b) if $p_e(r, H) = p_e(r, L)$, then $b[r, p_e(r, H)] = r$, $b[r, p_e(r, L)] = 1 - r$.

Condition 4(a) means that, if in equilibrium an entrant producing a high-quality product would price differently from an entrant producing a low-quality product, then the consumer correctly infers the quality of the entrant's product by observing the entrant's price. These are separating equilibria.

Condition 4(b) means that, if in equilibrium an entrant producing a high-quality product and an entrant producing a low-quality product would charge the same price, then the consumer gains no information from observing the entrant's price and simply carries over prior beliefs after observing p_e. These are pooling equilibria.

In addition to these definitional requirements, Bagwell restricts the analysis to pure strategies which call for price to be at least as great as marginal cost: $p_e(r, H) \geq c(H)$, $p_e(r, L) \geq c(L)$, $p_i(r) \geq c(L)$.

Separating equilibria

There are separating equilibria for this game. In such equilibria, the incumbent and an entrant producing a low-quality product price at marginal cost

$$p_i(r) = p_e(r, L) = c(L), \tag{11.76}$$

while an entrant producing a high-quality product sets

$$p_e(r, H) = U(H) - [U(L) - c(L)]. \tag{11.77}$$

In separating equilibrium, beliefs have the consumer think that the entrant's product is high quality if it sees the equilibrium $p_e(r, H)$ (that is, $b[p_e(r, H)] = 1$), but that the entrant's product is of low quality if it sees any other price ($b(p_e) = 0$ for any $p \neq p_e(r, H)$).

In separating equilibrium, the consumer never buys from an entrant producing a high-quality product. The consumer may or may not buy from an entrant producing a low-quality product.

To see that separating equilibrium has these properties, suppose first that $p_i(r) \neq p_e(r, L)$ in equilibrium. If $p_e(r, L) < p_i(r)$ and $p_e(r, L) < U(L)$, an entrant producing a low-quality variety could raise price without losing the sale to the incumbent; such a $p_e(r, L)$ could not be an equilibrium. But if $p_e(r, L) < p_i(r)$ and $p_e(r, L) = U(L)$, the incumbent could undercut $p_e(r, L)$ slightly and get the sale. Such a $p_i(r)$ could not be an equilibrium. This rules out $p_e(r, L) < p_i(r)$ in separating equilibrium.

Now suppose that $p_e(r, L) > p_i(r)$. An entrant producing a low-quality product could profitably undercut $p_i(r)$ and make the sale if $p_i(r) > c(L)$, so that cannot occur in equilibrium. But if $p_e(r, L) > p_i(r)$ and $p_i(r) = c(L)$, the incumbent could profitably raise price a little bit without losing the sale to an entrant producing a low-quality product.

This rules out $p_e(r, L) > p_i(r)$ in separating equilibrium, and the only remaining possibility is $p_e(r, L) = p_i(r)$. But if $p_e(r, L) = p_i(r)$, it must also be that $p_e(r, L) = p_i(r) = c(L)$. Having $p_e(r, L) = p_i(r) < c(L)$ is ruled out, since it would require the firms to lose money (a fate that could be avoided by setting price equal to marginal cost and losing the sale). $p_e(r, L) = p_i(r) > c(L)$ cannot be an equilibrium, since either firm could profitably undercut the other without losing the sale.

An entrant producing a high-quality product cannot make the sale in separating equilibrium. If this occurred, it would have to be for a price $p_e(r, H) \geq c(H)$. But since $c(H) > c(L)$, it would then be profitable for an incumbent producing a low-quality product to set $p_e(r, L) = p_e(r, H)$ and mimic an incumbent producing a high-quality product. But then we would no longer have a separating equilibrium.

Since the consumer must maximize expected utility and an entrant producing a high-quality product cannot make the sale, the consumer must receive at least as great an expected utility purchasing from the incumbent or the entrant producing the low-quality product as from an entrant producing a high-quality product: $U(L) - c(L) \geq U(H) - p_e(r, H)$. But if $U(L) - c(L) > U(H) - p_e(r, H)$, the incumbent could profitably raise price without expecting (with probability r) to lose the sale. Hence $U(L) - c(L) = U(H) - p_e(H)$.

At these values, the consumer receives utility $U(L) - c(L)$ whether it purchases from the incumbent or the entrant, regardless of the quality of the product produced by the entrant. It is therefore an equilibrium strategy for the consumer not to purchase from an entrant producing a high-quality product and to be indifferent between purchasing from the incumbent or an entrant producing a low-quality product.

Pooling equilibria

Write

$$U_r = rU(H) + (1 - r)U(L) \tag{11.78}$$

for the consumer's expected utility when it purchases a unit of unknown quality at the prior probability r that the unit is of high quality. Then there are pooling equilibria if $U_r - c(H) \geq U(L) - c(L)$. These equilibria are of two types:

1 either $p_i(r) = c(L), p_e(r, L) = p_e(r, H) = U_r - U(L) + c(L)$ and the incumbent makes the sale; or
2 $p_e(r, L) = p_e(r, H), p_e(r, H) \leq p_i(r) \leq c(L), c(H) \leq p_e(r, H) \leq U_r - U(L) + c(L)$, and the incumbent does not make the sale.

Consider first the case of a pooling equilibrium in which the incumbent makes the sale. For the incumbent to make the sale, the consumer must get greater utility by purchasing from an incumbent known to be selling a low-quality product than the expected utility from purchasing from an entrant whose product is of unknown quality: $U(L) - p_e(r) \geq U_r - p_e$. Payoff maximization requires that the incumbent set the largest price that satisfies this inequality, and so it will hold with equality. At the same time, if $p_i(r) > c(L)$, it would be profitable for an entrant producing a low-quality product to undersell the incumbent slightly. Hence $p_i(r) = c(L)$ if there is a pooling equilibrium and the incumbent makes the sale.

If there is a pooling equilibrium and the incumbent does not make the sale, then it must be that $p_e(r, H) = p_e(r, L) \geq p_i(r)$; if $p_i(r)$ were greater than $p_e(r, L)$, it would be profitable for an entrant producing a low-quality product to raise price. And if $U(L) - c(L) > U_r - p_e$, it would be possible and profitable for the incumbent (known to be producing a low-quality product) to make the sale at a price slightly greater than $c(L)$. This implies $U(L) - c(L) \leq U_r - p_e$, or $p_e \leq U_r - U(L) + c(L)$.

Finally, note that if

$$U(L) - c(L) > U_r - c(H), \tag{11.79}$$

it is profitable for an entrant producing a low-quality product to reveal that it is producing a low-quality product instead of mimicking an entrant producing a high-quality product. Hence pooling equilibria exist only if $U_r - c(H) \geq U(L) - c(L)$.

Qualifications and generalizations

In separating equilibrium, uncertainty about product quality precludes entry by a firm producing a high-quality product. Uncertainty about product quality acts as a barrier to entry. This result is obtained in a highly stylized model. As Bagwell notes, it seems particularly important to try to relax the assumption that there is only a single consumer.

Bagwell also presents a two-period extension of the model. In this extended version, there are some pooling equilibria in which an entrant producing a high-quality product can make the sale in the first period. Uncertainty about product quality need not create a barrier to entry.

However, the equilibrium first-period price for the entrant may be below $c(H)$, and so the equilibrium strategy might call for an entrant producing a high quality product to price below marginal cost. There are also pooling equilibria in which the incumbent makes the sale in both periods. In such cases, informational uncertainty does create a barrier to entry.

11.5   FINANCIAL MARKETS

Bain (1956) argued that absolute capital requirements are a source of barriers to entry. This is the case if entrants must finance greater amounts than incumbents or if the cost of capital is systematically higher for entrants than for incumbents. Poitevin (1989) develops a signaling model which offers another explanation for entry barriers based on the functioning of financial markets.[24] In the model, financial markets know the marginal cost of the incumbent but not the marginal cost of the entrant. In some equilibria, a low-cost entrant finances investment with bonds as a signal to financial markets. This reveals that the entrant has low cost, but the entrant comes into the market with a greater debt–equity ratio than the incumbent. In so doing, the entrant exposes itself to predatory behavior. The optimal strategy for the incumbent is to expand output and increase the probability that the entrant will go bankrupt. Uncertainty in financial markets makes it profitable for incumbents to behave in a way that makes it less likely that entry will be successful.

11.6   EMPIRICAL STUDIES OF MARKET STRUCTURE

11.6.1   Market concentration

The most common specification of empirical concentration equations assumes a lagged adjustment of concentration to a long-run level that depends on various aspects of market structure and firm conduct.[25] In first-difference form, such an equation is

$$CR - CR_{-1} = \lambda[CR^*(structure, conduct) - CR_{-1}], \qquad (11.80)$$

which is equivalent to

$$CR = \lambda CR^*(structure, conduct) + (1 - \lambda)CR_{-1}. \qquad (11.81)$$

CR^* is the long-run level of concentration and CR_{-1} is the concentration level one period in the past. Current concentration is a weighted average of past concentration and the long-run concentration level, with λ as a weighting or speed of adjustment parameter. The greater is

---

[24] See also Williamson (1974), Benoit (1984), Brander and Lewis (1986), and Martin (1988b, 1989).

[25] See Curry and George (1983) for a survey, and also the March 1987 issue of the *International Journal of Industrial Organization*.

λ, the greater is the weight given CR^* in any period and the more rapid is convergence to the long-run level.

Most such studies estimate an equation like (11.80) or (11.81) for a sample of different industries over a single time period. Levy (1985), for example, analyzes the change in the four-firm seller concentration ratio from 1963 to 1971 for a sample of 197 US manufacturing industries.

One of the equations that he estimates is[26]

$$CR472 - CR463 = 0.26 + 0.0019MES + 1.20ACR - 0.86ASR$$
$$\qquad\qquad (2.81)\qquad (2.00)\qquad\qquad (0.54)\qquad (0.63)$$
$$\qquad\quad - 0.45GR + 0.30CR463 \qquad\qquad R^2 = 0.073.$$
$$\qquad\quad (1.48)\qquad (3.03)\qquad\qquad\qquad\qquad\qquad (11.82)$$

The explanatory variables are MES, sales of a minimum efficient scale plant as a fraction of industry sales; ACR, absolute capital requirements of a minimum efficient scale plant; ASR, industry advertising–sales ratio; GR, growth rate of industry sales, 1963–72; and the lagged concentration variable $CR463$.

MES has a positive coefficient that is significant at the 95 percent level; GR has a negative coefficient that is significant at the 90 percent level. The coefficient of lagged concentration is significantly different from both 0 and 1, which is consistent with the hypothesis that there is a stable lagged adjustment process. The mean number of time periods for adjustment to the long-run concentration level is $(1 - \lambda)/\lambda$, or $[(1 - 0.3)/0.3] \times 9 = 21$ years. Lagged adjustment models usually find a slow adjustment of concentration to long-run levels.[27]

Geroski et al. (1987) estimate a nonlinear model in which the speed-of-adjustment parameter λ varies from industry to industry. They find a positive but not quite statistically significant impact of lagged profitability on λ, which suggests some impact of profitability in attracting entry and inducing the adjustment of concentration toward long-run levels. They also find the rate of adjustment to be significantly slower, the greater is the minimum efficient scale and the longer the time needed to build a new plant. The mean estimated value of λ for their sample was 0.123, implying a mean adjustment time to long-run concentration of 28.5 years. The value of λ one standard deviation less than the mean was 0.06, yielding a mean adjustment time to long-run concentration of 62.7 years. The value of λ one standard deviation more than the mean was 0.183, implying adjustment to the long-run concentration level in only(!) 17.9 years.

There is clearly substantial variation in adjustment rates across industries, but concentration appears on balance to adjust very slowly to its long-run level.

Sleuwaegen and Yamawaki (1988) use a logarithmic lagged adjustment equation to examine the impact of the formation of the common market on national concentration in West Germany, France, Italy, Belgium, and the Netherlands. For every country except the Netherlands, reductions in tariffs had a significant positive impact on the change in concentration over 1963–8. This is consistent with the argument that increasing cross-border

---

[26] t-statistics are reported in parentheses under the coefficient estimates. The dependent variable in this equation is subjected to a transformation designed to take account of the fact that $CR4$ must lie between 0 and 1. See Levy (1985, p. 67).

[27] The estimated t-statistic is 2.121. See Goldberger (1964, pp. 124–5).

competition leads to a concentration of sales in the hands of the largest, most efficient firms.

Amel and Liang (1990) estimate a nonlinear lagged adjustment model for concentration in regional US banking markets for various subperiods of the period 1966–86. They use the Herfindahl index as a measure of market concentration. For the period 1966–71, they estimate a speed-of-adjustment parameter

$$\lambda = 0.188 + 0.154 DPROF, \tag{11.83}$$

where $DPROF$ is the squared deviation of market profits from normal profits. Both coefficients are highly significant. This estimate (and others, which are similar) suggests that concentration adjusts more rapidly if profitability is either very high or very low. But adjustment is still very slow. A regional banking market with normal profitability would adjust to its long-run concentration level in 21.6 years. A regional banking market with $DPROF$ at the sample mean value would adjust to its long-run concentration level in 20.6 years. A regional banking market with $DPROF$ one standard deviation above the mean would adjust to its long-run concentration level in 18.1 years.

11.6.2   Market share

Using a sample of observations on 2,297 1975 lines of business,[28] Martin (1983b) estimates the following equation explaining market share:[29]

$$\begin{aligned}
MS = {} & -0.0545 & -0.000076 PCM_{-1} & + 0.0689 FS & -0.000419 IASR \\
& (8.3214) & (3.2905) & (16.4698) & (1.5339) \\
& + 0.000426 FOSR & + 0.002701 MES & -0.000298 LBRD \\
& (2.7014) & (8.9801) & (2.4581) \\
& -0.00048 FRD & + 0.019187 \log(FKAP). \\
& (2.9744) & (37.9691)
\end{aligned} \tag{11.84}$$

The results show a significant negative effect of lagged profitability (PCM_{-1}) on market share. Lines of business which earned higher profitability in the past tended to see their market share erode over time.

Several variables describing the firm of which the line of business is a part have significant effects on line of business market share. Firm share (FS) is the fraction of line of business sales in firm sales (defined by analogy with market share, which is the fraction of line-of-business sales in industry sales). Lines of business that are large in their firm also tend to be large in their market, all else equal. Parent-firm spending on sales efforts other than advertising ($FOSR$), per dollar of sales, has a positive effect on line of business market share (which suggests a barrier to entry effect). High parent-firm spending on research and development (FRD) and high line-of-business spending on research and development, tend to reduce

---

[28]   Line-of-business data was collected by the Federal Trade Commission for a few years in the mid-1970s and reports industry by industry on the operations of major US firms.

[29] t-statistics are in parentheses. The complete equation included 22 explanatory variables; only a portion of the results are reported here.

market share. If the parent firm has a large capital stock ($FKAP$), the line of business tends to have a larger market share.

Some industry characteristics are also significant in explaining differences in market share. If industry spending on advertising per dollar of sales ($IASR$) is higher, market share tends to be lower, all else equal. If minimum efficient scale (MES) is larger, market share tends to be larger.

11.6.3 Endogenous sunk costs and the bounds approach

Sutton (1991, 1998) paints the empirical implications of game-theoretic models of market structure with a broad brush, and distinguishes between two general types of industries.[30] In one class, the sunk costs that must covered to enter the industry are largely exogenous, given by the technology. In such industries, the minimum equilibrium value of seller concentration goes to zero as the market becomes large.[31] In the other class, sunk costs are endogenous, covering the costs of advertising (Sutton, 1991) and research and development (Sutton, 1998). For such industries, Sutton's model predicts that the minimum equilibrium value of seller concentration remains positive as the market becomes large.

Sutton applies what is in many ways a game-theory-inspired extension of Bain's small-sample, case study methodology. He finds support for his theoretical predictions in international comparisons of food industries in six industrialized countries.

Robinson and Chiang (1996) use a cross-section sample derived from the PIMS database[32] to test Sutton's predictions about the seller-concentration market size relationship. With some qualifications, their results seem to confirm the importance of the distinction between endogenous sunk cost industries and exogenous sunk cost industries.[33]

11.7 ENTRY

11.7.1 Oligopolistic interaction among entrants

It is usual to model the long-run number of firms in an industry by assuming that the number of firms adjusts until economic profit or the expected value of economic profit is zero. This

---

[30] For reviews, see Bresnahan (1992), Schmalensee (1992), and Scherer (2000).

[31] In a Cournot model with linear demand and a quadratic cost function, (11.19) gives the equilibrium number of plants. As market size becomes large, holding minimum efficient plant size fixed, MES goes to zero and the long-run market equilibrium number of firms goes to infinity. This type of model does not endogenize the number of plants per firm, and in this sense the model produces an expression for the minimum level of seller concentration (the maximum long-run equilibrium number of firms). But unless the equilibrium number of plants per firm rises as rapidly or more rapidly than market size, standard measures of seller concentration will go to zero as market size goes to infinity.

[32] See fn. 21, chapter 6.

[33] Robinson and Chiang find that seller concentration does not go to zero as market size rises in exogenous sunk cost industries that they classify as having tough price competition. This classification is based on structural factors (whether the product is standardized or not, whether the product is a raw or semi-finished material, whether orders are frequent or infrequent), and the toughness of price competition is an aspect of conduct. See Symeonidis (2000) for a clearer test of the impact of the toughness of price competition on market structure.

Table 11.4 A payoff matrix, Farrell cheap talk
entry game; $M > B > 0, L > 0$

| | Player 2 | |
Player 1	IN	OUT
IN	$-L, -L$	M, B
OUT	B, M	$0, 0$

makes sense for a perfectly competitive industry (Howrey and Quandt, 1968). It may make sense for oligopoly, particularly if uncertainty is minor and the technology does not require important sunk investments. But if the demand structure of a market is uncertain and firms are uncertain about their own or rivals' costs, one needs to model oligopolistic interaction in a pre-entry stage to analyze the long-run equilibrium number of firms.[34]

An entry game model

Farrell (1987) models pre-entry communication in a game between two potential entrants. In the final period of the game, in which entry decisions are made, payoffs are as shown in table 11.4. If both firms enter the market, each loses money. If only one firm enters, both firms receive positive payoffs, but the firm that enters receives a larger payoff than the firm that stays out. If both firms stay out, each breaks even.

With this payoff structure, each firm would prefer to be the unique entrant. But if a firm is not the unique entrant, it would prefer to have the other firm enter, so that it receives the payoff $B > 0$.

MIXED STRATEGY EQUILIBRIUM – THE ENTRY GAME

There are two pure-strategy equilibria for the game illustrated in table 11.4: (IN, OUT) and (IN, OUT). There is also a mixed-strategy equilibrium in which each player comes in with probability

$$p = Pr(IN) = \frac{M}{B + L + M} \tag{11.85}$$

and stays out with complementary probability.

If player 1 comes in with probability p and stays out otherwise, player 2's expected payoff is

$$u_1 = \frac{M}{B + L + M}(-L) + \left(1 - \frac{M}{B + L + M}\right)M = \frac{BM}{B + L + M} \tag{11.86}$$

---

[34] For a survey of this literature, see Geroski (1991b); see also Krouse (1991).

if it enters and

$$u_1 = \frac{M}{B+L+M}(B) + \left(1 - \frac{M}{B+L+M}\right)(0) = \frac{BM}{B+L+M} \tag{11.87}$$

if it does not. If player 1 comes in with probability p, player 2 receives the same payoff whether he comes in or stays out, and is therefore willing to play the indicated mixed strategy. But, by the same argument, if player 2 comes in with probability p and stays out otherwise, player 1 receives the same payoff whether he comes in or stays out, and is therefore willing to play the mixed strategy. This establishes that it is a noncooperative equilibrium for both players to come in with probability p and stay out with probability $1 - p$.

MIXED STRATEGY EQUILIBRIUM WITH CHEAP TALK

Now suppose that the entry game is preceded by a single round of nonbinding communication between the two firms – each firm announces that it intends to enter or to stay out once the entry period is reached. Announcement is not costly, and it is not binding – it is cheap talk.

Farrell (1987) restricts his attention to the equilibrium for the two–period game in which:

1 both players use the same mixed strategy;
2 if one player says IN and the other says OUT in the announcement period, those are the moves that are made in the entry period;
3 if both firms announce IN or both firms announce OUT, then in the entry period they each come in with probability p (11.85) and stay out with complementary probability.

If both players are to follow a mixed strategy in the announcement period, there must be some probability $q_1 = \Pr(\text{say } IN)$ which, if used by one player, makes the other indifferent between saying IN or OUT. If player 1 says IN with probability q_1 and OUT with probability $1 - q_1$, player 2's expected payoff from saying IN is

$$u_2 = q_1 u_1 + (1 - q_1)M, \tag{11.88}$$

where it will be recalled from (11.87) and (11.88) that u_1 is the payoff from the entry game if both firms play IN. On the other hand, player 2's expected payoff from saying OUT in the announcement period is

$$u_2 = q_1 B + (1 - q_1)u_1. \tag{11.89}$$

For q_1 to characterize a noncooperative equilibrium mixed strategy, the payoffs in (11.88) and (11.89) must be equal. This implies that

$$q_1 = \frac{M - u_1}{M + B - 2u_1}, \tag{11.90}$$

or, substituting $u_1 = pB$,

$$q_1 = \frac{M - pB}{M + B - 2u_1}. \tag{11.91}$$

From (11.91), we obtain

$$1 - q_1 = (1 - p)\left(\frac{B}{M + B - 2u_1}\right). \tag{11.92}$$

This in turn implies

$$(1 - p) - (1 - q_1) = (1 - p)\frac{M - 2pB}{M + B - 2pB} > 0. \tag{11.93}$$

But $(1 - p) > (1 - q_1)$ is the same as

$$q_1 > p. \tag{11.94}$$

Thus the mixed-strategy equilibrium probability that a firm says *IN* during the announcement game is greater than the probability that a firm actually plays *IN* in the entry game, if mixed strategies are followed once the entry period is reached.

We can say that entry is coordinated if only one firm plays *IN* during the entry period. If firms simply play the mixed equilibrium strategies from the entry game, the probability of a coordination failure is the probability that both firms play *IN* plus the probability that both firms play *OUT*:

$$p^2 + (1 - p)^2. \tag{11.95}$$

If there is one period of cheap talk, the equilibrium probability of a coordination failure is the probability that both firms make the same announcement multiplied by the probability that both firms take the same action in the entry period,

$$[q_1^2 + (1 - q_1)^2][p^2 + (1 - p)^2] < p^2 + (1 - p)^2. \tag{11.96}$$

A single period of cheap talk reduces the probability of a coordination failure. A preliminary announcement period gives firms an additional chance to agree, and if (playing mixed announcement strategies) they agree, then it is a noncooperative equilibrium for them to match actions to words in the entry period, because the firm that stays out gets B by carrying out its announcement, while it risks a zero payoff by deviating.

The natural generalization of this model is to have $T > 1$ periods of cheap talk, followed by an entry period. There is a mixed-strategy equilibrium in which the two firms follow their announcements if in some announcement period they make different announcements, and they play the mixed strategy described by (11.88) and (11.89) in the entry period otherwise. Farrell shows that there is a mixed strategy equilibrium for this generalized model. Expected payoffs using this strategy approach B from below as T rises, so that cheap talk makes players better off in an expected value sense. The probability of coordination failure decreases as the number of periods of cheap talk rises, but it does not go to zero.

11.7.2   Entry and exit – description

The kind of entry that one meets in theoretical models is not especially complicated. If there is a profit to be had by entry, new firms spring into existence. Sometimes the new firms have access to the same cost function as old firms, sometimes not. But the essential difference between new firms and old firms is that the new firms are new, while old firms are old.

The kind of entry one meets in empirical analysis is quite different. Some firms enter by buying existing plants from established firms; some firms enter by building entirely new plants. Some entrants are established in other industries or in other countries; some entrants are completely new entities. The important differences between new firms and old firms are that new firms are new, small, and (for the most part) doomed, while old firms are larger and are much more likely to survive.[35]

United States

Dunne et al. (1988) present a comprehensive description of entry and exit from US manufacturing industries using data for the five Census of Manufactures years 1963, 1967, 1972, 1977, and 1982. They find entrants and exitors to be many and small. Entrants (since the previous Census year) averaged 38.6 percent of the number of firms in a four-digit SIC manufacturing industry, but entrants' combined market share averaged only 15.8 percent of industry output. Between 30 and 40 percent of firms exit from one Census year to the next, but these firms are about one-third the size of firms that do not exit.

They also report substantial variations in entry and exit rates across industries, and that entry and exit rates or shares tend to be correlated across industries. In other words, industries that had high entry rates or shares also tended to have high exit rates or shares. At the same time, if the entry rate was above the industry average entry rate over the four Census periods, the exit rate tended to be below the industry average.

Entry is also unlikely to be successful. Firms entering US manufacturing in 1967, for example, averaged 13.9 percent of their industry's output in 1967, 8.3 percent in 1972, 6.7 percent in 1977, and 5.3 percent in 1982. Of firms entering in 1967, 63.9 percent had exited by 1972, 79 percent by 1977, and 87.6 percent by 1982.

Firms that survive, however, grow larger. Firms entering in 1967 were on average 35.2 percent of the average firm size for their industry in 1967; those firms that survived to 1982 were on average 132 percent of the average firm size for their industry.

Germany

Schwalbach (1991) reports entry and exit statistics for 183 four-digit German manufacturing industries for the period 1983–85. The number of entrants ranged from zero (for 17 industries) to 231 (plastics), with an average of about 21 entrants per industry. Entrants were small, either in number (averaging $11\frac{1}{2}$ percent of incumbent firms) or market share (4.9 percent combined entrants' share of sales). The typical entrant averaged 69.9 percent of the sales of the typical incumbent.

The statistics for exit are similar. The number of exitors varied from zero (12 industries) to 187 (wooden furniture), with an average of nearly 25. The number of exiting firms averaged

---

[35] For surveys, see Sutton (1997) and Caves (1998).

Table 11.5   Entry/exit data: Canada and UK

	UK			Canada		Percentage of 1974 entrants that exit in	
	Number of entrants (mean)	Entry share (mean)	Net entry share (mean)	Entry rate (mean)	Exit rate (mean)	Buy	Build
1974	96	0.0636	0.0103	0.062	0.074	5.26	10.69
1975	62	0.0255	−0.0108	0.036	0.057	8.77	9.82
1976	58	0.0285	0.0022	0.021	0.062	3.51	9.14
1977	35	0.0218	−0.0119	0.053	0.067	7.02	8.55
1978	31	0.0186	−0.0098	0.045	0.054	12.28	3.30
1979	18	−0.0052	−0.0052	0.058	0.064	1.75	5.15
Still alive in 1982						49.12	41.40

UK: for a sample of 87 three-digit industries; entry share = sales of new firms/(industry production + imports − exports); net entry share = (sales of entrants minus sales of exitors)/(industry production + imports − exports). Canada: for all Canadian four-digit manufacturing industries; entry rate = new firms/industry number of firms; "buy" refers to firms that entered by acquisition, "build" refers to firms that entered by building a new plant.

Sources: UK, Geroski, 1991a; Canada, Baldwin and Gorecki, 1989

13.8 percent of the number of firms in the industry, and their share of sales averaged 8.3 percent. The typical exiting firm averaged 55.3 percent of the sales of an incumbent firm.

In addition, entry and exit flows were correlated (correlation coefficients from 0.342 to 0.550, depending on the exact measure used).

Canada and the United Kingdom

A similar picture emerges from consideration of entry and exit data for other industrialized countries. Typical entry and exit statistics for Canada and UK are shown in table 11.5. The statistics for UK show a large number of entrants in a year (the decline over the sample period reflects worsening macroeconomic conditions). But entrants, on average, are small: in 1974 the average three-digit UK manufacturing industry had 96 entrants, but such entrants had a combined market share of only 6.36 percent, an average of one-fifteenth of 1 percent apiece. In the short run, entry on such a scale seems unlikely to place much of a limit on the conduct of established firms.

The impact of entry is even less if one considers net entry – entry minus exit – rather than gross entry. For both UK and Canada, the net share or rate of entry is often negative. Canadian data reveal that most entry is unsuccessful. Of firms that entered Canadian manufacturing in 1974, only half of the firms that entered by purchasing an established plant were in the industry eight years later, and only 40 percent of firms that entered by building a new plant were in the industry eight years later.

The picture of entry and exit in modern industry that emerges is aptly summarized by Geroski (1991b, p. 31):

> The consequence of most entry is a rather temporary displacement of small incumbents. Life in the bottom end of the industry size distribution is, no doubt, nasty, brutish and short. To reach a position remotely comparable to the mean sized firm ... requires a relatively long and highly risky expansion programme that most entrants quite simply fail to achieve.

11.8 EXIT

The analysis of the evolution of market structure inevitably draws attention to the analysis of market structure in the final phases of an industry's existence. Ghemawat and Nalebuff (1985) develop a model which yields the striking result that the equilibrium strategy of larger firms is to exit first from a declining industry.[36]

Two firms produce a homogeneous product. The industry inverse demand curve at time t is $p(Q, t)$, with negative first derivatives. Holding output constant, price declines over time. As t goes to infinity, $p(Q, t)$ goes to zero. The two firms supply a declining market.

Firms have capacities K_1 and K_2, with $K_1 > K_2$. There is a known rental cost c per unit of capital. The costs cK_1 and cK_2 are fixed but not sunk: they can be avoided by leaving the market. All costs are fixed; there is no variable cost. Thus if firms produce at all, they produce at capacity.

It will never be optimal for a firm to exit if price is greater than average cost. The analysis therefore begins at time zero, defined by the condition that at time zero price with both firms selling at capacity just equals the rental cost of capital:

$$p(K_1 + K_2, 0) = c. \tag{11.97}$$

Firm i's strategy at time t is the probability that firm i exits the industry at time t. Write $D_1(t, 1, 2)$ for the probability that firm 1 exits at time t, given that firms 1 and 2 are both in the market. $D_1(t, 1, 2) = 0$ means that firm 1 stays in the market at time t; $D_1(t, 1, 2) = 1$ means that firm 1 leaves the market at time t. $D_2(t, 1, 2)$ has a similar interpretation.

Single-firm exit times, t_1^* and t_2^*, satisfy

$$p(K_i, t_i^*) = c, \qquad i = 1, 2. \tag{11.98}$$

Since $K_1 > K_2$ and demand declines over time, $t_1^* < t_2^*$.

---

[36] In addition to the models discussed below, see Fudenberg and Tirole (1986), Frank (1988), and Ghemawat and Nalebuff (1990).

Let z be the last instant at which both firms are in the market. If firm j exits first, the value of firm i's payoffs, before and after firm j's exit, discounted back to time 0, are

$$C_i(z) = \int_0^z e^{-rt}[p(K_1 + K_2, t) - c]K_i \, dt \tag{11.99}$$

and

$$V_i(z, t_i^*) = \int_z^{t_i^*} e^{-rt}[p(K_i, t) - c]K_i \, dt \tag{11.100}$$

respectively (if z is less than t_i^*; otherwise, $V_i(z, t_i^*) = 0$).

If both firms operate until time z, and firm j exits first, the payoffs of the two firms are

$$\pi_i(z) = C_i(z) + V_i(z, t_i^*) \tag{11.101}$$

and

$$\pi_j(z) = C_j(z) \leq 0. \tag{11.102}$$

Each firm is just breaking even at time 0. Both firms lose money from time 0 to time z.

One of the firms exits at time z, and from that instant until it leaves the market, the survivor firm earns economic profits. The incentive to endure the period of losses is the profit that is to be had after the rival leaves the market. But the firm that leaves first has every incentive to make its period of losses as short as possible, which can be accomplished by exiting at time 0.

It follows that there are at most two possible noncooperative equilibria: either firm 1 exits at time 0 and firm 2 exits at time t_2^*, or firm 2 exits at time 0 and firm 1 exits at time t_1^*. Formally, the noncooperative equilibrium strategies are

$$D_i(t, 1, 2) = \begin{cases} 0 & t < t_i^* \\ 1 & t \geq t_i^* \end{cases}, \qquad i = 1, 2;$$

$$D_j(t, 1, 2) = 1 \qquad t \geq 0, \qquad j \neq i. \tag{11.103}$$

Although there are two noncooperative equilibria to this game, only one of them is subgame perfect. Consider the noncooperative equilibrium that calls for firm 2 to exit at time 0 and for firm 1 to stay in the market until time t_1^*. If, somehow or other, firm 2 stays in the market until a time very close to t_1^*, it will be profitable for firm 2 to stay in the market until t_1^*, when firm 1 will exit in any event, and enjoy economic profits over the period (t_1^*, t_2^*). But this means that firm 1's noncooperative equilibrium strategy for the game is not a noncooperative equilibrium in subgames that have firm 2 in the market sufficiently close to t_1^*. Hence the noncooperative equilibrium that calls for firm 2 to exit at time 0 is not subgame perfect.

The same argument does not apply to the noncooperative equilibrium that calls for firm 1 to leave the market at time 0, because firm 1 will not profit by staying in the market after t_1^*.

Ghemawat and Nalebuff extend their result to n-firm oligopoly. Keeping other aspects of their model the same, if there are n suppliers with $K_1 > K_2 > \cdots > K_n$, then firm 1 exits first, firm 2 exits second, and so on.

They also show that the order of exit may be reversed if there are economies of scale. If there are economies of scale in duopoly, the smaller firm will operate at a variable cost disadvantage with respect to the larger firm. If the cost disadvantage of the smaller firm is sufficiently great, it will begin to lose money before the large firm does, and its equilibrium strategy will be to exit first.

Whinston (1988) extends the Ghemawat and Nalebuff model to allow for multiplant firms, and shows that their results do not generalize to the extended model. Consider a duopoly in which firm 1 owns the largest plant and firm 2 owns two smaller plants. If it is to be an equilibrium strategy for firm 1 to exit first, firm 1 must believe that firm 2 will find it most profitable to hold open both plants. But if firm 2 closes one of its two plants, there is a price increase that benefits firm 2, in proportion to the output from its remaining plant. Under some circumstances (see Whinston, 1988, proposition 2), this may make it a subgame perfect equilibrium strategy for firm 2 to shut down one of its two plants before firm 1 exits the market.

Fishman (1990) extends the Ghemawat and Nalebuff duopoly model to consider the entire industry life-cycle–expansion and entry, decline and exit.[37] Each firm has a single plant, so the Ghemawat and Nalebuff results regarding the order of exit continue to hold. But in a model that covers the entire industry life-cycle, the capacities that firms have when the industry goes into decline are endogenous, resulting from decisions that firms make upon entry. This means that the payoff from installing a given capacity at the moment of entry is the result of an income stream that depends on exit times that are themselves endogenous (although determined by the Ghemawat–Nalebuff exit rule).

In Fishman's model, the first firm to move acts as a capacity-leader, picking the point on the second firm's capacity best-response curve that is most profitable for the first firm. Incentives for the first mover to limit entry by holding a high capacity are reduced compared with models that do not take the strategic implications of the declining phase of an industry's life-cycle into account, because a high capacity level makes the first entrant the first exitor as well.

11.9 EMPIRICAL STUDIES OF ENTRY AND EXIT

11.9.1 Canada

Shapiro and Khemani (1987) examine entry and exit flows over the period 1972–76 for a sample of 143 four-digit Canadian manufacturing industries.[38] They investigate the hypothesis that industry characteristics that impede entry also impede exit (1987, pp. 15–6):

> Durability and specificity, singly or in combination, give rise to sunk costs. Sunk costs in turn create barriers to entry because entrants must duplicate assets whose opportunity cost is higher than that for incumbent firms and because the assets have limited scrap value which increases the risk of entry (owing to the large losses associated with unsuccessful entry). However, the sunk cost characteristic of the assets also represents a barrier to exit for incumbent firms since the committed assets represent non-recoverable costs. Incumbents are therefore bound to their markets by the inability to divest.

---

[37] See Londregan (1990) for another such model.
[38] See also Gorecki (1976) and Baldwin and Gorecki (1987, 1989).

Their specification – which follows Orr (1974) and is typical of that used in the empirical literature on entry – uses the logarithm of the gross number of firms that entered/exited as a dependent variable and various entry/exit barrier and industry structural variables as explanatory variables, most often entered linearly.

Their results show that industry profitability has a significant positive effect on entry, while high market concentration has a significant negative effect on both entry and exit.

High absolute capital requirements, large minimum efficient scale relative to market size, and a high percentage of multiplant firms all tend to reduce entry and exit flows significantly. A high advertising–sales ratio and a high percentage of scientists and engineers in the work force tend to reduce entry and exit flows. High advertising intensity has a significant negative effect on entry, while research and development intensity has a significant negative effect on exit. Entry and exit flows both tend to be significantly greater, the larger is the industry. These results are consistent with the argument that it is investment in sunk assets that tends to discourage entry, and that entry barriers and exit barriers are the same.

Shapiro and Khemani re-estimate their exit equation to take account of the possibility that entry may displace some incumbent firms. Their estimate of the elasticity of exit with respect to entry, which is statistically significant, is 0.78. In their sample, a 1 percent increase in entry is associated with a 0.78 percent increase in exit, all else equal. This is consistent with the descriptive data that depict entry and exit flows essentially as a revolving door at the bottom of the industry size distribution.

11.9.2   The United States[39]

Sunk cost

In a study of entry into 266 US industries, Kessides (1986) finds evidence that the need to invest in advertising is a sunk cost of entry.[40] This is plausible, as advertising creates an asset – goodwill or reputation – that is subject to extremely limited resale upon exit. At the same time, he finds that net entry rises with the industry advertising–sales ratio. This is consistent with the hypothesis that advertising is a device that entrants can employ to inform customers and carve out a niche in the marketplace.

Kessides highlights the role of sunk costs as an entry barrier (1990a, p. 223):

> For the new entrant, the act of entry requires the conversion of liquid assets into frozen physical capital, only part of which is recoverable in the event of failure. For the incumbent, however, who is already beyond the regime of potential failure, either these commitments have already been made (initial capital investment), or they constitute a normal cost of doing business (advertising). There exists, therefore, an asymmetry in the incremental cost and risk faced by a potential entrant and the incumbent firms – and in this sense sunk costs constitute a barrier to entry.

---

[39] See Deutsch (1975) for an early study, as well as Bresnahan and Reiss (1987) and Shaanan (1988).

[40] The industries are defined at the four-digit Standard Industrial Classification (SIC) level. The study examines net entry – the number of entrants minus the number of exits – between 1972 and 1977 for industries where net entry was positive.

To test the impact of investment in sunk assets on entry, Kessides develops measures of industry-average investment in buildings and investment in machinery and equipment, for a sample of 264 US four-digit SIC manufacturing industries. These are used as explanatory variables in equations explaining the net number of entrants per industry between 1972 and 1977. Other explanatory variables are the growth rate of industry sales, a measure of industry-average plant size, and the pre-entry industry price–cost margin.

His empirical results suggest that it is investment in machinery and equipment, not investment in buildings, that deters entry. Investment in machinery and equipment is much more likely to be industry specific, and sunk, than investment in buildings.

He also finds that incumbent firms are more likely to react aggressively to entry, the more profitable they are and the more concentrated is the industry. The expected cost of entry into a concentrated industry will therefore be higher, all else equal, because the probability of a hostile reaction from incumbents is greater.

Entry also tends to rise with pre-entry profit and with industry growth, and to fall as average plant size rises. These results are consistent with the mainstream analysis of barriers to entry.

Small firms

Acs and Audretsch (1989) examine the determinants of entry by small firms into 247 four-digit US industries over the period 1978–80. Industry capital intensity and industry advertising intensity, which might be expected to deter entry on the basis of the results of studies of entry by all firms, have no significant impact on entry by small firms.

Small-firm entry is significantly greater, the greater is the rate of growth of industry sales and the greater is industry profitability. Profitability significantly affects entry only for firms with at least 250 employees, not for extremely small firms.

The rate of entry is significantly less, the greater is industry-average spending on research and development per dollar of sales (investment in a sunk asset, knowledge) and the more concentrated are industry sales. These results are similar to those of studies of entry by firms of all sizes.

Small-firm entry is significantly greater for industries where small firms are highly innovative, where small-firm labor productivity has been increasing, and where a larger percentage of employees are unionized (small firms, which are more likely to be able to avoid unionization, would thereby enjoy a cost advantage). Small-firm entry is significantly less into industries in which an important share of industry sales already accounted for by small firms.

Exit

Lieberman uses a sample describing producers of 30 chemical products to subject the theoretical literature on exit to empirical testing (1990, p. 538):

> The analysis is framed in terms of two contrasting sets of predictions. The first set of predictions is based on the observation that larger firms are often more efficient; size may convey economies of scale or reflect a process of more rapid growth by superior firms. Such differences in efficiency would cause smaller firms to be "shaken out" relatively early if prices fall during the decline

phase. The second set of predictions is based on the Cournot–Nash result that in the absence of cost differences, smaller firms can remain profitable over a longer period as demand tapers off to zero. Given this superior ability of small firms to "stake out" as the industry devolves, larger firms would rationally choose to exit early or to mimic their smaller rivals by drastically cutting capacity.

Lieberman examines the evolution of market structure after demand for the products begins to decline. Markets for the products are all highly concentrated, and the Herfindahl index tends to increase as demand declines.

Examination of exit rates shows that smaller firms were more likely to exit, all else equal. Of firms in the sample 38 percent exited, but only three of the 30 largest firms (the largest firm for each of the 30 products) exited. This is not consistent with the Ghemawat–Nalebuff "large firm first" exit rule. On the other hand, large firms tended to undertake more capacity reductions than small firms.

Lieberman also estimates a logit model of the probability that a plant will be closed, using as a sample plants producing the 17 products for which demand declined more than 35 percent over the sample period. A plant is more likely to close, all else equal, the smaller it is relative to the largest plant in the industry. A plant is more likely to close, the larger the share of its firm in industry capacity. Subsequent analysis reveals that this effect occurs only for multiplant firms. For single-plant firms, the probability of exit does not rise with size.

Lieberman summarizes his results as follows (1990, p. 552):

> These findings are consistent with multiple theories of divestment in declining industries. As predicted by the "shakeout" theory, small-share firms exhibited high rates of exit, and small-scale plants were most likely to close. Other findings support the "stakeout" models . . . . Controlling for plant size, the probability of plant closure increased with the firm's capacity share, assuming that the firm operated multiple plants. Within the cohort of surviving firms, large producers cut capacity by a greater percentage than small producers . . . . There is no support for the more extreme prediction of [Ghemawat and Nalebuff] that large producers would be most likely to exit.

11.9.3   The United Kingdom[41]

Geroski (1991a) distinguishes between foreign entry and entry by domestic firms. The distinction is potentially critical for policy purposes in an age of increasingly open economies. If the threat of foreign competition prevents domestic firms from exercising market power, domestic policy-makers have fewer reasons to be concerned about domestic market structure.

Geroski treats domestic and foreign entry as functions of expected profit, market size, and the industry growth rate. The intercepts of the entry rate equations are allowed to differ from industry to industry, which is a way of allowing for differences in entry conditions across industries. Estimated entry equations are reproduced in table 11.6.

The only significant coefficient which is of *a priori* expected sign is that of expected profit in the domestic entry equation. It is positive, and four times as large as the coefficient of the same variable in the foreign entry equation.

---

[41] See also Gorecki (1975) and Geroski and Murfin (1991).

Table 11.6 Domestic and foreign entry equations, UK, 1983–4

$$E^d = \cdots + \underset{(2.192)}{1.684\Pi^e} + \underset{(0.494)}{0.074SIZE_{-1}} - \underset{(1.83)}{0.2599GR_{-1}} \quad R^2 = 0.589$$

$$E^f = \cdots + \underset{(1.06)}{0.448\Pi^e} + \underset{(0.0542)}{0.003SIZE_{-1}} - \underset{(1.21)}{0.0505GR_{-1}} \quad R^2 = 0.618$$

Intercepts differ from industry to industry; E^d, domestic entry; E^f, foreign entry; Π^e, expected profit; $SIZE$, industry sales; GR denotes growth rate of industry sales; for a sample of 95 UK Minimum List Heading industries. Subscript, -1 denotes previous time period; t-statistics in parentheses.
Source: Geroski, 1991a

Despite the low significance of the coefficients reported in table 11.6, the explanatory power of the equations is quite high (by the standard of cross-section regressions). The explanatory power of the equations, by and large, comes from the industry-specific intercept terms, not from the explanatory variables that are common to all industries. What this suggests is that there are substantial variations in barriers to entry across industries, and that the effect of these barriers is being captured by the estimated intercept terms.

The results of this study do not support the view that foreign competition is an important determinant of domestic market performance (Geroski, 1991a, pp. 84–5):

> neither type of entrant appears to provide much in the way of a substantive challenge to incumbents in most markets.... the fact that the heights of entry barriers facing each of the two types of entrant are broadly similar across industries means that neither is a substitute for the other (judged as a competitive force).... (at least in the UK) the mere possibility of import competition does not obviate the need to be concerned with domestic market structure.

11.9.4 Germany

Schwalbach (1991)[42] estimates the following entry equation for a sample of 183 four-digit German manufacturing industries for 1983–5:

$$E = \cdots + \underset{(2.15)}{0.226\pi_{-1}} - \underset{(3.36)}{0.932Scale_{-1}} + \underset{(1.85)}{0.0512PD_{-1}} - \underset{(1.37)}{0.0518R\&D}$$
$$+ \underset{(0.08)}{0.0001ACR} + \underset{(2.00)}{0.0639GR_{-1}} - \underset{(1.64)}{0.0107SIZE} \tag{11.104}$$

($R^2 = 0.591$; separate intercepts for each industry are not reported; subscript, -1 denotes the previous time period; t-statistics in parentheses).

---

[42] See also Schwalbach (1987).

For this sample of industries, high profits attract entry, while economies of scale and investment in research and development discourage entry. Entry is also larger, the more rapid is industry growth. In contrast with other studies, entry is significantly greater the more important is product differentiation. Entry is smaller for larger industries, which is counterintuitive.

11.9.5   Japan

Yamawaki (1991) examines macroeconomic as well as microeconomic determinants of entry rates. For a sample of 135 Japanese three-digit industries over the period 1979–84, he estimates the net entry equation

$$NE = \ldots + 0.162PCM + 0.221GR_{-1} + 0.005GNPGR_{-1}$$
$$(1.704)\qquad (11.878)\qquad (2.987)$$
$$-0.040PINV \quad -008DISC$$
$$(9.661)\qquad (6.104)\qquad\qquad\qquad (11.105)$$

($R^2 = 0.696$; separate industry intercept terms are not reported; subscript -1 denotes the previous time period; t-statistics are in parentheses).

As far as industry variables are concerned, net entry into Japanese industries is significantly and positively affected by both lagged profitability and lagged industry growth. The effect of lagged industry growth is especially significant. These results parallel those for other countries.

The growth rate of gross national product ($GNPGR$) has an independent and significantly positive effect on industry net entry, while net entry is less, the higher the price index of investment goods ($PINV$) and the discount rate ($DISC$). The cost of capital ought to be greater, all else equal, the greater are $PINV$ and $DISC$, and it should be expected that higher values will be associated with slower net entry.

11.10   CONCLUSION

It is traditional to model market concentration as being determined by entry barriers, although formal models of market structure now proceed directly from the costs faced by entrants to resulting short-run and long-run equilibrium market structures. Whatever the underlying model, economies of scale, the extent of product differentiation, and absolute capital requirements for entry at minimum efficient scale are important determinants of the long-run degree of market concentration. Concentration of sales appears to adjust over time to a long-run level that depends on entry conditions. The rate of adjustment varies from industry to industry.

Theoretical models treat entry and exit as flows that take place more or less automatically in response to levels of profit or expected profit that differ from the long-run equilibrium value. Among other things, this implies that one should observe either entry or exit for a single industry, but not both.

Real-world data suggest that entry is a hazardous enterprise. In most industries, firms enter and exit simultaneously through what amounts to a revolving door, but few firms make it into the lobby and manage to maintain an enduring presence in the industry. Most entrants have little if any influence on market performance because most entrants exit, and fairly quickly. Far from being an automatic adjustment mechanism, entry and exit are part of a selection process that winnows out ill-suited firms and winnows in firms able to carve out a niche for themselves in a market.

PROBLEMS

11.1 In the Farrell and Shapiro model of Cournot oligopoly with industry-specific assets, let the inverse demand curve be linear,

$$p = a - bQ,$$

and let firm i's variable cost function be quadratic,

$$c^i(q_i, k_i) = cq + d\frac{q_i^2}{k_i}, \qquad i = 1, 2, \ldots, n.$$

Show that equilibrium firm outputs, industry output, and price are

$$q_i = \frac{\kappa_i}{1+\kappa}\frac{a-c}{b}, \qquad i = 1, 2, \ldots, n,$$

$$Q = \frac{\kappa}{1+\kappa}\frac{a-c}{b} \quad \text{and} \quad p = c + \frac{a-c}{1+\kappa},$$

respectively, where $\kappa_i = k_i/(k_i + \delta)$, $\delta = d/b$, and $\kappa = \kappa_1 + \kappa_2 + \cdots + \kappa_n$.

11.2 With the inverse demand curve and cost functions of Problem 11.1, show that (11.51) becomes

$$\chi_i = \frac{c^i_{qk_i}}{c^i_{qq} - p'} = \frac{p-c}{b} = \frac{2\delta}{(k_i + 2\delta)^2}.$$

CHAPTER TWELVE

FIRM STRUCTURE, MERGERS, AND JOINT VENTURES

An outsider to the field of economics would probably take it for granted that economists have a highly developed theory of the firm.

Hart (1989, p. 1757)

12.1 INTRODUCTION

The neoclassical theory of the firm is not so much the theory of the firm as a theory of markets supplied by firms. In these models, what firms do is well specified: they buy inputs and they produce outputs.[1] How firms do this – how activities are organized within firms, and how that organization affects firm and market performance – is a topic that is not addressed in neoclassical economics, and painfully little in traditional industrial economics.

Depending on the topic at hand, it may well be sufficient to include in the specification of a model "assume marginal cost is a constant *c*" or perhaps "let the cost function be $c(q)$" without dwelling on the conditions that are necessary for this to be the case. But for topics that involve the impact of the structure within firms and relations among firms on market performance, it seems essential to work with models that look within the firm. Such topics include the determinants of business efficiency and the causes and consequences of mergers and joint ventures, which we deal with in this chapter, and also the analysis of manufacturer–distributor relationships, which we take up in chapter 13.

12.2 WHY ARE THERE FIRMS?

Coase (1937) is the precursor of the new theory of the firm, which has come into its own only since the 1970s.[2] He anticipated the modern position that the firm and the market should be

---

[1] Most often, one assumes that firms are privately owned profit maximizers. Leading alternatives are public firms, regulated firms, and labor-managed firms.

[2] For surveys, see Caves (1980), Marris and Mueller (1980), Williamson (1981), Joskow (1988), Levinthal (1988), Milgrom and Roberts (1988), and Hart (1989). See also symposium articles in the Fall 1998 issue of the *Journal of*

viewed as alternative ways of organizing transactions (Coase, 1937/52, p. 333; see also Coase, 1972, pp. 63–4):

> Outside the firm, price movements direct production, which is co-ordinated through a series of exchange transactions on the market. Within a firm, these market transactions are eliminated and in place of the complicated market structure with exchange transactions is substituted the entrepreneur–co-ordinator, who directs production. It is clear that these are alternative methods of co-ordinating production.

Coase highlighted the costs – broadly defined – of carrying out transactions in the market as the reason for locating some productive activity within firms. He emphasized costs associated with imperfect information, such as the cost of discovering relevant prices and the costs to risk-averse economic agents of negotiating long-term contracts when the future is uncertain.[3] He asked as well the logical follow-up question, namely: given that it is efficient to locate some productive activity within firms, why are there markets? His answer was that just as there were costs to organizing economic activity across markets, so there were costs to organizing economic activity within firms. Here he pointed to managerial diseconomies of scale and the resulting failure to minimize costs (Coase, 1937/52, p. 340):

> it may be that as the transactions which are organised increase, the entrepreneur fails to place the factors of production in the uses where their value is greatest, that is, fails to make the best use of the factors of production.

He concluded that the limits to firm size were determined by relative transaction costs (1937/52, p. 341):[4]

> a firm will tend to expand until the costs of organising an extra transaction within the firm become equal to the costs of carrying out the same transaction by means of an exchange on the open market or the costs of organising another firm.

This is, of course, a very neoclassical answer – the boundary between firm and market lies where the marginal cost of organizing an activity in one sphere equals the marginal cost of organizing the same activity in the other sphere – to a question that neoclassical economists did not much ask. Much of the modern theory of the firm involves delving into the nature and consequences of the costs of organizing activity in one sphere or the other.

Economic Perspectives and correspondence between Richard Brooks – Susan Helper and Patrick Bolton – David S. Scharfstein in the Spring 2000 issue of the *Journal of Economic Perspectives*.

[3] For an interpretation of Coase (1937) in terms of the theory of contracts, see Cheung (1983).

[4] See Leibenstein (1987) for an extended analysis of transaction costs within the firm.

12.2.1   Bounded rationality and opportunism

Coase's contribution[5] failed to trigger a systematic, sustained study of firm organization by economists. That takeoff waited for the work of Oliver Williamson.[6] Like Coase, Williamson explains the existence of the firm in terms of the cost of carrying out transactions across markets (1981, p. 1537):

> the modern corporation is mainly to be understood as the product of a series of organizational innovations that have had the purpose and effect of economizing on transaction costs.

Williamson elaborated a transaction cost theory of the firm based on the twin assumptions of bounded rationality and opportunism in the presence of uncertainty.

Williamson follows Simon (1947, p. xxiv), who defined bounded rationality as behavior which is "intendedly rational, but only limitedly so." Human beings do not have unlimited calculating ability. The internal organization of real-world firms is in part a response to costs that would not exist if owners or managers of a firm had unlimited reasoning power.

Opportunism, which Williamson defines as "self-interest plus guile" (1975, p. 26; 1981, p. 1545) is essentially the assumption that economic agents noncooperatively pursue their own self-interest. In such a world, economic agents will not assume that contracts made across markets will automatically be honored, if it is costly to enforce a contract or to seek damages for violation of a contract. Rather, they will expect individuals or firms with whom or which they have negotiated a contract to break it if the expected benefit from breaking the contract, net of expected penalties, exceeds the expected benefit from adhering to the contract. Some transactions will be brought within the firm because it is easier to monitor performance of the transaction if the transaction is carried out by employees, rather than via a contract between independent opportunistic agents.

It is the combination of bounded rationality and opportunism that renders transaction cost economics interesting (Williamson, 1981, p. 1545):

> But for the simultaneous existence of both bounded rationality and opportunism, all economic contracting problems are trivial . . . Thus, but for bounded rationality, all economic exchange could be effectively organized by contract . . . .
>
>   Ubiquitous, albeit incomplete, contracting would nevertheless be feasible if economic agents were completely trustworthy.

Williamson and the literature that has developed from his work have highlighted asset specificity and subgoal pursuit as characteristics of transactions that determine whether or not a transaction within the firm is efficient.

Assets are highly specific to a particular transaction or class of transactions if the marginal productivity of the asset for other uses is negligible. An asset is specific to a particular kind of transaction if the asset could not be used productively in other activities of the firm.

---

[5] As well as later work by Simon (1947), Chandler (1962), Cyert and March (1963), and others.
[6] Williamson (1967, 1970, 1975, 1981, 1985, among others). See Englander (1988) for a critical review and Williamson (1988b) for a rejoinder.

If a firm must invest in highly specific assets to carry out a particular kind of transaction, then by that investment it gives up the opportunity of carrying out the transaction across a competitive market (Williamson, 1981, p. 1546):

> The reason why asset specificity is critical is that, once the investment has been made, buyer and seller are effectively operating in a bilateral exchange relation for a considerable period thereafter.

Transactions that require investment in highly specific assets are more likely to be brought into the firm, all else equal, to guard against possible exploitative behavior by an opportunistic trading partner after the investment has been made. This ties into the notion of subgoal pursuit (Williamson, 1981, p. 1547):

> in the course of executing contracts, agents also pursue private goals which may be in some degree inconsistent with the contract's intended purpose.

Bounded rationality – hierarchical control and firm size

OLIGOPOLY

In the transaction cost literature on firm structure, it is often assumed that firm structure is devoid of strategic purpose and is determined solely to minimize cost.[7] Thus Williamson (1967) examines the relationship between hierarchical control and firm size in an industry of price-taking firms. This specification is unnecessarily restrictive. Oligopolistic firms have an internal structure, and in oligopoly firm structure may have strategic as well as efficiency purposes.

We can extend Williamson's model by embedding it in a model of Cournot oligopoly. In a market supplied by n identical firms, let the market inverse demand curve be

$$p = a - b(q_1 + q_2 + \cdots + q_n). \tag{12.1}$$

A firm has m administrative layers. The span of administrative control is s – each employee can supervise s subordinates. There is one employee in the first administrative layer, there are s employees in the second administrative layer, s^2 employees in the third administrative layer, . . . , s^{m-1} employees in the final, mth layer. α is a control loss parameter that lies between 0 and 1; productivity falls by a fraction $1 - \alpha$ for each administrative layer. With m hierarchical layers, $q_i = \theta(\alpha s)^{m_i-1}$ is firm i's output. Firm i's profit is

$$\pi_i = (p - r)q_i - w_0 \frac{s^m - \beta^m}{s - \beta}, \tag{12.2}$$

where r is nonlabor costs per unit of output.

[7] Williamson (1981, p. 1540; 1985, p. 28). The first sentence of Fama and Jensen (1983) is an unambiguous statement of this position, no doubt reflecting the usual Chicago school position that departures from long-run competitive equilibrium are at most temporary. The need to expand the analysis of organization forms to include strategic motives is emphasized by Boyer and Jacquemin (1985).

Maximization of (12.2) with respect to m_i gives firm i's hierarchy best-response function:

$$\theta b \left\{ \frac{a-r}{b} - \theta \left[\sum_{j \neq i} (\alpha s)^{m_j - 1} + 2(\alpha s)^{m_i - 1} \right] \right\} (\alpha s)^{m_i - 1} \ln (\alpha s)$$

$$- w_0 \frac{s^{m_i} \ln s - \beta^{m_i} \ln \beta}{s - \beta} \equiv 0. \tag{12.3}$$

Imposing partial symmetry in (12.3) – letting $m_j = m_{-i}$ for all $i \neq j$ – one can show that hierarchy best-response curves slope downward. Imposing complete symmetry – letting $m_i = m_j = m$ for all i and j – we obtain the equation that defines the equilibrium number of hierarchical layers in n-firm Cournot oligopoly:

$$\theta b \left[\frac{a-r}{b} - \theta(n+1)(\alpha s)^{m-1} \right] (\alpha s)^{m-1} \ln (\alpha s) - w_0 \frac{s^m \ln s - \beta^m \ln \beta}{s - \beta} \equiv 0. \tag{12.4}$$

Differentiating (12.4) with respect to n gives

$$\frac{\partial m}{\partial n} = \frac{b\theta [\ln (\alpha s)](\alpha s)^{2(m-1)}}{DET}, \tag{12.5}$$

where DET is an expression that is negative provided that the second-order condition for profit maximization holds. Since the numerator is positive, the comparative statics effect of an increase in the number of firms in the industry is to reduce the equilibrium number of hierarchical layers per firm. When firm structure is treated as endogenous, there are links between firm structure and market structure.

ASSET SPECIFICITY

Riordan and Williamson (1985) model the impact of asset specificity on firm structure. The fundamental economic idea of the model is disarmingly simple: transactions across markets are carried out by means of (formal or informal) contracts that are inevitably incomplete, because the future is uncertain and the cost of working out a contract that provides for all possible contingencies is prohibitive.

There are some states of the world in which the contract must be renegotiated. If one of these states of the world occurs, and one party to the market transaction has invested in highly specific assets, it opens itself up to the possibility of opportunistic behavior by the other party.

If the value of the specific assets is low, the amount at risk due to possible contract renegotiation is not very great. But if a transaction must be supported by a substantial investment in highly specific assets, the expected cost of contract negotiation is large.

This cost can be avoided by bringing the transaction within the firm. But this is also costly – there will be a fixed cost of setting up an internal administrative structure, and the additional possibility of bureaucratic control loss. Choice of the profit-maximizing organizational form for a transaction is the result of a comparison between the expected cost of carrying out the transaction across the market and the cost of carrying out the transaction within the firm.

But the expected cost of carrying out the transaction across the market will be greater, the more specific are the assets in which the firm must invest to carry out the transaction. Hence internalization is more likely, the greater is asset specificity.

Formally, let a firm's revenue from producing output q be $R(q)$. We shall be vague about the type of market in which the firm operates, except to assume that it is not perfectly competitive. The cost of production is $c(q)$. Production requires the services of an asset, and the rental cost of the services of the asset is part of the cost function $c(q)$. But purchase of the services of the asset on an imperfectly competitive factor market involves a governance cost

$$G^m = W(s), \qquad W' > 0, \tag{12.6}$$

which is over and above the rental cost of asset services. s is an asset specificity parameter.

Without loss of generality, let $0 \leq s \leq 1$. If $s = 0$, the investment the firm makes to acquire asset services on the market is not at all specific to that transaction; it could be used to acquire similar asset services from some other supplier. If $s = 1$, the investment the firm makes to acquire asset services on the market is completely specific to that transaction, has no other use, and could not be used to acquire substitute services from some other supplier.

Alternatively, the firm may acquire the services of the productive asset by purchasing it and setting up an internal governance structure at cost

$$G^i = \beta > 0 \tag{12.7}$$

to manage use of the asset. Assume that

$$W(0) < \beta < W(1). \tag{12.8}$$

It costs less to acquire asset services across the market if supporting assets are not at all specific, but it costs less to internalize the use of the productive asset if supporting assets are completely specific to the particular supplier.

Since $W' > 0$, there is some critical level of s, defined by

$$W(s^*) = \beta, \tag{12.9}$$

which is the limit above which the least costly way of organizing the transaction is to bring it within the firm.

The firm's profit is

$$\pi^m = R(q) - c(q) - W(s) \tag{12.10}$$

if it acquires asset services across markets, and

$$\pi^i = R(q) - c(q) - \beta \tag{12.11}$$

if it internalizes management of the productive asset.

In this version of the model, profit-maximizing output is independent of the choice of input transactional form. The first-order condition for maximization of (12.10) and (12.11) is

$$R'(q) - c'(q) \equiv 0. \tag{12.12}$$

Given this result, if $s \geq s^*$ the firm will internalize the transaction. Otherwise, it will acquire asset services across the market.

There is a generalization of this model in which the degree of asset specificity that supports the transaction enters the cost function (with a negative derivative) and is a choice variable of the firm. By choosing to support a transaction with more specific assets, the firm reduces production cost. In this version of the model, the level of output and organizational form are no longer independent.[8]

Managerial incentives

Awareness of the implications of the separation of firm ownership from firm control for market performance can be found in *The Wealth of Nations* (Adam Smith, 1937, pp. 699–700), but modern treatments of the topic trace their lineage to Berle and Means (1932).[9] If ownership and control are separate, owners' influence over the operating decisions of the firm, if any, are indirect. What are the implications for market performance if owners determine the function that determines managers' payoffs, but managers make the operating decisions that determine firms' outputs?[10]

A central aspect of Williamson's analysis of market transaction costs and the existence of firms is opportunism – the idea that economic agents pursue their own self-interest at all times, and that this will sometimes make them unreliable partners in arm's length transactions. The rest of the argument is that managers will be better able to monitor and control the performance of subordinates than that of independent trading partners.

Principal–agent models analyze the relationship between a superior (the principal) who manipulates the actions of an opportunistic subordinate (the agent) by setting the fee schedule that determines the agent's reward as a function of the agent's effort. Consider the case of a single principal and a single agent. The agent's utility function is[11]

$$t[\phi(x)] - u(z), \tag{12.13}$$

where $t' > 0$, $t'' < 0$, $u' > 0$, and $u'' > 0$. z is the agent's effort or work. Monitoring by the principal is imperfect. If the agent performs work z, the principal perceives the agent as performing work $x = z + (\varepsilon/\xi)$. ε is a random variable with zero mean and density function $g(\varepsilon)$. $\xi > 0$ is the amount of effort by the principal to monitor the actions of the agent. More intense monitoring by the principal reduces the error with which the agent's work is measured.

The fee schedule $\phi(x)$ is set by the principal. The agent's compensation depends on his perceived effort, not his actual effort. $t(\phi)$ gives the agent's utility from income ϕ. u is the agent's disutility from making an effort z.

---

[8] See Joskow (1988) for a survey of empirical work on asset specificity. Experimental evidence reported by Whyte (1994) suggests that sunk costs alone, independent of any effect of sunk assets on transactions costs, are conducive to vertical integration.

[9] See also Marshall (1920, p. 253) and the June 1983 issue of the *Journal of Law and Economics* for contributions to a symposium held on the 50th anniversary of the publication of *The Modern Corporation and Private Property*.

[10] See also Sklivas (1987), which is a treatment very close to that of Fershtman and Judd (1987), as well as Fershtman (1985) and Bull and Ordover (1987).

[11] This section follows Mirrlees (1976); see also Holmström (1979). For surveys, see Rees (1987a,b) and Levinthal (1988). Williamson (1988a) compares the transaction cost and agency approaches to firm organization.

Although the agent is paid according to his perceived effort, the utility of the principal depends on the agent's actual effort, net of compensation, and on the disutility associated with monitoring the agent. The principal's utility function is

$$v[z - \phi(x)] - w(\xi), \tag{12.14}$$

with $v' > 0$, $v'' < 0$, $w' > 0$, and $w'' > 0$.

THE AGENT'S PROBLEM

The agent picks effort z to maximize expected utility

$$\int_x t[\phi(x)]g[\xi(x - z)]\,\mathrm{d}x - u(z), \tag{12.15}$$

where the relation $\varepsilon = \xi(x - z)$ has been used to eliminate ε and express the agent's maximization problem in terms of the random variable x. The first-order condition that characterizes the solution to the agent's utility-maximization problem is

$$-\xi \int_x t[\phi(x)]g'[\xi(x - z)]\,\mathrm{d}x - u'(z) \equiv 0. \tag{12.16}$$

THE PRINCIPAL'S PROBLEM

The principal seeks to pick the fee schedule $\phi(x)$ and monitoring effort ξ to maximize expected utility

$$\int_x v[z - \phi(x)]g[\xi(x - z)]\,\mathrm{d}x - w(z), \tag{12.17}$$

subject to two constraints.

The first constraint is that the agent's utility be at least as great as his reservation utility; that is, the utility he could receive in his next best alternative employment,

$$\int_x t[\phi(x)]g[\xi(x - z)]\,\mathrm{d}x - u(z) \geq \bar{u}. \tag{12.18}$$

If this constraint is not met, the agent will not work at all.

The second constraint is that the agent's effort z, given ϕ and ξ, maximize the agent's utility:

$$z = \operatorname{argmax} \int_x t[\phi(x)]g[\xi(x - z)]\,\mathrm{d}x - u(z). \tag{12.19}$$

Thus the principal acts to maximize his own utility, assuming that the agent will do the same. By setting the fee schedule, the principal induces the agent to make the effort which is most beneficial for the principal, given that the agent is acting noncooperatively to maximize his own utility.

Given the economist's familiarity with constrained optimization techniques, it is natural
to describe the principal's problem by a Lagrangian,

$$\mathcal{L} = \int_x v[z - \phi(x)]g[\xi(x - z)]\,dx - w(z) + \lambda \left\{ \int_x t[\phi(x)]g[\xi(x - z)]\,dx - u(z) - \bar{u} \right\}$$

$$- \mu \left\{ \xi \int_x t[\phi(x)]g'[\xi(x - z)]\,dx + u'(z) \right\}, \tag{12.20}$$

that incorporates the reservation utility constraint (12.18) and the first-order condition from
the agent's optimization problem, (12.16), in the principal's optimization problem.

This approach is not generally valid. For one thing, the first-order condition (12.16) does
not take account of the second-order condition that must be satisfied for (12.16) to identify
a local maximum of the agent's utility function. While every local maximum of the agent's
utility will satisfy (12.16), there may be values of z that satisfy (12.16) without being local
maxima; points of inflection and local minima are examples.

Even if this difficulty does not arise, there remains the possibility that the agent's problem
will have multiple equilibria for a fee schedule ϕ that solves the principal's problem. If there
are multiple equilibria to the agent's problem, then the solution to the principal's problem
would have to induce the agent to make the effort that is a global maximum for the agent's
problem. But there is nothing in (12.20) to ensure that the solution will move the agent to a
global maximum.[12]

But the first-order formalization of the principal–agent problem is valid if the solution to
(12.20) produces an agent's problem that has a unique solution.[13] In what follows, we assume
that this condition is met, and pursue the implications of the solution for the principal–agent
problem implied by (12.20).

Suppose first that $\phi > 0$. The first-order condition for maximization of (12.20) with
respect to ϕ is

$$\int_x (- v'g + \lambda t'g - \mu\xi t'g')\,dx \equiv 0. \tag{12.21}$$

This condition must hold for every value of the random variable x. The only way for this
to be true is if the term in parentheses under the integral sign is identically equal to zero. For
$\phi > 0$, therefore, the first-order condition for maximization of (12.20) is

$$\lambda - \frac{v'[z - \phi(x)]}{t'[\phi(x)]} = \mu\xi \frac{g'[\xi(x - z)]}{g[\xi(x - z)]}. \tag{12.22}$$

The first-order condition for optimization of (12.20) with respect to z is

$$\int_x (v'g - v\xi g')\,dx - \lambda \left(\xi \int_x tg'\,dx + u' \right) + \mu \left(\xi^2 \int_x tg''\,dx - u'' \right) \equiv 0. \tag{12.23}$$

But the coefficient of λ in (12.23) is zero, by the first-order condition for the agent's
problem, (12.16). Hence (12.23) can be solved for μ. It is generally the case that μ is greater

[12] For discussions, see Grossman and Hart (1983, pp. 7–9) or Rees (1987a, pp. 60–1).
[13] Grossman and Hart (1983, p. 8) attribute this result to Mirrlees (1975).

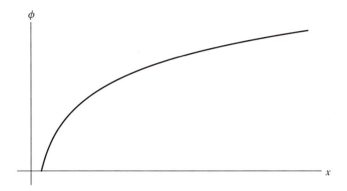

Figure 12.1 An optimal principal–agent fee schedule.

than 0, which implies that the reservation utility constraint is binding (Holmström, 1979). Optimization implies that the principal allows the agent to receive no more utility than would be possible in the agent's next best possible employment.

As an example, suppose that the random variable ε has a standard normal distribution, so that $g'/g = -\varepsilon$. Further, let the utility functions t and v exhibit constant absolute risk aversion, say[14]

$$t(\phi) = -\frac{1}{\alpha}e^{-\alpha\phi}, \qquad v(z-\phi) = -\frac{1}{\beta}e^{-\beta(z-\phi)}. \tag{12.24}$$

Substituting in (12.22) and rearranging terms, we obtain an expression for the fee schedule $\phi(x)$:

$$\phi = \frac{\beta z + \ln[\lambda + \mu(x-z)]}{\alpha + \beta}. \tag{12.25}$$

On the right in (12.25), λ, μ, and z are to be evaluated at the values implied by the solution to (12.20). The typical fee schedule of form (12.25) is shown in figure 12.1.

But (12.25) holds only if $\phi \geq 0$. If this is not the case, a Kuhn–Tucker-like argument shows that we must replace the equality in (12.21) by the inequality $\leq$. From (12.25), for the example that produces (12.24), $\phi \geq 0$ if and only if

$$x \geq z - \frac{\lambda - e^{-\beta z}}{\mu} \equiv x_0. \tag{12.26}$$

EXTENSIONS

Mirrlees (1976, pp. 127–30) outlines an adaptation of this model to address the questions of firm hierarchy and firm size. From the case of a single principal and a single agent, one can move to the case of a single principal and n agents. The principal selects the number of agents

---

[14] See, for example, Pratt (1964).

and sets a common fee schedule ϕ and a common level of monitoring effort ξ to maximize his own utility.

This model of a two-level organization can in turn be extended to a principal–agent model of hierarchy – the principal can monitor n first-level agents, each of which monitors n second-level agents, each of which monitors n third-level agents, and so on, until a final level of producing agents is reached. This is a principal–agent version of the Williamson (1967) model of hierarchy and firm size. It is a much more general model, since it endogenizes the span of control and makes explicit the way in which monitoring affects perceived effort. The formal structure of the model is also much more complex, and produces less general results. Although diseconomies of hierarchy may set in, and thus limit the size of the firm, this is not a necessary result. For some kinds of utility functions and monitoring technologies, control loss does not limit the size of the firm.

RESERVATIONS

Principal–agent models capture some of the central elements of the transaction cost theory of the firm. There is imperfect information, in that the principal cannot accurately observe the effort of the agent. There is the possibility of opportunistic behavior: the agent is assumed to act to maximize his own utility.

But the principal is assumed to know the agent's utility function, and to have enough calculating ability to devise a fee schedule that will induce the agent to do what the principal wants. Principal-agent models do not incorporate the bounded rationality aspect of the transaction cost theory of the firm.

It is probably accurate to describe the principal–agent approach as "the neoclassical response to questions regarding the behavior of an organization of self-interested agents with conflicting goals in a world of incomplete information" (Levinthal, 1988, p. 154). As a formalization of the transaction cost theory of the firm, it remains incomplete.

12.3 CORPORATE GOVERNANCE

12.3.1 The M-form hypothesis

The central argument of transaction cost theory is that firms rather than markets will be the vehicle for productive activity if it is more efficient – less costly – to carry out transactions within firms. But some ways of organizing transactions within firms may be more efficient than others.

There are many ways to organize transactions within firms. A small firm may be run by an owner–manager who makes all decisions for the firm. Other firms may be run as partnerships, and some such firms are quite large. For large industrial firms in particular, however, a more elaborate internal organization is likely to be needed.

Chandler (1962) traces the organizational development of management structure in large corporations in US industry.[15] A stylized version of his analysis is that:

1   a large firm requires a central administrative office to maintain operational efficiency;
2   a natural form of internal organization for a firm that operates mainly in one product or geographic market is along functional lines, with one production division, one sales division, one finance division, and so on;
3   but as a firm expands to several product or geographic markets, central management becomes so tied up in making operating decisions that strategic planning is neglected;
4   so it becomes more efficient to set up a separate operating division for each of the firm's product or geographic markets; operating decisions are taken at the division level, and corporate management occupies itself with strategic planning.

Williamson explains the efficiency advantage of the multidivisional, or M-form, firm in transaction cost terms (1975, p. 150):[16]

> The organization and operation of the large enterprise along the lines of the M-form favors goal pursuit and least-cost behavior more nearly associated with the neoclassical profit maximization hypothesis than does the U-form organizational alternative.

By allowing management to specialize (operating decisions taken at the divisional level, strategic decisions taken at corporate headquarters), the M-form of internal organization reduces the problem of bounded rationality, compared with a functional or unitary U-form of internal organization. The central office also enjoys advantages in monitoring divisional activities, allowing it to manage the problems of opportunism and subgoal pursuit. The corporate management of an M-form firm is also able to operate an internal capital market, collecting economic profits from all divisions of the firm and allocating them where, within the firm, they will yield the greatest return.

The operational superiority of the M-form firm over the U-form firm, at least for large firms, is a central tenet of transaction cost economics. Williamson is careful to emphasize the importance of substance over form. It is not enough to design an organization chart that shows a corporate headquarters with several independent operating divisions. Management responsibilities must actually be specialized in the way called for by the M-form hypothesis. A multidivisional organizational structure without strategic control from corporate headquarters is a holding company, an H-form firm, rather than an M-form firm.

12.3.2   Empirical evidence

Steer and Cable (1978) analyze the impact of organizational form and other variables on the profitability of a sample of 83 UK firms for the period 1967–71. Typical of their results is

---

[15] See also Bhargava (1973) and Chandler (1982).
[16] See Hill (1985a) for a critical summary of the M-form hypothesis.

the price–cost margin (PCM) or rate of return on sales equation:[17]

$$PCM = 0.0689 + 0.0233 \begin{cases} 1 \text{ if M-form} \\ 0 \text{ otherwise} \end{cases} + 0.00008 Size - \frac{0.0063}{KSR}, \tag{12.27}$$

where KSR is the firm's capital–sales ratio. The average price–cost margin in the sample was 6 percent. Steer and Cable's estimates imply that an M-form firm has a price–cost margin that is 2.33 percent greater than an otherwise identical firm with a U-form of internal organization. Their other results are consistent with this, and therefore provide strong support for the M-form hypothesis.

Teece (1981) puts together a sample of 20 US industries and, for each industry, measures the profitability of first and second leading firms to adopt the M-form of internal organization. Profitability is measured before and after the second firm adopted the M-form. If the M-form hypothesis is correct, the difference in profitability of the two firms should be reduced after the second firm adopts the M-form. Using nonparametric tests, Teece finds evidence that suggests that this is the case.

Cable and Dirrheimer (1983) present contrasting evidence for a sample of 48 West German firms for the early 1970s. They find a statistically significant reduction in the rate of return on capital for firms in the process of adopting an M-form, with a negative but statistically insignificant effect for firms with an M-form in place. They explain their results in terms of differences in management practices between West Germany and the UK or USA. In West Germany, they argue, there is a greater level of owner control and more profound involvement of banks in formulating corporate strategy. These factors tend to reduce discretionary behavior by management and promote the effective allocation of capital within the firm, even if an M-form of internal organization is not in place. But this reduces the differential efficiency of the M-form of internal organization.

12.4   BUSINESS GROUPS

Perhaps because the M-form hypothesis was developed by US scholars, it is formulated in a way that reflects the landscape of US economy in the late 20th century. But a kind of business group existed in US before the First World War. Investment banking firms took an active role in carrying out mergers that formed dominant industrial firms. Representatives of investment banking firms held seats on the boards of directors of horizontally and vertically related industrial companies, and took an active role in checking the performance of management.[18] De Long (1991) argues that the involvement of investment bankers served as a certification of management quality to investors. This is not unlike the strategic management role ascribed to corporate management in the M-form firm.

The Glass–Steagall Act of 1933[19] enforced a divorce between financial and industrial firms in USA. But the business group remains a characteristic form of organization in other

---

[17] Steer and Cable report a variety of alternative specifications; only statistically significant coefficients are reported here. Thompson (1981) reworks the Steer and Cable study using a stock market measure of profitability and concludes that it reflects frequent crises among H-form firms. Hill (1985b) is another study based on UK data.

[18] See Chernow (1990).

[19] Repealed in November 1999.

mature industrialized economies, even though it does not currently arise in USA. This is most prominently the case with Japan, where the zaibatsu and postwar keiretsu collected legally independent firms in webs of mutual shareholding, with a financial firm performing a prominent coordinating role (see Hirschmeier and Yui, 1981). Business groups also occur in Korea, Sweden, Germany, and France.

Chandler (1982) characterizes the M-form firm as the American version of a business group. Goto argues that the business group should be thought of as a way of organizing transactions that is intermediate between the firm and the market (1982, p. 61):

> From the standpoint of the firm, by forming or joining a group, it can economize on the transaction costs that it would have incurred if the transaction had been done through the market, and at the same time, it can avoid the scale diseconomies or control loss that would have occurred if it had expanded internally and performed that transaction within the firm.

Enderwick (1988) offers a similar interpretation of the role of Japanese general trading companies, which act to coordinate the activities of independent but loosely related supplying firms.

Cable and Yasuki (1985) carry out a test of the effects of internal organization and group membership on the profitability of 89 Japanese firms. They expect the potential gains from adoption of the M-form to be less in Japan than in UK or USA. This expectation is confirmed: there is no significant difference between the profitability of M-form firms and other firms, all else equal. In a regression with a large number of group-affiliation dummy variables, individual coefficients of the dummy variables were generally insignificant. An F-test did not reject deletion of all group dummy variables. Cable and Yasuki summarize their findings as follows (1985, p. 417):

> These results do not necessarily mean that M-firm, diversification and group membership are devoid of beneficial effects, but rather that . . . these do not systematically exceed those of alternative strategies and modes of organization available to Japanese firms.

Chang and Choi (1988) use a sample of data for 182 Korean firms to test the effect of group membership on profitability. They distinguish three types of groups:

- the four largest groups, which are vertically integrated and have an organization that mimics a multidivisional firm
- 20 groups with a multidivisional structure
- six groups without a multidivisional structure

When Chang and Choi measure profitability as a rate of return on equity, they estimate positive and significant coefficients for all three group membership dummies. Membership in one of the four largest groups has the largest and most significant coefficient. When they measure profitability as a rate of return on assets, it is only membership in one of the four largest groups that has a statistically significant positive effect on profitability.

They interpret their results as showing that, for Korean firms, group membership, particularly for groups that have a central strategic planning office, results in superior economic performance. Their results cannot distinguish the underlying cause of this superior economic performance. It could reflect a reduction in transaction costs, which is the interpretation that would be suggested by analogy with the M-form hypothesis. It could also reflect the barrier to entry effect of vertical integration, a factor emphasized by Chandler (1977, p. 364; 1982, pp. 6–7).[20]

Overall, empirical tests seem to indicate that the M-form of internal organization reduces transactions costs that stem from bounded rationality and opportunistic behavior. It also seems clear, however, that the merit of the M-form, relative to market transactions or to organizational links between quasi-independent firms, is highly culture-specific. For large US and UK firms, there appear to be efficiency advantages associated with the M-form. It is less clear that such advantages exist in other mature, industrialized economies.

12.5   X-INEFFICIENCY

Leibenstein[21] argues that welfare losses arising from the failure of firms to minimize cost substantially exceed welfare losses due to market power. In real-world firms, he argues, the contracts that define the employment relationship are inevitably incomplete. As a result, employees have some discretion in the way they carry out their jobs. Because monitoring by supervisors is imperfect, because supervisors have some discretion in the way they carry out their jobs, and because work involves disutility, employees will not carry out their jobs with maximum efficiency – they will not minimize costs. Firms' operations will therefore be inefficient, to some extent. The more competitive the market environment, however, the greater the pressure on employees up and down the firm hierarchy to minimize cost. Inefficiency ought to be less, therefore, the more competitive the market in which the firm operates.

Stigler (1976)[22] criticizes the theory of X-inefficiency. His reasoning is that, in the real world, it is costly to enforce contracts. What this means is that it will be efficient to monitor employees' performances until the value to the firm of a marginal increase in efficiency equals the marginal cost of an increase in monitoring effort. If there are costs of monitoring, Stigler argues, it is illogical to label the difference between the level of efficiency that is attainable in the real world and the level of efficiency that would be attainable if monitoring costs were zero "inefficiency."

It is only recently that economists have attempted to incorporate X-inefficiency into conventional models of oligopoly. We consider here two formal models. The first assumes the existence of X-inefficiency in a Cournot oligopoly model and examines the welfare consequences of entry. The results are broadly consistent with Leibenstein's arguments. The second is a principal–agent model of endogenous employee effort in Cournot oligopoly, which yields rather different results.

---

[20] See Joeng and Masson (1990) for a structure–conduct–performance analysis of Korean industrial profitability.
[21] See Leibenstein (1966, 1973, 1975, 1978, 1983) and Leibenstein and Maital (1994).
[22] See also De Alessi (1983) and Ashton (1987).

12.5.1 Organizational slack

Following Selten (1986), consider an n-firm Cournot oligopoly. The product is homogeneous and the inverse demand curve is linear:

$$p = a - b(q_1 + q_2 + \cdots + q_n). \tag{12.28}$$

Firm i's cost function is

$$c(q_i) = (c + \sigma_i)q_i + F, \qquad i = 1, 2, \ldots, n, \tag{12.29}$$

where F is fixed cost, c is the minimum value of marginal cost, and $\sigma_i \geq 0$ is organizational slack per unit of output for firm i.

This is a model of n-firm oligopoly with different marginal costs. Equilibrium output is found by solving the equations of the best-response curves of the n firms as a system of simultaneous equations. The result is

$$q_i = S_i - \frac{n}{n+1}\bar{S}, \tag{12.30}$$

where $S_i = (a - c - \sigma_i)/b$ and $\bar{S}$ is the average of the S_is. Firm i's profit is

$$\pi_i = b\,(q_i)^2 - F. \tag{12.31}$$

Suppose first that organizational slack is zero for all firms. Then if entry occurred until economic profit were zero, the number of firms in the market would be

$$n_{\max} = \frac{S_c}{\sqrt{F/b}} - 1, \tag{12.32}$$

for $S_c = (a - c)/b$.

To investigate the consequences of organizational slack, we now impose a strong form of symmetry: the slack rate is the same for all firms. Further, slack rates adjust until firm profit is zero. It follows from (12.31) that, in equilibrium,

$$\sigma = b\left[S_c - (n+1)\sqrt{\frac{F}{b}}\right]. \tag{12.33}$$

Correspondingly, equilibrium firm and market output are

$$q = \sqrt{\frac{F}{b}}, \qquad Q = n\sqrt{\frac{F}{b}}. \tag{12.34}$$

The equilibrium cost of organizational slack is σQ. Since organizational slack results from a failure on the part of employees to minimize cost, it is reasonable to regard some of the cost of this slack as generating utility for employees – inefficiency is in this sense consumption of the workplace. With this in mind, define a partial-equilibrium welfare measure for n-firm Cournot oligopoly with organizational slack as

$$W_n = CS + \sum_{i=1}^{n} \pi_i + \alpha \sigma Q, \tag{12.35}$$

where $CS = bQ^2/2$ is consumers' surplus, π_i is the profit of firm i, and α, $0 \leq \alpha \leq 1$, is a parameter that measures the extent to which employees derive utility from organizational slack.

Since we assume that organizational slack completely crowds out profit, (12.35) becomes

$$W_n = \tfrac{1}{2}n^2 F + n\alpha \left[S_c \sqrt{bF} - (n+1)F \right]. \tag{12.36}$$

Taking the derivative of W_n with respect to n gives

$$\frac{1}{F} \frac{\partial W_n}{\partial n} = (1 - \alpha)n + \alpha(n_{max} - n) \geq 0. \tag{12.37}$$

In this model, entry increases social welfare, so long as the number of firms is less than the maximum. This conclusion does not depend on the assumption that organizational slack is to some extent a consumption good. Even if $\alpha = 0$ in (12.37), W_n rises as n rises.

In Cournot oligopoly without organizational slack, economic profit falls as the number of firms increases. In this model, economic profits are frittered away in the form of organizational slack. As the number of firms increases, however, the leeway for such a failure to minimize cost is reduced. The result is that social welfare goes up as the number of firms goes up.

The weakness of this model is that it makes the degree of organizational slack exogenous. If the degree of organizational slack were endogenous, the way entry affects welfare would depend on the way entry affected the degree of organizational slack. If slack falls as the number of firms rises, however, the essential result of the model holds up: entry improves social welfare.

12.5.2   A principal–agent model of X-inefficiency[23]

Consider an industry supplied by n firms. The product is homogeneous and the inverse demand curve is linear. For each firm, there is an owner and a manager. Average and marginal cost for firm i is

$$c_i(i) = \alpha + \varepsilon_i e^{-L_i}, \tag{12.38}$$

where $\alpha > 0$ is a constant, ε_i is a nonnegative random variable, and L_i is the labor of the manager of firm i. Without loss of generality, suppose that $\underline{\varepsilon} \leq \varepsilon_i \leq \bar{\varepsilon}$ and that ε_i has a continuous density function $f(\varepsilon_i)$.

The manager of the firm observes ε_i and L_i, and the owner of the firm observes neither. The owner of the firm indirectly controls the manager's actions by establishing a cost target

[23] Martin (1993a); see also Baron and Myerson (1982), Willig (1987), and Bartoletti and Poletti (1996) for a comment and extension.

$c(\hat{\varepsilon}_i)$ and a fee schedule $\phi(\hat{\varepsilon}_i)$ that depend on the value of the random variable that the manager reports to the owner.

The manager must achieve the cost target if he is to receive any fee at all. Thus

$$c(\hat{\varepsilon}_i) = \alpha + \varepsilon_i e^{-L_i}, \tag{12.39}$$

so that the manager's labor is

$$L_i = \ln \varepsilon_i - \ln[c(\hat{\varepsilon}_i) - \alpha]. \tag{12.40}$$

If the true value of the random cost element is ε_i and the manager reports a value $\hat{\varepsilon}_i$, the manager's utility is

$$U(\hat{\varepsilon}_i \mid \varepsilon_i) = \phi(\hat{\varepsilon}_i) - \lambda L_i. \tag{12.41}$$

The manager selects L_i to maximize (12.41). The owner of the firm, unable to observe ε_i directly, maximizes his expected payoff, which equals firm profits minus the fee $\phi(\hat{\varepsilon}_i)$ paid to the manager.

Feasibility

Analysis of the problem is much simplified by use of the revelation principle, which is that the solution to the owner's problem can be obtained by restricting the owner to fee schedules that induce the manager to report the random cost component truthfully.[24]

Assume that the manager's reservation utility is zero. A fee schedule $\phi_i(\hat{\varepsilon}_i)$ and cost target $c_i(\hat{\varepsilon}_i)$ are feasible if

$$U(\varepsilon_i \mid \varepsilon_i) \geq U(\hat{\varepsilon}_i \mid \varepsilon_i), \underline{\varepsilon} \leq \hat{\varepsilon}_i \leq \bar{\varepsilon} \tag{12.42}$$

and

$$U(\varepsilon_i \mid \varepsilon_i) \geq 0. \tag{12.43}$$

From (12.41), we obtain

$$U(\hat{\varepsilon}_i \mid \varepsilon_i) - U(\hat{\varepsilon}_i \mid \hat{\varepsilon}_i) = \lambda(\ln \hat{\varepsilon}_i - \ln \varepsilon_i). \tag{12.44}$$

Then (12.42) gives

$$U(\varepsilon_i \mid \varepsilon_i) \geq U(\hat{\varepsilon}_i \mid \hat{\varepsilon}_i) + \lambda(\ln \hat{\varepsilon}_i - \ln \varepsilon_i), \tag{12.45}$$

from which

$$U(\varepsilon_i \mid \varepsilon_i) - U(\hat{\varepsilon}_i \mid \hat{\varepsilon}_i) \geq \lambda(\ln \hat{\varepsilon}_i - \ln \varepsilon_i). \tag{12.46}$$

If we run through the same arguments, reversing the roles of ε_i and $\hat{\varepsilon}_i$, we obtain

$$\lambda(\ln \hat{\varepsilon}_i - \ln \varepsilon_i) \geq U(\varepsilon_i \mid \varepsilon_i) - U(\hat{\varepsilon}_i \mid \hat{\varepsilon}_i). \tag{12.47}$$

---

[24] The following explanation is due to Baron and Myerson (1982, p. 913). For any fee schedule ϕ, let $\Psi(\varepsilon)$ be the value of ε that the manager reports if the true value of the random cost component is ε. Then consider a new fee schedule: if the manager reports $\hat{\varepsilon}_i$, the owner computes $\Psi(\hat{\varepsilon}_i)$, and pays the manager the fee that would have been paid under the original fee schedule ϕ if $\Psi(\hat{\varepsilon}_i)$ had been reported. This will induce the manager to report truthfully. See also Dasgupta, Hammond, and Maskin (1979).

But (12.46) and (12.47) can both be true only if both hold with equality; thus any feasible fee function and cost structure must produce a manager's utility that satisfies

$$U(\varepsilon_i \mid \varepsilon_i) - U(\hat{\varepsilon}_i \mid \hat{\varepsilon}_i) = \lambda(\ln \hat{\varepsilon}_i - \ln \varepsilon_i). \tag{12.48}$$

Since (12.48) is true for all ε_i and $\hat{\varepsilon}_i$, it is true for $\hat{\varepsilon}_i = \bar{\varepsilon}$. Substituting $\hat{\varepsilon}_i = \bar{\varepsilon}$ in (12.48) and rearranging terms, we obtain

$$U(\varepsilon_i \mid \varepsilon_i) = U(\bar{\varepsilon} \mid \bar{\varepsilon}) + \lambda \ln \left(\frac{\bar{\varepsilon}}{\varepsilon_i} \right). \tag{12.49}$$

Since $\bar{\varepsilon} \geq \varepsilon_i$, the last term on the right-hand side in (12.49) is positive. A feasible fee schedule and cost target will give the manager greater utility, the closer ε_i is to the lowest possible value. No fee schedule with $U(\bar{\varepsilon} \mid \bar{\varepsilon}) > 0$ could be optimal for the principal, since the principal could always switch to a less costly feasible fee schedule that would make $U(\bar{\varepsilon} \mid \bar{\varepsilon}) = 0$ and still satisfy $U(\varepsilon_i \mid \varepsilon_i) > 0$ for all ε_i.

An optimal feasible fee schedule therefore satisfies

$$U(\varepsilon_i \mid \varepsilon_i) = \lambda(\ln \bar{\varepsilon} - \ln \varepsilon_i). \tag{12.50}$$

Any feasible fee schedule/cost target pair satisfies (12.50). Now let a fee schedule satisfy (12.50). It is immediate that $U(\varepsilon_i \mid \varepsilon_i) > 0$, which is one of the elements of feasibility. Combining (12.40) and (12.41) gives

$$U(\hat{\varepsilon}_i \mid \varepsilon_i) = \phi(\hat{\varepsilon}_i) - \lambda \ln \varepsilon_i + \lambda \ln[c(\hat{\varepsilon}_i) - \alpha]. \tag{12.51}$$

Using (12.51), one finds that

$$U(\hat{\varepsilon}_i \mid \varepsilon_i) - U(\hat{\varepsilon}_i \mid \hat{\varepsilon}_i) = \lambda(\ln \hat{\varepsilon}_i - \ln \varepsilon_i). \tag{12.52}$$

But (12.50) and (12.52) yield

$$U(\hat{\varepsilon}_i \mid \varepsilon_i) = \lambda[\ln \bar{\varepsilon} - \ln \varepsilon_i] = U(\varepsilon_i \mid \varepsilon_i). \tag{12.53}$$

But this is the other element of feasibility. This establishes that a fee schedule/cost target pair is feasible if and only if it satisfies (12.50).

Using (12.40) and (12.41), we obtain a relation between a feasible fee schedule, cost target pair:

$$\phi_i(\varepsilon_i) = \lambda \ln \left[\frac{\bar{\varepsilon}}{c_i(\varepsilon_i) - \alpha} \right]. \tag{12.54}$$

This will be used to express the principal's optimization problem in terms of the cost target alone.

Product–market equilibrium

The market is an n-firm Cournot oligopoly with cost differences. The realized value of firm 1's profit is

$$V_1 = b\left(S_1 - \frac{n}{n+1}\bar{S}\right)^2 - \phi(\varepsilon_i), \tag{12.55}$$

where $S_1 = [a - c(\varepsilon_i)/b]$ and $\bar{S}$ is the average of all the S_i or, equivalently,

$$V_1 = \frac{1}{b(n+1)^2}\left\{a - \alpha - n[c(\varepsilon_1) - \alpha] + \sum_{j=2}^{n}[c(\varepsilon_j) - \alpha]\right\}^2 - \lambda\ln\bar{\varepsilon} + \lambda\ln[c(\varepsilon_1) - \alpha], \tag{12.56}$$

if profit is expressed in terms of the cost target.

Imputing Cournot-like behavior to the principal of firm 1, we suppose that he picks a cost target $c_1(\varepsilon_1)$ to maximize his expected payoff, taking the cost targets of other firms as given.

The principal of firm 1 thus seeks to maximize

$$E(V_1) = \frac{1}{b(n+1)^2}$$

$$\times \int_{\varepsilon_1}\cdots\int_{\varepsilon_n}\left\{a - \alpha - n[c_1(\varepsilon_1) - \alpha] + \sum_{j=2}^{n}[c_j(\varepsilon_j) - \alpha]\right\}^2 f(\varepsilon_n)\dots f(\varepsilon_1)\,\mathrm{d}\varepsilon_n\dots\mathrm{d}\varepsilon_1$$

$$- \lambda\ln\bar{\varepsilon} + \lambda\int_{\varepsilon_1}\ln[c_1(\varepsilon_1) - \alpha]f(\varepsilon_1)\,\mathrm{d}\varepsilon_1. \tag{12.57}$$

The Euler equation of the calculus of variations shows that the first-order necessary condition for maximization of (12.57) is found by differentiating under the integral signs with respect to $c_1(\varepsilon_1)$ and setting the result equal to zero. The first-order condition is

$$-\frac{2n}{(b+1)^2}\left\{a - \alpha - n[c_1(\varepsilon_1) - \alpha] + \sum_{j=2}^{n}[E(c_j(\varepsilon_j)) - \alpha]\right\} + \frac{\lambda}{c_1(\varepsilon_1) - \alpha} \equiv 0, \tag{12.58}$$

where E denotes expected value.

For notational simplicity, write

$$a^* = a - \alpha, \qquad c_j^* = c_j - \alpha. \tag{12.59}$$

Then (12.58) can be rewritten as a quadratic equation in c_1^*:

$$n(c_1^*)^2 - \left[a^* + \sum_{j=2}^{n}E(c_j^*)\right]c_1^* + \frac{(n+1)^2}{2n}b\lambda = 0. \tag{12.60}$$

This is the equation of firm 1's cost target best-response surface.

Table 12.1 Equilibrium values,
Cournot principal–agent model ($b = 1$,
$a = 10, \alpha = 1, \bar{\varepsilon} = 1$)

n	c^*	ϕ	V
2	0.2574	1.3573	7.1354
3	0.3068	1.1817	3.5416
4	0.3618	1.0168	1.9680
5	0.4196	0.8686	1.1766

Equation (12.60) defines the principal's payoff-maximizing c_1^* as a function of n, a^*, and the expected values of the fees offered to other firms' managers. But this equation holds for all values of ε_1 in the interval $(\underline{\varepsilon}, \bar{\varepsilon})$. Thus for the technology (12.38) the optimal cost target is a constant, independent of the realized value of ε_1. By (12.54), the fee schedule that is optimal for the principal is also constant.

Since the optimal cost target is a constant, $c_1^* = E(c_1^*)$. Substituting in (12.60) yields the equation of a best-response surface that defines principal 1's payoff-maximizing fee as a function of n, a^*, and the fees offered to other firms' managers.

Since firms are identical as regards the distribution of the random part of cost, managers' utility functions, and principals' utility functions, in equilibrium all principals select the same cost target. Imposing symmetry in (12.60) gives an equation that is satisfied by the cost target that is optimal for the principals:

$$\left(c^*\right)^2 - a^*c^* + \frac{(n+1)^2}{2n}b\lambda = 0. \tag{12.61}$$

The root of (12.61) that maximizes principals' payoffs is

$$c^* = \tfrac{1}{2}\left\{ a^* - \sqrt{(a^*)^2 - 2\frac{(n+1)^2}{n}b\lambda} \right\}. \tag{12.62}$$

From (12.62),

$$2\frac{\partial c^*}{\partial n} = \left(b\lambda\frac{n^2 - 1}{n^2}\right)\left[(a^*)^2 - 2\frac{(n+1)^2}{n}b\lambda\right]^{-1/2} > 0. \tag{12.63}$$

In this principal–agent model of managerial effort to minimize costs, costs rise with the number of firms.

A numerical example is shown in table 12.1. In this Cournot principal–agent model, the cost target rises as the number of firms rises. The manager's fee and the principal's payoff fall as the number of firms rises.

These results are just opposite to those which would be predicted by X-inefficiency theory. But, in the context of the model, they are not hard to understand. The principal sets a fee schedule, cost target pair that maximizes his expected return. The profit-maximizing pair will set the principal's marginal revenue equal to the marginal increase in the agent's fee, subject to constraints. But marginal revenue will be less, all else equal, the greater is the number of firms in the market. The greater the number of firms, therefore, the smaller is the incentive of the principal to set a high fee schedule and induce the agent to invest a great deal of labor in minimizing cost.

12.6 HORIZONTAL MERGERS[25]

12.6.1 Losses from horizontal merger?

Following Salant et al. (1983), consider an n-firm Cournot oligopoly with a homogeneous product, market inverse demand curve $p = a - bQ$, and constant marginal and average cost c per unit. From Problem 2.1, equilibrium price, output per firm, and profit per firm are

$$p = c + \frac{S}{n+1}, \qquad q = \frac{S}{n+1}, \qquad \pi = b\left(\frac{S}{n+1}\right)^2, \qquad (12.64)$$

for $S = (a - c)/b$.

Suppose that firms 1 through m, for $m < n$, merge. The new firm picks $q_1, q_2, \ldots,$ and q_m to maximize profit

$$\pi(m) = \sum_{i=1}^{m} (p - c)q_i = (p - c)\sum_{i=1}^{m} q_i = (p - c)Q_m, \qquad (12.65)$$

where $Q_m = q_1 + q_2 + \cdots + q_m$ is total output of the post-merger firm. From the equation of the inverse demand curve is

$$p - c = b[S - (Q_m + q_{m+1} + \cdots + q_n)]. \qquad (12.66)$$

It follows that the best-response function of the post-merger firm is

$$2Q_m + q_{m+1} + \cdots + q_n = S. \qquad (12.67)$$

But this is just the best-response function of a single firm in an $(n - m + 1)$-firm Cournot oligopoly. The best-response functions of the independent firms are unchanged by the merger, and the post-merger equilibrium is that of Cournot oligopoly with $n - m + 1$ equally sized firms. Selected equilibrium characteristics of the post-merger market are shown in table 12.2.

Firms that are outside the merger are better off because of the merger – they produce more, and they earn a greater profit on every unit they sell. But the firms that merge are

---

[25] See the March 1989 issue of the *International Journal of Industrial Organization* and the symposium on horizontal mergers and antitrust in the Fall 1987 issue of the *Journal of Economic Perspectives*.

Table 12.2   Selected post–merger equilibrium
characteristics, Salant–Switzer–Reynolds model

Price	$c + \dfrac{bS}{n - m + 2}$	
Firms	$1, \ldots, m$	$m + 1, \ldots, n$
Output	$\dfrac{1}{m} \dfrac{S}{n - m + 2}$	$\dfrac{S}{n - m + 2}$
Profit	$\dfrac{b}{m} \left(\dfrac{S}{n - m + 2} \right)^2$	$b \left(\dfrac{S}{n - m + 2} \right)^2$

Table 12.3   The smallest profitable merger size, Cournot
oligopoly; n = number of firms in industry; m = smallest
number of firms for which a merger would be privately
profitable

n	3	4	5	6	7	8	9	10	11	12
m	3	4	5	6	6	7	8	9	10	10

better off only if

$$\frac{b}{m} \left(\frac{S}{n - m + 2} \right)^2 > b \left(\frac{S}{n + 1} \right)^2 \tag{12.68}$$

or if

$$(n + 1)^2 > m(n - m + 2)^2. \tag{12.69}$$

This condition is quite restrictive. As shown in table 12.3, if there are six or fewer firms, a merger must include all firms to be profitable for participating firms. If there are seven through 11 firms, at most one firm can be excluded from a merger if it is to be profitable for participating firms.[26]

But this sort of combination is decidedly unlike real-world mergers. In the linear inverse demand, constant marginal cost Cournot model, m firms combine and in the post-merger market produce together as much as a firm that does not participate in the merger. It is the response of firms outside the merger to this output restriction that renders the merger unprofitable unless it includes all or almost all firms in the industry. It is more realistic to expect that merging firms will produce more, after the merger, than firms that do not combine.

Perry and Porter (1985) model this type of merger. In their model, a firm's cost function depends on the amount of capital it owns, and capital is in fixed supply to the industry. A merger combines the capital of the constituent firms in the survivor firm. In equilibrium, the survivor firm is larger than firms not involved in the merger.

---

[26] Deneckere and Davidson (1985) show that mergers in price-setting oligopoly with product differentiation are profitable, if demand is linear.

12.6.2   Welfare effects of horizontal mergers

A merger might be profitable because the survivor firm, without being more efficient than parent firms, has greater market power. In this case, a merger is likely to reduce consumer welfare and social welfare. Or a merger might be profitable because the survivor firm is more efficient than parent firms. Even if such a merger increases market power, cost savings create the possibility that the overall effect of the merger on market performance will be positive.

Farrell and Shapiro (1990a) conclude that mergers are likely to harm consumers unless cost savings are very great.[27] In their model, the profit of a single firm is

$$\pi_i = p(q_i + Q_{-i})q_i - c_i(q_i), \tag{12.70}$$

where Q_{-i} is the output of all firms except firm i. Cost functions are allowed to differ across firms. The first-order condition for maximization of π_i,

$$p(Q) + q_i p'(Q) - c_i'(q_i) \equiv 0, \tag{12.71}$$

(where Q is total output and a prime denotes the derivative) implicitly defines firm i's best-response function.

Differentiating (12.71), the slope of firm i's best-response function is

$$\frac{dq_i}{dQ_{-i}} = -\frac{p' + q_i p''}{2p' + q_i p'' - c_i''} < 0. \tag{12.72}$$

The denominator of the fraction on the right-hand side in (12.72) is negative by the second-order condition for profit maximization. The numerator is the derivative of firm i's marginal revenue, $MR_i = p + q_i p'$, with respect to the output of other firms. We assume that this is negative. This means that an increase in the output of all other firms reduces firm i's marginal revenue and guarantees that firm i's best-response curve slopes downward.

It is useful to investigate the relation between a change in one firm's output and the resulting change in total output. From (12.72),

$$\frac{dQ}{dQ_{-i}} = 1 + \frac{dq_i}{dQ_{-i}} = \frac{p' - c_i''}{2p' + q_i p'' - c_i''} > 0. \tag{12.73}$$

The numerator of (12.73) is negative if the firm's residual demand curve intersects its marginal cost curve from above, which we henceforth assume. Given this assumption, if all firms but one increase output, total output increases, even though the remaining firm reduces its output.

Using (12.72) and (12.73), we define

$$\lambda_i = -\frac{dq_i/dQ_{-i}}{dQ/dQ_{-i}} = \frac{p' + q_i p''}{p' - c_i''} > 0. \tag{12.74}$$

λ_i is the decrease in firm i's output as a fraction of the increase in total output if all other firms increase their output.

---

[27] See also Werden (1991) and Farrell and Shapiro (1991).

The fact that the λ_is are positive implies that if firm i changes its output and all other firms adjust output along their best response curves, total output changes in the same direction as firm i's output, but the absolute value of the change in total output is less than the absolute value of the change in firm i's output.[28] It follows that to analyze the impact of a merger on total output, and therefore on price, it is necessary only to determine the impact of the merger on the output of the firms involved in the merger.

Now suppose that the first m firms merge. Let pre-merger outputs be q_i, $i = 1, \ldots, n$, with total pre-merger output $\bar{Q}$ and Q_M the pre-merger output of the firms that merge. At the pre-merger output, the marginal revenue of the survivor firm is

$$MR_M(Q_M) = p(\bar{Q}) + \bar{Q}_M p'(\bar{Q}). \tag{12.75}$$

The firm produced by the merger will reduce output, compared with the combined pre-merger output of its component firms, if and only if its marginal cost exceeds its marginal revenue, or if and only if

$$c'_M(\bar{Q}_M) > p(\bar{Q}) + Q_M p'(\bar{Q}), \tag{12.76}$$

which is the same as

$$-\bar{Q}_M p'(\bar{Q}) > p(\bar{Q}) - c'_M(\bar{Q}_M). \tag{12.77}$$

But the pre-merger first-order condition for firm i implies

$$p(\bar{Q}) - c'_i(\bar{q}_i) = -\bar{q}_i p'(\bar{Q}) \tag{12.78}$$

for $i = 1, 2, \ldots, m$, which in turn gives

$$-\bar{Q}_M p'(\bar{Q}) = -\left(\sum_{i=1}^{m} \bar{q}_i\right) p'(\bar{Q}) = \sum_{i=1}^{m} [p(\bar{Q}) - c'_i(\bar{q}_i)]. \tag{12.79}$$

Substituting (12.79) in (12.77), the firm formed by merger will raise price, and consumer welfare will fall, if and only if

$$\sum_{i=1}^{m} [p(\bar{Q}) - c'_i(\bar{q}_i)] > p(\bar{Q}) - c'_M(\bar{Q}_M). \tag{12.80}$$

But the cost reductions that followed from a merger would have to be very large indeed for this condition to be violated. Consider a merger of two firms. The condition (12.80) implies

---

[28] Since $dq_j = -\lambda_j dQ$, $dQ_{-i} = \sum_{j \neq i} q_j = -\left(\sum_{j \neq i} \lambda_j\right) dQ$. Then $dQ = dq_i + dQ_{-i} = dq_i - \left(\sum_{j \neq i} \lambda_j\right) dQ$, from which

$$\frac{dQ}{dq_i} = \left(1 + \sum_{j \neq i} \lambda_j\right)^{-1}.$$

Since the λ_j coefficients are positive, $0 < dQ/dq_i < 1$.

that the post-merger price will fall, benefiting consumers, if and only if

$$p(\bar{Q}) - c'_M(\bar{q}_i) \geq p(\bar{Q}) - c'_1(\bar{q}_1) + p(\bar{Q}) - c'_2(\bar{q}_2) \qquad (12.81)$$

or if

$$c'_1(\bar{q}_1) - c'_M(\bar{q}_i) \geq p(\bar{Q}) - c'_2(\bar{q}_2). \qquad (12.82)$$

Without loss of generality, let $c'_1(\bar{q}_1) < c'_2(\bar{q}_2)$. Relation (12.82) implies that for a merger to reduce price and benefit consumers, the marginal cost of the most efficient pre-merger firm would have to exceed the marginal cost of the post-merger firm by at least the profit margin of the least efficient pre-merger firm, with costs and margins evaluated at pre-merger outputs.[29]

This suggests that mergers will almost always harm consumers. The net welfare effect of a merger will therefore usually depend on a tradeoff between harm to consumers and benefit to the owners of the firms involved in the merger (Williamson, 1968b).

12.6.3   Empirical evidence on the effects of horizontal mergers[30]

Baker and Bresnahan (1988) estimate demand curves for Anheuser-Busch, the leading US beer brewer, and two smaller firms in the same industry, Pabst and Coors. Their results imply that a merger between either of the smaller firms and Anheuser-Busch would increase market power for Anheuser-Busch, without increasing market power for the other party to the merger. Similarly, a merger between the two smaller firms is not predicted to yield an increase in market power. These results suggest that competition from these smaller firms limits the ability of Anheuser-Busch to exercise market power.

Additional evidence that horizontal mergers can reinforce market power comes from Barton and Sherman (1984), who examine the effect of two successive mergers on the relative price of differentiated brands of microfilm. A 1976 merger increased the market share of the industry's dominant firm in the diazo microfilm market from 40 to 55 percent, and the price of diazo microfilm products rose nearly 10 percent, relative to the price of vesicular microfilm products. In 1979, a second merger increased the dominant firm's share of the vesicular microfilm market from 67 to 93 percent, and the price of vesicular microfilm products rose more than a third relative to the price of diazo microfilm products.

---

[29] For the left-hand side of (12.82) to be positive, the merger must reduce marginal cost, in the sense that $c'_1(q_1) > c'_M(Q_M)$. If this does not happen, the merger must raise price and leave consumers worse off. Farrell and Shapiro obtain a stronger result: if the merger creates no new efficiencies, in the sense that the post-merger cost function is the lower envelope of the sum of the cost functions of the constituent firms, then the merger causes price to increase.

[30] See Dutz (1989) for an analysis of mergers in declining industries, with applications to the US steel, railroad, brewing, and auto parts industries.

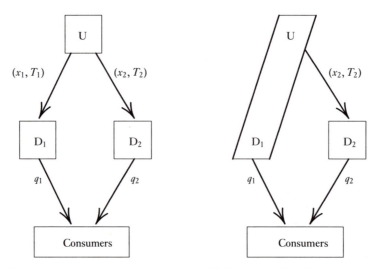

Figure 12.2 Alternative vertical market structures. (a) Nonintegration; (b) integration.

12.7 VERTICAL MERGERS AND VERTICAL FORECLOSURE[31,32]

A common theme of recent work on tight vertical relationships between manufacturers and distributors views them as a precondition for the exercise of market power at either vertical level. Without tight vertical relationships, a producer with some market power is unable to make a credible commitment to downstream distributors that it will restrict output. The inability of a producer to commit not to sell to multiple distributors limits the willingness of any one distributor to accept its portion of an overall package of offers that would yield the producer monopoly profit.[33] Vertical integration – or vertical contracts that have the effect of credibly committing the producer to limit its own future actions – allows the producer to fully exploit its market power.

In the market of figure 12.2(a), an upstream firm U produces an input at constant average and marginal cost, which we normal to zero. Each unit of the input is costlessly transformed by downstream firms D_1 and D_2 into a unit of a homogeneous final good. The final good is sold to consumers with decreasing inverse demand $P(q)$, where $q = q_1 + q_2$ and q_i is the output of D_i. Firms D_1 and D_2 engage in Cournot competition. U makes take-it-or-leave-it contract offers (x_i, T_i) simultaneously to D_i, $i = 1, 2$, where x_i is the quantity of input offered to D_i and T_i is the payment demanded for the bundle.

If the contract offers are public, so that D_1 observes the contract U offers to D_2 and vice versa, then U can obtain the monopoly profit by offering half the monopoly output to each

---

[31] This section follows Martin et al. (1999), which in turn relies on Rey and Tirole (forthcoming).

[32] Modeling vertical mergers in a linear Cournot framework tends to be tedious, involving as it does models of two vertically related oligopolies. See Salinger (1988, 1989), Ordover et al. (1990), and Martin and Schrader (1998).

[33] This is similar to the problem facing a durable-good monopolist, where an inability to commit to high future prices limits the current price that can be charged.

downstream firm for a flat fee that is half the monopoly profit – contracts $(q_m/2, \Pi_m/2)$ to each D_i, where q_m and Π_m respectively denote the monopoly quantity and profit in the market. Each downstream firm breaks even if it accepts the contract (buying the amount of the input offered, transforming it into final product and selling everything they produce at the monopoly price), so it should be willing to do so.

If the contracts are secret, the upstream firm cannot obtain the monopoly profit. Consider a case in which U offers $(q_m/2, \Pi_m/2)$ to D_2, and D_2 accepts the contract. U is then in the position of one party in a collusive agreement: taking D_2's sales as given and equal to $q_m/2$, U then can offer D_1 the quantity that maximizes U's payoff along the residual demand curve left after D_2 has sold the output for which it has contracted (and offering D_1 a fee T_2 that will allow D_1 a small positive profit). Such a deviation from the offer pair $(q_m/2, \Pi_m/2)$ would leave both U and D_1 better off.[34] Realizing this, D_2 would not accept the offer $(q_m/2, \Pi_m/2)$ in the first place. With secret contract offers, it is not an equilibrium for the downstream firms to accept contract offers $(q_m/2, \Pi_m/2)$.

The nature of equilibrium in the secret-contracts case depends on the beliefs of a downstream firm that receives an out-of-equilibrium offer. If a downstream firm faced with an out-of-equilibrium offer believes that its rival has received the equilibrium offer – which Rey and Tirole call passive beliefs – then in equilibrium the producer offers each downstream firm an amount of the input that just allows it to produce the Cournot duopoly equilibrium output, charging a fee that is just equal to the Cournot duopoly profit of a single firm. The distributors break even by accepting such a contract offer, so they should be willing to accept it. But the producer could increase its profit from the Cournot duopoly to the monopoly level if it can commit to output restriction.

One way for the producer to make such a commitment is by using public contracts. Yet another commitment mechanism is to use an exclusive dealing arrangement with a single distributor. Another is to integrate vertically, as in figure 12.2(b). Vertical merger can enable a producer to increase its ability to exercise market power.

12.7.1 Other market power explanations of vertical integration

A vertically integrated firm that controls or influences the upstream price of a necessary input can place nonintegrated rivals in the downstream market at a competitive disadvantage by increasing the price of the intermediate good. Adams and Dirlam (1964) present a classic analysis of this type of vertical price squeeze in the US steel industry.

Chandler emphasizes the entry-barrier creating effect of vertical integration, particularly forward integration into distribution (1977, p. 364).[35] In his review of US business history, he finds that few firms achieved horizontal dominance without integrating vertically. The combination of production and distribution within a single enterprise constituted a barrier

---

[34] This is easy to see for the case of linear inverse demand; Rey and Tirole (forthcoming) show that it holds in the case of concave inverse demand.
[35] See also Adams (1974).

to entry that successful rivals were obliged to imitate, leading in turn to high levels of concentration on the supply side of the market.

12.7.2   Distortions in input choice

In the model of market foreclosure outlined above, the technology is one of fixed coefficients, in the sense that exactly one unit of the intermediate good is required to produce a unit of the final product. If the technology for production of the final good permits substitution among inputs, then an intermediate good producer that raises price will induce substitution away from its own product. By integrating forward into final good production, such a producer can guarantee input choice based on relative marginal costs at the final good level, increasing efficiency and its own profit.[36]

12.7.3   Information and uncertainty

Arrow (1975) shows that if input supply is random and upstream producers have more information about realized supply, downstream producers will have an incentive to integrate backward to improve the quality of their information about the input market. Carlton (1979) presents a model in which it is final demand that is uncertain. Uncertain final demand translates into uncertain input demand. There is thus the possibility that aggregate input production and aggregate derived demand will be "out of sync": either too much of the input will be produced, in which case it would have to be discarded or stored in inventory, or else not enough of the input will be produced, implying an input shortage and a constraint on production of the final product. This potential lack of synchronization between input supply and input demand creates an incentive for firms to integrate vertically.

12.7.4   Price discrimination[37]

If a firm has market power, it is profitable to discriminate in price between classes of customers with different price elasticities of demand. This provides an explanation for the fact that Japanese automobiles cost more in Japan than in Europe, an explanation that has nothing to do with dumping. A necessary condition for this practice to be possible is that higher-elasticity consumers, who are offered a lower price, be unable to engage in arbitrage – unable to purchase for resale to lower-elasticity consumers. If an input-producing firm sells to firms with different elasticities, it can effectively price discriminate by integrating forward to high-elasticity segments of the final market and supplying low-elasticity segments at a profit-maximizing, higher, price. If input proportions are variable, this explanation for vertical integration overlaps with the explanation for vertical integration based on avoidance of distortions in input choice.

---

[36] See Vernon and Graham (1971) and Schmalensee (1973).
[37] See Gould (1977), Perry (1978), or Romano (1988).

12.7.5   Transaction costs

The transaction cost theory of the firm, which we have discussed above, is in one application a theory of vertical integration.[38] When repeated transactions involve the investment
of sunk assets by the purchaser, what was initially the selection of one of many potential suppliers is transformed into a bilateral monopoly situation. Given the expectation of
opportunistic behavior by the supplier, the purchaser should expect the supplier to seek to
renegotiate the terms of the agreement, over time, to the benefit of the supplier. To avoid
the potential loss of investment in sunk assets, there is an incentive to take the supplier into
the firm.[39]

12.7.6   Empirical studies of vertical integration[40]

Hennart (1988a, pp. 282–3) uses transaction cost theory to compare the extent of upstream
vertical integration in the aluminum and tin industries. Transaction cost theory predicts
greater vertical integration the smaller the number of actual or potential trading partners,
the greater the investment in sunk assets necessary to support a type of transaction, and the
greater the uncertainty associated with the transaction. Vertical integration should be less,
all else equal, the greater the differences between upstream and downstream markets and the
greater the cost of monitoring employees within the firm.

The aluminum industry is virtually a paradigmatic example of the transaction cost theory
of vertical integration. Operation of a minimum efficient scale bauxite mine requires a
substantial and largely sunk investment. Because bauxite is bulky and costly to ship, it is
not economically feasible to ship it to distant refineries.

At the same time, bauxite is a heterogeneous ore, and alumina refineries tend to be designed
for a specific type of ore. A bauxite supplier and an independent alumina refiner would
very quickly find themselves locked into a bilateral monopoly relationship, with large sunk
investments at stake. Not surprisingly, Hennart reports that, in 1976, 91 percent of bauxite,
by volume, was refined within vertically integrated firms.

There are two main types of tin-bearing deposits. Erosion of tin-bearing rock builds up
low-grade alluvial deposits that lie near the surface and can be refined with a standardized
technology. Mineral deposits tend to be underground, requiring a greater investment for
efficient operation and producing an ore that requires specific tailoring of refining operations.
As the transaction cost theory would predict, extraction and refining of alluvial deposits tend
to be carried out by independent firms, while processing of mineral deposits is for the most
part vertically integrated.

Masten et al. (1989) emphasize the importance of investment in specific human capital
as an incentive to integrate vertically. Using information on 118 motor vehicle components

---

[38] See Williamson (1971; 1985, chs 4 and 5; 1986), Crocker (1983), and Casson (1984).

[39] See, however, Bonanno and Vickers (1988) and Lin (1988), who develop models in which it is profitable for
manufacturers to sell through independent distributors. See also the Mathewson and Winter (1985) and Minkler
(1990) discussions of franchising.

[40] See also Anderson and Schmittlein (1984).

used by Chrysler, Ford, and General Motors, they estimate the equation

$$VI1 = 10.47 + 4.45HC + 0.92ASSET - 2.29SITE, \qquad R^2 = 0.36. \qquad (12.83)$$

The dependent variable, $VI1$, is the percentage of the company's component needs that are produced within the firm. The independent variables are measured on a scale from 1 (low) to 10 (high). HC measures the extent to which a transaction requires transaction specific human capital. Similarly, $ASSET$ measures the importance of transaction-specific physical assets, and $SITE$ measures the importance of locating successive stages of production close to one another.

The estimated coefficient of HC is statistically significant at the 1 percent level. No other estimated coefficient is statistically significant at even the 5 percent level. This test therefore suggests that it is the need to invest in highly specific human capital that promotes vertical integration. This in turn suggests that a critical advantage of vertical integration is the efficient limitation of opportunistic behavior by bringing critical employees within the firm.

Caves and Bradburd (1988) construct an index of forward vertical integration for a sample of 83 US four-digit Standard Industrial Classification producer good industries. The index ($VI2$) is a weighted average of the fraction of companies in the supplying industry that are integrated forward into customer industries in 1975. The weight applied to the fraction of companies integrated into a particular industry is the fraction of supplying industry shipments going to that industry.

$$VI2 = -4.99 + 0.29SCR4 + 0.37BCR4 + 8.66IMP$$
$$+ 0.21BSRD + 0.27BSKL. \qquad (12.84)$$

Their results ((12.84) is an example) indicate that vertical integration rises with supplying industry and buying industry market concentration ($SCR4$ and $BCR4$, respectively) and with an index of share of the supplying industry's product in costs of customer industries (IMP). This is consistent with the argument that small-numbers bargaining problems induce vertical integration.

They also find that vertical integration rises with indices of buying-industry and supplying-industry spending on research and development (a measure of investment in highly specific human capital) and with an index of buying-industry and supplying-industry capital–labor ratios (an index of investment in specific physical capital). All of these coefficient estimates are statistically significant, in varying degrees, and support the transaction cost theory of vertical integration.[41]

---

[41] Coefficients of some explanatory variables are omitted from (12.84). See Caves and Bradburd (1988) for complete results.

12.8 DIVERSIFICATION AND CONGLOMERATE MERGERS

Scott argues that conglomerate mergers can create or reinforce market power because they facilitate tacit collusion (1989b, p. 37):[42],[43]

> Consider two markets, each with only two sellers. In the first and the second we find seller A. In the first, we find seller B competing with seller A. In the second, seller A competes with seller C. If sellers B and C merge, even though they are not competitors, the merger creates a situation in which . . . tacit cooperation . . . is more easily attained. Since the same set of sellers meets in two markets, there are twice as many opportunities to come to understand one another. The process of reaching a consensus on price is facilitated because there is more contact.

Scott presents two case studies of conglomerate mergers that had the effect of increasing multimarket contact among competitors. He also reports a cross-sectional statistical analysis of 95 large US conglomerate mergers for 1977, and finds that they served to increase multimarket contact with competitors for firms involved in the mergers.

Teece (1980, 1982) applies the transaction cost theory of the firm to conglomerate diversification.[44] He highlights the common use of knowhow and specialized indivisible physical assets as a factor favoring diversification. Knowhow is knowledge which involves learning-by-doing as an essential feature. Transactions that involve knowhow are therefore open to opportunistic exploitation, which encourages bringing them within the firm. As regards highly specialized physical assets, markets for their services are likely to be thin, precisely in proportion to the extent that they are specialized. To cope with the possibility of market failure, it is often cost effective for a firm to diversify across industries in which the asset can be utilized.

Teece discusses the relatively recent diversification of petroleum firms into markets for alternative fuels, and suggests that this diversification is consistent with the desire to spread the use of technological knowhow across several industries. To the extent that petroleum firms have a similar pattern of diversification across alternative fuels – and it appears from Teece's table 1 that this is the case – then the diversification of petroleum firms is also

---

[42] It is customary to trace the origin of the literature on multimarket contact to Edwards (1955), and interesting to speculate that his attention may have been turned to the subject in part as a result of his experience in occupied Japan after the Second World War. Kahn has a strong claim as a precursor (1950, p. 208):

> Analysis of chemical markets requires something more than a consideration of the number of sellers in each, separately. The great, diversified companies share the bulk of output in field after field, sometimes among themselves, sometimes with one or a few large specialized manufacturers. This situation influences the pattern of competition and cooperation in all markets.

and (p. 209)

> Economic theory and experience alike suggest that this is a situation conducive to conservatism, with respect both to "excessive" investment, which may endanger satisfactory price and profit levels, and to price competition or similar "unfriendly" acts which might provoke retaliation.

[43] See Bernheim and Whinston (1990) for a formal theoretical treatment.
[44] See also Levy and Haber (1986) and Montgomery and Hariharan (1991).

consistent with Scott's (1989b) argument that the desire to promote multimarket contact is an engine for diversification.[45]

12.9   THE MARKET FOR CORPORATE CONTROL[46]

It is to Marris (1963) that we owe the observation that managers who do not vigilantly tend to the interests of the firm's owners open themselves up to the threat of being replaced. This leads to the notion of the market for corporate control and the merger, in particular the takeover, as an efficiency-enhancing and efficiency-enforcing device.

In principle, such mergers could be horizontal, vertical, or conglomerate: if a firm's management maximizes sales, growth, managerial prerogatives, or any target other than the expected present-discounted value of the income stream of the firm, it becomes profitable for a more efficient management team to mount a takeover bid that will offer shareholders a lump sum equal to the shortfall of the actual from the potential value of the firm. To avoid the possibility of such a takeover, management is induced to maximize the value of the firm.

There are transaction costs in the market for corporate control (Williamson, 1974, pp. 1481–2). Some of these transaction costs are associated with imperfect and impacted information. It is possible for managers to diverge from strategies that maximize present-discounted value because they have an information advantage over shareholders. But this means that incumbent managers have an information advantage over management teams that might mount a takeover attempt. In addition, there are expenses associated with a takeover attempt – shareholders must be contacted and convinced that the new management team offers them better value than incumbent management. Further, there are strategies open to incumbent managers to raise the cost of a takeover attempt – golden parachute retirement schemes for displaced management, for example.

12.9.1   Event studies

Considerations of this kind lead one to suspect that the managements of publicly owned companies will have some leeway to deviate from present-value-maximizing strategies. This is confirmed by Smiley's (1976) study of the impact of takeover offers on the share price of target firms. His results suggest that the market value of a firm can fall to 87 percent of the maximum value before triggering a takeover attempt.

Financial economists have tested the efficiency explanation of mergers by examining the impact of the announcement of a merger or takeover attempt on the stock prices of firms involved in the merger. The results are quite consistent (Caves, 1989, p. 153):[47]

> Acquisitions always entail a large gain for the target firm's shareholders over the market value of the free-standing entity. The proportional gain . . . amounts to 30 percent for the change in

---

[45] Stewart et al. (1984) report significant positive correlations between advertising intensity and research and development intensity of acquired and acquiring firms, results that seem consistent with the Teece hypothesis.

[46] See Ravenscraft and Scherer (1987), Scherer (1988), Caves (1989), and Helm (1989).

[47] See also Jarrell et al. (1988) and Scherer (1988).

corporate control via tender offer or takeover, 20 percent via merger...The average return to the bidding firm's shareholders is less clear. Some studies have found small but statistically significant gains, others small losses. It seems safe to conclude that the bidder's shareholders approximately break even.

If takeovers produce a clear gain for stockholders of the target firm, and leave the owners of the firm mounting the takeover about as well off as before, they seem to produce a net gain for society. But this is a conclusion that should be treated as tentative at best.

One of the underlying premises of these event studies is that the stock market value of the firm is the best possible estimate of the present-discounted value of the firm, given available information.[48] If this assumption is not met, then some takeover attempts may have nothing to do with replacing an inefficient management. If a firm with a perfectly effective management is undervalued by the stock market, that firm may be the target of a takeover attempt simply because it is a good buy.

The idea that the stock market value of the firm is an efficient distillation of all available information, and that mergers and takeovers are a rational response to this information, is difficult to reconcile with the record of 1980s takeover attempts, which more often seemed a speculative game of musical chairs than a rationality-driven search for efficiency.

It also seems hard to reconcile the idea that mergers and takeovers have efficiency motives and effects with the number of takeovers that end up being undone through divestiture. Mention should be made of the Ravenscraft and Scherer (1987) case studies of such mergers.

Sometimes the mergers did not work because of problems with the acquiring firm that were discovered only after merger – which confirms the importance of imperfect information about firms' performances in the merger process. Sometimes the mergers did not work because the acquiring firm was unable to establish effective or improved control over the acquired firm. The blending of internal organizations did not work – which makes clear that takeover of one firm by another does not automatically mean that a less efficient management team is being replaced by a more efficient team.

12.9.2 Studies of post-merger performance

While financial economists have used event studies to evaluate mergers, industrial economists have tended to examine the impact of mergers on measures of performance – profitability or market share.

Mueller (1985) studies the impact of mergers on market share for samples of companies drawn from the 1,000 largest US firms of 1950 and 1972. Using a simple autoregressive specification, he estimates equations of the form shown in table 12.4. The results exhibit regression toward the mean – high market shares tend to decline – whether or not a firm is involved in a merger. But the market share of acquired firms tend to decline much more rapidly than the market share of firms that remain independent, and this result occurs whether the merger was horizontal or conglomerate. This result hardly suggests that merger improves the efficiency of the acquired firm.

---

[48] For discussion, see Summers (1986).

Table 12.4   Mergers and market share: $MS72$ is 1972 market share; $MS50$ is 1950 market share; all coefficients are statistically significant

Conglomerate	$MS72 = 0.011 + 0.885MS50 - 0.705MS50 \begin{cases} 1 \text{ if acquired} \\ 0 \text{ if not} \end{cases}$
Horizontal	$MS72 = 0.027 + 0.547MS50 - 0.403MS50 \begin{cases} 1 \text{ if acquired} \\ 0 \text{ if not} \end{cases}$

Source: Mueller, 1985, tables 2 and 3

Table 12.5   Acquired company pre-merger excess profitability, by merger type: profitability is measured by operating income as a percentage of end-of-period assets; excess profitability is line-of-business profitability minus average profitability of the two-digit industry in which the line of business is classified

Merger type	*Excess* Π/A
Horizontal	11.8
Vertical	−7.0
Related industry	5.4
Conglomerate	9.9
Mixed horizontal/other	8.2
All	9.3

Source: Ravenscraft and Scherer, 1989, table 2

Ravenscraft and Scherer use a sample of observations on 2,732 US lines of business[49] to test two hypotheses about the effect of mergers on profitability (1989, p. 101):

> First, if mergers displace managers who have performed poorly at the task of profit maximization, acquired companies should have lower average pre-merger profitability than their home industry peers. Second, if mergers lead to economies of scale or scope, post-merger profits should rise relative to pre-merger profits and/or peer industry averages, other relevant variables held equal.

As shown in table 12.5, acquired companies tended to have a profitability that was greater than the industry average, before acquisition. This is true overall, and for all types of mergers except vertical.

In a series of cross-section regressions, Ravenscraft and Scherer examine the impact of differences in acquired firm characteristics on line-of-business profitability. When they regress line-of-business profitability on the share of line-of-business assets acquired by merger, the

---

[49]   That is, operations of diversified firms, classified by industry at something between the three- and the four-digit standard industrial classification level.

estimated coefficient is negative and statistically significant. In other regressions, market share has a statistically significant positive impact on profitability, but different variables measuring the share of assets acquired by merger continue to have negative or statistically insignificant coefficients. Only if assets were acquired in a merger between firms of roughly equal size was there any indication that the effect on profitability of the post-merger line of business was positive.

Ravenscraft and Scherer also compare the change in profitability over time of two samples of similar firms, one of firms acquired by merger and the other of firms that remained independent. In both groups, profitability of high-profit firms tended to fall over time – a regression toward the mean effect. But the profitability of firms acquired in mergers fell much more rapidly over time than the profitability of firms that remained independent.

Ravenscraft and Scherer's results do not support the efficiency interpretation of mergers. Acquired firms were not, in general, less profitable before takeover than the average of their industries. Merger did not, in general, raise post-merger profitability, and the profitability of acquired lines of business tended to decline at an accelerated rate. They conclude (1989, pp. 115–6):

> The . . . explanation for acquired units' sharp profit decline must be control loss owing to more complex organizational structures and lessened managerial competence and/or motivation. This control loss explanation is consistent with the high incidence of divestiture following acquisition and the tendency for sold-off units to have negative operating income in the year before their divestiture.

12.9.3   Determinants of merger activity

Taken together, the results of event studies and of studies of post-merger performance leave us up in the air. If the immediate payoff from a merger – the benefit at the time the merger takes place – goes to shareholders of the acquired firm, and post-merger performance is worse than would have been the case without merger, why do mergers take place at all? And why is it that acquired firms are able to attract such high prices?

Marris (1963) provides the theoretical foundation for a model of growth-maximizing behavior. In this framework, managerial utility is related to the size of the firm, but managers' desire for security implies a minimum profitability constraint, to reduce the possibility of a hostile takeover.

Mueller (1972), on the other hand, outlines a life-cycle theory of mergers. This model relies on bounded rationality of managers to argue that, early in the life of any firm, expansion is likely to be by internal growth rather than merger – mergers are a drain of limited management resources that a firm cannot afford while it seeks to develop a strong market position. The life-cycle model also relies on imperfect information in capital markets – a relatively young firm, without an established reputation, would be able to finance a merger by borrowing only at a differentially high interest rate. And a firm that is still establishing its market position in its basic market is unlikely to have enough of a cash flow to finance important mergers without borrowing.

But none of these constraints applies to a mature firm. Once market position is established in the firm's home industry, its operations will be relatively routine, freeing up management attention for other enterprises; its operations will establish a larger cash flow; and its reputation will allow it to raise funds at the lowest commercially available interest rate.

Schwartz (1984) models firms' desire to merge as a consequence of managers' growth-maximizing behavior, tempered by life-cycle effects, and constrained by available cash flow. Using samples of US firms, Schwartz estimates an econometric model of the probability that a firm will make an acquisition for four different time periods, corresponding to different levels of general merger activity in the economy as a whole (spanning the overall period 1962–77). In three of the four time periods, his results indicate that a firm is more likely to make an acquisition, the smaller the average number of shares of stock per shareholder. This is consistent with the hypothesis that managerial discretion will be greater when ownership of the firm is widely dispersed.

Older firms were significantly more likely to make an acquisition in only one of the four time periods. The probability of an acquisition was significantly less, the less important mergers had been in accomplishing past growth. The firm's cash flow has a significant positive effect on the probability of a merger in only one of the four time periods. Firms with high dividend sales are significantly less likely to make an acquisition, all else equal. Schwartz's results do not highlight any single factor as the overriding cause of mergers.

Slusky and Caves (1991) examine the influence of various firm characteristics on the size of the stock price induced by a successful takeover – the merger premium to the owners of the acquired firm. They use a sample of 100 mergers that took place over the period 1986–88.

They view the potential real gains from mergers as a phenomenon arising primarily from the indivisibility of corporate assets. A merger that allows fuller exploitation of "overhead" distribution facilities, production equipment, and so on will allow the post-merger firm to produce at lower cost, all else equal, than the pre-merger firm. In principle, therefore, merger premia should be greater, the more the operations of the acquiring and acquired firms create the potential for common use of productive assets. However, Slusky and Caves' empirical results do not confirm this hypothesis – variables that measure the closeness of fit between the operations of the two firms have no significant effect on the size of the merger premium.

According to Slusky and Caves' results, it is financial and managerial control factors that have the most significant effect on the size of merger premia. Merger premia are greater, the larger the debt–equity ratio of the target firm is relative to the debt–equity ratio of the acquiring firm. The potential gain comes from using the capital of the acquiring firm to retire the debt of the target firm.

Merger premia are less, all else equal, the more the ownership of the acquiring firm is concentrated in the hands of management and the board of directors; that is, the more the interests of acquiring firm management and shareholders coincide. Merger premia are also less the more the ownership of the target firm is concentrated in the hands of individual shareholders (not management or directors) with large blocks of stock – the greater the incentive of target firm shareholders to monitor management.

Merger premia are larger, all else equal, if payments to target firm shareholders are made in cash and if there were bids by more than one potential acquiring firm for the target firm. The latter result shows the effect of competition in driving up the price of the target firm.

12.10 JOINT VENTURES AND EQUITY INTERESTS

12.10.1 Incentives to form joint ventures

Hennart (1988b, p. 363) cites four motives for the formation of joint ventures that have appeared in the literature:

1 taking advantage of economies of scale and diversifying risk;
2 overcoming entry barriers into new markets;
3 pooling complementary bits of knowledge;
4 allaying xenophobic reactions when entering a foreign market.

Hennart himself argues that inefficiencies in input markets are a necessary condition for the formation of joint ventures. What he calls "scale joint ventures" arise if one market in a vertical chain fails and minimum efficient scale in that market is much larger than minimum efficient scale at other levels – a joint venture allows parent firms to maintain independent operations at other levels while benefiting from efficient operations at the point at which the market fails. "Link joint ventures" arise when two markets fail – for example, when one firm wishes to exploit knowledge in another country, but exploitation requires country-specific knowledge about retail distribution that is held by another firm. A joint venture allows firms to overcome the joint market failure.

Kogut (1989) finds that joint ventures are more likely to be stable and endure if the parties to the joint venture have some sort of contact in other markets. The implication is that the threat of strategic reactions in other markets allows nominally competitive firms to cooperate through the joint venture.

12.10.2 Joint ventures and market performance

We begin with the same sort of model used above to evaluate the effects of mergers on market performance:[50] Cournot oligopoly with a homogeneous product, market inverse demand curve $p = a - bQ$, and constant marginal and average cost c per unit. There are n parent firms, identified with a superscript P. These n firms form n joint ventures, identified with a superscript J. The ownership share of parent i in joint venture j is ϕ_{ij}. Ownership shares sum to unity: $\phi_{1j} + \phi_{2j} + \cdots + \phi_{nj} = 1$, for all j.

It is natural to suppose that parent firm i picks its output, q_i^P, to maximize its total payoff, which consists of its operating profit plus the profit that it inherits from its joint ventures:

$$G_j^P = \pi_i^P + \sum_{j=1}^{J} \phi_{ij}\pi_{ij}^J = (p - c)\left(q_i^P + \sum_{j=1}^{J}\phi_{ij}q_{ij}^J\right). \tag{12.85}$$

---

[50] For theoretical treatments, see Bresnahan and Salop (1986), Reynolds and Snapp (1986), and Flath (1989). Adams and Brock (1991) review the incidence of joint ventures in three industries, and give a careful treatment of policy issues.

Several kinds of behavior might be imputed to the joint ventures. Here we explore the option that seems most innocuous from the point of view of market performance: we suppose that the management of each firm picks its output to maximize its own profit:

$$G_j^J = \pi_j^J = (p - c)q_j^J. \tag{12.86}$$

Other possibilities (among which, that a joint venture picks own output to maximize the sum of own profit plus parents' profits) are considered by Bresnahan and Salop (1986).

We assume Cournot conjectures for parent firms and joint ventures. When it takes each decision, a firm assumes that the output of all other firms is given.

From (12.85) and (12.86), we obtain the first-order conditions

$$2q_i^P + \sum_{k \neq i}^{n} q_k^P + \sum_{j=1}^{J}(1 + \phi_{ij})q_j^J \equiv S, \qquad i = 1, 2, \ldots, n, \tag{12.87}$$

$$2q_j^J + \sum_{i=1}^{n} q_i^P + \sum_{j=1, j \neq k}^{J} q_j^J = S, \qquad j = 1, 2, \ldots, J, \tag{12.88}$$

where $S = (a - c)/b$. By manipulating (12.87) and (12.88), it is possible to obtain firm-specific expressions for the Lerner index of market power, as well as an industry-average index of market power. This is left as an exercise. Instead, observe that if one adds the first-order conditions of the parent firms, one obtains

$$Q = \frac{n}{n+1}S. \tag{12.89}$$

But this is the equilibrium output for the same model if there are n Cournot firms. With Cournot conjectures and independent decisions by joint ventures, the formation of joint ventures has no effect on equilibrium output or price. The only effect of forming joint ventures is to create the appearance of a greater number of independent competitors in the market.

Partial equity interests and market performance

It is common for firms in a business group to hold shares in other firms that are members of the same group. This creates a commonalty of interest among group members which, as one might expect, tends to worsen market performance.

Results for this sort of model are sensitive to the specification of the firm's maximand. We consider two cases.

Payoffs to private shareholders

Begin with an n-firm Cournot oligopoly with homogeneous product and constant cost. Suppose that a fraction v of the shares of each firm is held by other firms, with the remaining

$1 - v$ fraction of the shares held by the general public. The ownership share of firm i in firm j is ϕ_{ij}, and $\phi_{1j} + \phi_{2j} + \cdots + \phi_{nj} = 1$. In this specification, ϕ_{ii} is normalized at zero.

Firm i's output is selected to maximize the overall payoff of the firm, which is the sum of its own profits and the fractions of the profits of other firms which it inherits by dint of its ownership of other firms. That is, q_i is selected to maximize

$$G_i = \pi_i + \sum_{j \neq i} \phi_{ij}\pi_j = b(S - Q)\left(q_i + \sum_{j \neq i} \phi_{ij}q_j\right). \tag{12.90}$$

The first-order condition for maximization of (12.90) is

$$2q_i + \sum_{j \neq i}(1 + \phi_{ij})q_j == S. \tag{12.91}$$

Adding the first-order conditions of all n firms and rearranging terms, we obtain

$$Q = \frac{nS}{n + 1 + v} < \frac{nS}{n + 1}. \tag{12.92}$$

Unless $v = 0$, so that partial equity holdings are zero, total output is less than Cournot equilibrium output without partial equity holdings. Partial equity holdings, therefore, act to reduce output, raise price, and worsen market performance.

Payoffs to managers

Now permit $\phi_{ii} > 0$, but interpret ϕ_{ij} as the share of the managers of firm i in the ownership of firm j, and suppose that the managers of firm i pick q^i to maximize their own income. Then q_i is chosen to maximize

$$G_i = \sum_{j=1}^{n} \phi_{ij}\pi_j = (p - c)\sum_{j=1}^{n} \phi_{ij}q_j. \tag{12.93}$$

The first-order condition for maximization of (12.93) with respect to q_i is

$$(S - Q)\phi_{ii} - (p - c)\sum_{j=1}^{n} \phi_{ij}q_j \equiv 0, \qquad i = 1, 2, \ldots, n. \tag{12.94}$$

Adding the first-order conditions for all firms, we obtain

$$(S - Q)\sum_{i=1}^{n} \phi_{ii} = vQ, \tag{12.95}$$

from which

$$Q = \frac{\sum_{i=1}^{n} \phi_{ii}}{v + \sum_{i=1}^{n} \phi_{ii}}S. \tag{12.96}$$

The impact of partial equity holdings by managers on market performance can be judged by evaluating the equilibrium output for different ownership patterns. Suppose first that

$\phi_{ii} = v = 1$, for all i. In this case, each firm is owned entirely by its own managers. From (12.96) we find that $Q = nS/(n + 1)$, which is the equilibrium output for n-firm Cournot oligopoly.

On the other hand, let v be greater than 0 and $\phi_{ii} = v/n$ for all i. Then (12.96) becomes $Q = S/2$, which is monopoly output. No matter how small the share of managers in firms, if that share is evenly distributed among managers, managers maximize their payoff by maximizing joint profit. In this case, partial equity holdings are a mechanism for complete noncooperative collusion.

It is also interesting to consider the case of partial equity holdings for a subgroup of firms in the industry. Suppose that ownership of a fraction $v > 0$ of the first m firms in the industry is evenly divided between the managers of those firms. The managers of firm i then pick q_i to maximize

$$G_i = (p - c) \sum_{j=1}^{m} \frac{v}{m} \pi_i = b(S - Q) \frac{v}{m} \sum_{j=1}^{m} q_j, \qquad i = 1, 2, \dots, m. \tag{12.97}$$

The first-order condition for maximization of (12.97) is

$$S \equiv Q + Q_{pe}, \tag{12.98}$$

where Q_{pe} is the total output of firms linked through partial equity holdings.

For a firm not in the partial equity group, the first order condition for profit maximization is

$$S = Q + q_j, \qquad j = m + 1, \dots, n. \tag{12.99}$$

In principle, (12.98) and (12.99) can be solved as a system of simultaneous equations to find equilibrium outputs. But there is no need to do this – they have the same form as the first-order conditions for an $(n - m + 1)$-firm Cournot oligopoly. Partial equity holdings among managers of a group of firms, if evenly distributed, are equivalent to a complete merger of those firms. The rest of the model develops along the lines of the Salant et al. (1983) "Losses from horizontal merger" model.

12.11 CONCLUSION

It would be pleasant to report the development of a neoclassical theory of the existence and internal organization of firms. It would also be premature. There is an elaborate but for the most part discursive transaction cost theory of the existence of firms. Its influence has been limited by the fact that it has not used the tools of formal microeconomic theory,[51] and its development has been limited by the assumption that firms are defined and organized to minimize costs, without strategic motives or consequences (Williamson, 1981, p. 1540). Attempts to formalize this theory have produced a collection of narrowly drawn formal models, but no generally accepted analytic framework has emerged.

Theoretical models predict that mergers will often be privately unprofitable, because of the reactions of firms outside the merger. If mergers are privately profitable – so that they

---

[51] See Arrow (1985, p. 303) and Riordan and Williamson (1985, pp. 366–7).

can be expected to occur – and beneficial to society as a whole, it is nonetheless unlikely that those benefits will be passed on to consumers in the form of lower prices.

Empirical evidence suggests that firms involved in mergers suffer reductions in market share and profitability compared with similar firms that are not involved in mergers. Takeovers yield a one-time benefit to shareholders of acquired firms but do not benefit shareholders of acquiring firms. Taken as a whole, these results suggest that the motives for mergers must be sought in non-profit-maximizing behavior, and that mergers cannot be interpreted as the market's way of enforcing profit-maximizing behavior.

Theoretical models of joint ventures and partial equity holdings suggest that such combinations have the same effect on market performance as tacit collusion.

PROBLEM

12.1 Using the fact that, for a linear inverse demand curve $p = a - bQ$, the price elasticity of demand is $\varepsilon_{Qp} = p/bQ$, show that (12.87) and (12.88) can be written as

$$\frac{p - c}{p} = \frac{s^P + \sum_{j=1}^{J} \phi_{ij} s_j^J}{\varepsilon_{Qp}}, \qquad i = 1, 2, \ldots, n$$

and

$$\frac{p - c}{p} = \frac{s_j^J}{\varepsilon_{Qp}}$$

respectively, where s denotes market share. Multiply each equation by the market share of the firm to which it applies and add the resulting expressions over all firms to obtain an expression for the price–cost margin in terms of market shares of all firms and joint venture shares.

CHAPTER THIRTEEN
VERTICAL
RESTRAINTS

It seems true, nevertheless, that manufacturers, singly or in concert, do sometimes main-
tain resale prices and require their resellers not to handle the goods of rival manufacturers.
An explanation is required but a further study of actual cases will be necessary to supply it.

Robert H. Bork (1966, p. 414)

13.1 Introduction[1]

Manufacturers in a variety of markets sometimes impose contractual restraints on wholesale and retail firms that distribute their products. Sometimes the vertical restraint sets a minimum retail price for the manufacturer's product, and less often a maximum price. Sometimes it binds a retailer to sell only in a certain territory or from a certain location. Sometimes the manufacturer grants a retailer the exclusive right to sell in a certain territory. Sometimes the restraint limits the distributor to certain classes of consumers, and sometimes it binds the distributor not to sell to certain classes of consumers. Sometimes it requires the distributor to sell a certain minimum quantity over a given period of time. There are other kinds of restraints as well.

The analysis of the causes and effects of such restraints has been hampered by the fact that they occur for many types of products and in markets with a wide variety of structures.

Vertical restraints have been imposed by the manufacturers of patent medicines, automobiles, books, and jeans, and other products. They have been imposed by new firms with small market shares, by established dominant firms, and by oligopolists in markets with intermediate concentration levels.

Traditionally, vertical restraints have been interpreted either as an instrument of market power or as a device for correcting failure in the market for distribution services. The policy implications of the two views are quite different. If vertical restraints are a way for manufacturers to enhance their own market power, or for dealers to induce a manufacturer

[1] See Caves (1980), Blair and Kaserman (1983), Lafferty et al. (1984), and Neven et al. (1998); see Mathewson and Winter (1984, 1986, 1988) and Waterson (1988) for spatial models.

to police a dealer cartel, then it seems safe to recommend that such restraints should be prohibited. But if vertical restraints are necessary to permit manufacturers to purchase services from dealers that they cannot otherwise obtain, then making a case against vertical restraints requires a demonstration that such restraints, on balance, reduce social welfare.

Empirical evidence, mostly of a case study nature, suggests that the collusion and market failure explanations for vertical restraints are in fact of limited applicability. As a result, recent work puts forth new explanations for vertical restraints. These approaches suggest that vertical restraints may serve to certify product quality, may serve to induce retailers to carry a greater range of products, or may be a response to uncertainty.

13.2 INCENTIVES TO IMPOSE VERTICAL RESTRAINTS

13.2.1 Market power in oligopoly[2]

Rey and Stiglitz (1988) outline a model in which manufacturing duopolists can increase their profits – exercise a greater degree of market power – by granting exclusive territories to their dealers and using franchise fees to recover all profits from the distribution stage.[3]

Let inverse demand be linear, with varieties of the product differentiated as in the Bowley model:

$$p_1 = a - (q_1 + \theta q_2), \qquad p_2 = a - (\theta q_1 + q_2). \qquad (13.1)$$

Both manufacturers produce with constant marginal cost c per unit. To reach the final consumer, the product must pass through a retail distribution stage. For simplicity, assume that retailers operate without cost.

It is useful to work with a model of price-setting firms, and it is convenient to measure price in deviations from marginal cost. If the cost of variety 1 to a retailer is w_1 per unit and the cost of variety 2 to a retailer is w_2 per unit, the demand functions implied by the inverse demand functions (13.1) satisfy

$$(1 - \theta^2)q_1 = a - w_1 - \theta(a - w_2) - (p_1 - w_1) + \theta(p_2 - w_2), \qquad (13.2)$$

$$(1 - \theta^2)q_2 = a - w_2 - \theta(a - w_1) + \theta(p_1 - w_1) - (p_2 - w_2). \qquad (13.3)$$

Consider first the vertical integration case, in which each manufacturer distributes its own product. Then $w_1 = w_2 = c$, and firm 1 selects p_1 to maximize π_1, where

$$(1 - \theta^2)\pi_1 = (p_1 - c)[a - c - \theta(a - c) - (p_1 - c) + \theta(p_2 - c)]. \qquad (13.4)$$

The first-order condition that defines firm 1's best-response price is

$$2(p_1 - c) - \theta(p_2 - c) \equiv (1 - \theta)(a - c). \qquad (13.5)$$

We can obtain the equilibrium price under vertical integration using the fact that, in equilibrium, both manufacturers charge the same price. Substituting $p_1 = p_2 = p_{vi}$ in (13.5)

---

[2] See also Comanor and Frech (1985, 1987), Mathewson and Winter (1987), and Lin (1990). For analyses of vertical restraints imposed by a monopolist manufacturer, see Dixit (1983) or Gallini and Winter (1983), among others.
[3] For a similar model, see Bonanno and Vickers (1988).

and rearranging terms,

$$p_{vi}(\theta) = c + \frac{1-\theta}{2-\theta}(a-c). \tag{13.6}$$

If $\theta = 1$, which means that the product is standardized, equilibrium price equals marginal cost. This is the Bertrand (1883) result that we expect for price-setting oligopoly with standardized products. $\partial p_{vi}/\partial\theta < 0$, so that as θ falls and product differentiation increases, equilibrium price rises. When product differentiation is complete, $p_{vi}(\theta) = c+(a-c)/2 = p_m$, which is the monopoly price. Less obviously, one can show that for $0 < \theta \leq 1$, p_m is also the joint-profit-maximizing price.

We want these results to compare with cases in which manufacturing and distribution are not vertically integrated. When manufacturing and distribution are separate, manufacturers 1 and 2 sell their products to retailers at wholesale prices w_1 and w_2, respectively, and the equilibrium retail prices p_1 and p_2 are determined by interactions among retailers.

Consider first the case in which there are a large number of price-setting retailers who distribute each variety of the product. The retailers that distribute variety 1 form a group of price-setting firms that distribute a homogeneous product. Intrabrand competition among these retailers will drive their retail prices for variety 1 to their marginal cost, so that in equilibrium $p_1 = w_1$. (Recall that for simplicity we have assumed that retailers operate with zero marginal cost.) By a corresponding argument, in equilibrium $p_2 = w_2$. But this means that manufacturers, by setting wholesale prices w_1 and w_2, determine retail prices. From firm 1's point of view, the best value for $p_1 = w_1$, given p_2, is determined by (13.5), and there is a similar best-response curve for firm 2. Equilibrium wholesale (and retail) prices are as in the vertically integrated case. Using equilibrium prices from (13.6) to evaluate the quantities demanded, from (13.2) and (13.3), we find equilibrium manufacturing firm profit if production and distribution are separate and the retailing sector has at least two firms with Bertrand expectations distributing each variety:

$$\pi_1 = \frac{1-\theta}{1+\theta}\left(\frac{a-c}{2-\theta}\right)^2. \tag{13.7}$$

This is also equilibrium firm profit if production and distribution are vertically integrated.

Now consider an alternative scenario in which each manufacturer grants the exclusive right to distribute its variety to a single retailer. The retail market is then a duopoly of price-setting firms, each selling one variety of a differentiated product. The retail firm distributing variety 1 has marginal cost w_1; the retail firm distributing variety 2 has marginal cost w_2.

From the demand curves ((13.2) and (13.3)) we obtain an expression for retailer 1's profit 1:

$$(1-\theta^2)\pi_1 = (p_1-w_1)[(a-w_1) - \theta(a-w_2) - (p_1-w_1) + \theta(p_2-w_2)]. \tag{13.8}$$

The first-order condition for maximization of (13.8) yields the equation of retailer 1's price best-response curve, which satisfies

$$2(p_1-w_1) - \theta(p_2-w_2) = (a-w_1) - \theta(a-w_2). \tag{13.9}$$

There is a corresponding expression for retailer 2's price best-response function. Equilibrium retail prices, written as deviations from wholesale prices, satisfy

$$(4 - \theta^2)(p_1 - w_1) = (2 - \theta^2)(a - w_1) - \theta(a - w_2), \tag{13.10}$$

$$(4 - \theta^2)(p_2 - w_2) = (2 - \theta^2)(a - w_2) - \theta(a - w_1). \tag{13.11}$$

This allows us to express equilibrium retail prices as deviations from manufacturers' marginal cost, c per unit:

$$p_1(w_1, w_2) = c + \frac{(2 + \theta)(1 - \theta)(a - c) + 2(w_1 - c) + \theta(w_2 - c)}{4 - \theta^2}, \tag{13.12}$$

$$p_2(w_1, w_2) = c + \frac{(2 + \theta)(1 - \theta)(a - c) + \theta(w_1 - c) + 2(w_2 - c)}{4 - \theta^2}. \tag{13.13}$$

From (13.12), increases in either wholesale price raise both equilibrium retail prices:

$$\frac{\partial p_1}{\partial w_1} \geq \frac{\partial p_2}{\partial w_2} > 0 \tag{13.14}$$

(and a similar expression holding for p_2). An increase in w_1 has a greater effect on p_1 than does an increase in w_2.

Before proceeding to the analysis of the wholesale pricing decision, we need to consider how retailers' behavior is altered if manufacturers 1 and 2 impose franchise fees F_1 and F_2, respectively, on the retail firms to which they grant exclusive distributorships. The franchise fees reduce retail profit, but for any F_1 and F_2, retailers' best-response prices continue to be given by (13.10) and (13.11). Equilibrium retail prices, given by (13.12) and (13.13), are unchanged by the imposition of franchise fees. This means that we can analyze the determination of wholesale prices on the assumption that franchise fees allow manufacturers to appropriate all profit from the retailers to which they grant exclusive distributorships.

Substituting from (13.12) and (13.13) into the demand function (13.2), we obtain the equilibrium quantity demanded of variety 1, given w_1 and w_2 and our assumptions about retailers' behavior:

$$q_1(w_1, w_2) = \frac{(2 - \theta^2)(a - w_1) - \theta(a - w_2)}{(1 - \theta^2)(4 - \theta^2)}. \tag{13.15}$$

By choice of w_1 and F_1, manufacturer 1 appropriates all economic profit in the vertical chain that connects production and distribution. It therefore picks w_1 to maximize

$$\pi_{1P}(w_1, w_2) = [p_1(w_1, w_2) - c]q_1(w_1, w_2). \tag{13.16}$$

The first-order condition for maximization of (13.16) with respect to w_1 yields the equation of firm 1's wholesale price best-response function:

$$w_1 = c + \theta^2 \frac{(1 - \theta)(2 + \theta)(a - c) + \theta(w_2 - c)}{4(2 - \theta^2)}. \tag{13.17}$$

Best-response curves are upward-sloping, as we expect with linear demand curves, price-setting firms, and constant marginal cost.

In equilibrium, both manufacturers charge the same price. Setting $w_1 = w_2 = w$ in (13.17) yields the equilibrium wholesale price:

$$w = c + \frac{\theta^2}{4 - 2\theta - \theta^2}(a - c). \tag{13.18}$$

Substituting w from (13.18) into (13.16) gives equilibrium retail prices:

$$p_1 = c + \frac{2(1 - \theta)}{4 - 2\theta - \theta^2}(a - c). \tag{13.19}$$

Then using p_{vi} from (13.6), we find that

$$p_1 - p_{vi} = \frac{\theta^2(1 - \theta)(a - c)}{(2 - \theta)(4 - 2\theta - \theta^2)}. \tag{13.20}$$

p_1 is less than the joint-profit-maximizing price p_m:

$$p_m - p_1 = \frac{\theta(2 - \theta)}{4 - 2\theta - \theta^2}(a - c) > 0. \tag{13.21}$$

Distribution through retailers who have been granted exclusive distributorships allows manufacturers to obtain a retail price which is closer to the joint-profit-maximizing level than if manufacturers were vertically integrated. By suitable choice of franchise fee, manufacturers can appropriate the resulting incremental profit for themselves. Substituting (13.16) into (13.17), when distribution is through retailers with exclusive distributorships a manufacturer's profit is

$$\pi_P = 2\frac{1 - \theta}{1 + \theta}(2 - \theta^2)\left(\frac{a - c}{4 - 2\theta - \theta^2}\right)^2. \tag{13.22}$$

Using (13.7) and (13.22) to compare π_1 and π_P, we find that

$$\pi_P - \pi_1 = \frac{1 - \theta}{1 + \theta}\theta^3\frac{4 - 3\theta}{(2 - \theta^2)(4 - 2\theta - \theta^2)^2}(a - c)^2 > 0. \tag{13.23}$$

It is more profitable for manufacturers to grant exclusive territories than to distribute through a Bertrand oligopoly retail sector.

13.2.2   Free riding

The dealer services market failure explanation for vertical restraints is usually attributed to Telser (1960), although the same argument appears in Yamey (1954), Bowman (1955), and Bork (1966).[4]

---

[4] See Telser (1960, fns 1 and 4) for other references.

Telser's formulation is as follows. Suppose that:

1 final demand is positively affected by services that must be provided by the retail distributor;
2 that these services are specific to the product, not just part of the usual business operations of the retailer;
3 that it is costly to provide the service; and
4 that consumption of the services and purchase of the product are separable, in the sense that a consumer can visit one retailer, take advantage of pre-sale services, and then purchase the product from another retailer.

In these circumstances a manufacturer is not, in equilibrium, able to induce dealers to provide the special services. If some dealers should offer such services, consumers would take the services from one such dealer but take the product from some other dealer, at a price that would not cover the cost of providing the services. Thus dealers providing the service would lose money. Dealers would not, in equilibrium, provide the costly separable services.

This free-riding problem would not arise if it were possible to charge the consumer separately for the product and the service. Hence, post-sale maintenance service does not create an opportunity for free riding. Nor would the free-riding problem arise if the manufacturer could pay the retailer to perform the special services in question. But it will often be difficult for the manufacturer to monitor retailers' performance. In such cases, there is a failure in the market for dealer services: the manufacturer cannot buy a distribution network in which retailers provide special services that are profitable for the manufacturer.

By imposing a resale price maintenance scheme, however, the manufacturer can eliminate the retail-level price competition that is the root of the free-riding problem. By setting a retail price that is enough above the wholesale price to cover the cost of providing special services, the manufacturer makes it possible for retailers to provide the special services that the manufacturer wants. Since it is costly to provide the special services, individual retailers continue to have an incentive not to provide them. But under a resale price maintenance scheme, retailers who do not provide special services are unable to compensate consumers for the absence of the services with a lower price. Consumers who value the special services have no incentive to patronize retailers who do not provide them.

The free-rider argument is one explanation for the private profitability of resale price maintenance and, more generally, vertical restraints. But Scherer (1983), Comanor (1985), and Comanor and Kirkwood (1985) point out that the private profitability of vertical restraints does not mean that they are socially desirable.

Under the free-rider argument, the private profitability of resale price maintenance depends on the fact that marginal consumers are willing to pay the higher price required to induce distributors to supply special services. If all consumers place equal value on the special services, then resale price maintenance is socially beneficial: consumers value the special services enough to pay for them, and manufacturers' profit goes up. But it may well be the case that inframarginal consumers place less value on special services than marginal consumers. The first-time purchaser of a personal computer, a stereo system, or a round-the-world cruise may place great value on extensive pre-sales service. Experienced consumers of those products are likely to place much less value on the same services. Inframarginal consumers are made worse off if a system of resale price maintenance compels them to pay a higher price for the product in return for services that they neither need nor want.

13.2.3 Quality certification

Marvel and McCafferty point out the limited applicability of the market power and free-rider explanations of resale price maintenance.[5] As regards the former, they observe that (1984, p. 347):[6]

> Economists have long expressed hostility toward RPM and have concurred with the position of the courts that RPM was identical in effect to horizontal price-fixing, hence anticompetitive. As popular as this price-fixing analogy is, it falls far short of explaining the characteristics of RPM use . . . . it cannot explain why RPM was often adopted by new entrants to apparently competitive industries, and why RPM appears to have been more popular with producers of high-quality products than with manufacturers of similar but inferior goods. There is, in addition, the question of how retailers engaged in price-fixing could expect to retain any monopoly rents generated, given the apparent ease of entry. Finally, . . . it is unclear why manufacturers would tolerate high retail margins that were apparently inimical to their own interests.

With respect to the argument that resale price maintenance is designed to prevent free riding by some dealers on services provided by other dealers, they say (1984, p. 348)

> Since RPM has been common in grocery, drug, and apparel markets – markets in which services provided by dealers are difficult to identify – one is led to question whether efficiency explanations for RPM apply to only a small subset of the uses of the practice.

Their own explanation for resale price maintenance is a generalization of the free-riding argument to allow for the impact of dealers' reputations on manufacturers' profits (1984, p. 347):

> we propose a model of retailing in which a retailer serves as the consumer's agent in ascertaining the quality or stylishness of commodities. Our argument does not require that dealers provide tangible services, but rests instead on the mere willingness of dealers to stock the product in question. So long as consumers regard some dealers as having superior abilities to certify the characteristics of branded products, such certification will be valuable to manufacturers. But the branding of the product means that the retailer's certification is subject to free-riding.

The retail sector

Products are differentiated by quality, and retail outlets are differentiated by their reputation for quality. Let quality be measured by an index χ, which lies between zero and one. Consider the marketing decision of the manufacturer of a product of quality $\chi = 1$. Suppose that

---

[5] See also Springer and Frech (1986).
[6] See also Marvel and McCafferty (1985, 1986).

available retailers are uniformly distributed over the whole quality range, and that retailers will not carry products with quality index less than their own quality reputation.[7]

Retail costs of distributing a particular product include the cost of purchasing the product from the manufacturer, operating costs associated with the product, and the cost of maintaining a quality reputation. Let the cost of selling q units from a retail outlet of reputation χ be

$$C(q, \chi) = wq + cq + f\chi, \tag{13.24}$$

where w is the wholesale price, f is cost per unit of quality, and $c' > 0$, $c'' > 0$.

Suppose also that the product in question is sold by many retail outlets, so that each retail outlet takes the retail price as given and maximizes profit

$$\pi^r = (p - w)q - c(q) - f\chi. \tag{13.25}$$

Inversion of the first-order condition for maximization of π^r,

$$p - w = c'(q), \tag{13.26}$$

yields the retail firm supply function

$$q = (c')^{-1}(p - w) \equiv g(p - w), \tag{13.27}$$

where $g' = 1/c' > 0$.

Since cost rises with an outlet's quality reputation, there is some maximum quality level $\bar{\chi}$ at which a retail outlet carrying the product earns zero profit. This breakeven quality level is defined by

$$(p - w)q = c(q) + f\bar{\chi} = c[g(p - w)] + f\bar{\chi}, \tag{13.28}$$

or, equivalently, and writing $m = p - w$ for notational convenience,

$$\bar{\chi} = \frac{mg(m) - c[g(m)]}{f} \equiv \bar{\chi}(m). \tag{13.29}$$

From (13.29), we obtain

$$\frac{\partial \bar{\chi}}{\partial m} = \frac{(p - w - c')g' + g}{f} = \frac{g}{f} > 0, \tag{13.30}$$

using the first-order condition (13.26).

---

[7] Marvel and McCafferty later address the question of the impact of resale price maintenance on retail market structure, recognizing that in the long run the distribution of retail outlets over quality space is endogenous.

Retail equilibrium

Suppose that the manufacturer willingly distributes his product through stores with reputation $\underline{\chi}$ or greater. Then since retailers are uniformly distributed over reputation space, total supply of the product to final consumers is

$$Q^s = (\bar{\chi} - \underline{\chi})g(p - w). \tag{13.31}$$

We suppose that the quantity demanded of the product depends on price, quality, and availability:

$$Q^d = Q^d(p, \bar{\chi}, \bar{\chi} - \underline{\chi}), \tag{13.32}$$

where $Q_1^d < 0$, $Q_2^d > 0$, and $Q_3^d > 0$. In equilibrium, therefore,

$$\left[\bar{\chi}(m) - \underline{\chi}(m)\right]g(m) = Q^d\left[m + w, \bar{\chi}(m), \bar{\chi}(m) - \underline{\chi}(m)\right]. \tag{13.33}$$

This is a condition that determines the equilibrium price p or, equivalently, the equilibrium dealer margin $m = p - w$, as a function of the choice variables of the manufacturer, w and $\underline{\chi}$. From (13.33), we obtain the partial derivatives of the equilibrium dealer margin:

$$\frac{\partial m}{\partial w} = \frac{Q_1^d}{DEN}, \qquad \frac{\partial m}{\partial \underline{\chi}} = \frac{g - Q_3^d}{DEN}, \tag{13.34}$$

where the denominator DEN is

$$DEN = \left(\bar{\chi} - \underline{\chi}\right)g' + g\bar{\chi}' - Q_1^d - (Q_2^d + Q_3^d)\bar{\chi}'. \tag{13.35}$$

To evaluate the sign of DEN, observe that from (13.31) and (13.32), we have

$$Q^d - Q^s = Q^d\left[m + w, \bar{\chi}(m), \bar{\chi}(m) - \underline{\chi}\right] - \left[\bar{\chi}(m) - \underline{\chi}(m)\right]. \tag{13.36}$$

This in turn yields

$$\frac{\partial(Q^d - Q^s)}{\partial m} = -DEN. \tag{13.37}$$

Hence $DEN > 0$ if an increase in price acts to reduce excess demand.

Assuming this to be the case, we have, from (13.34), $\partial m/\partial w < 0$: increases in the wholesale price reduce the retail margin. This in turn implies that an increase in the wholesale price causes a less than proportional increase in the equilibrium retail price:

$$\frac{\partial p}{\partial w} = 1 + \frac{\partial m}{\partial w} < 1. \tag{13.38}$$

The manufacturer's profit depends on the quantity sold,

$$Q^s = \left[\bar{\chi}(m) - \underline{\chi}(m) \right] g(m). \tag{13.39}$$

From (13.39), we obtain

$$\frac{\partial Q^s}{\partial w} = \left[\left(\bar{\chi} - \underline{\chi} \right) g' + g \bar{\chi}' \right] \frac{\partial m}{\partial w} < 0, \tag{13.40}$$

$$\frac{\partial Q^s}{\partial \underline{\chi}} = \left[\left(\bar{\chi} - \underline{\chi} \right) g' + g \bar{\chi}' \right] \frac{\partial m}{\partial \underline{\chi}}$$

$$= \frac{[Q_1^d + (Q_2^d + Q_3^d)\bar{\chi}']g - Q_3^d \left[\left(\bar{\chi} - \underline{\chi} \right) g' + g \bar{\chi}' \right]}{DEN}. \tag{13.41}$$

If the manufacturer produces with constant marginal cost z per unit, he seeks to maximize

$$\pi^m = (w - z)Q^s(w, \underline{\chi}) \tag{13.42}$$

subject to the constraint that $\underline{\chi} \geq 0$. The first-order conditions for this problem are

$$\frac{\partial \pi^m}{\partial w} = (w - z)\frac{\partial Q^s}{\partial w} + Q^s(w, \underline{\chi}), \tag{13.43}$$

$$\frac{\partial \pi^m}{\partial \underline{\chi}} = (w - z)\frac{\partial Q^s}{\partial \underline{\chi}} \geq 0, \qquad \left[(w - z)\frac{\partial Q^s}{\partial \underline{\chi}} \right] \underline{\chi} \equiv 0, \qquad \underline{\chi} \geq 0. \tag{13.44}$$

The profitability of resale price maintenance

We now ask whether or not the manufacturer would find it profitable to depart from the equilibrium determined by (13.43) and (13.44) by imposing a resale price maintenance scheme on the retail sector. If the manufacturer fixes a retail price $\bar{p}$, the quantity demanded is

$$Q^d = Q^d(\bar{p}, \bar{\chi}, \bar{\chi} - \underline{\chi}), \tag{13.45}$$

where demand is distributed evenly over all retailers. $\bar{\chi}$ is now defined by

$$(\bar{p} - w)\frac{Q^d(\bar{p}, \bar{\chi}, \bar{\chi} - \underline{\chi})}{\bar{\chi} - \underline{\chi}}x = c(x) + f\bar{\chi}. \tag{13.46}$$

The impact of a change in the maintained price on demand is of ambiguous sign:

$$\frac{\partial Q^d}{\partial \bar{p}} = Q_1^d + \left(Q_2^d + Q_3^d \right)\bar{\chi}' = Q_1^d + \left(Q_2^d + Q_3^d \right)\frac{g(\bar{p} - w)}{f}. \tag{13.47}$$

The first term on the right is negative: a higher retail price drives some consumers from the market. The second term is positive, unless the highest quality retail outlet already carries the product. A higher retail price increases the quality of the retail output that just breaks even carrying the product. This increases demand for two reasons: it improves the product's reputation, and it expands the availability of the product.

The manufacturer's profit is

$$\pi^m = (w - z)Q^d(\bar{p}, \bar{\chi}, \bar{\chi} - \underline{\chi}), \tag{13.48}$$

so that

$$\frac{\partial \pi^m}{\partial \bar{p}} = (w - z)\frac{\partial Q^d}{\partial \bar{p}}. \tag{13.49}$$

Thus the effect of a resale price maintenance scheme on the manufacturer's profit depends on its effect on demand. Although this effect is in general ambiguous, it can be shown to be positive if the market equilibrium choice of the manufacturer is to set $\chi > 0$ – to refuse to supply low-quality outlets.

If $\chi > 0$, the first-order condition (13.44) implies that $\partial Q^2/\partial \underline{\chi} = 0$. Using (13.41), this in turn gives

$$Q_1^d + \left(Q_2^d + Q_3^d\right)\bar{\chi}' = \frac{Q_3^d}{g}\left[\left(\bar{\chi} - \underline{\chi}\right)g' + g\bar{\chi}'\right] > 0. \tag{13.50}$$

This makes (13.47) positive, which in turn makes (13.49) positive.

Hence, if it is optimal for the manufacturer to refuse to deal with low-reputation dealers in free market equilibrium, it is profitable for the manufacturer to impose a resale price maintenance scheme. Essentially, the manufacturer refuses to deal with low-quality outlets and uses resale price maintenance to attract high reputation outlets.

The effect of resale price maintenance on manufacturer profitability is ambiguous if the manufacturer supplies all retail outlets. Even in this case, resale price maintenance may be profitable for the manufacturer if the net effect of resale price maintenance on demand, given by (13.47), is positive.

The Net Book Agreement

Efficiency arguments for vertical restraints cannot explain practices such as resale price maintenance in markets where tangible pre-sales service or quality certification are unimportant. An example is the retail book market.[8]

A resale price maintenance scheme – the Net Book Agreement – was introduced in Great Britain in July 1890 and lasted until September 1995. Ironically, the first book marketed under the Net Book Agreement was Alfred Marshall's *Principles of Economics*. The explanation given at that time for instituting a resale price maintenance program was the desire to eliminate price competition at the retail level. But this in turn was motivated by the desire to induce retailers to carry greater stocks of books, and to permit retailers in out-of-the-way markets to

---

[8] For a related analysis, see Shaffer (1991).

stay in business (Frederick Macmillan writing to Alfred Marshall in April 1890; reproduced in Guillebaud, 1965, p. 522):

At present . . . it is usual for booksellers to allow their customers a discount of 2d. and sometimes 3d. in the 1s. from advertised prices. This system is the cause of two evils: in the first place books have to be made (nominally) ridiculously expensive in order that there may be plenty of margin for taking off discounts, and in the second place the system of allowing discounts to retail purchasers has fostered a spirit of competition among booksellers so keen that there is not enough profit in the business to enable booksellers to carry good stocks or to give their attention to bookselling proper. They have to supplement their profits by selling "fancy goods," Berlin wool, etc., and are in many cases, in the country especially, driven out of business altogether.

To analyze the impact of a resale price maintenance scheme in such a market, consider a discrete-time model. Suppose for simplicity that all books are sold by publishers to retailers at a wholesale price w, and are resold to the general public at a retail price p. Suppose also that associated with each bookstore is a parameter λ, lying between zero and one, which is the probability that a book in that store sells in the following period. λ depends on store characteristics, among which location, and is taken as given for each store. $1/\lambda$ can be thought of as an average turnover rate for books at a particular store.

A bookstore's capacity is the number of books that it can keep in stock. At the start of each period, a bookstore buys enough books to bring its stock up to capacity K. At the end of the period, the bookstore sells books and pays workers. The number of workers L is a function of capacity K, with $L' > 0$ and $L'' > 0$.

Expected sales are λK. If books are paid for at the start of the period and receipts collected and inputs paid at the end of the period, the expected present-discounted payoff of a bookstore is

$$E(PDV) = -w(\lambda K) + \frac{1}{1+r}\left[p(\lambda K) - gL(K) - rp^k K\right]$$
$$= [p - (1+r)w]\lambda K - gL(K) - rp^k K, \qquad (13.51)$$

where g is the wage rate and rp^k is the rental cost of capacity.

The first-order condition for maximization of $E(PDV)$ with respect to capacity K is

$$[p - (1+r)w]\lambda - gL'(K) - rp^k \equiv 0, \qquad (13.52)$$

from which the profit-maximizing capacity level is

$$K = (L')^{-1}\left\{\frac{[p - (1+r)w]\lambda - rp^k}{g}\right\}. \qquad (13.53)$$

There is a breakeven sales probability $\underline{\lambda}$, defined by

$$[p - (1+r)w]\underline{\lambda}K - gL(K) - rp^k K \equiv 0. \qquad (13.54)$$

For given wholesale and retail prices, and profit-maximizing choice of capacity, a retailer with turnover rate $1/\underline{\lambda}$ has a zero expected discounted present value. Firms with more rapid turnover rates earn a positive economic rent that is recorded as an accounting profit.

For a breakeven retailer, we can substitute from the first-order condition (13.52) into the breakeven constraint to eliminate $p - (1 + r)w$ and obtain

$$\frac{K}{L(K)}L'(K) = 1.$$

(13.55)

For the breakeven firm, the profit-maximizing capacity level makes the elasticity of labor input with respect to capacity equal to unity. In particular, for the breakeven firm, the profit-maximizing level of capacity is independent of λ.

However, from (13.54) we find that an increase in retail price reduces the breakeven $\underline{\lambda}$:

$$\frac{\partial \underline{\lambda}}{\partial p} = -\frac{\lambda}{p - (1+r)w} < 0.$$

(13.56)

In addition, from the first-order condition for capacity (13.52) we find that the effect of an increase in retail price on the capacity of inframarginal firms is positive:

$$\frac{\partial K}{\partial p} = \frac{\lambda}{gL''(K)} > 0.$$

(13.57)

It follows that a maintained retail price above the market equilibrium price increases the number of retail outlets and induces existing outlets to increase their stocks. Both effects tend to increase the publisher's sales, and therefore profits. An increase in the retail price tends to reduce sales. The private profitability of a resale price maintenance scheme depends on whether or not the net effect is to increase sales. If manufacturers impose a maintained retail price scheme in equilibrium, the inference is that the net effect of the scheme is to increase sales, and therefore manufacturers's profits. Because the product is differentiated, one cannot conclude from the fact that sales increase that consumer welfare is increased.[9]

13.2.4   Vertical restraints under uncertainty

Rey and Tirole (1986) set up a spatial model of production and distribution (although most of the results are for the case of zero transportation cost). They emphasize that manufacturers and retailers are likely to operate under conditions of imperfect information. The usual assumption is that manufacturers and retailers have complete and perfect information about the market. In the models that we have considered to this point, it is the assumption of complete and perfect information that allows the manufacturer to set a franchise fee that appropriates all retail-level profit. It is more realistic to assume that retailers have better information about final demand and about their own costs than manufacturers.

Rey and Tirole analyze a market in which consumers are uniformly distributed on a line segment of unit length. There are two retailers, one located at each end of the line segment.

[9] To address the question of consumer welfare in the context of the present model would require modeling the determinants of λ.

Each consumer has demand curve $q = d - p$, where p is the retail price and d is a random variable, with $\underline{d} \leq d \leq \bar{d}$.[10]

Retailers operate with marginal cost γ per unit, where $\underline{\gamma} \leq \gamma \leq \bar{\gamma}$. There is a single manufacturer, who charges retailers a franchise fee A and a wholesale price w per unit of output.

The manufacturer must set A and w before d and γ are observed; retailers are able to set the retail price (unless a resale price maintenance scheme is imposed) after d and γ are observed.

It is also assumed that manufacturers are risk neutral. Retailers, however, are so risk averse they must be guaranteed a positive profit in the worst possible state of the world ($d = \underline{d}$, $\gamma = \underline{\gamma}$).[11]

Nonintegration

We consider three cases in turn. In the first, production and distribution are carried out separately. The retail sector consists of two price-setting firms. When transportation costs are zero, the firms sell a homogeneous good, and Bertrand competition implies that the equilibrium retail price equals the retailers' marginal cost, $p^{\text{nvi}} = w^{\text{nvi}} + \gamma$. Since retailers just break even at this retail price, the equilibrium franchise fee is $A^{\text{nvi}} = 0$.

The manufacturer's problem is then to select the retail price that maximizes his expected profit,

$$\pi^{\text{nvi}} = \max_{w} E[(w - c)(d - w - \gamma)], \tag{13.58}$$

where E denotes expected value. The profit-maximizing wholesale price is

$$w^{\text{nvi}} = \tfrac{1}{2}[E(d - \gamma) + c], \tag{13.59}$$

with corresponding retail price

$$p^{\text{nvi}} = w^{\text{nvi}} + \gamma = \tfrac{1}{2}[E(d + \gamma) + c]. \tag{13.60}$$

Substitution into (13.58) gives the manufacturer's expected profit,

$$\pi_m^{\text{nvi}} = \tfrac{1}{4}[E(d - \gamma) + c]^2. \tag{13.61}$$

The realized value of consumers' surplus is

$$CS = \tfrac{1}{2}(d - p)^2. \tag{13.62}$$

The appropriate measure of social welfare is the sum of expected consumers' surplus and the manufacturer's expected profit (recall that retailers' profits are zero).

---

[10] With positive transportation cost, the demand curve is $q = d - (p + ty)$, where t is transportation cost per unit and y is the distance from the customer to the retail outlet.

[11] See Rey and Tirole (1986) for a discussion of changes in results if retailers are risk neutral.

Evaluating (13.62) for the nonvertically integrated equilibrium values, expected consumers' surplus is

$$E(CS)^{\text{nvi}} = \tfrac{1}{8}[E(d) - c - E(\gamma)]^2 + \tfrac{1}{2}[\sigma_d^2 + \sigma_\gamma^2]. \tag{13.63}$$

Equations (13.61) and (13.63) together imply that expected net social welfare if production and distribution are separate is

$$NSW^{\text{nvi}} = \tfrac{3}{8}[E(d) - c - E(\gamma)]^2 + \tfrac{1}{2}[\sigma_d^2 + \sigma_\gamma^2]. \tag{13.64}$$

Exclusive territories

With exclusive territories, each retailer is a monopolist over half the linear market. After observing d and γ (which have the same values for both retailers), each retailer picks retail price p to maximize profit

$$\tfrac{1}{2}(p - w - \gamma)(d - p). \tag{13.65}$$

The resulting retail price is

$$p = \tfrac{1}{2}(d + \gamma + w), \tag{13.66}$$

and so the quantity demanded is

$$d - p = \tfrac{1}{2}(d - \gamma - w). \tag{13.67}$$

From (13.66) and (13.67), a single retailer's profit is

$$\pi_r = \tfrac{1}{8}(d - \gamma - w)^2 - A. \tag{13.68}$$

The manufacturer will set the highest possible franchise fee, subject to the constraint that the retailer must earn nonnegative profit in the worst possible state of the world. Hence

$$A^{\text{et}} = \tfrac{1}{8}(\underline{d} - \bar{\gamma} - w)^2, \tag{13.69}$$

which gives a retailer zero profit if demand is as small as possible and average cost is as large as possible. The manufacturer's problem then is to maximize his expected payoff,

$$\pi_m^{\text{et}} = \max_w \left[2A^{\text{et}} + \tfrac{1}{2}(w - c)E(d - w - \gamma) \right]$$
$$= \max_w \left\{ \tfrac{1}{4}\left[\underline{d} - (w + \bar{\gamma}) \right]^2 + \tfrac{1}{2}(w - c)E(d - w - \gamma) \right\}. \tag{13.70}$$

The manufacture's profit-maximizing wholesale price is

$$w^{\text{et}} = c + [E(d) - \underline{d}] + [\bar{\gamma} - E(\gamma)]. \tag{13.71}$$

Other equilibrium values can be derived in a straightforward way from (13.71).

Resale price maintenance

If the manufacturer is able to fix the retail price, a retailer's profit is

$$\pi_r^{\text{rpm}} = \tfrac{1}{2}(p - w - \gamma)(d - p) - A.$$

The maximum franchise fee that leaves retailers with guaranteed nonnegative profit is

$$A^{\text{rpm}} = \tfrac{1}{2}(p - w - \bar{\gamma})(\underline{d} - p). \tag{13.72}$$

The manufacturer's problem is then to pick p and w to maximize

$$\pi_m^{\text{rpm}} = \max_{p,w} \{2A^{\text{rpm}} + (w - c)[E(d) - p]\}$$

$$= \max_{p,w} \{(\underline{d} - p)(p - w - \bar{\gamma}) + (w - c)[E(d) - p]\} \tag{13.73}$$

subject to the constraint that $p \geq w + \bar{\gamma}$.

Although it is possible to deal with this formally using a Lagrangian and Kuhn–Tucker conditions, it is simpler to remark that it is never optimal for the manufacturer to give retailers any larger margin than is absolutely necessary.[12] It must therefore be the case that, in equilibrium,

$$p = w + \bar{\gamma}. \tag{13.74}$$

Substituting (13.74) into (13.73) allows us to rewrite the manufacturer's maximand as a function of p alone,

$$\pi_m^{\text{rpm}} = \max_p [E(d) - p](p - \bar{\gamma} - c). \tag{13.75}$$

π_m^{rpm} is maximized for

$$p^{\text{rpm}} = \tfrac{1}{2}[E(d) + \bar{\gamma} + c]. \tag{13.76}$$

Other equilibrium values follow directly from (13.76).

Results for demand uncertainty

Suppose that there is no cost uncertainty, so that $\underline{d} = d = \bar{d}$ and $\sigma_\gamma^2 = 0$. Then

$$\pi_m^{\text{nvi}} = \pi_m^{\text{rpm}} > \pi_m^{\text{et}} \quad \text{and} \quad NSW^{\text{nvi}} = NSW^{\text{rpm}} > NSW^{\text{et}}. \tag{13.77}$$

In the presence of demand uncertainty alone, resale price maintenance and nonintegration are privately and socially equivalent, and are preferable to the use of exclusive territories.

These results are sensitive to the assumption that transportation costs are zero (that products are homogeneous). Rey and Tirole indicate that if transportation costs are small and positive, the profitability ranking is $\pi_m^{\text{rpm}} > \pi_m^{\text{nvi}} > \pi_m^{\text{et}}$, with a similar ranking for net social welfare.

---

[12] This argument would not go through if the retailers performed some product-specific service or invested in a quality image that benefited the manufacturer. But such factors do not appear in this model.

Results for cost uncertainty

If there is no demand uncertainty, so $\underline{d} = \bar{d} = d$ and $\sigma_d^2 = 0$,

$$\pi_m^{nvi} > \pi_m^{et} > \pi_m^{rpm} \quad \text{and} \quad NSW^{nvi} > NSW^{et} > NSW^{rpm}. \tag{13.78}$$

In their discussion of these results, Rey and Tirole make the following points:

1 exclusive distribution induces retailers to take full account of demand and cost shocks, since each retailer is a monopolist in his half of the retail market;
2 when production and distribution are not integrated, retailers earn zero profit, which means the manufacturer bears the brunt of demand and cost fluctuations;
3 under resale price maintenance, manufacturers bear the burden of demand fluctuations, but retailers bear the burden of cost fluctuations.

13.2.5   Exclusive dealing

Aghion and Bolton (1987) model equilibrium exclusive dealing contracts between a seller and a buyer. The buyer can be thought of as a final consumer, as a producer who uses the good as an input to purchase some other good, or as a wholesale or retail distributor.

For simplicity, consider the case of a single seller, a single buyer, and one potential entrant. The buyer purchases at most one unit of the product, and has a reservation price equal to one.

The incumbent's unit cost c is less than one. The entrant's unit cost, which is unknown to the incumbent and the buyer, is c_e. c_e is uniformly distributed on the interval $[0, 1]$.

If entry occurs, the two producers compete in prices. Hence the post-entry price is the larger of c and c_e (the firm with lower unit cost could get the sale by pricing infinitesimally less than the unit cost of the other firm). In the absence of an exclusive dealing contract, entry occurs only if $c_e \le c$. The probability that entry occurs is the probability that $c_e \le 1$. Since c_e is uniformly distributed on $[0, 1]$, $\Pr(entry|no\ contract) = c$.

The sequence of play is as follows:

1 the seller and buyer negotiate an exclusive dealing contract;
2 the potential entrant comes in or stays out;
3 trade occurs.

If the buyer is to sign an exclusive dealing contract, it must offer him at least as great a payoff as he would obtain in the absence of a contract. If there is no contract and entry does not occur, the buyer pays his reservation price, 1, for the product. If there is no contract and entry does occur, the buyer pays price c for the product (entry does not occur unless $c_e \le c$, and $price = \max(c, c_e)$). The benefit to the buyer if entry occurs is $1 - c$, the difference between the price actually paid and his reservation price. The buyer's expected payoff if there is no contract is therefore

$$(1 - c)(0) + c(1 - c) = c(1 - c). \tag{13.79}$$

Now suppose that an exclusive dealing contract is completely described by the parameters (p, d). p is the price that the buyer pays if he buys from the incumbent. d is the amount of damages that the buyer pays to the incumbent if he buys from the entrant.

If a contract (p, d) is signed and entry does not occur, the buyer's payoff is $1 - p$. It follows that if entry occurs, the entrant must offer the buyer a payoff of at least $1 - p$ to get the sale. It would never pay the entrant to offer the buyer any more than this (the entrant could get the sale by offering the buyer a price infinitesimally less than p). Hence if a contract (p, d) is signed, the buyer's payoff, whether or not entry occurs, is $1 - p$.

If a contract (p, d) has been signed, it is profitable for the entrant to come into the market only if the entrant's price p_e plus the damages d are no greater than p; that is, only if $p_e + dp$.

But if entry occurs, the entrant will take the largest price he can get, so that $p_e = p - d$. Hence if a contract (p, d) has been signed, entry occurs only if $p - d \geq c_e$, and this occurs with probability $p - d$ (provided that $p - d \geq 0$; otherwise the probability of entry is zero).

From this discussion, the incumbent's problem is to offer the contract (p, d) to the buyer that maximizes his own expected payoff,

$$(p - d)d + [1 - (p - d)](p - c), \tag{13.80}$$

subject to the constraint that the buyer's payoff be at least as great as it would be without the contract (see relation (13.79)):

$$1 - p \geq c(1 - c). \tag{13.81}$$

The Lagrangian for this constrained optimization problem is

$$L = (p - d)d + [1 - (p - d)](p - c) + \lambda[1 - p - c(1 - c)], \tag{13.82}$$

with corresponding first-order conditions

$$\frac{\partial L}{\partial p} = 2d + 1 - 2p + c - \lambda \equiv 0, \tag{13.83}$$

$$\frac{\partial L}{\partial d} = 2p - 2d - c \equiv 0, \tag{13.84}$$

$$\frac{\partial L}{\partial \lambda} = 1 - p - c(1 - c) \geq 0, \qquad \lambda \frac{\partial L}{\partial \lambda} \equiv 0, \qquad \lambda \geq 0. \tag{13.85}$$

The solution is straightforward. Equation (13.84) implies

$$p - d = \tfrac{1}{2}c > 0. \tag{13.86}$$

Then (13.83) implies that $\lambda = 1$. And if $\lambda = 1$, then (13.85) implies

$$p = c + (1 - c)^2. \tag{13.87}$$

Equations (13.86) and (13.87) together imply

$$d = 1 - \tfrac{3}{2}c + c^2.$$ (13.88)

Hence

$$\frac{\mathrm{d}p_e}{\mathrm{d}c} = -1 + 2c, \qquad \frac{\mathrm{d}d}{\mathrm{d}c} = -2\left(\tfrac{3}{4} - c\right).$$ (13.89)

p falls as c falls. d falls as c falls, if $c < 3/4$.

If there were no exclusive dealing contract, entry would occur only if $c_e \leq c$. Such entry would be socially desirable, since it would shift production to a lower-cost producer. With the exclusive dealing contract, entry occurs only if $c_e \leq p - d = c/2$. The exclusive dealing contract therefore cuts the probability of entry in half.

By construction, the contract leaves the buyer as well off as he would be if no contract were signed. It remains to examine the payoff of the incumbent.

Evaluating (13.82) for the optimal values (13.86)–(13.88), the incumbent's expected payoff under the exclusive dealing contract is

$$L^* = 1 - 2c - \tfrac{5}{4}c^2 = \left(1 + \tfrac{1}{2}c\right)\left(1 - \tfrac{5}{2}c\right).$$ (13.90)

If no contract is offered, the incumbent's payoff is 0 with probability $1 - c$ (if entry occurs) and $1 - c$ with probability c (if entry does not occur), or

$$c(1 - c).$$ (13.91)

It follows that the incumbent earns at least as great a profit offering an exclusive dealing contract if

$$1 - 2c - \tfrac{5}{4}c^2 \geq c(1 - c)$$ (13.92)

– a condition which is met for $0 \leq c \leq 2[\sqrt{10} - 3] \approx 0.32$. If the incumbent's unit cost falls in this range, it is privately profitable for the incumbent to offer an exclusive dealing contract that leaves the buyer as well off as before and discourages socially desirable entry.

The reason why the buyer is willing to enter into such a contract is clear: in an expected value sense, he is as well off with the contract as he is without it. The incumbent offers the contract because entry only occurs if the entrant has very low unit cost, and the penalty d allows the incumbent to appropriate part of those low costs.

Once the contract is offered, the incumbent gets a payoff $p - c = 1 - 2c + c^2$ if entry does not occur, and a payoff $d = 1 - \tfrac{3}{2}c + c^2$ if entry does occur. Since $d - (p - c) = c/2 > 0$, once a contract is offered, the incumbent strictly prefers that entry occur. The incumbent earns a greater return by collecting the penalty than he does by producing and selling on his own.

13.2.6   Tying and bundling[13]

Tying and bundling have strategic effects because they change the substitution relationships between the goods among which consumers choose. Tying and bundling in appropriate proportions is privately profitable, reduces rivals' profits and overall welfare, and may drive rivals from the market.

We work with a simple and standard model of consumer behavior. Let market demand for two goods be as in the Bowley (1924) representative consumer model, with inverse demand curves:

$$p_1 = a - (Q_1 + \theta Q_2) \tag{13.93}$$

and

$$p_2 = a - (\theta Q_1 + Q_2). \tag{13.94}$$

Let there be two firms, A and B. Firm A is a monopolist of product 1,

$$Q_1 = q_{A1}. \tag{13.95}$$

Both firms produce product 2:

$$Q_2 = q_{A2} + q_{B2}. \tag{13.96}$$

Suppose now that firm A sells its products only in the proportion k_A of good 1 to one unit of good 2; that is, firm A offers b_A bundles

$$(k_A, 1). \tag{13.97}$$

Firm B, which does not produce product 1, sells a "bundle" that consists only of one unit of good 2,

$$(0, 1). \tag{13.98}$$

The relationships between the bundles and the underlying variables are

$$Q_1 = k_A b_A \tag{13.99}$$

and

$$Q_2 = b_A + b_B, \tag{13.100}$$

respectively, where b_A is the number of bundles sold by firm 1 and b_B is the number of bundles sold by firm 2.

---

[13] Martin (1999). See also Burstein (1960), Adams and Yellen (1976), McGee (1987), Whinston (1990), and Slade (1998).

The implied inverse demand functions for bundles are[14]

$$P_A = (k_A + 1)a - [(1 + 2\theta k_A + k_A^2)b_A + (1 + \theta k_A)b_B], \qquad (13.101)$$

$$P_B = a - [(1 + \theta k_A)b_A + b_B]. \qquad (13.102)$$

Tying and bundling have strategic effects because they alters – indeed, may even create – substitutability relationships. If $\theta = 0$, so that there is no demand relationship between goods 1 and 2, the bundled goods are nonetheless demand substitutes.

Henceforth, for simplicity, let $\theta = 0$, so the two goods are independent in demand. This is not essential to the qualitative nature of the results that follow. Assume also that marginal cost is constant, c per unit, for both goods. For the moment, leave the nature of fixed costs unspecified. Finally, assume that the firms act as Cournot quantity-setting oligopolists. Noncooperative equilibrium outputs if firm 1 does not bundle are

$$q_{A1} = \tfrac{1}{2}(a - c), \qquad q_{A2} = q_{B2} = \tfrac{1}{3}(a - c). \qquad (13.103)$$

q_{A1} is monopoly output for good 1. q_{A2} and q_{B2} are Cournot duopoly outputs for good 2. Equilibrium payoffs, before allowing for fixed costs, are

$$\pi_A = \left(\tfrac{1}{4} + \tfrac{1}{9}\right)(a - c)^2 = \tfrac{13}{36}(a - c)^2, \qquad (13.104)$$

$$\pi_B = q_{B2}^2 = \tfrac{1}{9}(a - c)^2. \qquad (13.105)$$

Noncooperative equilibrium consumers' surplus plus economic profit is

$$\tfrac{59}{72}(a - c)^2. \qquad (13.106)$$

Let $k_A = 1$. This is sufficient to bring out the strategic and welfare effects of bundling. Noncooperative equilibrium outputs of bundles are

$$b_A = \tfrac{3}{7}(a - c), \qquad b_B = \tfrac{2}{7}(a - c). \qquad (13.107)$$

These translate into output levels

$$q_1 = \tfrac{3}{7}(a - c) < \tfrac{1}{2}(a - c) \qquad (13.108)$$

and

$$q_2 = \tfrac{5}{7}(a - c) > \tfrac{2}{3}(a - c) \qquad (13.109)$$

of the underlying goods.

Bundling reduces the output of good 1 and increases the output of good 2. Firm A produces $\tfrac{3}{7}(a - c)$ units of good 2, more than without bundling. Firm B produces $\tfrac{2}{7}(a - c)$ units of good 2, less than without bundling. This reflects the fact that bundles are strategic as well as demand substitutes.

---

[14] Substitute (13.99) and (13.100) into the equation of the representative consumer utility function that yields (13.93) and (13.94) (see (3.34) and the associated text). This expresses utility in terms of bundles. Constrained optimization of this transformed utility function yields (13.101) and (13.102).

The increase in output of good 2 means that the price of firm B's "bundle" is less than the equilibrium price of good 2 without bundling. Bundling by firm A means that firm 2 sells less and at a lower price, compared with a situation in which A does not bundle. Bundling therefore lowers firm 2's profit. Payoffs with bundling are

$$\Pi_A = \tfrac{18}{49}(a - c)^2 > \tfrac{13}{36}(a - c)^2 = \pi_A, \tag{13.110}$$

$$\Pi_B = \tfrac{4}{49}(a - c)^2 < \tfrac{1}{9}(a - c)^2 = \pi_B. \tag{13.111}$$

These expressions are for payoffs gross of fixed costs. If B's fixed costs fall in the appropriate range, it will be profitable for B to operate if A does not bundle, and become unprofitable for B to operate if A does bundle. In such cases, bundling will allow A to extend a (possibly legal) monopoly over product 1 to product 2.

In the model as specified to this point, net welfare with bundling is

$$\tfrac{39}{49}(a - c)^2 < \tfrac{59}{72}(a - c)^2. \tag{13.112}$$

Firm A's privately profitable bundling therefore reduces social welfare, compared with the case in which firm A does not bundle.

13.3 EMPIRICAL EVIDENCE

13.3.1 Econometric analysis

Gilligan (1986) distinguishes four explanations of resale price maintenance:

1   The dealer cartel hypothesis[15] – dealers induce a manufacturer to use resale price maintenance as a device to police a dealer cartel. Removal of resale price maintenance should increase, or at least not decrease, the price of shares of the manufacturer's stock.
2   The manufacturer cartel hypothesis – manufacturers use resale price maintenance to make it more difficult for members of a manufacturer cartel to undercut cartel prices. Removal of resale price maintenance should reduce the price of shares of the manufacturer's stock.
3   The price discrimination hypothesis – by preventing resale across groups of consumers with different price elasticities of demand, resale price maintenance favors profitable price discrimination. Removal of resale price maintenance should reduce the price of shares of the manufacturer's stock.
4   The market failure hypothesis[16] – resale price maintenance is a way of correcting for failure in the market for distribution services due to free-riding problems. Removal of resale price maintenance should reduce the price of shares of the manufacturer's stock. However, if managerial inertia has caused use of resale price maintenance to persist

---

[15] See also Comanor and Rey (2000).
[16] Which Gilligan describes as "transactional hypotheses."

after it ceases to be an optimal marketing strategy, removal of resale price maintenance may cause an increase in the price of shares of the manufacturer's stock.

Gilligan first tests these hypotheses by examining the impact of the announcement of a resale-price-maintenance-related antitrust complaint on the price of a company's stock. He uses a sample of 43 such complaints. His description of the results is as follows (Gilligan, 1986, p. 551):

> Some of the results are inconsistent with the dealer cartel, manufacturer cartel, and price discrimination hypotheses. The hypothesis that RPM is used solely for transactions cost reasons is not refutable . . . Thus, the results . . . suggest either that RPM has a wide variety of effects or that RPM is used exclusively to mitigate moral hazard problems.

In a follow-up analysis, Gilligan relates the stock-market response to a resale price maintenance complaint to retail market concentration, manufacturing market concentration, and the firm's market share. Results from this analysis are consistent with the dealer cartel, manufacturer cartel, and market failure with marketing inertia explanations of resale price maintenance.

Resale price maintenance, it would appear from this study, is a many-splendored thing.

13.3.2   Case studies

A 1984 Federal Trade Commission report (FTC) (Lafferty et al., 1984) contains case studies of five episodes of resale price maintenance. They demonstrate the diverse causes and effects of vertical restraints, but lend special support to the quality certification explanation.

The Levi Strauss company introduced a resale price maintenance program in the early 1960s, as a way of inducing high-quality retailers to carry Levi's jeans. This seems to be an example of the Marvel–McCafferty quality-certification theory of vertical restraints. The strategy was successful, but Levi Strauss maintained its resale price maintenance program long after customers had became familiar with its product. After an FTC legal challenge, Levi Strauss abandoned its price maintenance program. Stores specializing in jeans cut price, and Levi Strauss's sales and stock-market value increased sharply. Oster (1984) estimated that the shift away from resale price maintenance resulted in a gain of $3 million a year in consumers' surplus, with another $72 million a year benefit to consumers in reduced income transfers from consumers to Levi Strauss.

This example illustrates one of the inefficiencies attributed to resale price maintenance. By preventing retailers from experimenting with different prices, it prevents the manufacturer from learning whether or not demand is highly elastic, so that price reductions would be profitable.

Florsheim Shoes imposed a resale price maintenance program, and limited the number of dealers. The motive seems to have been to induce dealers to provide a high-quality image and a high level of in-store service. Florsheim used this marketing strategy to hold a market segment between consumers of low-priced shoes imported from Third World countries and high-price imports from Europe. The most important elements of "service" were carrying a full inventory and maintaining a high-quality ambience. In the words of Greening (1984, p. 129):

> we needn't understand why and how ambience is important to shoppers, only that it is expensive to provide and requires high margins on merchandise.

Components of stereo systems – turntables, amplifiers, radio receivers, and the like – were commonly marketed under a system of resale price maintenance. When this type of product was new and unknown to most consumers, quality certification was important (McEachern and Romeo, 1984, p. 24):

> RPM during the early days of the product life cycle was the quid pro quo, the bribe to secure shelf space and to encourage retailers to acquaint a relatively affluent subset of the consuming public with both an unfamiliar product and an unfamiliar brand.

The prevention of free riding on pre-sales dealer service may have been a motive. By the time FTC action induced manufacturers to give up resale price maintenance, the whole class of products was well established. As with Levi's jeans, it seems likely that inertia and imperfect information allowed an established distribution pattern to persist after it ceased to be optimal.

Marvel (1981) provides what may be an example of free riding, but free riding on services provided by manufacturers, not retailers. He analyzes the market for hearing aids, which were sold door-to-door by salesmen working from lists of potential clients provided by the manufacturer. If a single salesman had represented more than one manufacturer, lists of potential clients provided by one manufacturer could have been used to generate sales for other manufacturers. This would have reduced the incentive of any one manufacturer to invest in the national advertising that produced lists of potential clients in the first place. Manufacturers combated this potential market failure by imposing an exclusive dealing system on their salesmen.

In the late 1960s, established manufacturers of industrial gases faced increasing competition from entrants utilizing new technologies. They responded by imposing requirements contracts on their distributors, foreclosing entrants from access to established distributors. These requirements contracts probably raised the cost of entry and worsened market performance.

13.4   CONCLUSION

Vertical restraints are a multifaceted phenomenon. It now seems possible to reject both of the extreme positions that characterized the debate on vertical restraints in the 1970s. It is not correct that vertical restraints everywhere and always have an efficiency motive. Nor is it correct that vertical restraints are everywhere and always a consequence of or a support for market power.

Instead, we are left in a messy middle ground. Vertical restraints may be imposed by manufacturers who wish to guarantee the quality of the retail outlets that distribute their product.

When such restraints are imposed early in a product's life-cycle, in particular, they may be socially beneficial. But vertical restraints inhibit the kind of dealer experimentation with prices that produces information about demand. If imposed by manufacturers, they may have the effect of raising entry costs. Case study evidence supports the argument that vertical restraints are likely to outlast the period in which they are socially beneficial.

CHAPTER FOURTEEN

RESEARCH AND DEVELOPMENT

And I returned, and saw under the sun, that the race is not to the swift, nor the battle to the strong, neither yet bread to the wise, nor yet riches to men of understanding, nor yet favor to men of skill; but time and chance happeneth to them all.

Ecclesiastes 9:11

14.1 INTRODUCTION

The economic literature on research and development[1] continues to be shaped by the work of Joseph Schumpeter, who (in what must be one of the most frequently quoted passages in economics) emphasized (1943, p. 84) the importance of dynamic rather than static competition:

> Economists are at long last emerging from the stage at which price competition was all they saw. As soon as quality competition and sales effort are admitted into the sacred precincts of theory, the price variable is ousted from its dominant position. However, it is still competition within a rigid pattern of invariant conditions, methods of production and forms of industrial organization in particular, that practically monopolizes attention. But in capitalist reality as distinguished from its textbook picture, it is not that kind of competition which counts but competition from the new commodity, the new technology, the new source of supply, the new type of organization . . . competition which commands a decisive cost or quality advantage and which strikes not at the margins of the profits and outputs of existing firms but at their foundations and their very lives.

While the seminal nature of Schumpeter's contributions to the economics of innovation is universally recognized, what he thought and when he thought it remains a topic of interest. Winter (1984, pp. 294–7) emphasizes the distinction between what has come to be called

---

[1] For surveys, see Kamien and Schwartz (1982), Baldwin and Scott (1987), Dosi (1988), Reinganum (1989) and Beath et al. (1989).

Schumpeter Mark I – the Schumpeter of *The Theory of Economic Development* (1934) and Schumpeter Mark II – the Schumpeter of *Capitalism, Socialism, and Democracy* (1943).[2]

In Schumpeter Mark I, it is the new firm that is most often the vehicle of innovation (1934, p. 66):[3]

> it is not essential to the matter – though it may happen – that the new combinations should be carried out by the same people who control the productive or commercial process which is to be displaced by the new. On the contrary, new combinations are, as a rule, embodied, as it were, in new firms which generally do not arise out of the old ones but start producing beside them; . . . in general it is not the owner of stage-coaches who builds railways.

For the Mark II Schumpeter, however, it was the established firm that was responsible for technological progress (1943, p. 82):[4,5]

> As soon as we go into details and inquire into the individual items in which progress was most conspicuous, the trail leads not to the doors of those firms that work under conditions of comparatively free competition but precisely to the doors of the large concerns . . . and a shocking suspicion dawns upon us that big business may have had more to do with creating that standard of life than with keeping it down.

Static market power might be a prerequisite for rivalry based on innovation, but the Schumpeter Mark II view is that the overall welfare effect of innovation, taking welfare losses due to the exercise of static market power into account, is positive.

Schumpeter's visions of the forces that drive innovation continue to guide economists' analysis of research and development. Is large size a prerequisite for innovation? Is market power a prerequisite for innovation? Should society disapprove of static market power if it encourages innovation? Should society grant a legal monopoly (a patent) to the successful innovator? If so, on what terms? Can patents be effective, or is it always possible to invent around them? If patents are not effective, why do firms bother to take them out? It is a tribute to the profound nature of Schumpeter's work that economists still debate the answers to the questions he raised.

---

[2] The evolution of Schumpeter's views is noted by Kamien and Schwartz (1982, pp. 7–11). For the bulk of the literature (Baldwin and Scott, 1987; Tirole, 1988; Cohen and Levin, 1989), Schumpeter's views are those of Schumpeter Mark II.

[3] Schumpeter (1934, p. 66) defined "the carrying out of new combinations" as including the introduction of new products or new varieties of existing products, the introduction of new production processes, the opening of new markets, the development of new sources of supplies, and the development of new organizational forms (for example, creation or destruction of a monopoly position).

[4] The view that innovation is the province of established firms with leading market positions is put forward even more forcefully by Galbraith (1952, p. 86), who associated his conclusions with those of Schumpeter:

> Technical development has long since become the preserve of the scientist and the engineer. Most of the cheap and simple inventions have, to put it bluntly, been made. Not only is development now sophisticated and costly but it must be on a sufficient scale so that successes and failures will in some measure average out. Few can afford it if they must expect all projects to pay off.

[5] For views on the formal modeling of Schumpeter Mark II, see Fisher and Temin (1973) and Kohn and Scott (1982).

14.2   STYLIZED FACTS

14.2.1   Rate of return to innovation

There are many practical difficulties in measuring either the private or the social rate of return to innovation.[6] In measuring the private rate of return to innovation, estimates should account not only for the cost of a successful project, but also the cost of unsuccessful projects at the same firm with the same target. The private benefits of new product should make allowance for any profits lost on displaced products produced by the same firm. The social benefits of a new product should make allowance for profits lost on displaced products produced by any firm. Private benefits from either product or process innovation should allow for the fact that the innovation may itself be displaced by further innovation. The social return to investment in R&D that leads to one innovation includes not only incremental consumers' surplus from that innovation but also, in some measure, the benefits from follow-up, incremental innovations.

Keeping such qualifications in mind, a large literature suggests that private and social rates of return to innovation are larger than rates of return to more conventional types of investment. These results in turn suggest that there is underinvestment in innovation from a social point of view.[7]

Mansfield et al. (1977) report the results of case studies of four process and 13 product innovations. They estimate private rates of return ranging from negative to 214 percent, with a median of 25 percent. Estimated social rates of return range from negative to 307 percent, with a median of 56 percent. The estimated social rate of return tends to exceed the private rate of return, although this is not always the case.

Griliches (1986) uses firm-level data to estimate Cobb–Douglas production functions that include as an argument a constructed measure of the firm's R&D capital stock. His estimates imply rates of return to investment in R&D that range from 33 to 62 percent.[8] He also finds that basic research has a differentially positive impact on firm productivity, and that company-financed R&D spending has a greater impact on productivity than R&D spending financed by the US Federal government.

Bernstein (1989) reports estimates of the private and social rates of return of cost-reducing R&D for nine Canadian industries. The methodology is based on estimates of the parameters of industry cost functions that include as arguments industry R&D capital stocks. Time series for an industry's R&D capital stock are constructed from available data on industry R&D expenditures. He estimates private rates of return to R&D capital ranging from 24 to 47 percent, while private rates of return to physical capital range from 9 to 12 percent.

---

[6] For a survey of the literature on returns to R&D and R&D spillovers, see Griliches (1992).

[7] The rent-seeking literature (Fudenberg and Tirole, 1987) suggests the possibility of what Baldwin and Scott (1987) call the "overbidding problem": competing firms may spend more seeking private advantage from first innovation than an innovation is worth from a social point of view. Evidence does not support the existence of overbidding; see Cockburn and Henderson (1994).

[8] Applying a similar methodology to Japanese manufacturing, Goto and Suzuki (1989) estimate the marginal rate of return to investment in R&D at about 40 percent.

Estimated social rates of return on investment (which allow for spillovers of knowledge in one industry to reduce cost in other industries) range from 29 to 94 percent.

Many studies measure the social rate of return to R&D by including some measure of R&D input or R&D output as an explanatory variable in an estimating equation that explains total factor productivity growth. The estimated coefficient of the R&D variable indicates how much greater productivity growth would be if R&D activity were increased.

Jones and Williams (1997) survey this literature, and conclude that it shows an R&D rate of return of about 30 percent, considering only the returns to R&D within the industry carrying out the R&D. If returns in other industries are also taken into account, estimates of the rate of return are as high as 100 percent.

The results of Pakes and Schankerman (1984) sound a cautionary note. They estimate that the rate of depreciation of the revenue that flows from successful innovation is substantially larger than the rate of depreciation of physical assets.[9] They find that the private rate of return to innovation falls in a range from essentially the same as to perhaps twice the private rate of return to physical assets.

14.2.2   Spillovers

For 48 US new product innovations, Mansfield et al. (1981) report that 60 percent of successful patented innovations were imitated within four years of introduction. For a sample of 100 US manufacturing firms, Mansfield (1985) reports survey evidence indicating that rivals have information about R&D decisions in 12–18 months, and information about new products or processes in 12 months or less. Such leakages occur (Mansfield, 1985, p. 221) because

> [i]n some industries there is considerable movement of personnel from one firm to another, and there are informal communications networks among engineers and scientists working at various firms, as well as professional meetings at which information is exchanged. In other industries, input suppliers and customers are important channels (since they pass on a great deal of relevant information), patent applications are scrutinized very carefully, and reverse engineering is carried out. In still other industries, the diffusion process is accelerated by the fact that firms do not go to great lengths to keep such information secret, partly because they believe it would be futile in any event.

In the same vein, Henderson and Cockburn (1996, pp. 35–6) write of the pharmaceutical industry that

> [it] is characterized by high rates of publication in the open scientific literature, and many of the scientists . . . stressed the importance of keeping in touch with the science conducted both within the public sector and by their competitors. Nearly all of them had a quite accurate idea of the nature of the research being conducted by their competitors, and they often described the ways in which their rivals' discoveries had been instrumental in shaping their own research.

---

[9] Comanor (1986, p. 1184) makes this same point with reference to the pharmaceutical industry.

Caballero and Jaffe (1993) use patent citation data for the United States to estimate the rate of diffusion of information about innovations. They find rates of diffusion to be so large that they can be regarded as being instantaneous.

For a sample of 133 Federal Trade Commission line-of-business industries, Scott (1993, p. 129) finds that an additional dollar of R&D spending per dollar of sales increases total factor productivity by 14 percent. When he reorganizes the data in 93 observations of technologically related industries, the result is 37 percent. This suggests that the R&D efforts in one industry spill over into technologically related industries.

Adams and Jaffe (1996) match plant, firm, and industry data for the US chemical industry[10] to analyze spillovers between plants and firms, while controlling for geographic and technological distance.[11] Their results are that spillovers are important but local in nature (1996, p. 718):

> the broad picture painted by our results is one in which spillovers of R&D are important, both within and across firms . . . . these spillovers are significantly diluted as the number of recipients grows, calling into question the theoretical argument that R&D spillovers imply industrywide or economywide increasing returns to scale.

Similarly, Klette (1996) analyzes a sample of Norwegian plant-level data, and finds evidence of R&D spillovers among firms within a business group and among firms within the same line of business.

14.2.3 Summary

Empirical work suggests that the private return to investment in innovation is quite high – higher than other types of investments – and that the social rate of return to investment is higher than the private rate of return. This is evidence in favor of the view that in a market system there is underinvestment in innovation, relative to the social optimum.

At the same time, there appear to be substantial and fairly rapid information flows among firms operating in the same or related markets. In many sectors, firms have first access to the knowledge that they generate, but the lag before rivals access some form of that knowledge appears to be short. The theoretical literature has focused on the impact of such information flows on private levels of investment in innovation, and on the design of institutions (patents, subsidies, competition policy toward R&D joint ventures) to promote innovation.

---

[10] Standard Industrial Classification code 28.

[11] The technological distance between two firms measured is measured by the correlation between the distributions of the firms' R&D distribution vectors over the 32 National Science Foundation product categories (Adams and Jaffe, 1996, p. 707).

14.3   Deterministic Innovation

14.3.1   Fully noncooperative behavior

d'Aspremont and Jacquemin

d'Aspremont and Jacquemin (1988) (henceforth, AJ) present a widely generalized two-stage duopoly model of cost-saving innovation.[12] In the first stage, firms 1 and 2 pick cost reductions which they pay for as specified below. The cost reductions that are realized in the second stage depend on the cost reductions that are paid for in the first stage and on the nature of spillovers. In the second stage, firms play a Cournot game with (potentially) cost differences (although in equilibrium unit costs turn out to be the same).

The product is homogeneous, with linear inverse demand function

$$p = a - b(q_1 + q_2). \tag{14.1}$$

If there is no research and development, average cost is c per unit. In the first stage of the game, firms 1 and 2 pay for cost reductions x_1 and x_2, respectively, reducing their units costs to[13,14]

$$c_i = c - \left(x_i + \sigma x_j\right). \tag{14.2}$$

The output spillover parameter σ lies between zero and one. σ indicates the extent to which a cost reduction at one firm reduces unit cost at the other. $\sigma = 0$ implies that a firm benefits only from its own investment in cost reduction; $\sigma = 1$ means that each firm benefits as much from the other's investment in cost reduction as from its own.

The cost of R&D is quadratic: for a direct reduction in unit cost of x_i firm i must pay

$$\tfrac{1}{2}\gamma x_i^2. \tag{14.3}$$

There are thus increasing costs or decreasing returns to scale in directly paid for cost reductions.

When firms pick their R&D levels in the first stage, they do so noncooperatively to maximize own profit, anticipating the nature of the product market game that will be played in the second stage. To solve the game, therefore, we work backward from the second stage, first determining product–market equilibrium for given levels of x_1 and x_2, then determining the equilibrium values of x_1 and x_2.

---

[12] As noted by Amir (2000), this entire literature is anticipated by Ruff (1969). See also Spence (1984) and, for a survey, DeBondt (1997). Suzumura (1992) generalizes the AJ model to the case of n firms and general functional forms.

[13] In what follows, unless otherwise noted, subscripts $i, j = 1, 2$ and $i \neq j$.

[14] Evidently, this formulation makes sense only if the equilibrium values of c_1, c_2 are nonnegative, and this is henceforth assumed. This amounts to requiring that the cost of R&D be sufficiently great, relative to the size of the market, that firms do not undertake "too much" innovation.

THE SECOND STAGE

x_1 and x_2 are determined in the first stage. In the second stage, firm i picks output q_i to maximize its payoff

$$\pi_i = [a - c + x_i + \sigma x_j - b(q_1 + q_2)]q_i - \tfrac{1}{2}\gamma x_i^2. \tag{14.4}$$

The first-order conditions for profit maximization can be rewritten as the equations of the product-market best-response functions,

$$q_i = \frac{1}{2b}\left[a - c + x_i + \sigma x_j - q_j\right]. \tag{14.5}$$

Equilibrium output levels are

$$q_i = \frac{a - c + (2 - \sigma)x_i + (2\sigma - 1)x_j}{3b}, \tag{14.6}$$

and the other properties of product–market equilibrium can be derived in a straightforward way from the equilibrium output levels.

THE FIRST STAGE

Equation (14.6) gives equilibrium outputs in the second-stage game, as functions of the first-stage cost reductions x_1 and x_2. Substituting from (14.6) into (14.4) yields a reduced-form expression for firm i's payoff in terms of direct cost reductions alone:

$$\pi_i = bq_i^2 - \tfrac{1}{2}\gamma x_i^2. \tag{14.7}$$

In the first stage, each firm noncooperatively picks its direct cost reduction to maximize its reduced form payoff.

The first-order condition to maximize (14.7) can be rewritten as the equation of firm i's cost-reduction best-response function:

$$x_i = \tfrac{2}{9}(2 - \sigma)\frac{a - c + (2\sigma - 1)x_j}{b\gamma - \tfrac{2}{9}(2 - \sigma)^2}. \tag{14.8}$$

The second-order condition for profit maximization ensures that the denominator on the right is positive.

The slope of the best-response function is

$$\left.\frac{\mathrm{d}x_i}{\mathrm{d}x_j}\right|_{\mathrm{brf}} = \frac{2}{9}\frac{(2 - \sigma)(2\sigma - 1)}{b\gamma - \tfrac{2}{9}(2 - \sigma)^2}, \tag{14.9}$$

which has the same sign as $2\sigma - 1$. R&D best-response functions slope upward for $\sigma > \tfrac{1}{2}$ and downward for $\sigma < \tfrac{1}{2}$.[15]

[15] From section 2.6.2, stability requires that the slope of the R&D best-response function be less than one in absolute value. The stability condition is violated if γ is too small (Henriques, 1990; d'Aspremont and Jacquemin, 1990; Suzumura, 1992, fn. 6).

Equilibrium is symmetric; setting $x_1 = x_2 = x_{NN}$ in (14.8) and collecting terms gives the equilibrium cost reduction paid for by each firm:[16]

$$x_{NN} = \frac{2}{9} \frac{2 - \sigma}{b\gamma - \frac{2}{9}(1 + \sigma)(2 - \sigma)}(a - c). \tag{14.10}$$

Taking spillovers into account, the cost reduction realized by each firm is

$$(1 + \sigma)x_{NN} = \frac{2}{9} \frac{(1 + \sigma)(2 - \sigma)}{b\gamma - \frac{2}{9}(1 + \sigma)(2 - \sigma)}(a - c). \tag{14.11}$$

Substituting from (14.10) into (14.6) gives equilibrium outputs:

$$q(x_{NN}, x_{NN}) = \frac{b\gamma}{b\gamma - \frac{2}{9}(1 + \sigma)(2 - \sigma)} \frac{a - c}{3b}. \tag{14.12}$$

From (14.7), equilibrium payoffs per firm are

$$\pi_{NN}^{AJ} = \frac{1}{9}\gamma \frac{b\gamma - \frac{2}{9}(2 - \sigma)}{\left[b\gamma - \frac{2}{9}(1 + \sigma)(2 - \sigma)\right]^2}(a - c)^2. \tag{14.13}$$

With linear inverse demand, consumers' surplus is $\frac{1}{2}b(2q)^2$,

$$CS_{NN}^{AJ} = 2b\left[\frac{b\gamma}{b\gamma - \frac{2}{9}(1 + \sigma)(2 - \sigma)} \frac{a - c}{3b}\right]^2. \tag{14.14}$$

Net social welfare is the sum of consumers' surplus and profit,

$$NSW_{NN}^{AJ} = \frac{4}{9}\gamma \frac{b\gamma - \frac{1}{9}(2 - \sigma)^2}{\left[b\gamma - \frac{2}{9}(1 + \sigma)(2 - \sigma)\right]^2}(a - c)^2. \tag{14.15}$$

Since in this discussion the number of firms is fixed at two, the interesting comparative static question that can be asked is the impact of changes in σ, the degree of spillovers, on equilibrium values. From (14.11),

$$\frac{\partial(1 + \sigma)x_{NN}}{\partial\sigma} = \frac{2}{9}b\gamma \frac{1 - 2\sigma}{\left[b\gamma - \frac{2}{9}(1 + \sigma)(2 - \sigma)\right]^2}(a - c). \tag{14.16}$$

Increases in spillovers increase equilibrium cost reductions if $\sigma < \frac{1}{2}$, and reduce equilibrium cost reductions if $\sigma > \frac{1}{2}$. In the AJ model, high spillover levels worsen technological performance.

[16] The condition for $x_{NN} > 0$ is that the denominator on the right in (14.10) be positive. For any value of σ, the condition is satisfied if $b\gamma$ is sufficiently great.

Equilibrium output per firm and consumers' surplus rise with equilibrium cost reductions. Hence increases in spillovers increase output and consumers' surplus if $\sigma < \frac{1}{2}$, reduce them if $\sigma > \frac{1}{2}$. Although the impact of an increase in spillovers on profit is ambiguous, one can show that an increase in spillovers increases equilibrium firm profit for σ in a range from 0 to an upper limit that is greater than $\frac{1}{2}$. It follows that increases in spillovers increase net social welfare at least for $\sigma < \frac{1}{2}$, since in this range increases in σ increase both consumers' surplus and profits. For some range above $\sigma = \frac{1}{2}$, further increases in σ increase equilibrium profit per firm but leave consumers worse off.

We now compare x_{NN} with a second-best welfare standard, the cost saving that maximizes net social welfare, assuming noncooperative product–market behavior in the second stage.[17]

Equation (14.6) gives equilibrium outputs as a function of the first-stage cost reductions. If both firms pay for a cost reduction x,[18] output per firm is

$$q = \frac{a - c + (1 + \sigma)x}{3b}.$$

(14.17)

Net social welfare for this output level is

$$\tfrac{1}{2}b(2q)^2 + 2\left(bq^2 - \tfrac{1}{2}\gamma x^2\right) = 4b\left[\frac{a - c + (1 + \sigma)x}{3b}\right]^2 - \gamma x^2.$$

(14.18)

The cost reduction that maximizes (14.18) is

$$x_{SB} = \tfrac{4}{9}\frac{1 + \sigma}{b\gamma - \tfrac{4}{9}(1 + \sigma)^2}(a - c),$$

(14.19)

and x_{SB} is greater than the equilibrium cost reductions that emerge from the AJ model:

$$x_{SB} - x_{NN} = \tfrac{2}{9}\frac{3\sigma b\gamma(a - c)}{\left[b\gamma - \tfrac{4}{9}(1 + \sigma)^2\right]\left[b\gamma - \tfrac{2}{9}(1 + \sigma)(2 - \sigma)\right]} > 0.$$

(14.20)

In the AJ model, a market system results in an insufficient level of innovation, relative to the second-best optimum.

Kamien, Muller, and Zang

d'Aspremont and Jacquemin (1988) model spillovers of R&D outputs. Kamien, Muller, and Zang (1992) (henceforth, KMZ) model spillovers of R&D inputs. Using the functional forms

---

[17] The first-best R&D level would be found by maximizing net social welfare with respect to both cost savings and output. This would introduce the issue of welfare losses due to output restriction into the discussion. The analysis of such welfare losses is not without interest, but they are themselves the subject of a large literature and are distinct from the assessment of technological performance. Nor is it clear that policy-makers have the means to bring about first-best output levels.

[18] See Salant and Shaffer (1998) for analysis of asymmetric R&D allocations.

of Amir (2000),[19] if firms 1 and 2 spend amounts y_1 and y_2 on cost-reducing R&D, the realized cost reduction of firm i in the KMZ model is

$$\sqrt{\frac{2}{\gamma}\left(y_i + sy_j\right)}. \tag{14.21}$$

If $s = 0$ there are no input spillovers, so that to obtain a cost reduction x_i firm i must spend $y_i = \frac{1}{2}\gamma x_i^2$, as in the AJ model if there are no output spillovers ($\sigma = 0$). In the absence of spillovers, the two models are equivalent. In the presence of spillovers, they are not.

The method of solution of the KMZ model is the same as that of the AJ model: find noncooperative equilibrium second-stage payoffs as functions of first-stage choice variables, and then find noncooperative equilibrium values of the first-stage choice variables. Details are left to Problem 14.3.

The equilibrium realized cost saving in the KMZ model is

$$\sqrt{\frac{2}{\gamma}(1+s)y_{\text{NN}}} = \frac{2}{9}\frac{2-s}{b\gamma - \frac{2}{9}(2-s)}(a-c). \tag{14.22}$$

If we compare this with (14.11), the corresponding value for the AJ model, for the case of identical spillover levels ($\sigma = s$), we find

$$(1+\sigma)x_{\text{NN}} - \sqrt{\frac{2}{\gamma}(1+\sigma)y_{\text{NN}}} = \frac{2}{9}\frac{\sigma(2-\sigma)\,b\gamma\,(a-c)}{\left[b\gamma - \frac{2}{9}(1+\sigma)(2-\sigma)\right]\left[b\gamma - \frac{2}{9}(2-\sigma)\right]} > 0. \tag{14.23}$$

For the same spillover levels, the AJ model predicts systematically greater equilibrium cost reductions than the KMZ model.

We may also investigate the impact of changes in the spillover level on the equilibrium realized cost reduction in the KMZ model:

$$\frac{\partial}{\partial s}\left(\sqrt{\frac{2}{\gamma}(1+s)y_{\text{NN}}}\right) = -\frac{2}{9}\frac{b\gamma}{\left[b\gamma - \frac{2}{9}(2-s)\right]^2}(a-c) < 0. \tag{14.24}$$

In the KMZ model, increases in input spillovers worsen technological performance for all spillover levels. This may be contrasted with the corresponding result for the AJ model, in which increases in output spillovers worsen technological performance only for $\sigma > \frac{1}{2}$ (see (14.16)).

In the KMZ model, as in the AJ model, the market underprovides cost reductions compared with the second-best optimum. If we repeat the exercise that led to (14.20) for the AJ model, we find, for the KMZ model,

$$\sqrt{\frac{2}{\gamma}(1+s)y_{\text{SB}}} - \sqrt{\frac{2}{\gamma}(1+s)y_{\text{NN}}} = \frac{2}{9}\frac{3sb\gamma(a-c)}{\left[b\gamma - \frac{4}{9}(1+s)\right]\left[b\gamma - \frac{2}{9}(2-s)\right]} > 0. \tag{14.25}$$

---

[19] Upon which this section is based.

14.3.2   R&D joint ventures

The AJ and KMZ models both predict that noncooperative market behavior will under-provide cost-saving innovation. This prediction is consistent with the bulk of the empirical literature as well. Motivated by considerations of this kind,[20] economists turned to the analysis of policy measures that seek to improve technological performance.

Such measures might include subsidies (cash payments, low-interest loans, favorable tax treatment), a relaxed competition policy toward R&D joint ventures, subsidies to R&D joint ventures,[21] and the design of appropriate patent policy.

In this section we consider (in the context of the AJ and KMZ models) the case of an *operating-entity* (OE) research and development joint venture, in which the two firms set up a single R&D laboratory, each paying half the cost. In the post-innovation market, both firms have access to the new technology on the same terms, and firms behave noncooperatively on the output market.[22]

d'Aspremont and Jacquemin

If in the AJ model the two firms form an operating entity R&D joint venture,[23] the post-innovation market is a Cournot duopoly in which firms have identical unit cost, $c - x_{OE}$. Each firm's Cournot equilibrium payoff in the second-stage market is

$$b \left[\frac{a - (c - x_{OE})}{3b} \right]^2 . \tag{14.26}$$

In the first stage, firms pick x_{OE} to maximize the sum of second-stage payoffs, taking noncooperative second-stage behavior into account, net of the cost of R&D:

$$2b \left[\frac{a - (c - x_{OE})}{3b} \right]^2 - \tfrac{1}{2} \gamma x_{OE}^2 . \tag{14.27}$$

The privately optimal cost saving is

$$x_{OE} = \tfrac{4}{9} \frac{a - c}{b\gamma - \tfrac{4}{9}} . \tag{14.28}$$

---

[20] As well as by the rise of the new growth theory literature, which emphasizes (like the old growth theory, as far as that goes) innovation as a source of economic growth.

[21] On which, see Hinloopen (1997, 2000).

[22] See Ouchi (1989) and Vonortas (1994). The literature abounds with taxonomies of R&D cooperation, with definitions depending on the number of R&D operations, on whether or not formation of an R&D joint venture means an increase in the spillover parameter, and on whether or not firms cooperate in production as well as R&D. For alternative classifications, see d'Aspremont and Jacquemin (1988), Hagedoorn (1990), Kamien et al. (1992), and Amir (2000).

[23] In duopoly, if there is an R&D joint venture, it includes all firms in the industry. With more than two firms, some firms may form an R&D joint venture, others not; there may be competing R&D joint ventures. See Martin (1994), Yi (1998), Greenlee and Cassiman (1999), and Yi and Shin (2000).

x_{OE} is less than the realized cost saving with fully noncooperative behavior:

$$(1 + \sigma)x_{NN} - x_{OE} = \frac{\sigma(1 - \sigma)b\gamma}{\left[b\gamma - \frac{2}{9}(1 + \sigma)(2 - \sigma)\right]\left(b\gamma - \frac{4}{9}\right)} > 0. \tag{14.29}$$

In the AJ model, R&D cooperation in the form of an operating entity joint venture worsens technological performance. Unit costs are higher in the second stage with an OE joint venture than with fully noncooperative behavior; it follows that an OE joint venture means that output is smaller and consumers are worse off in the second stage.

Because an OE joint venture reduces spending on R&D, it may give firms greater profit than would fully noncooperative behavior. Comparing fully noncooperative and OE joint venture per-firm profit, if $b\gamma$ is sufficiently large that x_{NN} and x_{OE} are both positive,[24] it is not privately profitable for the two firms to form an OE joint venture for $0 \leq \sigma \leq 1 - \frac{1}{3}\sqrt{3} \approx 0.42265$. For higher values of σ, it is privately profitable to form an OE joint venture if $b\gamma$ is sufficiently large. In such cases, forming an OE joint venture may be socially beneficial, if the increase in firms' profit outweighs the loss of consumers' surplus. But if the OE joint venture is socially beneficial, it is not because it improves technological performance.

Kamien, Muller, and Zang

Since spillovers do not arise with an OE joint venture, the realized cost reduction with an OE joint venture is the same in the AJ and the KMZ models. If we compare x_{OE} and the realized cost saving with noncooperative behavior in the KMZ model, we have

$$x_{OE} - \sqrt{\frac{2}{\gamma}(1 + s)y_{NN}} = \frac{2}{9}\frac{sb\gamma(a - c)}{\left(b\gamma - \frac{4}{9}\right)\left[b\gamma - \frac{2}{9}(2 - s)\right]} > 0. \tag{14.30}$$

An OE joint venture improves technological performance in the KMZ model if there are input spillovers. Thus it increases output and leaves consumers better off than they would be with fully noncooperative behavior.

Comparing per-firm profits under the two regimes, an OE joint venture is privately profitable with input spillovers if

$$b\gamma \geq \frac{2(1 - s)(2 - s)^2}{9(2 - 4s + 3s^2)}. \tag{14.31}$$

The equality version of (14.31) is graphed as a solid line in figure 14.1, along with a dashed line showing the lower limit of values of $b\gamma$ for which y_{NN} is positive. For any spillover level s, an OE joint venture is privately profitable for values of $b\gamma$ above both these lines. For any value of $b\gamma$, an OE joint venture is privately profitable for spillover levels to the right of both these lines. For high values of $b\gamma$ and large input spillovers, private and social interests are in

---

[24] Linear-quadratic examples are often used for their tractability, and they are often valid only over limited regions of parameter space. It is as well to remember that d'Aspremont and Jacquemin labeled their model "an example."

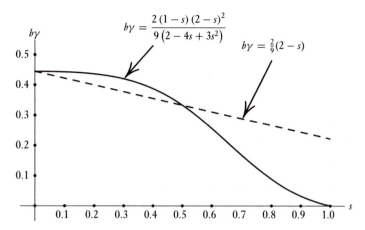

Figure 14.1 Regions of relative profitability in $(s, b\gamma)$-space, full noncooperation versus OE joint venture, KMZ model.

harmony in the sense that firms will find it privately profitable to form an OE joint venture that is socially beneficial. In the region

$$\tfrac{2}{9}(2 - s) \leq b\gamma \leq \frac{2(1 - s)(2 - s)^2}{9(2 - 4s + 3s^2)},$$

which occurs for $0 \leq s \leq \tfrac{1}{2}$ (that is, low $b\gamma$, low s), an OE joint venture will benefit consumers, may be socially beneficial, but will not be privately profitable. In such cases, incentives would be needed to induce firms to form a socially beneficial OE joint venture.

14.4   STOCHASTIC INNOVATION

Innovation is inherently uncertain (Tapon and Cadsby, 1996, pp. 389–90, quoting a researcher in the pharmaceutical sector):

> There are thought experiments that you can do and you can try and predict outcomes but the actuality of the thing is always determined by the data generated. That sometimes is not as predictable as you would like it to be. You cannot think about all the variables that go into even the simplest of systems.... But, you're not going to be able to predict 100%... of the outcome. You're always going to have things that happen that nobody really foresaw and you look back in hindsight and say that there is no way that we could have predicted that outcome...

The comparative advantage of the AJ and KMZ models is that they permit analysis of market structure – technological performance relationships in a minimalist and tractable framework. A limitation is that they treat innovation as deterministic: provided that a firm is willing to pay the cost, it can obtain any cost reduction that it wants. The model outlined in this section[25] treats input and output spillovers separately, and examines their impact on an uncertain innovation process.

14.4.1   Input spillovers

Let there be two firms, 1 and 2. Initially, both firms produce with unit cost c_A. Successful completion of a research project allows production at a lower unit cost c_B; research projects have a random success date.[26] We examine here the case of modest innovation, in the sense that it would be profitable for both firms to operate in the market with one using the old technology and one the new technology.[27]

Firm i, seeking to develop the lower-cost technology, engages in costly research. If firm i's research intensity is h_i, its effective research intensity is

$$g_i = h_i + s h_j, \tag{14.32}$$

s is the R&D input spillover parameter; it has the same properties ($0 \leq s \leq 1$) and general interpretation as the input spillover parameter in the KMZ model.

Firm i's random discovery time τ_i has a Poisson distribution,

$$\Pr(\tau_i \leq t) = 1 - e^{-g_i t}, \tag{14.33}$$

that has a hazard rate firm i's effective research intensity g_i.

The R&D cost function $z(h)$ has positive first and second derivatives:

$$z'(h) > 0, \qquad z''(h) > 0. \tag{14.34}$$

Assume that firms behave noncooperatively both with respect to R&D and on the product market. Firm i picks its R&D intensity h_i to maximize its expected present-discounted value,

$$V_i^N = \int_{t=0}^{\infty} e^{-(r+g_1+g_2)t} \left[\pi_N(c_1) - z(h_i) + \frac{g_i \pi_W + g_j \pi_L}{r} \right] dt. \tag{14.35}$$

Firm i's payoff if neither firm has innovated is $\pi_N(c_1) - z(h_i)$, and the probability that no firm has innovated at time t is $\exp[-(g_1 + g_2)t]$. If firm i is the first to innovate, its value from the moment of innovation is π_W/r (where the winner's instantaneous payoff π_W will be examined shortly). The probability density that firm i is the first to innovate and that this occurs at time t is $g_i \exp[-(g_1 + g_2)t]$. If firm j is the first to innovate, firm i's value from the moment of innovation is π_L/r. The probability density that firm j is the first to innovate and that first innovation is at time t is $g_j \exp[-(g_1 + g_2)t]$. Payoffs in alternative states of the

---

[25] Following Martin (2001). See Athey and Schmutzler (1995) for an alternative formalization of uncertain benefits from innovation.

[26] When account is taken of the stochastic nature of innovation, it might be a profit-maximizing strategy for firms to run several research projects that are seeking the same goal; see Scott (1993, chapter 8).

[27] If innovation is drastic, so that only one firm supplies the market after innovation, the issue of output spillovers does not arise.

world are multiplied by the appropriate probabilities, added together, and discounted by the factor $\exp(-rt)$, under the integral sign in (14.35).

Carrying out the integration and using (14.35) to express the firm's expected value in terms of research intensities, firm i's expected present-discounted value function is

$$V_i^N(h_1, h_2) = \left[\pi_N(c_1) - z(h_i) + \frac{(\pi_W + s\pi_L)h_i + (s\pi_W + \pi_L)h_j}{r} \right] \bigg/ [r + (1 + s)(h_i + h_j)].$$

$$(14.36)$$

When firm i increases its own research effort h_i it increases not only the probability that it will discover first, but also (because of input spillovers) the probability that firm j will discover first. Thus the coefficient of h_i/r in the numerator on the right in (14.36) is the sum of π_W and $s\pi_L$.

14.4.2 Appropriability

The extent to which a firm that invests in knowledge can profit from its investment poses a dilemma for innovation in a market system. On the one hand, the expected profit from investing in R&D is less if knowledge, once produced, becomes common knowledge. The inability to appropriate the profit that flows from successful innovation thus reduces private incentives to invest in innovation.

To promote appropriability, society establishes institutions that establish property rights in knowledge, at least for a limited period of time. Such property rights are necessarily imperfect (Arrow, 1962, p. 615):

> no amount of legal protection can make a thoroughly appropriable commodity of something so intangible as information. The very use of the information in any productive way is bound to reveal it, at least in part. Mobility of personnel among firms provides a way of spreading information. Legally imposed property rights can provide only a partial barrier, since there are obviously enormous difficulties in defining in any sharp way an item of information and differentiating it from similar sounding items.

Even if society could establish institutions that would guarantee complete appropriability, this would not eliminate the problems that knowledge poses for a market system. Optimal resource allocation requires that goods be made available at their marginal cost. The marginal cost of knowledge, once produced, is the cost of transmission. For the kinds of knowledge that can be described specifically enough to benefit from patent protection, the cost of transmission, compared to the cost of production, should be very close to zero. It follows that any set of institutions that ensures enough appropriability to induce private investment in knowledge will almost always ensure that knowledge, once produced, is distributed in a suboptimal way.

To incorporate imperfect appropriability – R&D output spillovers – in the model, assume that the first firm to successfully discover receives a patent that is intended to control the use of the new technology.[28] If the patent is completely effective, the patent-holder licenses

---

[28] For simplicity, assume that the patent has infinite duration. We examine the question of patent design in section 14.6.

use of the new technology to the loser at a rate $c_A - c_B$ per unit of output produced by the licensing firm.[29] If the patent is only partially effective, the license fee is $\alpha(c_A - c_B)$, for $0 \leq \alpha \leq 1$. α is the degree of appropriability of the rents that flow from innovation; $1 - \alpha$ is the size of output spillovers.

The unit cost of the losing firm is

$$c_L = c_B + \alpha(c_A - c_B) = \alpha c_A + (1 - \alpha)c_B. \tag{14.37}$$

Post-innovation static payoff functions are

$$\pi_W = (p - c_B)q_W + \alpha(c_A - c_B)q_L \tag{14.38}$$

and

$$\pi_L = (p - c_L)q_L. \tag{14.39}$$

If outputs are strategic substitutes and the output market is stable, one can show that

$$\frac{\partial \pi_W}{\partial \alpha} > 0, \qquad \frac{\partial \pi_L}{\partial \alpha} < 0. \tag{14.40}$$

Ex post, the successful innovator will prefer stronger appropriability, while rivals will prefer weaker appropriability.

14.4.3   Noncooperative R&D

The first-order condition to maximize (14.36) is

$$V_i^N = \left[\pi_N(c_1) - z(h_i) + \frac{(\pi_W + s\pi_L)h_i + (s\pi_W + \pi_L)h_j}{r}\right] \Big/ [r + (1 + s)(h_A + h_B)]$$

$$= \frac{1}{1 + s}\left[\frac{\pi_W + s\pi_L}{r} - z'(h_i)\right]. \tag{14.41}$$

The second-order condition for a maximum is that $z''(h_i) > 0$, which is met by (14.34).

Differentiating (14.41) gives the slope of firm i's R&D-intensity best-response function,

$$\frac{\partial h_i}{\partial h_j} = \left[(1 - s)\frac{\pi_W - \pi_L}{r} - z'(h_i)\right] \Big/ \left[\left(\frac{r}{1 + s} + h_1 + h_2\right)z''(h_i)\right]. \tag{14.42}$$

The second-order condition for expected value maximization implies that the denominator is positive.

Rewrite the second equality in (14.41) as

$$V_i^N = \frac{\pi_L}{r} + \frac{1}{1 + s}\left[\frac{\pi_W - \pi_L}{r} - z'(h_i)\right]. \tag{14.43}$$

If innovation is privately profitable, $V_i^N > \pi_L/r$ (one element of V_i^N is the value of the firm if it discovers first, weighted by the appropriate probability). It follows that the numerator

---

[29]   One might also consider alternative royalty schemes, such as allowing for a fixed as well as a per-unit fee.

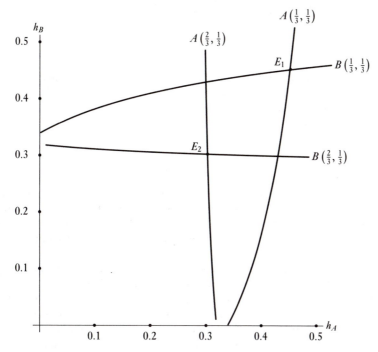

Figure 14.2 R&D best-response curves, alternative spillover levels: $p = 110 - Q$, $z(h) = 10h + 1000h^2$, $c_A = 10$, $c_B = 5$, $r = 1/10$; $A(\frac{2}{3}, \frac{1}{3})$ indicates A's best-response function for $s = \frac{2}{3}$, $\alpha = \frac{1}{3}$.

of (14.42) is positive for s near 1, and negative for s near zero. See figure 14.2 for examples of both cases.

Stability requires that the slope of the best-response function be less than one in absolute value in the neighborhood of equilibrium (Seade, 1980b). Setting $h_i = h_j = h_N$ in (14.42), the stability condition is

$$D = \left(\frac{r}{1+s} + 2h_N\right) z''(h_N) - \left[(1-s)\frac{\pi_W - \pi_L}{r} - z'(h_N)\right] > 0, \qquad (14.44)$$

which we assume is met.

14.4.4 Comparative statics

Setting $h_i = h_j = h_N$ in (14.41) and rearranging terms, noncooperative equilibrium R&D intensity satisfies the condensed first-order condition

$$\frac{\pi_W + s\pi_L}{1+s} - \pi_N + (1-s)\frac{\pi_W - \pi_L}{r}h_N + z(h_N) - \left(\frac{r}{1+s} + 2h_N\right) z'(h_N) = 0. \qquad (14.45)$$

Differentiating (14.45) and using the stability condition (14.44), one finds that

$$\frac{\partial h_N}{\partial s} < 0, \qquad \frac{\partial h_N}{\partial \alpha} > 0. \qquad (14.46)$$

The first part of (14.46) is illustrated in figure 14.2 for a linear demand – quadratic R&D cost example: as input spillovers increase, R&D best-response functions shift inward (changing slope from positive to negative) and equilibrium R&D intensity falls.

The equilibrium expected time to discovery is

$$E = \frac{1}{2(1+s)h}. \qquad (14.47)$$

From (14.46), $\partial E/\partial \alpha < 0$, while $\partial E/\partial s$ is of ambiguous sign. Greater post-innovation appropriability (smaller output spillovers) reduces the expected time to discovery. Greater R&D input spillovers mean that equilibrium per-firm R&D effort is less, but effective R&D effort per firm, $(1+s)h$, may rise as s rises, even if h falls as s rises. Expected time to discovery may well be less with greater input spillovers.

The comparative static effect of changes in α on firm value, on the expected present-discounted value of consumers' surplus, and on net social welfare[30] are all ambiguous. For the linear inverse demand, quadratic R&D cost example of figure 14.2, equilibrium firm value is maximized for $\alpha = 1$ (zero output spillovers) and $s = 0.91$ (high input spillovers). The expected present-discounted value of consumers' surplus, on the other hand, is maximized for $\alpha = 0$, $s = 1$. Consumer welfare is maximized when input spillovers are as large as possible (maximizing the social effectiveness of such R&D as does take place) and post-innovation appropriability as small as possible (meaning that both firms produce at marginal cost c_B in the post-innovation market). For this example (modest cost reduction, linear inverse demand, quadratic R&D cost), net social welfare is maximized for $\alpha = 0$, $s = 1$.

14.4.5   R&D joint ventures

With deterministic R&D, once firms have decided to establish an R&D joint venture, they would never set up more than one R&D project. With stochastic innovation, it may be optimal for firms to maintain more than one research project, since that may increase the chance that at least one of the projects succeeds.[31]

Here we examine secretariat R&D joint ventures with stochastic innovation: each firm maintains its own research project, s is increased from its noncooperative value to 1 (firms fully share information generated during the R&D process),[32] and if either firm discovers, both firms have access to the new technology on the same terms in the post-innovation

---

[30] The sum of firm values and the expected present-discounted value of consumers' surplus.

[31] A frequent argument put forward in favor of R&D joint ventures is that they reduce "wasteful duplication." Once the stochastic of innovation is recognized, it is clear that this argument is, in general, incorrect. For discussion, see Cockburn and Henderson (1994, pp. 488–9).

[32] This is one of the specifications considered by Kamien et al. (1992). Some case study evidence suggests that firms, although participating in an R&D joint venture, may strategically withhold proprietary information; see Sigurdson's (1986, pp. 45–6) discussion of Japan's VLSI project. See also De Fraja (1993).

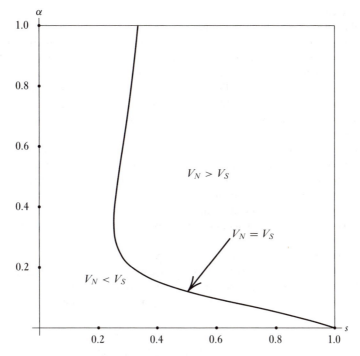

Figure 14.3 A comparison of noncooperative and secretariat joint venture equilibrium firm values: $a = 110$, $c_1 = 10$, $c_2 = 5$, $b = 1$, $r = 1/10$, $u = 10$, $v = 1,000$.

market. Since both firms have equal access to the innovation, once it is realized, the degree of appropriability has no impact on post-innovation payoffs. Firm 1's expected present-discounted value is

$$V_{S1} = \int_{t=0}^{\infty} e^{-(r+g_{S1}+g_{S2})t} \left[\pi_N(c_A) - z(h_{S1}) + (g_{S1} + g_{S2})\frac{\pi_N(c_B)}{r} \right] dt$$

$$= \frac{1}{r + 2(h_{S1} + h_{S2})} \left[\pi_N(c_A) - z(h_{S1}) + 2(h_{S1} + h_{S2})\frac{\pi_N(c_B)}{r} \right], \qquad (14.48)$$

where firm 1's effective R&D intensity is

$$g_{S1} = h_{S1} + h_{S2}. \qquad (14.49)$$

Firm 1 maximizes V_{S1} by choice of h_{S1}, taking h_{S2} as given. This determines firm 1's R&D best-response function. Firm 2 behaves in an analogous way. Noncooperative equilibrium R&D levels, firm value, consumer surplus, and net social welfare with a secretariat R&D joint venture do not depend on s or α.

Equilibrium R&D and welfare levels with fully noncooperative behavior do depend on s and α. Figure 14.3 shows typical regions in (s, α)-space where a secretariat joint venture yields greater firm value than noncooperative R&D.

Cooperative R&D yields firms a greater equilibrium firm value for low appropriability at all input spillover levels and low input spillover levels for all appropriability levels.

In the formulation used here, one advantage of a secretariat joint venture is that s rises from its noncooperative level to one. This advantage is smaller, the larger is s. One disadvantage of a secretariat joint venture is that a member loses the possibility of collecting royalties in the event that it is the first to discover. The lost income that this implies is greater, the greater is α. Noncooperative R&D thus yields greater firm values than cooperative R&D for high values of s and/or α; low R&D output spillovers discourage the formation of R&D joint ventures, all else equal.

In much of (s, α)-space, firms have a greater value with independent than with cooperative R&D, and one would not expect firms to voluntarily form R&D joint ventures.

For the parameter values of figure 14.3, consumer surplus is greater with a secretariat R&D joint venture than with noncooperative R&D for all s and α. One factor in this result is that post-innovation market performance is better with a secretariat joint venture, since both firms have access to the new technology on the same terms, neither paying royalties to the other.

With noncooperative behavior in the post-innovation product market, net social welfare is also greater with a secretariat R&D joint venture than with noncooperative R&D, for all s and α. Thus, with high input spillovers and high appropriability (low output spillovers) firms will not voluntarily form R&D joint ventures that would be socially beneficial.

14.5   ABSORPTIVE CAPACITY

Taking a position somewhat at odds with that of Arrow (see p. 459), Cohen and Levinthal (1989, pp. 569–70) emphasize that information often does not flow freely from innovator to other users:

> . . . we argue that while R&D obviously generates innovations, it also develops the firm's ability to identify, assimilate, and exploit knowledge from the environment—what we call a firm's 'learning' or 'absorptive' capacity. While encompassing a firm's ability to imitate new process or product innovations, absorptive capacity also includes the firm's ability to exploit outside knowledge of a more intermediate sort, such as basic research findings that provide the basis for subsequent applied research and development.

14.5.1   Deterministic innovation

Kamien and Zang (2000) extend the AJ model to allow for absorptive capacity by specifying firm i's realized cost reduction as

$$x_i + (1 - \delta_i)(1 - \delta_j)\beta x_i^{\delta_i} x_j^{1-\delta_i}, \tag{14.50}$$

rather than simply $x_i + \sigma x_j$. The second term in (14.50), the R&D output spillovers component, depends multiplicatively on x_i and is zero if $x_i = 0$ (for $\delta_i > 0$). If a firm does no R&D of its own, it cannot benefit from R&D carried on by other firms.

Kamien and Zang endogenize spillovers by making δ_i a choice variable of firm i in a three-stage game (pick δ_i; pick x_i; compete on the product market). For fully noncooperative behavior, they find that the need to maintain absorptive capacity increases equilibrium spending on R&D, compared with an otherwise equivalent model in which a firm costlessly enjoys complete absorptive capacity.

The fully noncooperative model is characterized by multiple equilibria in the choice of δs, but one set of subgame perfect equilibrium values is $\delta_i = \delta_j = 1$, so that output spillovers do not occur in equilibrium.

On the other hand, for a secretariat joint venture – each firm carrying out its own R&D, picking with own cost reductions picked to maximize joint profit in the final stage of the game – the unique subgame perfect equilibrium has $\delta_i = \delta_j = 0$, maximizing R&D output spillovers in the context of this model.

14.5.2   Stochastic innovation

Martin (2001) introduces absorptive capacity to a stochastic innovation model by firm i's effective R&D effort,

$$g_i = h_i + m(h_i)sh_j, \tag{14.51}$$

while the loser's unit cost in the post-innovation market is

$$c_A - (1 - \alpha)m(h_L)(c_A - c_B) = c_B + [1 - (1 - \alpha)m(h_L)](c_A - c_B), \tag{14.52}$$

for an absorption function $m(h)$, with $m'(h) \geq 0$, $m''(h) \leq 0$, $0 \leq m(h) \leq 1$, and $\lim_{h \to \infty} m(h) = 1$.[33]

With stochastic innovation, as with deterministic innovation, with fully noncooperative behavior the need to create absorptive capacity increases equilibrium R&D levels, compared with the costless and complete absorptive capacity case. Firms do more R&D, all else equal, to maintain the ability to absorb information about the cost reduction in the post-innovation market if the other firm should discover first.

With endogenous absorptive capacity of this type, it remains the case that for high input spillovers (s) and high appropriability (α), equilibrium firm profitability is greater with fully noncooperative behavior than with R&D cooperation, while secretariat joint ventures are always beneficial for consumers and for society as a whole. In industries described by a wide range of spillover–appropriability combinations, firms will not profit by forming socially beneficial secretariat R&D joint ventures.

---

[33] Of course, one might specify one absorption function for input spillovers and another for output spillovers.

14.6   PATENTS[34]

14.6.1   Patent length

Deterministic innovation

The seminal model of Nordhaus (1969) is useful for setting out the issues involved in the determination of the optimal length of the legal monopoly granted by a patent.[35] Initially, the market is in long-run perfectly competitive equilibrium. All firms produce with constant average and marginal cost c_1 per unit. The demand function is linear ($p = a - bQ$), price is c_1 per unit, and the quantity demanded is $S_1 = (a - c_1)/b$. A single firm develops a new technology with marginal cost $c_2 < c_1$. Letting $\Delta c = c_1 - c_2$ denote the benefit of the innovation, the R&D cost function is

$$c(\Delta c) = \alpha \Delta c^{1+\delta}, \tag{14.53}$$

with $\delta > 0$. There are therefore increasing costs or decreasing returns to scale in R&D: it costs more than twice as much to obtain a cost reduction which is twice as great.

The successful firm receives a patent that grants it a legal monopoly on the use of the new technology for a period of length T. After the patent expires, the new technology is available to all firms, the market is again competitive, and all firms use the new technology.

If the cost reduction is very great, the most profitable strategy for the innovator is to use the technology itself and act as a monopolist. If the cost reduction is less drastic, however, it will be most profitable for the innovator to license the use of the new technology to existing firms for a fee $\Delta c = c_1 - c_2$ per unit. Total output is slightly greater than S_1, and the innovator will collect revenue $\Delta c S_1$ per time period for the duration of the patent. We consider here the case in which the innovation is not drastic, so that the innovator prefers to license the use of the new technology. The present-discounted value of the innovator's profit is[36]

$$\pi = (1 - e^{-rT}) \frac{\Delta c S_1}{r} - \alpha \Delta c^{1+\delta}. \tag{14.54}$$

This is maximized for

$$\Delta c = \left\{ \frac{[1 - \exp(-rT)]S_1}{\alpha(1 + \delta)r} \right\}^{1/\delta}. \tag{14.55}$$

The benefit of innovation is greater, the longer the duration of the patent:

$$\frac{\partial \Delta c}{\partial T} = \left[\frac{S_1}{\alpha(1 + \delta)r} \right]^{1/\delta} \frac{r}{\delta} [1 - \exp(-rT)]^{(1-\delta)/\delta} \exp(-rT) > 0. \tag{14.56}$$

---

[34] See also Scotchmer and Green (1990), Gilbert and Shapiro (1990), Scotchmer (1991), Gallini (1992), Chiang (1995), Green and Scotchmer (1995), and Matutes et al. (1996).

[35] See Scherer (1972), Nordhaus (1972), and Kaufer (1989) for discussions of the Nordhaus model. The version of the model here is dual to Nordhaus' formulation (that is, it uses a cost function for R&D instead of a production function for R&D). For related contributions, see Kamien and Schwartz (1974) and DeBrock (1985).

[36] The innovator prefers to license if the maximized value of the expression in (14.54) is greater than the monopoly profit using the new technology, $bS_2^2/2$. Whether or not this is the case is endogenous, since it depends on the size of the innovator's control variable, $B = c_1 - c_2$.

The policy-maker's problem is pick the value of T that maximizes social welfare, given that Δc and T are related according to (14.55).

Social welfare is the sum of consumers' surplus plus economic profit. The present-discounted value of consumers' surplus is

$$CS = \frac{bS_1^2}{2r}[1 - \exp(-rT)] + \frac{bS_2^2}{2r}\exp(-rT), \tag{14.57}$$

where the first term measures consumers' surplus while the patent is in force and the second term measures consumers' surplus after the patent expires. It is convenient to rewrite (14.57) to express consumers' surplus in terms of S_1 and Δc:

$$CS = \frac{b}{2r}\left[S_1^2 + \exp(-rT)\frac{\Delta c}{b}\left(2S_1 + \frac{\Delta c}{b}\right)\right]. \tag{14.58}$$

We can then write

$$NSW = CS + \pi, \tag{14.59}$$

and optimal patent length is determined by the condition

$$\frac{\partial NSW}{\partial T} = \frac{\partial CS}{\partial T} + \frac{\partial CS}{\partial \Delta c}\frac{d\Delta c}{dT} + \frac{\partial \pi}{\partial T} = 0. \tag{14.60}$$

Equation (14.60) makes explicit the welfare tradeoffs inherent in extending patent life. The first term on the right-hand side in (14.60) is negative: making patent life longer postpones the time when consumers receive the full benefit of the new technology, and reduces expected consumer welfare.

But the remaining terms on the right-hand side in (14.60) are positive. Increasing Δc makes consumers better off, because price is lower in the post-patent period, and increasing T induces the innovator to make Δc larger (this is (14.56)). Increasing T increases the innovator's profit (choice of Δc being adjusted according to (14.55)) and makes the innovator better off.

The optimal length of patent makes the marginal loss of consumers' surplus from delaying competitive use of the new technology equal to the marginal gain in consumers' surplus from having a lower price, once the patent expires, plus the marginal gain in economic profit to the innovator.

Evaluating the various expressions in (14.60), we obtain

$$\frac{\Delta c^2}{2b} = \frac{\exp(-rT)}{r}\left(S_1 + \frac{\Delta c}{b}\right)\left[\frac{S_1}{a(1+\delta)r}\right]^{1/\delta}\left(\frac{r}{\delta}\right)^{(1-\delta)/\delta}. \tag{14.61}$$

This is one of two equations that determine optimal patent length. The other is (14.55), which defines Δc as a function of T. These equations are sufficiently nonlinear that the path of least resistance is to evaluate the solution numerically for different parameter values. For a discussion along these lines, see Nordhaus (1969).

The Nordhaus model makes clear what the tradeoffs are in determining optimal patent life, but it leaves out essential aspects of the R&D process. R&D is deterministic: for a specific cost, the innovator can immediately get a new technology that operates at the desired lower unit cost. There is only one innovating firm. The model does not explain why one firm is the innovator while others are not.

Stochastic innovation

We therefore examine the issue of optimal patent life in a stochastic innovation model. Consider once again an oligopoly of n quantity-setting oligopolists that use a technology with constant marginal and average cost c_1 per unit and compete to discover a new technology with constant marginal and average cost $c_2 < c_1$. The demand function is linear, $p = a - bQ$. The R&D technology – the relation between research effort and the probability of success – is given by

$$\Pr(\tau_i \leq t) = 1 - e^{-h_i t}; \tag{14.62}$$

the R&D cost function $z(h)$ has positive first and second derivatives, as in (14.34).

The successful innovator receives a patent for T periods. After the patent expires, the new technology is available to all firms.

If an innovation is not drastic, the market goes through three phases. First, it is a Cournot oligopoly in which all firms operate with marginal cost c_1 per unit. Then it is a Cournot oligopoly in which one firm has lower marginal cost than all others.[37] Finally, it is a Cournot oligopoly in which all firms have marginal cost c_2 per unit.

For a drastic innovation, the market is a monopoly in the second phase. Analysis of market performance in the third phase is dominated by treatment of the entry decision rather than by economic aspects of R&D. In this section, therefore, we confine our attention to innovations that are not drastic.

Acting noncooperatively, each firm selects its research intensity to maximize its own expected value, taking the research intensities of other firms as given. Firm i's expected value is

$$V^i = \left(r + \sum_j h_j\right)^{-1} \left\{ \pi_N(c_1) - z(h_i) + \frac{h_i \pi_W + \sum_{j \neq i} \pi_L}{r} [1 - \exp(-rT)] \right.$$

$$\left. + \frac{\pi_N(c_1)}{r} \exp(-rT) \sum_j h_j \right\}. \tag{14.63}$$

The first term in braces allows for income flows before successful innovation. The second reflects income flows while the patent is in force. The third reflects income flows after the patent has expired.

---

[37] Alternatively, the successful innovator could license the new technology to other firms, for a license fee of $c_1 - c_2$ per unit of output. Output would be same as in Cournot oligopoly with price differences, but the payoff of the innovator would be increased by the amount of the license fee (an income transfer from input suppliers to the innovator).

The first-order condition for expected value maximization is

$$\left(r + \sum_j h_j\right)\left\{[1 - \exp(-rT)]\frac{\pi_W}{r} - z'(h_i) + \frac{\pi_N(c_2)}{r}\exp(-rT)\right\}$$

$$= \pi_N(c_1) - z(h_i) + \frac{h_i\pi_W + \sum_{j\neq i}\pi_L}{r}[1 - \exp(-rT)]$$

$$+ \frac{\pi_N(c_1)}{r}\exp(-rT)\sum_j h_j. \tag{14.64}$$

The first-order condition implies that anywhere along its best-response function, and in particular in equilibrium, firm i's value is[38]

$$V^i = \frac{\pi_L}{r} + \frac{\pi_W - \pi_L}{r}[1 - \exp(-rT)] - z'(h_i). \tag{14.65}$$

Equilibrium is symmetric. Setting $h_i = h$ for all i and collecting terms somewhat, we obtain the equation that implicitly defines equilibrium research intensity:

$$[r + (n-1)h]\left\{\frac{\pi_W}{r}[1 - \exp(-rT)] - z'(h)\right\}$$

$$= \pi_N(c_1) + hz'(h) - z(h) - \pi_N(c_2)\exp(-rT)$$

$$+ (n-1)h\frac{\pi_L}{r}[1 - \exp(-rT)]. \tag{14.66}$$

In equilibrium, expected consumers' surplus is

$$CS_{ND} = \frac{b}{2}\frac{1}{r+nh}\left\{\left(\frac{nS_1}{n+1}\right)^2 + nh\left[\frac{S_2 + (n-1)S_1}{n+1}\right]^2\frac{[1 - \exp(-rT)]}{r}\right.$$

$$\left. + \left(\frac{nS_2}{n+1}\right)^2\frac{\exp(-rT)}{r}\right\}. \tag{14.67}$$

The terms in braces on the right measure consumers' surplus before innovation, while the patent is in force, and after the patent expires, in that order.

---

[38] Equation (14.64) also implies that

$$V^i = \frac{\pi_N(c_2)}{r} + \frac{\pi_W - \pi_N(c_2)}{r}[1 - \exp(-rT)] - z'(h_i).$$

The first term on the right-hand side is the present value of oligopoly profit at the lower cost level, over all future time. The second term is the present value of the excess of the winner's profit over the oligopoly profit, for the period that the patent is in force.

Expected net social welfare is the sum of expected consumers' surplus and the value of firms in the market:

$$NSW = CS_{ND} + nV. \tag{14.68}$$

Differentiating (14.68) with respect to patent length T, we obtain

$$\frac{\partial NSW}{\partial T} = \frac{\partial CS_{ND}}{\partial T} + \frac{\partial CS_{ND}}{\partial h}\frac{\partial h}{\partial T} + n\left(\frac{\partial V}{\partial T} + \frac{\partial V}{\partial h}\frac{\partial h}{\partial T}\right). \tag{14.69}$$

Because research intensity is chosen to maximize value, $\partial V/\partial h = 0$. Increasing the length of the patent increases the length of the period within which only one firm has access to the lower-cost technology, and postpones the start of the final period within which all firms have access to the lower-cost technology. Increasing T therefore reduces expected consumers' surplus, increases expected firm value, and increases equilibrium research intensity:[39]

$$\frac{\partial CS_{ND}}{\partial T} = -\frac{bh\exp(-rT)}{r+nh}\frac{n(n-1)}{(n+1)^2}(S_2 - S_1)[(n+1)S_2 + (n-1)S_1] < 0. \tag{14.70}$$

$$\frac{\partial V}{\partial T} = (\pi_W - \pi_L)\exp(-rT) > 0. \tag{14.71}$$

$$\frac{\partial h}{\partial T} = \frac{\exp(-rT)\{r[\pi_W - \pi_N(c_2)] + (n-1)h(\pi_W - \pi_L)\}}{(r+nh)z''(h) - (n-1)\{((\pi_W - \pi_L)/r)[1 - \exp(-rT)] - z'(h)\}} > 0. \tag{14.72}$$

An increase in equilibrium research intensity, which reduces the expected time to discovery, increases expected consumers' surplus:

$$\frac{\partial CS_{ND}}{\partial h} = \frac{bn(S_2 - S_1)}{2(n+1)^2(r+nh)^2}$$
$$\times \{S_2 + (2n-1)S_1 + \exp(-rT)[(n+1)S_2 - (n-1)S_1]\} > 0. \tag{14.73}$$

The first term on the right-hand side in (14.69) is therefore negative, while the remaining terms are positive. However, a little algebra shows that[40]

$$\frac{\partial CS}{\partial T} + n\frac{\partial V}{\partial T} = \frac{2bh\exp(-rT)}{r+nh}\frac{n(n-1)}{(n+1)^2}S_1(S_2 - S_1) > 0. \tag{14.74}$$

In this model, therefore, an increase in patent length always increases net social welfare. The socially optimal patent grants a permanent monopoly.

14.6.2   Patent breadth

A patent is characterized not only by its duration but by the extent of the monopoly that it grants. At one extreme, a patent on a new method of production might cover all techniques

---

[39] The first term in braces in (14.72) is positive. A stability argument establishes that the denominator is positive.

[40] For the derivation of (14.74) it is convenient to express firm value as in (14.63) rather than (14.65).

even remotely related to the innovative technology – a patent on the first airplane would grant a legal monopoly over all flying machines. At the other extreme, even a slight variation might be sufficient to exempt a competing technology from the coverage of the patent.

Without specifying the economic consequences of greater patent breadth in any detail, we can model breadth in terms of the profitability it permits.[41] Suppose, therefore, that a patent is characterized by its duration T and the flow rate of profit π that the holder of the patent can collect while the patent is in force.

Once the patent expires, the product or technology covered by the patent is in the public domain, and competition drives economic profit to zero. The present-discounted value of successful innovation is

$$V(\pi, T) = [1 - \exp(-rT)]\frac{\pi}{r}. \qquad (14.75)$$

Let $W(\pi)$ be instantaneous net social welfare – the sum of consumers' surplus and economic profit. The present-discounted value of net social welfare is

$$NSW = [1 - \exp(-rT)]\frac{W(\pi)}{r} + \exp(-rT)\frac{W(0)}{r}. \qquad (14.76)$$

If a minimum reward $\bar{V}$ is needed to induce innovation, the socially optimal patent maximizes net social welfare subject to the constraint that $V(\pi, T) = \bar{V}$ (it is never optimal to give a greater reward than necessary to bring forth the innovation). Then the flow rate of profit, given T, is

$$\pi = \frac{r\bar{V}}{1 - \exp(-rT)}, \qquad (14.77)$$

and net social welfare can be expressed in terms of T alone:

$$NSW = \frac{1 - \exp(-rT)}{r} W\left[\frac{r\bar{V}}{1 - \exp(-rT)}\right] + \frac{\exp(-rT)}{r} W(0). \qquad (14.78)$$

Taking the derivative of (14.78) with respect to T, we have

$$\frac{dNSW}{dT} = \exp(-rT)\left\{1 - \frac{\pi}{W - W(0)}\frac{d[W - W(0)]}{d\pi}\right\}. \qquad (14.79)$$

But this is positive, since $W'(\pi) < 0$. Increasing T always increases net social welfare. The optimal patent has infinite length and is no broader than absolutely necessary to bring forth innovation (from (14.77), $\pi = r\bar{V}$).

A weakness of this model is that breadth is not defined in terms of the characteristics of the market within which innovation takes place. In a spatial model, Klemperer (1990) models breadth as the minimum distance between a patent-holder's location and rivals' locations. In his model, narrow patents of long duration are optimal if all consumers have identical transportation costs. Broad patents of short duration are optimal if the maximum price that a consumer will pay for his or her most desired variety of the product is the same for all consumers.

---

[41] This section follows Gilbert and Shapiro (1990). See also La Manna et al. (1989).

14.7   EMPIRICAL STUDIES OF R&D

14.7.1   Market structure and R&D

Demand-pull versus technology-push

Jacob Schmookler (1966, 1972) advanced the hypothesis that resources are allocated to innovative activity in proportion to the profit expected to flow from successful innovation. For
this reason, he expected more innovative activity to be aimed at larger, potentially more
profitable markets.

Underlying this demand-pull explanation for the location of innovative activity is the
belief that the potential for innovation is more or less uniform throughout the economy. An
alternative view is that the potential for innovation is concentrated in a few sectors of the
economy that are high in technological opportunity, and that innovation tends to occur in
these sectors because the cost of innovation is less there than elsewhere in the economy.

The most comprehensive test of these hypotheses is due to Scherer (1982). His research
group classified all patents granted over a ten-month period in 1976–7 to a sample of large
US corporations operating in 245 industries, according to the industry in which the patent
originated and the industry or industries in which it could be used. One of Scherer's tests of
the demand-pull hypothesis is to regress the number of patents of capital goods capable of
being used in an industry on industry capital good investment. A typical result is

$$Usable\ Patents = -0.8 + 0.228Investment, \qquad R^2 = 0.544$$
$$(17.538) \tag{14.80}$$

(*t*-statistic in parentheses). It is clear that capital goods investment has a significant positive
impact on the number of patents that can be used in an industry. Logarithmic regressions
with the same data suggest decreasing returns to demand: a doubling of demand is estimated
to accompany an increase in the number of usable patents of from 44 to 69 percent.

To test the role of technological opportunity, Scherer reclassifies patents according to
industry of origin and regresses the number of patents originating in each industry against
industry sales, but using dummy variables designed to allow the sales coefficient to differ
across fairly broad industry groups. The patent-sales coefficient for industries in the organic
chemicals and electronics groups is significantly greater than the coefficient for general industry. The patent-sales coefficient for the traditional technology and metallurgical technology
industries is significantly less than the coefficient for general industry. When the patent-sales
coefficient in a linear regression is allowed to vary according to industry groups defined in
terms of technological opportunity, $R^2 = 0.809$.

On balance, these results provide support for both the demand-pull and the technology-
push models of the allocation of resources to R&D. The two explanations should be thought
of as complementary rather than mutually exclusive.

In another study of patents, Griliches (1989) examines the determinants of the number
of US patents granted to US residents over the period 1953–87. The number of patents
is negatively affected by defense spending and the cost of R&D, but positively affected by
industrial spending on R&D and by spending on basic R&D in universities. Changes in these

variables explain between 60 and 70 percent of the intertemporal variation in the number of patents granted.

Farber (1981) reports an econometric study of differences across industries in the share of engineers and scientists in the total workforce. He finds that the share of such personnel in the workforce rises with market concentration if the concentration in buying markets is sufficiently large (if the estimated share of the largest four buying firms exceeds 17 percent). This result is consistent with the argument that, if buying markets are relatively concentrated, firms invest in R&D only if they have enough market power of their own to appropriate the profits that flow from R&D. In the market concentration – R&D relationship, therefore, product market concentration is seen as a corrective for failure in the market for knowledge.

Firm size

Acs and Audretsch test the Schumpeterlich hypothesis (1987, p. 567):

> that large firms have the innovative advantage in markets characterized by imperfect competition, but that small firms have the innovative advantage in markets more closely approximating the competitive model.

They analyze samples of 142 innovative and 42 highly innovative US four-digit Standard Industrial Classification industries. The dependent variable in their study is the difference in annual number of innovations per employee in large and small firms. For highly innovative industries, large firms are relatively more innovative the more capital intensive the industry, the more concentrated the industry, and the greater the industry-average advertising–sales ratio. These are all variables that are traditionally associated with imperfect competition. These results therefore suggest that market power has a positive impact on technological performance. Market power variables generally lose their significance in the sample of innovative industries.

Acs and Audretsch's results are consistent with the Schumpeter Mark II hypothesis that market power and large firm size promote desirable dynamic market performance. They also indicate that rivalry and small firm size sometimes promote desirable dynamic market performance.[42]

Firm characteristics

Kraft (1989) analyzes the relation between market structure, firm structure, and innovation for a sample of 57 (West) German metal-working firms. The dependent variable is the percentage of sales due to products developed within the most recent five years in total firm sales. This percentage is larger, the smaller the number of important competitors and the greater the firm capital–sales ratio. It is also larger if management owns at least 25 percent

---

[42] It would be interesting to see separate regression results for large firms and small firms for the Acs and Audretsch sample. It should also be noted that it is risky to divide a sample in terms of an endogenous variable. Whether industries are innovative or highly innovative is precisely what one is trying to explain, and if the sample is divided according to observed innovation rates, there is undoubtedly some misclassification in both samples.

of the firm. Firm size has no significant impact on the share of new products in total sales (Kraft notes that the sample does not include large firms). These results are consistent with the Schumpeter Mark II hypothesis. They also confirm that firm characteristics, as well as market characteristics, influence innovative performance.

Multinational rivalry

Veugelers and Vanden Houte (1990) examine R&D spending per dollar of sales for a cross-section time-series sample describing 47 Belgian firms. They find R&D intensity to be less where multinational firms have a greater share of industry sales. Neither firm size nor market concentration have very significant effects on R&D intensity. Given the construction of their dependent variable, this suggests that R&D spending is roughly proportional to sales for their sample. For the presence of large firms to be conducive to desirable technological performance, R&D spending would have to rise more than proportionately to firm size. Thus their results are not particularly comforting to the Schumpeter Mark II view of the world.

14.7.2   Cooperative research and development

In the United States, the National Cooperative Research Act (NCRA) of 1984 sanctioned a relatively permissive attitude to R&D joint ventures.[43] One of the motivations for this attitude is the belief that a single firm, unable to fully appropriate the returns from R&D, will have less of an incentive to invest in R&D than is socially desirable. If the possibility of joint research increases expected appropriability and therefore the expected payoff to R&D, it can be expected to encourage investment in R&D and improve technological performance.

Scott (1988) points out that diversification across industries, especially across industries in which the innovation expected from an R&D program might be applied, is a strategy which might enhance the extent to which a single firm could appropriate the profit that flows from investment in R&D. He reports patterns of diversification of firms across industries that are consistent with the hypothesis that firms diversify into industries where they expect to be able to apply the results of innovative activity. He also reports evidence that cooperative R&D under the NCRA tends to occur in concentrated high-productivity industries in which companies had financed relatively large R&D programs and had been diversified in ways that seemed to be aimed at appropriating R&D output. Cross-industry R&D joint ventures seem, to a considerable extent, to substitute for cross-industry diversification by firms with active individual R&D programs.

Scott (1996) studies R&D joint ventures prompted by the US Clean Air Act Amendments of 1990, which tightened controls on air pollutants. Here he finds that the combination of a government "stick" – tougher regulatory standards – and a government "carrot" – a positive attitude toward R&D cooperation – leads to improved innovative performance. Thus there

---

[43] R&D joint ventures that filed with the government would be subject to single rather than treble damages for subsequent antitrust violations; whether or not antitrust laws had been violated would be decided under a rule of reason rather than a *per se* rule. See Scott (1989a) for further discussion.

is evidence that government policies to promote innovation in specifically targeted areas can achieve the desired result.

14.8   FINAL REMARKS

The Schumpeter Mark II view is that society ought to be willing to accept static market power for the desirable technological market performance that it brings. Sometimes, the argument is that large firms which earn economic profits are better able to finance risky R&D programs. Sometimes, the argument is that large diversified firms are more willing to invest in R&D because they are more likely to be able to apply a successful innovation in some of the markets in which they operate. Sometimes, the argument is that firms with market power are more likely to invest in R&D because, having fewer rivals, they are more likely to be able to appropriate the revenue that the flows from successful innovation.

Depending on the details of specification, formal models of R&D under uncertainty can yield either a positive or a negative predicted relationship between the number of firms and equilibrium per-firm research intensity. Stochastic models generally predict that the expected time to discovery falls, and expected social welfare rises, as the number of firms rises. In stochastic models, formation of R&D joint ventures tends to delay innovation – R&D effort is less if firms cooperate – but overall market performance is better as static market performance is better, all else equal, in the post-innovation market.

There is some empirical support for the claim that there is greater investment in R&D in more concentrated industries. Whether this is due to market power or simply to the advantages of large size is unclear. Nor is it clear that the relationship survives, once differences in technological oppurtunity across industries are controlled for. It is clear that the lure of profit and the ease of technological innovation also affect the degree of R&D.

PROBLEMS

14.1 (Exogenously determined prize, one-time expenditure on research and development; Loury, 1979) Let n firms undertake rival research projects aiming at successful development of a new product. The first firm to bring its research project to conclusion receives a lump-sum payoff V. Other firms receive nothing.

Let the random variable τ_i denote the uncertain time of discovery, and assume that the relationship between research effort h_i and the probability of success is exponential,

$$G_i(t) = \Pr(\tau_i \leq t) = 1 - e^{-h_i t}, \tag{14.81}$$

where to set up a research project at intensity h a firm must make a lump-sum payment $F(h)$ at time $t = 0$. The fixed-cost function $F(h)$ satisfies

$$F'(h) > 0, \qquad (\bar{h} - h)F''(h) < 0. \tag{14.82}$$

(a)   Write out the expression for the expected present-discounted value of a single firm, $E(\Pi_1)$.

(b)   Find first- and second-order necessary conditions to maximize $E(\Pi_1)$.

(c)   Differentiating the equation of the first-order condition with respect to h_1, find the equation of the slope of firm 1's R&D intensity best-response function.

(d)   Taking advantage of the fact that firms are identical, find the equation that is satisfied by equilibrium R&D intensity.

(e)   (Ignoring the fact that the number of firms is an integer) how is equilibrium R&D intensity affected by a change in the number of firms?

(f)   (Ignoring the fact that the number of firms is an integer) how is expected time to discovery affected by a change in the number of firms?

14.2 (Continuous expenditure on research and development; Lee and Wilde, 1980) Keeping all other aspects of Problem 14.1 unchanged, suppose that running an R&D project at intensity h requires an expenditure $z(h)$ per unit time as long as the project is under way.[44] Let the properties of the cost function $z(h)$ be

$$z'(h) > 0, \qquad (\bar{h} - h)z''(h) < 0. \tag{14.83}$$

Answer parts (a)–(f) of Problem 14.1 with this altered specification.

14.3 The second-stage payoff function in the section 14.3.1 version of the Kamien–Muller–Zang model is

$$\pi_i = \left(a - c + \sqrt{\frac{2}{\gamma}\left(y_i + s y_j\right)} - b(q_1 + q_2) \right) q_i - y_i.$$

Show that:

(a)   second-stage output as a function of R&D spending levels is

$$q_i = \frac{a - c + \sqrt{2/\gamma}\left(2\sqrt{(y_i + sy_j)} - \sqrt{(sy_i + y_j)}\right)}{3b};$$

(b)   the first-stage first-order condition for profit maximization can be rewritten as

$$\frac{1}{9b}\left(a - c + \sqrt{\frac{2}{\gamma}\left(2\sqrt{(y_1 + sy_2)} - \sqrt{(sy_1 + y_2)}\right)} \right)$$

$$\times \sqrt{\frac{2}{\gamma}}\left(\frac{2\sqrt{(sy_1 + y_2)} - s\sqrt{(y_1 + sy_2)}}{\sqrt{(y_1 + sy_2)}\sqrt{(sy_1 + y_2)}} \right) = 1;$$

(c)   the first-stage second-order condition for profit maximization, evaluated at the equilibrium, is

$$b\gamma > \frac{2\,(2 - s)^3}{9\,(2 - s^2)};$$

---

[44] Of course, one may consider the case in which an R&D project requires both an initial (setup) cost and continuous expenditure over the period of operation.

(d)   the equilibrium realized cost saving is

$$\sqrt{\frac{2}{\gamma}(1+s)y_{NN}} = \frac{2}{9}\frac{(2-s)(a-c)}{b\gamma - \frac{2}{9}(2-s)};$$

(e)   equilibrium output per firm is

$$q_i = \frac{b\gamma}{b\gamma - \frac{2}{9}(2-s)}\frac{a-c}{3b};$$

(f)   equilibrium profit per firm is

$$\pi_i = \frac{1}{9}\gamma\frac{b\gamma - \frac{2}{9}(2-s)^2/(1+s)}{\left[b\gamma - \frac{2}{9}(2-s)\right]^2}(a-c)^2;$$

(g)   equilibrium consumers' surplus is

$$2b\left[\frac{b\gamma}{b\gamma - \frac{2}{9}(2-s)}\frac{a-c}{3b}\right]^2;$$

(h)   equilibrium net social welfare is

$$\frac{4}{9}\gamma\frac{b\gamma - \frac{1}{9}(2-s)^2/(1+s)}{\left[b\gamma - \frac{2}{9}(2-s)\right]^2}(a-c)^2.$$

14.4 Suppose that a firm can carry out more than one research project, the probability of success of each of which obeys the exponential distribution

$$F(t) = \Pr(\tau \le t) = 1 - e^{-ht}.$$

If firm i carries out m_i such projects, what is the distribution function for the event "success by the firm"? (For simplicity, assume that the probability of success of individual experiments is independent, although this is an assumption that one might wish to abandon.) Reformulate the patent race models of the text to allow for multiple research projects by individual firms.

REFERENCES

Abbott, Edwin A. 1884: *Flatland: a Romance of Many Dimensions*, 2nd and revised edn. London.

Abreu, Dilip, Pearce, David, and Stacchetti, Ennio 1986: Optimal cartel equilibria with imperfect monitoring. *Journal of Economic Theory*, 39, 251–69.

Acs, Zoltan J., and Audretsch, David B. 1987: Innovation, market structure, and firm size. *Review of Economics and Statistics*, 69(4), 567–74.

—, and — 1989: Small-firm entry in US manufacturing. *Economica*, 56, 255–65.

Adams, James D., and Jaffe, Adam B. 1996: Bounding the effects of R&D: an investigation using matched establishment-firm data. *Rand Journal of Economics*, 27(4), 700–21.

Adams, Walter, and Brock, James W. 1991: Joint ventures, antitrust and transnational cartelization. *Northwestern Journal of International Law & Business*, 11(3), 433–83.

Adams, Walter, and Dirlam, Joel B. 1964: Steel imports and vertical oligopoly power. *American Economic Review*, 54(5), 626–55.

Adams, William James 1974: Market structure and corporate power: the horizontal dominance hypothesis reconsidered. *Columbia Law Review*, 74, 1276–97.

Adams, William James, and Yellen, Janet L. 1976: Commodity bundling and the burden of monopoly. *Quarterly Journal of Economics*, 90(3), 475–98.

Adelman, Morris A. 1966: *A&P: A Study in Price–Cost Behavior and Public Policy*. Cambridge, MA: Harvard University Press.

— 1969: Comment on the "H" concentration measure as a numbers equivalent. *Review of Economics and Statistics*, 51, 99–101.

Aghion, Philippe, and Bolton, Patrick 1987: Contracts as a barrier to entry. *American Economic Review*, 77(3), 388–401.

Akerlof, George A. 1970: The market for "lemons": quality uncertainty and the market mechanism. *Quarterly Journal of Economics*, 89(3), 345–64.

Albæk, Svend, and Lambertini, Luca 1998: Collusion in differentiated oligopolies revisited. *Economics Letters*, 59, 305–8.

Albæk, Svend, Møllgaard, Peter, and Overgaard, Per Balzer 1997: Government-assisted oligopoly coordination? A *Concrete* Case. *Journal of Industrial Economics*, 45(4), 429–43.

Allen, R. G. D. 1938: *Mathematical Analysis for Economists*. London: Macmillan.

al-Nowaihi, Ali, and Norman, George 1994: Product selection by quantity-setting firms. *International Journal of Industrial Organization*, 12, 473–94.

Amato, Louis, and Wilder, Ronald P. 1988: Market concentration, efficiency, and antitrust policy: Demsetz revisited. *Quarterly Journal of Business and Economics*, 24(4), 3–19.

Amel, Dean, and Froeb, Luke 1991: Do firms differ much? *Journal of Industrial Economics*, 39(3), 323–31.

Amel, Dean F., and Liang, Nellie J. 1990: Dynamics of market concentration in U.S. banking. *International Journal of Industrial Organization*, 8(3), 375–84.

Amir, Rabah 2000: Modelling imperfectly appropriable R&D via spillovers. *International Journal of Industrial Economics*, 18(7), 1013–32.

Amir, Rabah, and Lambson, Val E. 2000: On the effects of entry in Cournot markets. *Review of Economic Studies*, 67(2), 235–54.

Amoroso, Luigi 1921: *Lezioni di Economia Mathematica*. Bologna: Zanichelli.

Anderhub, Vita, Güth, Werner, Kameke, Ulrich, and Normann, Hans-Theo 2000: Capacity choices and price competition in experimental markets. March.

Anderson, Erin, and Schmittlein, David C. 1984: Integration of the sales force: an empirical examination. *Rand Journal of Economics*, 15(3), 385–95.

Anderson, Otto, and Rynning, Marjo-Riitta 1991: An empirical illustration of an alternative approach to measuring the market power and high profits hypothesis. *International Journal of Industrial Organization*, 9(2), 239–49.

Anderson, Simon P. 1986: Equilibrium existence in the circle model of product differentiation. In George Norman (ed.), *Spatial Pricing and Differentiated Markets*. Norwich: Page Brothers Limited, 19–29.

— 1987: Spatial competition and price leadership. *International Journal of Industrial Organization*, 5(4), 369–98.

— 1988: Equilibrium existence in the linear model of spatial competition. *Economica*, 55, 479–91.

Anderson, Simon P., and Engers, M. 1994: Spatial competition with price-taking firms. *Economica*, 61, 125–36.

Anderson, Simon P., and Neven, Damien J. 1991: Cournot competition yields spatial agglomeration. *International Economic Review*, 32, 793–808.

Anderson, Simon P., de Palma, André, and Thisse, Jacques-François 1992: *Discrete Choice Theory of Product Differentiation*. Cambridge, MA: The MIT Press.

Anglin, Paul M. 1992: The relationship between models of horizontal and vertical differentiation. *Bulletin of Economic Research*, 44(1), 1–20.

Appelbaum, Elie 1979: Testing price taking behavior. *Journal of Econometrics*, 9, 283–94.

— 1982: The estimation of the degree of oligopoly power. *Journal of Econometrics*, 19, 187–299.

Archibald, G. C., Eaton, B. C., and Lipsey, R. G. 1986: Address models of value theory. In Joseph E. Stiglitz and G. Frank Mathewson (eds), *New Developments in the Analysis of Market Structure*. Cambridge, MA: The MIT Press.

Arndt, J., and Simon, J. L. 1983: Advertising and economies of scale: critical comments and evidence. *Journal of Industrial Economics*, 32(2), 229–42.

Arrow, Kenneth J. 1962: Economic welfare and the allocation of resources for invention. In *The Rate and Direction of Inventive Activity: Economic and Social Factors*. Princeton, NJ: NBER, Princeton University Press, 609–25.

— 1975: Vertical integration and communication. *Bell Journal of Economics*, 6(1), 173–83.

— 1985: Informational structure of the firm. *American Economic Review*, 75(2), 303–7.

Arvan, Lanny 1986: Sunk capacity costs, long-run fixed costs, and entry deterrence under complete and incomplete information. *Rand Journal of Economics*, 17(1), 105–21.

Ashton, R. K. 1987: X-inefficiency and market power. *Managerial and Decision Economics*, 8(4), 333–8.

d'Aspremont, Claude, and Gabszewicz, Jean-Jaskold 1986: On the stability of collusion. In Joseph E. Stiglitz and G. Frank Mathewson (eds), *New Developments in the Analysis of Market Structure*. Cambridge, MA: The MIT Press, 243–61.

d'Aspremont, Claude, and Jacquemin, Alexis 1988: Cooperative and noncooperative R&D in duopoly with spillovers. *American Economic Review*, 78(5), 1133–7.

—, and — 1990: Cooperative and noncooperative R&D in duopoly with spillovers: erratum. *American Economic Review*, 80(3), 641–2.

d'Aspremont, Claude, Gabszewicz, Jean-Jaskold, and Thisse, Jacques-François 1979: On Hotelling's "Stability in Competition." *Econometrica*, 47(5), 1145–50.

—, —, and — 1983a: Product differences and prices. *Economics Letters*, 11, 19–23.

d'Aspremont, Claude, Jacquemin, Alexis, Gabszewicz, Jean-Jaskold, and Weymark, John A. 1983b: On the stability of collusive price leadership. *Canadian Journal of Economics*, 16(1), 17–25.

Athey, S., and Schmutzler, A. 1995: Product and process flexibility in an innovative environment. *Rand Journal of Economics*, 26, 557–74.

Aumann, Robert J. 1987: Game theory. In John Eatwell, Murray Milgate, and Peter Newman (eds), *The New Palgrave*. London: Macmillan Press, vol. 2, 460–83.

Ausubel, Lawrence M., and Deneckere, Raymond J. 1987: One is almost enough for monopoly. *Rand Journal of Economics*, 18(2), 255–74.

Bagwell, Kyle 1990: Informational product differentiation as a barrier to entry. *International Journal of Industrial Organization*, 8(2), 207–23.

Bagwell, Kyle, and Ramey, Garey 1988: Advertising and limit pricing. *Rand Journal of Economics*, 19(1), 59–71.

—, and — 1991: Oligopoly limit pricing. *Rand Journal of Economics*, 22(2), 155–72.

—, and — 1996: Capacity, entry, and forward induction. *Rand Journal of Economics*, 27(4), 660–80.

—, and — 1997: Collusion over the business cycle. *Rand Journal of Economics*, 28(1), 82–106.

Bain, Joe S. 1941: The profit rate as a measure of monopoly power. *Quarterly Journal of Economics*, 55(1), 272–92.

— 1949a: Price and production policies. In Howard S. Ellis (ed.), *A Survey of Contemporary Economics*. Philadelphia: The Blakiston Company, 129–73.

— 1949b: A note on pricing in monopoly and oligopoly. *American Economic Review*, 39(1), 448–69.

— 1950: Workable competition in oligopoly. *American Economic Review*, 40, 35–47.

— 1951: Relation of profit rate to industry concentration: American manufacturing, 1936–1940. *Quarterly Journal of Economics*, 65(3), 293–324.

— 1956: *Barriers to New Competition*. Cambridge, MA: Harvard University Press.

Baker, Jonathan B. 1989: Identifying cartel policing under uncertainty: the U.S. steel industry, 1933–39. *Journal of Law & Economics*, 32(2), Part 2, S47–76.

— 1993: Two Sherman Act Section 1 dilemmas: parallel pricing, the oligopoly problem, and contemporary economic theory. *Antitrust Bulletin*, 38(1), 143–219.

Baker, Jonathan B., and Bresnahan, Timothy F. 1988: Estimating the residual demand curve facing a single firm. *International Journal of Industrial Organization*, 6(3), 283–300.

Balder, Erik J. 1995: A unifying approach to existence of Nash equilibria. *International Journal of Game Theory*, 24, 79–94.

Baldwin, John R., and Gorecki, Paul K. 1987: Plant creation versus plant acquisition. The entry process in Canadian manufacturing. *International Journal of Industrial Organization*, 5(1), 27–41.

—, and — 1989: Firm entry and exit in the Canadian manufacturing sector. Business and Labour Market Analysis Group, Analytical Studies Branch, Statistics Canada, Research Paper Series No. 23, Fall.

Baldwin, William L., and Scott, John T. 1987: *Market Structure and Technological Change*. Chur: Harwood Academic Publishers.

Baron, David P., and Myerson, Roger B. 1982: Regulating a monopolist with unknown costs. *Econometrica*, 50(4), 911–30.

Bartoletti, Paolo, and Poletti, Clara 1996: A note on endogenous efficiency in Cournot models of incomplete information. *Journal of Economic Theory*, 71, 303–10.

Barton, David M., and Sherman, Roger 1984: The price and profit effects of horizontal merger. *Journal of Industrial Economics*, 33(2), 165–77.

Baumol, William J., Panzar, John C., and Willig, Robert D. 1982: *Contestable Markets and the Theory of Industry Structure*. New York: Harcourt Brace Jovanovich.

—, —, and — 1983: Contestable markets: an uprising in the theory of industry structure: reply. *American Economic Review*, 73(3), 491–6.

Beath, John, Katsoulacos, Yannis, and Ulph, David 1989: The game-theoretic analysis of innovation: a survey. *Bulletin of Economic Research*, 41(3), 163–84.

Belton, Terrence M. 1987: A model of duopoly and meeting or beating competition. *International Journal of Industrial Organization*, 5(4), 399–417.

Benoit, Jean-Pierre 1984: Financially constrained entry in a game with incomplete information. *Rand Journal of Economics*, 15(4), 490–9.

Benoit, Jean-Pierre, and Krishna, Vijay 1985: Finitely repeated games. *Econometrica*, 53(4), 905–22.

Benston, George J. 1982: Accounting numbers and economic values. *Antitrust Bulletin*, 27(1), 161–215.

— 1985: The validity of profits–structure studies with particular reference to the FTC's Line of Business data. *American Economic Review*, 75(1), 37–67.

— 1987: The validity of studies with line of business data: reply. *American Economic Review*, 76(5), 218–23.

Berle, Adolf A., and Means, Gardiner C. 1932: *The Modern Corporation and Private Property*. New York: Macmillan.

Bernheim, B. Douglas 1984: Strategic entry deterrence of sequential entry into an industry. *Rand Journal of Economics*, 15(1), 1–11.

Bernheim, B. Douglas, and Whinston, Michael D. 1985: Common marketing agency as a device for facilitating collusion. *Rand Journal of Economics*, 16(2), 260–81.

—, and — 1990: Multimarket contact and collusive behavior. *Rand Journal of Economics*, 21(1), 1–26.

Bernstein, Jeffrey I. 1989: The structure of Canadian interindustry R&D spillovers and the rates of return to R&D. *Journal of Industrial Economics*, 21, 324–47.

Berry, Steven, Levinsohn, James, and Pakes, Ariel 1995: Automobile prices in market equilibrium. *Econometrica*, 63(4), 841–90.

Bertrand, Joseph 1883: Review. *Journal des Savants*, 68, 499–508; reprinted in English translation by James W. Friedman in Andrew F. Daughety (ed.), *Cournot Oligopoly*. Cambridge: Cambridge University Press, 1988, 73–81; and by Margaret Chevaillier in an Appendix to Magnan de Bornier (1992).

Besanko, David, and Lyon, Thomas P. 1993: Equilibrium incentives for most-favored customer clauses in an oligopolistic industry. *International Journal of Industrial Organization*, 11(3), 347–67.

Bester, Helmut, de Palma, André, Leininger, Wolfgang, von Thadden, Ernst-Ludwig, and Thomas, Jonathan 1991: The missing equilibria in Hotelling's location game. Discussion Paper 9163, CentER, December.

Bhargava, Narottam 1973: The impact of organization form on the firm: experience of 1920–1970. Ph.D. dissertation, University of Pennsylvania.

Binmore, Ken 1996: Introduction. In John F. Nash, Jr., *Essays on Game Theory*. Cheltenham, UK and Brookfield, US: Edward Elgar.

Bishop, Robert L. 1962: The stability of the Cournot oligopoly solution: further comment. *Review of Economic Studies*, 29, (4), 332–6.

Blackorby, Charles, Donaldson, David, and Weymark, John A. 1982: A normative approach to industrial performance evaluation and concentration indices. *European Economic Review*, 19, 89–122.

Blair, Roger D., and Kaserman, David L. 1983: *Law and Economics of Vertical Integration and Control*. New York: Academic Press.

Bloch, Harry 1974: Advertising and profitability: a reappraisal. *Journal of Political Economy*, 82(2), Part 1, 267–86.

Bloch, Harry 1994: Sample-selection procedures for estimating the relationship between concentration and profitability from cross-industry data. *Review of Industrial Organization*, 9(1), 71–84.

Boccard, Nicolas, and Wauthy, Xavier 1998: Strategic trade policies with endogenous mode of competition: a comment. Manuscript, October.

Böckem, Sabine 1994: A generalized model of horizontal product differentiation. *Journal of Industrial Economics*, 42(3), 287–98.

Bonanno, Giacomo 1988: Entry deterrence with uncertain entry and uncertain observability of commitment. *International Journal of Industrial Organization*, 6(3), 351–62.

Bonanno, Giacomo, and Brandolini, Dario 1990: Introduction. In Giacomo Bonano and Dario Brandolini (eds), *Industrial Structure in the New Industrial Economics*. Oxford: Clarendon Press.

Bonanno, Giacomo, and Vickers, John, 1988: Vertical separation. *Journal of Industrial Economics*, 36(3), 257–65.

Border, Kim C. 1985: *Fixed Point Theorems with Applications to Economics and Game Theory*. Cambridge: Cambridge University Press.

Borenstein, Severin, and Netz, Janet, 1999: Why do all the flights leave at 8 AM? Competition and departure – time differentiation in airline markets. *International Journal of Industrial Organization*, 17(5), 611–40.

Bork, Robert H. 1966: The rule of reason and the per se concept: price fixing and market division. *Yale Law Journal*, 75(3), 373–475.

— 1978: *The Antitrust Paradox: a Policy at War with Itself*. New York: Basic Books.

Bosch, J. C. 1989: Alternative measures of rates of return: some empirical evidence. *Managerial and Decision Economics*, 10(3), 229–39.

Bothwell, James, and Keeler, Theodore E. 1976: Profits, market structure and portfolio risk. In Robert T. Masson and P. David Qualls (eds), *Essays in Industrial Organization in Honor of Joe S. Bain*. Cambridge, MA: Ballinger, 71–88.

Boulding, Kenneth E. 1966: *Economic Analysis: I, Microeconomics*, 4th edn. New York: Harpers.

Bowley, A. L. 1924: *The Mathematical Groundwork of Economics*. Oxford: Oxford University Press.

Bowman, Ward S. Jr. 1955: The prerequisites and effects of resale price maintenance. *University of Chicago Law Review*, 22(4), 825–73.

Boyer, Kenneth D. 1974: Informative and goodwill advertising. *Review of Economics and Statistics*, 56(4), 541–8.

— 1979: Industry boundaries. In Terry Calvani and John J. Siegfried (eds), *Economic Analysis and Antitrust*. Boston: Little, Brown.

— 1984: Is there a principle for defining industries? *Southern Economic Journal*, 50(3), 761–70.

— 1996: Can market power really be estimated? *Review of Industrial Organization*, 11(1), 115–24.

Boyer, Kenneth D., and Lancaster, Kent M. 1986: Are there scale economies in advertising. *Journal of Business*, 59(3), 509–26.

Boyer, Marcel, and Jacquemin, Alexis 1985: Organizational choices for efficiency and market power. *Economics Letters*, 18, 79–82.

Brack, John 1987: Price adjustment within a framework of symmetric oligopoly. *International Journal of Industrial Organization*, 5, 289–301.

Bramness, Gunnar 1979: The general conjectural model of oligopoly – some classical results revisited. Warwick Economic Research Papers No. 142, February.

Brander, James A., and Lewis, T. R. 1986: Oligopoly and financial structure: the limited liability effect. *American Economic Review*, 76(5), 956–70.

Brannman, Lance, Klein, J. Douglass, and Weiss, Leonard W. 1987: The price effects of increased competition in auction markets. *Review of Economics and Statistics*, 69(1), 24–32; reprinted in Leonard W. Weiss (ed.), *Concentration and Price*. Cambridge, MA: The MIT Press, 1989.

van Breda, Michael F. 1984: The misuse of accounting rates of return: comment. *American Economic Review*, 74(3), 507–17.

Brennan, Timothy J. 1988: Understanding "raising rivals' costs". *Antitrust Bulletin*, 33(1), 95–113.

Bresnahan, Timothy F. 1980: Three essays on the American automobile oligopoly. Ph.D. dissertation, Princeton University, June.

— 1981a: Departures from marginal-cost pricing in the American automobile industry. *Journal of Econometrics*, 17, 201–27.

— 1981b: Duopoly models with consistent conjectures. *American Economic Review*, 71(5), 934–43.

— 1982: The oligopoly solution is identified. *Economics Letters*, 10, 87–92.

— 1987: Competition and collusion in the American automobile oligopoly: the 1955 price war. *Journal of Industrial Economics*, 35, 457–82.

— 1992: Sutton's *Sunk Costs and Market Structure: Price Competition, Advertising, and the Evolution of Concentration. Rand Journal of Economics*, 23(1), 137–52.

Bresnahan, Timothy F., and Reiss, P. C. 1987: Do entry conditions vary across markets? *Brookings Papers on Economic Activity*, 1987:3, 833–81.

Bresnahan, Timothy F., and Salop, Steven C. 1986: Quantifying the competitive effects of production joint ventures. *International Journal of Industrial Organization*, 4(2), 155–75.

Bresnahan, Timothy F., and Schmalensee, Richard C. 1987: The empirical renaissance in industrial economics: an overview. *Journal of Industrial Economics*, 35(4), 371–8.

Brooks, D. G. 1973: Buyer concentration: a forgotten element in market structure models. *Industrial Organization Review*, 1(3), 151–63.

Brown, R. S. 1978: Estimating advantages to large-scale advertising. *Review of Economics and Statistics*, 60(3), 428–37.

Brozen, Yale 1969a: Significance of profit data for antitrust policy. In J. Fred Weston and Sam Peltzman (eds), *Public Policy Toward Mergers*. Pacific Palisades, CA: Goodyear Publishing, 110–27.

— 1969b: Barriers facilitate entry. *Antitrust Bulletin*, 14, 851–4.

— 1969c: Significance of profit data for antitrust policy. *Antitrust Bulletin*, 14, 119–39.

— 1970: The Antitrust Task Force recommendation for deconcentration. *Journal of Law and Economics*, 13(2), 279–92.

— 1971: Bain's concentration and rates of return revisited. *Journal of Law and Economics*, 14, 351–69.

— 1974: Entry barriers: advertising and product differentiation. In Harvey J. Goldschmid, H. Michael Mann, and J. Fred Weston (eds), *Industrial Concentration: the New Learning*. Boston: Little, Brown.

Bucklin, Randolph E., Caves, Richard E., and Lo, Andrew W. 1989: Games of survival in the US newspaper industry. *Applied Economics*, 21(5), 631–49.

Bull, Clive, and Ordover, Janusz A. 1987: Market structure and optimal management organizations. *Rand Journal of Economics*, 18(4), 480–91.

Bulow, Jeremy, Geanakoplos, John, and Klemperer, Paul D. 1985: Multimarket oligopoly: strategic substitutes and complements. *Journal of Political Economy*, 93(3), 488–511.

Burns, Malcolm R. 1986: Predatory pricing and the acquisition cost of competitors. *Journal of Political Economy*, 94(2), 266–96.

Burstein, M. L. 1960: The economics of tie-in sales. *Review of Economics and Statistics*, 42(1), 68–73.

Butters, Gerald R. 1977: Equilibrium distributions of sales and advertising prices. *Review of Economic Studies*, 44(3), 465–91.

Buzzell, R. D., and Gale, Bradley T. 1987: *The PIMS Principles*. New York: The Free Press.

Caballero, Ricardo J., and Jaffe, Adam B. 1993: How high are the giants' shoulders: an empirical assessment of knowledge spillovers and creative destruction in a model of economic growth. *NBER Macroeconomics Annual*, 15–74.

Cable, John 1972: Market structure, advertising policy and interindustry differences in advertising intensity. In Keith Cowling (ed.), *Market Structure and Corporate Behavior: Theory and Empirical Analysis of the Firm*. London: Grey-Mills, 105–24.

Cable, John, and Dirrheimer, Manfred J. 1983: Hierarchies and markets: an empirical test of the multidivisional hypothesis in West Germany. *International Journal of Industrial Organization*, 1(1), 43–62.

Cable, John, and Yasuki, Hirohiko 1985: Internal organization, business groups and corporate performance. *International Journal of Industrial Organization*, 3(4), 401–20.

Cabral, Luis M. B. 1995: Conjectural variations as a reduced form. *Economics Letters*, 49, 397–402.

Cairns, Robert D. 1996: Toward measuring market power. *Review of Industrial Organization*, 11(1), 125–33.

Caminal, Ramon, and Matutes, Carmen 1990: Endogenous switching costs in a duopoly model. *International Journal of Industrial Organization*, 8(3), 353–73.

Capozza, Dennis R., and Van Order, Robert 1982: Product differentiation and the consistency of monopolistic competition: a spatial perspective. *Journal of Industrial Economics*, 31(1/2), 27–39.

Carlton, Dennis W. 1979: Vertical integration in competitive markets under uncertainty. *Journal of Industrial Economics*, 27(3), 189–209.

Casson, Mark 1984: The theory of vertical integration: a survey and synthesis. *Journal of Economic Studies*, 11(2), 3–43.

Caves, Richard E. 1980: Industrial organization, corporate strategy and structure. *Journal of Economic Literature*, 18(1), 64–92.

— 1989: Mergers, takeovers, and economic efficiency: foresight vs. hindsight. *International Journal of Industrial Organization*, 7(1), 151–74.

— 1998: Industrial organization and new findings on the turnover and mobility of firms. *Journal of Economic Literature*, 36(4), 1947–82.

Caves, Richard E., and Bradburd, Ralph M. 1988: The empirical determinants of vertical integration. *Journal of Economic Behavior and Organization*, 9, 265–79.

Caves, Richard E., Gale, Bradley T., and Porter, Michael E. 1977: Interfirm profitability differences: comment. *Quarterly Journal of Economics*, 91(4), 667–75.

Caves, Richard E., Khalilzadeh-Shirazi, J., and Porter, Michael E. 1975: Scale economies in statistical analyses of market power. *Review of Economics and Statistics*, 57(2), 133–40.

Caves, Richard E., Whinston, Michael D., and Hurwitz, Mark A. 1991: Patent expiration, entry, and competition in the U.S. pharmaceutical industry. *Brookings Papers on Economic Activity*, Microeconomics 1991, 1–48.

Chamberlin, Edward H. 1929: Duopoly: value where sellers are few. *Quarterly Journal of Economics*, 44, 63–100.

— 1933: *The Theory of Monopolistic Competition*. Cambridge, MA: Harvard University Press.

— 1953: The product as an economic variable. *Quarterly Journal of Economics*, 67(1), 1–29.

Champsaur, Paul, and Rochet, Jean-Charles 1989: Multiproduct duopolists. *Econometrica*, 57(3), 533–57.

Chandler, Alfred D., Jr. 1962: *Strategy and Structure: Chapters in the History of Industrial Enterprise*. Cambridge, MA: The MIT Press.

— 1977: *The Visible Hand: the Managerial Revolution in American Business*. Cambridge, MA: Harvard University Press.

— 1982: The M-form: industrial groups, American style. *European Economic Review*, 19, 3–23.

Chang, Sea Jin, and Choi, Unghwan 1988: Strategy, structure and performance of Korean business groups. *Journal of Industrial Economics*, 37(2), 141–58.

Cheng, Leonard 1985: Comparing Bertrand and Cournot equilibria: a geometric approach. *Rand Journal of Economics*, 16(1), 146–52.

Cheng, Myong-Hun 1991: The effects of product differentiation on collusive pricing. *International Journal of Industrial Organization*, 9(3), 453–69.

Chernow, Ron. 1990: *The House of Morgan*. London: Simon & Schuster.

Cherriman, John Bradford 1857: Review of Cournot (1838). *Canadian Journal of Industry, Science, and Art* n.s. 2, 185–94 (reprinted in Dimand, 1995).

Cheung, S. N. S. 1983: The contractual nature of the firm. *Journal of Law and Economics*, 26(1), 1–22.

Chiang, Alpha C. 1984: *Fundamental Methods of Mathematical Economics*, 3rd edn. New York: McGraw-Hill.

Chiang, H. 1995: Patent scope, antitrust policy, and cumulative innovation. *Rand Journal of Economics*, 26, 34–57.

Churchill, Winston S. 1930: *My Early Life: a Roving Commission*. London: Scribner.

Clarke, Darral G. 1976: Econometric measurement of the duration of advertising effect on sales. *Journal of Marketing Research*, 13(4), 345–57.

Clarke, Roger, and Davies, Stephen W. 1982: Market structure and price–cost margins. *Economica*, 49, 277–87.

Clarke, Roger, Davies, Stephen W., and Waterson, Michael 1984: The profitability–concentration relation: market power or efficiency? *Journal of Industrial Economics*, 32(4), 435–50.

Clyde, Paul S., and Reitzes, James D. 1998: Market power and collusion in the ocean shipping industry: is a bigger cartel a better cartel? *Economic Inquiry*, 36(2), 292–304.

Coase, R. H. 1935: The problem of duopoly reconsidered. *Review of Economic Studies*, 2(2), 137–43.

—— 1937: The nature of the firm. *Economica*, New Series IV, 386–405; reprinted in George J. Stigler and Kenneth E. Boulding (eds), *Readings in Price Theory*. Chicago: Richard D. Irwin, 1952, 331–51.

—— 1972: Industrial organization: a proposal for research. In Victor R. Fuchs (ed.), *Policy Issues and Research Opportunities in Industrial Organization*. New York: National Bureau of Economic Research, 59–73.

Coate, Malcolm B. 1989: The dynamics of price-cost margins in concentrated industries. *Applied Economics*, 21(2), 261–72.

—— 1991: The effect of dynamic competition on price-cost margins. *Applied Economics*, 23(6), 1065–76.

Cockburn, Iain, and Henderson, Rebecca 1994: Racing to invest? The dynamics of competition in ethical drug discovery. *Journal of Economics & Management Strategy*, 3(3), 481–519.

Cohen, Wesley M., and Levin, Richard C. 1989: Empirical studies of innovation and market structure. In Richard C. Schmalensee and Robert D. Willig (eds), *Handbook of Industrial Organization*. Amsterdam: North-Holland, 1059–107.

Cohen, Wesley M., and Levinthal, Daniel A. 1989: Innovation and learning: the two faces of R&D. *Economic Journal*, 99(397), 569–96.

Collie, David 1992: International trade and Cournot equilibrium: existence, uniqueness and comparative statics. *Bulletin of Economic Research*, 44(1), 55–66.

Collins, Norman R., and Preston, Lee E. 1969: Price–cost margins and industry structure. *Review of Economics and Statistics*, 51, 271–86.

Collins, Richard, and Sherstyuk, Katerina 2000: Spatial competition with three firms: an experimental study. *Economic Inquiry*, 38(1), 73–94.

Comanor, William S. 1971: Comments. In M. D. Intriligator (ed.), *Frontiers of Quantitative Economics*. Amsterdam: North-Holland, 403–8.

—— 1985: Vertical price-fixing, vertical market restrictions, and the new antitrust policies. *Harvard Law Review*, 98(5), 983–1002.

—— 1986: The political economy of the pharmaceutical industry. *Journal of Economic Literature*, 24(3), 1178–217.

Comanor, William S., and Frech, H. E. III 1985: The competitive effects of vertical agreements. *American Economic Review*, 75(3), 539–46.

——, and —— 1987: The competitive effects of vertical agreements: reply. *American Economic Review*, 77(5), 1069–72.

Comanor, William S., and Kirkwood, John B. 1985: Resale price maintenance and antitrust policy. *Contemporary Policy Issues*, III(3), Part 1, 9–16.

Comanor, William S., and Rey, Patrick 2000: Vertical restraints and the market power of large distributors. *Review of Industrial Organization*, 17(2), 135–53.

Comanor, William S., and Wilson, Thomas A. 1967: Advertising market structure and performance. *Review of Economics and Statistics*, 49(4), 423–40.

—, and — 1974: *Advertising and Market Power*. Cambridge, MA: Harvard University Press.

Connolly, Robert A., and Schwartz, Steven 1985: The intertemporal behavior of economic profits. *International Journal of Industrial Organization*, 3(4), 379–400.

Constantatos, Christos, and Perrakis, Stylianos 1997: Vertical differentiation: entry and market coverage with multiproduct firms. *International Journal of Industrial Organization*, 16(1), 81–103.

Contini, Bruno 1989: Organization, markets and persistence of profits in Italian industry. *Journal of Economic Behavior and Organization*, 12(2), 181–95.

Cooley, Thomas F. 1982: Specification analysis with discriminating priors: an application to the concentration profits debate. *Econometric Reviews*, 1(1), 97–128.

Cooper, Thomas E. 1986: Most-favored-customer pricing and tacit collusion. *Rand Journal of Economics*, 17(3), 377–88.

Corts, Kenneth S. 1997: On the competitive effects of price-matching policies. *International Journal of Industrial Organization*, 15(3), 283–99.

— 1999: Conduct parameters and the measurement of market power. *Journal of Econometrics*, 88, 227–50.

Cotterill, Ronald W. 1986: Market power in the retail food industry: evidence from Vermont. *Review of Economics and Statistics*, 68(3), 379–86.

Cournot, Augustin *Researches into the Mathematical Principles of the Theory of Wealth*. Original Paris: L. Hachette, 1838. English translation by Nathaniel T. Bacon (New York: The Macmillan Company, 1897); reprinted 1927 by The Macmillan Company, New York, with notes by Irving Fisher; reprinted 1960, 1964, 1971, by Augustus M. Kelley, New York.

Cowling, Keith 1976: On the theoretical specification of industrial structure–performance relationships. *European Economic Review*, 8, 1–14.

Cowling, Keith, and Waterson, Michael 1976: Price-cost margins and market structure. *Economica*, 43, 267–74.

Coyte, Peter C., and Lindsey, C. Robin 1988: Spatial monopoly and spatial monopolistic competition with two-part pricing. *Economica*, 55, 461–77.

Cremer, Helmuth, and Thisse, Jacques-François 1991: Location models of horizontal diversification: a special case of vertical differentiation models. *Journal of Industrial Economics*, 39(4), 383–90.

Crocker, Keith J. 1983: Vertical integration and the strategic use of private information. *Bell Journal of Economics*, 14, 236–48.

Cubbin, John S. 1981: Advertising and the theory of entry barriers. *Economica*, 48, 289–98.

— 1983: Apparent collusion and conjectural variations in differentiated oligopoly. *International Journal of Industrial Organization*, 1(2), 155–65.

— 1988: *Market Structure and Performance – the Empirical Research*. Chur, Switzerland: Harwood Academic Publishers.

Cubbin, John S., and Domberger, Simon 1988: Advertising and post-entry oligopoly behavior. *Journal of Industrial Economics*, 37(2), 123–40.

Cubbin, John S., and Geroski, Paul A. 1987: The convergence of profits in the long run: inter-firm and inter-industry comparisons. *Journal of Industrial Economics*, 35(4), 427–42.

Curry, B., and K. George 1983: Industrial concentration: a survey. *Journal of Industrial Economics*, 31(3), 203–55.

Cyert, Richard M., and DeGroot, Morris H., 1973: An analysis of cooperation and learning in a duopoly context. *American Economic Review*, 63, 24–37.

Cyert, Richard M., and March, James G. 1963: *A Behavioral Theory of the Firm*. Englewood Cliffs, NJ: Prentice-Hall.

Dansby, Robert E., and Willig, Robert D. 1979: Industry performance gradient indexes. *American Economic Review*, 69(3), 249–60.

Dasgupta, Partha, and Maskin, Eric 1986: The existence of equilibrium in discontinuous economic games, II: applications. *Review of Economic Studies*, 53, 27–41.

Dasgupta, Partha, Hammond, Peter, and Maskin, Eric 1979: The implementation of social choice rules: some results on incentive compatibility. *Review of Economic Studies*, 46(2), 185–216.

Daughety, Andrew F. 1985: Reconsidering Cournot: the Cournot equilibrium is consistent. *Rand Journal of Economics*, 16(3), 368–79; reprinted in Andrew F. Daughety (ed.), *Cournot Oligopoly*. Cambridge: Cambridge University Press, 1988, 161–78.

— 1988: Introduction, purpose, and overview. In Andrew F. Daughety (ed.), *Cournot Oligopoly: Characterizations and Applications*. Cambridge: Cambridge University Press, 3–44.

— 1990: Beneficial concentration. *American Economic Review*, 80(5), 1231–7.

Davidson, Carl 1984: Cartel stability and tariff policy. *Journal of International Economics*, 17, 219–37.

Davidson, C., and Deneckere, R. 1986: Long–run competition in capacity, short–run competition in price, and the Cournot model. *Rand Journal of Economics*, 17, 404–15.

Davies, Stephen W. 1979: Choosing between concentration indices: the isoconcentration curve. *Economica*, 46(181), 67–75.

De Alessi, Louis 1983: Property rights, transaction costs, and X-efficiency: an essay in economic theory. *American Economic Review*, 73(1), 64–81.

DeBondt, Raymond 1997: Spillovers and innovative activities. *International Journal of Industrial Organization*, 15(1), 1–28.

DeBrock, Lawrence M. 1985: Market structure, innovation, and optimal patent life. *Journal of Law and Economics*, 28(1), 223–44.

De Fraja, Giovanni 1993: Strategic spillovers in patent races. *International Journal of Industrial Organization*, 11(1), 139–46.

De Long, J. Bradford 1991: Did J. P. Morgan's men add value? An economist's perspective on financial capitalism. In Peter Temin (ed.), *Inside the Business Enterprise: Historical Perspectives on the Use of Information*. Chicago: University of Chicago Press, 205–36.

Demsetz, Harold 1973: Industry structure, market rivalry, and public policy. *Journal of Law and Economics*, 16(1), 1–9.

— 1974: Two systems of belief about monopoly. In Harvey J. Goldschmid, H. Michael Mann, and J. Fred Weston (eds), *Industrial Concentration: the New Learning*. Boston: Little, Brown.

Deneckere, Raymond J. 1983: Duopoly supergames with product differentiation. *Economics Letters*, 11, 37–42.

— 1984: Corrigendum. *Economics Letters*, 15, 385–7.

Deneckere, Raymond J., and Davidson, Carl 1985: Incentives to form coalitions with Bertrand competition. *Rand Journal of Economics*, 16(4), 473–86.

Dernburg, Thomas, and McDougall, Duncan 1976: *Macroeconomics*, 5th edn. New York: McGraw-Hill.

Deutsch, Larry L. 1975: Structure, performance and the net rate of entry into manufacturing industry. *Southern Economic Journal*, 41, 450–6.

Dick, Andrew R., and Lott, John R. Jr. 1990: Comment on "The role of potential competition in industrial organization." *Journal of Economic Perspectives*, 4(2), 213–5.

Dickson, V. A. 1979: The Lerner index and measures of concentration. *Economics Letters*, 3(3), 275–9.

— 1981: Conjectural variation elasticities and concentration. *Economics Letters*, 7, 281–5.

— 1982: Collusion and price–cost margins. *Economica*, 43(193), 39–42.

— 1991: The relationship between concentration and prices and concentration and costs. *Applied Economics*, 23(1A), 101–6.

Dimand, Robert W. 1995: Cournot, Bertrand, and Cherriman. *History of Political Economy*, 27(3), 563–78.

Dixit, Avinash 1979: A model of duopoly suggesting a theory of entry barriers. *Bell Journal of Economics*, 10(1), 20–32.

— 1980: The role of investment in entry-deterrence. *Economic Journal*, 90, 95–106.

— 1983: Vertical integration in a monopolistically competitive industry. *International Journal of Industrial Organization*, 1(1), 63–78.

— 1986: Comparative statics for oligopoly. *International Economic Review*, 27(1), 107–22.

Dixit, Avinash, and Norman, Victor, 1978: Advertising and welfare. *Bell Journal of Economics*, 9(1), 1–17.

—, and — 1980: Advertising and welfare: another reply. *Bell Journal of Economics*, 11(2), 753–4.

Dixit, Avinash, and Stiglitz, Joseph E. 1977: Monopolistic competition and optimum product diversity. *American Economic Review*, 67, 297–308.

Dixon, Huw 1986: Strategic investment with consistent conjectures. *Oxford Economic Papers*, 38, Supplement, November, 111–28.

— 1987: The general theory of household and market contingent demand. *The Manchester School*, 55, 287–304.

— 1990: Bertrand–Edgeworth equilibria when firms avoid turning customers away. *Journal of Industrial Economics*, 39(2), 131–46.

Dobson, Paul W., and Sinclair, Donald C. 1990: On the possibility of price wars when firms use a "tit-for-tat" strategy. *Economics Letters*, 32(2), 115–19.

Dockner, E. J. 1992: A dynamic theory of conjectural variations. *Journal of Industrial Economics*, 40, 377–95.

Domowitz, Ian, Hubbard, R. Glenn, and Petersen, Bruce C. 1986: Business cycles and the relationship between concentration and price–cost margins. *Rand Journal of Economics*, 17(1), 1–17.

—, —, and — 1987: Oligopoly supergames: some empirical evidence on prices and margins. *Journal of Industrial Economics*, 35(4), 379–98.

—, —, and — 1988: Market structure and cyclical fluctuations in U.S. manufacturing. *Review of Economics and Statistics*, 70(1), 55–66.

Donnenfeld, Shabtai, and White, Lawrence J. 1988: Product variety and the inefficiency of monopoly. *Economica*, 55, 393–401.

Donsimoni, Marie-Paule 1985: Stable heterogeneous cartels. *International Journal of Industrial Organization*, 3(4), 451–67.

Donsimoni, Marie-Paule, Economides, Nicolas S., and Polemarchakis, H. M. 1986: Stable cartels. *International Economic Review*, 27(2), 317–27.

Dorfman, Robert, and Steiner, Peter O. 1954: Optimal advertising and optimal quality. *American Economic Review*, 44(5), 826–36.

Dos Santos Ferreira, Rodolphe, and Thisse, Jacques-François 1996: Horizontal and vertical differentiation: the Launhardt model. *International Journal of Industrial Organization*, 14(4), 485–506.

Dosi, Giovanni 1988: Sources, procedures, and microeconomic sources of innovation. *Journal of Economic Literature*, 26, 1120–71.

Dowrick, Steve 1986: Von Stackelberg and Cournot duopoly: choosing roles. *Rand Journal of Economics*, 17(2), 251–60.

Doyle, Christopher 1988: Different selling strategies in Bertrand oligopoly. *Economic Letters*, 28, 387–90.

— 1989: Strategy variables and theories of industrial organization. In Frank H. Hahn (ed.), *The Economics of Missing Markets, Information and Games*. Cambridge: Oxford University Press, 149–62.

Dunne, Timothy, Roberts, Mark J., and Samuelson, Larry 1988: Patterns of firm entry and exit in U.S. manufacturing industries. *Rand Journal of Economics*, 19(4), 495–515.

Dutz, Mark A. 1989: Horizontal mergers in declining industries: theory and evidence. *International Journal of Industrial Organization*, 7(1), 11–33.

Easley, David, Masson, Robert T., and Reynolds, Robert J. 1985: Preying for time. *Journal of Industrial Economics*, 33(4), 445–60.

Easterbrook, Frank H. 1981: Predatory strategies and counterstrategies. *University of Chicago Law Review*, 48(2), 263–337.

Eaton, B. Curtis 1972: Spatial competition revisited. *Canadian Journal of Economics*, 5(2), 268–78.

Eaton, B. Curtis and Lipsey, Richard G. 1975: The principle of minimum differentiation reconsidered: some new developments in the theory of spatial competition. *Review of Economic Studies*, 42(1), 27–49.

—, and — 1978: Freedom of entry and the existence of pure profit. *Economic Journal*, 88(351), 455–69.

Eaton, B. Curtis, and Ware, Roger 1987: A theory of market structure with sequential entry. *Rand Journal of Economics*, 18(1), 1–16.

Eckbo, B. E. 1983: Horizontal mergers, collusion, and stockholder wealth. *Journal of Financial Economics*, 11, 241–73.

Eckbo, B. E., and Wier, P. 1985: Antimerger policy under the Hart–Scott–Rodino Act: a reexamination of the market power hypothesis. *Journal of Law and Economics*, 28(1), 119–49.

Economides, Nicholas 1984: The principle of minimum differentiation revisited. *European Economic Review*, 24, 345–68.

Edgeworth, F. Y. 1881: *Mathematical Psychics*. London: Kegan Paul.

— 1922: The mathematical economics of Professor Amoroso. *Economic Journal*, 32(127), 400–7.

— 1925: The pure theory of monopoly. In *Papers Relating to Political Economy*, vol. I. London: Royal Economic Society, 111–42 (translation of Teoria pura del monopolio. *Giornale degli Economisti*, July 1897, 13–31; October 1897, 307–20; November 1897, 405–14).

— 1925–6: Cournot. In Henry Higgs (ed.), *Palgrave's Dictionary of Political Economy*, 2nd edn. New York: Sentry Press, I. 445–7.

Edwards, Corwin D. 1955: Conglomerate bigness as a source of power. In National Bureau of Economic Research conference report, *Business Concentration and Price Policy*. Princeton, NJ: Princeton University Press, 331–59.

Edwards, Jeremy, Kay, John A., and Mayer, Colin 1987: *The Economic Analysis of Accounting Profitability*. Oxford: Clarendon Press.

Ekelund, Robert B., and Hébert, Robert F. 1990a: Cournot and his contemporaries: is an obituary the only bad review? *Southern Economic Journal*, 57(1), 139–49.

—, and — 1990b: Chamberlin and contemporary industrial organisation theory. *Journal of Economic Studies*, 17(2), 20–31.

Ellison, Glenn 1994: Theories of cartel stability and the Joint Executive Committee. *Rand Journal of Economics*, 25(1), 37–57.

Elzinga, Kenneth G., and Hogarty, Thomas F. 1973: The problem of geographic market definition in antimerger suits. *Antitrust Bulletin*, 18(1), 45–81.

—, and — 1978: The problem of geographic market delineation revisited: the case of coal. *Antitrust Bulletin*, 23(1), 1–18.

Encaoua, David, and Jacquemin, Alexis 1980: Degree of monopoly, indices of concentration and threat of entry. *International Economic Review*, 21(1), 87–105.

Encaoua, David, Geroski, Paul A., and Jacquemin, Alexis 1986: Strategic competition and the persistence of dominant firms: a survey. In Joseph E. Stiglitz and G. Frank Mathewson (eds), *New Developments in the Analysis of Market Structure*. Cambridge, MA: The MIT Press, 55–86.

Enderwick, Peter 1988: Between markets and hierarchies: the multinational operations of Japanese general trading companies. *Managerial and Decision Economics*, 9(1), 35–40.

Englander, Ernest J. 1988: Technology and Oliver Williamson's transaction cost economics. *Journal of Economic Behavior and Organization*, 10, 339–53.

Esposito, Louis, and Esposito, Frances Ferguson 1971: Foreign competition and domestic industry profitability. *Review of Economics and Statistics*, 53, 343–53.

Fama, Eugene, and Jensen, Michael C. 1983: The separation of ownership and control. *Journal of Law and Economics*, 26(2), 301–25.

Farber, Stephen 1981: Buyer market structure and R&D effort: a simultaneous equations model. *Review of Economics and Statistics*, 63(3), 336–45.

Farrell, Joseph 1986: Moral hazard as an entry barrier. *Rand Journal of Economics*, 17(3), 440–9.

— 1987: Cheap talk, coordination, and entry. *Rand Journal of Economics*, 18(1), 34–9.

Farrell, Joseph, and Maskin, Eric 1989: Renegotiation in repeated games. *Games and Economic Behavior*, 1(4), 327–60.

Farrell, Joseph, and Shapiro, Carl 1988: Dynamic competition with switching costs. *Rand Journal of Economics*, 19(1), 123–37.

—, and — 1990a: Horizontal mergers: an equilibrium analysis. *American Economic Review*, 80(1), 107–26.

—, and — 1990b: Asset ownership and market structure in oligopoly. *Rand Journal of Economics*, 21(2), 275–92.

—, and — 1991: Horizontal mergers: reply. *American Economic Review*, 81(4), 1007–11.

Feenstra, Robert C., and Levinsohn, James A. 1995: Estimating markups and market conduct with multidimensional product attributes. *Review of Economic Studies*, 62(1), 19–52.

Feinberg, Robert M. 1989: Imports as a threat to cartel stability. *International Journal of Industrial Organization*, 7(2), 281–8.

Fellner, William 1949: *Competition Among the Few*. New York: Knopf.

Ferguson, Charles 1969: *The Neoclassical Theory of Production and Distribution*. Cambridge: Cambridge University Press.

Fershtman, Chaim 1985: Managerial incentives as a strategic variable in a duopolistic environment. *International Journal of Industrial Organization*, 3(2), 245–53.

Fershtman, Chaim, and Judd, Kenneth L. 1987: Equilibrium incentives in oligopoly. *American Economic Review*, 77(5), 927–40.

Fisher, Franklin M. 1961: On the stability of the Cournot oligopoly solution: the effects of speeds of adjustment and increasing marginal cost. *Review of Economic Studies*, 28(2), 125–35.

— 1966: *The Identification Problem in Econometrics*. New York: McGraw-Hill.

— 1984: On the misuse of accounting rates of return to infer monopoly profits: reply. *American Economic Review*, 74(3), 509–17.

— 1987: On the misuse of the profit-sales ratio to infer monopoly power. *Rand Journal of Economics*, 18(3), 384–96.

— 1989: Games economists play. *Rand Journal of Economics*, 20(1), 113–24.

— 1991: Organizing industrial organization: reflections on the *Handbook of Industrial Organization*. *Brookings Papers on Economic Activity* Microeconomics 1991, 201–25.

Fisher, Franklin M., and McGowan, John J. 1979: Advertising and welfare: comment. *Bell Journal of Economics*, 10(2), 726–7.

—, and — 1983: On the misuse of accounting rates of return to infer monopoly profits. *American Economic Review*, 73, 82–97.

Fisher, Franklin M., and Temin, Peter 1973: Returns to scale in research and development: What does the Schumpeterian hypothesis imply? *Journal of Political Economy*, 81(1), 56–70.

Fisher, I. N., and Hall, G. R. 1969: Risk and corporate rates of return. *Quarterly Journal of Economics*, 83(1), 79–92.

Fisher, Irving 1898a: Cournot and mathematical economics. *Quarterly Journal of Economics*, 12, 119–38.

— 1898b: Notes on Cournot's mathematics. *Quarterly Journal of Economics*, 12, 238–44.

Fishman, Arthur 1990: Entry deterrence in a finitely-lived industry. *Rand Journal of Economics*, 21(1), 63–71.

Flath, David 1989: Vertical integration by means of shareholding interlocks. *International Journal of Industrial Organization*, 7(3), 369–80.

Fontenay, R. de 1864: Principes de la théorie des richesses. *Journal des Économistes*, 43, 231–51.

Frank, Charles R. Jr., and Quandt, Richard E. 1963: On the existence of Cournot equilibrium. *International Economic Review*, 4(1), 92–6.

—, and — 1964: Satic Cournot equilibrium: reply. *International Economic Review*, 5(3), 337–8.

Frank, Murray Z. 1988: An intertemporal model of industrial exit. *Quarterly Journal of Economics*, 103(2), 333–44.

Freeman, Donald B., and Dungey, Frances L. 1981: A spatial duopoly: competition in the western Canadian fur trade, 1770–1835. *Journal of Historical Geography*, 7(3), 252–70.

Friedman, James W. 1971: A non-cooperative equilibrium for supergames. *Review of Economic Studies*, 38(1), 1–12; reprinted in Andrew F. Daughety (ed.), *Cournot Oligopoly: Characterization and Applications*. Cambridge: Cambridge University Press, 1988, 142–57.

— 1979: On entry preventing behavior and limit price models of entry. In S. J. Brams and G. Schwodiauer (eds), *Applied Game Theory*. Wurzburg–Wien: Physica-Verlag, 236–53.

— 1983a: Advertising and oligopolistic equilibrium. *Bell Journal of Economics*, 14(2), 464–73.

— 1983b: *Oligopoly Theory*. Cambridge: Cambridge University Press.

— 1985: Cooperative equilibria in finite horizon noncooperative supergames. *Journal of Economic Theory*, 35: 390–8.

— 1986: *Game Theory with Applications to Economics*. Oxford: Oxford University Press.

— 1988: On the strategic importance of prices versus quantities. *Rand Journal of Economics*, 19(4), 607–22.

— 1992: Price-quantity oligopoly with adjustment costs. In Reinhard Selten (ed.), *Rational Interaction Essays in Honor of John C. Harsanyi*. Berlin: Springer-Verlag, 225–44.

Friedman, James W., and Samuelson, Larry 1990: Subgame perfect equilibrium with continuous reaction functions. *Games and Economic Behavior*, 2, 304–24.

Friedman, James W., and Thisse, Jacques–François 1993: Partial collusion fosters minimum product differentiation. *Rand Journal of Economics*, 24(4), 631–45.

Friedman, Milton, and Schwartz, Anna J. 1991: Alternative approaches to analyzing economic data. *American Economic Review*, 81(1), 39–49.

Frisch, Ragnar 1933: Monopole – polypole – la notion de force dans l'économie. *Nationalokonomisk Tidsskrift* 241–59; reprinted in English translation in *International Economic Papers* No. 1, London: Macmillan/New York: The Macmillan Company, 1951, 23–35.

Fuchs, Victor R. (ed.) 1972: *Policy Issues and Research Opportunities in Industrial Organization*. New York: National Bureau of Economic Research.

Fudenberg, Drew, and Levine, David K. 1990: An approximate folk theorem with imperfect private information. *Journal of Economic Theory*, 54(1), 26–47.

Fudenberg, Drew and Maskin, Eric 1986: The folk theorem in repeated games with discounting and with incomplete information. *Econometrica*, 54(3), 533–54.

—, and — 1990: Nash and perfect equilibria of discounted repeated games. *Journal of Economic Theory*, 51(1), 194–206.

Fudenberg, Drew, and Tirole, Jean 1983: Capital as a commitment: strategic investment to deter entry. *Journal of Economic Theory*, 31, 227–50.

—, and — 1984: The fat-cat effect, the puppy-dog ploy, and the lean and hungry look. *American Economic Review*, 74(2), 361–6.

—, and — 1986: A theory of exit in duopoly. *Econometrica*, 54(4), 943–60.

—, and — 1987: Understanding rent dissipation: on the use of game theory in industrial organization. *American Economic Review*, 77(2), 176–83.

Fudenberg, Drew, Levine, David K., and Maskin, Eric 1989: The folk theorem with imperfect public information. Department of Economics, Massachusetts Institute of Technology Working Paper No. 523, May.

Furth, Dave, and Kovenock, Dan 1993: Price leadership in a duopoly with capacity constraints and product differentiation. *Journal of Economics*, 57(1), 1–35.

Gabay, Daniel, and Moulin, Hervé 1980: On the uniqueness and stability of Nash-equilibria in non-cooperative games. In Alain Benoussan, Paul Kleindorfer, and Charles S. Tapiero (eds), *Applied Stochastic Control in Econometrics and Management Science*. Amsterdam: North-Holland, 271–93.

Gabszewicz, Jean-Jaskold, and Garella, Paolo G. 1987: Price search and spatial competition. *European Economic Review*, 31, 827–42.

Gabszewicz, Jean-Jaskold, and Thisse, Jacques-François 1979: Price competition, quality, and income disparities. *Journal of Economic Theory*, 20(3), 340–59.

—, and — 1980: Entry (and exit) in a differentiated industry. *Journal of Economic Theory*, 22, 327–38.

—, and — 1982: Product differentiation with income disparities: an illustrative model. *Journal of Industrial Economics*, 31(1/2), 115–29.

—, and — 1986: On the nature of competition with differentiated products. *Economic Journal*, 96, 160–72.

Galbraith, John K. 1952: *American Capitalism: the Concept of Countervailing Power*. Boston: Houghton–Mifflin.

Gallet, Craig A. 1999: The effect of the 1971 advertising ban on behavior in the cigarette industry. *Managerial and Decision Economics*, 20(6), 299–303.

Gallini, N. 1992: Patent policy and costly imitation. *Rand Journal of Economics*, 23, 52–63.

Gallini, Nancy T., and Karp, Larry 1989: Sales and consumer lock-in. *Economica*, 56, 279–94.

Gallini, Nancy T., and Winter, Ralph A. 1983: On vertical control in monopolistic competition. *International Journal of Industrial Organization*, 1(3), 275–86.

Gal-Or, Esther 1982: Hotelling's spatial competition as a model of sales. *Economics Letters*, 9, 1–6.

Gasmi, Farid, and Vuong, Quang H. 1991: An econometric analysis of some duopolistic games in prices and advertising. In George F. Rhodes, Jr. (ed.), *Advances in Econometrics*, 9, 225–54.

Gasmi, Farid, Laffont, Jean-Jacques, and Vuong, Quang H. 1992: Econometric analysis of collusive behavior in a soft-drink market. *Journal of Economics & Management Strategy*, 1(2), 277–311.

Geithman, Frederick E., Marvel, Howard P., and Weiss, Leonard W. 1981: Concentration, price and critical concentration ratios. *Review of Economics and Statistics*, 63(3), 346–53.

Genesove, David, and Mullin, Wallace P. 1998a: Testing static oligopoly models: conduct and cost in the sugar industry, 1890–1914. *Rand Journal of Economics*, 29(2), 355–77.

—, and — 1998b: Narrative evidence on the dynamics of collusion: the Sugar Institute case. Manuscript, May 31.

—, and — 1999: The Sugar Institute learns to organize information exchange. In Naomi Lamoreaux, Daniel M. G. Raff, and Peter Temin (eds), *Learning by Doing in Markets, Firms, and Countries*. Chicago: University of Chicago Press.

Geroski, Paul A. 1981: Specification and testing the profits–concentration relationship: some experiments for the U.K. *Economica*, 48, 279–88.

— 1982: Simultaneous equations models of the structure–performance paradigm. *European Economic Review*, 19, 145–58.

— 1983: Some reflections on the theory and application of concentration indices. *International Journal of Industrial Organization*, 1(1), 79–94.

— 1990: Modeling persistent profitability. In Dennis C. Mueller (ed.), *The Dynamics of Company Profits: an Intertemporal Comparison*. Cambridge: Cambridge University Press.

— 1991a: Domestic and foreign entry in the UK: 1983–84. In Paul A. Geroski and Joachim Schwalbach (eds), *Entry and Market Contestability: An International Comparison*, Oxford: Basil Blackwell.

— 1991b: *Market Dynamics and Entry*. London: Basil Blackwell.

Geroski, Paul A., and Jacquemin, Alexis 1988: The persistence of profits: a European comparison. *Economic Journal*, 98, 375–89.

Geroski, Paul A., and Mueller, Dennis C. 1990: The persistence of profits in perspective. In Dennis C. Mueller (ed.), *The Dynamics of Company Profits: an International Comparison*. Cambridge: Cambridge University Press.

Geroski, Paul A., and Murfin, A. 1991: Entry and intra-industry mobility in the U.K. car market. *Oxford Bulletin of Economics and Statistics*, 53(4), 341–59.

Geroski, Paul A., Masson, Robert T., and Shaanan, Joseph 1987: The dynamics of market structure. *International Journal of Industrial Organization*, 5(1), 93–100.

Ghemawat, Pankaj, and Caves, Richard E. 1986: Capital commitment and profitability: an empirical investigation. *Oxford Economic Papers*, 38, Supplement, November, 94–110.

Ghemawat, Pankaj, and Nalebuff, Barry 1985: Exit. *Rand Journal of Economics*, 16(2), 184–94.

—, and — 1990: The devolution of declining industries. *Quarterly Journal of Economics*, 105(1), 167–86.

Gibbons, Robert 1992: *Game Theory for Applied Economists*. Princeton, NJ: Princeton University Press.

Gilbert, Richard J. 1986: Preemptive competition. In Joseph E. Stiglitz and G. Frank Mathewson (eds), *New Developments in the Analysis of Market Structure*. Cambridge, MA: The MIT Press, 90–123.

— 1989: Mobility barriers and the value of incumbency. In Richard C. Schmalensee and Robert D. Willig (eds), *Handbook of Industrial Organization*. Amsterdam: North-Holland, 475–535.

Gilbert, Richard J., and Lieberman, Marvin B. 1987: Investment and coordination in oligopolistic industries. *Rand Journal of Economics*, 18(1), 17–33.

Gilbert, Richard J., and Shapiro, Carl 1990: Optimal patent length and breadth. *Rand Journal of Economics*, 21, 106–12.

Gilbert, Richard J., and Vives, Xavier 1986: Entry deterrence and the free rider problem. *Review of Economic Studies*, 53, 71–83.

Gilligan, Thomas W. 1986: The competitive effects of resale price maintenance. *Rand Journal of Economics*, 17(4), 544–56.

Gisser, Micha 1991: Advertising, concentration and profitability in manufacturing. *Economic Inquiry*, 29(1), 148–65.

Glick, Mark, and Ehrbar, Hans 1990: Long-run equilibrium in the empirical study of monopoly and competition. *Economic Inquiry*, 28(1), 151–62.

Goddard, J. A., and Wilson, J. O. S. 1999: The persistence of profit: a new empirical interpretation. *International Journal of Industrial Organization*, 17(5), 663–87.

Goldberg, Pinelopi Koujianou 1995: Product differentiation and oligopoly in international markets: the case of the U.S. automobile industry. *Econometrica*, 63(4), 891–951.

Goldberg, Victor, and Moirao, Sharon 1973: Limit pricing and potential competition. *Journal of Political Economy*, 81, 1460–6.

Goldberger, Arthur S. 1964: *Econometric Theory*. New York: John Wiley.

Goldschmid, Harvey J., Mann, H. Michael, and Weston, J. Fred, (eds) 1974: *Industrial Concentration: the New Learning*. Boston: Little, Brown & Company.

Gorecki, Paul K. 1975: The determinants of entry by new and diversifying enterprises in the U.K. manufacturing sector, 1958–1963: some tentative results. *Applied Economics*, 7(2), 139–47.

— 1976: The determinants of entry by domestic and foreign enterprises in Canadian manufacturing industries: some comments and empirical results. *Review of Economics and Statistics*, 58(4), 485–8.

Goto, Akira 1982: Business groups in a market economy. *European Economic Review*, 19, 53–70.

Goto, Akira, and Suzuki, Kazuyuki 1989: R&D capital, rate of return on R&D investment and spillover of R&D in Japanese manufacturing industries. *Review of Economics and Statistics*, 71(4), 555–64.

Gould, J. R. 1977: Price discrimination and vertical control: a note. *Journal of Political Economy*, 85(5), 1063–71.

Graddy, Kathryn 1995: Testing for imperfect competition at the Fulton fish market. *Rand Journal of Economics*, 26, 75–92.

Green, Edward J., and Porter, Robert H. 1984: Noncooperative collusion under imperfect price information. *Econometrica*, 52(1), 87–100.

Green, J., and Scotchmer, S. 1995: On the division of profit in sequential innovation. *Rand Journal of Economics*, 26, 20–33.

Green, Richard J., and Newbery, David M. 1992: Competition in the British electricity spot market. *Journal of Political Economy*, 100(5), 929–53.

Greenhut, Melvin L., and Ohta, H. 1973: Spatial configurations and competitive equilibrium. *Weltwirtschaftliches Archiv*, 109, 87–104.

Greenhut, Melvin L., Norman, George, and Hung, Chao–Shun 1987: *The Economics of Imperfect Competition; a Spatial Approach.* Cambridge: Cambridge University Press.

Greening, Timothy 1984: Analysis of the impact of the *Florsheim Shoe* Case. In Ronald N. Lafferty, Robert H. Lande, and John B. Kirkwood, *Impact Evaluation of Federal Trade Commission Vertical Restraints Cases.* Washington, DC: Federal Trade Commission.

Greenlee, Patrick, and Cassiman, Bruno 1999: Product market objectives and the formation of research joint ventures. *Managerial and Decision Economics*, 20, 115–30.

Greer, Douglas F. 1971: Advertising and market concentration. *Southern Economic Journal*, 38(1), 19–32.

Grether, E. T. 1970: Industrial organization: past history and future problems. *American Economic Review*, 60(2), 83–9.

Griliches, Zvi 1986: Productivity, R&D, and basic research at the firm level in the 1970s. *American Economic Review*, 76, 141–54.

—— 1989: Patents: recent trends and puzzles. *Brookings Papers on Economic Activity*, Microeconomics 1989, 291–328.

—— 1992: The search for R&D spillovers. *Scandinavian Journal of Economics*, 94 (Supplement), 29–47.

Grossack, Irvin M. 1965: Towards an integration of static and dynamic measures of industry concentration. *Review of Economics and Statistics*, 47(3), 301–8.

—— 1972: The concept and measurement of permanent industrial concentration. *Journal of Political Economy*, 80(4), 745–60.

Grossman, Sanford J., and Hart, Oliver D. 1983: An analysis of the principal–agent problem. *Econometrica*, 50(1), 7–45.

Guillebaud, C. W. 1965: The Marshall–Macmillan correspondence over the net book system. *Economica*, 75(299), 518–38.

Gul, Faruk 1987: Noncooperative collusion in durable goods oligopoly. *Rand Journal of Economics*, 18(2), 248–54.

Gupta, B., Pal, Debashis, and Sarkar, J. 1997: Cournot competition and agglomeration in a model of location choice. *Regional Science and Urban Economics*, 27, 261–82.

Güth, Werner 1995: A simple justification of quantity competition and the Cournot-oligopoly solution. *ifo–Studien*, 41(2), 245–57.

Häckner, Jonas 1996: Optimal symmetric punishments in a Bertrand differentiated products duopoly. *International Journal of Industrial Organization*, 14(5), 611–30.

Hagedoorn, John 1990: Organizational modes of inter-firm co-operation and technology transfer. *Innovation*, 10(1), 17–30.

Hahn, Frank H. 1962: Comments on the stability of the Cournot oligopoly solution. *Review of Economic Studies*, 29(4), 329–31.

Hall, Marshall, and Weiss, Leonard W. 1967: Firm size and profitability. *Review of Economics and Statistics*, 49, 319–31.

Hall, Robert E. 1986: Market structure and macroeconomic fluctuations. *Brookings Papers on Economic Activity*, 1986:2, 285–322.

—— 1988: The relation between price and marginal cost in U.S. industry. *Journal of Political Economy*, 96(5), 921–47.

Hamilton, J. H., and Slutsky, S. M. 1990: Endogenous timing in duopoly games: Stackelberg or Cournot equilibria. *Games and Economic Behavior*, 2, 29–46.

Hamilton, J. H., Klein, J. F., Sheshinski, E., and Slutsky, S. M. 1994: Quantity competition in a spatial model. *Canadian Journal of Economics*, 27, 903–17.

Hansen, Robert G. 1985: Empirical testing of auction theory. *American Economic Review*, 75(2), 156–9.

Harcourt, G. C. 1965: The accountant in a golden age. *Oxford Economic Papers*, 17, 66–80.

Harrington, Joseph E. Jr. 1987a: Collusion in multiproduct oligopoly games under a finite horizon. *International Economic Review*, 28(1), 1–14.

— 1987b: Oligopolistic entry deterrence under incomplete information. *Rand Journal of Economics*, 18(2), 211–31.

— 1989: Collusion and predation under (almost) free entry. *International Journal of Industrial Organization*, 7(3), 381–401.

— 1991: The joint profit maximum as a free-entry equilibrium outcome. *European Economic Review*, 35(5), 1087–101.

Harris, Frederick H. deB. 1988: Testing competing hypotheses from structure–performance theory: efficient structure versus market power. *Journal of Industrial Economics*, 36(3), 267–80.

Harstad, Ronald, Martin, Stephen, and Normann, Hans-Theo 1998: Experimental tests of consciously parallel behavior in oligopoly. In Louis Phlips (ed.), *Applied Industrial Economics*. Cambridge: Cambridge University Press, 123–51.

Hart, Oliver 1989: An economist's perspective on the theory of the firm. *Columbia Law Review*, 89, 1757–74.

Hart, P. E. 1975: Moment distributions in economics: an exposition. *Journal of the Royal Statistical Society*, Series A 138, Part 3, 423–34.

Hathaway, N. J., and Rickard, J. A. 1979: Equilibria of price-setting and quantity-setting duopolies. *Economics Letters*, 3, 133–7.

Hay, George A. 2000: The meaning of "agreement" under the Sherman Act: thoughts from the "facilitating practices" experience. *Review of Industrial Organization*, 16(2), 113–29.

Hay, George A., and Kelley, Daniel 1974: An empirical survey of price fixing conspiracies. *Journal of Law and Economics*, 17(1), 13–38.

Hayward, E. J. R. 1941: H. von Stackelberg's work on duopoly. *Economic Record*, 99–106.

Hazledine, Tim 1984: The possibility of price umbrellas in Canadian manufacturing industries. *International Journal of Industrial Organization*, 2(3), 251–62.

Helm, Dieter 1989: Mergers, takeovers, and the enforcement of profit maximization. In James A. Fairburn and John A. Kay (eds), *Mergers and Merger Policy*. Oxford: Oxford University Press, 133–47.

Henderson, Rebecca, and Cockburn, Ian 1996: Scale, scope and spillovers: the determinants of research productivity in drug discovery. *Rand Journal of Economics*, 27(1), 32–59.

Hennart, Jean-François 1988a: Upstream vertical integration in the aluminum and tin industries. *Journal of Economic Behavior and Organization*, 9, 281–99.

— 1988b: A transaction costs theory of equity joint ventures. *Strategic Management Journal*, 9, 361–74.

Henriques, Irene 1990: Cooperative and noncooperative R&D in duopoly with spillovers: comment. *American Economic Review*, 80(3), 638–40.

Herfindahl, Orris C. 1950: Concentration in the steel industry. Unpublished Ph.D. dissertation, Columbia University.

Heywood, John S. 1987: Market share and efficiency: a reprise. *Economics Letters*, 24, 171–5.

Hicks, J. R. 1935: Annual survey of economic theory: the theory of monopoly. *Econometrica*, 3(1), 1–20.

Hill, C. W. L. 1985a: Oliver Williamson and the M-form firm: a critical review. *Journal of Economic Issues*, 19(3), 731–51.

— 1985b: Internal organization and economic performance: an empirical analysis of profitability of principal firms. *Managerial and Decision Economics*, 6(4), 210–16.

Hinloopen, Jeroen 1997: Subsidizing cooperative and noncooperative R&D in duopoly with spillovers. *Journal of Economics*, 66, 151–75.

Hinloopen, Jeroen 2000: Subsidizing cooperative and noncooperative R&D: an equivalence result? *Economics of Innovation and New Technology*, 9, 317–29.

Hinloopen, Jeroen, and van Marrewijk, Charles 1999: On the limits and possibilities of the principle of minimum differentiation. *International Journal of Industrial Organization*, 17(5), 735–50.

Hirschman, A. O. 1964: The paternity of an index. *American Economic Review*, 54(5), 761–2.

Hirschmeier, Johannes, and Yui, Tsunehiko 1981: *The Development of Japanese Business*, 2nd edn. London: Allen & Unwin.

Hobbs, Benjamin F. 1986: Mill pricing versus spatial price discrimination under Bertrand and Cournot spatial competition. *Journal of Industrial Economics*, 35(2), 173–91.

Holahan, William L. 1975: The welfare effects of spatial price discrimination. *American Economic Review*, 65(5), 498–503.

Holmström, Bengt 1979: Moral hazard and observability. *Bell Journal of Economics*, 10, 74–91.

Holt, Charles A. 1985: An experimental test of the consistent-conjectures hypothesis. *American Economic Review*, 75(3), 314–25.

Holt, Charles A., and Scheffman, David T. 1987: Facilitating practices: the effects of advance notice and best-price policies. *Rand Journal of Economics*, 18(2), 187–97.

Hoover, Edgar M. Jr. 1937: Spatial price discrimination. *Review of Economic Studies*, IV(3), 182–91.

Horowitz, Ira 1984: The misuse of accounting rates of return: comment. *American Economic Review*, 74(3), 492–3.

Horstmann, Ignatius, and MacDonald, Glenn M. 1994: When is advertising a signal of product quality? *Journal of Economics & Management Strategy*, 3(3), 561–84.

Horstmann, Ignatius, and Slivinski, Alan 1985: Location models as models of product choice. *Journal of Economic Theory*, 36, 367–86.

Hotelling, Harold H. 1929: Stability in competition. *Economic Journal*, 39, 41–57; reprinted in George J. Stigler and Kenneth E. Boulding (eds), *A. E. A. Readings in Price Theory*. Chicago: Richard D. Irwin, 1952.

Howrey, E. P., and Quandt, R. E. 1968: The dynamics of the number of firms in an industry. *Review of Economic Studies*, 35(3), 349–53.

Huang, Cliff J. and Crooke, Philip S. 1997: *Mathematics and Mathematica for Economists*. Oxford: Blackwell.

Hubbard, R. Glenn 1986: Comment. *Brookings Papers on Economic Activity*, 1986:2, 328–36.

Hviid, Morten 1991: Capacity constrained duopolies, uncertain demand and non-existence of pure strategy equilibria. *European Journal of Political Economy*, 7, 183–90.

Hyde, Charles E., and Perloff, Jeffrey M. 1995: Can market power be estimated? *Review of Industrial Organization*, 10(4), 465–85.

Iwata, Gyoichi 1974: Measurement of conjectural variations in oligopoly. *Econometrica*, 42(5), 947–66.

Jarrell, Gregg A., Brickley, James A., and Netter, Jeffry M. 1988: The market for corporate control: the empirical evidence since 1980. *Journal of Economic Perspectives*, 2(1), 49–68.

Jenks, J. W. 1925–6: Monopolies in the United States. In Henry Higgs (ed.), *Palgrave's Dictionary of Political Economy*, revised edn. New York: Augustus M. Kelley, reprinted 1963, II, 803–5.

Jevons, W. Stanley 1879: *The Theory of Political Economy*, 2nd edn. London: Macmillan.

Joeng, Kap-Young, and Masson, Robert T. 1990: Market structure, entry, and performance in Korea. *Review of Economics and Statistics*, 72(3), 455–62.

Johansen, Leif 1982: On the status of the Nash type of noncooperative equilibrium in economic theory. *Scandinavian Journal of Economics*, 84(3), 421–41.

Jones, Charles I., and Williams, John C. 1997: Measuring the social return to R&D. Finance and Economics Discussion Series Staff Working Paper 1997-12, Federal Reserve Board, Washington, DC, February.

Joskow, Paul L. 1988: Asset specificity and the structure of vertical relationships: empirical evidence. *Journal of Law, Economics, and Organization*, 4(1), 95–117.

Jung, Yun Joo, Kegel, John H., and Levin, Dan 1994: On the existence of predatory pricing: an experimental study of reputation and entry deterrence in the chain-store game. *Rand Journal of Economics*, 25(1), 72–93.

Kadiyali, Vrinda 1996: Entry, its deterrence, and its accommodation: a study of the U.S. photographic film industry. *Rand Journal of Economics*, 27(3), 452–78.

Kahn, Alfred E. 1950: The chemicals industry. In Walter Adams (ed.), *The Structure of American Industry*. New York: The Macmillan Company, 197–230.

Kaldor, Nicolas 1950–1: The economic aspects of advertising. *Review of Economic Studies*, 18, 1–27.

Kamerschen, David R. 1968: The influence of ownership and control on profit rates. *American Economic Review*, 58, 432–47.

Kamien, Morton I. 1987: Limit pricing. In John Eatwell, Murray Milgate, and Peter Newman (eds), *The New Palgrave*. London: Macmillan Press Limited, vol. 3, 189–92.

Kamien, Morton I., and Schwartz, Nancy L. 1974: Patent life and R & D rivalry. *American Economic Review*, 64, 183–7.

—, and — 1982: *Market Structure and Innovation*. Cambridge: Cambridge University Press.

—, and — 1983: Conjectural variations. *Canadian Journal of Economics*, 16(2), 191–211.

Kamien, Morton I., and Zang, Israel 2000: Meet me halfway: research joint ventures and absorptive capacity. *International Journal of Industrial Organization*, 18(7), 995–1012.

Kamien, Morton I., Muller, Eitan, and Zang, Israel 1992: Research joint ventures and R&D cartels. *American Economic Review*, 82(5), 1293–306.

Kania, John J. 1987: Profitability and market power in industries with regional–local markets. *American Economist*, 31(2), 29–34.

Kaplan, Todd R. 2001: Effective price-matching. *International Journal of Industrial Organization*, forthcoming.

Katz, Amoz 1995: More on Hotelling's stability in competition. *International Journal of Industrial Organization*, 13, 89–93.

Kaufer, Erich 1989: *The Economics of the Patent System*. Chur: Harwood Academic Publishers.

Kaul, Anil, and Wittink, Dick R. 1995: Empirical generalizations about the impact of advertising on price sensitivity and price. *Marketing Science*, 14(3), G151–60.

Kay, John A. 1976: Accountants, too, could be happy in a golden age: the accountant's rate of profit and the internal rate of return. *Oxford Economic Papers*, NS, 28(3), 447–60.

Kaysen, Carl 1956: *United States v. United States Shoe Machinery Corporation: an economic analysis of an antitrust case*. Cambridge, MA: Harvard University Press.

Keating, Barry 1991: An update on industries ranked by average rates of return. *Applied Economics*, 23(5), 897–902.

Kessides, Ioannis N. 1986: Advertising, sunk costs, and barriers to entry. *Review of Economics and Statistics*, 68(1), 84–95.

— 1989: Do firms differ much? Some additional evidence. Mimeo.

— 1990a: Internal versus external market conditions and firm profitability: an exploratory model. *Economic Journal*, 100(402), 773–92.

— 1990b: Towards a testable model of entry: a study of the US manufacturing industries. *Economica*, 57, 219–38.

Kihlstrom, R., and Riordan, Michael H. 1984: Advertising as a signal. *Journal of Political Economy*, 92(3), 427–50.

Kirman, William I., and Masson, Robert T. 1986: Capacity signals and entry deterrence. *International Journal of Industrial Organization*, 4(1), 25–42.

Klemperer, Paul D. 1987: Entry deterrence in markets with consumer switching costs. *Economic Journal*, 97, Conference 1987, 99–117.

— 1989: Price wars caused by switching costs. *Review of Economic Studies*, 56, 405–20.

— 1990: How broad should the scope of patent protection be? *Rand Journal of Economics*, 21(1), 113–30.

Klemperer, Paul D., and Meyer, Margaret A. 1988: Consistent conjectures equilibria: a reformulation showing non-uniqueness. *Economics Letters*, 27, 111–15.

— 1989: Supply function equilibria in oligopoly under uncertainty. *Econometrica*, 57(6), 1243–77.

Klette, Tor Jakob 1996: R&D, scope economies, and plant performance. *Rand Journal of Economics*, 27(3), 502–22.

— 1999: Market power, scale economies and productivity: estimates from a panel of establishment data. *Journal of Industrial Economics*, 48(4), 451–76.

Klock, Mark, Thies, Clifford F., and Baum, Christopher F. 1991: Tobin's q and measurement error: caveat investigator. *Journal of Economics and Business*, 43(3), 241–52.

Kogut, Bruce 1989: The stability of joint ventures: reciprocity and competitive rivalry. *Journal of Industrial Economics*, 38(2), 183–98.

Kohn, Meir, and Scott, John T. 1982: Scale economies in research and development. *Journal of Industrial Economics*, 30(3), 239–49.

Kolstad, Charles D., and Mathiesen, Lars 1987: Necessary and sufficient conditions for uniqueness of a Cournot equilibrium. *Review of Economic Studies*, 54(4), 681–90.

Kraft, Kornelius 1989: Market structure, firm characteristics and innovative activity. *Journal of Industrial Economics*, 37(3), 329–36.

Krattenmaker, Thomas G., and Salop, Steven C. 1986: Anticompetitive exclusion: raising rivals' costs to achieve power over price. *Yale Law Journal*, 96(2), 209–93.

Krepps, Mathew B. 1999: Facilitating practices and the path-dependence of collusion. *International Journal of Industrial Organization*, 17(6), 887–901.

Kreps, David M., and Scheinkman, José 1983: Quantity precommitment and Bertrand competition yield Cournot outcomes. *Bell Journal of Economics*, 14(2), 326–37.

Kreps, David M., and Wilson, Robert 1982: Reputation and imperfect information. *Journal of Economic Theory*, 27, 253–79.

Krouse, Clement G. 1991: Competition for monopoly II: entry and exit. *Bulletin of Economic Research*, 43(3), 197–222.

Kwoka, John E. Jr. 1979: The effect of market share distribution on market performance. *Review of Economics and Statistics*, 61(1), 101–9.

— 1981: Does the choice of concentration measure really matter? *Journal of Industrial Economics*, 29(4), 445–53.

— 1985: The Herfindahl index in theory and practice. *Antitrust Bulletin*, 30, 915–47.

Lafferty, Ronald N., Lande, Robert H., and Kirkwood, John B. 1984: *Impact Evaluation of Federal Trade Commission Vertical Restraints Cases*. Washington, DC: Federal Trade Commission.

La Manna, Manfredi, Macleod, Ross, and David de Meza 1989: The case for permissive patents. *European Economic Review*, 33(7), 1427–33.

Lambin, Jean-Jacques 1970: Optimal allocation of competitive marketing efforts: an empirical study. *Journal of Business*, 43(4), 468–84.

Lambson, Val Eugene 1991: Industry evolution with sunk costs and uncertain market conditions. *International Journal of Industrial Organization*, 9, 171–96.

Lancaster, Kelvin J. 1979: *Variety, Equity, and Efficiency*. New York: Columbia University Press.

— 1980: Intra-industry trade under perfect monopolistic competition. *Journal of International Economics*, 10, 151–75.

Lapham, Beverly and Ware, Roger 1994: Markov puppy dogs and related animals. *International Journal of Industrial Organization*, 12(4), 569–93.

Lau, Lawrence J. 1982: On identifying the degree of competitiveness from industry price and output data. *Economics Letters*, 10, 93–9.

Launhardt, W. 1885: *Mathematische Begründung der Volkswirtschaftslehre*. Leipzig: B. G. Teubner.

— 1993: *Principles of Mathematical Economics*. Aldershot: Edward Elgar.

Lazear, Edward P. 2000: Economic imperialism. *Quarterly Journal of Economics*, 115(1), 99–146.

Ledwidge, Bernard 1982: *De Gaulle*. London: Weidenfeld and Nicolson.

Lee, Tom, and Wilde, Louis L. 1980: Market structure and innovation: a reformulation. *Quarterly Journal of Economics*, 94(2), 429–36.

Leibenstein, Harvey 1966: Allocative efficiency vs. "X-efficiency." *American Economic Review*, 56(3), 392–415.

— 1973: Competition and X-efficiency: reply. *Journal of Political Economy*, 81(3), 765–77.

— 1975: Aspects of the X-efficiency theory of the firm. *Bell Journal of Economics*, 6(2), 580–606.

— 1978: X-inefficiency Xists – Reply to an Xorcist. *American Economic Review*, 68(1), 203–11.

— 1983: Property rights and X-efficiency: comment. *American Economic Review*, 73(4), 831–42.

— 1987: *Inside the Firm: the Inefficiencies of Hierarchy*. Cambridge, MA: Harvard University Press.

Leibenstein, Harvey, and Maital, Shlomo 1994: The organizational foundations of X-inefficiency. *Journal of Economic Behavior and Organization*, 23, 251–68.

Leonard, Robert J. 1994: Reading Cournot, reading Nash: the creation and stabilisation of the Nash equilibrium. *Economic Journal*, 104, 492–511.

Leone, Robert P. 1995: Generalizing what is known about temporal aggregation and advertising carryover. *Marketing Science*, 14(3), G141–50.

Leontief, Wassily 1936: Stackelberg on monopolistic competition. *Journal of Political Economy*, 44(4), 554–9.

Lerner, Abba P. 1934: The concept of monopoly and the measurement of monopoly power. *Review of Economic Studies*, 1, 157–75.

Lerner, Abba P., and Singer, H. W. 1937: Some notes on duopoly and spatial competition. *Journal of Political Economy*, 45(2), 145–86.

Levinstein, Margaret C. 1997: Price wars and the stability of collusion: a study of the pre-World War I bromine industry. *Journal of Industrial Economics*, 45(2), 117–37.

Levinthal, Daniel 1988: A survey of agency models of organizations. *Journal of Economic Behavior and Organization*, 9, 153–85.

Levitan, R., and Shubik, Martin. 1978: Duopoly with price and quantity as strategic variables. *International Journal of Game Theory*, 7(1), 1–11.

Levy, David T. 1985: Specifying the dynamics of industry concentration. *Journal of Industrial Economics*, 34(1), 55–68.

Levy, David T., and Haber, Lawrence J. 1986: An advantage of the multiproduct firm: the transferability of firm-specific capital. *Journal of Economic Behavior and Organization*, 7, 291–302.

Liang, J. Nellie 1989: Price reaction functions and conjectural variations: an application to the breakfast cereal industry. *Review of Industrial Organization*, 4(2), 31–58.

Lieberman, Marvin B. 1987a: Excess capacity as a barrier to entry: an empirical appraisal. *Journal of Industrial Economics*, 35(4), 607–27.

— 1987b: Postentry investment and market structure in the chemical processing industries. *Rand Journal of Economics*, 18(4), 533–49.

— 1990: Exit from declining industries: "shakeout" or "stakeout"? *Rand Journal of Economics*, 21(4), 538–54.

Liebowitz, S. 1982: What do census price–cost margins measure? *Journal of Law and Economics*, 25(2), 231–46.

Lin, Y. Joseph 1988: Oligopoly and vertical integration: a note. *American Economic Review*, 78(1), 251–4.

— 1990: The dampening-of-competition effect of exclusive dealing. *Journal of Industrial Economics*, 39(2), 209–23.

Lindenberg, Eric, and Ross, Stephen 1981: Tobin's *q* ratio and industrial organization. *Journal of Business*, 54(1), 1–32.

Lindh, Thomas 1992: The inconsistency of consistent conjectures: coming back to Cournot. *Journal of Economic Behavior and Organization*, 18, 69–90.

Lipman, Barton P. 1990: Delaying or deterring entry: a game theoretic analysis. *Journal of Economic Dynamics and Control*, 14(3/4), 685–708.

Lofaro, Andrea 1999: When imperfect collusion is profitable. *Journal of Economics*, 70(3), 235–59.

Logan, John W., and Lutter, Randall W. 1989: Guaranteed lowest prices: Do they facilitate collusion? *Economics Letters*, 31, 189–92.

Londregan, J. 1990: Entry and exit over the industry life cycle. *Rand Journal of Economics*, 21(3), 446–58.

Long, William, and Ravenscraft, David J. 1984: The misuse of accounting rates of return: comment. *American Economic Review*, 74(3), 494–500.

Lösch, A. 1938: The nature of economic regions. *Southern Economic Journal*, 5, 71–8.

—— 1944: *Die raumliche Ordnung der Wirtschaft*, 2nd edn. Iena: G. Fisher.

—— 1954: *The Economics of Location*. New Haven: Yale University Press.

Loury, Glenn C. 1979: Market structure and innovation. *Quarterly Journal of Economics*, 93(3), 395–10.

Luce, R. D., and Raiffa, H. 1957: *Games and Decisions*. New York: John Wiley.

Lustgarten, Steven R. 1975: The impact of buyer concentration in manufacturing industry. *Review of Economics and Statistics*, 57(2), 125–32.

Lustgarten, Steven R., and Thomadakis, Stavros 1987: Mobility barriers and Tobin's *q*. *Journal of Business*, 60(4), 519–37.

Lydall, H. F. 1955: Conditions of new entry and the theory of price. *Oxford Economic Papers*, 7, 300–11.

MacLeod, W. Bentley 1985: A theory of conscious parallelism. *European Economic Review*, 27(1), 25–44.

Madden, Paul 1998: Elastic demand, sunk costs and the Kreps–Scheinkman extension of the Cournot model. *Economic Theory*, 12, 199–212.

Maggi, Giovanni 1996: Strategic trade policies with endogenous mode of competition. *American Economic Review*, 86(1), 237–58.

Magnan de Bornier, Jean 1992: The "Cournot–Bertrand debate": a historical perspective. *History of Political Economy*, 24(3), 623–56.

Mailath, George J. 1998: Do people play Nash equilibrium? Lessons from evolutionary game theory. *Journal of Economic Literature*, 36, 1347–74.

Majerus, David W. 1988: Price vs. quantity competition in oligopoly supergames. *Economics Letters*, 27, 293–7.

Maksimovic, Vojislav 1988: Captial structure in repeated oligopolies. *Rand Journal of Economics*, 19(3), 389–407.

Malueg, David A., and Schwartz, Marius 1991: Preemptive investment, toehold entry, and the mimicking principle. *Rand Journal of Economics*, 22(1), 1–13.

Mancke, R. B. 1974: Causes of interfirm profitability differences: a new interpretation. *Quarterly Journal of Economics*, 88(2), 181–93.

Mankiw, N. Gregory, and Whinston, Michael D. 1986: Free entry and social efficiency. *Rand Journal of Economics*, 17(1), 48–58.

Mann, H. Michael 1966: Seller concentration, barriers to entry, and rates of return in thirty industries, 1950–1960. *Review of Economics and Statistics*, 48, 296–307.

—— 1969: A note on barriers to entry and long run profitability. *Antitrust Bulletin*, 14, 845–9.

Mann, H. Michael, and Meehan, James W. Jr. 1969: Concentration and profitability: an examination of a recent study. *Antitrust Bulletin*, 385–95.

Mansfield, Edwin 1985: How rapidly does new industrial technology leak out? *Journal of Industrial Economics*, 34(2), 217–23.

Mansfield, Edwin, Schwartz, Mark, and Wagner, Samuel 1981: Imitation costs and patents: an empirical study. *Economic Journal*, 91, 907–18.

Mansfield, Edwin, Rapoport, John, Romeo, Anthony, Wagner, Samuel, and Beardsley, George 1977: Social and private rates of return from industrial innovations. *Quarterly Journal of Economics*, 91(2), 221–40.

Marion, Bruce W. 1989: The concentration–price relationship in food retailing. In Leonard W. Weiss (ed.), *Concentration and Price*. Cambridge, MA: The MIT Press.

Marion, Bruce W., Mueller, Willard F., Cotterill, Ronald W., Geithman, Frederick E., and Schmelzer, J. R. 1979a: *The Food Retailing Industry: Market Structure, Profits, and Prices*. New York, Praeger.

—, —, —, —, and — 1979b: The price and profit performance of leading food chains. *American Journal of Agricultural Economics*, 79, 420–33.

Marris, Robin 1963: A model of the "managerial" enterprise. *Quarterly Journal of Economics*, 77, 185–209.

Marris, Robin, and Mueller, Dennis C. 1980: The corporation, competition, and the invisible hand. *Journal of Economic Literature*, 18(1), 32–63.

Marshall, Alfred 1920: *Principles of Economics*, 8th edn. London: The Macmillan Press.

Martin, Stephen 1979: Advertising, concentration, and profitability: the simultaneity problem. *Bell Journal of Economics*, 10(2), 639–47.

— 1983a: Vertical relationships and industrial performance. *Quarterly Review of Economics and Business*, 23(1), 6–18.

— 1983b: *Market, Firm, and Economic Performance*. Salomon Brothers Center for the Study of Financial Institutions Monograph Series 1983-1.

— 1984a: Comment on the specification of structure–performance relationships. *European Economic Review*, 24(2), 197–201.

— 1984b: A Bainsian interpretation of von Weizsäcker's model of scale economies. *Southern Economic Journal*, 50(4), 1192–5.

— 1984c: The misuse of accounting rates of return: comment. *American Economic Review*, 74(3), 501–6.

— 1988a: Market power and/or efficiency? *Review of Economics and Statistics*, 70(2), 331–5.

— 1988b: The measurement of profitability and the diagnosis of market power. *International Journal of Industrial Organization*, 6(3), 301–21.

— 1988c: *Industrial Economics*. New York: Macmillan.

— 1989: Sunk cost, financial markets, and contestability. *European Economic Review*, 33(6), 1089–113.

— 1990: Fringe size and cartel stability. Department of Economics, European University Institute, Working Paper 90/16, November.

— 1993a: Endogenous firm efficiency in a Cournot principal–agent model. *Journal of Economic Theory*, 59(2), 445–50.

— 1993b: On the divergence between the legal and economic meanings of collusion. Manuscript, European University Institute, Florence, Italy, 1993; http://www.fee.uva.nl/fo/sm/cr/diverge.pdf

— 1994: Private and social incentives to form R&D joint ventures. *Review of Industrial Organization*, 9(2), 157–71.

— 1995: Oligopoly limit pricing: strategic substitutes, strategic complements. *International Journal of Industrial Organization*, 13(1), 41–65.

— 1996: R&D joint ventures and tacit product market collusion. *European Journal of Political Economy*, 11(4), 733–41.

— 1998: Competition policy: publicity vs. prohibition & punishment. In Stephen Martin (ed.), *European Competition Policies*. Elsevier – North-Holland.

— 1999: Strategic and welfare implications of bundling. *Economics Letters*, 62, 371–76.

— 2001: Spillovers, appropriability, and R&D. *Journal of Economics*, forthcoming.

Martin, Stephen, and Ravenscraft, David J. 1982: Aggregation and studies of industrial profitability. *Economics Letters*, 10, 161–5.

Martin, Stephen, and Schrader, Alexander 1998: Vertical market participation. *Review of Industrial Organization*, 13(3), 321–31.

Martin, Stephen, Snyder, Christopher M., and Normann, Hans-Theo 1999: Vertical foreclosure in experimental markets. Manuscript, October 9.

Martinelli, César 1997: Small firms, borrowing constraints, and reputation. *Journal of Economic Behavior & Organization*, 33, 91–105.

Marvel, Howard P. 1981: Vertical restraints in the hearing aids industry. Manuscript, April; reprinted in Ronald N. Lafferty, Robert H. Lande, and John B. Kirkwood, *Impact Evaluation of Federal Trade Commission Vertical Restraints Cases*. Washington, DC: Federal Trade Commission, 1984.

— 1989: Concentration and price in gasoline retailing. In Leonard W. Weiss (ed.), *Concentration and Price*. Cambridge, MA: The MIT Press.

Marvel, Howard P., and McCafferty, Stephen 1984: Resale price maintenance and quality certification. *Rand Journal of Economics*, 15(3), 346–59.

—, and — 1985: The welfare effects of resale price maintenance. *Journal of Law and Economics*, 28(2), 363–79.

—, and — 1986: The political economy of retail price maintenance. *Journal of Political Economy*, 94(5), 1074–95.

Mason, Edward S. 1939: Price and production policies of large-scale enterprise. *American Economic Review*, 29(1), 61–74; reprinted in Edward S. Mason, *Economic Concentration and the Monopoly Problem*. Cambridge, MA: Harvard University Press, 1959.

Masson, Robert T., and Shaanan, Joseph 1986: Excess capacity and limit pricing: an empirical test. *Economica*, 53, 365–78.

Masten, Scott E., Meehan, James W. Jr., and Snyder, Edward A. 1989: Vertical integration in the U.S. auto industry. *Journal of Economic Behavior and Organization*, 12, 265–73.

Mathewson, G. Frank, and Winter, Ralph A. 1984: An economic theory of vertical restraints. *Rand Journal of Economics*, 15(1), 27–38.

—, and — 1985: The economics of franchise contracts. *Journal of Law and Economics*, 28(3), 503–26.

—, and — 1986: The economics of vertical restraints in distribution. In Joseph E. Stiglitz and G. Frank Mathewson (eds), *New Developments in the Analysis of Market Structure*. Cambridge, MA: The MIT Press, 211–39.

—, and — 1987: The competitive effects of vertical agreements: comment. *American Economic Review*, 77(5), 1057–62.

—, and — 1988: Vertical restraints and the law: a reply. *Rand Journal of Economics*, 19(2), 298–301.

Matutes, Carmen, Rockett, Katherine, and Regibeau, Pierre 1996: Optimal patent design and the diffusion of innovation. *Rand Journal of Economics*, 27, 60–83.

McEachern, William A., and Romeo, Anthony A. 1984: Vertical restraints in the audio components industry: an economic analysis of FTC intervention. In Ronald N. Lafferty, Robert H. Lande, and John B. Kirkwood, *Impact Evaluation of Federal Trade Commission Vertical Restraints Cases*. Washington, DC: Federal Trade Commission.

McFarland, Henry 1988: Evaluating q as an alternative to the rate of return in measuring profitability. *Review of Economics and Statistics*, 70(4), 614–22.

McGahan, Anita M. 1999: The performance of US corporations: 1981–1994. *Journal of Industrial Economics*, 47(4), 373–98.

McGee, John S. 1958: Predatory price cutting: the Standard Oil (N.J.) case. *Journal of Law and Economics*, 1, 137–69.

— 1980: Predatory pricing revisited. *Journal of Law and Economics*, 23(2), 289–330.

— 1987: Compound pricing. *Economic Inquiry*, 25(2), 315–39.

McGucken, Robert, and Chen, Heng 1976: Interactions between buyer and seller concentration and industry price–cost margins. *Industrial Organization Review*, 4, 123–33.

McKinnon, Ronald 1966: Stigler's theory of oligopoly: a comment. *Journal of Political Economy*, 74(3), 281–5.

McLean, Richard P., and Riordan, Michael H. 1989: Industry structure with sequential technology choice. *Journal of Economic Theory*, 47(1), 1–21.

McManus, Maurice 1962: Numbers and size in Cournot oligopoly. *Yorkshire Bulletin of Economic and Social Research*, 14(1), 14–22.

— 1964a: A note on static Cournot equilibrium. *International Economic Review*, 5(3), 335–6.

— 1964b: Static Cournot equilibrium: rejoinder. *International Economic Review*, 5(3), 339–40.

— 1964c: Equilibrium, numbers and size in Cournot oligopoly. *Yorkshire Bulletin of Economic and Social Research*, 16(2), 68–75.

Meehan, James W. Jr., and Larner, Robert 1989: The structural school, its critics, and its progeny: an assessment. In Robert J. Larner and James W. Meehan (eds), *Economics and Antitrust Policy*. New York: Quorum Books, 179–208.

Messerlin, Patrick A. 1990: Anti-dumping regulations or pro-cartel law? The EC chemical cases. *World Economy*, 13, 465–92.

Milgrom, Paul 1987: Predatory pricing. In John Eatwell, Murray Milgate, and Peter Newman (eds), *The New Palgrave*. London: Macmillan Press, vol. 3, 937–8.

Milgrom, Paul, and Roberts, John 1982a: Limit pricing and entry under incomplete information. *Econometrica*, 50(2), 443–66.

— 1982b: Predation, reputation, and entry deterrence. *Journal of Economic Theory*, 27(2), 280–312.

— 1986: Price and advertising as signals of product quality. *Journal of Political Economy*, 94(4), 796–821.

— 1988: Economic theories of the firm: past, present, and future. *Canadian Journal of Economics*, 21(3), 444–58.

Miller, Richard A. 1967: Marginal concentration ratios and industrial profit rates: some empirical results of oligopoly behavior. *Southern Economic Journal*, 34, 259–67.

Milyo, Jeffrey, and Waldfogel, Joel 1999: The effect of advertising on prices: evidence in the wake of *44 Liquormart*. *American Economic Review*, 89(5), 1081–96.

Minkler, Alanson P. 1990: An empirical analysis of a firm's decision to franchise. *Economics Letters*, 34, 77–81.

Mirrlees, James A. 1975: The theory of moral hazard and unobservable behavior – part I. Nuffield College, Oxford, mimeo.

— 1976: The optimal structure of incentives and authority within an organization. *Bell Journal of Economics*, 7(1), 105–31.

Modigliani, Franco 1958: New developments on the oligopoly front. *Journal of Political Economy*, 66(3), 215–32.

Mohr, Ernst 1988: On the incredibility of perfect threats in repeated games: note. *International Economic Review*, 20(3), 551–5.

Montgomery, Cynthia A., and Hariharan S. 1991: Diversified expansion by large established firms. *Journal of Economic Behavior and Organization*, 15(1), 71–89.

Morgan, Theodore 1988: Theory versus empiricism in academic economics. *Journal of Economic Perspectives* (2), 4, 159–64.

Morgenstern, Oskar 1948: Demand theory reconsidered. *Quarterly Journal of Economics*, 165–201.

Motta, Massimo 1993: Endogenous quality choice: price vs. quantity competition. *Journal of Industrial Economics*, 41(3), 113–31.

Mueller, Dennis C. 1972: A life cycle theory of the firm. *Journal of Industrial Economics*, 20(3), 199–219; reprinted in Mueller, Dennis C. 1986: *The Modern Corporation*. Lincoln, NE: University of Nebraska Press.

— 1977: The persistence of profits above the norm. *Economica* 44, 176, 369–80; reprinted in Mueller, Dennis C. 1986: *The Modern Corporation*. Lincoln, NE: University of Nebraska Press.

— 1985: Mergers and market share. *Review of Economics and Statistics*, 47(2), 259–67.

— 1986: *Profits in the Long Run*. Cambridge: Cambridge University Press.

Mueller, Dennis C., and Raunig, Burkhard 1999: Heterogeneities within industries and structure–performance models. *Review of Industrial Organization*, 15(4), 303–20.

Mullin, George L., Mullin, Joseph C., and Mullin, Wallace P. 1995: The competitive effects of mergers: stock market evidence from the U.S. Steel dissolution suit. *Rand Journal of Economics*, 26(2), 314–30.

Mussa, Michael, and Rosen, Sherwin 1978: Monopoly and product quality. *Journal of Economic Theory*, 18, 301–17.

Myerson, Roger B. 1999: Nash equilibrium and the history of economic theory. *Journal of Economic Literature*, 37(3), 1067–82.

Nash, John F. Jr. 1950: Non–cooperative games. Ph.D. dissertation, Princeton University.

Neilson, William S., and Winter, Harold 1993: Bilateral most-favored-customer pricing and collusion. *Rand Journal of Economics*, 24(1), 147–55.

Nelson, Phillip 1970: Information and consumer behavior. *Journal of Political Economy*, 78(2), 311–29.

— 1974: Advertising and information. *Journal of Political Economy*, 82(4), 729–54.

Nerlove, Marc, and Waugh, Frederick V. 1961: Advertising without supply control. *Journal of Farm Economics*, 42(4), 813–37.

Neumann, Manfred, and Haid, Alfred 1985: Concentration and economic performance: a cross–section analysis of West German industries. In Joachim Schwalbach (ed.), *Industry Structure and Performance*. Berlin: Edition Sigma Rainer Bohn Verlag.

Neven, Damien 1986: "Address" models of differentiation. In George Norman (ed.), *Spatial Pricing and Differentiated Markets*. London: Pion, 5–18.

— 1989: Strategic entry deterrence: recent developments in the economics of industry. *Journal of Economic Surveys*, 3(3), 213–33.

Neven, Damien, Papandropoulos, Penelope, and Seabright, Paul 1998: *Trawling for Minnows: European Competition Policy and Agreements Between Firms*. London: Centre for Economic Policy Research.

Nevo, Aviv 2001: Measuring market power in the ready-to-eat cereal industry. *Econometrica*, 69(2), 307–42.

Newmark, Craig M. 1990: A new test of the price–concentration relationship in grocery retailing. *Economics Letters*, 33, 369–73.

Nordhaus, William D. 1969: *Invention, Growth, and Welfare: A Theoretical Treatment of Technological Change*. Cambridge, MA. The MIT Press.

— 1972: The optimum life of a patent: reply. *American Economic Review*, 62(3), 428–31.

Norrbin, S. C. 1993: The relation between price and marginal cost in U.S. industry: a contradiction. *Journal of Political Economy*, 101(6), 1149–64.

Novshek, William 1980: Equilibrium in simple spatial (or differentiated product) models. *Journal of Economic Theory*, 22, 313–26.

— 1985: On the existence of Cournot equilibrium. *Review of Economic Studies*, 52, 85–98.

Odagiri, Hiroyuki, and Yamawaki, Hideki 1986: A study of company profit-rate time series: Japan and the United States. *International Journal of Industrial Organization*, 4(1), 1–23.

Okuguchi, Koji 1987: Equilibrium prices in the Bertrand and Cournot oligopolies. *Journal of Economic Theory*, 42(1), 128–39.

Oliveira Martins, Joaquim, Scarpetta, Stefano, and Pilat, Dirk 1996: Mark-up ratios in manufacturing industries. Estimates for 14 OECD countries. Economics Department Working Papers No. 162, OECD, Paris.

Ordover, Janusz A., and Saloner, Garth 1989: Predation, monopolization, and antitrust. In Richard C. Schmalensee and Robert D. Willig (eds), *Handbook of Industrial Organization*. Amsterdam: North-Holland, 537–96.

Ordover, Janusz A., Saloner, Garth, and Salop, Steven C. 1990: Equilibrium vertical foreclosure. *American Economic Review*, 80(1), 127–42.

Ornstein, Stanley I. 1975: Empirical uses of the price–cost margin. *Journal of Industrial Economics*, 24(2), 105–17.

— 1977: *Industrial Concentration and Advertising Policy*. Washington, DC: American Enterprise Institute for Public Policy Research.

Orr, Dale 1974: The determinants of entry: a study of the Canadian manufacturing industries. *Review of Economics and Statistics*, 56(1), 58–66.

Osborne, Martin J., and Pitchik, Carolyn 1986: Price competition in a capacity-constrained duopoly. *Journal of Economic Theory*, 38, 238–60.

—, and — 1987: Equilibrium in Hotelling's model of spatial competition. *Econometrica*, 55(4), 911–22.

Oster, Sharon 1984: The *FTC v. Levi Strauss*: an analysis of the economic issues. In Ronald N. Lafferty, Robert H. Lande, and John B. Kirkwood, *Impact Evaluation of Federal Trade Commission Vertical Restraints Cases*. Washington, DC: Federal Trade Commission.

Ouchi, W. G. 1989: The new joint R&D. *Proceedings of the IEEE*, 77(9), 1318–26.

Pakes, Ariel 1987: Mueller's *Profits in the Long Run*. *Rand Journal of Economics*, 18(2), 319–32.

Pakes, Ariel, and Schankerman, Mark 1984: The rate of obsolescence of patents, research gestation lags, and the private rate of return to research resources. In Zvi Griliches (ed.), *R&D, Patents, and Productivity*. Chicago: The University of Chicago Press, 73–88.

Palda, Kristain 1964: *The Measurement of Cumulative Advertising Effects*. Englewood Cliffs, NJ: Prentice-Hall.

de Palma, André, Ginsburgh, Victor, and Thisse, Jacques-François 1987: On existence of location equilibria in the 3-firm Hotelling problem. *Journal of Industrial Economics*, 36(2), 245–52.

de Palma, André, Ginsburgh, Victor, Papageorgiou, Y. Y., and Thisse, Jacques-François 1985: The principle of minimum differentiation holds under sufficient heterogeneity. *Econometrica*, 53(4), 767–81.

Panzar, John C., and Rosse, James N. 1987: Testing for "monopoly" equilibrium. *Journal of Industrial Economics*, 35(4), 443–56.

Paraskevopoulos, D., and Pitelis, Christos N. 1995: An econometric analysis of the determinants of capacity expansion investment in the Western European chemical industry. *Managerial and Decision Economics*, 16(6), 619–32.

Peacock, Alan T. 1950: Recent German contributions to economics. *Economica*, n.s., 17, 175–87.

Peles, Yoram 1971: Rates of amortization of advertising expenditure. *Journal of Political Economy*, 79(5), 1032–58.

Peltzman, Sam 1969: Profit data and public policy. In J. Fred Weston and Sam Peltzman (eds), *Public Policy Toward Mergers*. Pacific Palisades, CA: Goodyear Publishing, 128–36.

— 1991: *The Handbook of Industrial Organization*: a review article. *Journal of Political Economy*, 99(1), 201–17.

Perrakis, Stylianos, and Warskett, George, 1983: Capacity and entry under demand uncertainty. *Review of Economic Studies*, 50, 495–511.

—, and — 1986: Uncertainty, economies of scale, and barrier to entry. *Oxford Economic Papers*, 38, Supplement, November, 58–73.

Perry, Martin K. 1978: Price discrimination and forward integration. *Bell Journal of Economics*, 9(1), 209–17.

— 1982: Oligopoly and consistent conjectural variations. *Bell Journal of Economics*, 13(1), 197–205.

Perry, Martin K., and Porter, Robert H. 1985: Oligopoly and the incentive for horizontal merger. *American Economic Review*, 75(1), 219–27.

Phillips, Almarin 1974: Commentary. In Harvey J. Goldschmid, H. Michael Mann, and J. Fred Weston (eds), *Industrial Concentration: the New Learning*. Boston: Little, Brown, 408–13.

— 1976: A critique of empirical studies of relations between market structure and profitability. *Journal of Industrial Economics*, 24(4), 241–9.

Phillips, Almarin, and Stevenson, Rodney E. 1974: The historical development of industrial organization. *History of Political Economy*, 6(3), 324–42.

Phlips, Louis 1983: *The Economics of Price Discrimination*. Cambridge: Cambridge University Press.

Phlips, Louis 1993: Basing point pricing, competition, and market integration. In Hiroshi Ohta and Jacques-François Thisse (eds), *Does Economic Space Matter? Essays in Honour of Melvin L. Greenhut.* London: The Macmillan Press, 303–15.

Phlips, Louis, and Thisse, Jacques-François 1982: Spatial competition and the theory of differentiated markets. *Journal of Industrial Economics*, 31(1/2), 1–9.

Pigou, A. C. 1955: *Alfred Marshall and Current Thought.* London: Macmillan.

— (ed.) 1956: *Memorials of Alfred Marshall.* New York: Kelley & Millman.

Pigou, A. C., and Robertson, D. H. 1931: *Economic Essays and Addresses.* London: P. S. King.

Pitelis, Christos N. 1990: Neoclassical models of industrial organization. In Ben Dankbaar, John Groenewegen, and Hans Schenk (eds), *Perspectives in Industrial Organization*, vol. II. Amsterdam: North-Holland, ch. 19, 1109–76.

Poitevin, Michel 1989: Financial signalling and the "deep-pocket" argument. *Rand Journal of Economics*, 20(1), 26–40.

Porter, Michael E. 1974: Consumer behavior, retailer power, and market performance in consumer good industries. *Review of Economics and Statistics*, 56(4), 419–36.

Porter, Robert H. 1983a: Optimal cartel trigger price strategies. *Journal of Economic Theory*, 29, 313–38.

— 1983b: A study of cartel stability: the Joint Executive Committee, 1880–1886. *Bell Journal of Economics*, 14(2), 2, 301–14.

— 1983c: On the rationality of buying from a price predator. *Economics Letters*, 11, 385–9.

Posner, Richard A. 1975: The social costs of monopoly and regulation. *Journal of Political Economy*, 83(4), 807–27.

— 1979: The Chicago School of economic analysis. *University of Pennsylvania Law Review*, 127(4), 925–48.

Pratt, John W. 1964: Risk aversion in the small and in the large. *Econometrica*, 32(1–2), 122–36.

Puu, T. 1998: The chaotic duopolists revisited. *Journal of Economic Behavior & Organization*, 33, 385–94.

Radner, Roy 1980: Collusive behavior in noncooperative epsilon-equilibria of oligopolies with long but finite lives. *Journal of Economic Theory*, 22(2), 136–54; reprinted in Andrew F. Daughety (ed.), *Cournot Oligopoly: Characterization and Applications.* Cambridge: Cambridge University Press, 1988 122–41.

Rasmusen, Eric 1988: Entry for buyout. *Journal of Industrial Economics*, 36(3), 281–99.

— 1989: *Games and Information.* Oxford: Basil Blackwell.

Rath, Kali P., and Zhao, Gongyun 2001: Two–stage equilibrium and product choice with elastic demand. *International Journal of Industrial Organization*, 19, forthcoming.

Ravenscraft, David J. 1983: Structure–profit relationships at the line of business and industry level. *Review of Economics and Statistics*, 65(1), 22–31.

— 1984: Collusion vs. superiority: a Monte Carlo analysis. *International Journal of Industrial Organization*, 2(4), 385–402.

Ravenscraft, David J., and Scherer, F. M. 1987: *Mergers, Sell-offs, and Economic Efficiency.* Washington, DC: Brookings Institution.

—, and — 1989: The profitability of mergers. *International Journal of Industrial Organization*, 7(1), 101–16.

Ravenscraft, David J., and Wagner, Curtis L. III 1991: The role of the FTC's Line of Business data in testing and expanding the theory of the firm. *Journal of Law and Economics*, 34(1), Part 2, 703–39.

Rees, Ray 1985: Cheating in a duopoly supergame. *Journal of Industrial Economics*, 33(4), 387–400.

— 1987a: The theory of principal and agent: part I. In John D. Hey and Peter J. Lambert (eds), *Surveys in the Economics of Uncertainty.* Basil Blackwell: Oxford, 46–69.

— 1987b: The theory of principal and agent: part 2. In John D. Hey and Peter J. Lambert (eds), *Surveys in the Economics of Uncertainty.* Basil Blackwell: Oxford, 70–90.

— 1993: Collusive equilibrium in the great salt duopoly. *Economic Journal*, 103(419), 833–48; reprinted in Louis Phlips (ed.), *Applied Industrial Economics*. Cambridge: Cambridge University Press, 1998.

Reinganum, Jennifer F. 1989: The timing of innovation: research, development, and diffusion. In Richard C. Schmalensee and Robert D. Willig, *Handbook of Industrial Organization*. Amsterdam: North Holland, vol. 1, 849–908.

Rey, Patrick, and Stiglitz, Joseph E. 1988: Vertical restraints and producers' competition. *European Economic Review*, 32(2/3), 561–88.

Rey, Patrick, and Tirole, Jean 1986: The logic of vertical restraints. *American Economic Review*, 76(5), 921–39.

— forthcoming: A primer on foreclosure. In *Handbook of Industrial Organization*, vol. III. New York: Elsevier–North-Holland.

Reynolds, Robert J., and Snapp, Bruce R. 1986: The competitive effects of partial equity interests and joint ventures. *International Journal of Industrial Organization*, 4(2), 141–53.

Riordan, Michael H., and Williamson, Oliver E. 1985: Asset specificity and economic organization. *International Journal of Industrial Organization*, 3(4), 365–78.

Roberts, John 1986: A signaling model of predatory pricing. *Oxford Economic Papers*, 38, Supplement, November, 75–83.

— 1987: Battles for market share: incomplete information, aggressive strategic pricing, and competitive dynamics. In Truman F. Bewley (ed.), *Advances in Economic Theory*. Cambridge: Cambridge University Press, 157–95.

Roberts, John, and Sonnenschein, Hugo 1976: On the existence of Cournot equilibrium without concave profit functions. *Journal of Economic Theory*, 13, 112–17.

Roberts, Mark J. 1984: Testing oligopolistic behaviour: an application of the variable profit function. *International Journal of Industrial Organization*, 4(2), 367–84.

Roberts, Mark J., and Samuelson, Larry 1988: An empirical analysis of dynamic, nonprice competition in an oligopolistic industry. *Rand Journal of Economics*, 19(2), 200–20.

Roberts, Mark J., and Supina, Dylan 1996: Output price, markups, and producer size. *European Economic Review*, 40(3–5), 909–21.

— 1997: Output price and markup dispersion in micro data: the roles of producer heterogeneity and noise. NBER Working Paper 6075, June.

Robinson, Joan 1933: *The Economics of Imperfect Competition*, 2nd edn. London: Macmillan, St. Martin's Press.

Robinson, William T., and Chiang, Jeongwen 1996: Are Sutton's predictions robust? Empirical insights into advertising, R&D, and concentration. *Journal of Industrial Economics*, 44(4), 398–408.

Roeger, Werner 1995: Can imperfect competition explain the difference between primal and dual productivity measures? Estimates for U.S. manufacturing. *Journal of Political Economy*, 103(2), 316–30.

— 1996: Mark-ups and excess capacity in German manufacturing. Manuscript, April.

Röller, Lars-Hendrik, and Sickles, Robin C. 2000: Capacity and product market competition: measuring market power in a "puppy-dog" industry. *International Journal of Industrial Organization*, 18(6), 845–65.

Romano, Richard E. 1988: A note on vertical integration: price discrimination and successive monopoly. *Economica*, 55, 261–8.

Romano, Richard E., and Berg, Sanford V. 1985: The identification of predatory behavior in the presence of uncertainty. *International Journal of Industrial Organization*, 3(2), 231–43.

Ronnen, Uri 1991: Minimum quality standards, fixed costs, and competition. *Rand Journal of Economics*, 22(4), 490–504.

Rosenbaum, David I. 1986: A further test of a supergame-theoretic model of price wars during booms. Working Paper 86–9, Department of Economics, University of Nebraska, October.

Rosenbaum, David I. 1987: Predatory pricing and the reconstituted lemon juice industry. *Journal of Economic Issues*, 21(1), 237–58.

Rosenthal, Robert W. 1981: Games of perfect information, predatory pricing and the chain-store paradox. *Journal of Economic Theory*, 25, 92–100.

Ross, Thomas W. 1992: Cartel stability and product differentiation. *International Journal of Industrial Organization*, 10(1), 1–13.

Rotemberg, Julio J., and Saloner, Garth 1986: A supergame-theoretic model of price wars during booms. *American Economic Review*, 76(3), 390–407.

Rothschild, Kurt W. 1942: The degree of monopoly. *Economica*, 24, 24–39.

Rothschild, R. 1982: Competitive behavior in chain–linked markets. *Journal of Industrial Economics*, 31(1/2), 57–67.

— 1995: Sustaining collusion when the choice of strategic variable is endogenous. *Journal of Economic Behavior and Organization*, 28, 373–85.

— 1999: Cartel stability when costs are heterogeneous. *International Journal of Industrial Organization*, 17(5), 717–34.

Ruff, Larry E. 1969: Research and technological progress in a Cournot economy. *Journal of Economic Theory*, 1(4), 397–415.

Ruffin, R. J. 1971: Cournot oligopoly and competitive behavior. *Review of Economic Studies*, 38(4), 493–502.

Rumelt, Richard P. 1991: "How much does industry matter?" *Strategic Management Journal*, 12, 167–85.

Sabourian, Hamid 1992: Rational conjectural equilibrium and repeated games. In Partha Dasgupta, Douglas Gale, Oliver Hart, and Eric Maskin (eds), *Economic Analysis of Markets and Games: Essays in Honor of Frank Hahn*. Cambridge, MA: The MIT Press, 228–57.

Salamon, G. 1970: Relationship between the accounting and the internal rate of return measure: a synthesis and an analysis. *Journal of Accounting Research*, 8, 199–216.

Salant, Stephen W., and Shaffer, Greg 1998: Optimal asymmetric strategies in research joint ventures. *International Journal of Industrial Organization*, 16, 195–208.

Salant, Stephen W., Switzer, S., and Reynolds, Robert J. 1983: Losses from horizontal merger: the effects of an exogenous change in industry structure on Cournot–Nash equilibrium. *Quarterly Journal of Economics*, 98(2), 185–213.

Salinger, M. A. 1984: Tobin's q, unionization and the concentration–profits relationship. *Rand Journal of Economics*, 15(2), 159–70.

— 1988: Vertical mergers and market foreclosure. *Quarterly Journal of Economics*, 103(2), 345–56.

— 1989: The meaning of "upstream" and "downstream" and the implications for modeling vertical mergers. *Journal of Industrial Economics*, 37(4), 373–87.

Saloner, Garth 1985: Excess capacity as a policing device. *Economics Letters*, 18, 83–6.

— 1987: Predation, mergers, and incomplete information. *Rand Journal of Economics*, 18(2), 165–86.

Salop, Steven C. 1979: Monopolistic competition with outside goods. *Bell Journal of Economics*, 10(1), 141–56.

— 1986: Practices that (credibly) facilitate oligopoly co-ordination. In Joseph E. Stiglitz and G. Frank Mathewson (eds), *New Developments in the Analysis of Market Structure*. Cambridge, MA: The MIT Press, 265–94.

Salop, Steven C., and Scheffman, David T. 1983: Raising rivals' costs. *American Economic Review*, 73(2), 267–71.

— 1987: Cost-raising strategies. *Journal of Industrial Economics*, 36(1), 19–34.

Samuelson, Paul A. 1947: *Foundations of Economic Analysis*. Cambridge, MA: Harvard University Press.

— 1967: The monopolistic competition revolution. In R. E. Kuenne (ed.), *Monopolistic Competition Theory: Studies in Impact. Essays in Honor of Edward H. Chamberlin*. New York: John Wiley; reprinted in Robert C. Merton (ed.), *The Collected Scientific Papers of Paul A. Samuelson*. vol. III Cambridge, MA: The MIT Press, 1972, 18–51. (Page references are to reprinted version.)

Saving, T. 1970: Concentration ratios and the degree of monopoly. *International Economic Review*, 11, 139–46.

Sawyer, Malcolm W. 1982: On the specification of structure–performance relationships. *European Economic Review*, 17, 295–306.

Scarpa, Carlo 1998: Minimum quality standards with more than two firms. *International Journal of Industrial Organization*, 16(5), 665–76.

Scherer, F. M. 1967: Research and development resource allocation under rivalry. *Quarterly Journal of Economics*, 81(3), 359–94.

—— 1970: *Industrial Market Structure and Economic Performance*. Chicago: Rand McNally.

—— 1972: Nordhaus' theory of optimal patent life: a geometric reinterpretation. *American Economic Review*, 62(3), 422–7; reprinted in F. M. Scherer, *Innovation and Growth*. Cambridge, MA: The MIT Press, 1984.

—— 1982: Demand-pull and technological invention: Schmookler revisited. *Journal of Industrial Economics*, 30(3), 225–37.

—— 1983: The economics of vertical restraints. *Antitrust Law Journal*, 52(3), 687–18.

—— 1988: Corporate takeovers: the efficiency arguments. *Journal of Economic Perspectives*, 2(1), 69–82.

—— 1996: Heinrich von Stackelberg's "Marktform und Gleichgewicht." *Journal of Economic Studies*, 23(5–6), 58–70.

—— 2000: Professor Sutton's "Technology and Market Structure." *Journal of Industrial Economics*, 48(2), 215–23.

Scherer, F. M., Long, William F., Martin, Stephen, Mueller, Dennis C., Pascoe, George, Ravenscraft, David J., and Weiss, Leonard W. 1987: The validity of studies with line of business data: comment. *American Economic Review*, 77(1), 205–17.

Schlee, Edward E. 1993a: A curvature condition ensuring uniqueness of Cournot equilibrium, with applications to comparative statics. *Economics Letters*, 41, 29–33.

—— 1993b: Corrigenda. *Economics Letters*, 43, 239.

Schmalensee, Richard C. 1972: *The Economics of Advertising*. Amsterdam: North-Holland.

—— 1973: A note on the theory of vertical integration. *Journal of Political Economy*, 81(2), Part I, 442–9.

—— 1977: Using the H-index of concentration with published data. *Review of Economics and Statistics*, 59(2), 186–93.

—— 1979: On the use of economic models in antitrust: the ReaLemon case. *University of Pennsylvania Law Review*, 127(4), 994–1050.

—— 1981: Economies of scale and barriers to entry. *Journal of Political Economy*, 89(6), 1228–38.

—— 1982: The new industrial organization and the economic analysis of modern markets. In Werner Hildebrand (ed.), *Advances in Economic Theory*. Cambridge: Cambridge University Press, 253–84.

—— 1985: Do markets differ much? *American Economic Review*, 75(3), 341–51.

—— 1987a: Industrial organization. In John Eatwell, Murray Milgate, and Peter Newman (eds), *The New Palgrave*. London: Macmillan Press, vol. 2, 803–8.

—— 1987b: Competitive advantage and collusive optima. *International Journal of Industrial Organization*, 5(4), 351–67.

—— 1988: Industrial economics: an overview. *Economic Journal*, 98(392), 643–81.

—— 1989: Inter-industry studies of structure and performance. In Richard C. Schmalensee and Robert D. Willig (eds), *Handbook of Industrial Organization*. Amsterdam: North-Holland, vol. II, ch. 16, 951–1009.

—— 1990: Empirical studies of rivalrous behavior. In Giacomo Bonanno and Dario Brandolini (eds), *Industrial Structure in the New Industrial Economics*. Oxford: Clarendon Press.

—— 1992: Sunk costs and market structure: a review article. *Journal of Industrial Economics*, 40, 125–34.

Schmookler, Jacob 1966: *Invention and Economic Growth*. Cambridge, MA: Harvard University Press.

Schmookler, Jacob 1972: In Zvi Griliches and Leonid Hurwicz (eds), *Patents, Invention, and Economic Change: Data and Selected Essays*. Cambridge, MA: Harvard University Press.

Schneider, Erich 1962: *Pricing and Equilibrium*, 2nd edn. London: George Allen & Unwin.

Schnitzer, Monika 1994: Dynamic duopoly with best-price clauses. *Rand Journal of Economics*, 25(1), 186–96.

Schohl, Frank 1990: Persistence of profits in the long run: a critical extension of some recent findings. *International Journal of Industrial Organization*, 8(3), 385–403.

Schroeter, John R., Azzam, Azzeddine M., and Zhang, Mingxia 2000: Measuring market power in bilateral oligopoly: the wholesale market for beef. *Southern Economic Journal*, 66(3), 526–47.

Schulz, Norbert 2000: A comment on Yin and Ng. *Australian Economic Papers*, 39(1), 108–12.

Schumpeter, Joseph A. 1934: *The Theory of Economic Development*. Cambridge, MA: Harvard University Press.

— 1943: *Capitalism, Socialism and Democracy*. London: Allen & Unwin; New York: Harper & Row, Colophon edition, 1975.

— 1954: *History of Economic Analysis*. New York: Oxford University Press.

Schwalbach, Joachim 1987: Entry by diversified firms into German industries. *International Journal of Industrial Organization*, 5(1), 15–26.

— 1991: Entry, concentration, and market contestability. In Paul A. Geroski and Joachim Schwalbach (eds), *Entry and Market Contestability: an International Comparison*. London: Basil Blackwell, 121–42.

Schwartz, Marius 1989: Investments in oligopoly: welfare effects and tests for predation. *Oxford Economic Papers*, 41, 698–719.

Schwartz, Steven 1984: An empirical test of a managerial, life-cycle, and cost of capital model of merger activity. *Journal of Industrial Economics*, 32(3), 265–76.

Schwartzman, David 1959: The effect of monopoly on price. *Journal of Political Economy*, 67(4), 352–62.

Schwartzman, David, and Bodoff, Jean 1971: Concentration in regional and local industries. *Southern Economic Journal*, 37(3), 343–8.

Scotchmer, S. 1991: Standing on the shoulders of giants: cumulative research and the patent law. *Journal of Economic Perspectives*, 29–41.

Scotchmer, S., and Green, J. 1990: Novelty and disclosure in patent law. *Rand Journal of Economics*, 21, 131–46.

Scott, John T. 1988: Diversification versus co-operation in R&D investment. *Managerial and Decision Economics*, 9(3), 173–86.

— 1989a: Historical and economic perspectives of the National Cooperative Research Act. In Albert N. Link and Gregory Tassey (eds), *Cooperative Research and Development: The Industry–University–Government Relationship*. Dordrecht: Kluwer.

— 1989b: Purposive diversification as a motive for merger. *International Journal of Industrial Organization*, 7(1), 35–47.

— 1991: Multimarket contact among diversified oligopolists. *International Journal of Industrial Organization*, 9(2), 225–38.

— 1993: *Purposive Diversification and Economic Performance*. Cambridge: Cambridge University Press.

— 1996: Environmental research joint ventures among manufacturers. *Review of Industrial Organization*, 11(5), 655–79.

Scott, John T., and Pascoe, George 1986: Beyond firm and industry effects on profitability in imperfect markets. *Review of Economics and Statistics*, 68(2), 284–92.

Seade, Jesus 1980a: On the effects of entry. *Econometrica*, 48(2), 479–9.

— 1980b: The stability of Cournot revisited. *Journal of Economic Theory*, 23(1), 15–27.

Segerstrom, Paul S. 1988: Demons and repentance. *Journal of Economic Theory*, 45(1), 32–52.

Selten, Reinhard 1973: A simple model of imperfect competition where four are few and six are many. *International Journal of Game Theory*, 2, 141–201; reprinted in Reinhard Selten, *Models of Strategic Rationality*. Dordrecht: Kluwer, 1988.

—— 1978: The chain store paradox. *Theory and Decision*, 9, 127–59; reprinted in Reinhard Selten, *Models of Strategic Rationality*. Dordrecht: Kluwer, 1988; page references are to reprinted version.

—— 1986: Elementary theory of slack-ridden imperfect competition. In Joseph E. Stiglitz and G. Frank Mathewson (eds), *New Developments in the Analysis of Market Structure*. Cambridge, MA: The MIT Press, 126–44.

—— 1988: A model of oligopolistic size structure and profitability. In Reinhard Selten, *Models of Strategic Rationality*. Dordrecht: Kluwer, ch. 6, 157–81.

Shaanan, Joseph 1988: Welfare and barriers to entry: an empirical study. *Southern Economic Journal*, 54(3), 746–62.

Shaffer, Greg 1991: Slotting allowances and resale price maintenance: a comparison of facilitating practices. *Rand Journal of Economics*, 22(1), 120–35.

Shaffer, Sherrill 1982: Competition, conduct and demand elasticity. *Economics Letters*, 10, 167–71.

—— 1983: The Rosse–Panzar statistic and the Lerner index in the short run. *Economics Letters*, 11, 175–8.

—— 1995: Stable cartels with a Cournot fringe. *Southern Economic Journal*, 61(3), 744–54.

Shaked, A. 1982: Existence and computation of mixed strategy Nash equilibrium for 3-firms location problem. *Journal of Industrial Economics*, 31, 93–7.

Shaked, Avner, and Sutton, John 1982: Relaxing price competition through product differentiation. *Review of Economic Studies*, 49(1), 3–13.

Shapiro, Carl 1980: Advertising and welfare: comment. *Bell Journal of Economics*, 11(2), 749–52.

Shapiro, D., and Khemani, R. S. 1987: The determinants of entry and exit reconsidered. *International Journal of Industrial Organization*, 5(1), 15–26.

Shepherd, William G. 1972: The elements of market structure. *Review of Economics and Statistics*, 54(1), 25–37.

—— 1976: Bain's influence on research into industrial organization. In Robert T. Masson and P. David Qualls (eds), *Essays on Industrial Organization in Honor of Joe S. Bain*. Cambridge, MA: Ballinger, 1–17.

—— 1986: Tobin's *q* and the structure–performance relationship: comment. *American Economic Review*, 76(6), 1205–10.

—— 2000: Market structure and profits, market power and Cournot: a comment. *Review of Industrial Organization*, 16(3), 247–50.

Sherman, Roger, and Willet, Thomas D. 1967: Potential entrants discourage entry. *Journal of Political Economy*, 75, 400–3.

Shinnar, Reuel, Dressler, Ofer, Feng, C. A., and Avidan, Alan I. 1989: Estimation of the economic rate of return for industrial companies. *Journal of Business*, 62(3), 417–45.

Shubik, Martin 1987: Cournot. In John Eatwell, Murray Milgate, and Peter Newman (eds), *The New Palgrave*. London: Macmillan Press, vol. 1, 708–12.

Shubik, Martin, and Levitan, Richard 1980: *Market Structure and Behavior*. Cambridge, MA: Harvard University Press.

Shy, Oz 2001: A quick-and-easy method for estimating switching costs. *International Journal of Industrial Economics*, 19, forthcoming.

Siegfried, John J., and Weiss, Leonard W. 1974: Advertising, concentration, and corporate taxes revisited. *Review of Economics and Statistics*, 56, 195–200.

Sigurdson, Jon 1986: *Industry and State Partnership in Japan: the Very Large Scale Integrated (VLSI) Circuit Project*. Lund: Swedish Research Policy Institute, University of Lund.

Simon, Herbert A. 1947: *Administrative Behavior: a Study of Decision-making Processes in Administrative Organization*. New York: Macmillan.

Singh, N. and Vives, Xavier 1984: Price and quantity competition in a differentiated oligopoly. *Rand Journal of Economics*, 15(4), 546–54.

Sklivas, Steven D. 1987: The strategic choice of managerial incentives. *Rand Journal of Economics*, 18(3), 452–8.

Slade, Margaret E. 1987: Interfirm rivalry in a repeated game: an empirical test of tacit collusion. *Journal of Industrial Economics*, 35(4), 499–516.

— 1989: Price wars in price-setting supergames. *Economica*, 56, 295–310.

— 1990: Cheating on collusive agreements. *International Journal of Industrial Organization*, 8(4), 519–43.

— 1995: Product rivalry with multiple strategic weapons. *Journal of Economics & Management Strategy*, 4(3), 445–76.

— 1998: The leverage theory of tying revisited: evidence from newspaper advertising. *Southern Economic Journal*, 65(2), 204–22.

Sleuwaegen, Leo, and Dehandschutter, Wim 1986: The critical choice between the concentration ratio and the H-index in assessing industry performance. *Journal of Industrial Economics*, 35(2), 193–208.

Sleuwaegen, Leo, and Yamawaki, Hideki 1988: The formation of the European common market and changes in market structure and performance. *International Journal of Industrial Organization*, 32(7), 1451–75.

Slusky, Alexander S., and Caves, Richard E. 1991: Synergy, agency and the determinants of premia paid in mergers. *Journal of Industrial Economics*, 39(3), 277–96.

Smiley, Robert 1976: Tender offers, transaction costs, and the theory of the firm. *Review of Economics and Statistics*, 58(1), 22–32.

Smirlock, M., Gilligan, Thomas W., and Marshall, W. 1984: Tobin's q and the structure–performance relationship. *American Economic Review*, 74(5), 1051–60.

—, —, and — 1986: Tobin's q and the structure–performance relationship: reply. *American Economic Review*, 76(6), 1211–13.

Smith, Adam 1937: *An Inquiry Into the Nature and Causes of the Wealth of Nations*, Edwin Cannan (ed.). New York: The Modern Library.

Smithies, Arthur 1941: Optimum location in spatial competition. *Journal of Political Economy*, 49, 423–39.

Solomon, Ezra 1970: Alternative rate of return concepts and their implications for utility regulation. *Bell Journal of Economics*, 1, 65–81.

Solow, Robert M. 1957: Technical change and the aggregate production function. *Review of Economics and Statistics*, 39(3), 312–20.

Spence, A. Michael 1976a: Product differentiation and welfare. *American Economic Review*, 66(2), 407–14.

— 1976b: Product selection, fixed costs, and monopolistic competition. *Review of Economic Studies*, 43(2), 217–35.

— 1977: Entry, capacity, investment oligopolistic pricing. *Bell Journal of Economics*, 8(2), 534–44.

— 1979: Investment strategy and growth in a new market. *Bell Journal of Economics*, 10(1), 1–19.

Spence, A. Michael 1984: Cost reduction, competition, and industry performance. *Econometrica*, 52(1), 101–21.

Spiller, Pablo T. 1985: Tobin's q and monopoly power, a capital asset pricing perspective. *Economic Letters*, 18, 261–3.

Spiller, Pablo T., and Favaro, Edgardo 1984: The effects of entry regulation oligopolistic interaction: the Uruguayan banking sector. *Rand Journal of Economics*, 15(2), 244–54.

Springer, Robert F., and Frech, H. E. III 1986: Deterring fraud: the role of resale price maintenance. *Journal of Business*, 59(3), 433–49.

Spulber, Daniel F. 1981: Capacity, output, and sequential entry. *American Economic Review*, 71(3), 503–14.

Srinagesh, Padmanabhan, and Bradburd, Ralph M. 1989: Quality distortion by a discriminating monopolist. *American Economic Review*, 79(1), 96–105.

Stackelberg, Heinrich von 1934: *Marktform und Gleichgewicht*. Vienna: Julius Springer.

— 1952: *The Theory of the Market Economy*, Alan T. Peacock, translator. London: William Hodge.

Stahl, Dale O. II 1994: Oligopolistic pricing and advertising. *Journal of Economic Theory*, 64(1), 162–77.

Stahl, Konrad 1982: Differentiated products, computer search, and locational oligopoly. *Journal of Industrial Economics*, 31(1/2), 97–113.

Stauffer, T. R. 1971: The measurement of corporate rates of return: a generalized formulation. *Bell Journal of Economics*, 2, 434–69.

Steen, Frode, and Salvanes, Kjell G. 1999: Testing for market power using a dynamic oligopoly model. *International Journal of Industrial Organization*, 17(2), 147–77.

Steer, Peter, and Cable, John 1978: Internal organization and profit: an empirical analysis of large U.K. companies. *Journal of Industrial Economics*, 27(1), 13–30.

Stegeman, Mark 1991: Advertising in competitive markets. *American Economic Review*, 81(1), 210–23.

Stevens, Jerry L. 1990: Tobin's q and the structure–performance relationship: comment. *American Economic Review*, 80(3), 618–21.

Stewart, John F., Harris, Robert F., and Carleton, Willard T. 1984: The role of market structure in merger behavior. *Journal of Industrial Economics*, 32(3), 293–312.

Stigler, George J. 1940: Notes on the theory of duopoly. *Journal of Political Economy*, 48(4), 521–41.

— 1949: Monopolistic competition in retrospect. In *Five lectures on Economic Problems*. London: London School of Economics; reprinted in George J. Stigler, *The Organization of Industry*. Homewood, IL: Richard D. Irwin, 1968.

— 1963: *Capital and Rates of Return in Manufacturing*. Princeton, NJ: Princeton University Press.

— 1964: A theory of oligopoly. *Journal of Political Economy*, 72(1), 44–61; reprinted in George J. Stigler, *The Organization of Industry*. Homewood, IL: Richard D. Irwin, 1968, 39–63.

— 1967: Imperfections in the capital market. *Journal of Political Economy*, 75(3), 287–92; reprinted in George J. Stigler, *The Organization of Industry*. Homewood, IL: Richard D. Irwin, 1968.

— 1968a: The measurement of concentration. In George J. Stigler, *The Organization of Industry*. Homewood, IL: Richard D. Irwin.

— 1968b: *The Organization of Industry*. Homewood, IL: Richard D. Irwin.

— 1974: Henry Calvert Simons. *Journal of Law and Economics*, 17(1), 1–5.

— 1976: The Existence of X-efficiency. *American Economic Review*, 66(1), 213–16.

Stillman, R. 1983: Examining antitrust policy towards horizontal mergers. *Journal of Financial Economics*, 11, 225–40.

Summers, Lawrence H. 1986: Does the stock market rationally reflect fundamental values? *Journal of Finance*, 41, 591–601.

Sumner, Daniel A. 1981: Measurement of monopoly behavior: an application to the cigarette industry. *Journal of Political Economy*, 89(5), 1010–19.

Suslow, Valerie Y. 1986: Estimating monopoly behavior with competitive recycling: an application to Alcoa. *Rand Journal of Economics*, 17(3), 389–403.

Sutton, C. J. 1974: Advertising, concentration and competition. *Economic Journal*, 88(333), 56–69.

Sutton, John 1991: *Sunk Costs and Market Structure*. Cambridge, MA: The MIT Press.

— 1997: Gibrat's legacy. *Journal of Economic Literature*, 35(1), 40–59.

— 1998: *Technology and Market Structure*. Cambridge, MA: The MIT Press.

Suzumura, Kotaro 1992: Cooperative and noncooperative R&D in an oligopoly with spillovers. *American Economic Review*, 82(5), 1307–20.

Suzumura, Kotaro, and Kiyono, Kazuharu 1987: Entry barriers and economic welfare. *Review of Economic Studies*, 54(1), 157–67.

Svizzero, Serge 1997: Cournot equilibrium with convex demand. *Economics Letters*, 54, 155–8.

Sylos-Labini, Paolo 1957: *Oligopolio e progresso tecnico*. Milan: Giuffrè; published in English translation as *Oligopoly and Technical Progress*. Cambridge, MA: Harvard University Press, 1962.

Symeonidis, George 1998: The evolution of UK cartel policy and its impact on conduct and structure. In Stephen Martin (ed.), *Competition Policies in Europe*. Amsterdam: North-Holland.

— 1999a: Cartel stability in advertising-intensive and R&D-intensive industries. *Economics Letters*, 62, 121–9.

— 1999b: In which industries is collusion more likely? Evidence from the UK. CEPR Discussion Paper No. 2301, November.

— 2000: The effects of competition: cartel policy and the evolusion of strategy and market structure in British industry. Manuscript, May.

Szidarovszky, F., and Yakowitz, S. 1977: A new proof of the existence and uniqueness of the Cournot equilibrium. *International Economic Review*, 18(3), 787–9.

Takahashi, Takaaki, and de Palma André 1993: A unified treatment of the segment and circular market models. In Hiroshi Ohta and Jacques-François Thisse (eds), *Does Economic Space Matter? Essays in Honour of Melvin L. Greenhut*. London: The Macmillan Press.

Tapon, Francis, and Cadsby, Charles Bram 1996: The optimal organization of research: evidence from eight case studies of pharmaceutical firms. *Journal of Economic & Behavioral Organization*, 31, 381–99.

Teece, David J. 1980: Economies of scope and the scope of the enterprise. *Journal of Economic Behavior and Organization*, 1, 223–47.

— 1981: Internal organization and economic performance: an empirical analysis of profitability of principal firms. *Journal of Industrial Economics*, 30(2), 173–99.

— 1982: Towards an economic theory of the multiproduct firm. *Journal of Economic Behavior and Organization*, 3, 39–63.

Telser, Lester G. 1960: Why should manufacturers want fair trade? *Journal of Law and Economics*, 3(1), 86–105.

— 1962: Advertising and cigarettes. *Journal of Political Economy*, 70(5), 471–98.

Theil, Henri 1971: *Principles of Econometrics*. New York: John Wiley.

Theocharis, R. D. 1959–60: On the stability of the Cournot solution of the oligopoly problem. *Review of Economic Studies* 27(2), 133–4.

Thisse, Jacques-François and Vives, Xavier 1988: Spatial pricing schemes. *American Economic Review*, 78, 122–37; reprinted in Louis Phlips (ed.), *Applied Industrial Economics*. Cambridge: Cambridge University Press, 1998.

Thomas, Louis A. 1999: Incumbent firms' response to entry: price, advertising, and new product introduction. *International Journal of Industrial Organization*, 17(4), 527–55.

Thompson, R. S. 1981: Internal organization and profit: a note. *Journal of Industrial Economics*, 30(2), 201–11.

Tirole, Jean 1988: *The Theory of Industrial Organization*. Cambridge, MA: The MIT Press.

Tremblay, Carol Horton, and Tremblay, Victor J. 1995: Advertising, price and welfare: evidence from the U.S. brewing industry. *Southern Economic Journal*, 62(2), 367–81.

Tyagi, Rajeev K. 1999: On the relationship between product substitutability and tacit collusion. *Managerial and Decision Economics*, 20(6), 293–8.

von Ungern–Sternberg, Thomas 1988a: Cartel stability in sealed bid second price auctions. *Journal of Industrial Economics*, 36(3), 351–8.

— 1988b: Excess capacity as a commitment to promote entry. *Journal of Industrial Economics*, 37(2), 113–22.

— 1991: Monopolistic competition on the pyramid. *Journal of Industrial Economics*, 39(4), 355–68.

von Ungern-Sternberg, Thomas, and von Weizsäcker, Carl Christian 1981: Marktstruktur und marktverhalten bei qualitätsunsicherheit. *Zeitschrift für Wirtschafts- und Sozialwissenschaften*, 101(6), 609–26.

Vanlommel, E., de Brabander, B., and Liebaers, D. 1977: Industrial concentration in Belgium: empirical comparison of alternative seller concentration measures. *Journal of Industrial Economics*, 26(1), 1–20.

Verboven, Frank 1997: Collusive behavior with heterogeneous firms. *Journal of Economic Behavior & Organization*, 33(1), 121–36.

Vernon, John M., and Graham, Daniel A. 1971: Profitability of monopolization by vertical integration. *Journal of Political Economy*, 79, 924–5.

Vernon, John M., and Nourse, Robert E. 1973: Profit rates and market structure of advertising intensive firms. *Journal of Industrial Economics*, 22(1), 1–20.

Verma, Kiran 1990: Effects of accounting techniques on the study of market power. *International Journal of Industrial Organization*, 8(4), 587–98.

Veugelers, Reinhilde, and Vanden Houte, Peter 1990: Domestic R&D in the presence of multinational enterprises. *International Journal of Industrial Organization*, 8(1), 1–15.

Vickers, John 1985: Strategic competition among the few – some recent developments in the economics of industry. *Oxford Review of Economic Policy*, 1(3), 39–62.

—— 1989: The nature of costs and the number of firms at Cournot equilibrium. *International Journal of Industrial Organization*, 7(4), 503–9.

Vickrey, W. S. 1964: *Microstatics*. New York: Harcourt, Brace and World.

Vives, Xavier 1984: On the efficiency of Bertrand and Cournot equilibria with product differentiation. *Journal of Economic Theory*, 36, 166–75.

Vonortas, Nicholas S. 1994: Inter-firm cooperation with imperfectly appropriable research. *International Journal of Industrial Organization*, 12(3), 413–35.

Waldman, Michael 1987: Noncooperative entry deterrence, uncertainty, and the free rider problem. *Review of Economic Studies*, 54(2), 301–10.

Waldmann, Robert J. 1991: Implausible results or implausible data? Anomalies in the construction of value-added data and implications for estimates of price–cost markups. *Journal of Political Economy*, 99(6), 1315–28.

Wallace, Donald H. 1937: *Market Control in the Aluminum Industry*. Cambridge: MA: Harvard University Press.

Walras, Léon 1954: *Elements of Pure Economics*. 4th edn (1926), translated by Williamé Jaffé. Homewood, IL: Richard D. Irwin.

Ward, James A. 1995: *The Fall of the Packard Motor Car Company*. Stanford, CA: Stanford University Press.

Ware, R. 1984: Sunk costs and strategic commitment: a proposed three-stage equilibrium. *Economic Journal*, 94, 370–8.

Waring, Geoffrey F. 1996: Industry differences in the persistence of firm-specific returns. *American Economic Review*, 86(5), 1253–65.

Waterson, Michael 1988: Vertical restraints and the law: a note. *Rand Journal of Economics*, 19(2), 293–7.

—— 1989: Models of product differentiation. *Bulletin of Economic Research*, 41(1), 1–27.

Wauthy, Xavier 1996: Quality choice in models of vertical differentiation. *Journal of Industrial Economics*, 44(3), 345–53.

Weinstock, David S. 1982: Using the Herfindahl index to measure concentration. *Antitrust Bulletin*, 27, 285–301.

—— 1984: Some little-known properties of the Herfindahl–Hirschman index: problems of translation and specification. *Antitrust Bulletin*, 29, 705–17.

Weiss, Leonard W. 1963: Average concentration ratios and industrial performance. *Journal of Industrial Economics*, 11, 233–54.

—— 1966: Concentration and labor earnings. *American Economic Review*, 56(1), 96–117.

—— 1969: Advertising, profits, and corporate taxes. *Review of Economics and Statistics*, 54(4), 421–30.

Weiss, Leonard W. 1971: Quantitative studies of industrial organization. In M. D. Intriligator (ed.), *Frontiers of Quantitative Economics*. Amsterdam: North-Holland, ch. 9, 362–403.

— 1974: The concentration–profits relationship and antitrust. In Harvey J. Goldschmid, H. Michael Mann, and J. Fred Weston (eds), *Industrial Concentration: the New Learning*. Boston: Little, Brown.

— 1985: Concentration and price – a possible way out of the box. In Joachim Schwalbach (ed.), *Industry Structure and Performance*. Berlin: Edition Sigma Rainer Bohn Verlag.

— 1989: Why study concentration and price? In Leonard W. Weiss (ed.), *Concentration and Price*. Cambridge, MA: The MIT Press, 1–14.

von Weizsäcker, C. C. 1980a: A welfare analysis of barriers to entry. *Bell Journal of Economics*, 11(2), 399–420.

— 1980b: *Barriers to Entry*. Berlin: Springer-Verlag.

Wenders, John T. 1971: Excess capacity as a barrier to entry. *Journal of Industrial Economics*, 20, 14–19.

Werden, Gregory J. 1991: Horizontal mergers: comment. *American Economic Review*, 81(4), 1002–6.

Wernerfelt, Birger 1989: Tacit collusion in differentiated Cournot games. *Economics Letters*, 29, 303–6.

Whinston, Michael D. 1988: Exit with multiplant firms. *Rand Journal of Economics*, 19(4), 74–94.

— 1990: Tying, foreclosure, and exclusion. *American Economic Review*, 80(4), 837–59.

White, Lawrence J. 1976: Searching for the critical concentration ratio: an application of the "switching of regimes" technique. In S. M. Goldfeld and R. E. Quandt (eds), *Studies in Nonlinear Estimation*. Cambridge, MA: Ballinger, ch. 3, 61–75.

Whyte , Glen 1994: The role of asset specificity in the vertical integration decision. *Journal of Economic Behavior and Organization*, 23, 287–302.

Williamson, Oliver E. 1967: Hierarchical control and optimum firm size. *Journal of Political Economy*, 75(2), 123–38; reprinted in Douglas Needham (ed.), *Readings in the Economics of Industrial Organization*. New York: Holt, Reinhart and Winston, 1970.

— 1968a: Wage rates as a barrier to entry: the Pennington case. *Quarterly Journal of Economics*, 85, 85–116.

— 1968b: Economies as an antitrust defense: the welfare tradeoffs. *American Economic Review*, 58(1), 18–36.

— 1970: *Corporate Control and Business Behavior: an Inquiry into the Effects of Organization Form on Enterprise Behavior*. Englewood Cliffs, NJ: Prentice-Hall.

— 1971: The vertical integration of production: market failure considerations. *American Economic Review*, 61, 112–23.

— 1974: The economics of antitrust: transaction cost considerations. *University of Pennsylvania Law Review*, 122(6), 1439–96.

— 1975: *Markets and Hierarchies*. New York: The Free Press.

— 1981: The modern corporation: origins, evolution, attributes. *Journal of Economic Literature*, 19(4), 1537–68.

— 1985: *The Economic Institutions of Capitalism*. New York: The Free Press.

— 1986: Vertical integration and related variations on a transaction–cost economics theme. In Joseph E. Stiglitz and G. Frank Mathewson (eds), *New Developments in the Analysis of Market Structure*. Cambridge, MA: The MIT Press, 149–74.

— 1988a: Corporate finance and corporate governance. *Journal of Finance*, 43(3), 567–91.

— 1988b: Technology and transaction cost economics: a reply. *Journal of Economic Behavior and Organization*, 10, 355–63.

Willig, Robert D. 1987: Corporate governance and market structure. In Assaf Razin and Efriam Sadka (eds), *Economic Policy in Theory and Practice*. London: Macmillan Press, 481–94.

Winn, Daryl N., and Leabo, Dick A. 1974: Rates of return, concentration and growth – question of disequilibrium. *Journal of Law and Economics*, 17(1), 97–115.

Winter, Sidney G. 1984: Schumperian competition in alternative technological regimes. *Journal of Economic Behavior and Organization*, 5, 287–320.

Yamawaki, Hideki 1991: The effects of business conditions on net entry: evidence from Japan. In Paul A. Geroski and Joachim Schwalbach (eds), *Entry and Market Contestability: an International Comparison*. London: Basil Blackwell, 168–86.

Yamey, Basil S. 1954: *The Economics of Resale Price Maintenance*. London: Sir Isaac Pitman.

Yang, Bill Z. 1996: Learning, reputation and entry deterrence: a chain-store game with correlated entrants. *International Journal of Industrial Organization*, 14(5), 561–73.

Yi, Sang-Seung 1998: Endogenous formation of joint ventures with efficiency gains. *Rand Journal of Economics*, 29(3), 610–31.

Yi, Sang-Seung, and Shin, Hyukseung 2000: Endogenous formation of research coalitions with spillovers. *International Journal of Industrial Organization*, 18(2), 229–56.

Yin, Xiangkang, and Ng, Yew-Kwang 1997: Quantity precommitment and Bertrand competition yield Cournot outcomes: a case with product differentiation. *Australian Economic Papers*, 36, 14–22.

—, and — 2000: Quantity precommitment and Bertrand competition yield Cournot outcomes: a case with product differentiation reply. *Australian Economic Papers*, 39(1), 113–19.

INDEX OF NAMES

INDEX OF SUBJECTS